Performance-Based Budgeting

ASPA Classics

Conceived and sponsored by the American Society for Public Administration (ASPA), the ASPA Classics series will publish volumes on topics that have been, and continue to be, central to the contemporary development of public administration. The ASPA Classics are intended for classroom use and may be quite suitable for libraries and general reference collections. Drawing from the Public Administration Review and other journals related to the ASPA sections, each volume in the series is edited by a scholar who is charged with presenting a thorough and balanced perspective on an enduring issue. These journals now represent some six decades of collective wisdom. Yet, many of the writings collected in the ASPA Classics might not otherwise easily come to the attention of future public managers. Given the explosion in research and writing on all aspects of public administration in recent decades, these ASPA Classics anthologies should point readers to definitive or groundbreaking authors whose voices should not be lost in the cacophony of the newest administrative technique or invention.

Public servants carry out their responsibilities in a complex, multidimensional environment. The mission of ASPA Classics is to provide the reader with a historical and firsthand view of the development of the topic at hand. As such, each ASPA Classics volume presents the most enduring scholarship, often in complete, or nearly complete, original form on the given topic. Each volume will be devoted to a specific continuing concern to the administration of all public sector programs. Early volumes in the series address public sector performance, public service as commitment and diversity and affirmative action in public service. Future volumes will include equally important dialogues on classic ideas as enduring ideas, reinventing government, public budgeting and public service ethics.

The volume editors are to be commended for volunteering for the substantial task of compiling and editing these unique collections of articles that might not otherwise be readily available to scholars, teachers, and students.

Books in This Series

Performance-Based Budgeting,
ed. by Gerald J. Miller, W. Bartley Hildreth, and Jack Rabin

Public Sector Performance: Management, Motivation, and Measurement,
ed. by Rochard C. Kearney and Evan M. Berman

Diversity and Affirmative Action in the Public Service,
ed. by Walter D. Broadnax

Public Service: Callings, Commitments and Constraints,
ed. by Marc Holzer

Performance-Based Budgeting

An ASPA Classic

Gerald J. Miller

W. Bartley Hildreth

Jack Rabin

Rutgers University, Wichita State University,
Pennsylvania State University

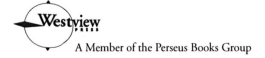

Westview
PRESS

A Member of the Perseus Books Group

Copyright © 2001 by Westview Press, A Member of the Perseus Books Group

Published in 2001 in the United States of America by Westview Press, 5500 Central Avenue, Boulder, Colorado 80301-2877, and in the United Kingdom by Westview Press, 12 Hid's Copse Road, Cumnor Hill, Oxford OX2 9JJ

Find us on the World Wide Web at www.westviewpress.com

Performance based budgeting / Gerald J. Miller, W. Bartley Hildreth, Jack Rabin.
　　p.　cm. — (ASPA classics)
　Includes bibliographical references and index.
　ISBN 0-8133-9774-X
　1. Program budgeting—United States.　2. Budget—United States.　3. Local budgets—United States.　I. Miller, Gerald.　II. Hildreth, W. Bartley, 1949– .　III. Rabin, Jack, 1945– .　IV. Series.

HJ2031.5.U6 P467　2000
352.4'8214'0973—dc21

00-043789

The paper used in this publication meets the requirements of the American National Standard for Permanence of Paper for Printed Library Materials Z39.48-1984.

10　　9　　8　　7　　6　　5　　4　　3　　2　　1

CONTENTS

TABLES AND ILLUSTRATIONS

Figures

EDITOR BIOGRAPHIES

Gerald J. Miller is Associate Professor of Public Administration, Rutgers, the State University of New Jersey, Campus at Newark. The author of forty-five research articles and eighteen books, his work includes *Government Financial Management Theory*. His research and teaching cover the area of resource allocation and control, especially government budgeting and financial management.

* * *

W. Bartley Hildreth, Regents Distinguished Professor of Public Finance in the Hugo Wall School of Urban and Public Affairs and the W. Frank Barton School of Business at Wichita State University, is a prolific author, former city finance director, and member of the National Advisory Council of State and Local Budgeting.

* * *

Jack Rabin is Professor of Public Administration and Public Policy at the Pennsylvania State University at Harrisburg. He is the author/editor of nearly thirty books and editor of eight peer-reviewed journals. Rabin also is Executive Editor of the Marcel Dekker Public Administration and Public Policy book Series, the largest book series in the field.

INTRODUCTION

From budgeting's inception, public budgeteers have tried to connect funding decisions with accountability. Cleveland's idea of the budget-making process (1915) as a responsible executive openly questioned by representatives became the essence of Willoughby's view of the larger purpose of a budget (1918), namely, to conduct government in conformity with the will of the people. Burkhead (1961, 14) developed the idea of accountability:

> The budget was conceived as a major weapon for instilling responsibility in the governmental structure: the budget system rests on popular control; the budget will publicize what government is doing and make for an informed and alert citizenry; the budget will destroy the rule of invisible government.

Budgeteers also profess an obligation to broader goals: "to serve the public by upholding justice, ensuring law and order, providing a common defense, protecting the helpless, preserving the environment, and advancing the health and welfare of the public" (Caiden, 1998, 36). The question that follows for all of us in budgeting emerges immediately: How well has budgeting met professional standards of accountability, and how well has it achieved its broader obligations? With the reaction to the growth of government in an environment of mixed levels of economic growth, broad and fundamental changes brought about by globalization, and the evolving bases by which we judge a good and moral society, a crisis has developed in which views of government's role as necessary and important have come into doubt. Many reforms have been designed to reinstate the belief among taxpayers, citizens, and clients that governments perform well and spend money wisely.

Current reform efforts have striven to strengthen government accountability by tightening the link between budget decisions and government performance. The belief in tightening the link, widely held, rests on the idea that the public, recognizing and understanding the performance-funding linkage and the success professionals in the public sector have in achieving results, will see the public sector, and public managers, as a productive, necessary, and important part of society.

The current spate of reforms, which we call performance-based reforms, hail from some obvious places. Critics constantly beset governments with the complaint, Why can't you operate like a business? Many have rebutted the notion behind the question: by the very nature of their work, government managers aim for efficiency as only one goal among several. The fact remains that taxpayers, even politicians and managers, need a bottom line to tell them quickly whether their decisions are probably right or probably wrong and whether they are succeeding in their efforts to do their jobs well.

The Traditional Concentration on Communicating How Well We're Doing

Much of the taxpayer revolt and one major response to it, the "reinventing government" movement, stems from the public servants' extreme discomfort when they think traditionally and find that they do not know how to communicate how well or how poorly their work serves the public.

The history of efforts to bottom-line government operations goes back at least a century. Almost every decade has seen the introduction of federal efforts, usually as a commission of business people and academic experts, and now and then as a presidential initiative that plays well in the political arena, along with hundreds of state commissions and gubernatorial and legislative initiatives and thousands of local government efforts of the same kind. These various commissions and initiatives have all pointed out ways to strengthen budgeting while differing in what the budget focus should be.

Initially budgets focused on inputs or dollars, positions and salaries, materials, and supplies. This approach employed before-the-fact controls, a short-term horizon, and an emphasis on cutting waste and economizing. Later attention focused on outputs, or the tasks actually completed—immediately observable products and services related to the work done. Outputs data were supplemented by information on the desired quality, cost, and timeliness. The work was measured in terms of productivity, as the input-output ratio. The output emphasis lay on the process of work, as it proceeded, and forced managers to commit themselves to account for efficiency.

Later still, the focus broadened to outcomes. With the establishment of program budgeting, attention moved to goals actually met. That attention has homed in on two issues—measurability, or knowing that one has either achieved the goal or not, and validity, or knowing what difference achieving the goal itself would make. Cost-effectiveness and program effectiveness dominated the methods of judgment. Managers learned management techniques to achieve these outcomes, often without shedding their prior emphases and their efforts to economize (strong input controls) and to be efficient (strong work process controls).

What reforms all seem to do is to widen the scope for budgeting. The focus on inputs led to efforts to control budget increases and to control spending while executing the budget through structures, procedures, and people concerned with fraud, waste, and abuse. Output-focused budgets widened attention to management improvement or to the productivity and efficiency of programs. Finally, outcomes budgeting connected the process with policy formulation, strategic planning, program goal formulation, and program evaluation.

The Present Concern for Citizen Participation and Democratic Governance of Budgeting

One definition of the current problem—"We just do not know how to communicate how well we're doing at what we think the citizens want"— reflects an insider view. As many have observed, the citizen often is very far away from the issue of concern, the manager and elected official somewhere between citizen and issue (King, Feltey, and Susel, 1998). As tax revolts and citizen complaints have mounted, the issues that most citizens, managers, and officials are alarmed about have surfaced in the budget. The budget directly or indirectly reflects every issue, with a power to force action in the direction citizens desire. Citizens, having penetrated the budgeting process—a not inconsiderable task—have established their rightful place there.

The present performance-based reforms have focused attention more than ever on sharing information and decision making in budgeting. Sharing information about what governments do well, through performance measurement and reporting, can go a long way in reducing cynicism (Berman, 1997). Broader participation in trading off various goals and means to achieve them, as well as in developing performance measures, will yield better decisions and a sharing of risks among citizens, public managers, and elected officials.

Expansion to deal with inputs, outputs, and outcomes with citizen participation in understanding and framing issues characterizes budgeting at the beginning of the twenty-first century. Recommendations have come from the National Advisory Council on State and Local Budgeting, a group of state and local practitioners, elected officials, and academics backed by the Government Finance Officers Association and other local and state government budgeting and management professional organizations. More prominently, President Clinton and Vice President Gore implemented the National Performance Review, and Congress passed the Government Performance and Results Act of 1993.

What Is a Budget?

The current reform efforts reflect similar concerns in the private sector. A private-sector model of budgeting takes a definite input-output-outcome form (Lazere, 1998; Churchill, 1984; Hax and Majluf, 1984; Knight, 1981; Trapani, 1982). First, forecasts of the economy, regulations governing business, and markets—customers and competitors—establish some horizon of opportunities and threats. Strategic goal setting follows with analysis of organization strengths and weaknesses. The result is the formulation of specific goals, including what market share the business and its business units can achieve over five or so years and what new business units might be created with what new products or services. The goals translate into annual or tactical performance plans—essentially what and who should do what this year. Plans include targets so that one knows whether one is making progress in achieving strategic business unit goals. The business unit also establishes measurable outputs and outcomes, called substantive and financial scorecards, weighting them in such a way that they balance emphasis and focus attention as intended. Budgets, in lump sum and having few process controls, follow plans and give considerable discretion to lower-level managers. Budgets also count in accrual terms, in that future spending is discounted to the present. Finally, individual employee performance plans follow from annual plans. Just as important, these individual plans and their measurable objectives tie into each individual's compensation. Needless to say, finance underlies and integrally relates all of these components: What does it cost and how much will that cost lever in earnings? The private-sector budget model differs from the public-sector model we have known. There is accrual of spending and a multiyear period that budgets must span; previously hidden future spending is recorded in the present. Present decisions must accord with long-term goals. Structures are decentralized and budgets lump sums, especially where performance measures are adequate, policies farsighted, and managers adept.

In comparison, what have reformers proposed as criteria for a good, modern, government budget? According to the National Advisory Council on State and Local Budgeting (1997), a budget should clearly define policy direction; translate taxes and revenues received into concrete levels of service; show consequences of increases or decreases in service and communicate this to stakeholders; facilitate control over expenditures; motivate and give feedback to employees; and evaluate employee and organization performance and make adjustments.

A similar picture develops in the operation of the Government Performance and Results Act of 1993 (Radin, 1998), and likewise in state and local results acts and executive orders (Melkers and Willoughby, 1998). Implementation of the federal act began only recently but emphasizes program results and holding federal government agencies accountable for them. The act focuses managers' attention on setting goals, measuring program performance against those goals, and reporting publicly on progress made. Obviously one of the foremost purposes of the act is to instill confidence in the public about federal government managers' ability to solve problems and meet citizen-taxpayers' needs.

To implement the federal Results Act, each agency must first develop strategic plans covering a period of at least five years. The strategic plan must include a mission statement, outcome-related measurable goals and objectives, and plans that agency managers and professionals intend to follow to achieve these goals through their activities and through their human, capital, information, and other resources. Those in the agency must consult Congress and others interested in or affected by the plans; in other words, they must consult stakeholders. As with the private-sector budget model, agency managers and professionals must develop annual performance plans that include performance indicators that will cover relevant outputs, service levels, and outcomes. With these performance plans, "Congress intended . . . to establish a direct annual link between plans and budgets" (GAO, 1999, 3) and to capture the long-range implication of choices and decisions with new methods of recognizing and measuring transactions in the budget (GAO, 2000; see also GASB, 1999). The U.S. Office of Management and Budget in the Executive Office of the President consolidates these measures in the federal budget each year. Agency managers and professionals provide, in annual performance reports to Congress, information on how well they have achieved their goals and performance measures in the previous fiscal year. Thus, from both private and public prototype budgets and guidelines, we find more emphasis on strategic planning with measurable results, annual plans with measurable results, costed-out annual plans or performance budgets, and plans broken down ultimately to the individual level with the goal of compensating individuals accordingly.

Given the history of reform movements in the United States at all levels of government, we may ask, how is this reform similar to the past? Larkey and Devereux (1999, 167) categorize past reforms in five different ways:

> First there are the rationalizing reforms that emphasize enhanced analysis and reason. Second, there are ad hoc norms such as balance and annularity that have been evolving over the last 150 years or so in Western democracies and have been expressed in a variety of administrative reforms. Third, there are democratizing reforms that seek to open the decision processes to inform and involve citizens better. Fourth, there are power shifting reforms such as line-item vetoes that adjust authority and responsibility for budgeting, particularly

between executives and legislatures. Fifth, there are control reforms such as auditing, tax limitations, and balanced budget amendments that attempt to impose external constraints on decisional behaviors.

These budget process reforms, with their emphasis on economic analysis of costs and benefits or marginal utility, especially Planning, Programming Budgeting System (PPBS) and zero-based budgeting (ZBB), belong to the rationalizing reforms category. The concepts of budget balance, comprehensiveness, and annularity belong to the ad hoc norm tradition. Freedom of information and sunshine laws are part of the democratizing movement. The line-item veto is one of a number of reforms in the power shifting tradition, in which reform shifted some element of control among executives, legislators, and public managers. The fifth tradition, greater control, usually developed to address "the problems of fraud, waste, and abuse in the handling of public money . . . [with] audits auditing the auditors who audit the auditors, all overseen by legislators looking for political advantage and a sporadically attentive public" (1999, 178).

The performance-based reforms, however, combine elements of all five movements. Additional elements cover the inclusion of planning, relative value comparisons, and productivity analysis. Ad hoc norms among performance-based reforms include what Larkey and Devereux call "decisional efficiency," primarily the savings in time and effort that come with decentralization, and "feasible comparisons"—the stimulation of competition or cooperation, as appropriate, among agencies in solving particular problems. Democratizing reforms come from the wider scope of accountability problems the reforms try to tackle with explicit attention to greater stakeholder and citizen participation and involvement. Power-shifting reforms entail broad decentralization of power over budgets, implicit incentives to reallocate funds from lower to higher priority programs, and the retention of savings when improvements in efficiency provide them. Finally, performance-based reforms produce a reversal of the traditional reform emphasis on increasing input controls to provide greater output controls. Thus, performance-based reforms clearly signal a massive effort to reform government.

The present concern for results or performance nevertheless builds on the past while contributing much that is new. According to Cothran (1993, 450),

the latest trends in budgeting contain elements of the earlier reforms. They contain performance measures from performance budgeting, functional categories from program budgeting, negotiation of objectives from management by objectives, and ranking of objectives from zero-base budgeting. But there are some differences between the old reforms and the latest ones. The latter are generally simpler, more streamlined, and require less paperwork and analysis. They involve more discretion by line managers than did the earlier reforms, and there is a much greater emphasis on accountability than under the older formats. Finally, the recent reforms are motivated by a desire to change fundamentally the culture of public management by turning bureaucrats into entrepreneurs. Previous budgetary reforms pursued legality, efficiency, and effectiveness. The present wave of budgetary reform aims to stimulate motivation. The new approaches incorporate most of the goals of the previous reforms, but they seek to achieve them through decentralized incentives that give program managers greater authority to combine resources as they think best but that hold the managers accountable for the results.

The performance-based reforms also have come at a time of clashing national priorities and movements at all levels of government. The setting for reform has been a period of change that has seen budget cutting and surplus dividing, sometimes at the same time, making this a different era for reform. As Radin observes (1998, 311), "[The Results Act accentuates] planning. The tradition of planning is embedded in an era of growth; plans are most often used as a way to choose new directions or to expand programs." Strategic plans in performance-based reforms, therefore, must deal with issues not as new initiatives added to existing programs but as reallocations that eliminate an existing program if a new one is proposed.

The nature of government service delivery now runs counter to the direction traditional reforms took. Devolution and privatization, compounding the existing fragmentation in decision making, play against strategic planning's usual emphasis on centralization. The fundamental nature of entitlements and block grants reduces much of the budget's ability to force compliance with state and national spending and performance priorities.

The mixed ideological motives of those who support performance-based reforms also looms large. Again, Radin observes (1998, 311–312, quoting Shin, 1997): "It is clear that some proponents of the legislation are those who advocate good government for its own sake, but . . . '[while] performance measures could give an agency that's targeted for extinction proof of its effectiveness, such standards could also provide Members [of Congress] determined to sink an agency just the ammo they need'."

Performance-based reforms deal widely with organization change, so why the emphasis on budget reform too? From the earliest days of management improvement programs, and especially with recent efforts to reinvent government programs and organizations and orient them to getting results, budgeting has played an integral role. Consider this range of opinions why: First, no other decision-making system has the leverage to pressure departments to improve program management like the budget. Second, the budget process has always been and always will be the place where everyone raises questions of the efficiency, economy, effectiveness, productivity, impact, and results of government activities. Third, the power of the purse is a formidable weapon in getting results. And, finally, only budget offices can stimulate, goad, and even inspire agencies to strengthen their programs, operating systems, and organizational structures (Schick, 1966; Caiden, 1998).

Overall, the aim of Results Acts is high, intuitive, and in keeping with traditional reform ideas of accountability and governance. The aim is high given the consolidation of information that a performance budget would provide—everything everyone accomplished, how they accomplished it, and how much it cost. The aim is intuitive, as Niskanen simply states (1971, 42): "[A] bureau that performs better than expected is likely to be rewarded by higher future budgets." The aim is in keeping with traditional reform in that "systematic presentation of performance information alongside budget amounts will improve budget decision-making" (GAO, 1999, 2).

The Lack of a Budgetary Theory

The budget theory underlying Results Acts is not beyond dispute, however, and therein lies the eventual path these performance-based reforms will take toward budgeting success or failure. Since empirical research began to accumulate, some have warned budgeteers to "avoid too good results" (Wildavsky, 1964, 93). Why?

> The danger of claiming superb accomplishments is that Congress and the Budget Bureau may reward the agency by ending the program. "Why would you need five more people in the supervisory unit?" John Rooney inquired of the Justice Department. "Since you are doing so well, as we have heard for fifteen minutes, you surely do not need any more supervision." However good it may be said that results are, it is advisable to put equal stress on what remains to be done. "Progress has been realized in the past," the Civil Defense agency asserted, "but we cannot permit these past accomplishments to lull us into a false sense of security (Wildavsky, 1964, 93).

At least one empirical test confirms Wildavsky's view and rejects Niskanen's assertion (Warren, 1975). Other budget behavior observers, such as Schick (1978, 179), have agreed, pointing out that the "budget process conventionally confronts managers with the uncomfortable risk of a loss of funds if they try to purge inefficiencies from their agencies." The fact that an agency performs well does not inform the decision about the need for additional resources: "[S]hould it be provided with more resources to do an even better job, or should it be cut back on the grounds that its purpose has been achieved and it is no longer needed? ... If a program is doing badly, and showing few results, does this mean it should be terminated, or provided with more resources to do a better job?" (Caiden, 1998, 44). In broader issues of resource allocation, Caiden finds performance somewhat irrelevant in deciding "whether a given sum of money is too little, too much, or just right to preserve a species, operate a system of trauma centers, or monitor or control contagious diseases." Political popularity and the necessity of balancing budgets often become the sole reasons for budget decisions. In addition, the technology of performance measurement has not, on the whole, developed beyond the superficial.

Joyce (1993) nevertheless predicts slow but eventual acceptance of performance-based reforms and budgets. He notes (p. 14) that many governments' experiences suggest limited success using performance information for anything more than understanding trade-offs. For an example, he argues that

> if the choice were between a job training and an air pollution program, we might know that adding $100 million more to the EPA budget would make the air cleaner by X amount, while costing Y amount of lost wages from workers who had not been trained. If we had all of these data (and we believed them), that would make decisions more informed; it would not necessarily make the choices easier.

Given how budgeting works now, many find performance-based reforms success hard to envision. Joyce, for one (1993, 14), says, "A system that affords less control over individual line items in order to hold agencies solely accountable for results would be a fundamental change from the current system." The current budget system tends to encourage micromanagement of resources by political leaders rather than the macromanagement of values that Key (1940) suggests as the sole prerogative and most important function of politics.

How, then, will performance-based reforms influence budgets? Joyce argues that eventual acceptance will come as the result of "a culture change" brought about by valid information—to which we would add agreed-upon measures of results, clearly articulated authorizations and appropriations, and the delegation of management to public administrators whose discretion the budget rewards. This is a tall order.

Reforms will also change budgeting by not forcing performance information into a decisive role in budgeting but forcing budgeteers to oversee management improvements. The reforms have forced management improvement functions into the budget office when federal, state, and local government budget offices became OMBs—offices of management and budget. At the same time, budget offices have become more independent of finance offices—traditionally the tax collection, accounting, purchasing, debt management, and budgeting office, and more allied with the chief administrative or operating officer or the chief executive officer. Questions quickly emerge about the capacity of a budget office—possibly knowledgeable about costs and concerned most with overall spending and tax levels—to review managerial issues and performance. Can a budget office cope with management improvement on top of budget examination and control? Should the budget manager be responsible for management improvement? Hildreth (1983) suggests that existing professional disclosure standards, with which most financial officers are quite familiar, serve as a ready basis for productivity analysis, making many aspects of performance-based management reform amenable to existing technologies and ways of thinking.

Others are not as optimistic and even see a period in which budget offices may drift and lose their comfortable anchors. At the federal level, the Results Act came after reductions on the management side in the U.S. Office of Management and Budget (Moe, 1994). What will budget officers do? According to Schick (1990, 33),

> [t]he old controller role is slipping away and, along with it, the leverage that budget officials exercised over departments as well as a part of their data base for monitoring expenditures. Central staff understand that it does not suffice for them to make the big decisions while ceding all the details to spenders. They hope that performance measures will substitute for the lost information and controls while giving them an important niche in the management process. Yet they are not sure things will work out this way. While the budget offices . . . generally support decentralization, they worry that the new performance-based system will leave them without effective roles or controls. They are not confident that performance measurement will go beyond technique to the behavior of managers. Departments will "take the money and run," one budget official protested. But he also conceded that the old controls are no longer viable.

Thus decentralization and devolution as well as a results orientation in performance-based reforms are replacing traditional structures and institutions. The budget theory is not clear, although eventual use of performance information in budgeting seems likely.

What role budget offices will play and with what tools remain matters to be worked out over time. From Schick's analysis, it is possible to propose broad outlines, and four crucial roles suggest themselves so far. First, budget officers will become forecasters of far more phenomena to support agency planning and target setting, just as is typical of private sector budgeting. Second, budget officers will be asked at least to compile and probably to verify performance information. Third, budget officers will act to encourage the maximization of performance in spending choices. Finally, budget officers will play a greater role in the design of controls that force the identification of objectives and intended results in advance and ensure that the results managers obtain are achieved through lawful means.

Performance-based reforms have become a major movement and are now often compared with the reform movement at the last turn of the century. For budgeting, however, this reform movement resembles much that has happened in previous budget reform episodes. Budget offices in the past have changed from staffs of accountants to staffs of economists. Will they now be staffed with organization and management theorists, or will they be mere record keepers and reporters? Will the basic forces of budgetary decision making remain the same?

Focus of This Book and Overview of Its Contents

This book provides the classic ideas that underlie the reforms linking budgeting decisions with the performance of government agencies found in the journals sponsored by the American Society for Public Administration. The first section of the book provides the conceptual rationale for the linkage between performance and budgeting. The positive and negative aspects are laid out, the section closes with several reviews of current practices that provide something of an optimistic sense of eventual accomplishment.

The second section of the book deals directly with the issues related to performance-based budgeting and its relationship to larger management issues. We break down the parts of the performance model into three components—strategic planning, performance management, and pay-for-performance—and illustrate with discussion from the literature.

References

Berman, Evan (1997). Dealing with cynical citizens. *Public Administration Review* 57(2), 105–112.

Burkhead, Jesse (1961). *Government budgeting*. New York: Wiley.

Caiden, Naomi (1998). Public service professionalism for performance measurement and evaluation. *Public Budgeting and Finance* 18(2), 35–52.

Churchill, Neil C. (1984). Budget choice: Planning vs. control. *Harvard Business Review* 62(4), 150–164.

Cleveland, Frederick A. (1915). Evolution of the budget idea in the United States. *Annals of the American Academy of Political and Social Science*, 15–35.

Cothran, Dan A. (1993). Entrepreneurial budgeting: An emerging reform? *Public Administration Review* 53(5), 445–454.

General Accounting Office (GAO) (1999). *Performance budgeting: Initial agency experiences provide a foundation to assess future directions* (GAO/T-AIMD-GGD-99-216, July 1). Washington, DC: General Accounting Office.

General Accounting Office (GAO) (2000). *Accrual budgeting: Experiences of other nations and implications for the United States* (GAO/AIMD-00-57, February). Washington, DC: General Accounting Office.

Government Accounting Standards Board (GASB) (1999). *Statement No. 34: Basic financial statements—and management's discussion and analysis—for state and local governments.* Norwalk, CT: GASB.

Hax, Arnoldo C., and Nicholas S. Majluf (1984). The corporate strategic planning process. *Interfaces* 14(1), 47–60.

Hildreth, W. Bartley (1983). Applying professional disclosure standards to productivity financial analyses. *Public Productivity Review* 7(3), 269–287.

Joyce, Philip G. (1993). Using performance measures for federal budgeting: Proposals and prospects. *Public Budgeting and Finance* 13(4), 3–17.

Key, V. O. (1940). The lack of a budgetary theory. *American Political Science Review* 34, 1137–1144.

King, Cheryl Simrell, Kathryn M. Feltey, and Bridget O'Neill Susel (1998). The question of participation: Toward authentic public participation in public administration. *Public Administration Review* 58(4), 317–326.

Knight, Henry C. (1981). Budgeting: A contrast of preaching and practice. *Cost and Management* 55(6), 42–46.

Larkey, Patrick D., and Erik A. Devereux (1999). Good budgetary decision processes. In *Public management reform and innovation: Research, theory, and application*, ed. H. George Frederickson and Jocelyn M. Johnston. Tuscaloosa: University of Alabama Press, 166–188.

Lazere, Cathy (1998). All together now: Why you must link budgeting and forecasting to planning and performance. *CFO* 14(2), 28–36.

Melkers, Julia, and Katherine Willoughby (1998). The state of the states: Performance-based budgeting requirements in 47 out of 50. *Public Administration Review* 58(1): 66–73.

Moe, Ronald (1994). The reinventing government exercise: Misinterpreting the problem, misjudging the consequences. *Public Administration Review* 54(2): 111–122.

National Advisory Council on State and Local Budgeting (1997). *A framework for improved state and local government budgeting and recommended budget practices.* Chicago: Government Finance Officers Association.

Niskanen, William A. (1971) *Bureaucracy and representative government.* Chicago: Aldine-Atherton.

Radin, Beryl A. (1998). The Government Performance and Results Act (GPRA): Hydra-headed monster or flexible management tool." *Public Administration Review* 58(4), 307–315.

Schick, Allan (1966). The road to PPB. *Public Administration Review* 26(6), 243–258.

Schick, Allan (1978). The road from ZBB. *Public Administration Review* 38(2), 177–180.

Schick, Allan (1990). Budgeting for results: Recent developments in five industrialized countries. *Public Administration Review* 50(1), 26–34.

Shin, Annya (1997). On the front burner. *National Journal* 21 (June), 1289.

Trapani, Cosmo S. (1982). Six critical areas in the budgeting process. *Management Accounting* 64(5), 52–56.

Warren, Ronald S. (1975). Bureaucratic performance and budgetary reward. *Public Choice* 24, 51–57.

Wildavsky, Aaron (1964). *The politics of the budgetary process.* Boston: Little, Brown.

Willoughby, William F. (1918). *The movement for budgetary reform in the states.* New York: D. Appleton and Company for the Institute for Government Research.

Part I

Origins and Development

Introduction

Each route budget reform has taken has implied a rationale for budgeting and, therefore, a normative theory. This book first describes three basic normative theories for budgeting that have appeared. Lewis's "Toward a Theory of Budgeting" provides an *economic* rationale for budgeting. Lindblom's observations in "The Science of Muddling Through" yield a stark contrast to Lewis in creating an opposed *administrative* rationale for decisions (and, by implication, for budgeting). Finally, in "The Political Implications of Budget Reform," Wildavsky portrays budgeting as inherently *political*.

Beyond normative theories, accounts of actual reforms have appeared. In "The Road to PPB" Schick describes three stages of reform and provides a conceptual understanding of which normative theories gained ascendancy at what times. With a different view of reform and the routes taken, Wildavsky, in "Why the Traditional Budget Lasts," suggests less movement than a cursory observation would uncover.

Despite the ebb and flow of theory and reform, the bedrock question of what matters in budgeting remains: On what factors do budget outcomes depend? Grizzle, in "Does Budget Format Really Govern the Actions of Budget Makers?" surveys budget actors to determine whether the various budget reform frameworks or "formats" really have any influence on outcomes.

Budget reforms continue to unfold across the world, many taking the form of "results-oriented" budget processes. What is a results-oriented budget? Three observers provide answers. First, Schick looks at the reform movement in the West in "Budgeting for Results: Recent Developments in Five Industrialized Countries." Thompson delves deeply into federal budget reform in the United States following the National Performance Review in "Mission-Driven, Results-Oriented Budgeting: Fiscal Administration and the New Public Management" and proposes ways to make present budget practice "permissive, continuous, and selective." Finally, Cothran examines events at the local level in the United States, in "Entrepreneurial Budgeting: An Emerging Reform?"

Budgeting has often been the lever through which reform in government institutions, and particularly management practices, has sprung. Significant questions exist, however, about the present performance movement in government management and the place budgeting holds in its unfolding. Is results- or performance-oriented management—the new public management as Thompson called it—a reform that ignores budgeting? How friendly is budgeting as practiced with a performance or productivity emphasis? In various ways, Lauth ("Budgeting and Productivity in State Government: Not Integrated But Friendly"), Grizzle ("Linking Performance to Funding Decisions: What Is the Budgeter's Role?"), and Klay ("Management Through Budgetary Incentives") explain that budgeting at all levels of government exists for reasons of performance accountability as well as other, more fundamentally important reasons, such as control, particularly legislative control, of administration.

Section I.A

THEORY, CONCEPTUALIZATION, AND CRITIQUE

1

TOWARD A THEORY OF BUDGETING

Verne B. Lewis

The $64.00 question on the expenditure side of public budgeting is: On what basis shall it be decided to allocate X dollars to Activity A instead of allocating them to Activity B, or instead of allowing the taxpayer to use the money for his individual purposes? Over a decade ago V. O. Key called attention to the lack of a budgetary theory which would assist in arriving at an answer to this question.[1] Pointing out that budgeting is essentially a form of applied economics, since it requires the allocation of scarce resources among competing demands, Professor Key urged that this question be explored from the point of view of economic theory.

The purpose of this article is to analyze three propositions which are derived from economic theory[2] which appear to be applicable to public budgeting and to be appropriate building blocks for construction of an economic theory of budgeting. In brief, the three principles are:

1. Since resources are scarce in relation to demands, the basic economic test which must be applied is that the return from every expenditure must be worth its cost in terms of sacrificed alternatives. Budget analysis, therefore, is basically a comparison of the relative merits of alternative uses of funds.

1952. Toward a theory of budgeting. Lewis, Verne B. **Public Administration Review** 12 (Winter): 43–45.

2. Incremental analysis (that is, analysis of the additional values to be derived from an additional expenditure) is necessary because of the phenomenon of diminishing utility. Analysis of the increments is necessary and useful only at or near the margin; this is the point of balance at which an additional expenditure for any purpose would yield the same return.
3. Comparison of relative merits can be made only in terms of relative effectiveness in achieving a common objective.

Part I of this article will be devoted to consideration of these principles. In Part II a proposal, which will be called the alternative budget procedure, will be outlined and analyzed in terms of the three principles. Primary emphasis throughout will be placed on the applicability of concepts developed by the economists to methods of analyzing budget estimates. The discussion is pointed specifically at problems of the federal government; the general ideas, however, should be equally applicable to state and local governmental units.

I

Relative Value. Budget decisions must be made on the basis of relative values. There is no absolute standard of value. It is not enough to say that an expenditure for a particular purpose is desirable or worth while. The results must be worth their cost. The results must be more valuable than the results would be if the money were used for any other purpose.

Comparison of relative values to be obtained from alternative uses of funds is necessary because our resources are inadequate to do all the things we consider desirable and necessary. In fact, public budgeting is necessary only because our desires exceed our means. The desires of human beings are virtually unlimited. Although the supply of resources has been greatly expanded in recent decades, the supply is still short in relation to demands. It would be nice if we had enough to go around, but we do not have. Some demands can be met only in part, some not at all.

Scarcity of resources in relation to demands confronts us at every level of public budgeting. Public services consume scarce materials and manpower which have alternative uses. If used for governmental activities, they cannot be used for private purposes. If used for Activity A of the government, they cannot be used for Activity B. Expressed in terms of money, the problem of scarcity arises in connection with appropriations. As individual taxpayers, we put pressures on Congress to hold down federal taxes so that a larger proportion of our already inadequate personal incomes will be available to satisfy our individual desires. In view of these pressures, Congress usually appropriates less than is requested by the President and interest groups. The President in turn usually requests the Congress to appropriate less than the total of the estimates submitted to him by agency heads. Rarely does an agency have sufficient funds to do all the things it would like to do or that it is requested to do by citizen groups.

Confronted with limited resources, congressmen and administrative officials must make choices. The available money will buy this *or* that, but not *both*. On what basis should the choice be made?

The economists, who specialize in problems of scarcity, have a general answer to this question. It is found in the doctrine of marginal utility. This doctrine, as applied to public budgeting, has been formulated by Professor Pigou as follows:

> As regards the distribution, as distinct from the aggregate cost, of optional government expenditure, it is clear that, just as an individual will get more satisfaction out of his income by maintaining a certain balance between different sorts of expenditure, so also will a community through its government. The principle of balance in both cases is provided by the postulate that resources should be so distributed among different uses that the marginal return of satisfaction is the same for all of them. . . . Expenditure should be distributed between battleships and poor relief in such wise that the last shilling devoted to each of them yields the same real return. We have here, so far as theory goes, a test by means of which the distribution of expenditure along different lines can be settled.[3]

Other aspects of the marginal utility concept will be considered in later sections; here we want to note that this concept poses the problem in terms of relative values rather than absolutes. To determine the distribution of funds between battleships and poor relief we must weigh the relative value of the results to be obtained from these alternative uses. Is it worth while to spend an additional $1,000,000 for battleships? We can answer "yes" only if we think we would get more valuable results than would be obtained by using that $1,000,000 for poor relief.

When the economists approach the problem in terms of costs rather than results they arrive at the same conclusion. Fundamentally, as the economists indicate in their "opportunity" or "displacement" concept of costs, "the cost of a thing is simply the amount of other things which has to be given up for its sake."[4] If Robinson Crusoe finds he has time to build a house *or* catch some fish, but not *both*, the cost of the house is the fish he does not catch or vice versa. The cost of anything is therefore the result that would have been realized had the resources been used for an alternative purpose.

Of what significance from the point of view of budget analysis are these concepts of relative value and displacement cost? They indicate that the ba-

sic objective of budget analysis is the comparison of the relative value of results to be obtained from alternative uses of funds. If an analyst is convinced after reading the usual argument supporting a budget request that
the activity in question is desirable and necessary, his task has just begun.
To be justifiable in terms of making the most advantageous use of resources, the returns from an expenditure for any activity must be more desirable and more necessary than for any alternative use of the funds. On
the other hand, a budget request for an activity cannot legitimately be
turned down solely on the basis that the activity costs too much. Costs and
results must be considered together. The costs must be judged in relation to
the results and the results must be worth their costs in terms of alternative
results that are foregone or displaced.

Incremental Analysis. If the basic guide for budget analysis is that results
must be worth their costs, budget analysis must include a comparison of
relative values. How can such a comparison of values be made?

The marginal utility concept suggests a way of approaching the problem.
The method, briefly, is to divide available resources into increments and
consider which of the alternative uses of each increment would yield the
greatest return. Analysis of increments is necessary because of the phenomenon of diminishing utility. This means, roughly, that as we acquire more
and more units of anything, the additional units have less and less use
value. If enough units are acquired, an added unit may be of no value at all
and may even be objectionable. To illustrate, four tires on a car are essential, a fifth tire is less essential but is handy to have, whereas a sixth tire
just gets in the way. Although a sixth tire will cost as much as any of the
first five, it has considerably less use value. In deciding how many tires to
buy, we must therefore consider the use value to be derived from each *additional* tire.

Because of the phenomenon of diminishing utility, there is no point in
trying to determine the *total* or *average* benefits to be obtained from total
expenditures for a particular commodity or function. We must analyze the
benefits by increments. If one million bazookas make a valuable contribution toward winning a war, we cannot assume that the contribution would
be doubled if we had two million. Perhaps there are not enough soldiers to
use that many. No matter how valuable bazookas might be toward winning a war, a point would be reached sometime on the diminishing scale of
utility where additional expenditures for bazookas would be completely
wasted. Since we do not have enough resources to do all the things we
would like to do, we certainly should not produce anything that will not or
cannot be used.

But we cannot assume that we would make best use of resources even if
we produced no more bazookas than could be used. Perhaps the manpower and materials consumed in producing the last thousand bazookas

would serve a more valuable purpose if they were used for producing additional hand grenades or some other item. This reasoning leads us back to the basic criterion for deciding how much should be spent for each activity. We should allocate enough money for bazookas so that the last dollar spent for bazookas will serve as valuable a purpose as the last dollar for hand grenades or any other purpose. If more than this amount is spent for bazookas, we sacrifice a more valuable alternative use. Thus, as is suggested by the marginal utility theory, maximum returns can be obtained only if expenditures are distributed among different purposes in such a way that the last dollar spent for each yields the same real return.

The marginal utility concept also indicates that a comparison of incremental values is meaningful and necessary only at or near the margins. When analyzing the value of the returns by increments of expenditure near the margins we would ask: How much will be sacrificed if proposed expenditures for Function A are reduced by $1,000? Can efficiency be increased so that output will not have to be reduced? What would be the consequences of lowering standards of quality? Of reducing quantities? Of postponing some portion of the work?

When these issues are explored, the pay-off question can be tackled. Would the sacrifices be greater or less if the $1,000 cut is applied to Function B rather than to Function A? This question brings up the most difficult and most critical problem. How can the values of unlike functions be compared? How can the value of an atom bomb and cancer research be compared? Or public roads and public schools? So far we have not indicated how this question can be answered. We have only narrowed the field by indicating that the value of functions must be compared by increments rather than in total and that the value of increments need only be compared near the marginal point of balance. Incremental analysis at the margins is just a tool, though a useful one, we believe. It does not supply the answers, but it helps to focus attention on the real points at issue.

Relative Effectiveness. The relative value of different things cannot be compared unless they have a common denominator. The common aspect of an atom bomb and cancer research, of public roads and public schools, is the broad purpose each is designed to serve. These items, as well as all other public and private activities, are undertaken to serve human needs and desires. We can only compare their values by evaluating their relative effectiveness in serving a common objective.

To revert to a previously used example, we do not make bazookas just for the sake of making bazookas. We make them because they help win wars. Although bazookas, hand grenades, and K-rations are unlike things, they serve a common military purpose. The relative values of these items can be weighed in terms of their relative effectiveness in fighting a war. We do not fight wars for their own sake either. They are fought for a larger purpose of national security. Economic aid to foreign countries also serves this purpose. Since they share a common objective, the relative value of military activities and economic aid can also be compared in terms of their effectiveness in achieving this objective.

Let us take a different type of case which is less general and more tangible than national security. Purchasing officers and engineers perform quite different functions. Yet, if they are working in an organization which does construction work, for example, they share the common objective of that organization. Operating within a ceiling on total expenditures, the head of the agency might be faced with this question: Would a part of the money allocated to the procurement section yield greater returns if transferred to the engineering section? This question involves value comparisons of unlike things, whether for a private firm or for a government agency. Moreover, the firm or the agency usually cannot express the contributions of procurement officers and engineers in terms of precise numbers. Nevertheless, reasonable men who are reasonably well informed arrive at substantially the same answer to such questions provided the basic objective has been decided in advance. If the objective is to build a structure according to prescribed specifications in X months and at not to exceed Y dollars, this objective provides a common basis for evaluation. The answer will depend upon forecasts of facts and will also be influenced by relative need. For example, if design is on schedule but construction is being delayed because purchase orders are not being issued on schedule, additions to the procurement staff would probably yield greater returns than additions to the design staff. On the other hand, if design is behind schedule and, as a consequence, the procurement staff has no material requisitions to process, more design engineers would yield the greater return.

Evaluation in terms of relative effectiveness in achieving a common objective is, therefore, a second fundamental method of budget analysis.[5]

Evaluation in terms of common purposes is another way of saying that alternative means can be evaluated in terms of the end they are designed to achieve. That end can be considered, in turn, as a means of achieving a broader end. This process requires, of course, that the ultimate ends be somehow established. How can these fundamental decisions be made? In a democracy we are not so much concerned with how they are made as by whom they are made. The ideal of democracy is that the desires of the people, no matter how they are arrived at or how unwise they may be, should control the actions of the government. The representatives of the people in Congress make the fundamental decisions as to the ultimate aims of governmental services. These decisions, in the form of laws and appropriation acts, provide the basis for economic calculation by administrative agencies in the same way as consumer action in the market place provides the basis for decisions in the private economy.

We now have some basic elements of an economic theory of budgeting. The economic aim of budgeting is to achieve best use of our resources. To meet this test, the benefits derived from any expenditure must be worth their cost in terms of sacrificed or displaced alternatives. As a first step in applying that test, we can use incremental analysis at the margins as a means of concentrating attention at the areas where comparison of values is necessary and meaningful. These values can be compared by determining their relative effectiveness in achieving a common purpose. Analysis in terms of common purposes requires a set of basic premises which are found in the ultimate ends or purposes established by the Congress acting for the people. This means that Congress is charged by the people with the basic responsibility for deciding what constitutes the "best use of resources," so far as the federal government is concerned.

Practical Limitations. Although the propositions outlined above concerning relative value, incremental analysis, and relative effectiveness constitute, in a sense, a formula for budget analysis which appears to be theoretically sound, the formula is not always easy to apply. Precise numbers to use in the equations are frequently unavailable. Although the formula will work in a theoretically valid manner, even if one has to guess the numbers to put into the equation, the practical usefulness of the answers will depend upon the accuracy of the numbers.

One area where firm numbers are hard to get involves forecasts of future needs and conditions. As we have noted, value is a function of need and need changes from time to time. In comparing the relative value of guns and butter, for example, we will strike a balance between them at different points at different times depending upon whether we are engaged in a hot war, a cold war, or no war at all. The balance between public health and police will be struck at one point if communicable diseases are rampant at a time when the traffic accident rate is low. The balance will be struck at a different point if the state of public health is good but the accident rate is alarming.

Budgetary decisions have to be based not only on relative needs as they are today but also on forecasts of what the needs will be tomorrow, next year, or in the next decade. The point is illustrated most dramatically by the decision made by the federal government during World War II to try to develop an atomic bomb. At the time, no one knew whether a bomb could be made, or if it could be made in time to help win the war. Hence, the government in deciding to divert tremendous quantities of scarce resources to this purpose had to take a calculated risk. Its decision was based not on firm facts but on forecasts and hopes as to the values to be realized.

There are probably as many budget arguments over forecasts of needs as there are over the relative merits of the expenditures which are proposed to meet those needs.

Not only must budget decisions be based, in some cases, on sheer guesses as to future needs and future accomplishments, but oftentimes the nature of governmental activities is such that accomplishments in relation to costs cannot be precisely measured even after the fact. How can one tell, for example, how much fire damage was prevented for each $1,000 spent by the fire department for fire prevention?

Perhaps it was the frequent difficulty in obtaining precise numbers that led Professor Key to question the applicability of the marginal utility theory to public budgeting. He concluded:

> ... The doctrine of marginal utility, developed most finely in the analysis of the market economy, has a ring of unreality when applied to public expenditures. The most advantageous utilization of public funds resolves itself into a matter of value preferences between ends lacking a common denominator. As such, the question is a problem of political philosophy. . . .[6]

Whether firm numbers are available or not, judgments and decisions have to be made. The lack of precise numbers does not invalidate the basic principles or methods of calculation which we have outlined. The methods have to be judged on the basis of whether or not they lead to proper conclusions *if* it is assumed that the numbers used in the equations are the right ones. Obtaining the right numbers, though a fundamental and difficult problem, is separate and distinct from the problem of developing methods of calculation.

On the other hand, Professor Key may have been questioning the basic principle. It is perfectly true, as Key points out, that budgeting involves questions of value preferences which must be based on philosophy rather than science or logic. We agree that it is a problem for philosophers, but not exclusively, since the methods of the economists can also be applied. The problem of value has long been one of the central topics on the agenda of the economists. They do not approach the problem from the point of view of trying to develop an absolute standard of value or from the point of view of trying to prescribe which ends, goals, or objectives men should strive for. Rather they concentrate on methods to be used to achieve the most valuable use of scarce resources as judged by whatever standard of value men embrace. While the philosopher helps us decide which goals we should strive for, the economist helps us achieve those goals most efficiently. Thus, I believe, the economists' approach to the problem of value as expressed in the marginal utility theory can be accepted as a useful approach for public budgeting.

The views outlined in this article concerning the applicability of the methods of the economists to public budgeting run sharply counter to the views of some economists. Ludwig von Mises, for example, contends, in his book *Bureaucracy,*[7] that there is no method of economic calculation which can be applied to government. It can be shown, I think, that the problem in government, so far as it exists, arises out of the lack of firm numbers rather than out of the lack of a method.

Dr. Mises' central argument is that bureaucrats have no means of calculating the relative usefulness of governmental activities because these activities have no price in the market place. Therefore, he contends, government agencies have no criterion of value to apply. In private business, he points out (p. 26), "the ultimate basis of economic calculation is the valuation of all consumers' goods on the part of all the people" in the market place. Further, "economic calculation makes it possible for business to adjust production to the demands of the consumers." (p. 27) On the other hand, he argues, ". . . if a public enterprise is to be operated without regard to profits, the behavior of the public no longer provides a criterion of its usefulness." (p. 61) Therefore, he concludes, "the problem of bureaucratic management is precisely the absence of such a method of calculation." (p. 49)

We can agree with the part of his argument that says market prices provide a criterion of value which serves as a basis for economic calculation in private business; but we cannot agree that government agencies are completely lacking such a criterion. As has been noted, appropriations, like market prices, indicate in quantitative terms how much the representatives of the people are willing to pay for goods and services rendered by the government. In appropriating funds, congressmen express their attitudes concerning the usefulness of governmental activities as definitely as individuals do when they buy bread at the corner bakery. Congressmen, in effect, are serving as purchasing agents for the American people.

What function does the market price criterion serve in determining whether an activity is worth its cost? One function is to provide the numbers necessary for determining how the cost of doing a particular job can be reduced to a minimum. Nothing, of course, is worth its cost if the same result can somehow be achieved at a lower cost. Market prices are as useful in government as they are in business in this regard. In constructing a road, a building, or a dam—even in running an office—the government has to pay market prices for the raw material and manpower it uses just as a private businessman does. If the guide to economic calculation is the market price, the government engineer has numbers to put into his equations just as his engineering brother in private industry has. Market prices provide the data he needs to calculate which combination of available materials, men, and machines will be least costly.

After all corners have been cut and the cost of doing a job has been reduced to the minimum, we face a broader question. Is the job worth doing? Dr. Mises undoubtedly would answer that a job is worth doing in private business if it yields a profit. In attempting to calculate whether a given activity will yield a profit, a businessman, however, faces some of the problems faced by government. He has to forecast market conditions. The numbers he forecasts may or may not be right. Likewise, a businessman cannot always determine even after the fact whether an individual activity has been profitable or not. No method has yet been found, for example, of measuring precisely how much of a company's profit or loss results from such activities as advertising, research, and employee welfare programs. Moreover, a businessman, if he wants to maximize profits, cannot engage in an activity just because it is profitable. It must be more profitable than alternative activities open to him. Thus, he is faced with the same problem of relative value as is the government official. Suppose it costs $1.00 a pound to recover scrap materials in a private factory and that the scrap can be sold on the market for $1.10 a pound, thereby yielding a profit of 10 per cent. Does it automatically follow that the scrap should be recovered? Not at all, since the firm might make a profit of 20 per cent if the men and materials were used instead for making new products.

The method of calculation by a government agency for a similar situation would be exactly the same. In fact, if government appropriations specified precisely the quantities, quality, standards, and maximum permissible unit prices for each government service, the problem of economic calculation would not only be exactly the same but the answers could be expressed in terms of a profit equivalent. If the agency could produce at a lower unit cost than specified by Congress, the funds saved would be comparable to profit and would be returned to the Treasury as a dividend to the taxpayers.

In many cases, however, government services are of such a nature that Congress cannot enact precise specifications. For example, the production of plutonium by the Atomic Energy Commission has not yet reached the stage where such specifications can be written. Congress, in effect, tells the commission to produce as much plutonium as it can, according to specifications deemed most suitable by the commission, with a total expenditure of not to exceed X million dollars. The commission then has no basis of knowing exactly what dollar value is placed on a pound of plutonium by the Congress. Nevertheless, the commission is not without means of making economic decisions. The problem might be to decide whether it is worth spending Y dollars to recover scrap plutonium which accumulates during the manufacturing process. The decision can be made on the basis of comparison of alternative means of accomplishing a common objective. This objective is to produce the maximum amount of usable plutonium during a specified period within the limits of available funds and other resources. In the light of this objective the commission can afford to spend as much per pound for recovery as it has to spend to produce a pound of new plutonium. If it spent either more or less than this amount, the total usable quantity of plutonium produced during a period would be less than the potential maximum. Faced with this kind of problem, a private business would calculate in precisely the same way. The common objective of new production and recovery operations might be expressed in terms of dollars of profit rather than pounds of product, but the answer would be the same.

When the problem facing the government involves activities such as education, foreign relations, and public recreation where the goals are less tangible, where the results are less subject to measurement, and where the amount of results arising from an increment of expenditures is more difficult to determine, the numbers used in the equations will be less firm. Even so, we conclude, Dr. Mises arguments notwithstanding, that the differences between business and government in economic calculation lie not so much in the methods of calculation as in the availability of precise numbers with which to calculate.

II

In the foregoing analysis of economic ideas in relation to public budgeting, we have stressed the importance of looking upon budgeting as a problem of relative values and have examined the applicability of two methods—incremental analysis and evaluation of relative effectiveness in achieving a common objective—to budget analysis.

On the administrative implications of these ideas, Professor Key has said, "Perhaps the approach toward the practical working out of the issue lies in canalizing of decisions through the governmental machinery so as to place alternatives in juxtaposition and compel consideration of relative values."[8]

The budget machinery of the federal government does accomplish this purpose. The federal budget forces a simultaneous, or nearly simultaneous, consideration of all the competing claims by the President and the Congress. Moreover, at each level in the administrative hierarchy, the budget forces consideration of the relative merits of competing claims within each jurisdiction.[9]

Budget estimates and justifications are rarely prepared in a manner, however, which makes it easy to compare relative merits. We shall, therefore, now outline a budget system designed to facilitate such comparisons and to apply other ideas derived from the preceding economic analysis. After outlining this system, we shall compare it with other budget methods now being used.

The system to be described will be called the alternative budget system. Under this procedure, each administrative official who prepares a budget estimate, either as a basis for an appropriation request or an allotment request after the appropriation is made, would be required to prepare a basic budget estimate supplemented by skeleton plans for alternative amounts. If the amount of the basic estimate equals 100, the alternatives might represent, respectively, 80, 90, 110, and 120 per cent of that amount. The number of alternatives might vary with the situation. Ordinarily, three alternatives would seem to secure a sufficient range of possibilities. In the interest of providing a safety valve, each subordinate might be permitted to prepare one or more additional alternative budgets totaling more than the top figure prescribed by his superior. In order to focus attention on problems near the margins, the amounts of the alternative budgets should range from a little less than the lowest amount that is likely to be approved to a little more than the recommended amount. Increments of 10 per cent might be appropriate in some cases; larger or smaller increments might be required in others.

The establishment of the alternative levels would have to start with the President. He would select several alternative levels of overall governmental expenditure, and he would establish corresponding alternative levels for each department or agency. The head of each department or agency would, in turn, establish alternative levels for each of his subordinates which would be consistent with the prescribed departmental levels.

In preparing the alternative budgets, the subordinate official would first indicate, as he does under present procedures, the nature, quantity, and quality of services his agency could render the taxpayers if the amount of the basic budget were approved. In addition, he would indicate the recommended revisions in the plan of service for each of the alternative amounts and the benefits or sacrifices which would result.

At each superior level the responsible official would review the alternative proposals submitted by his several subordinates and select from them the features that would be, in his opinion, the most advantageous to the taxpayers for each alternative amount set for him by the next highest organization level. Finally, the President would submit alternative budgets to the Congress. At this level the alternatives would reflect the major issues involved in determining the work program for the entire government.

The advantages of the alternative budget procedure will be brought out by comparing it with other budget methods and techniques now in use. For convenience, the other techniques will be labeled (a) open-end budgeting, (b) fixed-ceiling budgeting, (c) work measurement and unit costing, (d) increase-decrease analysis, (e) priority listings, and (f) item-by-item control. These methods are not mutually exclusive; some of them could very well be incorporated as features of the alternative budget plan. Some are used primarily in budget estimating, others in budget control.

Open-End Budgeting. Some agencies of the federal government (and in some years the Bureau of the Budget) permit subordinate officials to submit a single budget estimate for whatever amount the subordinate decides to recommend. This method has been used not only for preparing requests for appropriations but also for submission of allotment requests to agency heads after the appropriations have been made. This single estimate represents, by and large, the official's judgment as to optimum program for his agency for the ensuing year, tempered perhaps by his judgment as to what the traffic will bear in view of the general political and economic climate existing at the time. No restrictions are placed on him; the sky is the limit so far as the amount he can request is concerned. For this reason, we have selected the short title "open-end budgeting" as being descriptive of this method.

In the justification for such a budget estimate, the official, in effect, says, "I think it is desirable (or important, or essential) that the taxpayers be given the services outlined in this budget. Such a program will cost X dollars. Any reductions in the amount requested will deprive the public of exceedingly valuable services." While such general statements are, of course, backed up by more-or-less specific facts and figures, the information provided leaves many gaps from the point of view of what the superior official needs in order to weigh the importance of each dollar requested by one subordinate against each dollar requested by other subordinates.

Statements which merely prove that a program is desirable do not fulfill the needs of a superior who is faced with the necessity of reducing the total amount requested by the subordinates, not because he thinks the requests are for undesirable or unnecessary purposes, but simply because the pattern is too big for the cloth. The subordinate's budget estimates and justifications, submitted to him under the open-end procedure, are deficient because they do not indicate specifically how plans would be changed if a smaller amount were available or specifically the subordinate's judgment as to the consequences of such a change in plans. Almost the entire burden, then, of ascertaining where the reductions can be made with the least harmful consequences is placed on the superior official, who naturally is less well informed on the details than are his subordinates.

In what way would the assistance rendered by the subordinate to his superior be enhanced if the alternative budget method were used? Under any circumstances the contribution of a subordinate official is limited by the fact that he is concerned with a segment rather than with the whole. His advice as to how much should be appropriated for his particular sphere of activities obviously cannot be accepted without careful scrutiny. He lacks information about other activities which would be necessary to make a comparison of relative importance. Even if he had complete information, he would be quite unique if he did not place a higher valuation on his own activities than others do. This generalization is borne out by the fact that the aggregate of requests from subordinate officials is invariably more than the public, acting through Congress, is willing to devote to public services.

The subordinate administrative official can be expected, however, to make a substantial contribution in advising the Congress and the President on the relative merits of competing demands within his own jurisdiction, even though he cannot be expected to weigh those demands against demands in other jurisdictions. The subordinate official can perform an indispensable service by comparing the relative effectiveness of each activity in achieving the goals of his agency and by indicating how he thinks any specified amount of money can best be distributed among the programs of his agency. His service in this respect is valuable not only because considerable technical knowledge and experience usually is required as a basis for arriving at such judgments, but also because the pressure of time may force the President and the Congress to rely greatly on his judgment.

This phase of the contribution of the subordinate official to budget making is comparable to services I can get from an architect if I should decide to build a house. The architect's advice as to whether I should spend eight, twelve, or sixteen thousand dollars for a house is not very helpful. On the other hand, the architect can be very helpful in advising me as to how I can get the most of what I want in a house for any given sum I choose to spend.

Another way in which a subordinate can be of service is in advising his superiors on probable gains or losses from appropriating more or less for his portion of the government's work. This kind of contribution is comparable to the assistance an architect can render by analyzing the additional features in a house which can be obtained for each increment of cost, and by indicating the features that would have to be sacrificed if costs were reduced by specified amounts.

Alternative budgets prepared by subordinates would take advantage of both of these types of assistance. The subordinate would indicate his judgment as to the best way of using several alternative amounts and in addition he would analyze the benefits to be gained by each increment of funds.

Fixed-Ceiling Budgeting. If the open-end procedure is one extreme, the fixed-ceiling method represents the opposite pole. Under this plan, a fixed-ceiling is established in advance which the subordinate's budget estimate cannot exceed. Such a ceiling creates for the subordinate a situation similar to that facing the President if he should decide to recommend a balanced budget. Then the amount of anticipated revenues constitutes the ceiling on the amount of expenditures he can recommend.

Whatever the merits, or lack thereof, of allowing revenues to determine the total amount to be spent by the government, working to a set ceiling does have the advantage of forcing consideration at the presidential level of relative merits to a greater extent than is likely to prevail under open-end budgeting. In open-end budgeting, it is easy to keep adding items that appear to be desirable and thereby pass the buck to the next level of review in the event the total cost of the "desirable" items exceeds an acceptable figure. But prescribing a single fixed ceiling in advance for subordinate levels of the executive branch involves the danger of judging a case before the evidence is heard. The basic reason for requiring estimates from subordinate officials is that higher officials do not have enough detailed information, time, or specialized skill to prepare the plans themselves. How can these officials judge the merits of the experts' plans before they are submitted? In setting the ceiling figures in advance, how can one be sure that the ceiling for one function is not set too high and the ceiling for another too low?

The alternative budget plan, like the fixed-ceiling practice, forces consideration of relative merits within a given amount at each organization level, but the final decision as to amount does not have to be made by the superior until the evidence is in.

Work Load Measurement and Unit Costing. Increasing emphasis has been placed in recent years on work load measurement and unit costing for budgetary purposes. The ultimate goal is to devise units of work and to determine unit costs wherever possible so that budget requests can be stated in this fashion: "It costs X dollars to perform each unit of this type of work. If you want us to perform 100 units, the cost will be 100 times X dollars. If you want only 50 units the cost will be 50 times X dollars."

This approach is useful for budgeting in many situations. It supplies some of the numbers needed for the economic calculation discussed in Part I above. Precise, quantitative measures, if pertinent and feasible, are better than vague generalities. Some budget questions cannot be answered, however, in terms of work load and unit cost data. These data will show how many units are being done, but not how many should be done. They show what unit costs are, but not what they should be. They may or may not give an indication of the quality of the work, but they leave unanswered the question of the proper quality standards.

A further limitation on use of work load measurement is that the end product of many agencies is not measurable by any means yet devised. In other cases, the amount of work performed is not a measure of its significance or value. Some work is stand-by in character. Some facilities, for example, are maintained to meet emergencies if and when they arise. In such cases the less work there is to be done the better. Much of the work of military agencies and fire-fighters is of this type. In other cases, too, the amount of work performed is inadequate as an index of results. This is true with respect to many research projects and enforcement activities. In the case of research, it is the final result that counts, not the amount of work required to achieve the result. In enforcement work, the number of infractions dealt with is not an adequate measure since the ideal would be to have no infractions at all.

Lacking an adequate way of measuring or even identifying the end product in precise terms, it is still possible in many cases to develop significant measures of work load of subsidiary activities that contribute to the end product. Examples are number of letters typed, miles patrolled, or purchase orders processed. Detailed data of this type are useful in budgeting but their use is largely confined to the lower organization levels. The sheer mass of such data precludes their extensive use at higher levels.

The alternative budget proposal would permit use of work load and unit cost data to the extent feasible in each case. Under each alternative total figure, the number of units of work that could be performed, the quality standards, and unit costs could be shown. Thus the benefits to be derived from work load measurement would be fully utilized under the alternative budget procedure. In addition, the judgment of subordinates would be obtained on questions which cannot be answered by work load data alone. Such questions involve, for example, the gains or losses of performing alternative amounts of work, the achievement of alternative quality standards, and the effects of spending more or less per unit of work.

Increase-Decrease Analysis. A common technique in the federal government is to require in budget estimates identification of the items representing increases and decreases as compared with the prior year's budget. Special explanations are required for the increases. Budget reviewers are frequently criticized for concentrating on the increases and giving too little attention to items in the base amount. This criticism is justified in part because the amount appropriated last year is not necessarily appropriate for this year and the activities carried on last year are not necessarily appropriate for this year. However, the sheer mass of work involved in reviewing budget estimates precludes examination of every detail every year. Even if it were possible, it would not be necessary, for conditions do not change so fast that every issue has to be rehashed every year.

The basic fault of the increase-decrease method is the fact that it does not require comparison of the relative values of the old and the new. While the proposed increase may be for an eminently desirable purpose, it does not necessarily follow that the appropriation of the agency should be increased. Perhaps other programs of the agency should be cut back enough, or more, to make room for the new. The alternative budget approach has all the advantages of the increase-decrease method without having this basic fault. It would require agencies to weigh the relative merits of all proposals, whether old or new, and thus would reflect the agency's evaluation of the importance of the proposed additions to the spending program in relation to the items composing the base.

Priority Listings. Subordinates are required, in some cases, to indicate priorities of items included in their budget estimates or allotment requests to assist reviewers in determining where cutbacks should be made. Budgets for construction of physical facilities, for example, might contain a listing in priority order of the facilities proposed. The assumption underlying this method is that a budget reduction would be met by eliminating enough projects at the lower end of the list to bring the estimates down to the desired level. When that is the case priority listings are useful. Elimination of the lowest priority items, however, is only one of several means of reducing estimates. Some of the other types of adjustments are as follows: cheaper materials may be used in some or all of the facilities; the size, strength, or durability of the facilities may be decreased; or certain features may be eliminated or postponed until a later date. All of these types of adjustments can be reflected in alternative budgets since they all affect dollar requirements. The priority approach reflects only the one kind of adjustment.

Item-by-Item Control. Approval of individual items of expenditure by higher authority is a common budgetary control technique. Equipment purchases, additions to staff, travel, expensive types of communications as well as entire projects, are frequently subjected to this type of control. An actual case will illustrate the problems involved. During World War II, the Secretary of the Navy was concerned about the expansion of the physical plant of the Navy in the continental United States. In an effort to assure that no facilities would be built unless vitally needed for war purposes and that costs and use of scarce materials would be minimized, the Secretary of the Navy required that all proposed construction projects should be subject to his approval. Prior to this approval they had to be screened at several different levels in the Navy Department. The projects were reviewed by officials in the sponsoring bureau, by the Bureau of Yards and Docks (to insure conformity to wartime engineering standards), by the Chief of Naval Operations (to determine their military necessity), and by a special committee in the Secretary's office composed mainly of civilian businessmen (to determine their over-all justification). Even with this series of reviews, the Secretary apparently was not convinced that outlays for facilities were being held down as much as they should be. The process was something less than satisfactory to subordinate officials, too, but for different reasons. They complained of the delays involved in getting a decision and of the amount of time and effort required to justify and rejustify each proposal at the several screening points.

The root of the difficulty, if the thesis of this article is sound, is that controls of individual items do not require or facilitate systematic consideration of relative desirability. Item-by-item control poses the problem at each level of review in these terms: Is the proposal desirable, or essential, or justified? A more pertinent question is: Is the proposal more essential than any alternative use of the funds?

The alternative budget procedure could be applied to this situation in the following manner: bureau chiefs, as well as officials at lower levels, if desired, would be asked to prepare alternative programs for construction of facilities for the period in question. The bureau chiefs in presenting these alternatives would, in effect, tell the Chief of Naval Operations and the Secretary, "If only X dollars are available, I recommend using the money this way . . . ; if 2 X dollars are available, I think the money should be used this way. . . . The advantages and disadvantages of each plan are as follows: . . . " Having an opportunity to see the picture as a whole, having before him alternatives from which to choose, and having the judgment of his subordinates as to gains and losses resulting from each alternative, the Secretary, it would seem, would be able to make his decision fairly readily and with assurance. It is unlikely that he would have to spend as much time reviewing details as is necessary under the item-by-item approach. He would be in a better position to exercise his responsibilities while the subordinates would be freed from the delays, burdens, and irritations invariably involved in piece-by-piece screening processes.

In addition to the specific points discussed above, the alternative budget plan appears to have certain general advantages. It would, we believe, make budgeting a little more palatable to the technically minded operating official who must prepare and justify budgets. His role will be less that of a special pleader for THE plan he thinks should be accepted and more that of an expert adviser. He will be less like an architect who tries to sell a client on a single plan costing a certain sum and more like an architect advising the client on the relative merits of several house plans and suggesting how the client can get the most for his money regardless of the amount he decides to spend.

Budget analysts under this plan would have a frame of reference which would enable them to operate more effectively. At present, much of their effort is directed toward determining desirability or necessity and not enough attention is given to issues of relative desirability. Under the plan suggested here, the primary job of the budget analyst would be to assist his superior in weighing the relative value of alternative uses of each increment of funds as a step in developing the alternatives to be submitted to the next higher level in the organization. Another aspect of his work would be to explore some of the many possible variations and combinations of features that could not be reflected in the limited number of alternatives formally submitted by the lower officials. Moreover, the analyst would have to check for accuracy, objectivity, and general adequacy the subordinate official's statements of the advantages and disadvantages of the alternatives submitted.

Another significant advantage of the alternative budget proposal is that it would make budgeting somewhat less authoritarian. It would make the budget recommendations of administrative officials less final without weakening in any way their usefulness.

At present, an item screened out of a budget by any administrative official even though it is of major importance is not considered at later stages unless it is brought to the attention of higher executive officials or the Congress by some method which is prohibited by the prevailing rules. To put it mildly, quite definite steps are taken to discourage later consideration. A bureau chief, for example, would be considered out of bounds if he appealed to the President for consideration of an item screened out of his budget by his departmental head. Any administrative officer is prohibited from recommending congressional consideration of any alternatives to the single proposal contained in the President's budget unless specifically requested to do so by a member of Congress. Publication of requests submitted by the departments to the President is also banned.

It is not at all unlikely that superior administrative officials or the Congress would want to adopt some of these screened-out items if they had an opportunity to consider them. Since Congress, in our form of government, is largely responsible for deciding what shall or shall not be done by the executive agencies, the wisdom of such strict censoring of proposals submitted for consideration by Congress seems questionable. Since the President's budget estimates are only recommendations, there would seem to be no disadvantage in his outlining the major alternatives from which he made his selection. In this way the views of subordinates who may have an honest difference of opinion with the President could be submitted to Congress for consideration openly and without subterfuge. After considering the evidence pertaining to each alternative, Congress could then take its choice. Since the making of such choices is involved in exercising congressional control over the purse strings—a control which historically and currently is a basic cornerstone of democratic government—the provision of information which will assist Congress in evaluating the major alternative courses is of vital importance.[10]

In general, the alternative budget plan is designed to emphasize throughout the budget process the economic ideas discussed in Part I of this article. Its purpose is to pose budget questions at every level in terms of relative value. It also is designed to make maximum use of the expert knowledge and judgment of officials at the lower organization levels by having them analyze, incrementally, the estimates of their agencies and evaluate the relative effectiveness of their several activities in achieving the goals of their organizations.

In proposing this system, I am not particularly concerned with detailed mechanics. There are undoubtedly other ways of accomplishing substantially the same results as this plan is designed to achieve. More important than the precise mechanics is the way of looking at budget problems, the approach to budget analysis and control which this plan reflects.

How practical is the alternative budget plan? How well will it work in practice? The answers to these questions depend in large measure on the relationships between superior and subordinate and between the Administration and the Congress. Neither this system nor any other can work satisfactorily if the relations are strained, if the reviewer lacks confidence in the integrity or judgment of the official who is submitting the estimate, or if those who prepare the estimates are not sincerely interested in providing information which the reviewers need to form an intelligent judgment on the merits of the issues.

Perhaps undue faith in the rationality of man underlies the approach to budgeting outlined in this article. In real life, budget decisions are undoubtedly influenced to a greater or lesser extent by such non-economic and non-rational factors as pride and prejudice, provincialism and politics. These aspects deserve consideration, but they lie beyond the scope of this article. My primary purpose herein has been to stimulate further consideration of the economic aspects of budgeting.[11]

Notes

1. V. O. Key, Jr., "The Lack of a Budgetary Theory," 34 *American Political Science Review* 1137–44 (December, 1940).

2. Ideas derived from Herbert A. Simon's works as to the applicability of economic concepts to administration have been particularly useful for this purpose. See his *Administrative Behavior* (Macmillan Co., 1947).

3. As quoted by Key, *op. cit.*, p. 1139.

4. L. M. Fraser, *Economic Thought and Language* (A. and C. Black Ltd., 1937), p. 103.

5. This method, as it applies to public administration in general, has been extensively analyzed by Herbert A. Simon under the heading of the "criterion of efficiency," *op. cit.*, pp. 172–97.

6. Key, *op. cit.*, p. 1143.

7. Ludwig von Mises, *Bureaucracy* (Yale University Press, 1944), p. 47.

8. *Op. cit.*, p. 1142.

9. See also, Simon, *op. cit.*, p. 214.

10. Simon also has recommended submission of alternative budget plans to legislatures for substantially the same reason. *Op. cit.*, p. 195.

11. Note on Relation to a Performance Budget. A performance budget, as proposed by the Hoover Commission, would give primary emphasis to the result or end product to be obtained with the money spent by the government. The commission wisely criticized budget presentations that deal only with the ingredients that are required to produce the end product. Certainly first attention should be given to what is to be accomplished rather than to the people who have to be employed, or the materials which have to be bought, in order to accomplish the basic purpose.

Emphasizing performance or end results does not require us to ignore the ingredients or the means to the ends. It should not lead to that result. Important budget issues often times involve only the means. While the purpose may be agreed to, the methods may be in dispute. For example, a conservation agency may be responsible for inducing producer conservation of some natural resource. Should the objective be accomplished by an educational program, by regulatory action, or by subsidy?

The alternative budget plan is flexible enough to be adapted to the situation. Alternative purposes as well as alternative methods could and should be reflected in the alternative budget estimates. Whether greater emphasis would be placed on purposes than on methods would depend upon the nature of the problem.

2

THE SCIENCE OF "MUDDLING THROUGH"

Charles E. Lindblom

Suppose an administrator is given responsibility for formulating policy with respect to inflation. He might start by trying to list all related values in order of importance, e.g., full employment, reasonable business profit, protection of small savings, prevention of a stock market crash. Then all possible policy outcomes could be rated as more or less efficient in attaining a maximum of these values. This would of course require a prodigious inquiry into values held by members of society and an equally prodigious net of calculations on how much of each value is equal to how much of each other value. He could then proceed to outline all possible policy alternatives. In a third step, he would undertake systematic comparison of his multitude of alternatives to determine which attains the greatest amount of values.

In comparing policies, he would take advantage of any theory available that generalized about classes of policies. In considering inflation, for example, he would compare all policies in the light of the theory of prices. Since no alternatives are beyond his investigation, he would consider strict central control and the abolition of all prices and markets on the one hand and elimination of all public controls with reliance completely on the free market on the other, both in the light of whatever theoretical generalizations he could find on such hypothetical economies.

1959. The science of "muddling through." Lindblom, Charles E. **Public Administration Review** 19 (Spring): 79–88.

39

Finally, he would try to make the choice that would in fact maximize his values.

An alternative line of attack would be to set as his principal objective, either explicitly or without conscious thought, the relatively simple goal of keeping prices level. This objective might be compromised or complicated by only a few other goals, such as full employment. He would in fact disregard most other social values as beyond his present interest, and he would for the moment not even attempt to rank the few values that he regarded as immediately relevant. Were he pressed, he would quickly admit that he was ignoring many related values and many possible important consequences of his policies.

As a second step, he would outline those relatively few policy alternatives that occurred to him. He would then compare them. In comparing his limited number of alternatives, most of them familiar from past controversies, he would not ordinarily find a body of theory precise enough to carry him through a comparison of their respective consequences. Instead he would rely heavily on the record of past experience with small policy steps to predict the consequences of similar steps extended into the future.

Moreover, he would find that the policy alternatives combined objectives or values in different ways. For example, one policy might offer price level stability at the cost of some risk of unemployment; another might offer less price stability but also less risk of unemployment. Hence, the next step in his approach—the final selection—would combine into one the choice among values and the choice among instruments for reaching values. It would not, as in the first method of policymaking, approximate a more mechanical process of choosing the means that best satisfied goals that were previously clarified and ranked. Because practitioners of the second approach expect to achieve their goals only partially, they would expect to repeat endlessly the sequence just described, as conditions and aspirations changed and as accuracy of prediction improved.

By Root or by Branch

For complex problems, the first of these two approaches is of course impossible. Although such an approach can be described, it cannot be practiced except for relatively simple problems and even then only in a somewhat modified form. It assumes intellectual capacities and sources of information that men simply do not possess, and it is even more absurd as an approach to policy when the time and money that can be allocated to a policy problem is limited, as is always the case. Of particular importance to public administrators is the fact that public agencies are in effect usually instructed not to practice the first method. That is to say, their prescribed functions and constraints—the politically or legally possible—restrict their attention to relatively few values and relatively few alternative policies among the countless alternatives that might be imagined. It is the second method that is practiced.

Curiously, however, the literatures of decision-making, policy formulation, planning, and public administration formalize the first approach rather than the second, leaving public administrators who handle complex decisions in the position of practicing what few preach. For emphasis I run some risk of overstatement. True enough, the literature is well aware of limits on man's capacities and of the inevitability that policies will be approached in some such style as the second. But attempts to formalize rational policy formulation—to lay out explicitly the necessary steps in the process—usually describe the first approach and not the second.[1]

The common tendency to describe policy formulation even for complex problems as though it followed the first approach has been strengthened by the attention given to, and successes enjoyed by, operations research, statistical decision theory, and systems analysis. The hallmarks of these procedures, typical of the first approach, are clarity of objective, explicitness of evaluation, a high degree of comprehensiveness of overview, and, wherever possible, quantification of values for mathematical analysis. But these advanced procedures remain largely the appropriate techniques of relatively small-scale problem-solving where the total number of variables to be considered is small and value problems restricted. Charles Hitch, head of the Economics Division of RAND Corporation, one of the leading centers for application of these techniques, has written:

> I would make the empirical generalization from my experience at RAND and elsewhere that operations research is the art of sub-optimizing, i.e., of solving some lower-level problems, and that difficulties increase and our special competence diminishes by an order of magnitude with every level of decision making we attempt to ascend. The sort of simple explicit model which operations researchers are so proficient in using can certainly reflect most of the significant factors influencing traffic control on the George Washington Bridge, but the proportion of the relevant reality which we can represent by any such model or models in studying, say, a major foreign-policy decision, appears to be almost trivial.[2]

Accordingly, I propose in this paper to clarify and formalize the second method, much neglected in the literature. This might be described as the method of *successive limited comparisons*. I will contrast it with the first approach, which might be called the rational-comprehensive method.[3] More impressionistically and briefly—and therefore generally used in this article—they could be characterized as the branch method and root method, the former continually building out from the current situation, step-by-step and by small degrees; the latter starting from fundamentals anew each time, building on the past only as experience is embodied in a theory, and always prepared to start completely from the ground up.

Let us put the characteristics of the two methods side by side in simplest terms.

Rational-Comprehensive (Root)

1. Clarification of values or objectives distinct from and usually prerequisite to empirical analysis of alternative policies.
2. Policy-formulation is therefore approached through means-end analysis: First the ends are isolated, then the means to achieve them are sought.
3. The test of a "good" policy is that it can be shown to be the most appropriate means to desired ends.
4. Analysis is comprehensive; every important relevant factor is taken into account.
5. Theory is often heavily relied upon.

Successive Limited Comparisons (Branch)

1. Selection of value goals and empirical analysis of the needed action are not distinct from one another but are closely intertwined.
2. Since means and ends are not distinct, means-end analysis is often inappropriate or limited.
3. The test of a "good" policy is typically that various analysts find themselves directly agreeing on a policy (without their agreeing that it is the most appropriate means to an agreed objective).
4. Analysis is drastically limited:
    a. Important possible outcomes are neglected.
    b. Important alternative potential policies are neglected.
    c. Important affected values are neglected.
5. A succession of comparisons greatly reduces or eliminates reliance on theory.

Assuming that the root method is familiar and understandable, we proceed directly to clarification of its alternative by contrast. In explaining the second, we shall be describing how most administrators do in fact approach complex questions, for the root method, the "best" way as a blueprint or model, is in fact not workable for complex policy questions, and administrators are forced to use the method of successive limited comparisons.

Intertwining Evaluation and
Empirical Analysis (1b)

The quickest way to understand how values are handled in the method of successive limited comparisons is to see how the root method often breaks down in *its* handling of values or objectives. The idea that values should be clarified, and in advance of the examination of alternative policies, is appealing. But what happens when we attempt it for complex social problems? The first difficulty is that on many critical values or objectives, citizens disagree, congressmen disagree, and public administrators disagree. Even where a fairly specific objective is prescribed for the administrator, there remains considerable room for disagreement on subobjectives. Consider, for example, the conflict with respect to locating public housing, described in Meyerson and Banfield's study of the Chicago Housing Authority[4]—disagreement which occurred despite the clear objective of providing a certain number of public housing units in the city. Similarly conflicting are objectives in highway location, traffic control, minimum wage administration, development of tourist facilities in national parks, or insect control.

Administrators cannot escape these conflicts by ascertaining the majority's preference, for preferences have not been registered on most issues; indeed, there often *are* no preferences in the absence of public discussion sufficient to bring an issue to the attention of the electorate. Furthermore, there is a question of whether intensity of feeling should be considered as well as the number of persons preferring each alternative. By the impossibility of doing otherwise, administrators often are reduced to deciding policy without clarifying objectives first.

Even when an administrator resolves to follow his own values as a criterion for decisions, he often will not know how to rank them when they conflict with one another, as they usually do. Suppose, for example, that an administrator must relocate tenants living in tenements scheduled for destruction. One objective is to empty the buildings fairly promptly, another is to find suitable accommodation for persons displaced, another is to avoid friction with residents in other areas in which a large influx would be unwelcome, another is to deal with all concerned through persuasion if possible, and so on.

How does one state even to himself the relative importance of these partially conflicting values? A simple ranking of them is not enough; one needs ideally to know how much of one value is worth sacrificing for some of another value. The answer is that typically the administrator chooses—and must choose—directly among policies in which these values are combined in different ways. He cannot first clarify his values and then choose among policies.

A more subtle third point underlies both the first two. Social objectives do not always have the same relative values. One objective may be highly prized in one circumstance another in another circumstance. If, for example, an administrator values highly both the dispatch with which his agency can carry through its projects *and* good public relations, it matters little which of the two possibly conflicting values he favors in some abstract or general sense. Policy questions arise in forms which put to administrators such a question as: Given the degree to which we are or are not already achieving the values of dispatch and the values of good public relations, is it worth sacrificing a little speed for a happier clientele, or is it better to risk offending the clientele so that we can get on with our work? The answer to such a question varies with circumstances.

The value problem is, as the example shows, always a problem of adjustments at a margin. But there is no practicable way to state marginal objectives or values except in terms of particular policies. That one value is preferred to another in one decision situation does not mean that it will be preferred in another decision situation in which it can be had only at great sacrifice of another value. Attempts to rank or order values in general and abstract terms so that they do not shift from decision to decision end up by ignoring the relevant marginal preferences. The significance of this third point thus goes very far. Even if all administrators had at hand an agreed set of values, objectives, and constraints, and an agreed ranking of these values, objectives, and constraints, their marginal values in actual choice situations would be impossible to formulate.

Unable consequently to formulate the relevant values first and then choose among policies to achieve them, administrators must choose directly among alternative policies that offer different marginal combinations of values. Somewhat paradoxically, the only practicable way to disclose one's relevant marginal values even to oneself is to describe the policy one chooses to achieve them. Except roughly and vaguely, I know of no way to describe—or even to understand—what my relative evaluations are for, say, freedom and security, speed and accuracy in governmental decisions, or low taxes and better schools than to describe my preferences among specific policy choices that might be made between the alternatives in each of the pairs.

In summary, two aspects of the process by which values are actually handled can be distinguished. The first is clear: evaluation and empirical analysis are intertwined; that is, one chooses among values and among policies at one and the same time. Put a little more elaborately, one simultaneously chooses a policy to attain certain objectives and chooses the objectives themselves. The second aspect is related but distinct: the administrator focuses his attention on marginal or incremental values. Whether he is aware of it or not, he does not find general formulations of objectives very helpful and in fact makes specific marginal or incremental comparisons. Two policies, X and Y, confront him. Both promise the same degree of attainment of objectives *a, b, c, d,* and *e.* But X promises him somewhat more of *f* than does Y, while Y promises him somewhat more of *g* than does X. In choosing between them, he is in fact offered the alternative of a marginal or incremental amount of *f* at the expense of a marginal or incremental amount of *g.* The only values that are relevant to his choice are these increments by which the two policies differ; and, when he finally chooses between the two marginal values, he does so by making a choice between policies.[5]

As to whether the attempt to clarify objectives in advance of policy selection is more or less rational than the close intertwining of marginal evaluation and empirical analysis, the principal difference established is that for complex problems the first is impossible and irrelevant, and the second is both possible and relevant. The second is possible because the administrator need not try to analyze any values except the values by which alternative policies differ and need not be concerned with them except as they differ marginally. His need for information on values or objectives is drastically reduced as compared with the root method; and his capacity for grasping, comprehending, and relating values to one another is not strained beyond the breaking point.

Relations Between
Means and Ends (2b)

Decision-making is ordinarily formalized as a means-ends relationship: means are conceived to be evaluated and chosen in the light of ends finally selected independently of and prior to the choice of means. This is the means-ends relationship of the root method. But it follows from all that has just been said that such a means-ends relationship is possible only to the extent that values are agreed upon, are reconcilable, and are stable at the margin. Typically, therefore, such a means-ends relationship is absent from the branch method, where means and ends are simultaneously chosen.

Yet any departure from the means-ends relationship of the root method will strike some readers as inconceivable. For it will appear to them that only in such a relationship is it possible to determine whether one policy choice is better or worse than another. How can an administrator know whether he has made a wise or foolish decision if he is without prior values or objectives by which to judge his decisions? The answer to this question calls up the third distinctive difference between root and branch methods: how to decide the best policy.

The Test of "Good" Policy (3b)

In the root method, a decision is "correct," "good," or "rational" if it can be shown to attain some specified objective, where the objective can be

specified without simply describing the decision itself. Where objectives are
defined only through the marginal or incremental approach to values described above, it is still sometimes possible to test whether a policy does in
fact attain the desired objectives; but a precise statement of the objectives
takes the form of a description of the policy chosen or some alternative to
it. To show that a policy is mistaken one cannot offer an abstract argument
that important objectives are not achieved; one must instead argue that another policy is more to be preferred.

So far, the departure from customary ways of looking at problem-solving is not trouble-some, for many administrators will be quick to agree
that the most effective discussion of the correctness of policy does take the
form of comparison with other policies that might have been chosen. But
what of the situation in which administrators cannot agree on values or
objectives, either abstractly or in marginal terms? What then is the test of
"good" policy? For the root method, there is no test. Agreement on objectives failing, there is no standard of "correctness." For the method of successive limited comparisons, the test is agreement on policy itself, which remains possible even when agreement on values is not.

It has been suggested that continuing agreement in Congress on the desirability of extending old age insurance stems from liberal desires to
strengthen the welfare programs of the federal government and from conservative desires to reduce union demands for private pension plans. If so,
this is an excellent demonstration of the ease with which individuals of different ideologies often can agree on concrete policy. Labor mediators report a similar phenomenon: the contestants cannot agree on criteria for
settling their disputes but can agree on specific proposals. Similarly, when
one administrator's objective turns out to be another's means, they often
can agree on policy.

Agreement on policy thus becomes the only practicable test of the policy's correctness. And for one administrator to seek to win the other over
to agreement on ends as well would accomplish nothing and create quite
unnecessary controversy.

If agreement directly on policy as a test for "best" policy seems a poor
substitute for testing the policy against its objectives, it ought to be remembered that objectives themselves have no ultimate validity other than they
are agreed upon. Hence agreement is the test of "best" policy in both
methods. But where the root method requires agreement on what elements
in the decision constitute objectives and on which of these objectives
should be sought, the branch method falls back on agreement wherever it
can be found.

In an important sense, therefore, it is not irrational for an administrator to defend a policy as good without being able to specify what it is
good for.

Non-Comprehensive Analysis (4b)

Ideally, rational-comprehensive analysis leaves out nothing important. But it is impossible to take everything important into consideration unless "important" is so narrowly defined that analysis is in fact quite limited. Limits on human intellectual capacities and on available information set definite limits to man's capacity to be comprehensive. In actual fact, therefore, no one can practice the rational-comprehensive method for really complex problems, and every administrator faced with a sufficiently complex problem must find ways drastically to simplify.

An administrator assisting in the formulation of agricultural economic policy cannot in the first place be competent on all possible policies. He cannot even comprehend one policy entirely. In planning a soil bank program, he cannot successfully anticipate the impact of higher or lower farm income on, say, urbanization—the possible consequent loosening of family ties, possible consequent eventual need for revisions in social security and further implications for tax problems arising out of new federal responsibilities for social security and municipal responsibilities for urban services. Nor, to follow another line of repercussions, can he work through the soil bank program's effects on prices for agricultural products in foreign markets and consequent implications for foreign relations, including those arising out of economic rivalry between the United States and the U.S.S.R.

In the method of successive limited comparisons, simplification is systematically achieved in two principal ways. First, it is achieved through limitation of policy comparisons to those policies that differ in relatively small degree from policies presently in effect. Such a limitation immediately reduces the number of alternatives to be investigated and also drastically simplifies the character of the investigation of each. For it is not necessary to undertake fundamental inquiry into an alternative and its consequences; it is necessary only to study those respects in which the proposed alternative and its consequences differ from the status quo. The empirical comparison of marginal differences among alternative policies that differ only marginally is, of course, a counterpart to the incremental or marginal comparison of values discussed above.[6]

Relevance as Well as Realism

It is a matter of common observation that in Western democracies public administrators and policy analysts in general do largely limit their analyses to incremental or marginal differences in policies that are chosen to differ only incrementally. They do not do so, however, solely because they desperately need some way to simplify their problems; they also do so in order to be relevant. Democracies change their policies almost entirely through incremental adjustments. Policy does not move in leaps and bounds.

The incremental character of political change in the United States has often been remarked. The two major political parties agree on fundamentals; they offer alternative policies to the voters only on relatively small points of difference. Both parties favor full employment, but they define it somewhat differently; both favor the development of water power resources, but in slightly different ways; and both favor unemployment compensation, but not the same level of benefits. Similarly, shifts of policy within a party take place largely through a series of relatively small changes, as can be seen in their only gradual acceptance of the idea of governmental responsibility for support of the unemployed, a change in party positions beginning in the early 30's and culminating in a sense in the Employment Act of 1946.

Party behavior is in turn rooted in public attitudes, and political theorists cannot conceive of democracy's surviving in the United States in the absence of fundamental agreement on potentially disruptive issues, with consequent limitation of policy debates to relatively small differences in policy.

Since the policies ignored by the administrator are politically impossible and so irrelevant, the simplification of analysis achieved by concentrating on policies that differ only incrementally is not a capricious kind of simplification. In addition, it can be argued that, given the limits on knowledge within which policy-makers are confined, simplifying by limiting the focus to small variations from present policy makes the most of available knowledge. Because policies being considered are like present and past policies, the administrator can obtain information and claim some insight. Non-incremental policy proposals are therefore typically not only politically irrelevant but also unpredictable in their consequences.

The second method of simplification of analysis is the practice of ignoring important possible consequences of possible policies, as well as the values attached to the neglected consequences. If this appears to disclose a shocking shortcoming of successive limited comparisons, it can be replied that, even if the exclusions are random, policies may nevertheless be more intelligently formulated than through futile attempts to achieve a comprehensiveness beyond human capacity. Actually, however, the exclusions, seeming arbitrary or random from one point of view, need be neither.

Achieving a Degree of Comprehensiveness

Suppose that each value neglected by one policy-making agency were a major concern of at least one other agency. In that case, a helpful division of labor would be achieved, and no agency need find its task beyond its capacities. The shortcomings of such a system would be that one agency might destroy a value either before another agency could be activated to safeguard it or in spite of another agency's efforts. But the possibility that important values may be lost is present in any form of organization, even where agencies attempt to comprehend in planning more than is humanly possible.

The virtue of such a hypothetical division of labor is that every important interest or value has its watchdog. And these watchdogs can protect the interests in their jurisdiction in two quite different ways: first, by redressing damages done by other agencies; and, second, by anticipating and heading off injury before it occurs.

In a society like that of the United States in which individuals are free to combine to pursue almost any possible common interest they might have and in which government agencies are sensitive to the pressures of these groups, the system described is approximated. Almost every interest has its watchdog. Without claiming that every interest has a sufficiently powerful watchdog, it can be argued that our system often can assure a more comprehensive regard for the values of the whole society than any attempt at intellectual comprehensiveness.

In the United States, for example, no part of government attempts a comprehensive overview of policy on income distribution. A policy nevertheless evolves, and one responding to a wide variety of interests. A process of mutual adjustment among farm groups, labor unions, municipalities and school boards, tax authorities, and government agencies with responsibilities in the fields of housing, health, highways, national parks, fire, and police accomplishes a distribution of income in which particular income problems neglected at one point in the decision processes become central at another point.

Mutual adjustment is more pervasive than the explicit forms it takes in negotiation between groups; it persists through the mutual impacts of groups upon each other even where they are not in communication. For all the imperfections and latent dangers in this ubiquitous process of mutual adjustment, it will often accomplish an adaptation of policies to a wider range of interests than could be done by one group centrally.

Note, too, how the incremental pattern of policy-making fits with the multiple pressure pattern. For when decisions are only incremental— closely related to known policies, it is easier for one group to anticipate the kind of moves another might make and easier too for it to make correction for injury already accomplished.[7]

Even partisanship and narrowness, to use pejorative terms, will sometimes be assets to rational decision-making, for they can doubly insure that what one agency neglects, another will not; they specialize personnel to distinct points of view. The claim is valid that effective rational coordination of the federal administration, if possible to achieve at all, would require an agreed set of values[8]—if "rational" is defined as the practice of the root method of decision-making. But a high degree of administrative coordination occurs as each agency adjusts its policies to the concerns of the other agencies in the process of fragmented decision-making I have just described.

For all the apparent shortcomings of the incremental approach to policy alternatives with its arbitrary exclusion coupled with fragmentation, when compared to the root method, the branch method often looks far superior. In the root method, the inevitable exclusion of factors is accidental, unsystematic, and not defensible by any argument so far developed, while in the branch method the exclusions are deliberate, systematic, and defensible. Ideally, of course, the root method does not exclude; in practice it must.

Nor does the branch method necessarily neglect long-run considerations and objectives. It is clear that important values must be omitted in considering policy, and sometimes the only way long-run objectives can be given adequate attention is through the neglect of short-run considerations. But the values omitted can be either long-run or short-run.

Succession of Comparisons (5b)

The final distinctive element in the branch method is that the comparisons, together with the policy choice, proceed in a chronological series. Policy is not made once and for all; it is made and re-made endlessly. Policy-making is a process of successive approximation to some desired objectives in which what is desired itself continues to change under reconsideration.

Making policy is at best a very rough process. Neither social scientists, nor politicians, nor public administrators yet know enough about the social world to avoid repeated error in predicting the consequences of policy moves. A wise policy-maker consequently expects that his policies will achieve only part of what he hopes and at the same time will produce unanticipated consequences he would have preferred to avoid. If he proceeds through a *succession* of incremental changes, he avoids serious lasting mistakes in several ways.

In the first place, past sequences of policy steps have given him knowledge about the probable consequences of further similar steps. Second, he need not attempt big jumps toward his goals that would require predictions beyond his or anyone else's knowledge, because he never expects his policy to be a final resolution of a problem. His decision is only one step, one that if successful can quickly be followed by another. Third, he is in effect able to test his previous predictions as he moves on to each further step. Lastly, he often can remedy a past error fairly quickly—more quickly than if policy proceeded through more distinct steps widely spaced in time.

Compare this comparative analysis of incremental changes with the aspiration to employ theory in the root method. Man cannot think without classifying, without subsuming one experience under a more general category of experiences. The attempt to push categorization as far as possible and to find general propositions which can be applied to specific situations is what I refer to with the word "theory." Where root analysis often leans heavily on theory in this sense, the branch method does not.

The assumption of root analysts is that theory is the most systematic and economical way to bring relevant knowledge to bear on a specific problem. Granting the assumption, an unhappy fact is that we do not have adequate theory to apply to problems in any policy area, although theory is more adequate in some areas—monetary policy, for example—than in others. Comparative analysis, as in the branch method, is sometimes a systematic alternative to theory.

Suppose an administrator must choose among a small group of policies that differ only incrementally from each other and from present policy. He might aspire to "understand" each of the alternatives—for example, to know all the consequences of each aspect of each policy. If so, he would indeed require theory. In fact, however, he would usually decide that, *for policy-making purposes,* he need know, as explained above, only the consequences of each of those aspects of the policies in which they differed from one another. For this much more modest aspiration, he requires no theory (although it might be helpful, if available), for he can proceed to isolate probable differences by examining the differences in consequences associated with past differences in policies, a feasible program because he can take his observations from a long sequence of incremental changes.

For example, without a more comprehensive social theory about juvenile delinquency than scholars have yet produced, one cannot possibly understand the ways in which a variety of public policies—say on education, housing, recreation, employment, race relations, and policing—might encourage or discourage delinquency. And one needs such an understanding if he undertakes the comprehensive overview of the problem prescribed in the models of the root method. If, however, one merely wants to mobilize knowledge sufficient to assist in a choice among a small group of similar policies—alternative policies on juvenile court procedures, for example— he can do so by comparative analysis of the results of similar past policy moves.

Theorists and Practitioners

This difference explains—in some cases at least—why the administrator often feels that the outside expert or academic problem-solver is sometimes not helpful and why they in turn often urge more theory on him. And it explains why an administrator often feels more confident when "flying by the seat of his pants" than when following the advice of theorists. Theorists often ask the administrator to go the long way round to the solution of his problems, in effect ask him to follow the best canons of the scientific method, when the administrator knows that the best available theory will work less well than more modest incremental comparisons. Theorists do not realize that the administrator is often in fact practicing a systematic method. It would be foolish to push this explanation too far, for sometimes practical decision-makers are pursuing neither a theoretical approach nor successive comparisons, nor any other systematic method.

It may be worth emphasizing that theory is sometimes of extremely limited helpfulness in policy-making for at least two rather different reasons. It is greedy for facts; it can be constructed only through a great collection of observations. And it is typically insufficiently precise for application to a policy process that moves through small changes. In contrast, the comparative method both economizes on the need for facts and directs the analyst's attention to just those facts that are relevant to the fine choices faced by the decision-maker.

With respect to precision of theory, economic theory serves as an example. It predicts that an economy without money or prices would in certain specified ways misallocate resources, but this finding pertains to an alternative far removed from the kind of policies on which administrators need help. On the other hand, it is not precise enough to predict the consequences of policies restricting business mergers, and this is the kind of issue on which the administrators need help. Only in relatively restricted areas does economic theory achieve sufficient precision to go far in resolving policy questions; its helpfulness in policy-making is always so limited that it requires supplementation through comparative analysis.

Successive Comparison as a System

Successive limited comparisons is, then, indeed a method or system; it is not a failure of method for which administrators ought to apologize. None the less, its imperfections, which have not been explored in this paper, are many. For example, the method is without a built-in safeguard for all relevant values, and it also may lead the decision-maker to overlook excellent policies for no other reason than that they are not suggested by the chain of successive policy steps leading up to the present. Hence, it ought to be said that under this method, as well as under some of the most sophisticated variants of the root method—operations research, for example—policies will continue to be as foolish as they are wise.

Why then bother to describe the method in all the above detail? Because it is in fact a common method of policy formulation, and is, for complex problems, the principal reliance of administrators as well as of other policy analysts.[9] And because it will be superior to any other decision-making method available for complex problems in many circumstances, certainly superior to a futile attempt at superhuman comprehensiveness. The reaction of the public administrator to the exposition of method doubtless will be less a discovery of a new method than a better acquaintance with an old. But by becoming more conscious of their practice of this method, administrators might practice it with more skill and know when to extend or constrict its use. (That they sometimes practice it effectively and sometimes not may explain the extremes of opinion on "muddling through," which is both praised as a highly sophisticated form of problem-solving and denounced as no method at all. For I suspect that in so far as there is a system in what is known as "muddling through," this method is it.)

One of the noteworthy incidental consequences of clarification of the method is the light it throws on the suspicion an administrator sometimes entertains that a consultant or adviser is not speaking relevantly and responsibly when in fact by all ordinary objective evidence he is. The trouble lies in the fact that most of us approach policy problems within a framework given by our view of a chain of successive policy choices made up to the present. One's thinking about appropriate policies with respect, say, to urban traffic control is greatly influenced by one's knowledge of the incremental steps taken up to the present. An administrator enjoys an intimate knowledge of his past sequences that "outsiders" do not share, and his thinking and that of the "outsider" will consequently be different in ways that may puzzle both. Both may appear to be talking intelligently, yet each may find the other unsatisfactory. The relevance of the policy chain of succession is even more clear when an American tries to discuss, say, antitrust policy with a Swiss, for the chains of policy in the two countries are strikingly different and the two individuals consequently have organized their knowledge in quite different ways.

If this phenomenon is a barrier to communication, an understanding of it promises an enrichment of intellectual interaction in policy formulation. Once the source of difference is understood, it will sometimes be stimulating for an administrator to seek out a policy analyst whose recent experience is with a policy chain different from his own.

This raises again a question only briefly discussed above on the merits of like-mindedness among government administrators. While much of organization theory argues the virtues of common values and agreed organizational objectives, for complex problems in which the root method is inapplicable, agencies will want among their own personnel two types of diversification: administrators whose thinking is organized by reference to policy chains other than those familiar to most members of the organization and, even more commonly, administrators whose professional or personal values or interests create diversity of view (perhaps coming from different specialties, social classes, geographical areas) so that, even within a single agency, decision-making can be fragmented and parts of the agency can serve as watchdogs for other parts.

Notes

1. James G. March and Herbert A. Simon similarly characterize the literature. They also take some important steps, as have Simon's recent articles, to describe a less heroic model of policy-making. See *Organizations* (John Wiley and Sons, 1958), p. 137.

2. "Operations Research and National Planning—A Dissent," 5 *Operations Research* 718 (October, 1957). Hitch's dissent is from particular points made in the article to which his paper is a reply; his claim that operations research is for low-level problems is widely accepted.

For examples of the kind of problems to which operations research is applied, see C. W. Churchman, R. L. Ackoff and E. L. Arnoff, *Introduction to Operations Research* (John Wiley and Sons, 1957); and J. F. McCloskey and J. M. Coppinger (eds.), *Operations Research for Management*, Vol. II, (The Johns Hopkins Press, 1956).

3. I am assuming that administrators often make policy and advise in the making of policy and am treating decision-making and policy-making as synonymous for purposes of this paper.

4. Martin Meyerson and Edward C. Banfield, *Politics, Planning and the Public Interest* (The Free Press, 1955).

5. The line of argument is, of course, an extension of the theory of market choice, especially the theory of consumer choice, to public policy choices.

6. A more precise definition of incremental policies and a discussion of whether a change that appears "small" to one observer might be seen differently by another is to be found in my "Policy Analysis," 48 *American Economic Review* 298 (June, 1958).

7. The link between the practice of the method of successive limited comparisons and mutual adjustment of interests in a highly fragmented decision-making process adds a new facet to pluralist theories of government and administration.

8. Herbert Simon, Donald W. Smithburg, and Victor A. Thompson, *Public Administration* (Alfred A. Knopf, 1950), p. 434.

9. Elsewhere I have explored this same method of policy formulation as practiced by academic analysts of policy ("Policy Analysis," 48 *American Economic Review* 298 [June, 1958]). Although it has been here presented as a method for public administrators, it is no less necessary to analysts more removed from immediate policy questions, despite their tendencies to describe their own analytical efforts as though they were the rational-comprehensive method with an especially heavy use of theory. Similarly, this same method is inevitably resorted to in personal problem-solving, where means and ends are sometimes impossible to separate, where aspirations or objectives undergo constant development, and where

drastic simplification of the complexity of the real world is urgent if problems are to be solved in the time that can be given to them. To an economist accustomed to dealing with the marginal or incremental concept in market processes, the central idea in the method is that both evaluation and empirical analysis are incremental. Accordingly I have referred to the method elsewhere as "the incremental method."

3

POLITICAL IMPLICATIONS OF BUDGETARY REFORM

Aaron Wildavsky

A large part of the literature on budgeting in the United States is concerned with reform. The goals of the proposed reforms are couched in similar language—economy, efficiency, improvement, or just better budgeting. The President, the Congress and its committees, administrative agencies, even the interested citizenry are all to gain by some change in the way the budget is formulated, presented, or evaluated. There is little or no realization among the reformers, however, that any effective change in budgetary relationships must necessarily alter the outcomes of the budgetary process. Otherwise, why bother? Far from being a neutral matter of "better budgeting," proposed reforms inevitably contain important implications for the political system, that is for the "who gets what" of governmental decisions. What are some of the major political implications of budgetary reform and where should we look to increase our knowledge about how the budget is made? We begin with the noblest vision of reform: the development of a normative theory of budgeting that would provide the basis for allocating funds among competing activities.

A Normative Theory of Budgeting?

In 1940, in what is still the best discussion of the subject, V. O. Key lamented "The Lack of a Budgetary Theory." He called for a theory which

1961. Political implications of budgetary reform. Wildavsky, Aaron. **Public Administration Review** 21 (Autumn): 183–190.

would help answer the basic question of budgeting on the expenditure side: "On what basis shall it be decided to allocate X dollars to Activity A instead of Activity B?"[1] Although several attempts have been made to meet this challenge,[2] not one has come close to succeeding. No progress has been made for the excellent reason that the task, as posed, is impossible to fulfill.[3] The search for an unrealizable goal indicates serious weaknesses in prevailing conceptions of the budget.

If a normative theory of budgeting is to be more than an academic exercise, it must actually guide the making of governmental decisions. The items of expenditures which are passed by Congress, enacted into law, and spent must in large measure conform to the theory if it is to have any practical effect. This is tantamount to prescribing that virtually all the activities of government be carried on according to the theory. For whatever the government does must be paid for from public funds; it is difficult to think of any policy which can be carried out without money.

The budget is the life-blood of the government, the financial reflection of what the government does or intends to do. A theory which contains criteria for determining what ought to be in the budget is nothing less than a theory stating what the government ought to do. If we substitute the words "what the government ought to do" for the words "ought to be in the budget," it becomes clear that a normative theory of budgeting would be a comprehensive and specific political theory detailing what the government's activities ought to be at a particular time. A normative theory of budgeting, therefore, is utopian in the fullest sense of that word; its accomplishment and acceptance would mean the end of conflict over the government's role in society.

By suppressing dissent, totalitarian regimes enforce their normative theory of budgeting on others. Presumably, we reject this solution to the problem of conflict in society and insist on democratic procedures. How then arrive at a theory of budgeting which is something more than one man's preferences?

The crucial aspect of budgeting is whose preferences are to prevail in disputes about which activities are to be carried on and to what degree, in the light of limited resources. The problem is not only "how shall budgetary benefits be maximized?" as if it made no difference who received them, but also "who shall receive budgetary benefits and how much?" One may purport to solve the problem of budgeting by proposing a normative theory (or a welfare function or a hierarchy of values) which specifies a method for maximizing returns for budgetary expenditures. In the absence of ability to impose a set of preferred policies on others, however, this solution breaks down. It amounts to no more than saying that if you can persuade others to agree with you, than you will have achieved agreement. Or it begs the question of what kind of policies will be fed into the scheme by assuming that these are agreed upon. Yet we hardly need argue that a state of universal agreement has not yet arisen.

Another way of avoiding the problem of budgeting is to treat society as a single organism with a consistent set of desires and a life of its own, much as a single consumer might be assumed to have a stable demand and indifference schedule. Instead of revenue being raised and the budget being spent by and for many individuals who may have their own preferences and feelings, as is surely the case, these processes are treated, in effect, as if a single individual were the only one concerned. This approach avoids the central problems of social conflict, of somehow aggregating different preferences so that a decision may emerge. How can we compare the worth of expenditures for irrigation to certain farmers with the worth of widening a highway to motorists and the desirability of aiding old people to pay medical bills as against the degree of safety provided by an expanded defense program?

The process we have developed for dealing with interpersonal comparisons in Government is not economic but political. Conflicts are resolved (under agreed upon rules) by translating different preferences through the political system into units called votes or into types of authority like a veto power. There need not be (and there is not) full agreement on goals or the preferential weights to be accorded to different goals. Congressmen directly threaten, compromise, and trade favors in regard to policies in which values are implicitly weighted, and then agree to register the results according to the rules for tallying votes.

The burden of calculation is enormously reduced for three primary reasons: first, only the small number of alternatives which are politically feasible at any one time are considered; second, these policies in a democracy typically differ only in small increments from previous policies on which there is a store of relevant information; and, third, each participant may ordinarily assume that he need consider only his preferences and those of his powerful opponents since the American political system works to assure that every significant interest has representation at some key point. Since only a relatively few interest groups contend on any given issue and no single item is considered in conjunction with all others (because budgets are made in bits and pieces), a huge and confusing array of interests are not activated all at once.

In the American context, a typical result is that bargaining takes place among many dispersed centers of influence and that favors are swapped as in the case of log-rolling public works appropriations. Since there is no one group of men who can necessarily impose their preferences upon others within the American political system, special coalitions are formed to support or oppose specific policies. Support is sought in this system of fragmented power at numerous centers of influence—Congressional committees, the Congressional leadership, the President, the Budget Bureau, inter-departmental committees, departments, bureaus, private groups, and so on. Nowhere does a single authority have power to determine what is going to be in the budget.

The Politics in Budget Reform

The seeming irrationalities[4] of a political system which does not provide for even formal consideration of the budget as a whole (except by the President who cannot control the final result) has led to many attacks and proposals for reform. The tradition of reform in America is a noble one, not easily to be denied. But in this case it is doomed to failure because it is aimed at the wrong target. If the present budgetary process is rightly or wrongly deemed unsatisfactory, then one must alter in some respect the political system of which the budget is but an expression. It makes no sense to speak as if one could make drastic changes in budgeting without also altering the distribution of influence. But this task is inevitably so formidable (though the reformers are not directly conscious of it) that most adversaries prefer to speak of changing the budgetary process, as if by some subtle alchemy the irrefractible political element could be transformed into a more malleable substance.

The reader who objects to being taken thus far only to be told the obvious truth that the budget is inextricably linked to the political system would have a just complaint if the implications of this remark were truly recognized in the literature on budgeting. But this is not so. One implication is that by far the most significant way of influencing the budget is to introduce basic political changes (or to wait for secular changes like the growing industrialization of the South). Provide the President with more powers enabling him to control the votes of his party in Congress; enable a small group of Congressmen to command a majority of votes on all occasions so that they can push their program through. Then you will have exerted a profound influence on the content of the budget.

A second implication is that no significant change can be made in the budgetary process without affecting the political process. There would be no point in tinkering with the budgetary machinery if, at the end, the pattern of budgetary decisions was precisely the same as before. On the contrary, reform has little justification unless it results in different kinds of decisions and, when and if this has been accomplished, the play of political forces has necessarily been altered. Enabling some political forces to gain at the expense of others requires the explicit introduction and defense of value premises which are ordinarily missing from proposals for budgetary reform.

Since the budget represents conflicts over whose preferences shall prevail, the third implication is that one cannot speak of "better budgeting" without considering who benefits and who loses or demonstrating that no one loses. Just as the supposedly objective criterion of "efficiency" has been shown to have normative implications,[5] so a "better budget" may well be a cloak for hidden policy preferences. To propose that the President be given an item veto, for example, means an attempt to increase the influence of the particular interests which gain superior access to the Chief Executive rather than, say, to the Congress. Only if one eliminates the element of conflict over expenditures, can it be assumed that a reform which enables an official to do a better job from his point of view is simply "good" without considering the policy implications for others.

Arthur Smithies may stand as a typical proponent of a typical reform. Identifying rationality with a comprehensive overview of the budget by a single person or group, Smithies despairs of the fragmented approach taken by Congress and proposes a remedy. He suggests that a Joint (Congressional) Budget Policy committee be formed and empowered to consider all proposals for revenue and expenditure in a single package and that their decisions be made binding by a concurrent resolution. And he presents his reform as a moderate proposal to improve the rationality of the budget process.[6] If the proposed Joint Committee were unable to secure the passage of its recommendations, as would surely be the case, it would have gone to enormous trouble without accomplishing anything but a public revelation of futility. The impotence of the Joint Committee on the Legislative Budget,[7] the breakdown of the single Congressional attempt to develop a comprehensive legislative budget,[8] and the failure of Congressional attempts to control the Council of Economic Advisers[9] and the Budget Bureau,[10] all stem from the same cause. There is no cohesive group in Congress capable of using these devices to affect decision making by imposing its preferences on a majority of Congressmen. Smithies' budgetary reform presupposes a completely different political system from the one which exists in the United States. To be sure, there is a name for a committee which imposes its will on the legislature and tolerates no rival committees—it is called a Cabinet on the British model. In the guise of a procedural change in the preparation of the budget by Congress, Smithies is actually proposing a revolutionary move which would mean the virtual introduction of the British Parliamentary system if it were successful.

Smithies (pp. 188–225) suggests that his proposals would be helpful to the President. But the membership of the Joint Committee would be made up largely of conservatives from safe districts who are not dependent on the President, who come from a different constituency than he does, but with whom he must deal in order to get any money for his programs. Should the Joint Committee ever be able to command a two-thirds vote of the Congress, it could virtually ignore the President in matters of domestic policy and run the executive branch so that it is accountable only to them.

I do not mean to disparage in any way the important problem of efficiency, of finding ways to maximize budgetary benefits given a specified distribution of shares. In principle, there seems to be no reason why policy machinery could not be so arranged as to alter the ratio of inputs to outputs without changing the distribution of shares. One can imagine situations in which everyone benefits or where the losses suffered in one respect are made up by greater gains elsewhere. There may be cases where such losses as do exist are not felt by the participants and they may be happy to make changes which increase their felt benefits. The inevitable lack of full information and the disinclination of participants to utilize their political resources to the fullest extent undoubtedly leave broad areas of inertia and inattention open for change. Thus, the "slack" in the system may leave considerable room for ingenuity and innovation in such areas as benefit cost analysis and the comparability and interrelatedness of public works without running into outstanding political difficulties or involving large changes in the system. Most practical budgeting may take place in a twilight zone between politics and efficiency. Without presenting a final opinion on this matter, it does seem to me that the problem of distributing shares has either been neglected entirely or has been confused with the problem of efficiency to the detriment of both concerns. The statements in this paper should be understood to refer only to the question of determining shares in the budget.

What Do We Know About Budgeting?

The overriding concern of the literature on budgeting with normative theory and reform has tended to obscure the fact that we know very little about it. Aside from the now classical articles on Congressional oversight of administration by Arthur MacMahon,[11] an excellent study of internal budgetary procedures in the Army by Frederick C. Mosher,[12] and an interesting case history by Kathryn S. Arnow,[13] there is virtually nothing of substance about how or why budgetary decisions are actually made. Of course, the general literature on decision making in national government provides some valuable propositions, but it is not keyed-in to the budgetary process. Yet the opportunities for developing and testing important propositions about budgetary decisions are extraordinarily good and I would like to suggest a few of the many possible approaches here.

How do various agencies decide how much to ask for? Most agencies cannot simply ask for everything they would like to have. If they continually ask for much more than they can get, their opinions are automatically discounted and they risk a loss of confidence by the Budget Bureau and Appropriations subcommittees which damages the prospects of their highest priority items. The agencies cannot even ask for all that they are authorized to spend because their authorizations commonly run way ahead of any realistic expectation of achievement. At the same time, they do not wish to sell themselves short. The result is that the men who make this choice (an official title is no certain guide to whom they are) seek signals from the environment—supporting interests, their own personnel, current events, last year's actions, attitudes of Congressmen, and so on—to arrive at a composite estimate of "what will go." A combination of interviews, case studies, and direct observation should enable the researcher to determine what these signals are, to construct propositions accounting for the agencies budgetary position, and to generally recreate the environment out of which these choices come.

Once having decided what they would like to get, how do agencies go about trying to achieve their objectives? Today, we do not even have a preliminary list of the most common strategies used by participants in trying to influence budgetary outcomes. Again, the techniques listed above should bring the necessary data to light.

Perhaps a few examples will demonstrate the importance of understanding budgetary strategies. There are times when an agency wishes to cut its own budget because it has lost faith in a program, for internal disciplinary reasons, or because it would like to use the money elsewhere. If the agency is particularly well endowed with effective clientele groups, however, it may not only fail in this purpose but may actually see the appropriation increased as this threat mobilizes the affected interests. One budget officer informed me that he tried to convince the Budget Bureau to undertake two projects which the agency did not want but which several influential Congressmen felt strongly about. Otherwise, the official argued, the Congressmen would secure their desires by offering additional projects to their colleagues. The Budget Bureau turned him down and the result was nine unwanted projects instead of two.

The appearance of a budget may take on considerable importance, a circumstance which is often neglected by proponents of program budgeting. Suppose that an agency has strong clientele backing for individual projects. It is likely to gain by presenting them separately so that any cut may be readily identified and support easily mobilized. Lumping a large number of items together may facilitate cuts on an across-the-board basis. Items lacking support, on the other hand, may do better by being placed in large categories so that it is more difficult to single them out for deeper slashes.

We might also inquire (through questionnaires, interviews, direct observation, documentary research) about the participants' perceptions of their roles and the reciprocal expectations they have about the behavior of others. In speaking to officials concerned with budgeting I was impressed with how often the behavior they described was predicated on a belief about what others would do, how they would react in turn, how a third participant would react to this result and so on. Budgetary items are commonly adjusted on the basis of mutual expectations or on a single participant's notion of the role he is expected to play. I strongly suspect, on the basis of some interviewing, that if we studied conceptions of role prevalent on the House Appropriations Committee, their transmittal to new members and staff, and the consequent resistance of members to seeing party as relevant to choice, we would understand a great deal more about the characteristic behavior of many members as budget cutters.

My interviews suggest that the administrator's perception of Congressional knowledge and motivation helps determine the kind of relationships he seeks to establish. The administrator who feels that the members of his appropriations subcommittees are not too well informed on specifics and that they evaluate the agency's program on the basis of feedback from constituents, stresses the role of supporting interests in maintaining good relations with Congressmen. He may not feel the need to be too careful with his estimates. The administrator who believes that the Congressmen are well informed and fairly autonomous is likely to stress personal relationships and demonstrations of good work as well as clientele support. Priority in research should be given to study of these perceptions and the ways in which they determine behavior.

Another approach would be to locate and segregate classes of administrative officials who are found by observation to have or not to have the confidence of the appropriations committees and to seek to explain the differences. For if there is any one thing which participants in budgeting are likely to stress, it is the importance of maintaining relations of confidence and they are highly conscious of what this requires. Since it appears from preliminary investigation that the difference is not accounted for by the popularity of the agency or its programs, it is possible that applications of some gross psychological and skill categories would reveal interesting results.

Many participants in budgeting (in the agencies, Congress, the Budget Bureau) speak of somehow having arrived at a total figure which represents an agency's or an activity's "fair share" of the budget. The fact that a fair share concept exists may go a long way toward explaining the degree of informal coordination that exists among the participants in budgeting. Investigation of how these figures are arrived at and communicated would help us understand how notions of limits (ceilings and floors) enter into budgetary decisions. A minimum effort in this direction would require the compilation of appropriations histories of various agencies and programs rather than just individual case histories which concentrate on some specific event or moment in time. Investigation of the Tennessee Valley Authority's experience in securing electric power appropriations, over a twenty-five-year period, for example, reveals patterns and presents explanatory possibilities which would not otherwise be available.[14]

By its very nature the budgetary process presents excellent opportunities for the use of quantitative data although these must be used with great caution and with special attention to their theoretical relevance. Richard Fenno has collected figures on thirty-seven bureaus dealing with domestic policies from 1947 to 1958 from their initial estimates to decisions by the Budget Bureau, appropriations committees in both houses, conference committees, and floor action. Using these figures he expects to go beyond the usual facile generalizations that the House cuts and the Senate raises bureau estimates, to the much more interesting question of determining the conditions under which the patterns that do exist actually obtain.[15] Although such data do not by any means tell the whole story, they can be used to check generalizations about patterns of floor action or conference committee action which would not otherwise be possible.

After giving the matter considerable thought, I have decided that it would not be fruitful to devise a measure which would ostensibly give an objective rank ordering of bureaus and departments according to their degree of success in securing appropriations. The first measure which might be used would be to compare an agency's initial requests with its actual appropriations. The difficulty here is that agency estimates are not merely a measure of their desire but also include a guess as to what they can reasonably expect to get. The agency which succeeds in getting most of what it desires, therefore, may be the one which is best at figuring out what it is likely to get. A better measure, perhaps, would be an agency's record in securing appropriations calculated as percentages above or below previous years' appropriations. But this standard also leads to serious problems. There are fortuitous events—sputnik, a drought, advances in scientific knowledge—which are beyond the control of an agency but which may have a vital bearing on its success in getting appropriations. Indeed, some "affluent agencies" like the National Institutes of Health may find that there is little they can do to stop vast amounts of money from coming in; they may not even be able to cut their own budgets when they want to do so. Furthermore, agencies generally carry on a wide variety of programs and the total figures may hide the fact that some are doing very well and others quite poorly. Thus it would be necessary to validate the measure by an intensive study of each agency's appropriations history and this would appear to make the original computation unnecessary.

The purpose of this suggested research, much of which the author intends to pursue, is to formulate empirically valid propositions which will be useful in constructing theories (general explanations) accounting for the operation and outcomes of the budgetary process. A theory of influence would describe the power relationships among the participants, explain why some are more successful than others in achieving their budgetary goals, state the conditions under which various strategies are or are not efficacious, and in this way account for the pattern of budgetary decisions.

With such a theory, it would become possible to specify the advantages which some participants gain under the existing system, to predict the consequences of contemplated changes on the distribution of influence, and to anticipate sources of opposition. Possibly, those desiring change might then suggest a strategy to overcome the expected resistance. But they would not, in their scholarly role, accuse their opponents of irrationality in not wishing to have their throats cut.

It would also be desirable to construct a theory of budgetary calculation by specifying the series of related factors (including influence relationships) which affect the choice of competing alternatives by the decision makers. This kind of theory would describe how problems arise, how they are broken down, how information is fed into the system, how the participants are related to one another, and how a semblance of coordination is achieved. The kinds of calculations which actually guide the making of decisions would be emphasized. One would like to know, for example, whether long-range planning really exists or is merely engaged in for form's sake while decisions are really based on short-run indices like reactions to last year's appropriation requests. If changes in procedure lead to different kinds of calculations, one would like to be able to predict what the impact on decisions was likely to be.

The Goals of Knowledge and Reform

Concentration on developing at least the rudiments of a descriptive theory is not meant to discourage concern with normative theory and reform. On the contrary, it is worthwhile studying budgeting from both standpoints. Surely, it is not asking too much to suggest that a lot of reform be preceded by a little knowledge. The point is that until we develop more adequate descriptive theory about budgeting, until we know something about the "existential situation" in which the participants find themselves under our political system, proposals for major reform must be based on woefully inadequate understanding. A proposal which alters established relationships, which does not permit an agency to show certain programs in the most favorable light, which does not tell influential Congressmen what they want to know, which changes prevailing expectations about the behavior of key participants, or which leads to different calculations of an agency's fair share, would have many consequences no one is even able to guess at today. Of course, small, incremental changes proceeding in a pragmatic fashion of trial and error could proceed as before without benefit of theory; but this is not the kind of change with which the literature on budgeting is generally concerned.

Perhaps the "study of budgeting" is just another expression for the "study of politics"; yet one cannot study everything at once, and the vantage point offered by concentration on budgetary decisions offers a useful and much neglected perspective from which to analyze the making of policy. The opportunities for comparison are ample, the outcomes are specific and quantifiable, and a dynamic quality is assured by virtue of the comparative ease with which one can study the development of budgetary items over a period of years.

Notes

1. V. O. Key, Jr., "The Lack of a Budgetary Theory," 34 *American Political Science Review* 1137–44 (December 1940).

2. Verne B. Lewis, "Toward a Theory of Budgeting," 12 *Public Administration Review* 42–54 (Winter 1952); "Symposium on Budgetary Theory," 10 *Public Administration Review* 20–31 (Spring 1954); Arthur Smithies, *The Budgetary Process in the United States* (McGraw-Hill, 1955).

3. Key, in fact, shies away from the implications of his question and indicates keen awareness of the political problems involved. But the question has been posed by subsequent authors largely in the terms in which he framed it.

4. See Charles E. Lindblom, "The Science of 'Muddling' Through," 19 *Public Administration Review* 79–88 (Spring 1959), for a description and criticism of the comprehensive method. See also his "Decision-Making in Taxation and Expenditure" in National Bureau of Economic Research, *Public Finances: Needs, Sources, and Utilization* (Princeton University Press, 1961), pp. 295–327, and his "Policy Analysis," 48 *American Economic Review* 298–312 (June 1958).

5. Dwight Waldo, *The Administrative State* (Ronald Press, 1948); Herbert A. Simon, "The Criterion of Efficiency," in *Administrative Behavior*, 2nd ed. (Macmillan, 1957), pp. 172–97.

6. Smithies, *op. cit.*, pp. 192–93ff.

7. Avery Leiserson, "Coordination of the Federal Budgetary and Appropriations Procedures Under the Legislative Reorganization Act of 1946," 1 *National Tax Journal* 118–26 (June 1948).

8. Robert Ash Wallace, "Congressional Control of the Budget," 3 *Midwest Journal of Political Science* 160–62 (May 1959); Dalmas H. Nelson, "The Omnibus Appropriations Act of 1950," 15 *Journal of Politics* 274–88 (May 1953); Representative John Phillips, "The Hadacol of the Budget Makers," 4 *National Tax Journal* 255–68 (September 1951).

9. Roy Blough, "The Role of the Economist in Federal Policy-Making," 51 *University of Illinois Bulletin* (November 1953); Lester Seligman, "Presidential Leadership: The Inner Circle and Institutionalization," 18 *Journal of Politics* 410–26 (August 1956); Edwin G. Nourse, *Economics in the Public Service: Administrative Aspects of the Employment Act* (Harcourt Brace, 1953); Ronald C. Hood, "Reorganizing the Council of Economic Advisors," 69 *Political Science Quarterly* 413–37 (September 1954).

10. Fritz Morstein Marx, "The Bureau of the Budget: Its Evolution and Present Role II," 39 *American Political Science Review* 363–98 (October 1945); Richard Neustadt, "The Presidency and Legislation: The Growth of Central Clearance," 48 *Ibid.* 631–71 (September 1954); Seligman, *op. cit.*

11. Arthur McMahon, "Congressional Oversight of Administration," 58 *Political Science Quarterly* 161–90, 380–414 (June, September 1943).

12. Frederick C. Mosher, *Program Budgeting:* Theory and Practice, with Particular Reference to the U.S. Department of the Army (Public Administrative Service, 1954).

13. *The Department of Commerce Field Offices,* Inter-University Case Series No. 21 (University of Alabama Press, 1954).

14. See Aaron B. Wildavsky, "TVA and Power Politics," 55 *American Political Science Review* 576–90 (September 1961).

15. From a research proposal kindly lent me by Richard Fenno. See also his excellent paper, "The House Appropriations Committee as a Political System: The Problem of Integration," delivered at the 1961 meeting of the American Political Science Association.

4

THE ROAD TO PPB
The Stages of Budget Reform

Allen Schick

Among the new men in the nascent PPB [Planning-Programming-Budgeting System] staffs and the fellow travellers who have joined the bandwagon, the mood is of "a revolutionary development in the history of government management." There is excited talk about the differences between what has been and what will be; of the benefits that will accrue from an explicit and "hard" appraisal of objectives and alternatives; of the merits of multiyear budget forecasts and plans; of the great divergence between the skills and role of the analyst and the job of the examiner; of the realignments in government structure that might result from changes in the budget process.

This is not the only version, however. The closer one gets to the nerve centers of budget life—the Divisions in the Bureau of the Budget and the budget offices in the departments and agencies—the more one is likely to hear that "there's nothing very new in PPB; it's hardly different from what we've been doing until now." Some old-timers interpret PPB as a revival of the performance budgeting venture of the early 1950's. Others belittle the claim that—before PPB—decisions on how much to spend for personnel or supplies were made without real consideration of the purposes for which these inputs were to be invested. They point to previous changes that have been in line with PPB, albeit without PPB's distinctive package of techniques and nomenclature. Such things as the waning role of the "green sheets" in the central budget process, the redesign of the appropriation structure and the development of activity classifications, refinements in

1966. The road to PPB: The stages of budget reform. Schick, Allen. **Public Administration Review** 26 (December): 243–258.

work measurement, productivity analysis, and other types of output measurement, and the utilization of the Spring Preview for a broad look at programs and major issues.

Between the uncertain protests of the traditional budgeteer and the uncertain expectations of the *avant garde,* there is a third version. The PPB system that is being developed portends a radical change in the central function of budgeting, but it is anchored to half a century of tradition and evolution. The budget system of the future will be a product of past and emerging developments; that is, it will embrace both the budgetary functions introduced during earlier stages of reform as well as the planning function which is highlighted by PPB. PPB is the first budget system *designed* to accommodate the multiple functions of budgeting.

The Functions of Budgeting

Budgeting always has been conceived as a process for systematically relating the expenditure of funds to the accomplishment of planned objectives. In this important sense, there is a bit of PPB in every budget system. Even in the initial stirrings of budget reform more than 50 years ago, there were cogent statements on the need for a budget system to plan the objectives and activities of government and to furnish reliable data on what was to be accomplished with public funds. In 1907, for example, the New York Bureau of Municipal Research published a sample "program memorandum" that contained some 125 pages of functional accounts and data for the New York City Health Department.[1]

However, this orientation was not *explicitly* reflected in the budget systems—national, state, or local—that were introduced during the first decades of this century, nor is it *explicitly* reflected in the budget systems that exist today. The plain fact is that planning is not the only function that must be served by a budget system. The *management* of ongoing activities and the *control* of spending are two functions which, in the past, have been given priority over the planning function. Robert Anthony identifies three distinct administrative processes, strategic planning, management control, and operational control.

> **Strategic planning** is the process of deciding on objectives of the organization, on changes in these objectives, on the resources used to attain these objectives, and on the policies that are to govern the acquisition, use, and disposition of these reresources.
> **Management control** is the process by which managers assure that resources are obtained and used effectively and efficiently in the accomplishment of the organization's objectives.

Operational control is the process of assuring that specific tasks are carried out effectively and efficiently.[2]

Every budget system, even rudimentary ones, comprises planning, management, and control processes. Operationally, these processes often are indivisible, but for analytic purposes they are distinguished here. In the context of budgeting, *planning* involves the determination of objectives, the evaluation of alternative courses of action, and the authorization of select programs. Planning is linked most closely to budget preparation, but it would be a mistake to disregard the management and control elements in budget preparation or the possibilities for planning during other phases of the budget year. Clearly, one of the major aims of PPB is to convert the annual routine of preparing a budget into a conscious appraisal and formulation of future goals and policies. Management involves the programming of approved goals into specific projects and activities, the design of organizational units to carry out approved programs, and the staffing of these units and the procurement of necessary resources. The management process is spread over the entire budget cycle; ideally, it is the link between goals made and activities undertaken. *Control* refers to the process of binding operating officials to the policies and plans set by their superiors. Control is predominant during the execution and audit stages, although the form of budget estimates and appropriations often is determined by control considerations. The assorted controls and reporting procedures that are associated with budget execution—position controls, restrictions on transfers, requisition procedures, and travel regulations, to mention the more prominent ones—have the purpose of securing compliance with policies made by central authorities.

Very rarely are planning, management, and control given equal attention in the operation of budget systems. As a practical matter, planning, management, and control have tended to be competing processes in budgeting with no neat division of functions among the various participants. Because time is scarce, central authorities must be selective in the things they do. Although this scarcity counsels the devolution of control responsibilities to operating levels, the lack of reliable and relied-on internal control systems has loaded central authorities with control functions at the expense of the planning function. Moreover, these processes often require different skills and generate different ways of handling the budget mission, so that one type of perspective tends to predominate over the others. Thus, in the staffing of the budget offices, there has been a shift from accountants to administrators as budgeting has moved from a control to a management posture. The initial experience with PPB suggests that the next transition might be from administrators to economists as budgeting takes on more of the planning function.

Most important, perhaps, are the differential informational requirements of planning, control, and management processes. Informational
needs differ in terms of time spans, levels of aggregation, linkages with organizational and operating units, and input-out-put foci. The apparent solution is to design a system that serves the multiple needs of budgeting.
Historically, however, there has been a strong tendency to homogenize informational structures and to rely on a single classification scheme to serve
all budgetary purposes. For the most part, the informational system has
been structured to meet the purposes of control. As a result, the type of
multiple-purpose budget system envisioned by PPB has been avoided.

An examination of budget systems should reveal whether greater emphasis is placed *at the central levels* on planning, management, or control. A
planning orientation focuses on the broadest range of issues: What are the
long-range goals and policies of the government and how are these related
to particular expenditure choices? What criteria should be used in appraising the requests of the agencies? Which programs should be initiated or
terminated, and which expanded or curtailed? A *management orientation*
deals with less fundamental issues: What is the best way to organize for the
accomplishment of a prescribed task? Which of several staffing alternatives
achieves the most effective relationship between the central and field offices? Of the various grants and projects proposed, which should be approved? A *control orientation* deals with a relatively narrow range of concerns: How can agencies be held to the expenditure ceilings established by
the legislature and chief executive? What reporting procedures should be
used to enforce propriety in expenditures? What limits should be placed on
agency spending for personnel and equipment?

It should be clear that every budget system contains planning, management, and control features. A control orientation means the subordination,
not the absence, of planning and management functions. In the matter of
orientations, we are dealing with relative emphases, not with pure dichotomies. The germane issue is the balance among these vital functions at
the central level. Viewed centrally, what weight does each have in the design and operation of the budget system?

The Stages of Budget Reform

The framework outlined above suggests a useful approach to the study of
budget reform. Every reform alters the planning-management-control balance, sometimes inadvertently, usually deliberately. Accordingly, it is possible to identify three successive stages of reform. In the first stage, dating
roughly from 1920 to 1935, the dominant emphasis was on developing an
adequate system of expenditure control. Although planning and management considerations were not altogether absent (and indeed occupied a

prominent role in the debates leading to the Budget and Accounting Act of 1921), they were pushed to the side by what was regarded as the first priority, a reliable system of expenditure accounts. The second stage came into the open during the New Deal and reached its zenith more than a decade later in the movement for performance budgeting. The management orientation, paramount during this period, made its mark in the reform of the appropriation structure, development of management improvement and work measurement programs, and the focusing of budget preparation on the work and activities of the agencies. The third stage, the full emergence of which must await the institutionalization of PPB, can be traced to earlier efforts to link planning and budgeting as well as to the analytic criteria of welfare economics, but its recent development is a product of modern informational and decisional technologies such as those pioneered in the Department of Defense.

PPB is predicated on the primacy of the planning function; yet it strives for a multipurpose budget system that gives adequate and necessary attention to the control and management areas. Even in embryonic stage, PPB envisions the development of crosswalk grids for the conversion of data from a planning to a management and control framework, and back again. PPB treats the three basic functions as compatible and complementary elements of a budget system, though not as coequal aspects of central budgeting. In ideal form, PPB would centralize the planning function and delegate *primary* managerial and control responsibilities to the supervisory and operating levels respectively.

In the modern genesis of budgeting, efforts to improve planning, management, and control made common cause under the popular banner of the executive-budget concept. In the goals and lexicon of the first reformers, budgeting meant executive budgeting. The two were inseparable. There was virtually no dissent from Cleveland's dictum that "to be a budget it must be prepared and submitted by a responsible executive ... "[3] Whether from the standpoint of planning, management or control, the executive was deemed in the best position to prepare and execute the budget. As Cleveland argued in 1915, only the executive "could think in terms of the institution as a whole," and, therefore, he "is the only one who can be made responsible for leadership."[4]

The executive budget idea also took root in the administrative integration movement, and here was allied with such reforms as functional consolidation of agencies, elimination of independent boards and commissions, the short ballot, and strengthening the chief executive's appointive and removal powers. The chief executive often was likened to the general manager of a corporation, the Budget Bureau serving as his general staff.

Finally, the executive budget was intended to strengthen honesty and efficiency by restricting the discretion of administrators in this role. It was associated with such innovations as centralized purchasing and competitive bidding, civil service reform, uniform accounting procedures, and expenditure audits.

The Control Orientation

In the drive for executive budgeting, the various goals converged. There was a radical parting of the ways, however, in the conversion of the budget idea into an operational reality. Hard choices had to be made in the design of expenditure accounts and in the orientation of the budget office. On both counts, the control orientation was predominant.

In varying degrees of itemization, the expenditure classifications established during the first wave of reform were based on objects-of-expenditure, with detailed tabulations of the myriad items required to operate an administrative unit—personnel, fuel, rent, office supplies, and other inputs. On these "line-itemizations" were built technical routines for the compilation and review of estimates and the disbursement of funds. The leaders in the movement for executive budgeting, however, envisioned a system of functional classifications focusing on the work to be accomplished. They regarded objects-of-expenditure as subsidiary data to be included for informational purposes. Their preference for functional accounts derived from their conception of the budget as a planning instrument, their disdain for objects from the contemporary division between politics and administration.[5] The Taft Commission vigorously opposed object-of-expenditure appropriations and recommended that expenditures be classified by class of work, organizational unit, character of expense, and method of financing. In its model budget, the Commission included several functional classifications.[6]

In the establishment of a budget system for New York City by the Bureau of Municipal Research, there was an historic confrontation between diverse conceptions of budgeting.

In evolving suitable techniques, the Bureau soon faced a conflict between functional and object budgeting. Unlike almost all other budget systems which began on a control footing with object classifications, the Bureau turned to control (and the itemization of objects) only after trial-and-error experimentation with program methods.

When confronted with an urgent need for effective control over administration, the Bureau was compelled to conclude that this need was more critical than the need for a planning-functional emphasis. "Budget reform," Charles Beard once wrote, "bears the imprint of the age in which it originated."[7] In an age when personnel and purchasing controls were unreliable, the first consideration was how to prevent administrative improprieties.

In the opinion of those who were in charge of the development of a budget procedure, the most important service to be rendered was the establishing of central controls so that responsibility could be located and enforced through elected executives. . . . The view was, therefore, accepted, that questions of administration and niceties of adjustment must be left in abeyance until central control has been effectively established and the basis has been laid for careful scrutiny of departmental contracts and purchases as well as departmental work.[8]

Functional accounts had been designed to facilitate rational program decisions, not to deter officials from misfeasance. "The classification by 'functions' affords no protection; it only operates as a restriction on the use which may be made of the services."[9] The detailed itemization of objects was regarded as desirable not only "because it provides for the utilization of all the machinery of control which has been provided, but it also admits to a much higher degree of perfection than it has at present attained."[10]

With the introduction of object accounts, New York City had a threefold classification of expenditures: (1) by organizational units; (2) by functions; and (3) by objects. In a sense, the Bureau of Municipal Research was striving to develop a budget system that would serve the multiple purposes of budgeting simultaneously. To the Bureau, the inclusion of more varied and detailed data in the budget was a salutory trend; all purposes would be served and the public would have a more complete picture of government spending. Thus the Bureau "urged from the beginning a classification of costs in as many different ways as there are stories to be told."[11] But the Bureau did not anticipate the practical difficulties which would ensue from the multiple classification scheme. In the 1913 appropriations act

there were 3992 distinct items of appropriation. . . . Each constituted a distinct appropriation, besides which there was a further itemization of positions and salaries of personnel that multiplied this number several times, each of which operated as limitations on administrative discretion.[12]

This predicament confronted the Bureau with a direct choice between the itemization of objects and a functional classification. As a solution, the Bureau recommended retention of object accounts and the total "defunctionalization" of the budget; in other words, it gave priority to the objects and the control orientation they manifested. Once installed, object controls rapidly gained stature as an indispensable deterrent to administrative misbehavior. Amelioration of the adverse effects of multiple classifications was to be accomplished in a different manner, one which would strengthen the planning and management processes. The Bureau postulated a fundamental distinction between the purposes of budgets and appropriations, and between the types of classification suitable for each.

. . . an act of appropriation has a single purpose—that of putting a limitation on the amount of obligations which may be incurred and the amount of vouchers which may be drawn to pay for personal services, supplies, etc. The only significant classification of appropriation items, therefore, is according to persons to whom drawing accounts are given and the classes of things to be bought.[13]

Appropriations, in sum, were to be used as statutory controls on spending. In its "Next Steps" proposals, the Bureau recommended that appropriations retain "exactly the same itemization so far as specifications of positions and compensations are concerned and, therefore, the same protection."[14]

Budgets, on the other hand, were regarded as instruments of planning and publicity. They should include "all the details of the work plans and specifications of cost of work."[15] In addition to the regular object and organization classifications, the budget would report the "total cost incurred, classified by *functions*—for determining questions of policy having to do with service rendered as well as to be rendered, and laying a foundation for appraisal of results."[16] The Bureau also recommended a new instrument, a *work program,* which would furnish "a detailed schedule or analysis of each function, activity, or process within each organization unit. This analysis would give the total cost and the unit cost wherever standards were established."[17]

Truly a far-sighted conception of budgeting! There would be three documents for the three basic functions of budgeting. Although the Bureau did not use the analytic framework suggested above, it seems that the appropriations were intended for control purposes, the budget for planning purposes, and the work program for management purposes. Each of the three documents would have its specialized information scheme, but jointly they would comprise a multipurpose budget system not very different from PPB, even though the language of crosswalking or systems analysis was not used.

Yet the plan failed, for in the end the Bureau was left with object accounts pegged to a control orientation. The Bureau's distinction between budgets and appropriations was not well understood, and the work-program idea was rejected by New York City on the ground that adequate accounting backup was lacking. The Bureau had failed to recognize that the conceptual distinction between budgets and appropriations tends to break down under the stress of informational demands. If the legislature appropriates by objects, the budget very likely will be classified by objects. Conversely, if there are no functional accounts, the prospects for including such data in the budget are diminished substantially. As has almost always been the case, the budget came to mirror the appropriations act; in each, objects were paramount. It remains to be seen whether PPB will be able to break this interlocking informational pattern.

By the early 1920's the basic functions of planning and management were over-looked by those who carried the gospel of budget reform across the nation. First generation budget workers concentrated on perfecting and spreading the widely approved object-of-expenditure approach, and budget writers settled into a nearly complete preoccupation with forms and with factual descriptions of actual and recommended procedures. Although ideas about the use of the budget for planning and management purposes were retained in Buck's catalogs of "approved" practices,[18] they did not have sufficient priority to challenge tradition.

From the start, Federal budgeting was placed on a control, object-of-expenditure footing, the full flavor of which can be perceived in reading Charles G. Dawes' documentary on *The First Year of the Budget of The United States.* According to Dawes,

> the Bureau of the Budget is concerned only with the humbler and routine business of Government. Unlike cabinet officers, it is concerned with no question of policy, save that of economy and efficiency.[19]

This distinction fitted neatly with object classifications that provided a firm accounting base for the routine conduct of government business, but no information on policy implications of public expenditures. Furthermore, in its first decade, the Bureau's tiny staff (40 or fewer) had to coordinate a multitude of well-advertised economy drives which shaped the job of the examiner as being that of reviewing itemized estimates to pare them down. Although Section 209 of the Budget and Accounting Act had authorized the Bureau to study and recommend improvements in the organization and administrative practices of Federal agencies, the Bureau was overwhelmingly preoccupied with the business of control.

The Management Orientation

Although no single action represents the shift from a control to a management orientation, the turning point in this evolution probably came with the New Deal's broadening perspective of government responsibilities.

During the 1920's and 1930's, occasional voices urged a return to the conceptions of budgeting advocated by the early reformers. In a notable 1924 article, Lent D. Upson argued vigorously that "budget procedure had stopped halfway in its development," and he proposed six modifications in the form of the budget, the net effect being a shift in emphasis from accounting control to functional accounting.[20] A similar position was taken a decade later by Wylic Kilpatrick who insisted that "the one fundamental basis of expenditure is functional, an accounting of payments for the services performed by government."[21]

Meanwhile, gradual changes were preparing the way for a reorientation of budgeting to a management mission. Many of the administrative abuses that had given rise to object controls were curbed by statutes and regulations and by a general upgrading of the public service. Reliable accounting systems were installed and personnel and purchasing reforms introduced, thereby freeing budgeting from some of its watchdog chores. The rapid growth of government activities and expenditures made it more difficult and costly for central officials to keep track of the myriad objects in the budget. With expansion, the bits and pieces into which the objects were itemized became less and less significant, while the aggregate of activities performed became more significant. With expansion, there was heightened need for central management of the incohesive sprawl of administrative agencies.

The climb in activities and expenditures also signaled radical changes in the role of the budget system. As long as government was considered a "necessary evil," and there was little recognition of the social value of public expenditures, the main function of budgeting was to keep spending in check. Because the outputs were deemed to be of limited and fixed value, it made sense to use the budget for central control over inputs. However, as the work and accomplishments of public agencies came to be regarded as benefits, the task of budgeting was redefined as the effective marshalling of fiscal and organizational resources for the attainment of benefits. This new posture focused attention on the problems of managing large programs and organizations, and on the opportunities for using the budget to extend executive hegemony over the dispersed administrative structure.

All these factors converged in the New Deal years. Federal expenditures rose rapidly from $4.2 billion in 1932 to $10 billion in 1940. Keynesian economics (the full budgetary implications of which are emerging only now in PPB) stressed the relationship between public spending and the condition of the economy. The President's Committee on Administrative Management (1937) castigated the routinized, control-minded approach of the Bureau of the Budget and urged that budgeting be used to coordinate Federal activities under presidential leadership. With its transfer in 1939 from the Treasury to the newly-created Executive Office of the President, the Bureau was on its way to becoming the leading management arm of the Federal Government. The Bureau's own staff was increased tenfold; it developed the administrative management and statistical coordination functions that it still possesses; and it installed apportionment procedures for budget execution. More and more, the Bureau was staffed from the ranks of public administration rather than from accounting, and it was during the Directorship of Harold D. Smith (1939–46) that the Bureau substantially embraced the management orientation.[22] Executive Order 8248 placed the President's imprimatur on the management philosophy. It directed the Bureau to keep the President informed of the progress of activities by agencies of the Government with respect to work proposed, work actually initiated, and work completed, together with the relative timing of work between the several agencies of the Government; all to the end that the work programs of the several agencies of the executive branch of the Government may be coordinated and that the monies appropriated by the Congress may be expended in the most economical manner possible to prevent overlapping and duplication of effort.

Accompanying the growing management use of the budget process for the appraisal and improvement of administrative performance and the scientific management movement with its historical linkage to public administration were far more relevant applications of managerial cost accounting to governmental operations. Government agencies sought to devise performance standards and the rudimentary techniques of work measurement were introduced in several agencies including the Forest Service, the Census Bureau, and the Bureau of Reclamation.[23] Various professional associations developed grading systems to assess administrative performance as well as the need for public services. These crude and unscientific methods were the forerunners of more sophisticated and objective techniques. At the apogee of these efforts, Clarence Ridley and Herbert Simon published *Measuring Municipal Activities: A Survey of Suggested Criteria for Appraising Administration,* in which they identified five kinds of measurement—(1) needs, (2) results, (3) costs, (4) effort, and (5) performance—and surveyed the obstacles to the measurement of needs and results. The latter three categories they combined into a measure of administrative efficiency. This study provides an excellent inventory of the state of the technology prior to the breakthrough made by cost-benefit and systems analysis.

At the close of World War II, the management orientation was entrenched in all but one aspect of Federal budgeting—the classification of expenditures. Except for isolated cases (such as TVA's activity accounts and the project structure in the Department of Agriculture), the traditional object accounts were retained though the control function had receded in importance. In 1949 the Hoover Commission called for alterations in budget classifications consonant with the management orientation. It recommended "that the whole budgetary concept of the Federal Government should be refashioned by the adoption of a budget based upon functions, activities, and projects."[24] To create a sense of novelty, the Commission gave a new label—performance budgeting—to what had long been known as functional or activity budgeting. Because its task force had used still another term—program budgeting—there were two new terms to denote the budget innovations of that period. Among writers there was no uniformity in usage, some preferring the "program budgeting" label, others "performance budgeting," to describe the same things. The level of confusion has been increased recently by the association of the term "program budgeting" (also the title of the Rand publication edited by David Novick) with the PPB movement.

Although a variety of factors and expectations influenced the Hoover Commission, and the Commission's proposals have been interpreted in many ways, including some that closely approximate the PPB concept, for purposes of clarity, and in accord with the control-management-planning framework, performance budgeting *as it was generally-understood and applied* must be distinguished from the emergent PPB idea. The term "performance budgeting" is hereafter used in reference to reforms set in motion by the Hoover Commission and the term "program budgeting" is used in conjunction with PPB.

Performance budgeting is management-oriented; its principal thrust is to help administrators to assess the work-efficiency of operating units by (1) casting budget categories in functional terms, and (2) providing work-cost measurements to facilitate the efficient performance of prescribed activities. Generally, its method is particularistic, the reduction of work-cost data unto discrete, measurable units. Program budgeting (PPB) is planning-oriented; its main goal is to rationalize policy making by providing (1) data on the costs and benefits of alternative ways of attaining proposed public objectives, and (2) output measurements to facilitate the effective attainment of chosen objectives. As a policy device, program budgeting departs from simple engineering models of efficiency in which the objective is fixed and the quantity of inputs and outputs is adjusted to an optimal relationship. In PPB, the objective itself is variable; analysis may lead to a new statement of objectives. In order to enable budget makers to evaluate the costs and benefits of alternative expenditure options, program budgeting focuses on expenditure aggregates; the details come into play only as they contribute to an analysis of the total (the system) or of marginal trade-offs among competing proposals. Thus, in this macroanalytic approach, the accent is on comprehensiveness and on grouping data into categories that allow comparisons among alternative expenditure mixes.

Performance budgeting derived its ethos and much of its technique from cost accounting and scientific management; program budgeting has drawn its core ideas from economics and systems analysis. In the performance budgeting literature, budgeting is described as a "tool of management" and the budget as a "work program." In PPB, budgeting is an allocative process among competing claims, and the budget is a statement of policy. Chronologically, there was a gap of several years between the bloom of performance budgeting and the first articulated conceptions of program budgeting. In the aftermath of the first Hoover report, and especially during the early 1950's, there was a plethora of writings on the administrative advantages of the performance budget. Substantial interest in program budgeting did not emerge until the mid–1950's when a number of economists (including Smithies, Novick, and McKean) began to urge reform of the Federal budget system. What the economists had in mind was not the same thing as the Hoover Commission.

In line with its management perspective, the Commission averred that "the all-important thing in budgeting is the work or service to be accomplished, and what that work or service will cost."[25] Mosher followed this view closely in writing that "the central idea of the performance budget . . . is that the budget process be focused upon programs and functions—that is, accomplishments to be achieved, work to be done."[26] But from the planning perspective, the all-important thing surely is not the work or service to be accomplished but the objectives or purposes to be fulfilled by the investment of public funds. Whereas in performance budgeting, work and activities are treated virtually as ends in themselves, in program budgeting work and services are regarded as intermediate aspects, the process of converting resources into outputs. Thus, in a 1954 Rand paper, Novick defined a program as "the sum of the steps or interdependent activities which enter into the attainment of a specified objective. The program, therefore, is the end objective and is developed or budgeted in terms of all the elements necessary to its execution."[27] Novick goes on to add, "this is not the sense in which the government budget now uses the term."

Because the evaluation of performance and the evaluation of program are distinct budget functions, they call for different methods of classification which serves as an intermediate layer between objects and organizations. The activities relate to the functions and work of a distinct operating unit; hence their classification ordinarily conforms to organizational lines. This is the type of classification most useful for an administrator who has to schedule the procurement and utilization of resources for the production of goods and services. Activity classifications gather under a single rubric all the expenditure data needed by a manager to run his unit. The evaluation of programs, however, requires an end-product classification that is oriented to the mission and purposes of government. This type of classification may not be very useful for the manager, but it is of great value to the budget maker who has to decide how to allocate scarce funds among competing claims. Some of the difference between end-product and activity classifications can be gleaned by comparing the Coast Guard's existing activity schedule with the proposed program structure on the last page of Bulletin 66–3. The activity structure which was developed under the aegis of performance budgeting is geared to the operating responsibilities of the Coast Guard: Vessel Operations, Aviation Operations, Repair and Supply Facilities, and others. The proposed program structure is hinged to the large purposes sought through Coast

Guard operations: Search and Rescue, Aids to Navigation, Law Enforcement, and so on.

It would be a mistake to assume that performance techniques presuppose program budgeting or that it is not possible to collect performance data without program classifications. Nevertheless, the view has gained hold that a program budget is "a transitional type of budget between the orthodox (traditional) character and object budget on the one hand and performance budget on the other."[28] Kammerer and Shadoan stress a similar connection. The former writes that "a *performance* budget carries the program budget one step further: into *unit costs*."[29] Shadoan "envisions 'performance budgeting' as an extension of . . . the program budget concept to which the element of unit work measurement has been added."[30] These writers ignore the divergent functions served by performance and program budgets. It is possible to devise and apply performance techniques without relating them to, or having the use of, larger program aggregates. A cost accountant or work measurement specialist can measure the cost or effort required to perform a repetitive task without probing into the purpose of the work or its relationship to the mission of the organization. Work measurement—"a method of establishing an equitable relationship between the volume of work performed and manpower utilized"—[31] is only distantly and indirectly related to the process of determining governmental policy at the higher levels. Program classifications are vitally linked to the making and implementation of policy through the allocation of public resources. As a general rule, performance budgeting is concerned with the *process of work* (what methods should be used) while program budgeting is concerned with the *purpose of work* (what activities should be authorized).

Perhaps the most reliable way to describe this difference is to show what was tried and accomplished under performance budgeting. First of all, performance budgeting led to the introduction of activity classifications, the management-orientation of which has already been discussed. Second, narrative descriptions of program and performance were added to the budget document. These statements give the budget-reader a general picture of the work that will be done by the organizational unit requesting funds. But unlike the analytic documents currently being developed under PPB, the narratives have a descriptive and justificatory function; they do not provide an objective basis for evaluating the cost-utility of an expenditure. Indeed, there hardly is any evidence that the narratives have been used for decision making; rather they seem best suited for giving the uninformed outsider some glimpses of what is going on inside.

Third, performance budgeting spawned a multitude of work-cost measurement explorations. Most used, but least useful, were the detailed workload statistics assembled by administrators to justify their requests for additional funds. On a higher level of sophistication were attempts to apply the techniques of scientific management and cost accounting to the development of work and productivity standards. In these efforts, the Bureau of the Budget had a long involvement, beginning with the issuance of the trilogy of work measurement handbooks in 1950 and reaching its highest development in the productivity-measurement studies that were published in 1964. All these applications were at a level of detail useful for managers with operating or supervisory responsibilities, but of scant usefulness for top-level officials who have to determine organizational objectives and goals. Does it really help top officials if they know that it cost $0.07 to wash a pound of laundry or that the average postal employee processes 289 items of mail per hour? These are the main fruits of performance measurements, and they have an importance place in the management of an organization. They are of great value to the operating official who has the limited function of getting a job done, but they would put a crushing burden on the policy maker whose function is to map the future course of action.

Finally, the management viewpoint led to significant departures from PPB's principle that the expenditure accounts should show total systems cost. The 1949 National Security Act (possibly the first concrete result of the Hoover report) directed the segregation of capital and operating costs in the defense budget. New York State's performance—budgeting experiment for TB hospitals separated expenditures into cost centers (a concept derived from managerial cost accounting) and within each center into fixed and variable costs. In most manpower and work measurements, labor has been isolated from other inputs. Most important, in many states and localities (and implicitly in Federal budgeting) the cost of continuing existing programs has been separated from the cost of new or expanded programs. This separation is useful for managers who build up a budget in terms of increments and decrements from the base, but it is a violation of program budgeting's working assumption that all claims must be pitted against one another in the competition for funds. Likewise, the forms of separation previously mentioned make sense from the standpoint of the manager, but impair the planner's capability to compare expenditure alternatives.

The Planning Orientation

The foregoing has revealed some of the factors leading to the emergence of the planning orientation. Three important developments influenced the evolution from a management to a planning orientation.

1. Economic analysis—macro and micro—has had an increasing part in the shaping of fiscal and budgetary policy.

2. The development of new informational and decisional
   technologies has enlarged the applicability of objective analysis to
   policy making. And,
3. There has been a gradual convergence of planning and budgetary
   processes.

Keynesian economics with its macroanalytic focus on the impact of governmental action on the private sector had its genesis in the underemploy-
ment economy of the Great Depression. In calling attention to the opportunities for attaining full employment by means of fiscal policy, the
Keynesians set into motion a major restatement of the central budget function. From the utilization of fiscal policy to achieve economic objectives, it
was but a few steps to the utilization of the budget process to achieve fiscal
objectives. Nevertheless, between the emergence and the victory of the new
economics, there was a lapse of a full generation, a delay due primarily to
the entrenched balanced-budget ideology. But the full realization of the
budget's economic potential was stymied on the revenue side by static tax
policies and on the expenditure side by status spending policies.

If the recent tax policy of the Federal Government is evidence that the
new economics has come of age, it also offers evidence of the long-standing
failure of public officials to use the taxing power as a variable constraint
on the economy. Previously, during normal times, the tax structure was accepted as given, and the task of fiscal analysis was to forecast future tax
yields so as to ascertain how much would be available for expenditure. The
new approach treats taxes as variable, to be altered periodically in accord
with national policy and economic conditions. Changes in tax rates are not
to be determined (as they still are in virtually all States and localities) by
how much is needed to cover expenditures but by the projected impact of
alternative tax structures on the economy.

It is more than coincidental that the advent of PPB has followed on the
heels of the explicit utilization of tax policy to guide the economy. In
macroeconomics, taxes and expenditures are mirror images of one another; a tax cut and an expenditure increase have comparable impacts.
Hence, the hinging of tax policy to economic considerations inevitably led
to the similar treatment of expenditures. But there were (and remain) a
number of obstacles to the utilization of the budget as a fiscal tool. For one
thing, the conversion of the budget process to an economic orientation
probably was slowed by the Full Employment Act of 1946 which established the Council of Economic Advisers and transferred the Budget Bureau's fiscal analysis function to the Council. The institutional separation
between the CEA and the BOB and between fiscal policy and budget making was not compensated by cooperative work relationships. Economic
analysis had only a slight impact on expenditure policy. It offered a few

guidelines (for example, that spending should be increased during recessions) and a few ideas (such as a shelf of public works projects), but it did not feed into the regular channels of budgeting. The business of preparing the budget was foremost a matter of responding to agency spending pressures, not of responding to economic conditions.

Moreover, expenditures (like taxes) have been treated virtually as givens, to be determined by the unconstrained claims of the spending units. In the absence of central policy instructions, the agencies have been allowed to vent their demands without prior restraints by central authorities and without an operational set of planning guidelines. By the time the Bureau gets into the act, it is faced with the overriding task of bringing estimates into line with projected resources. In other words, the Bureau has had a budget-cutting function, to reduce claims to an acceptable level. The President's role has been similarly restricted. He is the *gatekeeper* of Federal budgeting. He directs the pace of spending increases by deciding which of the various expansions proposed by the agencies shall be included in the budget. But, as the gatekeeper, the President rarely has been able to look back at the items that have previously passed through the gate; his attention is riveted to those programs that are departures from the established base. In their limited roles, neither the Bureau nor the President has been able to inject fiscal and policy objectives into the forefront of budget preparation.

It will not be easy to wean budgeting from its utilization as an administrative procedure for financing ongoing programs to a decisional process for determining the range and direction of public objectives and the government's involvement in the economy. In the transition to a planning emphasis, an important step was the 1963 hearings of the Joint Economic Committee on *The Federal Budget as an Economic Document*. These hearings and the pursuant report of the JEC explored the latent policy opportunities in budget making. Another development was the expanded time horizons manifested by the multiyear expenditure projections introduced in the early 1960's. Something of a breakthrough was achieved via the revelation that the existing tax structure would yield cumulatively larger increments of uncommitted funds—estimated as much as $50 billion by 1970—which could be applied to a number of alternative uses. How much of the funds should be "returned" to the private sector through tax reductions and how much through expenditure increases? How much should go to the States and localities under a broadened system of Federal grants? How much should be allocated to the rebuilding of cities, to the improvement of education, or to the eradication of racial injustices. The traditional budget system lacked the analytic tools to cope with these questions, though decisions ultimately would be made one way or another. The expansion of the time horizon from the single year to a multiyear frame enhances the opportunity for planning and analysis to have an impact on future expenditure decisions. With a one-year perspective, almost all options have been foreclosed by previous commitments; analysis is effective only for the increments provided by self-generating revenue increases or to the extent that it is feasible to convert funds from one use to another. With a longer time span, however, many more options are open, and economic analysis can have a prominent part in determining which course of action to pursue.

So much for the macroeconomic trends in budget reform. On the microeconomic side, PPB traces its lineage to the attempts of welfare economists to construct a science of finance predicted on the principle of marginal utility. Such a science, it was hoped, would furnish objective criteria for determining the optimal allocation of public funds among competing uses. By appraising the marginal costs and benefits of alternatives (poor relief versus battleships in Pigou's classic example), it would be possible to determine which combination of expenditures afforded maximum utility. The quest for a welfare function provided the conceptual underpinning for a 1940 article on "The Lack of a Budgetary Theory" in which V. O. Key noted the absence of a theory which would determine whether "to allocate x dollars to activity A instead of activity B."[32] In terms of its direct contribution to budgetary practice, welfare economics has been a failure. It has not been possible to distill the conflicts and complexities of political life into a welfare criterion or homogeneous distribution formula. But stripped of its normative and formal overtones, its principles have been applied to budgeting by economists such as Arthur Smithies. Smithies has formulated a budget rule that "expenditure proposals should be considered in the light of the objectives they are intended to further, and in general final expenditure decisions should not be made until all claims on the budget can be considered."[33] PPB is the application of this rule to budget practice. By structuring expenditures so as to juxtapose substitutive elements within program categories, and by analyzing the costs and benefits of the various substitutes, PPB has opened the door to the use of marginal analysis in budgeting.

Actually, the door was opened somewhat by the development of new decisional and informational technologies, the second item on the list of influences in the evolution of the planning orientation. Without the availability of the decisional-informational capability provided by cost-benefit and systems analysis, it is doubtful that PPB would be part of the budgetary apparatus today. The new technologies make it possible to cope with the enormous informational and analytic burdens imposed by PPB. As aids to calculation, they furnish a methodology for the analysis of alternatives, thereby expanding the range of decision-making in budgeting.

Operations research, the oldest of these technologies, grew out of complex World War II conditions that required the optimal coordination of manpower, material, and equipment to achieve defense objectives. Operations research is most applicable to those repetitive operations where the opportunity for qualtification is highest. Another technology, cost-benefit analysis, was intensively adapted during the 1950's to large-scale water resource investments, and subsequently to many other governmental functions. Systems analysis is the most global of these technologies. It involves the skillful analysis of the major factors that go into the attainment of an interconnected set of objectives. Systems analysis has been applied in DOD to the choice of weapons systems, the location of military bases, and the determination of sealift-airlift requirements. Although the extension of these technologies across-the-board to government was urged repeatedly by members of the Rand Corporation during the 1950's, it was DOD's experience that set the stage for the current ferment. It cannot be doubted that the coming of PPB has been pushed ahead several years or more by the "success story" in DOD.

The third stream of influence in the transformation of the budget function has been a closing of the gap between planning and budgeting. Institutionally and operationally, planning and budgeting have run along separate tracks. The national government has been reluctant to embrace central planning of any sort because of identification with socialist management of the economy. The closest thing we have had to a central planning agency was the National Resources Planning Board in the 1939–1943 period. Currently, the National Security Council and the Council of Economic Advisors have planning responsibilities in the defense and fiscal areas. As far as the Bureau of the Budget is concerned, it has eschewed the planning function in favor of control and management. In many States and localities, planning and budgeting are handled by separate organizational units: in the States, because limitations on debt financing have encouraged the separation of the capital and operating budgets; in the cities, because the professional autonomy and land-use preoccupations of the planners have set them apart from the budgeteers.

In all governments, the appropriations cycle, rather than the anticipation of future objectives, tends to dictate the pace and posture of budgeting. Into the repetitive, one-year span of the budget is wedged all financial decisions, including those that have multiyear implications. As a result, planning, if it is done at all, "occurs independently of budgeting and with little relation to it."[34] Budgeting and planning, moreover, invite disparate perspectives: the one is conservative and negativistic; the other, innovative and expansionist. As Mosher has noted, "budgeting and planning are apposite, if not opposite. In extreme form, the one means saving; the other, spending."[35]

Nevertheless, there has been some *rapprochement* of planning and budgeting. One factor is the long lead-time in the development and procurement of hardware and capital investments. The multiyear projections inau-
gurated several years ago were a partial response to this problem. Another
factor has been the diversity of government agencies involved in related
functions. This has given rise to various *ad hoc* coordinating devices, but it
also has pointed to the need for permanent machinery to integrate dispersed activities. Still another factor has been the sheer growth of Federal
activities and expenditures and the need for a rational system of allocation.
The operational code of planners contains three tenets relevant to these
budgetary needs: (1) planning is future-oriented; it connects present decisions to the attainment of a desired future state of affairs; (2) planning, ideally, encompasses all resources involved in the attainment of future objectives. It strives for comprehensiveness. The *master plan* is the one that
brings within its scope all relevant factors; (3) planning is means-ends oriented. The allocation of resources is strictly dictated by the ends that are to
be accomplished. All this is to say that planning is an economizing process,
though planners are more oriented to the future than economists. It is not
surprising that planners have found the traditional budget system deficient,[36] nor is it surprising that the major reforms entailed by PPB emphasize the planning function.

Having outlined the several trends in the emerging transition to a planning orientation, it remains to mention several qualifications. First, the
planning emphasis is not predominant in Federal budgeting at this time.
Although PPB asserts the paramountcy of planning, PPB itself is not yet a
truly operational part of the budget machinery. We are now at the dawn of
a new era in budgeting; high noon is still a long way off. Second, this transition has not been preceded by a reorientation of the Bureau of the Budget. Unlike the earlier change-over from control to management in which
the alteration of budgetary techniques *followed* the revision of the Bureau's
role, the conversion from management to planning is taking a different
course—first, the installation of new techniques; afterwards, a reformula-
tion of the Bureau's mission. Whether this sequence will hinder reform efforts is a matter that cannot be predicted, but it should be noted that in the
present instance the Bureau cannot convert to a new mission by bringing in
a wholly new staff, as was the case in the late 1930's and early 1940's.

What Difference Does It Make?

The starting point for the author was distinguishing the old from the new
in budgeting. The interpretation has been framed in analytic terms, and
budgeting has been viewed historically in three stages corresponding to the
three basic functions of budgeting. In this analysis, an attempt has been

made to identify the difference between the existing and the emerging as a difference between management and planning orientations.

In an operational sense, however, what difference does it make whether the central budget process is oriented toward planning rather than management? Does the change merely mean a new way of making decisions, or does it mean different decisions as well? These are not easy questions to answer, particularly since the budget system of the future will be a compound of all three functions. The case for PPB rests on the assumption that the form in which information is classified and used governs the actions of budget makers, and, conversely, that alterations in form will produce desired changes in behavior. Take away the assumption that behavior follows form, and the movement for PPB is reduced to a trivial manipulation of techniques—form for form's sake without any significant bearing on the conduct of budgetary affairs.

Yet this assumed connection between roles and information is a relatively uncharted facet of the PPB literature. The behavioral side of the equation has been neglected. PPB implies that each participant will behave as a sort of Budgetary Man, a counterpart of the classical Economic Man and Simon's Administrative Man.[37] Budgetary Man, whatever his station or role in the budget process, is assumed to be guided by an unwavering commitment to the rule of efficiency; in every instance he chooses that alternative that optimizes the allocation of public resources.

PPB probably takes an overly mechanistic view of the impact of form on behavior and underestimates the strategic and volitional aspects of budget making. In the political arena, data are used to influence the "who gets what" in budgets and appropriations. If information influences behavior, the reverse also is true. Indeed, data are more tractable than roles; participants are more likely to seek and use data which suit their preferences than to alter their behavior automatically in response to formal changes.

All this constrains, rather than negates, the impact of budget form. The advocates of PPB, probably in awareness of the above limitations, have imported into budgeting men with professional commitments to the types of analysis and norms required by the new techniques, men with a background in economics and systems analysis, rather than with general administrative training.

PPB aspires to create a different environment for choice. Traditionally, budgeting has defined its mission in terms of identifying the existing base and proposed departures from it—"This is where we are; where do we go from here?" PPB defines its mission in terms of budgetary objectives and purposes—"Where do we want to go? What do we do to get there?" The environment of choice under traditional circumstances is *incremental*; in PPB it is *teletic*. Presumably, these different processes will lead to different budgetary outcomes.

A budgeting process which accepts the base and examines only the increments will produce decisions to transfer the present into the future with a few small variations. The curve of government activities will be continuous, with few zigzags or breaks. A budget-making process which begins with objectives will require the base to compete on an equal footing with new proposals. The decisions will be more radical than those made under incremental conditions. This does not mean that each year's budget will lack continuity with the past. There are sunk costs that have to be reckoned, and the benefits of radical changes will have to outweigh the costs of terminating prior commitments. Furthermore, the extended time span of PPB will mean that big investment decisions will be made for a number of years, with each year being a partial installment of the plan. Most important, the political manifestations of sunk costs—vested interests—will bias decisions away from radical departures. The conservatism of the political system, therefore, will tend to minimize the decisional differences between traditional and PPB approaches. However, the very availability of analytic data will cause a shift in the balance of economic and political forces that go into the making of a budget.

Teletic and incremental conditions of choice lead to still another distinction. In budgeting, which is committed to the established base, the flow of budgetary decisions is upward and aggregative. Traditionally, the first step in budgeting, in anticipation of the call for estimates, is for each department to issue its own call to prepare and to submit a set of estimates. This call reaches to the lowest level capable of assembling its own estimates. Lowest level estimates form the building blocks for the next level where they are aggregated and reviewed and transmitted upward until the highest level is reached and the totality constitutes a department-wide budget. Since budgeting is tied to a base, the building-up-from-below approach is sensible; each building block estimates the cost of what it is already doing plus the cost of the increments it wants. (The building blocks, then, are decisional elements, not simply informational elements as is often assumed.)

PPB reverses the informational and decisional flow. Before the call for estimates is issued, top policy has to be made, and this policy constrains the estimates prepared below. For each lower level, the relevant policy instructions are issued by the superior level prior to the preparation of estimates. Accordingly, the critical decisional process—that of deciding on purposes and plans—has a downward and disaggregative flow.

If the making of policy is to be antecedent to the costing of estimates, there will have to be a shift in the distribution of budget responsibilities. The main energies of the Bureau of the Budget are now devoted to budget preparation; under PPB these energies will be centered on what we may term *prepreparation*—the stage of budget making that deals with policy and is prior to the preparation of the budget. One of the steps marking the

TABLE 4.1 Some Basic Differences Between Budget Orientations

Characteristic	Control	Management	Planning
Personnel Skill	Accounting	Administration	Economics
Information Focus	Objects	Activities	Purposes
Key Budget Stage (central)	Execution	Preparation	Pre-preparation
Breadth of Measurement	Discrete	Discrete/ activities	Comprehensive
Role of Budget Agency	Ficuciary	Efficiency	Policy
Decisional-Flow	Upward- aggregative	Upward- aggregative	Downward- disaggregative
Type of Choice	Incremental	Incremental	Teletic
Control Responsibility	Central	Operating	Operating
Management Responsibility	Dispersed	Central	Supervisory
Planning Responsibility	Dispersed	Dispersed	Central
Budget-Appropriations Classifications	Same	Same	Different
Appropriations-Organizational Link	Direct	Direct	Crosswalk

advent of the planning orientation was the inauguration of the Spring Preview several years ago for the purpose of affording an advance look at departmental programs.

If budget-making is to be oriented to the planning function, there probably will be a centralization of policy-making, both within and among departments. The DOD experience offers some precedent for predicting that greater budgetary authority will be vested in department heads than heretofore, but there is no firm basis for predicting the degree of centralization that may derive from the relatedness of objectives pursued by many departments. It is possible that the mantle of central budgetary policy will be assumed by the Bureau; indeed, this is the expectation in many agencies. On the other hand, the Bureau gives little indication at this time that it is willing or prepared to take this comprehensive role.

Conclusion

The various differences between the budgetary orientations are charted in Table 4.1. All the differences may be summed up in the statement that the ethos of budgeting will shift from justification to analysis. To far greater extent than heretofore, budget decisions will be influenced by explicit statements of objectives and by a formal weighing of the costs and benefits of alternatives.

Notes

1. New York Bureau of Municipal Research, *Making a Municipal Budget* (New York: 1907), pp. 9–10.

2. Robert N. Anthony, *Planning and Control Systems: A Framework for Analysis* (Boston: 1965), pp. 16–18.

3. Frederick A. Cleveland, "Evolution of the Budget Idea in the United States," *Annals of the American Academy of Political and Social Science,* LXII (1915), 16.

4. *Ibid.,* p. 17.

5. See Frank J. Goodnow, "The Limit of Budgetary Control," *Proceedings of the American Political Science Association* (Baltimore: 1913), p. 72; also William F. Willoughby, "Allotment of Funds by Executive Officials, An Essential Feature of Any Correct Budgetary System," *ibid.,* pp. 78–87.

6. U.S., President's Commission on Economy and Efficiency, *The Need for a National Budget* (Washington: 1912), pp. 210–213.

7. Charles A. Beard, "Prefatory Note," *ibid.,* p. vii.

8. New York Bureau of Municipal Research, "Some Results and Limitations of Central Financial Control in New York City," *Municipal Research,* LXXXI (1917), 10.

9. "Next Steps . . . ," *op. cit.,* p. 39.

10. "Next Steps . . . ", *op. cit.,* p. 67.

11. "Some Results and Limitations . . . ", *op. cit.,* p. 9.

12. "Next Steps . . . ", *op. cit,* p. 35.

13. *Ibid,* p. 7.

14. "Next Steps . . . ", p. 39.

15. "Some Results and Limitations . . . ", *op. cit.,* p. 7.

16. *Ibid.,* p. 9.

17. "Next Steps . . . ", *op. cit.,* p. 30.

18. See A. E. Buck, *Public Budgeting* (New York: 1929), pp. 181–88.

19. Charles G. Dawes, *The First Year of the Budget of the United States* (New York: 1923), preface, p. ii.

20. Lent D. Upson, "Half-time Budget Methods," *The Annals of the American Academy of Political and Social Science,* CXIII (1924), 72.

21. Wylie Kilpatrick, "Classification and Measurement of Public Expenditure", *The Annals of the American Academy of Political and Social Science,* C.XXXIII (1936), 20.

22. See Harold D. Smith, *The Management of Your Government* (New York: 1945).

23. Public Administration Service, *The Work Unit in Federal Administration* (Chicago: 1937).

24. U.S. Commission on Organization of the Executive Branch of the Government, *Budgeting and Accounting* (Washington: 1949), 8.

25. *Ibid.*

26. Frederick C. Mosher, *Program Budgeting: Theory and Practice* (Chicago: 1954), p. 79.

27. David Novick, *Which Program Do We Mean in "Program Budgeting?"* (Santa Monica: 1954), p. 17.

28. Lennex L. Moak and Kathryn W. Killian, *A Manual of Techniques for the Preparation, Consideration, Adoption, and Administration of Operating Budgets* (Chicago: 1963), p. 11.

29. Gladys M. Kammerer, *Program Budgeting: An Aid to Understanding* (Gainesville: 1959), p. 6.

30. Arlene Theuer Shadean, *Preparation, Review, and Execution of the State Operating Budget* (Lexington: 1963), p. 13.

31. U.S. Bureau of the Budget, *A Work Measurement System* (Washington: 1950), p. 2.

32. V. O. Key, "The Lack of a Budgetary Theory," *The American Political Science Review,* XXXIV (1940), 1138.

33. Arthur Smithies, *The Budgetary Process in the United States* (New York: 1955), p. 16.

34. Mosher, *op, cit.,* p. 47–48.

35. *Ibid.,* p. 48.

36. See Edward C. Banfield, "Congress and the Budget: A Planner's Criticism," *The American Political Science Review,* XLIII (1949), 1217–1227.

37. Herbert A. Simon, *Administrative Behavior* (New York: 1957).

5

A BUDGET FOR ALL SEASONS?

Why the Traditional Budget Lasts

Aaron Wildavsky

PAR gratefully acknowledges, and is sincerely appreciative of the permission granted by Dr. Wildavsky, Dr. Benjamin Geist, deputy director general, State Comptroller's Office, State of Israel, and Macmillan of England to publish this article in *Public Administration Review.*

Almost from the time the caterpillar of budgetary evolution became the butterfly of budgetary reform, the line-item budget has been condemned as a reactionary throwback to its primitive larva. Budgeting, its critics claim, has been metamorphized in reverse, an example of retrogression instead of progress. Over the last century, the traditional annual cash budget has been condemned as mindless, because its lines do not match programs, irrational, because they deal with inputs instead of outputs, short-sighted, because they cover one year instead of many, fragmented, because as a rule only changes are reviewed, conservative, because these changes tend to be small, and worse. Yet despite these faults, real and alleged, the traditional budget reigns supreme virtually everywhere, in practice if not in theory. Why?

The usual answer, if it can be dignified as such, is bureaucratic inertia. The forces of conservatism within government resist change. Presumably

1978. A budget for all seasons? Why the traditional budget lasts. Wildavsky, Aaron. **Public Administration Review** 38 (November-December): 501–509.

the same explanation fits all cases past and present. How, then, explain why countries like Britain departed from tradition in recent years only to return to it? It is hard to credit institutional inertia in virtually all countries for a century. Has nothing happened over time to entrench the line-item budget?

The line-item budget is a product of history, not of logic. It was not so much created as evolved. Its procedures and its purposes represent accretions over time rather than propositions postulated at a moment in time. Hence we should not expect to find them either consistent or complementary.

Control over public money and accountability to public authority were among the earliest purposes of budgeting. Predictability and planning— knowing what there will be to spend over time—was not far behind. From the beginning, relating expenditure to revenue was of prime importance. In our day we have added macro-economic management to moderate inflation and unemployment. Spending is varied to suit the economy. In time the need for money came to be used as a level to enhance the efficiency or effectiveness of policies. He who pays the piper hopes to call the tune. Here we have it: Budgeting is supposed to contribute to continuity (for planning), to change (for policy evaluation), to flexibility (for the economy), and to provide rigidity (for limiting spending).

These different and (to some extent) opposed purposes contain a clue to the perennial dissatisfaction with budgeting. Obviously, no process can simultaneously provide continuity and change, rigidity and flexibility. And no one should be surprised that those who concentrate on one purpose or the other should find budgeting unsatisfactory or that, as purposes change, these criticisms should become constant. The real surprise is that traditional budgeting has not been replaced by any of its outstanding competitors in this century.

If traditional budgeting is so bad, why are there no better alternatives? Appropriate answers are unobtainable, I believe, so long as we proceed on this high level of aggregation. So far as I know, the traditional budget has never been compared systematically, characteristic for characteristic, with the leading alternatives.[1] By doing so we can see better which characteristics of budgetary processes suit different purposes under a variety of conditions. Why, again, if traditional budgeting does have defects, which I do not doubt, has it not been replaced? Perhaps the complaints are the clue: What is it that is inferior for most purposes and yet superior over all?

The ability of a process to score high on one criterion may increase the likelihood of its scoring low on another. Planning requires predictability and economic management requires reversibility. Thus, there may well be no ideal mode of budgeting. If so, this is the question: Do we choose a budgetary process that does splendidly on one criterion but terribly on others, or a process that satisfies all these demands even though it does not score brilliantly on any single one?

The Traditional Budget

Traditional budgeting is annual (repeated yearly) and incremental (departing marginally from the year before). It is conducted on a cash basis (in current dollars). Its content comes in the form of line-items (such as personnel or maintenance). Alternatives to all these characteristics have been developed and tried, though never, so far as I know, with success. Why this should be so, despite the obvious and admitted defects of tradition, will emerge if we consider the criteria each type of budgetary process has to meet.

What purpose is a public sector budget supposed to serve? Certainly one purpose is accountability. By associating government publicly with certain expenditures, opponents can ask questions or contribute criticisms. Here the clarity of the budget presentation in linking expenditures to activities and to responsible officials is crucial. Close to accountability is control: Are the funds which are authorized and appropriated being spent for the designated activities? Control (or its antonym "out of control") can be used in several senses. Are expenditures within the limits (a) stipulated or (b) desired. While a budget (or item) might be "out of control" to a critic who desires it to be different, in our terms "control" is lacking only when limits are stipulated and exceeded.

Budgets may be mechanisms of efficiency—doing whatever is done at least cost or getting the most out of a given level of expenditure—and/or of effectiveness—achieving certain results in public policy like improving the health of children or reducing crime.

In modern times, budgeting has also become an instrument of economic management and of planning. With the advent of Keynesian economics efforts have been made to vary the rate of spending so as to increase employment in slack times or to reduce inflation when prices are deemed to be rising too quickly. Here (leaving out alternative tax policies), the ability to increase and decrease spending in the short run is of paramount importance. For budgeting to serve planning, however, predictability (not variability) is critical. The ability to maintain a course of behavior over time is essential.

Now, as everyone knows, budgeting is not only an economic but a political instrument. Since inability to implement decisions nullifies them, the ability to mobilize support is as important as making the right choice. So is the capacity to figure out what to do—that is, to make choices. Thus, the effect of budgeting on conflict and calculation—the capacity to make and support decisions—has to be considered.

Unit of Measurement: Cash or Volume

Budgeting can be done not only in cash but by volume. Instead of promising to pay so much in the next year or years, the commitment can be made in terms of operations performed or services provided. Why might anyone want to budget in volume (or constant currency) terms? One reason, obviously, is to aid planning. If public agencies know they can count not on variable currency but on what the currency can buy, that is, on a volume of activity, they can plan ahead as far as the budget runs. Indeed, if one wishes to make decisions now that could be made at future periods, so as to help assure consistency over time, stability in the unit of effort—so many applications processed or such a level of services provided—is the very consideration to be desired.

So long as purchasing power remains constant, budgeting in cash or by volume remains a distinction without a difference. However, should the value of money fluctuate (and, in our time, this means inflation), the public budget must absorb additional amounts so as to provide the designated volume of activity. Budgeters lose control of money because they have to supply whatever is needed. Evidently, given large and unexpected changes in prices, the size of the budget in cash terms would fluctuate wildly. Evidently, also, no government could permit itself to be so far out of control. Hence, the very stability budgeting by volume is designed to achieve turns out to be its major unarticulated premise.

Who pays the price for budgeting by volume? The private sector and the central controller. Budgeting by volume is, first of all, an effort by elements of the public sector to invade the private sector. What budgeting by volume says, in effect, is that the public sector will be protected against inflation by getting its agreed level of services before other needs are met. The real resources necessary to make up the gap between projected and current prices must come from the private sector in the form of taxation or interest for borrowing. In other words, for the public sector volume budgeting is a form of indexing against inflation.

Given an irreducible amount of uncertainty in the system, not every element can be stabilized at one and the same time. Who, then, will be kept stable and who will bear the costs of change? Within the government the obvious answer is that spending by agencies will be kept whole. The central budget office (the Treasury, Ministry of Finance or the Office of Management and Budget, as it is variously called) bears the brunt of covering larger expenditures and takes the blame when the budget goes out of control, i.e., rises faster and in different directions than predicted. In Britain, where budgeting by volume went under the name of the Public Expenditure Survey, the Treasury finally responded to years of severe inflation by imposing cash limits, otherwise known as the traditional cold-cash budget. Of course, departmental cash limits include an amount for price changes, but this is not necessarily what the Treasury expects but the amount it desires. The point is that the spending departments have to make up deficits caused by inflation. Instead of the Treasury forking over the money automatically, as in the volume budget, departments have to ask and may be denied. The local spenders, not the central controllers, have to pay the price of monetary instability.[2]

Inflation has become not only an evil to be avoided but a (perhaps *the*) major instrument of modern public policy. Taxes are hard to increase and benefits are virtually impossible to decrease. Similar results may be obtained through inflation, which artificially elevates the tax brackets in which people find themselves and decreases their purchasing power. Wage increases that cannot be directly contested may be indirectly nullified (and the real burden of the national debt reduced) without changing the ostensible amount, all by inflation. The sensitivity of budgetary forms to inflation is a crucial consideration.

From all this, it follows that budgeting by volume is counter-productive in fighting inflation because it accommodates price increases rather than struggling against them. Volume budgeting may maintain public sector employment at the expense of taking resources from the private sector, thus possibly reducing employment there. There can be no doubt, however, that volume budgeting is for counter-cyclical purposes because the whole point is that the amount and quality of service do not vary over time; if they go up or down to suit short-run economic needs they are bound to be out of kilter over the long run.

How does volume budgeting stack up as a source of policy information? It should enable departments to understand better what they are doing, since they are presumably doing the same thing over the period of the budget, but volume budgeting does poorly as a method of instigating change. For one thing, the money is guaranteed against price changes, so there is less need to please outsiders. For another, volume budgeting necessarily leads to interest in internal affairs—how to do what one wishes—not to external advice—whether there are better things one might be doing. British departments that are unwilling to let outsiders evaluate their activities are hardly going to be motivated by guarantees against price fluctuations.

Time Span: Months, One Year, Many Years

Multi-year budgeting has long been proposed as a reform to enhance rational choice by viewing resource allocation in a long-term perspective. Considering one year, it has been argued, leads to short-sightedness—only the next year's expenditures are reviewed; over-spending—because huge disbursements in future years are hidden; conservatism—incremental changes do not open up larger future vistas; and parochialism—programs tend to be viewed in isolation rather than in comparison to their future costs in relation to expected revenue. Extending the time-span of budgeting to three or five years, it is argued, would enable long-range planning to overtake short-term reaction and substitute financial control for merely muddling through. Moreover, it is argued, the practice of rushing spending to use up resources by the end of the year would decline in frequency.

Much depends, to be sure, on how long budgetary commitments last. The seemingly arcane question of whether budgeting should be done on a cash or a volume basis will assume importance if a nation adopts multi-year budgeting. The longer the term of the budget, the more important inflation becomes. To the degree that price changes are automatically absorbed into budgets, a certain volume of activity is guaranteed. To the degree agencies have to absorb inflation, their real level of activity declines. Multi-year budgeting in cash terms diminishes the relative size of the public sector, leaving the private sector larger. Behind discussions of the span of the budget, the real debate is over the relative shares of the public and private sectors—which one will be asked to absorb inflation and which one will be allowed to expand into the other.

A similar issue of relative shares is created within government by proposals to budget in some sectors for several years, and, in others, for only one. Which sectors of policy will be free from the vicissitudes of life in the short term, the question becomes, and which will be protected from them? Like any other device, multi-year budgeting is not neutral but distributes indulgences differently among the affected interests.

Of course, multi-year budgeting has its positive parts. If control of expenditure is desired, for instance, a multi-year budget makes it necessary to estimate expenditures far into the future. The old tactic of the camel's nose—beginning with small expenditures while hiding larger ones later on—is rendered more difficult. Still, hard-in, as the British learned, often implies harder-out. Once an expenditure gets in a multi-year projection it is likely to stay in because it has become part of an interrelated set of proposals that could be expensive to disrupt. Besides, part of the bargain struck when agencies are persuaded to estimate as accurately as they can, is that they will gain stability, i.e., not be subject to sudden reductions according to the needs of the moment. Thus, control in a single year may have to be sacrificed to maintaining limits over the multi-year period; and, should the call come for cuts to meet a particular problem, British experience shows that reductions in future years, (which are always "iffy") are easily traded for maintenance of spending in the all-important present. By making prices more prominent due to the larger time period involved, moreover, large sums may have to be supplied in order to meet commitments for a given volume of services in a volatile world.[3]

Suppose, however, that it were deemed desirable to reduce significantly some expenditures in order to increase others. Due to the built-in pressure of continuing commitments, what can be done in a single year is extremely limited. Making arrangements over a three to five year period (with constant prices, five percent a year for five years compounded would bring about a one third change in the budget) would permit larger changes in amount in a more orderly way. This may be true, of course, but other things—prices, priorities, politicians—seldom remain equal. While the British were working under a five year budget projection, prices and production could hardly be predicted for five months at a time.

As Robert Hartman put it, "there is no absolutely right way to devise a long-run budget strategy."[4] No one knows how the private economy will be doing or what the consequences will be of a fairly wide range of targets for budget totals. There is no political or economic agreement on whether budget targets should be expressed in terms of levels required for full employment, for price stability, or for budget balancing. Nor is it self-evidently desirable either to estimate where the economy is going and devise a governmental spending target to complement that estimate or to decide what the economy should be doing and get the government to encourage that direction.

In any event, given economic volatility and theoretical poverty, the ability to outguess the future is extremely limited. Responsiveness to changing economic conditions, therefore, if that were the main purpose of budgeting, would be facilitated best with a budget calculated in months or weeks rather than years. Such budgets do exist in poor and uncertain countries. Naomi Caiden and I have called the process "repetitive budgeting" to signify that the budget may be made and remade several times during the year.[5] Because finance ministries often do not know how much is actually in the nation's treasury or what they will have to spend, they hold off making decisions until the last possible moment. The repetitive budget is not a reliable guide to proposed expenditure, but an invitation to agencies to "get it if they can." When economic or political conditions change, which is often, the budget is renegotiated. Adaptiveness is maximized but predictability is minimized. Conflict increases because the same decision is remade several times each year. Agencies must be wary of each other because they do not know when next they will have to compete. Control declines, partly because frequent changes make the audit trail difficult to follow, and partly because departments seek to escape from control so as to reestablish a modicum of predictability. Hence, they obfuscate their activities, thus reducing accountability, and actively seek funds of their own in the form of earmarked revenues, thus diminishing control. Both efficiency and effectiveness suffer. The former is either unnecessary (if separate funds exist) or impossible (without continuity), and the latter is obscured by the lack of relationship between what is in the budget and what happens in the world. Drastically shortening the time-frame wreaks havoc with efficiency, effectiveness, conflict, and calculation. However, if it is immediate responsiveness that is desired, as in economic management, the shorter the span the better.

Just as the annual budget on a cash basis is integral to the traditional process, so is the budgetary base—the expectation that most expenditures will be continued. Normally, only increases or decreases to the existing base are considered in any one period. If budgetary practices may be described as incremental, the main alternative to the traditional budget is one that emphasizes comprehensive calculation. So it is not surprising that the main modern alternatives are planning, programming and budgeting (PPB) and zero base budgeting (ZBB).

Calculation: Incremental or Comprehensive

Let us think of PPB as embodying horizontal comprehensiveness—comparing alternative expenditure packages to decide which best contributes to larger programmatic objectives. ZBB, by contrast, might be thought of as manifesting vertical comprehensiveness—every year alternative expenditures from base zero are considered for all governmental activities or objectives treated as discrete entities. In a word, PPB compares programs and ZBB compares alternative funding.

The strength of PPB lies in its emphasis on policy analysis to increase effectiveness. Programs are evaluated, found wanting, and presumably replaced with alternatives designed to produce superior results. Unfortunately, PPB engenders a conflict between error recognition and error correction. There is little point in designing better policies so as to minimize their prospects of implementation. But why should a process devoted to policy evaluation end up stultifying policy execution? Because PPB's policy rationality is countered by its organizational irrationality.

If error is to be altered, it must be relatively easy to correct,[6] but PPB makes it hard. The "systems" in PPB are characterized by their proponents as highly differentiated and tightly linked. The rationale for program budgeting lies in its connectedness—like-programs are grouped together. Program structures are meant to replace the confused concatenations of line-items with clearly differentiated, non-overlapping boundaries; only one set of programs to a structure. This means that a change in one element or structure must result in change reverberating throughout every element in the same system. Instead of alerting only neighboring units or central control units, which would make change feasible, all are, so to speak, wired together so the choice is effectively all or none.

Imagine one of us deciding whether to buy a tie or a kerchief. A simple task, one might think. Suppose, however, that organizational rules require us to keep our entire wardrobe as a unit. If everything must be rearranged when one item is altered, the probability we will do anything is low. The more tightly linked the elements, and the more highly differentiated they are, the greater the probability of error (because the tolerances are so small), and the less the likelihood the error will be corrected (because with change, every element has to be recalibrated with every other one that was previously adjusted). Being caught between revolution (change in everything) and resignation (change in nothing) has little to recommend it.

Program budgeting increases rather than decreases the cost of correcting error. The great complaint about bureaucracies is their rigidity. As things stand, the object of organizational affection is the bureau as serviced by the usual line-item categories from which people, money, and facilities flow. Viewed from the standpoint of bureau interests, programs, to some extent, are negotiable; some can be increased and others decreased while keeping the agency on an even keel or, if necessary, adjusting it to less happy times without calling into question its very existence. Line-item budgeting, precisely because its categories (personnel, maintenance, supplies) do not relate directly to programs, is easier to change. Budgeting by programs, precisely because money flows to objectives, makes it difficult to abandon objectives without abandoning the organization that gets its money for them. It is better that non-programmatic rubrics be used as formal budget categories, thus permitting a diversity of analytical perspectives, than that a temporary analytic insight be made the permanent perspective through which money is funneled.

The good organization is interested in discovering and correcting its own mistakes. The higher the cost of error—not only in terms of money but also in personnel, programs, and perogatives—the less the chance anything will be done about them. Organizations should be designed, therefore, to make errors visible and correctible—that is, noticeable and reversible—which, in turn, is to say, cheap and affordable.

The ideal, a-historical information system is zero-base budgeting. The past, as reflected in the budgetary base (common expectations as to amounts and types of funding), is explicitly rejected. There is no yesterday. Nothing is to be taken for granted. Everything at every period is subject to searching scrutiny. As a result, calculations become unmanageable. The same is true of PPB, which requires comparisons of all or most programs that might contribute to common objectives. To say that a budgetary process is a-historical is to conclude that it increases the sources of error while decreasing the chances of correcting mistakes. If history is abolished, nothing is settled. Old quarrels become new conflicts. Both calculation and conflict increase exponentially, the former worsening selection, and the latter, correction of error. As the number of independent variables grows, because the past is assumed not to limit the future, ability to control the future declines. As mistrust grows with conflict, willingness to admit and, hence, to correct error diminishes. Doing without history is a little like abolishing memory—momentarily convenient, perhaps, but ultimately embarrassing.

Only poor countries come close to zero-base budgeting, not because they wish to do so but because their uncertain financial position continually causes them to go back on old commitments. Because past disputes are part of present conflicts, their budgets lack predictive value; little stated in them is likely to occur. A-historical practices, which are a dire consequence of extreme instability and from which all who experience them devoutly desire to escape, should not be considered normative.

ZBB and PPB share an emphasis on the virtue of objectives. Program budgeting is designed to relate larger to smaller objectives among different programs, and zero base budgeting promises to do the same within a single program. The policy implications of these methods of budgeting, which distinguish them from existing approaches, derive from their overwhelming concern with ranking objectives. Thinking about objectives is one thing, however, and making budget categories out of them is quite another. Of course, if one wants the objectives of today to be the objectives of tomorrow, which is to say if one wants no change in objectives, then building the budget around objectives is a brilliant idea. However, if one wants flexibility in objectives (sometimes known as learning from experience) it must be possible to change them without simultaneously destroying the organization by withdrawing financial support.

Both PPB and ZBB are expressions of the prevailing paradigm of rationality in which reason is rendered equivalent to ranking objectives. Alas, an efficient mode of presenting results in research papers—find objectives, order them, choose the highest valued—has been confused with proper processes of social inquiry. For purposes of resource allocation, which is what budgeting is about, ranking objectives without consideration of resources is irrational. The question can not be "what do you want?" as if there were no limits, but should be "what do you want compared to what you can get?" (Ignoring resources is as bad as neglecting objectives as if one were not interested in the question "what do I want to do this for?"). After all, an agency with a billion dollars would not only do more than it would with a million dollars but might well wish to do different things. Resources affect objectives as well as the other way around, and budgeting should not separate what reason tells us belongs together.

For purposes of economic management, comprehensive calculations stressing efficiency (ZBB) and effectiveness (PPB) leave much to be desired. For one thing, comprehensiveness takes time and this is no asset in responding to fast-moving events. For another, devices that stress the intrinsic merits of their methods—this is (in)efficient and that is (in)effective—rub raw when good cannot be done for external reasons, i.e., the state of the economy. Cooperation will be compromised when virtue in passing one test becomes vice in failing another.

I have already said that conflict is increased by a-historical methods of budgeting. Here I wish to observe that efforts to reduce conflict only make things worse by vitiating the essential character of comprehensiveness. The cutting edge of competition among programs lies in postulating a range of policy objectives small enough to be encompassed and large enough to overlap so there are choices (trade-offs in the jargon of the trade) among them. Instead, PPB generated a tendency either to have only a few objectives, so anything and everything fit under them, or a multitude of objectives, so that each organizational unit had its own home and did not have to compete with any other.[78] ZBB worked it this way: Since a zero base was too threatening or too absurd, zero moved up until it reached, say, 80 per cent of the base. To be sure, the burden of conflict and calculation declined, but so did any real difference with traditional incremental budgeting.

Insofar as financial control is concerned, ZBB and PBB raise the question of control over what? Is it control over the content of programs or the efficiency of a given program or the total costs of government or just the legality of expenditures? In theory, ZBB would be better for efficiency, PPB for effectiveness, and traditional budgeting for legality. Whether control extends to total costs, however, depends on the form of financing, a matter to which we now turn.

Appropriations or Treasury Budgeting

A traditional budget, without saying much about it, depends on traditional practice—authorization and appropriation followed by expenditure post-audited by external authorities. In many countries traditional budgeting is not, in fact, the main form of public spending. Close to half of public spending in the United States as well as in other countries does not take the form of appropriations budgeting, but what I shall call treasury budgeting. I find this nomenclature useful in avoiding the pejorative connotations of what would otherwise be called "backdoor" spending, because it avoids the appropriations committees in favor of automatic disbursement of funds through the treasury.

For present purposes, the two forms of treasury budgeting that constitute alternatives to traditional appropriations are tax expenditures and mandatory entitlements. When concessions are granted in the form of tax reductions for home ownership or college tuition or medical expenses these are equivalent to budgetary expenditures except that the money is deflected at the source. In the United States, tax expenditures now amount to more than $100 billion a year. In one sense this is a way of avoiding budgeting before there is a budget. Whether one accepts this view is a matter of philosophy. It is said, for instance, that the United States government has a progressive income tax. Is that the real tax system or is it a would-be progressive tax as modified by innumerable exceptions? The budgetary process is usually described as resource allocation by the president and Congress through its appropriations committees. Is that the real budgetary process or is it that process together with numerous provisions for "back-door" spending, low interest loans, and other devices? From a behavioral or descriptive point-of-view actual practices constitute the real system. Then the exceptions are part of the rule. Indeed, since less than half of the budget passes through the appropriations committees, the exceptions must be greater than the rule, and some would say the same could be said about taxation. If the exceptions are part of the rule, however, tax expenditures stand in a better light. Then the government is not contributing or losing income but legitimately excluding certain private activities from being considered as income. There is no question of equity—people are just disposing of their own income as they see fit in a free society. Unless whatever is, is right, tax and budget reformers will object to sanctifying regrettable lapses as operating principles. To them the real systems are the ones which we ought to perfect—a progressive tax on income whose revenues are allocated at the same time through the same public mechanism. Tax expenditures interfere with both these ideals.

Mandatory, open-ended entitlements, our second category of treasury budgeting, provide that anyone eligible for certain benefits must be paid regardless of the total. Until the legislation is changed or a "cap" limits total expenditure, entitlements constitute obligations of the state through direct drafts on the treasury. Were I asked to give an operational definition of the end of budgeting, I would say "indexed, open-ended entitlements". Budgeting would no longer involve allocation within limited resources but only addition of one entitlement to another, all guarded against fluctuation in prices.

Obviously, treasury budgeting leaves a great deal to be desired in controlling costs of programs, which depend on such variables as levels of benefits set in prior years, rate of application, and severity of administration. Legal control is possible but difficult because of the large number of individual cases and the innumerable provisions governing eligibility. If the guiding principle is that no one who is eligible should be denied even if some who are ineligible must be included, expenditures will rise. They will decline if the opposite principle—no ineligibles even if some eligibles suffer—prevails.

Whether or not entitlement programs are efficient or effective, the budgetary process will neither add to nor subtract from that result simply because it plays no part. To the extent that efficiency or effectiveness are spurred by the need to convince others to provide funds, such incentives are much weakened or altogether absent. The political difficulties of reducing benefits or eliminating beneficiaries speak eloquently on this subject. No doubt benefits may be eroded by inflation. Protecting against this possibility is the purpose of indexing benefits against inflation (thus doing for the individual what volume budgeting does for the bureaucracy).

Why, then, in view of its anti-budgetary character, is treasury budgeting so popular? Because of its value in coping with conflict, calculation, and economic management. After a number of entitlements and tax expenditures have been decided upon at different times, usually without full awareness of the others, implicit priorities are produced *ipso-facto,* untouched as it were, by human hands. Conflict is reduced, for the time being at least, because no explicit decisions giving more to this group and less to another are necessary. Ultimately, to be sure, resource limits will have to be considered, but even then only a few rather than all expenditures will be directly involved, since the others go on, as it were, automatically. Similarly, calculation is contracted as treasury budgeting produces figures, allowing a large part of the budget to be taken for granted. Ultimately, of course, days of reckoning come in which there is a loss of flexibility due to the implicit pre-programming of so large a proportion of available funds. For the moment, however, the attitude appears to be "sufficient unto the day is the (financial) evil thereof."

For purposes of economic management, treasury budgeting is a mixed bag. It is useful in providing what are called automatic stabilizers. When it is deemed desirable not to make new decisions every time conditions change, as pertains to unemployment benefits, an entitlement enables funds to flow according to the size of the problem. The difficulty is that not all entitlements are counter-cyclical (child benefits, for example, may rise independently of economic conditions) and the loss in financial flexibility generated by entitlements may hurt when the time comes to do less.

Nevertheless, treasury budgeting has one significant advantage over appropriations budgeting, namely, time. Changes in policy are manifested quickly in changes in spending. In order to bring considerations of economic management to bear on budgeting, these factors must be introduced early in the process of shaping the appropriations budget. Otherwise, last-minute changes of large magnitude will cause chaos by unhinging all sorts of prior understandings. Then the money must be voted and preparations made for spending. In the United States under this process—from the spring previews in the Office of Management and Budget, to the president's budget in January, to congressional action by the following summer and fall, to spending, in the winter and spring—18 to 24 months have elapsed. This is not control but remote control.

"Fine-tuning expenditures", attempting to make small adjustments to speed up or slow down the economy, do not work well anywhere. Efforts to increase expenditure are as likely to decrease the expenditure in the short-run due to the effort required to expand operations. Efforts to reduce spending in the short run are as likely to increase spending due to severence pay, penalties for breaking contracts, and so on. Hence, even as efforts continue to make expenditures more responsive, the attractiveness of more immediate tax and entitlement increases is apparent.

The recalcitrance of all forms of budgeting to economic management is not so surprising; both spending programs and economic management cannot be made more predictable if one is to vary to serve the other. In an age profoundly influenced by Keynesian economic doctrines, with their emphasis on the power of government spending, however, continued efforts to link macro-economics with micro-spending are to be expected.

The Structural Budget Margin

One such effort is the "Structural Budget Margin" developed in the Netherlands. Due to dissatisfaction with the Keynesian approach to economic stabilization, as well as disillusionment with its short-term fine-tuning, the Dutch sought to develop a longer-term relationship between the growth of public spending and the size of the national economy. Economic management was to rely less on sudden starts and stops of taxation and expenditure, and greater effort was to be devoted to controlling public spending. (The closest the United States has come is through the doctrine of balancing the budget at the level of full employment which almost always would mean a deficit). The Dutch were particularly interested in a control device because of the difficulty of getting agreement to hold down expenditures in coalition governments. Thus, spending was to be related not to actual growth but to desired growth, with only the designated margin available for new expenditure.[9]

Needless to say there are differences in definition of the appropriate structural growth rate and it has been revised up and down. Since the year used as a base makes a difference, that has also been in dispute. As we would also expect, there are disagreements over calculation of cash or volume of services with rising inflation propelling a move toward cash. Moreover, since people learn to play any game, conservative governments used the structural budget margin to hold down spending and socialists used it to increase it, for then the margin became a mechanism for figuring out the necessary increases in taxation. Every way one turns, it appears, budgetary devices are good for some purposes and not for others.

Why the Traditional Budget Lasts

Every criticism of traditional budgeting is undoubtedly correct. It is incremental rather than comprehensive; it does fragment decisions, usually making them piecemeal; it is heavily historical looking backward more than forward; it is indifferent about objectives. Why, then, has traditional budgeting lasted so long? Because it has the virtue of its defects.

Traditional budgeting makes calculations easy precisely because it is not comprehensive. History provides a strong base on which to rest a case. The present is appropriated to the past which may be known, instead of the future, which cannot be comprehended. Choices that might cause conflict are fragmented so that not all difficulties need be faced at one time. Budgeters may have objectives, but the budget itself is organized around activities or functions. One can change objectives, then, without challenging organizational survival. Traditional budgeting does not demand analysis of policy but neither does it inhibit it. Because it is neutral in regard to policy, traditional budgeting is compatable with a variety of policies, all of which can be converted into line-items. Budgeting for one year at a time has no special virtue (two years, for instance might be as good or better) except in comparison to more extreme alternatives. Budgeting several times a year aids economic adjustment but also creates chaos in departments, disorders calculations, and worsens conflict. Multi-year budgeting enhances planning at the expense of adjustment, accountability, and possible price volatility. Budgeting by volume and entitlement also aid planning and efficiency in government at the cost of control and effectiveness. Budgeting becomes spending. Traditional budgeting lasts, then, because it is simpler, easier, more controllable, more flexible than modern alternatives like PPB, ZBB, and indexed entitlements.

A final criterion has not been mentioned because it is inherent in the multiplicity of others, namely, adaptability. To be useful a budgetary process should perform tolerably well under all conditions. It must perform under the unexpected—deficits and surpluses, inflation and deflation, economic growth and economic stagnation. Because budgets are contracts within governments signifying agreed understandings, and signals outside of government informing others of what government is likely to do so they can adapt to it, budgets must be good (though not necessarily great) for all seasons. It is not so much that traditional budgeting succeeds brilliantly on every criterion, but that it does not entirely fail on any one that is responsible for its longevity.

Needless to say, traditional budgeting also has the defects of its virtues. No instrument of policy is equally good for every purpose. Though budgets look back, they may not look back far enough to understand how (or why) they got where they are. Comparing this year with last year may not mean much if the past was a mistake and the future is likely to be a bigger one. Quick calculation may be worse than none if it is grossly in error. There is an incremental road to disaster as well as faster roads to perdition; simplicity may become simple-mindedness. Policy neutrality may degenerate into disinterest in programs. So why has it lasted? So far, no one has come up with another budgetary procedure that has the virtues of traditional budgeting but lacks its defects.

At once one is disposed to ask why it is necessary to settle for second or third best: Why not combine the best features of the various processes, specially selected to work under prevailing conditions? Why not multi-year volume entitlements for this and annual cash zero base budgeting for that? The question answers itself; there can only be one budgetary process at a time: Therefore, the luxury of picking different ones for different purposes is unobtainable. Again, the necessity of choosing the least worst, or the most widely applicable over the largest number of cases is made evident.

Yet almost a diametrically opposite conclusion also is obvious to students of budgeting. Observation reveals that a number of different processes do, in fact, co-exist right now. Some programs are single year but others are multi-year, some have cash limits while others are open-ended or even indexed, some are investigated in increments but others (where repetitive operations are involved) receive, in effect, a zero-base review. Beneath the facade of unity, there is, in fact, diversity.

How, then, are we to choose among truths that are self-evident (there can be only one form of budgeting at a time and there are many)? Both cannot be correct when applied to the same sphere but I think they are when applied to different spheres. The critical difference is between the financial form in which the budget is voted on in the legislature, and the different ways of thinking about budgeting. It is possible to analyze expenditures in terms of programs, over long periods of time, and in many other ways without requiring that the form of analysis be the same as the form of appropriation. Indeed, as we have seen, there are persuasive reasons for insisting that form and function be different. All this can be summarized: The more neutral the form of presenting appropriations, the easier to translate other changes—in program, direction, organizational structure— into the desired amount without making the categories into additional forms of rigidity, which will become barriers to future changes.

Nonetheless, traditional budgeting must be lacking in some respects or it would not be replaced so often by entitlements or multi-year accounts. Put another way, treasury budgeting must reflect strong social forces. These are not mechanisms to control spending but to increase it. "The Budget" may be annual, but tax expenditures and budget entitlements go on until changed. With a will to spend there is a way.

I write about auditing largely in terms of budgeting and budgeting largely in terms of public policy. The rise of big government has necessarily altered out administrative doctrines of first and last things. When government was small so was public spending. Affairs of state were treated as extensions of personal integrity, or the lack thereof. The question was whether spending was honest. If public spending posed a threat to society it was that private individuals would use government funds to accumulate fortunes as sources of power. State audit was about private avarice. As government grew larger, its manipulation meant more. Was it doing what it said it would do with public money? State audit became state compliance. However, when government became gigantic, the sheer size of the state became overwhelming. The issue was no longer control of the state—getting government to do what it was told—but the ability of the state to control society. Public policy, i.e., public measures to control private behavior, lept to the fore; and that is how auditing shifted from private corruption to governmental compliance to public policy.

Social forces ultimately get their way, but while there is a struggle for supremacy, the form of budgeting can make a modest difference. It is difficult to say, for instance, whether the concept of a balanced budget declined due to social pressure or whether the concept of a unified budget, including almost all transactions in and out of the economy, such as trust funds, makes it even less likely. In days of old when cash was cash, and perpetual deficits were not yet invented, a deficit meant more cash out than came in. Today, with a much larger total, estimating plays a much more important part, and it's anyone's guess within $50 billion as to the actual state of affairs. The lesson is that for purposes of accountability, and control, the simpler the budget the better.

Taking as large a view as I know how, the suitability of a budgetary process under varied conditions depends on how well diverse concerns can be translated into its forms. For sheer transparency, traditional budgeting is hard to beat.

Notes

1. But, for a beginning, see Allen Schick, "The Road to PPB: The Stages of Budget Reform," *Public Administration Review,* (Dec. 1966) pp 243–258.

2. Hugh Heclo, Aaron Wildavsky, *The Private Government of Public Money: Community and Policy Inside British Political Administration,* London, Macmillan; Berkeley and Los Angeles, University of California Press, (2nd edition forthcoming).

3. *Idem.*

4. Robert A. Hartman, "Multiyear Budget Planning," in Joseph A. Pechman, ed. *Setting National Priorities: The 1979 Budget.* (The Brookings Institution, Washington, D.C. 1978) p. 312.

5. Naomi Caiden, Aaron Wildavsky, *Planning and Budgeting in Poor Countries,* New York, John Wiley and Sons, 1974.

6. This and the next eight paragraphs are taken from my "Policy Analysis is What Information Systems are Not," *New York Affairs,* Vol. 4, No. 2 Spring 1977.

7. See Jeanne Nienaber, and A. Wildavsky, *The Budgeting and Evaluation of Federal Recreation Programs, or Money Doesn't Grow on Trees*, New York, Basic Books, 1973.

8. The importance of these principles is discussed in my book, *Speaking Truth to Power: The Art and Craft of Policy Analysis* (Boston, Little, Brown and Co. (forthcoming).

9. J. Diamond, "The New Orthodoxy in Budgetary Planning: A Critical Review of Dutch Experience," In *Public Finance*, Vol. XXXII, No. 1 (1977) pp 56–76.

6

DOES BUDGET FORMAT REALLY GOVERN THE ACTIONS OF BUDGETMAKERS?

Gloria A. Grizzle

For well over half a century students of budgeting have assumed that the format into which a budget is cast influences budget decisions. Yet as late as 1980 Hayes stated that "there is little or no material on the factors affecting outcomes in the budget process and, indeed, little basis for any judgment as to whether the character of the process has any significant impact on the results obtained. . . . The fundamental need is for analyses of experience,"[1] Since that time, several studies have analyzed budget outcomes quantitatively and related them to the budget formats used. This article provides a framework for integrating the results of these studies with earlier case descriptions of budget reforms. It then identifies an area that still needs exploring and presents the results of one study that addresses this need.

Budget Formats, Deliberations, and Decisions

Beginning in 1917 with the Bureau of Municipal Research's recommendations on format for the New York City budget, one can trace a series of authors who hold that the format in which a budget is cast importantly af-

1986. Does budget format really govern the actions of budgetmakers? Grizzle, Gloria A. **Public Budgeting and Finance** 6 (Spring): 60–70.

fects the ensuing budget deliberations and ultimately the allocation of funds.[2] With the advent of program or performance budgeting in the 1950s, both Burkhead and Mosher noted the importance of format.[3] In his study of performance budgeting in the U.S. Department of the Army, Mosher concluded that the way in which information is classified importantly affected the "kinds of treatment and kinds of decisions that can be made at various levels" because the classification framework "conditions our subsequent perspectives, understandings, and decisions made within the framework."[4]

In thinking about how the organization of data might affect budget decisions, it is useful to conceptualize a two-step process. In the first step, the format in which the proposed budget is cast would influence the content of discussions that budget makers hold during the budget review process. Anton emphasizes this influence in his description of the Illinois state budgeting process. He reports that the budgetary discourse was shaped by the informational categories established by the line-item format that Illinois used. In his words, "because these categories reflect a desire to know how much money was or will be spent for which things, budget presentation and review is rarely accomplished in any terms but these."[5]

In the second step, the content of budget deliberations, that is, "the nature of budgetary discourse," would influence the budget decisions that determine how much money is appropriated for what purposes. The planning-programming-budgeting system (PPBS) is perhaps the best known budget reform for which format was believed to affect budget decisions. For example, in studying the introduction of PPBS into the federal government's budgeting process, Fenno, Schick, and Wildavsky have stated that the budget format affects budgeting decisions.[6] Perhaps Schick expressed it most cogently when he said, "the case for PPB rests on the assumption that the form in which information is classified and used governs the actions of budgetmakers, and, conversely, that alterations in form will produce desired changes in behavior."[7]

Thus, the two-step process envisioned by budget reform proponents can be diagrammed as follows:

Some practitioners, however, do not agree that budget format has an important effect upon budget deliberations, especially where the legislature's deliberations are concerned. They believe that legislators base their budget decisions on "politics" and that changing budget format will not change legislative decisions. In his study of the Georgia zero-base budgeting (ZBB) process, Lauth reports that 84 percent of the agency budget officers and 88 percent of analysts in the governor's office believed that the appropriations committees rarely or never took evaluation measures into account in making budget decisions.[8] In their survey of state budget directors. Ramsey and Hackbart reported that legislatures often act as barriers to real change in budgetary emphasis because they insist "on knowing how specific monies are being spent and what is being bought with these monies."[9] Juszczak, a budgeter in the federal government, concluded that the structuring of supporting schedules is more important than the overall budget format.[10]

Only recently have students of budgeting attempted to quantify the ways in which new formats introduced through budget reform have in fact changed appropriations. Three studies of state budgeting systems have attempted to relate format to appropriations directly without examining in what ways, if any, format affected the intervening budget review deliberations. Two of these studies examine the change over time in the proportion of the total budget allocated to broad functions. Examining these proportions for Arkansas during a five-year period after the introduction of its priority budgeting system (a variant of ZBB), Carr concludes that budgetary decisions are incremental and that the budget format had no effect upon budgetary decisions.[11] In looking at Virginia's change to a program budget format, Hickman concludes that format is one of many factors that influence budget decision. He cites economic and demographic changes as more influential than format in causing shifts over time in the proportion of the total budget allocated to broad functions, such as education.[12]

Stutzman, in the third study, examines the extent to which the Michigan legislature's departmental appropriations agreed with the governor's recommendations over a 15-year period. She found that changes in budget format affected legislative behavior in a surprising way. During those years of major budget format change, the legislators reacted by making appropriations that departed radically from the governor's budget recommendations.[13]

While these studies represent a commendable step in moving from descriptive case studies to assessing quantitatively the effects of budget reforms, looking only at formats and appropriations for broad functions may leave several important questions unanswered. First, studies at such high levels of aggregation cannot capture programmatic shifts that may have taken place within broad functional areas. It is possible that format could have influenced how much was appropriated to particular programs within these broad functions.

Second, to demonstrate convincingly that a change in format did or did not change appropriations when studying a single state requires a time series of budget decisions that occurred both before and after the budget reform, as well as evidence that refutes other plausible causes of appropriation changes. To their credit, the Virginia and Michigan studies do take other causes into account. The Virginia study concludes that other factors are more important influences on budget decisions than format, and the Michigan study goes further by providing sufficient evidence to discount the other factors examined as being the cause of disagreement between gubernatorial recommendations and legislative appropriations.

Third, studies that focus only upon format and legislative appropriations leave unexplored the budget review process that occurs after proposed budgets are formatted and before the legislature appropriates funds. If we are to advocate budget formats as instruments of budget reform, we need to understand better the intervening process by which formats influence appropriations. Budget reforms are, we are told, expected to center legislative attention "on integrated related activities or programs rather than line-item objects of expenditure."[14] To what extent does format "center legislative attention"?

Case studies reported in the literature do give some attention to this intervening process. In studying the change from a line-item to a performance budget format in Los Angeles, Sherwood and Eghtedari concluded that the unanticipated effect was that legislators opted not to participate rather than to focus on broad policy.[15] In contrast, Hickman concluded that Virginia's shift to a program format resulted in more direct involvement by the legislature in shaping budget outcomes.[16] Based upon interviews with budget directors in five cities, Cope concluded that city councils used the parts of the format with which they were familiar or comfortable and ignored the rest.[17] Hrebenar reports a similar tendency on the part of the Washington Senate.[18] In sum, these case studies report conflicting results about the effect of format upon legislative deliberations.

In conclusion, we cannot, from the studies mentioned above, make any generalizations about how, or to what extent, budget format affects the nature of legislative deliberations. We might learn more about how the organization of the budget influences appropriations decisions if we would undertake a few studies that directly test Fenno's proposition that ". . . the form of the budget determines what the conversation will be about."[19] The sections below report one such study that compares the deliberations of legislative appropriations committees that used different budget formats.

Analytical Framework for
Describing Budget Deliberations

Surely the best known work asserting the influence of budget format on the character of the budgeting process is contained in Schick's "The Road to PPB."[20] The three classic orientations described in this article—control, management, and planning—provide appropriate analytical categories for classifying the nature of budget deliberations. The control orientation is believed to dominate budget reviews that use line-item formats. The management orientation best characterizes the performance budget; and the planning orientation best characterizes the program budget. Each of these orientations, and the content of deliberations expected to occur when they are used during the budget review process, is briefly described below.

A budget format containing detailed classification of objects of expenditure conforms to the control orientation. The range of concerns to which this format responds includes holding agencies to spending ceilings set by the legislature and chief executive, providing reporting that will enforce the propriety of spending, limiting an agency's spending in terms of the objects to be bought (e.g., equipment, office space, and personnel).

A budget format organized around a government's activities conforms to the management orientation. It focuses upon the work that operating units do and how efficiently they do it. Performance measures associated with this orientation include the quantity and quality of output and the unit cost of that output. The range of concerns includes how much work is to be done, how best to organize to accomplish the work to be done, and which grants and projects should be funded.

A budget format organized by program conforms to the planning orientation. The range of concerns includes long-range goals and policies and how these relate to initiating, terminating, expanding, or curtailing particular programs. Performance measures associated with this orientation include program outcomes, cost-effectiveness, and the extent to which program objectives are achieved. Cost-benefit studies, systems analyses, and long-range forecasts are sources of information expected to be associated with the planning orientation to a greater extent than with management and control.

Schick notes that "it should be clear that every budget system contains planning, management, and control features. A control orientation means the subordination, not the absence, of planning and management functions. In the matter of orientations, we are dealing with relative emphases, not with pure dichotomies."[21]

In a 1974 survey of 88 cities, Friedman found the control orientation to be most prevalent, as evidenced by scoring the presence of institutional practices related to each budgeting type for each city. The average presence of institutional practices related to each type of budgeting was 70 percent for control, 60 percent for management, and 42 percent for planning. He found that "one or another budget-making purpose tends to dominate and assume paramount importance in most cities. Although they are compatible, the three patterns of budgeting are not necessarily co-equal."[22]

Friedman's survey confirmed Axelrod's contention that the three orientations are not mutually exclusive and that governments have improved their budgets by strengthening management and planning without abandoning control.[23] As an illustration of the hybrid nature of budgeting in practice, note a Fort Worth budget participant's description of that city's "performance" budget:

Actually, the Fort Worth budgetary process is one which includes the elements of all three traditional types of budgets. It is a line-item budget, particularly in the control aspects, in that specific appropriations are made for each line item, and operating department heads are accountable by line item for variances between appropriations and actual expenditures. Elements of a performance budget are present because activity appropriations are based loosely on work to be performed, at least in the planning stages of the budget. However, the Fort Worth budgetary system could best be described as primarily a program budget because inputs to the process each year are defined in terms of existing, expanded, or reduced programs, and detailed descriptions of each program are provided in the budget document.[24]

Similarly, Howard, in reviewing state budgeting, finds it "virtually impossible to classify states' budgeting processes in unambiguous categories. The simple question—Is your state doing object-of-expenditure budgeting, program budgeting, PPBS, or zero-base budgeting?—cannot be answered simply. State budget systems are hybrids rather than purebreeds, distinguished by the adopted and adapted parts of recent reforms as well as by state-specific practices."[25]

Thus, we would not expect to find pure forms of budget formats in state or local governments. We can, however, characterize the extent to which a given government's budget format conforms to the three orientations and compare formats that differ in their dominant orientations.

How Do Formats Influence
"What the Conversation Will Be About"?

Ideally, one would like to address this question by exposing each of several budgeting groups to different budget formats (in their pure forms) and then comparing the nature of deliberations under the different formats. Barber's method of eliciting decision criteria from legislative groups would be useful, given such an experimental design. He was able to induce local government boards of finance to spend a half hour in a small-group laboratory on a budget-reducing task. He tape recorded and analyzed their deliberations and categorized them by the decision criteria used.[26] However, the laboratory approach has two serious disadvantages. First, gaining executive or legislative participation in such an experiment is unlikely. Moreover, budgeting behavior in a short laboratory exercise might differ from behavior in the budgeters' natural environment.

A more practical way of learning about the relationship of format to the nature of deliberations would be to compare deliberations according to format variations as they naturally occur in the real world. This approach is more likely to produce information of direct relevance to practitioners.

State governments have two advantages in this regard. First, states vary considerably in the formats they use. Second, a number of states tape record (but do not transcribe) their legislative appropriations committee meetings. The discussions in these meetings can be analyzed to compare the dominant orientations of legislative deliberations under different budget formats. The study reported below takes this approach, using the control, management, and planning orientations discussed above.

Florida and North Carolina were the two states selected for study. Appropriations committees for both houses of the legislature in both states were included in the analysis. During the 1979 and 1981 legislative sessions, the period included in the analysis, Florida appropriations committees used the organizational-unit format described below.

North Carolina is a particularly interesting state to study because its appropriations committees used two quite different formats. After the governor's recommended budget changed to a program format in the early 1970s, some appropriations committees used that format for a few years. Other committees, however, insisted that the governor provide them with a detailed line-item format. By 1981, all the committees used the line-item format. The North Carolina committee meetings examined occurred during the 1975, 1977, and 1981 legislative sessions.

A Description of the Budget Formats Studied

Table 6.1 summarizes the features of each budget format studied.[27] In order to illustrate how a department's budget would be structured under each format, we compare the structure used for a single department—the Department of Corrections. The program format presents pages for each of nine corrections programs. These programs are classified into 22 subprograms. Six of these 22 subprograms are further broken down into 16 program elements. Finally, four of the 16 elements are themselves broken down into 10 subelements. In contrast, the line-item budget is first classified by three accounting funds. One fund includes pages for each of 18 purposes; the second, for 11 purposes; and the third, for a single purpose. The organizational format presents pages for each of eight budget entities. Four entities are departmental divisions and four are organizational units one level below the division level.

None of these formats is a pure type. The program format described, for example, does not cut across departmental lines. However, the formats are sufficiently different from each other that we would expect them to influence deliberations differently.

Given our descriptions of the three formats, we would expect budget deliberations using the program format to focus on the range of concerns defined by the planning orientation. We would expect the deliberations

TABLE 6.1   A Comparison of the Characteristics of the Budget Formats Studied

	Format		
Characteristic	*Program*	*Line Item*	*Organization*
Overall structure of information	Program	Fund; purpose	Organizational unit
Dominant information focus	Lowest level of program structure	Purpose's detailed objects	Division's summary objects: issues
Narrative	Descriptions at each level of program structure	Brief descriptions of each purpose's function	None
Objective	For each program component	For some purposes	None
Statistical information presented	Lowest level of program structure	Each purpose	None
Comparative financial data presented	Last year's actual; this year's appropriation; governor's recommended	Last year's actual; this year's appropriation; governor's recommended	This year's estimate; agency request; governor's recommended
Separation of continuation level funding expansion funding	None	For each fund, purpose, and object	For each division
Funding source classification	Each program component; 3 categories	Each purpose; detailed itemization	Each division; 2 categories

using the line-item format to focus on those concerns included within the control orientation. Although the organizational-unit budget is not a performance budget, we would expect its focus on divisions and subdivisions to result in a greater management orientation than would the other two formats.

Analysis and Findings

For each of the three budget formats, 10 appropriations committee meetings were selected for analysis.[28] For each of these meetings, questions that legislators asked and comments they made during the meeting were coded according to their orientation. In addition to Schick's planning, management, and control orientations, a fourth category was added to capture funding-oriented questions. Frequently legislators wanted to know how an expenditure was to be funded. Would state funds be matched by federal funds? What proportion of the cost would be supported by user fees? Was state money required? Would state general fund revenues be required in the future?[29]

Table 6.2 distributes the questions by budget format and orientation. As expected, the program format deliberations contain a higher proportion of planning-oriented remarks by legislators than do the other two formats. Both the program and organizational-unit formats contain about the same proportion of management-oriented remarks, but substantially more than occur with line-item format deliberations. There is also a marked difference in the proportion of remarks that are control-oriented, with deliberations using the line-item format dominated by this orientation to a much greater extent than are program and organizational-unit format deliberations. Finally, all the committees demonstrate some concern for funding, but this concern does not dominate any committee's deliberations and variation across the three format types is not marked.[30]

There is an additional observation about the data in Table 6.2. The planning orientation does not dominate deliberations under the program format. In spite of this format, the management orientation dominates. Planning ranks third, after management and funding concerns. It appears that legislators do seek out additional information they believe important when a given format does not provide it.

To what extent does program format account for, or "explain" in a statistical sense, the variations in orientation that occurred among the 30 meetings? To address this question, we analyzed this variation across the committee meetings. As Table 6.3 shows, budget format was not a statistically significant factor in explaining the extent to which different committee meeting deliberations emphasized the funding orientation. Format did account for some significant proportion of the variation for the other three orientations. Format accounts for 64 percent of the variation in how much emphasis a committee placed upon control. It accounts for 32 percent of the variation in management emphasis and 20 percent of the variation in planning emphasis.

TABLE 6.2   Percentage of Legislators' Remarks Fitting Each Orientation, by Budget Format

		Format	
Orientation	*Program*	*Line Item*	*Organizational Unit*
Planning	9%	1%	3%
Management	69	40	70
Control	4	51	13
Funding	18	8	13

TABLE 6.3   Proportion of Variation in Orientations Across Meetings That Budget Format "Explained"

Orientation	*Proportion (Eta Squared)*	*Significance (F Value)*
Planning	.20	3.46*
Management	.32	6.24*
Control	.64	23.59*
Funding	.10	1.49

*Indicates explanation is statistically significant at the 0.5 alpha level.

Conclusion

These findings indicate that format is, as budget reform proponents have assumed, an important factor influencing the nature of budget delibera-tions. As Hickman suggested when analyzing the Virginia experience with program budgeting, format is not the only factor and, at least in this study, does not explain a majority of the variation in orientation among legisla-tive appropriations committee meetings. Clearly, however, format did in-fluence "what the conversation was about" during the legislatures' review of these states' proposed budgets.

Further research, extending this analytic approach both to executive as well as legislative deliberations and to additional states, might yield an-swers to questions this single study necessarily leaves unresolved. For in-stance, to what extent and in what direction do other formats influence legislative deliberations? To what extent do factors other than budget format affect the nature of the deliberations? For example, do deliberations differ in growth compared to no-growth or retrenchment years?

Once this intervening link between budget format and appropriations decision is better understood, a second step will be to link deliberations under different formats to appropriations decisions, controlling for other factors that influence appropriations. Eventually, we should be able to identify not only the ways in which format affects budget review, but also how these effects vary in the presence of other factors, such as fiscal condition and demographics. The practitioner could then be better guided in choosing the format that best suits the situation. Or, should it turn out that in many situations formats do not make much difference one way or the other, budgeting theory could be redirected toward more fruitful lines of inquiry.

Notes

1. Frederick O'R. Hayes, "Curriculum Needs in Public Sector Budgeting," (Boston: Boston University, Public Management Program), p. 3.

2. New York Bureau of Municipal Research, "Some Results and Limitations of Central Financial Control in New York City," *Municipal Research* 81 (1917). See also W.F. Willoughby, *Principles of Public Administration* (Washington, D.C.: Brookings, 1927), p. 454.

3. Jesse Burkhead, *Government Budgeting* (New York: John Wiley, 1956), p. viii; Frederick C. Mosher, *Program Budgeting: Theory and Practice* (Chicago: Public Administration Service, 1954).

4. Mosher, pp. 5 and 83.

5. Thomas J. Anton, *The Politics of State Expenditure in Illinois* (Urbana: University of Illinois Press, 1966), p. 73.

6. Richard F. Fenno, "The Impact of PPBS on the Congressional Appropriation Process" in *Information Support, Program Budgeting, and the Congress*, Robert L. Chartrand, Kenneth Janda, and Michael Hugo, eds. (New York: Spartan, 1968), p. 183; Allen Schick, "The Road to PPB: The Stages of Budget Reform," *Public Administration Review* 26 (December 1966), p. 257; Aaron Wildavsky, *The Politics of the Budgetary Process*, 2d ed. (Boston: Little, Brown, 1974), p. 136.

7. Schick, p. 257.

8. Thomas P. Lauth, "Performance Evaluation in the Georgia Budgetary Process," *Public Budgeting & Finance* 5 (Spring 1985), p. 72.

9. James R. Ramsey and Merlin M. Hackbart, "Budgeting: Inducements and Impediments to Innovations." *State Government* 52 (Spring 1979), p. 69.

10. Thad Juszczak, "Designing Budget Formats for Analysis" (presentation at the 1983 meeting of the American Society for Public Administration).

11. T. R. Carr, "An Evaluation of the Impact of the Priority Budgeting System of Arkansas on Budget Outcomes" (paper presented at the 1983 meeting of the American Society for Public Administration), p. 13.

12. Richard E. Hickman, Jr., "The Effect of Virginia's Program Budget Format on Budget Outcomes" (paper presented at the 1983 meeting of the American Society for Public Administration), p. 8.

13. Mary Patrick Stutzman, "Changing the Format of Budget Documents: The Effect on Budgeting Outcomes" (paper presented at the 1983 meeting of the American Society for Public Administration). p. 15.

14. Eli B. Silverman, "Public Budgeting and Public Administration: Enter the Legislature," *Public Finance Quarterly* 2 (October 1974), p. 477.

15. Frank Sherwood and Ali Eghtedari, "Performance Budgeting in Los Angeles," *Public Administration Review* 20 (Spring 1960), p. 66.

16. Hickman, "Virginia's Program Format," p. 8.

17. Glen Hahn Cope, "The Architecture of Budget Requests: Does Form Follow Function?" (paper presented at the 1983 meeting of the American Society for Public Administration), p. 11.

18. Ronald J. Hrebenar, "State Legislative Budgetary Review Processes: Utilization Patterns of Alternative Information Sources," *Midwest Review of Public Administration* 9 (April–July 1975), p. 140.

19. Fenno, "Impact of PPBS," p. 68.

20. Schick, "Road to PPB," pp. 245–256.

21. *Ibid.*, p. 245.

22. Lewis C. Friedman, "Control, Management, and Planning: An Empirical Examination," *Public Administration Review* 35 (November/December 1975), p. 627.

23. Donald Axelrod, "Post-Burkhead: The State of the Art or Science of Budgeting." *Public Administration Review* 33 (November/December 1973), p. 577.

24. Charles W. Binford, "Reflections on the Performance Budget: Past, Present and Future," *Governmental Finance* 1 (November 1972), p. 30.

25. S. Kenneth Howard, "State Budgeting" in *The Book of the States 1980–81*, vol. 23 (Lexington, Ky.: Council of State Governments), p. 199.

26. James David Barber, *Power in Committees: An Experiment in Governmental Process* (Chicago: Rand McNally, 1966), pp. 34–46.

27. Appendix A contains a more detailed description of the three budget formats studied.

28. Early in the appropriations process information sessions are held. Agency personnel give presentations and committee members ask questions. Later the process is more oriented to deciding how much the committee will recommend that the House and Senate appropriate for each program, budget entity, or line item. Meetings for each format were balanced in terms of the phase of the appropriations process in which they occurred.

An attempt was also made to examine deliberations in several different program areas. Meetings selected using the organizational-unit format were education, corrections, and human resource programs. Program-format meetings were education, human resource, transportation and general government programs. Line-item format meetings were education, human resources, and corrections.

29. A total of 1321 questions/comments were coded by type of concern expressed and then categorized by the orientation related to that concern. For example, questions about program goals., outcomes, and cost-effectiveness were catego-

rized as planning orientation. Questions asking for justifications of individual objects of expenditure were categorized as control orientation. Questions about a department's activities, the amount of work to be done, and the efficiency of agency operations were classified as management oriented.

30. A contingency table analysis showed these differences to be statistically significant at the .001 level. Chi square for the raw frequencies table was 310.06. Cramer's V, representing the degree of association between format and orientation was moderately positive, .34 (the possible range is .00 to 1.00). Because of differences in cell sizes, Chi square and Cramer's V were also calculated for a standardized contingency table. The calculations were similar to those for the raw frequencies table. Chi square was still significant at the .001 level, and Cramer's V was .36.

Note: A detailed description of the budget formats reviewed here is available from the author on request.

Section I.B

RECENT BUDGET PRACTICES REVEALED

7

BUDGETING FOR RESULTS: RECENT DEVELOPMENTS IN FIVE INDUSTRIALIZED COUNTRIES

Allen Schick

"The concept is simple—objectives, results, and resources should all be linked. The application is difficult."[1] This observation by the Auditor General of Canada in his 1987 annual report sums up the state of the art in contemporary efforts to budget for results. The ultimate objective is, in some countries, to mold the budget into a "contract for performance." In exchange for obtaining agreed-to resources, managers would be expected to achieve specified targets. To budget in this fashion requires that measures of performance be available in a form that can be related to resource decisions.

The measurement of performance is an old practice that is taking on a new lease. In the United States, progress in this area can be traced to the Ridley-Simon work in the 1930s, performance budgeting in the 1950s, and program budgeting in the 1960s.[2] It is in application, however, that performance measurement is breaking new ground. Governments are awash in data on what they are doing; what they lack, as the quote that leads this article states, is the competence to apply performance data to their budget and other managerial decisions. The main contemporary emphasis, therefore, is not so much on generating new measures—though some of this is

1990. Budgeting for results: Recent developments in five industrialized countries. Schick, Allen. **Public Administration Review** 50 (January-February): 26–34.

also underway—as on fostering a managerial environment which is attentive to performance when funds are parceled out.

This article reports on recent developments in five countries: Australia, Canada, Denmark, Sweden, and the United Kingdom. The material is drawn from documentary sources and interviews in all of the countries except Australia.[3] After describing each country's approach, the article analyzes common themes and differences.

The order in which country descriptions appear has been dictated by affinities in their approaches. The two Scandinavian countries comprise one group, the three Commonwealth countries another. In the latter, British activities are recounted first because they have strongly influenced Australian and Canadian innovations.

Britain: Financial Management Initiatives

The development and application of performance measures is a central feature of the financial management initiatives (FMI) launched in 1982 and continued through the decade.[4] FMI is a long-term effort to change the managerial culture of public departments. FMI aims for quantification wherever feasible so as to facilitate the assessment of whether programs are providing "value for money."[5]

FMI was introduced during a period of severe pressure on administrative expenditure and contraction in public employment. The number of civil servants dropped from 732,000 in 1979 when the Conservative Government took office to fewer than 600,000 in 1988. In announcing FMI, the Government sought "in each department an organisation and a system in which managers at all levels have . . . a clear view of their objectives and the means to assess, and wherever possible, measure outputs or performance in relation to those objectives."[6]

Inasmuch as it is intended to spur managerial initiative, FMI does not prescribe a uniform approach for all departments. Within broad guidelines, each department is free to develop the managerial style and system suited to its circumstances. One common element, however, is an insistence on delegated budgeting in which responsibility for resources is pushed down the line to "budget holders" (those who actually spend resources and carry out operations) who are to be given sufficient flexibility and incentive to produce value for money.[7]

Changing the culture of management has been slowed by difficulties in altering the relationships between spending departments and central agencies. Treasury has taken the position that delegation must proceed hand in hand with the spread of accountability within departments. "It is necessary," a Treasury report has insisted, "to recognize the Treasury's legitimate concerns and requirements arising from its responsibility for controlling the level of public expenditure . . . the central departments need evidence of robust new systems before they can sensibly relax their existing control mechanisms."[8] The Treasury has, nevertheless, progressively loosened its hold. A key move, taken in 1988, was the removal of central manpower ceilings on departments in favor of overall financial caps on administrative costs.

The government has found that divestiture of central controls has not always been accompanied by flexibility at operational levels.[9] Instead, headquarters in departments often take over the controls. Managerial flexibility has also been compromised by the recurring need to recapture funds for labor settlements in excess of budgeted levels. The government recognizes that altering managerial behavior will be a difficult, time-consuming task that depends on a steady infusion of top-level support. Treasury has prodded departments by issuing a steady stream of reports and working papers on FMI's progress. FMI has benefited from the longevity of the Thatcher Government; in office a full decade at the time this article was written, the government has not wavered in its determination to remake British management.

Output and Performance Measures

FMI conceives of budgeting as a "contract for performance" in which departments commit themselves to concrete targets in exchange for agreed-to resources. A 1986 Treasury report defined budgeting as:

> . . . a means of delivering value for money against a background of aims, objectives and targets. . . . Budgeting will only fully realise its full potential if it has the support and involvement of top management, if there are strong connections between budgets, outputs and results, and if it operates within a supportive central and managerial environment.[10]

Case studies issued by Treasury indicate that behavior has fallen short of this ideal. In many areas, objectives are not expressed with sufficient precision to allow assessment of whether the purposes are being achieved. The Government has noted measurement problems in its response to a critique of FMI by Parliament's Public Accounts Committee.[11] It is not yet the norm for managers to have approved budgets for outputs as well as inputs or for adjustments and responses to be made in tandem with changes in targeted levels of performance. In some cases, managers have been frustrated when agreed-to budget levels were reduced without commensurate adjustment in required levels of service.

The linkage of performance measures and budgets has been promoted by the extensive publication of such measures in the annual Public Expenditure White Paper. The 1988/1989–1990/1991 White Paper contains more than 1,800 output and performance measures, more than 50 percent above the level of two years before. Rather than further increase the number of such measures, Treasury has embarked on an effort to upgrade their quality, principally by emphasizing measures of effectiveness and specific targets.

Progress in reporting on performance can be seen in the indicators published for the Department of Transport. The department's chapter in the White Paper measures the performance of London Regional Transport in terms of passenger miles, load factors, cost per vehicle mile, and percentage of schedule operated. Performance statistics also cover the productivity of British Rail, cost-effectiveness measures of road construction, and traffic and price trends. Work underway in the department is concentrated on devising targets against which future performance may be compared. Thus, its internal management plan compares the outturn against target for the last completed fiscal year, presents the approved targets for the year in progress, and lists provisional targets for the next two years. Quantified measures are provided for future construction starts and completions, road repairs, lane closing due to construction, percentage of work completed on time and within budget, and so forth.

While the Transport Department may be somewhat more advanced than other units, recent White Papers exhibit performance data in many areas of public service. It has become the rule to include these measures in budget documents and to quantify what is being accomplished with the budgeted resources.

Canada: Increased Ministerial
Authority and Accountability

Departments in Canada have been required to measure and report on performance since the early 1970s, but compliance has not been satisfactory.[12] However, this requirement has been given substantially greater prominence by the Increased Ministerial Authority and Accountability (IMAA) reforms now being introduced into Canadian government.[13] IMAA gives departments discretion over many administrative matters previously requiring central approval. Departments have also been granted expanded authority to reallocate resources within approved funding levels, and they are now permitted to carry a portion of their capital funds into the next fiscal year. In exchange, IMAA demands enhanced accountability for results. Departments are to be held accountable for performance expectations set forth in memoranda of understanding agreed to by them and the Treasury Board.

IMAA was launched in 1986, and it is to be phased in over a number of years. The process is slow because memoranda of understanding (MOU) have to be individually negotiated with each department. The MOU process is initiated by a departmental proposal to modify Treasury Board rules, in addition to those relaxed for all agencies, and to establish accountability methods that ensure the integrity of public expenditure. It is intended that each MOU cover a three-year period within which the annual budget-appropriations cycle would operate. While Canada's governmental system does not permit multiyear commitments on the future resources to be provided, it may be possible to incorporate statements of intent, based on approved budget levels, in the MOUs. Each participating department prepares an annual management report which then triggers an assessment of performance geared to the targets and expectations set in the MOU. The assessment is a joint activity drawing in senior officials of the Treasury Board and the department. Although no department has yet gone through a complete MOU cycle, it is anticipated that every third year a major accountability review would be undertaken pursuant to which specific directives might be issued to improve the use of resources.[14]

The Treasury Board has taken an active role in designing and promoting IMAA. The Board envisions that IMAA will lead to significant changes in its own operations. It will be less concerned with how procedural rules are abided and more with what departments do by way of program results. By means of the MOUs, the Treasury Board hopes to establish contractual relationships with departments in which they obtain greater stability with respect to resources and relief from various controls but agree to achieve expected levels of performance. This contractual relationship depends on careful specification of the MOU after detailed negotiations with departments. The MOUs are not to be boilerplate or standard forms; each one is to be tailored to the individual department's circumstances. Not surprisingly, therefore, most Canadian departments are not yet covered by MOUs.

Performance Measures

The federal government has had extensive experience with performance measures, not all of it fruitful. Directives on this subject, which are still in force, date back to 1976. A key issue is the extent to which data on outputs and results should be linked to the budget. Taking the view that performance indicators should be used principally as a tool for resource allocation, the Canadian Auditor General has found "that decision makers do not have the information to ensure that they allocate resources in the most efficient or effective manner."[15] Treasury Board, however, views performance indicators more as support for departmental management and less as an activity to support central decisions on resources. It is in this light that IMAA conceives of performance data as an internal departmental management tool which has only secondary utility as a budgeting tool.

Rather than layering new measurement requirements on departments, IMAA seeks to integrate preexisting attempts to link resources and results. The key instrument is the Operational Plan Framework (OPF), introduced in the early 1980s, which provides for departments to establish objectives in a hierarchical order and to set forth means of monitoring and reporting on results.[16] The OPF is based on the assumption that objectives can be clearly stated in advance and that intended results can be identified. Almost all departments use the OPF structure; still, the Auditor General has found that "managers have considerable difficulty translating objectives into clear, measurable, and attainable statements of purpose."[17] The Treasury Board has acknowledged OPF's limitations, but it rejects the expectation that all results be stated in measurable terms and be directly related to program objectives and resources.

IMAA tries to make OPF and other previous innovations more useful by establishing a management environment and center-agency relationship conducive to accountability for performance. The process of negotiating an MOU entails a review of the affected department's OPF. Before entering into a memorandum of understanding, Treasury Board expects the OPF to contain a clear statement of objectives; the particular targets, results, and issues on which the department will render an accounting to the Treasury Board; and an agreed-upon plan for reporting key results.

IMAA guidelines offer a detailed discussion of the way in which results statements can be conveniently developed and reported.[18] The guidelines recognize that it is not always feasible to develop precise quantitative results statements, and they urge that, where appropriate, qualitative or proxy measures be used instead. The guidelines also suggest that departments be selective in reporting on results, and it advises them to concentrate on those indicators which Ministers would want to use in describing program accomplishments to the public or to the Treasury Board.

Australia: Decentralizing Financial Control

The development of performance indicators is proceeding under the aegis of two major reforms undertaken by the Australian government in the 1980s: the financial management improvement program (FMIP) and program management and budgeting (PMB).[19] FMIP/PMB is shifting the focus of budgeting from the inputs used to the results achieved. It seeks to change the operating culture of Australian public management from one which places a premium on compliance with externally-imposed rules to one which spurs managers to do the best they can with the resources at hand. The reforms are being phased in over a number of years; hence, the availability of performance indicators, while increasing, is still somewhat limited.[20]

Until the mid–1980s, financial control was highly centralized, and spending departments had little opportunity or incentive to manage their finances. A 1983 government study found that 94 percent of its senior managers perceived financial management to be merely spending the total allocated or controlling expenditures against appropriations.[21] These attitudes were rooted in the form of appropriation and the financial controls built up around it. Departments received separate administrative appropriations for as many as 21 line items. These itemized appropriations were backed by detailed estimates submitted to the Department of Finance, attention to inputs in Parliament, and central control of personnel actions.

Centralized control came under attack in the 1983 Review of Commonwealth Administration, which strongly urged central agencies to "place less emphasis on their detailed control activity. . . . The accent should be on the periodic assessment of departmental performance. . . ."[22] This attitude was endorsed by the Government's 1984 White Paper on Budget Reform, which gave the green light to pilot testing PMB and the implementation of FMIP.[23] These initiatives were viewed as part of a quid pro quo. In exchange for divesting many existing controls, a new performance-based accountability system would be established. This linkage of performance accountability and spending flexibility was explicit in a report on FMIP:

> More devolution of responsibility to agencies and, within them to line managers, seems to be the greatest incentive that can be provided for improved management performance. . . . It should also be understood and accepted that increased responsibility has to be matched with increased accountability.[24]

Devolution was inevitably the first step in the reform process, for, without it, there was no prospect of convincing managers that they had meaningful responsibility for resources and results. Among the initiatives taken thus far have been the consolidation of appropriations for operating expenses into two categories, the installation of a "corporate" planning process at the top of each department, decentralization of resource management within departments, and development of internal evaluation capacity.

Decentralization has been introduced during a period of fiscal constraint, in which the government has expressly pursued a "trilogy" policy of stabilizing budget outlays, tax revenue, and the deficit as a percentage of the gross domestic product. One element of fiscal restraint has been the imposition of an "efficiency dividend" of 3.75 percent over three years. The government views the dividend as one of the benefits of decentralization; departments have greater flexibility and opportunity for efficiency, and

they can retain any money saved in excess of the dividend. Some departments see the forced dividend, however, as a squeeze on resources.

Although Australia's Department of Finance has actively promoted
FMIP, it has had difficulty balancing the need for central direction with
FMIP's commitment to allow each department to set up its own management system. Finance is trying to "assist the managers to manage," but this
assistance is sometimes seen by departments as an intervention in internal
affairs. While Finance recognizes that it must avoid being seen as intrusive,
it still insists on having sufficiently detailed knowledge of an agency's activities to ensure a sound base for informed and objective advice to the agency
and Ministers.

Performance Measures

The pace of developing performance measures has been slowed by progress
in introducing program budgeting. Program Management and Budgeting
(PMB) is the key for identifying each organization's objectives and placing
them into a framework within which targets can be set for managers at all
levels. The program structure arrays objectives in hierarchical order, with
those at the lower levels more subject to being expressed in measurable
terms than those at the higher levels. The development of Australia's PMB
has been complicated by problems which should be familiar to those who
recall Planning, Programming, Budgeting (PPB) innovations in other countries. There has been difficulty in defining policy aims and in using performance indicators to measure results. An official report has found that
progress in developing indicators has been confined mainly to the more
easily measurable efficiency and workload targets. The report concluded
that this development will require prolonged effort by government agencies.[25]

The Department of Finance has mandated the use of performance measures in (1) evaluation plans, (2) policy initiatives, and (3) the Explanatory
Notes (ENs) that accompany the annual budget submitted to Parliament.
One set of ENs is prepared for each of the 17 portfolios into which the
budget is divided. The ENs are organized on a program basis so that each
category of expenditure is classified according to the program or element
with which it is associated. In view of the uneven implementation of program budgeting, it is to be expected that the ENs vary greatly in the
amount and quality of program information. Each EN is structured into
two parts, one providing "environmental" information on the problem or
need to be addressed, the other setting forth specific performance indicators for measuring the extent to which a particular program is impacting
on the identified need.

The Australian government recognizes the inadequacy of the measures currently in use and has made their improvement a key objective of FMIP/PMB. Because much of the Commonwealth's budget entails transfer payments to other levels of government, developing useful performance indicators will be a challenging task.

Denmark:
Budgeting for Productivity Improvement

Since 1983, the government of Denmark has adhered to a policy of zero real growth in public expenditure. Fiscal restraint has been accompanied by an ambitious program to modernize the public sector. Modernization has gone through two stages. The first (1983–1985) concentrated on relationships between spending ministries and the government; the second (1986–1987) focused on improving internal agency management. In the first phase, budget reforms gave state institutions greater flexibility in using financial and personnel resources, while holding them accountable for spending within fixed limits. As modernization progressed, increased emphasis was placed on productivity and financial management.[26]

Through most of the 1980s, the government has imposed a two-percent cut (below the inflation-adjusted level) on operating expenditures. The intention has been to force agencies to be more productive by squeezing the resources allocated to them. The 1985 Public Expenditure White Paper announced that future spending limits would be set in terms of desired improvements in productivity. Beginning with the 1987 budget, the government introduced a more selective method of establishing productivity targets. Public employees have been classified into a number of categories, and a separate annual target has been set for each category. These specific targets have been based on studies of productivity growth in both the public and private sectors.[27]

Each agency's productivity target is derived by determining its mix of personnel and computing the gain that each type is required to achieve. It should be noted that selective targets are applied only to salaries and personnel ceilings, not to other operating expenditures which are still subject to annual two-percent cuts. Moreover, the targets do not require that all programs and agencies have their budgets cut. Within the targets for each ministry, there is scope for reallocation. The targets are only one of the factors influencing budget decisions.

The data used in setting the targets are retrospective and highly aggregated: they report on past gains in an entire sector of category of employment. They do not shed light on how efficiently an agency is run or on the opportunities it has for improvement. The Department of Management and Personnel (DMP) has carried out pilot studies in six agencies, taking care to assure employees that it is the productivity of the organization which is being reviewed, not their individual performance. DMP has found that successful productivity analysis depends on, among other things, involvement of management and employees, careful specification of the unit being studied and of the outputs being measured, and sensitivity to the qualitative factors affecting productivity.

The Danish government recognizes that productivity increases comparable to those achieved in the private sector depend on the cooperation of managers and employees. To encourage their cooperation, it permits agencies to retain any savings realized by raising productivity above the budgeted target. It has also experimented with schemes to distribute a portion of above-target gains to employees and with collective bargaining agreements to authorize agencies to negotiate the payment of bonuses for productivity advances in excess of the normal improvement for the particular category of work.

The distribution of financial rewards to workers is contingent on a number of conditions. These include: prior agreement between management and employees as to the results to be achieved and the portion of the savings to be distributed; the gains must be measurable and the benefits must be substantiated; the gains must be directly related to the performance of those to be rewarded; and the agency making the rewards must adhere to strict financial limits. The Ministry of Finance has closely monitored the experiment, and it may withdraw an agency's authority to participate in it.

The Ministry has also encouraged productivity gains by lending money to agencies (to be repaid out of their future budgets) for acquisition of new technology. Investment has also been spurred by permitting agencies to carry forward unobligated funds to be used in subsequent years on approved productivity-enhancing projects.

Sweden: Triennial Budgeting

Performance measures are being linked to the budget in Sweden through three-year budget frames, a new means of allocating resources to encourage in-depth review of operations and performance. (In the Swedish budget, a "frame" is the total allocated to a major category of expenditure, such as a program or agency.) Triennial budgeting has been introduced following a long period, beginning in the late 1970s, during which annual across-the-board cuts of two percent (in real terms) were imposed on administrative expenditures. This "cheese slicer," as the two-percent cut is often referred to, has been made more flexible in recent years by requiring agencies to save five percent over a three-year period. There is reason to believe, however, that while the five-percent rule is uniform, its application is not, and actual allocations often vary from this starting point.

The enforced cutbacks reflect the government's determination to stabilize the size of public expenditure relative to the gross national product. This policy was articulated in the 1988 Revised Budget Statement, which declared that:

> The point has been reached where the public sector's share of the economy cannot continue to grow as it has in the past. . . . Never before have the resources for public activities been so great. The main task is not to increase these resources but to find methods for making activities more efficient and being able to redistribute resources by means of a continuous review of systems and organizational structures.[28]

Sustained pressure on resources and the need for reallocation have spurred the government to give agencies greater flexibility in using funds. The government has felt, however, that it could not allow more freedom without obtaining more information on performance in return. The two ideas—greater spending discretion and closer monitoring of results—have been brought together in the three-year budget frames that were pilot tested in approximately 20 state agencies before a decision was made in 1988 to extend them to almost all national agencies. (Military and civil defense are not covered, and selected agencies may be exempted.) The transition to the new process is to be made over a three-year period. Approximately one-third of the agencies will undertake triennial budgeting for the 1991/1992 budget; another third will be brought into the process for the 1992/1993 budget; and the process will be extended to all remaining agencies in the year after that.

Agencies receiving three-year frames will go through a more elaborate and lengthier process in formulating their budgets.[29] At the outset, agencies are to receive both general and specific directives, the former issued by the government or the Ministry of Finance, the latter by the competent ministry in their area of operation. The general directives require agencies to report on performance for the previous five years, assess current objectives and arrangements, and develop measurable targets for the work to be done and results to be achieved over the next three years. These directives also call upon agencies to apply productivity measures developed in recent years, so as to show whether they are becoming more or less efficient. The special directives are tailored to each agency's circumstances and pertain to the specific evaluations to be undertaken, priorities and alternatives, and the policy options to be considered.

Although the three-year frames cover only administrative costs, the review process will extend to program objectives and expenditures as well.

That is, agencies are expected to assess their total performance and the full range of activities. In effect, the government is offering increased flexibility in administrative management as an inducement for agencies to make a broad, probing assessment of their overall performance.

In the two intervening years of the triennial cycle, each participating agency is to submit a simplified budget request, unless developments warrant a change in the approved direction for the three-year period. Each agency also is to submit an annual outcomes report on expenditures, performance, productivity change, and the previous year's results. It is contemplated that at the end of the cycle, each agency would undergo a fresh, in-depth scrutiny which would eventuate in a new three-year budget frame and decisions on the agency's future objectives and activities.

It is premature, of course, to assess the quality of the performance data generated by triennial budgeting. As might be expected in a new process, the material submitted by the agencies participating in the pilot test has been quite uneven. Some agencies have had difficulty linking administrative resources, which are covered by the three-year frames, to broader program expenditures, which are not covered. The National Audit Bureau and the Swedish Agency for Administrative Development (SAFAD) have been tasked by the government to devise procedures for improved performance reporting.

Productivity Studies

The government has also given priority to productivity in the public sector. This emphasis has been spurred by various studies showing adverse productivity trends in Sweden.[30] The most ambitious studies have been undertaken by the Expert Study Group (ESO) affiliated with the Ministry of Finance. ESO measured changes in public sector productivity since 1960; the study covered eight service areas, encompassing 70 percent of the Swedish public sector.

With few exceptions, the studies showed a negative productivity trend for the 1960–1980 period.[31] In general, however, the trend has been favorable since about 1975. More recent studies updating the data through 1985 indicate some further improvements in productivity. The fact that productivity slipped during the high spending growth period of the 1960s and early 1970s, but improved during subsequent years of fiscal stress, was noted in the ESO report, from which the following excerpt is drawn:

> . . . productivity falls when the resources increase strongly and rises when the resources decrease. This indicates that it is easier to maintain a certain level of output despite dwindling resources than to raise the level at a rate correspond-

ing to an increase of resources. In other words, there is a lack of flexibility in the public sector, albeit explainable by overhead costs, personnel policies, etc.[32]

These and other productivity studies have become increasingly prominent in efforts to upgrade the efficiency of Swedish government. The findings have sensitized government officials to the need for special efforts such as triennial budgeting, and they have also provided justification to cheese slicer tactics that squeeze agency budgets.

Linking Budgets and Performance

It will be some time before the governments covered in this article have sufficient evidence to determine whether spenders have been remade into managers. This article focuses on what governments are striving for and the inducements they are offering. It should be kept in mind, however, that much of the story has yet to unfold. At present, there is much more to report about the procedures introduced than about behavioral adjustments.

The relationship of performance measurement and resource allocation is unsettled. In theory, it might seem advantageous to make a direct and explicit connection between the size of an agency's budget and the efficiency or effectiveness of its programs. This view is embraced in Australia's FMIP/PMB reform, a central aim of which "is to establish performance measurement as the basis of budget allocations. . . ."[33] As a contract for performance, the budget would be tied to achievement of precise targets, and incremental resources would be provided for incremental performance. Agencies requesting increased resources would have to show the measurable results of having more money.

In practice, none of the governments has forged a tight relationship between resources and results, nor is any likely to try. They have shied away from a strict linkup of resources and performance for a number of reasons. One is that they still are far from certain that agencies can deliver on promised improvements in performance. The more explicit the link, the more visible is the failure if departments fall short of agreed-to objectives. The state of the art in performance measurement is not so advanced as to warrant precise commitments on what will be accomplished with public funds.

Another reason for the loose relationship is that the measures are intended to have a broad managerial application. The objective is to change management styles and cultures, not just to make more rational or defensible budget decisions. It is believed that strong reliance on the measures would generate controversy and discourage managers from cooperating. If this were to occur, the supply of data would certainly dry up and the quality would be impaired.

Viewed solely as a measurement problem, the current spate of innovations is a throwback to the performance budgeting and PPB movements. But the spirit of reform is different this time around. Today's management-oriented reforms are concerned with what organizations do and produce, and they focus on means of holding them accountable for performance. The shift in emphasis is subtle but critical. Unlike past innovations, which strove to optimize programs, contemporary developments seek to improve organizations. They aim to give managers financial (and other) incentives that make them more aware of and accountable for costs and performance and more willing—and able—to shift resources to more productive activities.

Two of the more conspicuous features of contemporary performance measurement are the emphasis on productivity improvement and on setting advance targets against which results are to be compared. While broader effectiveness measures are the direction in which most of the governments would like to move, and although these measures are sometimes used or under development, they are generally viewed as attainable only after more modest performance objectives have been realized.

Productivity improvement is an attractive early step. Measuring productivity is less controversial and easier to implement than measuring the outcomes of public activity. Indeed, something is reassuring for public sector managers in productivity's unstated presumption that they are doing the right things, but that reorganizing their work might enable them to do more or take on high priority tasks that have been neglected for lack of resources. The underlying challenge of effectiveness measures, by contrast, is that government might be doing the wrong things or pursuing the wrong objectives. When measurement takes on these divisive questions, it is often unable to advance beyond the conceptual stage.

Productivity measurement can yield quicker and more visible payoffs than might investment in other approaches. By focusing on outputs, performance assessors grapple with matters in the purview of managers rather than with basic issues which may be more driven by exogenous factors than by matters controlled by the organization carrying out the activity. This is especially important because the thrust of contemporary reform is to make managers accountable for what they do.

The interest in productivity is clearly related to fiscal stress and to the squeeze imposed in the countries studied on administrative expenditure. As operating resources are tightened, governments must consider whether the pressures they are applying might lead to hidden reductions in the volume of services. By concentrating on productivity, governments can guard against this side effect.

Targets, the second feature of current innovations, refer to specific levels of performance to be achieved by a designated time. The targets may be more or less binding, closely linked to budget allocations or tied to other managerial processes. Because of their specificity, targets provide a reasonably clear basis for assessing performance. Targets—in contrast to objectives—must be reachable, both in the sense that their levels can be met and that success depends on the performance of managers rather than on outside factors.

The publication of targets for future performance is another unsettled issue. It is understandable that managers would not want to commit themselves openly to the precise performance to be achieved by a certain date. In the United Kingdom, only a small portion of the targets used internally by departments have found their way into the annual White Paper. The trend in that and other countries, however, is toward increased disclosure.

Decentralization

Decentralization is a common theme in modern management. It is seen as a precondition for holding managers to account for what they spend and do. But there is a realization at central levels that accountability cannot hinge solely on the expectation that, once given the opportunity, managers will take charge and turn their organizations into more productive workplaces. Letting managers manage, past experience has taught, does not mean that they will. The current emphasis is on making them manage by nailing down the performance levels to which they will be held.

Delegation of previously centralized controls has stirred a rethinking of the role of the central budget organization. The old controller role is slipping away and, along with it, the leverage that budget officials exercised over departments as well as a part of their data base for monitoring expenditures. Central staff understand that it does not suffice for them to make the big decisions while ceding all the details to spenders. They hope that performance measures will substitute for the lost information and controls while giving them an important niche in the management process. Yet they are not sure things will work out this way. While the budget offices consulted for this study generally support decentralization, they worry that the new performance-based system will leave them without effective roles or controls. They are not confident that performance measurement will go beyond technique to the behavior of managers. Departments will "take the money and run," one budget official protested. But he also conceded that the old controls are no longer viable.

Central staff view performance measures as a handle for reviewing and possibly intervening on other matters of management. The measures provide "talking points" in dealing with departments, move the discussion to a more objective plane, and enable budget makers to question what the departments have accomplished or intend to do. But they believe these measures will be fresh and relevant only if (a) the affected departments have the lead role in selecting them; (b) the measures are principally used for internal management rather than for central review; (c) the data are not turned into evidence for reducing budgets but are a means of spurring agencies to "spend better"; and (d) the measures are part of a larger framework which encourages managerial initiative and accountability, within which there is a clear definition of the expectations of both spending agencies and central budget staffs.

Balancing these requirements can be a difficult task. On the one hand, central budget experts must take an active role in designing and promoting managerial innovation; on the other, performance measures must be indigenous to departments and accepted by them. In the early stages of development, there is widespread understanding that central staff must take the lead in moving innovation along; if performance measurement matures, central budget staff will have to withdraw to a more circumscribed role. It remains to be seen whether they will be content to be supporting players.

Worrying about the role of budget makers and the uses of performance measures may prove to be needless if the current wave of reform exhausts itself in procedural adjustments, as previous ones did. What is the likelihood of this happening? One cannot know in advance because it is difficult to appraise managerial innovations during their developmental stage. When the reforms are new and still being actively promoted by the government—as are the five innovations discussed in this article—official reports tend to be upbeat and speak of the progress that has been made or that is forthcoming. When, as often happens, the government loses interest, the reform fades away or is abandoned with little advance notice.

Changing the culture of public management, getting finance staffs to divest the tools that have given them power and access, and prodding managers to reallocate resources for efficiency's sake are all difficult, time-consuming tasks. Shortly after the British Government launched FMI, a White Paper described it as "a programme for the life of a Parliament and beyond."[34] The Thatcher Government has now been in power for more than a decade, yet its FMI work is far from completed. Few democratic regimes govern long enough to have sufficient staying power to see their innovations come to fruition. It should occasion no surprise if the current reforms end up with a relaxation of financial controls and somewhat more performance information, but fail to bring about a real transformation in financial management.

Notes

1. Auditor General of Canada, *Annual Report to the House of Commons* (Ottawa: October 1987), paragraph 4.28.

2. A series of articles by Clarence E. Ridley and Herbert A. Simon, first published individually in 1938, were assembled into a volume: *Measuring Municipal Activities* (Chicago: International City Managers Association, 1943).

3. Documents on Australian practices were supplemented by interviews with senior officials from the Department of Finance posted to the Commonwealth delegation in London and the Australian Embassy in Washington, DC.

4. The initial concept of financial management initiatives was presented in *Efficiency and Effectiveness in the Civil Service*, Cmnd. 8616 (London: September 1982).

5. For those who may not be familiar with the term, "value for money" in Commonwealth countries commonly refers to efficient and/or effective public service.

6. Cmnd. 8616, *op. cit.*

7. The argument for decentralized, or "devolved," budgeting is made in HM Treasury, *Multi-departmental Review of Budgeting: Final Central Report* (London: March 1986).

8. *Ibid.*, p. 33.

9. These and other problems are discussed in HM Treasury, *Flexibility for Budget Holders* (London: August 1987).

10. HM Treasury, *Multi-departmental Review of Budgeting: Executive Summary* (London: March 1986), p. 8.

11. See House of Commons, Committee of Public Accounts, Thirteenth Report, *The Financial Management Initiative* (London: Her Majesty's Stationery Office, April 1987).

12. Treasury Board Secretariat, *Measurement of the Performance of Government Operations*, Circular No. 1976–25 (Ottawa: 22 July, 1976).

13. See Treasury Board of Canada, *Increased Ministerial Authority and Accountability: Introduction and Progress Report* (Ottawa: January 1988).

14. See Treasury Board Secretariat, *The IMAA Handbook: A Guide to Development and Implementation* (Ottawa: 1988).

15. Auditor General of Canada, *op. cit.*, paragraph 4.57. This paragraph also contains the following finding: "It is almost impossible to challenge budgets objectively. . . . Statements of results are imprecise. Information on the cost of products or services is still inadequate. There are few performance indicators. Service levels are often not defined."

16. The Canadian Government also issued instructions in 1982 for publication of Part III of the Estimates submitted to Parliament. The Part IIIs, as they are known, contain detailed data on planned and actual results as well as other performance data useful in justifying resource requirements. See Comptroller General of Canada, *Revisions to the Form of the Estimates*, Circular No. 1982–8 (Canberra: 12 February 1982).

17. Auditor General of Canada, *op. cit.*, paragraph, 4.78.

18. *The IMAA Handbook, op. cit.*, declares that "for some programs, it is not possible to develop precise quantitative results statements. In these cases, qualitative statements and proxy measures, if appropriate, should be used."

19. The reform was initially referred to as "program budgeting." It was subsequently relabeled "program management and budgeting" to emphasize the managerial aspects of the innovations.

20. These reforms are explained in Department of Finance, *FMIP and Program Budgeting: A Study of Implementation in Selected Agencies* (Canberra: Australian Government Publishing Service, 1987).

21. Australian Public Service Board and Department of Finance, *Financial Management Improvement Program: Diagnostic Study* (Canberra: February 1984).

22. Commonwealth of Australia, *Review of Commonwealth Administration* (Canberra: Australian Government Publishing Service, January 1983), p. xvi.

23. Commonwealth of Australia, *Budget Reform* (Canberra: Australian Government Publishing Service, April 1984).

24. *Diagnostic Study, op. cit.,* p. 17. The linkage of performance and flexibility was also made clear in the White Paper on Budget Reform: "As agreed program objectives and performance indicators develop, and improved management performance and control becomes evident, central agencies will be able to increase the managerial flexibility available to departments in the disposition of resources." *Budget Reform, op. cit.,* p. 21.

25. Thus, progress in developing performance measures "has been confined mainly to the more easily measurable efficiency aspects and workplan targets. . . ." Department of Finance, *FMIP and Program Budgeting, op. cit.,* p. 46.

26. Ministry of Finance, Department of Administration, "The Danish Programme for Modernisation of the Public Sector," typescript (Copenhagen: 11 April 1986).

27. See Ministry of Finance, Department of the Budget, *Improving Productivity in Central Government* (Copenhagen: 1987).

28. Ministry of Finance, *Renewing the Public Sector, Exerpts from the 1988 Revised Budget Statement,* (Stockholm: 1988), p. 3.

29. The triennial budget system is described in *ibid.*

30. See the Swedish Agency for Administrative Development, "Productivity and Efficiency in the Public Sector—Methods and Results from Studies in Sweden," presented to Council of Europe Seminar, November 1987.

31. Ministry of Finance, Expert Group on Public Finance, *Public Services—A Searchlight on Productivity and Users* (Stockholm: Swedish Government Printing, 1987).

32. *Ibid.,* p. 16.

33. *FMIP and Program Budgeting, op. cit.,* p. 7.

34. *Progress in Financial Management in Government Departments,* Cmnd. 9297 (London: July 1984), paragraph 32.

8

ENTREPRENEURIAL BUDGETING: AN EMERGING REFORM?

Dan A. Cothran

In a widely cited article, Aaron Wildavsky offered an answer to the question of "why the traditional budget lasts" (1978). He argued that despite all the efforts to reform budgeting in the past few decades, it has remained essentially incremental and line-item. Although this may be true, efforts to reform budgeting occur with such regularity that the question could easily be turned around: Why are attacks on traditional budgeting so persistent? Some shortcomings must exist in budgeting for reforms to be proposed so regularly. Although none of these efforts, such as performance, program, or zero-base budgeting, entirely supplanted incremental line-item budgeting, elements of these reforms endure in the budgeting process of many governments. Now a new challenge to traditional budgeting has appeared.

The process of government budgeting has changed significantly in the 20th century, beginning with the introduction of executive budgeting in the 1920s. Since the 1950s, a relatively major reform has been proposed about once each decade in an effort to overcome some of the perceived deficiencies of incremental line-item budgeting—performance budgeting in the 1950s, program budgeting in the 1960s, and zero-base budgeting in the 1970s. In the 1980s, there was a growth of what might be called "automatic control budgeting" in which voters and policy makers tried to im-

1993.   Entrepreneurial budgeting: An emerging reform? Cothran, Dan A. **Public Administration Review** 53 (September-October): 445–454.

pose statutorily prescribed formulas on revenues and expenditures, the most notable examples being Proposition 13-type laws, Gramm-Rudman-Hollings, and the movement for a federal balanced budget amendment to the Constitution.[1] In the 1990s, another type of budgetary reform is being proposed—entrepreneurial budgeting. In this article, I examine three examples of this type of budgeting. One is used by some local U.S. governments, another by the national governments of several industrial democracies, and the third is proposed as a way to improve defense budgeting in the United States. This article asks whether these methods have any qualities in common, why they are being proposed, and how likely they are to last. As disparate as they appear, they are remarkably similar in fundamental ways. Although they go by various names, all of these methods might be characterized as entrepreneurial budgeting because of their emphasis on decentralization and incentives.

Entrepreneurial Budgeting: Three Examples

Expenditure Control Budgeting[2]

One observer claims that since 1979, U.S. "cities have been experimenting with and slowly developing a new system for public budgeting" (Gaebler Group, 1988, p. 1), which has been called entrepreneurial budgeting, expenditure control budgeting, profit sharing, and various other things. Unlike traditional budgeting where policy makers wait for departments to make their requests, in this approach the city council begins by setting expenditure limits. This part of the budgetary process is very much top-down, rather than bottom-up as is often the case under traditional budgeting. The expenditure limits are frequently expressed by a formula, such as holding the increase in total spending to 7 percent over the current year. The council's budget plan is quite brief, perhaps no more than two pages, in contrast to the huge line-item document with which most city councils have traditionally struggled. The idea is to get the top policy makers to focus on the big picture, not the details. In doing this, the council tries to determine what citizens want their city government to do. From this information and their own preferences, the council members set the overall policy direction for the city. They may, for example, decide that the citizens are particularly concerned about the conditions of roads, and hence the city council may increase the road budget by 12 percent, rather than only 7 percent. The council then monitors the performance of the city government to ensure that policy goals are being met. It does not, however, get caught up in detailed scrutiny of line-item spending. In this way, the council, and to an extent the city manager, move away from micro-management and toward greater attention to broad policy questions. Governments that use this approach clearly are motivated by the constraints that voters have put on revenues since the late 1970s.

At the same time, the operating departments are given more discretion. Within the bounds of the centrally determined expenditure limits, each department is free to use funds as its professional managers think best (subject to the usual constraints of legality and political prudence, of course). For example, they are free to move money from salaries to supplies if they think that will allow their department to pursue its mission more effectively. In addition, the city manager maintains a contingency fund for the entire government, so that individual departments do not need to maintain such funds.

Perhaps the most significant change in this approach is what happens to funds left over at the end of the fiscal year. Instead of a year-end spending spree motivated by the "use it or lose it" rule, departments are allowed to carry over a significant portion of their unspent authority, usually 30 to 50 percent, but in some cases 100 percent. This form of "profit sharing" is seen by many as the most important departure from the traditional budget. Along with the general increase in discretion over the use of funds, it is supposed to improve both management and morale by giving more discretion to those who actually administer the program. The more decentralized approach gives line managers the flexibility to manage their resources in more creative ways and to respond to changing conditions. In that way, it allegedly departs from the rigidity frequently attributed to government bureaucracy and moves toward the flexibility often associated with private enterprise. That is why it is sometimes called entrepreneurial budgeting.

Basing their actions on organizational theory, policy makers hope that operating managers will exhibit greater productivity in return for the greater freedom. Carl Bellone examined four cities in California that used decentralized budgeting. He writes: "Instead of the department heads in each city submitting a detailed budget request which is then negotiated item by item with the city manager . . . each department is given a pot of money. . . . The department head is then free to spend the money allocated in the way that he or she feels is best." Bellone concludes, "This budgetary freedom fosters creativity and innovation" (1988, p. 84).

One of the earliest local governments to use the approach was the city of Fairfield, California. The city manager introduced the system after Proposition 13 devastated the city budget in 1978. It is a departure from the traditional way of building budgets from the bottom up, in which departments start with their expenditure levels for the current year and then try to increase that as much as possible for the following year, meanwhile quickly spending any balance left over at the end of the fiscal year. In expenditure control budgeting, the Fairfield city council examines a two-page budget proposal that highlights broad categories of spending. Department heads are, in effect, given block grants that demonstrate considerable trust in their judgment about the use of money and that allow a high level of autonomy in managing their departments. Any unspent balance at the end of the fiscal year is retained by the departments, so that managers have an incentive to save unspent funds for higher priority items in the new fiscal year, rather than spend the funds immediately for lower priority items. Under this system, however, the city council and city manager will expect evidence of achievement by the various programs. In fact, by reducing the amount of time that they spend examining detailed line-items, they will have more time to monitor actual program performance. This approach greatly simplifies budget preparation, as departments are generally given a lump-sum allocation based on the prior year's budget plus an increment for inflation and for the increase in population.[3] In 1982, the Fairfield city manager received the International City Managers Association Award for Outstanding Management Innovation for the new approach. Fairfield officials believe that the approach saved the city almost $5 million over a period of 8 years (*Cal-Tax News,* June 1, 1987, p. 10). Fairfield was still using this decentralized approach to budgeting in 1992, 13 years after its introduction. City officials believed that the system was more efficient than traditional line-item budgeting in that it made managers more responsible, reduced inter-departmental conflict at budget time, and encouraged thrift and efficiency in operations.

Dade County, Florida, has used a similar approach. Faced with a loss of federal revenue-sharing funds in fiscal year 1986–87 and constrained by its property tax limit, the county faced revenue growth of less than 1 percent for the next fiscal year. That meant an across-the-board cut of about 20 percent for all departments from the normal expected budget for the following year. At that point, the county instituted a budgetary approach that it called "profit sharing," in which each department was allowed greater autonomy in managing its funds, and could retain most of a year-end balance. County officials believe that the increased efficiency that resulted from the new approach saved or generated $11 million. Like Fairfield, Dade County also received a public administration award for its use of the new method (*Dade County News,* February 8, 1988).

The city of Chandler, Arizona, has also used expenditure control budgeting in recent years. In Chandler, the base budget is adjusted annually for population growth and inflation to produce a current services budget. Department managers are given maximum autonomy in managing their budgets, including carrying forward any unspent funds. Managers are expected to pursue efficiencies that will generate savings that can be used for future years' programs. Program managers generally are responsible for providing the funds to meet service levels that cannot be covered by the automatic annual adjustments for population and inflation. Unexpected demands on de-

partmental budgets can be handled by contingency fund transfers that require approval by the city manager and city council. Chandler city officials
believe that the new way of budgeting has motivated program managers to
pay greater attention to priorities and results. The city manager said that
the new approach saved the city over $2 million in fiscal year 1986–87.[4]

The city of Westminster, Colorado, uses what it calls a modified decentralized approach to budgeting. The city council appropriates by line-item
but then gives department managers considerable discretion to move funds
from one line-item to another. In a theoretical sense, one could argue that
line-item and decentralized budgeting are incompatible in that line-item is
a method of centralized control. But the relationship between centralization and decentralization can be seen as a continuum, not a sharp dichotomy. The use of line-items, but with greater latitude than in the past,
allows policy makers to grant more discretion while simultaneously retaining a comfortable vestige of central control in case they want to reassert
that control later. (Knowing that you have a way to retreat can make you
more willing to advance.) Westminster has found that giving department
heads the ability to transfer between line items provides greater flexibility
for them to acquire capital equipment, to hire temporary employees, and
generally to allocate resources efficiently throughout the year. At year's
end, the city council also allows departments to retain some of their savings, on a descending scale. A department can keep 100 percent of the first
25 percent of savings and a lesser percentage of any saving above that
level. Westminster officials believe that this provides an incentive for departments to save and to avoid the year-end spending spree.[5]

A similar modified approach is used by the San Diego campus of the
University of California. In contrast with the highly centralized budgetary
process at most of the other UC campuses, UCSD allocates by line-item but
then gives greater discretion to program directors over the use of the funds.
For example, deans and department chairs are given "the flexibility to
move funds more freely between line items than in the more centralized
past." In addition, limitations on carrying forward unexpended funds have
been relaxed somewhat, subject to state-imposed restrictions. However, the
university has no ability to transfer funds from the operating to the capital
budget, as the two are funded from different sources.[6] This points up a restriction that a state agency might face that a city government might not.
For a state agency, the decision to use the fuller version of decentralized
budgeting would have to be made at the state capitol.

Budgeting for Results

Recent studies of budgeting in several industrial democracies indicate that
a number of national governments are struggling toward a common

method that one author calls "budgeting for results." Allen Schick (1990) looked at national budgeting in Australia, Canada, Denmark, Sweden, and Britain, and from the richness of his descriptive detail, one can extract several qualities that virtually all of the governmental efforts have in common. In one form or another, each government is trying to achieve *central* control of total spending, *decentralization* of authority to departments in the use of the funds, and enhanced *accountability* for results.

In response to the fiscal stress and cutbacks of the 1970s and 1980s, the British government launched its "financial management initiatives" in 1982. Under this system, the cabinet decides overall spending limits with Treasury advice, but then the Treasury loosens its control somewhat more than in the past, giving departments more discretion over how to use the money. Within limits, each department is free to use the resources in the ways its managers believe will be most efficient and effective. For example, in 1988, the Treasury replaced central manpower ceilings for departments with overall financial limits on administrative costs; now each department can decide on its mix of personnel and equipment, as long as the total *cost* does not exceed the specified limit. However, that enhanced discretion is accompanied by increased accountability for results. In collaboration with the Treasury, each department is expected to develop measures of performance and, in fact, a recent government White Paper listed over 1,800 output and performance measures.

In 1979, the Canadian federal government took a major step toward giving high-level policy makers greater control over total spending and priorities with the introduction of what came to be known as "envelope budgeting." Programs were collected into broad policy sectors, or envelopes, such as defense, social development, and economic development. The cabinet then decided on the allocation of funds to the envelopes in an effort to gain enhanced control over both total spending and relative sectoral shares. Within their broad allocations, officials were granted some discretion to move funds around. Because funds for new initiatives generally had to be found within a sector's or program's overall allocation, managers had an incentive to delete unproductive activities so that funds could be made available for the new initiatives (McCaffery, 1984). In envelope budgeting, however, the emphasis was on sectoral allocation by the cabinet, rather than on decentralization of management and accountability for results. Perhaps for that reason, in 1986 the Canadian government introduced a more decentralized budgeting system called "Increased Ministerial Authority and Accountability" (IMAA). Although the cabinet decides on the overall budget and on the allocation for various broad categories, such as defense and health, departments have more "discretion over many administrative matters previously requiring central approval" (Schick, 1990, p. 27). For example, departments now have broader authority over the reallocation of resources without Treasury or cabinet approval. They can reallocate funds from one program to another and can carry some unused funds into the next fiscal year. In exchange for the enhanced discretion, however, IMAA requires greater accountability for results. "Memoranda of Understanding" are negotiated between the Treasury Board and the departments. These are virtually contractual relationships by which the departments receive greater stability of resources and greater discretion in the use of those resources in exchange for an agreement to achieve certain levels of performance. The departments set forth their specific objectives in hierarchical order and indicate how they will be measured and monitored. The Treasury Board recognizes that quantitative measures are not always feasible, and it also suggests that departments should be selective in reporting those indicators that ministers would find the most useful in describing the accomplishments of each program. Nonetheless, despite those brakes, there is an unmistakable move toward greater accountability for results.

Australia has followed a similar pattern. After decades of highly centralized financial control in government, a 1984 White Paper on budget reform recommended greater decentralization of managerial decision making and enhanced accountability by departments. This quotation from an Australian government study could almost have come from a discussion of entrepreneurial budgeting in one of the U.S. cities mentioned above: "More devolution of responsibility to agencies and, within them to line managers, seems to be the greatest incentive that can be provided for improved management performance. . . . [But] increased responsibility has to be matched with increased accountability" (Schick, 1990, p. 29). The Australian government has done this in three ways—the collapse of 21 line items into two, decentralization of resource management within each department, and development of an evaluation capacity within each department.

Like most of the other governments mentioned, Denmark has been motivated partly by fiscal limitations. In recent years, the government has cut the funds available to agencies, and so it is making a special effort to increase productivity as a way to avoid cutting services too starkly. To encourage greater productivity, the Danish government allows agencies to keep any savings that result from increases in productivity that exceed target levels. In one of the most dramatic innovations in budgeting in the world, it also has experimented with allowing the employees themselves to retain some of the savings resulting from unusually high productivity gains. The Ministry of Finance has also tried to spur productivity by lending money to agencies for the acquisition of new technology and by allowing agencies to carry forward some unspent funds if they are used for projects that will improve productivity.

New Zealand has also adopted a budget system that emphasizes achievement of objectives, rather than close monitoring of line-item expenditures.

This was part of a broad move away from traditional government provision of services and toward a situation in which many government functions were either privatized or made relatively independent of government control, numerous economic activities were deregulated, and the traditional civil service rules were loosened (Scott *et al.*, 1990).

In all of these countries, a major goal of decentralization is to encourage the development of a new administrative culture in which program managers see their objective as maximum achievement with the available resources, rather than as acquiring the largest possible budget for their programs and then spending all they get. However, further research is needed to determine if spenders have been turned into managers.

Mission Budgeting at the Pentagon

Recent proposals for reforming defense budgeting bear striking resemblances to the two approaches discussed above. In the five decades since it was created, the Defense Department has undergone two major changes in the way resources are allocated. In the Defense Reorganization Act of 1958, President Eisenhower and Congress tried to reform military structure by increasing the authority of the Office of the Secretary of Defense and reorganizing the combat commands along regional lines. In a passage that sounds like the justification for expenditure control budgeting in Fairfield, California, one author says:

> Eisenhower wanted to decentralize operational authority and responsibility to mission and theater commanders, because he believed that the combatant commanders were potentially best situated and motivated to plan operations and to determine the size and composition of forces required to accomplish their assigned combat missions, as well as to carry them out (Thompson, 1991, p. 55).

However, the reform did not have the intended result of increasing combat readiness, primarily because combatant commanders had to accept the military units the services chose to supply, and the uniformed services retained full administrative control over those forces. Therefore, because decentralization occurred in form only, the Eisenhower reforms merely made a very complex bureaucracy even more complex.

A similar development occurred during the McNamara years. PPBS was instituted in the Defense Department by Secretary Robert McNamara and Comptroller Charles Hitch in an effort to enhance the military's pursuit of national security goals. Instead of organizing budgets only by inputs (e.g., personnel) and administrative units (e.g., the army), PPBS organized the budget request by functions to be performed. The system was centralized in that the goals were established by top-level policy makers, but it was decentralized in that lower-level officials were given considerable discretion in the methods that could be used to achieve the goals. McNamara said that he wanted to push all decisions to the lowest appropriate level. In addition, the system sought to establish a clearer link between goals, performance, and rewards. Defense comptrollers Charles Hitch and later Robert Anthony tried to install "results-oriented operational budgeting." Anthony proposed an accounting structure that "was firmly grounded in the principles of responsibility budgeting and accounting" (Thompson 1991, p. 58).[7]

Although PPBS was probably more successful in the Defense Department than in most federal agencies, many of the reforms of the McNamara period did not become fully operational even in Defense, partly because of the Vietnam conflict. Various authors, however, argue that the essential elements of the Eisenhower-McNamara reforms should still be pursued. Jacques Gansler, for example, wants Congress to concern itself with large policy questions such as foreign policy goals, strategic choices, and the allocation of resources to broad military missions. He would "restructure the budget process so that Congress will be forced to vote on 'top-line dollars for the various 'mission areas' rather than on the details of specific programs and projects that are clearly identified with districts and states" (Gansler, 1989, p. 120). In his proposal, Congress would restrict itself to establishing broad policy guidelines. It would delegate more authority to the Department of Defense to choose among weapons systems, deploy military units, and so on. Gansler would even put an end to congressional apportionment of military expenditure by state and district as wasteful and irrational. Although it may be politically naive to think that Congress would delegate its authority to the degree that Gansler recommends, it is enlightening to see how often decentralization of decision making in defense budgeting is proposed. Finally, Gansler calls for more real evaluation to "allow decision makers to assess the outputs realized and the accomplishments achieved against the dollars expended" (Gansler, 1989, p. 329).

Another dramatic proposal to restructure defense spending along the lines of mission budgeting has been offered by L. R. Jones and R. B. Doyle (1989), professors of financial management at the Naval Postgraduate School. Under their scheme, the budget authority granted by President and Congress would be general, rather than detailed. The Joint Chiefs of Staff would have the authority to allocate funds to the combatant commands, rather than to the uniformed services. That would be the centralized aspect of their scheme. From that point, decision making would be more decentralized than it is now. The combatant commanders would use their funds to purchase personnel and equipment from training and support commands and to lease facilities and weapons systems from the private sector. Purchasing and leasing would be carried out in a set of markets that would operate much as a private economy does. Combatant commanders would bid for supplies and personnel; suppliers would sell their wares to the highest bidder, and prices would be raised or lowered to bring demand into line with supply.

Whether the Jones-Doyle and Gansler proposals are feasible or not, their commonalities are striking. They involve centralized priority setting, decentralized implementation, and enhanced accountability for results. They involve some centralization in the sense of having top-level decision makers such as the President, Congress, and Joint Chiefs focus more on policies and priorities and less on the details of micro-management. They involve considerable devolution of authority to line managers. Finally, they would require greater accountability from those line managers for the results achieved.

The timing of these proposals for defense decentralization may be partly a result of the fact that defense budgeting has actually become more centralized in recent years. Defense analyst J. Ronald Fox of the Harvard Business School believes that Congress asserted greater control of the weapons acquisitions process and other aspects of the defense budget after 1970 for a series of reasons, including Vietnam, Watergate, the growth of congressional staff, cost overruns, and spectacular incidents such as the $600 ashtray. Thus Congress saw micromanagement "as a necessary and natural response to the Defense Department's failure to manage its own affairs" (Fox, 1988, p. 85).

Common Qualities

Proposals for budgetary reform have emerged in the 1980s and 1990s for local budgeting in the United States, for defense budgeting, and for national budgeting in other industrial democracies. These proposals have at least three qualities in common.

Central Control of Goals

Entrepreneurial budgeting, mission budgeting, and budgeting for results all involve some centralization, usually in two ways. First, central decision makers maintain control over the *total* amount of spending. Different governments may mean different things by "control of the total." A local government may impose a total spending ceiling of $100 million for fiscal year 1993, while a national government may restrict the total budget increase next year to, say, 7 percent. For example, in recent years the Swedish government has tried to limit government spending to about 60 percent of gross national product. Second, central policy makers usually decide total spending for broad functions, such as health, public safety, or roads. A government may decide to allocate X percent for health, Y percent for income maintenance, and so on. The central control of totals and priorities is a salient characteristic of, and no doubt one of the major motivations for, these reform proposals.

Decentralization of Means

At the same time that budgeting remains or even becomes more centralized in the above ways, it is also decentralized in important ways. Once the overall total and the allocation to broad functions have been decided by central policy makers, program managers are then given considerably more discretion over how they spend their money. Government managers are treated more like business managers. They might be given more discretion to move money around among line items, such as from salaries to supplies, or to move money from operations to capital spending. In addition, they might be allowed to carry over a significant portion of a year-end surplus to the next fiscal year. The literature on entrepreneurial budgeting says that many local governments allow program managers to carry over about 30 to 50 percent of their year-end "surplus" to the new fiscal year in order to avoid the "waste" of the surplus in a year-end spending spree. Therefore, both the chief executive and the program managers supposedly benefit from the increased flexibility—the chief executive by contending with less waste and the program manager by enjoying greater discretion.

Accountability for Results

Of course, higher-level decision makers ask something in return for the increased discretion that they give to lower-level officials. Primarily, they want greater evidence of program achievement, particularly efficiency. Often an almost contractual agreement is negotiated between the central budget office and the operating departments in which each department lists and ranks its objectives, specifies indicators for measuring the achievement of those objectives, and quantifies the indicators as far as possible.

Paradoxically, these new approaches all call for additional centralization *and* decentralization at the same time. At first glance, these two qualities might appear to be incompatible, but, in fact, organizations often centralize in order to decentralize (Perrow, 1977). Once those at the top are confident that their goals will be pursued by those below, they are more willing to give those subordinates greater discretion to decide on the methods to employ. To be effective, such devolution of authority must be accompanied by a clear specification of goals, authority, and responsibilities. Decentralization requires prior clarification of the purpose of each administrative unit, procedures for setting objectives and for monitoring and rewarding performance, and a control structure that links each unit to the goals of the organization as a whole. That is, incentives are specified in advance in order to entice members to behave in ways consistent with the goals of the larger organization. Thus devolution comes at a price, namely some assurance that the units will efficiently pursue the goals of the larger organization. Hence centralization and decentralization can go together.[8]

Clearly, the latest trends in budgeting contain elements of the earlier reforms. They contain performance measures from performance budgeting, functional categories from program budgeting, negotiation of objectives from management by objectives, and ranking of objectives from zero-base budgeting. But there are some differences between the old reforms and the latest ones. The latter are generally simpler, more streamlined, and require less paperwork and analysis. They involve more discretion by line managers than did the earlier reforms, and there is a much greater emphasis on accountability than under the older formats. Finally, the recent reforms are motivated by a desire to change fundamentally the culture of public management by turning bureaucrats into entrepreneurs. Previous budgetary reforms pursued legality, efficiency, and effectiveness. The present wave of budgetary reform aims to stimulate motivation. The new approaches incorporate most of the goals of the previous reforms, but they seek to achieve them through decentralized incentives that give program managers greater authority to combine resources as they think best but that hold the managers accountable for the results. These two qualities are virtually a definition of entrepreneurship.

Reasons For Decentralization

To the extent that these proposals and reforms constitute a trend, what accounts for it? It appears that two factors are particularly important: fiscal stress and the perceived virtues of decentralization.

It is a common observation that governments throughout the world were faced with a more difficult fiscal problem in the 1970s and 1980s than in the 1950s and 1960s. This fiscal problem was a result of the combination of increased demand for public services and growing taxpayer resistance to higher taxes, a situation that has been called the "scissors crisis" in public finance (Tarschys, 1983). People in the industrial democracies wanted more and more government services, but they were not always willing to pay higher taxes to fund those services. Resistance to higher taxes began at the local level in the United States at least as early as the 1960s, as bond issues and tax overrides began to fail with greater frequency. Then the big bang came in 1978 with Proposition 13 in California, followed by similar measures in other states. The slowdown in economic growth after 1970 exacerbated the problem. This fiscal stress prompted adaptive behavior by governments, including more privatization, contracting out, increased user fees, and an array of other devices either to make government provision of services more efficient or to shift the burden for the financing of those services. Virtually every account of the decentralized approach to budgeting at the local level mentions fiscal stress as a major reason for its adoption (for example, Osborne and Gaebler, 1992, pp. 2, 119–120). The fiscal stress brought on by the combination of slower economic growth, taxpayer resistance, and ever-increasing demand for public services is also given as a major reason for the move to budgeting for results by industrialized countries (Schick, 1990, pp. 26, 29, 30). The cutbacks that are impending in the 1990s are also given by Thompson and other analysts as a reason for reviving and refining the proposals for decentralization of defense budgeting (Thompson, 1991, p. 64). If the decentralized approach has not attracted more support within the federal government to this point, perhaps it is partly because, unlike localities, the federal government can run a deficit and hence does not face the same fiscal discipline as do local governments.

One adaptation to fiscal stress was for policy makers to take greater control of total spending in order to retard incremental budget growth at the same time that they gave program managers greater discretion in the detailed use of the funds. In fact, to the extent that they get a firmer grip on total amounts, policy makers are often willing to grant greater discretion. They hope that the decentralization and more intensive accountability will lead to greater efficiency and effectiveness with the funds available. It is not an accident that these techniques emerged soon after the beginning of the taxpayer revolt in the late 1970s.

A second source of the budget reforms is the accumulating body of knowledge on the virtues of decentralized organization. The literature on organization[9] suggests a model of behavior something like this: If policy makers want an organization to pursue the policy-makers' goals efficiently, they should clearly specify the goals, and perhaps even involve subordinates in the setting of those goals. They should then create a structure of incentives that will motivate subordinates to pursue those goals but give them a high degree of autonomy in the choice of methods. In a mutually reinforcing way, this will allow workers to exercise their creativity, which will give them more satisfaction, thereby making them more productive, and allow them to generate better solutions to the problems that they face because they are closer to the problem and probably have better information about it. At the same time, the delegation of authority will leave those at the top more time to think about goals and to monitor performance.

The recent reforms of budgeting appear to be firmly grounded in the research on decentralization. The local managers emphasize incentives, participation, creativity, and other qualities that the research mentions as alleged virtues of decentralized management. Likewise, the budget leaders in the other industrial democracies base the recent reforms on organization theory. Although Schick does not explicitly address the question of the intellectual foundations of the latest reforms, it is clear that the reforms are an outgrowth of research on organization theory, and specifically on an analysis of the virtues of decentralization. Because the proposals for mission budgeting at the Pentagon are made by scholars who are familiar with the literature on organization theory and institutional economics, it is not surprising that their arguments are based explicitly on that literature. Citing William Niskanen, Robert Anthony, Frederick Mosher, and other scholars of organization, Thompson (1991) emphasizes the importance of a clear definition of purpose, devolution of decision making about means, and close accountability through responsibility budgeting and accounting. Indeed, he argues that: "It has been demonstrated to the satisfaction of most students of management that the effectiveness of large, complex organizations improves when authority is delegated down into the organization along with responsibility" (p. 53). Although the explicitness of the relationship between organization literature and the decision to propose decentralized budgeting varies by individual, most of the participants seem to be aware of the connection.

This is not to say that the trend described above has been universal. Robert D. Lee's (1991) study of developments in state budgeting over the past 20 years suggests that two of the three qualities discussed above have become more prominent at the state level, but not necessarily the third. He found that state policy makers and central budget officers had increased their control of goals and limits. Compared to 1970, they are now more apt to specify priorities and dollar ceilings and to provide other forms of policy guidance in telling agencies how to prepare their budget requests. This is consistent with our point about the centralization of goals. Likewise, they are now far more likely to require agencies to provide measures of productivity and effectiveness either in their budget requests or in subsequent documents. The proportion of state governments that required such data rose dramatically from about 25 percent in 1970 to about 90 percent in 1990. This is consistent with our point about the movement toward greater accountability of agencies for achieving results with the funds that they receive.

However, the computerization of accounting has made it possible for central budget offices to exercise greater central control over the details of spending than previously. Lee found that the proportion of states in which the central budget office exercised control over the transfer of funds from one major object of expenditure to another (such as from supplies to personnel) rose slightly from 59 percent in 1970 to 72 percent in 1990, and the number of budget offices that exercised control over transfer of funds from one *minor* object to another (e.g., from office supplies to painting) rose from 10 to 20 percent. While these figures run against any alleged trend toward decentralization of the means of administration, they are perhaps not very large increases in actual control in light of the greater capacity for control provided by the computerization of accounting. It can, therefore, be said that—with the exception mentioned here—state governments have also moved in the same direction as the local and national governments.

Conclusion

This article has examined an approach to budgeting that uses decentralized incentives as a way to stimulate entrepreneurial behavior by public administrators. After top policy makers have established their overall control through broad guidelines, the new methods decentralize decision making by providing agency managers with incentives to be both efficient and effective. In addition, the new methods aim to make administrators more accountable for the results of their decisions by monitoring actual performance more than in the past. The goal is to motivate managers to behave more in harmony with the purposes of the overall organization and to lessen the "suboptimization" that often characterizes public programs. Ultimately, a goal is to change the culture of public management.

If it is true, as Wildavsky (1978) has argued, that the traditional budget has lasted because it is workable and because it fulfills various functions for policy makers, it is also true that the traditional budget has persistently come under attack.[10] The fact that reforms are so regularly tried (about one each decade since the 1950s) suggests that something was wrong with traditional budgeting. Although budgetary reforms are often oversold and do not perform up to their advance billing, they almost always leave their mark. In fact, the degree to which the earlier reforms were rejected may have been overstated. A recent study indicated that a majority of municipal governments continue to use most of the tools created in recent years for increasing efficiency. For example, 75 percent use performance monitoring, 70 percent still use program budgeting at least to some degree, and over 30 percent even use elements of zero-base budgeting (Poister and Streib, 1989). Moreover, the decentralized approach is in harmony with the near consensus in management theory today—that a certain kind of decentralized organization can be efficient, accountable, and satisfying to workers. For these reasons, it seems likely that this emerging trend will have a lasting effect on budgeting, even if it does not transform the budgetary process as much as its advocates hope.

However, a number of cautions should be noted. Proposed reforms have almost always followed a pattern characterized by initial enthusiasm and subsequent disappointment, for at least two reasons. First, the reforms are often difficult to put into practice. Entrepreneurial budgeting is similar in various ways to performance budgeting, program budgeting, management by objectives, and zero-base budgeting. For example, it requires measures of performance and outcomes that are not always easy to construct for government programs. However, entrepreneurial budgeting is simpler than the earlier reforms, and, in fact, that is one of its attractions for policy makers. In addition, considerable progress has been made in the construction of performance measures, and it is possible that evaluation of programs can be done better today than in earlier decades. In any case, Lee's (1991) study of state budget developments shows that far more governments are conducting efficiency and effectiveness studies today than 20 years ago (also see Osborne and Gaebler, 1992; and Hatry *et al.,* 1990).

A second reason for eventual disappointment is that reforms sometimes fail to make any substantive difference in resource allocation or program performance. In this regard, many of the claims by local governments of greater efficiency and effectiveness from decentralized budgeting so far are vague and difficult to assess. Managers claim "savings" of various amounts, but it is seldom clear what they mean. They are truly savings only if efficiency is enhanced or if the new method allowed cuts that otherwise were not feasible to make (for example, managers and their interest group clients acquiesced in the cuts because they were given greater discretion in the use of the remaining funds). The alleged savings may be real, but further research is needed to test the claims. A related problem is that the available descriptions of the reforms generally do not provide data in forms that allow a clear calculation of the magnitude of the savings even if we could agree on the meaning of the term. For example, in addition to being told that a city's departments spent $6 million less than they were appropriated, we need to know how many years are covered by this figure, what the total budgeted amounts were (so percentage savings can be calculated), and so on. Moreover, the fact that entrepreneurial budgeting at the local level has been used mainly by relatively small governments raises the question of its applicability to larger cities and states. However, the fact that several national governments are using a similar approach takes some of the thrust out of this criticism. Logically, entrepreneurial budgeting should be even more appropriate for large and complex organizations than for small and simple ones precisely because, in decentralizing the middle step (implementation), it makes the first and third steps (goal setting and monitoring) more manageable for policy makers. Moreover, if this approach to budgeting is well grounded in organization theory, it should stand a good chance of being relatively successful. However, enthusiasts should keep in mind the checkered history of those earlier reforms.

In addition there is the question of whether decentralization is actually dangerous. Theodore Lowi (1979) is concerned about the proclivity of policy makers in the United States to delegate too much vague authority to administrators and to interest groups without clear indication of what they are authorized to do. With regard to the enormous delegation of authority granted by federal statutes since the 1930s, Lowi warned that "Delegation of power . . . turned out to be . . . a gift of sovereignty to private satrapies" (also McConnell, 1967). It is conceivable that entrepreneurial budgeting might beguile policy makers into abdicating responsibility to bureaucrats for the making of public policy. Even if they grant more discretion to administrators, policy makers must still decide on relative priorities, specify what they want accomplished with the funds, and develop measures of the results. In short, policy makers must be careful that in delegating more authority to administrators to decide *how* to pursue goals, they do not inadvertently delegate decisions about *what* goals to pursue. However, as Lowi points out, it is possible to delegate authority in ways that do not relinquish authority. A strong and clear rule has both centralizing and decentralizing effects; it centralizes authority in the hands of policy makers but decentralizes the implementation within clear guidelines for the use of the authority. Like Lowi's "juridical democracy," the proposals described here could give policy makers more control of overall policy direction while delegating more of the details of implementation to administrators. By relieving policy makers of the burden of detailed scrutiny of the process by which program goals are achieved, decentralized budgeting could allow them more time to devote to the goals themselves. Thus entrepreneurial budgeting, and decentralized management in general, can lead to an expansion of power, rather than to a redistribution of power. If entrepreneurial budgeting works as claimed, policy makers should have more of the power that is relevant to their task and subordinates should also have more power to do their jobs. In short, it could enhance governmental capacity, rather than redistribute governmental authority. Of course, unless superiors specify what activities are acceptable, subordinates may become too "creative" in their entrepreneurship. A few years ago, for example, California policy makers believed that the state's community colleges demonstrated excessive creativity in thinking of new ways to attract additional state funds (Cothran, 1981 and 1986).

As was true of the earlier budget reforms, this latest one is not likely to be the salvation of modern government as it struggles to provide the benefits that people expect while staying within the fiscal restraints that voters have imposed. However, this reform may have even more effect than the others because it actually involves less, not more, work by most participants and it is in keeping with the findings of research on organizational behavior in recent decades. If it fails, it probably will not do much damage, but if it succeeds, it could contribute to the creation of a new entrepreneurial management culture in public administration.

The budget reforms are part of a larger managerial revolution that includes such techniques as management by objectives, management information systems, performance monitoring, program evaluation, total quality management, and others. A consensus seems to be emerging among scholars of organization about what constitutes good management. For example, in their analysis of 70 studies of the use of management by objectives, Rodgers and Hunter (1992) found that MBO-type processes have become more widely used in both government and business and that they have almost always had a positive effect on productivity when supported by top management. What we have called entrepreneurial budgeting bears a striking resemblance to MBO. The latter usually comprises three processes—participatory decision making, goal setting, and objective feedback (Rodgers and Hunter, 1992), which are very similar to the three components of entrepreneurial budgeting. In turn, both MBO and entrepreneurial budgeting are similar to "total quality management," especially as modified for use in government (Swiss, 1992).

This managerial revolution seems to be part of a larger institutional transformation sweeping the world, a revolution of decentralization that includes the movement for choice in education, devolution of power to Indian tribes,[11] contracting out by local governments, privatization in Latin America, and even the decommunization of Eastern Europe. A major implication of these changes is that institutions characterized by overly centralized decision making and lack of accountability for socially useful results do not work very well.

These budgetary proposals can thus be seen as manifestations of a larger institutional revolution that has occurred in recent years. It is obvious that the "market" as a device for allocating resources has experienced a resurgence. After decades of movement toward centralized decision making as a way to allocate resources, governments in the United States and other countries are now contracting out services or privatizing public enterprises as never before. Whether one is as enthusiastic about this trend as its most zealous advocates (for example, Savas, 1987), the indisputable fact is that the use of market-like incentives has enjoyed a notable revival in recent years. Indeed, the return of largely centralized economies back to more decentralized arrangements is one of the great political-economic transformations of the late 20th century. Although Eastern Europe and the former Soviet Union have received the most attention, other areas of the world such as Latin America are also caught up in the enthusiasm for the market and for decentralization in general. Mexico, for example, reduced the number of its state-owned enterprises from about 1,200 in 1982 to about 300 by 1992. A similar trend toward decentralized incentives can be seen in business in the United States, where the idea of managers and workers personally gaining some of the benefits of their increased productivity is currently very much in favor. In fact, some business analysts are predicting that "gainsharing" as a way to improve productivity will become one of the fastest growing business strategies in the country in the 1990s (Graham-Moore and Ross 1990). The trend toward decentralized decision making and incentives is, therefore, spread across a number of countries and institutions. In budgeting as in political economy in general, this might be called the "age of incentives."

Notes

1. While the arrangement by decade makes a neater presentation and is approximately correct, the actual dates are not so orderly. For example, performance budgeting was proposed long before the 1950s, Proposition 13 was enacted in 1978, and the attempt to enact a balanced budget amendment continued at least until its defeat in Congress in 1992.

2. In addition to a survey of recent literature on budgeting, for this section I communicated with 20 local governments that were mentioned in the literature as having instituted decentralized budgeting.

3. David Creighton, city of Fairfield, letter to author, November 8, 1990.

4. Pat Walker, city of Chandler, telephone interview with author, April 22, 1991.

5. Alan Miller, city of Westminster, Colorado, letter to author, November 26, 1990.

6. Robert Brents, University of California at San Diego, letter to author, November 20, 1990.

7. Here Thompson draws upon Anthony (1962) and Anthony and Young (1988).

8. *Incentives* stated in advance should not be confused with *controls* put in place in advance, or *ex ante*. For a more elaborate discussion of *ex ante* controls and when they are appropriate, see Thompson and Jones (1986).

9. Austin and Larkey, 1992; Vining and Weimer, 1990; Marcus, 1988; Denhardt, 1984; Williamson, 1975; Rumelt, 1974; Turcotte, 1974; Golembiewski, 1972; Chandler, 1966; Crozier, 1964; Argyris, 1962; McGregor, 1960; Simon, 1957.

10. In his recent writings, Wildavsky (1988) seems to have relented a bit in his defense of traditional budgeting. See also Rubin (1989).

11. A proposal made by Senator Dennis DeConcini in 1990 (*Arizona Republic*, April 28, 1990).

References

Anthony, Robert, 1962. "New Frontiers in Defense Financial Management." *The Federal Accountant*, vol. 11 (June), pp. 13–32.

Anthony, Robert, and David Young, 1988. *Management Control in Nonprofit Organizations*, 4th ed. Homewood, IL: Irwin.

Argyris, Chris, 1962. *Interpersonal Competence and Organizational Effectiveness.* Homewood, IL: Dorsey Press.

Arizona Republic, 1990, April 28.

Austin, Robert, and Patrick Larkey, 1992. "The Unintended Consequences of Micromanagement: The Case of Procuring Mission Critical Computer Resources." *Policy Sciences,* vol. 25, no. 1 (February), pp. 3–28.

Bellone, Carl, 1988. "Public Entrepreneurship: New Role Expectations for Local Government." *Urban Analysis,* vol. 9, no. 1, pp. 71–86.

Cal-Tax News, June 1, 1987, p. 10.

Chandler, Alfred D., 1966. *Strategy and Structure.* Garden City, NY: Doubleday.

Cothran, Dan A., 1981. "Program Flexibility and Budget Growth." *Western Political Quarterly,* vol. 34 (December), pp. 593–610.

———, 1986. "Some Sources of Budgetary Uncontrollability: The Interaction of Automatic Funding and Program Flexibility." *Public Budgeting and Finance,* vol. 6 (Summer), pp. 45–62.

———, 1987. "Japanese Bureaucrats and Policy Implementation: Lessons for America?" *Policy Studies Review,* vol. 6, (February), pp. 439–458.

Crozier, Michel, 1964. *The Bureaucratic Phenomenon.* Chicago: University of Chicago Press.

Dade County News, 1988, February 8.

Denhardt, Robert, 1984. *Theories of Public Organization.* Monterey, CA: Brooks/Cole Publishing Co.

Fox, J. Ronald, 1988. *The Defense Management Challenge: Weapons Acquisition.* Cambridge, MA: Harvard Business School Press.

Gaebler Group, 1988. *Expenditure Control Budgeting System.* San Rafael, CA: Gaebler Group.

Gansler, Jacques, 1989. *Affording Defense.* Cambridge, MA: MIT Press.

Golembiewski, Robert, 1972. *Renewing Organizations.* Itasca, IL: Peacock.

Graham-Moore, Brian, and Timothy L. Ross, 1990. *Gainsharing: Plans for Improving Performance.* Washington, DC: Bureau of National Affairs.

Hatry, Harry, et al., 1990. *Service Efforts and Accomplishments Reporting: Its Time Has Come.* Norwalk, CT: Governmental Accounting Standards Board.

Jones, L. R., and R. B. Doyle, 1989. "Public Policy Issues in Budgeting for Defense." Paper Delivered at the 11th annual Research Conference of the Association for Public Policy and Management." Arlington, VA (November 3).

Lee, Robert D., 1991. "Developments in State Budgeting: Trends of Two Decades." *Public Administration Review,* vol. 51 (May-June), pp. 254–262.

Lowi, Theodore J., 1979. *The End of Liberalism: The Second Republic of the United States,* 2d ed. New York: W. W. Norton.

Marcus, Alfred, 1988. "Responses to Externally Induced Innovation: Their Effects on Organizational Performance." *Strategic Management Journal,* vol. 9 (July–August), pp. 387–402.

McCaffery, Jerry, 1984. "Canada's Envelope Budgeting: A Strategic Management System." *Public Administrative Review,* vol. 44 (July-August), pp. 316–323.

McConnell, Grant, 1967. *Private Power and American Democracy.* New York: Alfred A. Knopf.

McGregor, Douglas, 1960. *The Human Side of Enterprise.* New York: McGraw-Hill.

Osborne, David, and Ted Gaebler, 1992. *Reinventing Government*. Reading, MA: Addison-Wesley.

Perrow, Charles, 1977. "The Bureaucratic Paradox: The Efficient Organization Centralizes in Order to Decentralize." *Organization Dynamics* (Spring), pp. 3–14.

Poister, Theodore, and Gregory Streib, 1989. "Management Tools in Municipal Government: Trends Over the Past Decade." *Public Administration Review*, vol. 49 (May-June), pp. 240–248.

Rodgers, Robert, and John E. Hunter, 1992. "A Foundation of Good Management Practices in Government: Management by Objectives." *Public Administration Review*, vol. 52 (January-February), pp. 27–39.

Rubin, Irene, 1989. "Aaron Wildavsky and the Demise of Incrementalism." *Public Administration Review*, vol. 49 (January-February), pp. 78–81.

Rumelt, Richard, 1974. *Strategy, Structure, and Economic Performance*. Boston: Harvard Business School Press.

Savas, E. S., 1987. *Privatization: The Key to Better Government*. Chatham, NJ: Chatham House Publishers.

Schick, Allen, 1990. "Budgeting for Results: Recent Developments in Five Industrialized Countries." *Public Administration Review*, vol. 50 (January-February), pp. 26–34.

Scott, Graham, Peter Bushnell, and Nikiti Sallee, 1990. "Reform of the Core Public Sector: New Zealand Experience." *Governance: An International Journal of Policy and Administration*, vol. 3 (April), pp. 138–167.

Simon, Herbert, 1957. *Models of Man*. New York: John Wiley and Sons.

Swiss, James E., 1992. "Adapting Total Quality Management to Government." *Public Administration Review*, vol. 52 (July-August), pp. 356–362.

Tarschys, Daniel, 1983. "The Scissors Crisis in Public Finance." *Policy Sciences*, vol. 15, no. 3 (April), pp. 205–224.

Thompson, Fred, 1991. "Management Control and the Pentagon: The Organizational Strategy-Structure Mismatch." *Public Administration Review*, vol. 51 (January-February), pp. 52–66.

Thompson, Fred, and L. R. Jones, 1986. "Controllership in the Public Sector." *Journal of Policy analysis and Management*, vol. 51 (January-February), pp. 52–66.

Turcotte, William E., 1974. "Control Systems, Performance, and Satisfaction in Two State Agencies." *Administrative Science Quarterly*, vol. 19 (March), pp. 60–73.

Vining, Aidan, and David Weimer, 1990. "Government Supply and Government Production Failure: A Framework Based on Contestability." *Journal of Public Policy*, vol. 10, pp. 1–22.

Wildavsky, Aaron, 1978. "A Budget for All Seasons: Why the Traditional Budget Lasts." *Public Administration Review*, vol. 38 (November-December), pp. 501–509.

_____, 1988. *The New Politics of the Budgetary Process*. Glenview, IL: Scott-Foresman–Little, Brown.

Williamson, Oliver, 1975. *Markets and Hierarchies*. New York: Free Press.

9

MISSION-DRIVEN, RESULTS-ORIENTED BUDGETING

Fiscal Administration and the New Public Management

Fred Thompson

The *National Performance Review* (NPR) calls for inventing "a government that puts people first" by creating a sense of mission, delegating authority, replacing rules and regulations with incentives, developing budgets based upon results, exposing government operations to competition, searching for market rather than administrative solutions, and, whenever possible, by measuring the success in terms of customer satisfaction (Gore, 1993, p. 7). Taken together, these ideas comprise a coherent reform agenda that some describe as the "new public management" (Rhodes, 1991; see also Hood, 1991; Osborne and Gaebler, 1992; Barzelay, 1992).

Implementation of this agenda would profoundly affect the budgets, administrative controls, and financial management practices of the federal government. The NPR calls for the federal government to develop mission-driven, results-oriented budgets, emphasize monetary targets and incentives in those budgets, break up departments and agencies into entities that

1994. Mission-driven, results-oriented budgeting: Fiscal administration and the new public management. Thompson, Fred. **Public Budgeting and Finance** 14 (Fall): 90–105.

deal with each other on a user-pay basis, measure direct costs, use internal markets and contracting out to foster competition, establish a long-term, fixed-asset planning process and incorporate it into federal budgeting to insure that choices are not biased against long-term investments, and expand the capital investment fund and manage its operations in a more businesslike fashion (see Table 9.1).

In addition to these administrative reforms, the NPR also wants the legislative budget process to be simpler, more comprehensible, and more coherent. It wants to reduce overitemization, remove overly detailed restrictions and earmarks from appropriations, simplify the apportionment process, expedite reprogramming of funds, permit rollovers of unobligated balances, and increase the use of multi-year and no-year appropriations.

What the NPR fails to do, however, is show *how* its proposals would work in practice. There are vast discrepancies between the existing budgets, administrative controls, and financial-management practices of the federal government and those proposed by the NPR. These discrepancies would need to be resolved. Moreover, the NPR fails to clarify the linkages between its *administrative-reform* proposals and the changes it recommends for the *legislative* budget process, although these changes are critical and are intrinsically linked to administrative reform under the mission-driven, results-oriented budget concept.

In this article, I explain how the budgets, administrative controls, and financial-management practices proposed by the NPR differ from those that are currently used in the federal government and how the federal government's legislative budget process would need to be modified to accommodate the changes proposed by the NPR.

Public Budgets and Private Budgets

In contemporary management jargon, the process of identifying best practice in a specific area is called benchmarking. Boiled down to basics, the NPR calls for the federal government to adopt the practices used in benchmark organizations and taught in up-to-date schools of management. So far as budgeting and accounting practices are concerned, most benchmark organizations are now private firms. This does not mean that public agencies can not be benchmark organizations. At the turn of the century and again in 1950s and 1960s, many well-managed businesses adopted budgetary practices and procedures that originated in government. Nor does it mean that all businesses are benchmark organizations. Most are not. For example, it costs the average company about $20 to process travel and expense reports; the best do it for less than $2. The average for accounts receivable is $16; the best do it for $6. The average for accounts payable is $8; the best do it for $.80 (Gunn, Carberry, Frigo, & Behrens, 1993, p. 230).[1]

TABLE 9.1   Key *NPR* Recommendations on Budgeting and Finance

Key NPR Recommendations On Budgeting and Finance

- Develop mission-driven, results-oriented budgets: incorporate performance objectives and results as key elements in budget and management reviews; reduce over-itemization and excessive subdivision of funds in financial operating plans and remove overly detailed restrictions and earmarks from appropriations; measure direct costs; simplify the apportionment process, expedite reprogramming of funds, permit rollovers of unobligated balances; and increase the use of multi-year and no-year appropriations.
- Improve financial management by fully integrating budget, financial, and program information; use technology to streamline financial services; reduce financial regulations and requirements; simplify financial reporting; and "franchise" internal services.
- Establish a long-term fixed asset planning process and incorporate it into federal budgeting to insure that choices are not biased against long-term investments, and expand the capital investment fund and manage its operations in a more businesslike fashion.
- Redesign programs to cut cost and improve performance.
- Improve distribution systems to reduce costly inventories and provide incentives to dispose of excess property; allow managers and commanders to purchase the best value common supplies and services from public or private sources; and outsource non-core functions.
- Implement a systems design approach to management control: streamline the internal controls program; reduce internal regulations and management control positions at least 50 percent; and expand the use of waivers to encourage innovation.
- Use market mechanisms to solve problems—make service organizations compete, create market dynamics, and substitute market mechanisms for command and control type regulation where possible.

The existing budget, administrative control, and financial-management practices of the federal government have some of the attributes of the budget and management control systems used by benchmark organizations, but the differences are great and in several respects decisive. The biggest difference is that the federal government tries to make do with a single budget for all purposes. Trying to serve multiple purposes—macroeconomic planning, ranking alternatives and weighing choices, controlling operations, coordinating activities, motivating employees, and promoting economy and efficiency—with a single instrument means that each individual purpose is short-changed. Furthermore, successive attempts to fix the federal budget have left it excessively top heavy. Budgeting now dominates congressional attention as never before—almost to the exclusion of everything else. Indeed, the preoccupation with budgeting has nearly brought the process of governing in America to a creaking, grinding halt (Cothran, 1993; Pitsvada, 1988).

In contrast, benchmark organizations employ different budgets for different purposes: capital budgets, operating budgets, and cash budgets. In benchmark organizations, capital budgeting is *mission driven.* It is concerned with *all* decisions that have significant future consequences for the success of the organization's mission and not just those that involve the acquisition of facilities and equipment. Capital budgeting's time horizon is the life of the decision; its focus is the discounted present value of the decision alternative. Operating budgeting is *results oriented.* It is concerned with motivating responsibility center managers to maximize their contributions to the goals of the organization. Its time horizon is the operating cycle of the responsibility center in question, perhaps a month or even a week in the case of cost and revenue centers, usually longer where investment and profit centers are concerned. The capital budgeting focus is on the performance of the responsibility center, results accomplished and resources consumed. Where possible, these are measured in real dollars.

Cash budgeting is concerned with providing liquidity just when it is needed. Its time horizon is the organization's cash-flow cycle, the temporal pattern of receipts and outlays experienced by an entity. The one problem the federal budget and financial control system is well designed to solve is the liquidity problem, since the U.S. government's cash flow cycle has a period of one year and its accounts are maintained on a cash as well as an obligation and a purchases basis. Paradoxically, however, liquidity is *not* a serious problem for the U.S. government.

Government Budgeting and Capital Budgeting

Capital budgeting in benchmark organizations is selective, usually concerned only with new initiatives that materially enhance the entity's *capacity* to perform its mission or with changes in operations that are expected to yield benefits for longer than a year (Bower, 1970). In contrast, *the executive branch's requests to Congress for budget authority are comprehensive.* They reflect *all* planned asset acquisitions, including current assets as well as long-term assets.

Furthermore, *capital budgeting in benchmark organizations tends to be a continuous process.*[2] Most well-managed organizations always have a variety of investment proposals under development. The decision to go ahead with a proposal is usually made only once when the proposal is ripe, and is usually reconsidered only if it turns sour. *In most cases, the proposal's champion within the organization is given the authority and the responsibility for implementing it* (Bower, 1970). In contrast, *budgeting in the fed-*

eral government tends to be repetitive—most programs, entitlements aside, are reconsidered annually on the basis of a rigid schedule. New initiatives must be supported by elaborate analytical justifications and reviewed and approved by hundreds of people all along the line from the lowest to the highest echelon, including the president and the Office of Management and Budget (OMB), before they ever get to Congress. And the new initiative's principal advocate is seldom assigned responsibility for its implementation; instead, that responsibility is usually given to someone else, sometimes in an entirely different department!

Another difference is that *the objective of capital budgeting in benchmark organizations is the identification of options with positive net present values,* because in the absence of real limits on the availability of cash or managerial attention, the welfare of an organization's stakeholders will usually be maximized by the implementation of all projects offering positive net present values. The long-term fixed asset planning process in the Department of Defense, the Planning Programming and Budgeting System (PPBS) which was installed by Secretary Robert S. McNamara and remains the most sophisticated budgeting system in use by the federal government, mimics the benchmark process in that it shows the future implications of current decisions, albeit in a somewhat truncated manner (Jones, 1991). Moreover, many of government's programmatic spending and regulatory decisions are informed by cost-benefit and cost-effectiveness analysis. But *nothing in the executive branch's requests for budget authority depicts the future implications of current decisions in present value terms*—otherwise, Congress would not, for example, routinely stretch out weapons systems acquisition programs, often increasing program cost by as much as 60 percent, in order to reduce the deficit and to avoid borrowing at interest rates of less than 10 percent!

Government Budgeting and Operational Budgeting

The biggest difference, however, between the budget authority granted the executive branch by Congress and the capital budgets approved by top management in benchmark organizations lies in its relationship to the executive branch's management control structure (Anthony and Young, 1988, pp. 365–86). *In benchmark organizations, management control is results oriented. It is a process for motivating and inspiring people, especially subordinate managers, to serve the missions, policies, and purposes of the organizations to which they belong.* It is only secondarily a process for detecting and correcting unintentional performance errors and intentional irregularities such as theft or misuse of resources. The primary instrument of management control is operational budgeting which comprehends both the formulation of operating budgets and their execution. In the formulation of an operating budget, an organization's commitments (the results of all past capital budgeting decisions) are converted into terms that correspond to the sphere of responsibility of administrative units and their managers (Anthony and Young, 1988, p. 19). In budget execution, operations are monitored and subordinate managers evaluated and rewarded or penalized.

Again, there are critical differences between programming and budgeting in the federal government and standard practices in benchmark organizations: *operational budgets in the federal government are highly detailed spending or resource-acquisition plans which must be scrupulously executed just as they were approved.* In contrast, *operating budgets in benchmark organizations are remarkably sparing of detail*, often consisting of no more than a handful of quantitative performance standards.

This difference reflects the efforts made by benchmark organizations to delegate authority and responsibility down into the organization. Delegation of authority means giving departmental managers the maximum feasible authority needed to make their units productive or, in the alternative, subjecting them to a minimum of constraints. Hence, delegation of authority requires operating budgets to be stripped to the minimum needed in order to motivate and inspire subordinates to maximize their contribution to the organization as a whole—and, because only one thing can be maximized at a time, it also requires the specification of a single monetary or performance target (Hitch and McKean, 1960, pp. 254–68). Most large-scale benchmark organizations produce fairly comprehensive operating reports describing many relevant aspects of the performance of their component departments and managers, but only a few of these are used to evaluate operations or to motivate subordinates. Ideally, the operating budget of an operating unit, a mission or support center, would contain a single number or performance target (e.g., a "sales" quota, a unit cost standard, or a profit or return-on-investment target) for each administrative unit.

Responsibility budgeting is the most common results-oriented approach to operational budgeting used in benchmark organizations (Anthony and Young, 1988; Thompson, 1991, 1993). The fundamental construct of responsibility budgeting is an account (or control) structure that is oriented toward *responsibility centers.* According to Robert N. Anthony and David Young (1988, pp. 8–9), a responsibility center is an administrative unit headed by a manager who is responsible for its actions. Responsibility centers have purposes or objectives and they use inputs (resources) to produce outputs (goods or services). The outputs of a well-designed responsibility center will be closely related to its objectives.

Responsibility centers are classified according to two dimensions: (1) the integration dimension, i.e., the relationship between the responsibility center's objectives and the overall mission of the organization; and (2) the decentralization dimension, i.e., the amount of authority delegated to the responsibility manager, measured in terms of her discretion to acquire and use assets.

On the first dimension, a responsibility center can be either a *mission center* or a *support center*. The output of a mission center contributes directly to the organization's objectives. The output of a support center is an input to another responsibility center in the organization, another support center or a mission center.

On the second dimension, revenue and expense targets are found at one extreme and profit and investment targets at the other. Expense is a monetary *measure* of resources consumed; revenue is a monetary *measure* of services delivered; and profit is simply the difference between the two. A support center may be either an expense center, a profit center, or an investment center. If the latter, it "sells" its services to other responsibility centers and its "profit" is the difference between its expenses and the "revenue" it gets from the "sale" of its services. Most governmental support centers can be set up as quasi-profit or even investment centers. Examples include the Bureau of Motor Vehicle Repair in New York City (Anthony and Young, 1988, pp. 356–57), the Department of General Services in Minnesota (Barzelay, 1992), the Computer Store operated by California's Department of General Services (Gore, 1993, p. 166), the Naval Sea Systems Command's warehouses (Harr, 1989, 1990), and the DLA Mechanicsburg Depot (Harr and Godfrey, 1991).

In the context of responsibility budgeting, budget execution means monitoring a center's performance in terms of a specified monetary target and rewarding its manager accordingly. This is what the NPR must have had in mind when it called for the federal government to emphasize monetary targets and incentives in operating budgets, to break up departments and agencies into entities that deal with each other on a userpay basis, and to measure direct costs.[3]

How Capital Budgets Should Relate to Operating Budgets

Effective delegation of authority is possible in benchmark organizations in part because capital budgeting and operational budgeting are treated as related but distinct processes. Of course, an organization's operating budget must reflect all the commitments that affect its capacity to perform its mission or missions. Thus, decisions to invest resources in new initiatives that are expected to materially enhance the organization's capacity to perform its mission or that significantly change its operating procedures should be reflected in the operating budgets of all the responsibility centers affected by the decision to go ahead with a project. Operating budgets should be revised to account for the benefit and cost flows that justified the decision in the first place. Performance targets should be revised to take account of anticipated improvements and responsibility for realizing improvements specified. This process is called *programming* or, in the case of discrete, multi-period projects, project budgeting.

Programming helps to keep the purpose and the content of capital and operating budgets—deciding and doing—distinct.

Federal budgeting often reflects the form if not the content of budgets in benchmark organizations. The PPBS process, for example, starts with strategic plans (Jones, 1991). These are then broken down by function into broad missions (e.g., strategic retaliatory forces) and are then further subdivided into hundreds of subprograms or mission elements (e.g., the Midgetman system). Next comes programming—in the context of PPBS, programming comprises the identification of mission alternatives, forecasting and evaluating the consequences of program alternatives, and deciding which program alternatives to carry out. This exercise produces the future year defense plan, which details both continuing programmatic commitments (the "base") and new commitments ("increments" or "decrements") in terms of force structure (including sizes and types of forces) and readiness levels, inventories and logistical capabilities and the development of new weapons and support systems. The consequences of the Department of Defense's programming decisions are estimated in terms of the amount, character, and timing of inputs, including all acquisitions and construction, to be funded for each program package (assuming no change in commitments) during the next six-year period. They are expressed in terms of current dollars and arrayed by military department, object of expenditure, and function. These estimates constitute the financial management portion of the future year defense plan (Jones, 1991).

However, in most cases, federal budgeting does not distinguish between deciding what to do and actually doing it. What is decided is what gets done—budgets are executed the way they were enacted. For the most part, operating managers within the federal government may do only what their budget says they can do: buy certain things. Their budgets focus exclusively on resources to be acquired by individual administrative units and on the timing of those acquisitions; they focus on objects of expenditure or line items rather than performance targets, on many inputs rather than a few critical outputs or results. In other words, operating managers have no authority to acquire or use assets. But without authority, they cannot properly be held responsible for the performance of the administrative units they nominally head.

Many years ago in an important book on budgeting, the late Frederick C. Mosher advanced a proposal for a program budget that would have permitted elected officials to make essential policy decisions but, at the same time, would have permitted considerable decentralization of operations (Mosher, 1954, pp. 237–43). Like his counterparts at RAND who developed PPBS, Mosher proposed "mission packaging" to help top managers in the executive branch establish strategic priorities and ration capital between major missions. He also proposed a functional account structure to force alternatives to the surface and to help the top managers identify the most cost-effective service supplier. *Mosher, however, envisioned this upward-oriented, mission-driven budget operating in synchronization with a results-oriented operating budget, structured along administrative lines, which would have provided the primary vehicle for internal planning and control.* Unlike his RAND counterparts, Mosher clearly recognized that different kinds of budgets are needed for different purposes for which different processes and timing are appropriate. This insight is one of the keys to effective delegation of authority—providing discretion along with accountability—in any organization.

Robert N. Anthony, McNamara's second controller in the Department of Defense, also appreciated the significance of the distinction between deciding and doing, between planning and operating (Anthony, 1962). This distinction was reflected in the comprehensive resource management system he proposed for the federal government which had a separate results-oriented operational budgeting component. Anthony clearly saw the need for prior clarification of organizational purpose, boundaries, and relationships, and for an account structure that would tie the organization together. The account structure he proposed was firmly grounded in the principles of responsibility budgeting and accounting. Indeed, the only significant conceptual difference between Anthony's system and standard practice in benchmark private-sector organizations is that he proposed to establish separate funds to manage the acquisition, utilization, and disposition of fixed assets and some inventories, but this too is now standard practice in many not-for-profit organizations.

Reconciling Accountability with Discretion

In any organization, but especially in government, an important accountability problem arises because there are discrepancies between the timing of obligations, outlays, purchases, and consumption. Mission centers cannot meet all of their needs using spot market transactions. Given reasonable organizational relationships and institutional arrangements, mission centers are frequently required to enter into long-term, exclusive relationships with suppliers. Moreover, support centers within government must make long-term commitments involving highly specific assets. Regardless of how mission centers obtain the use of long-term assets—directly through lease or purchase from a supplier or indirectly through lease or purchase on the part of a support center—the employment of long-term assets gives rise to discrepancies between obligations and consumption. Their employment also gives rise to intertemporal spillovers from one budget period to the next. The existing cash-basis accounting system of the federal government deals with this problem by ignoring consumption. Unfortunately, this also means sacrificing responsibility budgeting.

Anthony believed that the federal government could deal with these spillovers without sacrificing mission-driven, results-oriented responsibility budgeting (Anthony, 1962). Anthony proposed that the federal government should:

1. Classify all administrative units as either mission or support centers.
2. Charge all costs accrued by support centers—including charges for the use of capital assets and inventory depletion—to the mission centers served by them.
3. Fund mission centers to cover all expected expenses—including support charges.
4. Establish a working capital fund to provide short-term financing for support units.
5. Establish a capital asset fund to provide long-term financing of capital assets and to encourage efficient management of their acquisition, utilization, and disposition.[4]

The revolving fund is the principal formal device by which a measure of intraorganizational decentralization is *now* accomplished within the federal government. These funds (e.g., the $40 billion Defense Business Operating Fund) involve buyer-seller arrangements internal to the government. They encourage efficient choice on the part of both support center managers and the support and mission centers that use their services by charging expenses against revenues earned delivering services rather than against a budget authorization. In revolving fund operations, the responsibility center manager is fully authorized to incur expenses provided only that his or her purchases are consistent with the center's stated purpose or objective (Bailey, 1967; Chaplin, 1991). Anthony would have expanded the scope of this device and enhanced its potency; so too would the NPR.

Thus, reconciling accountability with discretion under the NPR's administrative design would necessitate fundamental changes in the financial practices of the federal government. First of all, common accounting standards and pricing policies would have to be established. This is necessary for cost measurement and analysis used for purposes of internal control, but it is also prerequisite to effective revolving fund operations. This means that a unit would probably have to be created, perhaps in the Office of Management and Budget, to establish and enforce *the cost-accounting procedures and the internal pricing policies* to be followed by mission and support centers throughout the federal establishment. Its role would be similar to that played by a public utilities commission (see Barzelay, 1992; Chaplin, 1992). Of course, meaningful cost-accounting standards must be based on resources consumed rather than cash outlays or encumbrances.

Reconciling Mission-Driven, Results-Oriented Budgets with the Congressional Appropriations Process

Decentralizing the federal government, implementing mission-driven, results-oriented budgets, and using market mechanisms to solve problems also requires fundamental changes in the way Congress reviews and enacts budgets. This change is necessary to bring congressional review of the budget into line with the mission-driven, results-oriented budgeting.

Existing Congressional Budget Procedures

While the executive budget focuses on outlays, the legislative budget has traditionally emphasized the provision of budget authority. Under procedures established by the Congressional Budget and Impoundment Control Act of 1974, Congress now also adopts comprehensive outlay targets for the federal government before it takes action on individual spending proposals. Furthermore, the Budget Enforcement Act of 1990 sets ceilings (toplines) on both obligational authority and outlays (Doyle and McCaffery, 1991).

Outlays in any given fiscal year flow in part from current-year budget authority and in part from the unexpended balances of prior-year budget authority. Estimating these flows—scorekeeping, in congressional budget lingo—and battling over the estimates have become congressional preoccupations since the Budget Enforcement Act (Doyle and McCaffery, 1991).

This is actually quite remarkable because outlays have little real economic significance.[5] Most economists would accept the notion that the source of financing (e.g., debt or taxes) used to acquire publicly owned assets or the timing of payments has no discernible economic effects, except insofar as these choices influence long-term considerations arising from the level of savings or private-sector investment. For some reason, however, Congress has in recent years adopted the defunct Keynesian economics of the 1967 report of the President's Commission on Budget Concepts and now gives as much weight to outlays as to budget authority.

Purchase is the penultimate step in the existing federal budget and accounting process. Purchases are measured when goods and services are actually delivered to the government. Deliveries may follow outlays (as they generally do in the acquisition of major weapons systems and major construction projects, where firms performing work for the government are paid as the work is done rather than when the products produced by that work are delivered); they may occur in the same accounting period; or they may precede payment (as they generally do where off-the-shelf purchases are concerned).

The last stage of the federal budget and accounting process is audit and evaluation to determine whether agency spending has complied with the provisions of the authorization and appropriations acts. The objective is to verify that operating managers in the government did what the appropriations act said they were supposed do and did not do what they were not authorized to do.

Reforming the Congressional Budgetary Process

That Congress should provide budget authority to mission centers rather than to administrative units is the plain meaning of mission-driven budgeting. Beyond this obvious point, however, there is also the matter of item-by-item budget approval. If mission-driven, results-oriented budgeting means only that *existing* items will be grouped into new mission accounts rather than into departmental or appropriation accounts, then it is hard to see how this change would be more than cosmetic.

To give the mission-driven, results-oriented budget concept meaning, and to make decentralization perform as intended, Congress must delegate to responsibility center managers some of its authority to acquire and use assets. The question is how much and what kind of authority is needed. This question is extremely important because Congress has not in recent years been willing to delegate very much fiscal authority to the executive branch of government.

Jacques Gansler answers this question by denying that detailed line-item approval serves any legitimate purpose whatsoever. He argues that Congress should get entirely out of the business of choosing among objects of expenditure. He argues that Congress should concern itself with higher things—the determination of policy objectives and constraints, making strategic choices that have major political implications, and the allocation of resources to the major government missions:

> The answer, therefore, is to restructure the budget process so that Congress will be forced to vote on 'top line' (i.e., total budget) dollars for the various 'mission areas' rather than on the details of specific programs and projects that are clearly identified with districts and states. Such a move would restore Congress to a deliberative body acting in the national interest rather than a staff driven special-interest machine whose members see each budget action as a way to raise election funds and/or to obtain jobs for constituents. (Gansler, 1989, p. 120)

Although Gansler is ready to make radical changes in the scope and domain of congressional authority, he would leave the existing comprehensive, repetitive congressional budget process and its duplicative accounting procedures largely unchanged.

I think Gansler's proposal fundamentally misunderstands the role of Congress in the American system of government. My point is not Harvey Brooks's (1989–90, p. 176)—that Gansler is naive because his proposal "would deprive members of Congress of one of their principal opportunities to visibly serve their constituents—the main basis for their continuation in office." My point is, instead, that item-by-item budget approval is deeply rooted in the American constitutional order. It did not happen by accident or mistake.

The locus of Congress's power lies in its power over the purse and the details of administration, as exemplified by item-by-item approval (see Phaup, 1990, p. 9). More than any other institutional arrangement, item-by-item approval distinguishes congressional government from European-style parliamentary systems in which the legislature's power is largely a sham. In parliamentary systems, the budget documents handed down from cabinet to parliament are often cryptic and largely uninformative (if not totally obscure). Parliament must vote the budget of each department as proposed by cabinet either up or down. Party discipline is rarely breached and the entire budget is usually enacted right on schedule, following perfunctory debate, just as it was handed down. (In contrast, the Department of Defense's FY89 budget justification book, for example, ran 30,000 pages. Individual line items are adjusted at at least fourteen points in the legislative budget process. Also, the federal budget has been enacted on time only once in the last ten years.) Is it really necessary to transform Congress from a decision-making body into a debating society to give meaning to the mission-driven, results-oriented budget concept?

No, Congress could allow enough flexibility to make mission-driven, results-oriented budgeting work merely by adopting the NPR's legislative budget recommendations: by increasing an agency's discretion to transfer budget authority between lines and through time, by treating budget authority as permissive (i.e., permitting, but not requiring, the obligation of funds), and by restricting its propensity to fund long-term investment programs on a one-year-at-a-time basis (Gore, 1993, pp. 160–63). It might also be necessary to repeal the Anti-Deficiency Act.

Robert Anthony would go a little further. He would divide the budget into an operating portion and a capital portion. The operating budget would be appropriated annually or biannually and would be expressed in terms of the amount of expenses authorized for the period in question. The capital budget would be directed to the acquisition of long-lived assets and would, in essence, be unchanged from existing provisions of obligational authority (personal correspondence, 8 September 1990; see also Anthony, 1990, pp. 50–52, and Anthony and Young, 1988, pp. 543–46).

Anthony recognizes that responsibility centers cannot possibly meet all of their needs using spot-market transactions. They frequently need to enter into long-term, exclusive relationships with outside suppliers, and support centers have to make long-term commitments, involving highly specific assets, to supply other support and mission centers within government. Regardless of how mission centers obtain the use of long-term assets, directly from an outside supplier or indirectly through a support center, their employment will give rise to discrepancies between obligations, outlays, and consumption. The use of long-term assets and inventory depletion also give rise to intertemporal spillovers from one budget period to the next and, therefore, discrepancies between operating budget accounts and the Treasury's cash account. Reconciling these discrepancies under Anthony's proposal would necessitate the creation of an additional annual (or biannual) appropriation for changes in working capital (the mechanics of this process are explained in Anthony and Young, 1988, pp. 543–46). Presumably too, Anthony would have Congress set up a capital fund to provide both mission centers and their suppliers in government with financing for the acquisition of long-term capital assets.

My preference would be to go further still. I would like to make congressional budgeting even simpler, more comprehensible, and more coherent. I think *congressional budgeting should be a lot more like capital budgeting in benchmark organizations.*

Doing It the Way the Benchmark Organization Does It

To say that congressional budgeting should be more like capital budgeting in benchmark organizations means that it should be *permissive, continuous,* and *selective.*[6] It also means that congressional budgeting should focus on *all of the cash flows* that ensue from programmatic legislative decisions (operating expenditures and transfers as well as acquisitions and construction), and for the life of the decision, not just the cash flows that occur in the initial fiscal year. New obligational authority should be expressed in terms of the *discounted present values of those cash flows.*

If Congress wishes to emulate capital budgeting in benchmark organizations, then it would deemphasize the budget resolution, with its unhealthy fixation on outlays, and reemphasize obligational authority. The core of congressional power lies in its authority to decide to go ahead with a program, activity, or acquisition, which is what the authorization/appropriations process has always been about. Congress has more important things to worry about than scheduling cash flows. Congress had it right to begin with; it should go back to the way it used to do things.

Its next step would be to throw away the president's budget (see Pitsvada, 1988). Congress already treats the president's budget as little more than a policy statement and a summary report; it should in the future allow executive branch agencies to come forward at any time with proposals to change the scope, level, or timing of their operations.

Congress should consider proposals to try something new as soon as they are ready to be considered, but consider them only once. Once a project has been approved by Congress, it should be reconsidered only if circumstances change or the project goes bad. This means that obligational authority should be granted for the life of the project and should reflect the discounted present value of the project's cash-flows. Standing appropriations should be continuously adjusted to reflect these important decisions.

Congress currently takes about the right approach to providing budget authority for the acquisition of long-lived assets, although the system of one-year-at-a-time authorization and appropriation that Congress has adopted in recent years is inimical to sound project management. Nevertheless, where plant and equipment are concerned, current costs are present values. In contrast, where on-going activities are concerned, current costs greatly understate government's actual obligations.

The third step would be to make legislative budgeting more selective—this means that mission-driven budgeting should be more like the current process of authorization and appropriation for Social Security. Congressional budgeting should focus only on significant changes in operations, activities, and investments in fixed assets. Otherwise, congressional attention should not be necessary. It makes no sense for Congress to look at every purchase contemplated by the entire federal government every year.

To give meaning to mission-driven, results-oriented budgeting, mission centers should probably operate under permanent authority. They should have to seek budget authority from Congress only when they want to make changes with significant future consequences and, then, only if the changes increase the Treasury's liabilities. If Congress wants to reduce spending, then it would have to enact programmatic changes that reduce permanent appropriations (although performance-based spending cuts could be built into those appropriations, see Monden and Lee, 1993, for example).

Under this approach to mission-driven, results-oriented budgeting, support centers would still probably be required to obtain congressional authorization to make major new investments or changes in their corpus. And Congress would probably still want to reconsider funding levels for research and development on an annual or biannual basis. Aside from these exceptions, however, all new obligational authority would be expressed in terms of discounted net cash flows which, as I have noted, would dramatically change congressional authorizations and appropriations for operating purposes. Congress would probably also have to acknowledge formally that obligational authority is permissive rather than mandatory.

Fiscal control under this approach to congressional budgeting would remain more or less as it is now. Presumably, the Office of Management Budget's monthly apportionments to responsibility centers would remain at constant levels as long as Congress did not increase (or reduce) their budget authority. In addition, the Treasury should probably be authorized to buy and sell notes on behalf of agencies in order to provide it with short-term liquidity and to match cash inflows with the actual pattern of cash outflows (see Blum, 1993, pp. 14–18).

There is nothing new about any of these notions. Congressional budgeting has traditionally been permissive, continuous, and selective rather than comprehensive and repetitive. And while the idea of providing budget authority in present-value terms may seem outlandish, it would not be totally unprecedented. Congress currently funds the federal government's loan-guarantee and insurance programs in precisely that manner (see Redburn, 1992; Meyer, 1990; Kennedy, 1992; see also Scott *et al.*, 1990).

In essence, these changes would restore the congressional budget process that existed prior to the passage of the Budget Act in 1921, which proposed a comprehensive annual executive budget for the entire federal government, created what has become the Office of Management and Budget, and at the same time, reduced congressional power.

Notes

1. Of course, in some cases, the federal government is not even as good as the average firm. For example, it costs the Navy about $24 to process accounts payable. It takes the Navy twenty-six manual accounting transactions and nine reconciliations—thirty-five steps in all, instead of the three used by benchmark organizations—to process and pay for the things it buys (Hemingway, 1993, pp. 8–12). According to the NPR, this system is not only time consuming, it often leads to bad service and excessive investment. For example, it causes delays in obtaining repair parts that keep a high proportion of the Navy's cars and trucks out of commission and forces the taxpayer to buy 10 percent more vehicles than the Navy really needs (Gore, 1993, p. 12). The Navy's Byzantine system of accounting was designed to insure that neither ships' captains nor higher level authorities exceeded the spending authority granted them by Congress. (That authority is now divided into fifty accounts, 557 management codes, and 1,769 accounting lines.) Hence, it is largely a consequence of the *Anti-Deficiency Act* (33 U.S.C. s 1214, 1257 [1905]).

2. One might say that capital budgeting in this sense of the term is radically incremental (see Wildavsky, 1966).

3. It might be noted that if a target is high enough to elicit the manager's best efforts, then it cannot be achieved 100 percent of the time. As Andrew Stedry (1960) has observed, a target that can be achieved with certainty is necessarily too low.

4. Anthony no longer believes that it makes sense to include a charge for capital consumption in the cost of providing services, except perhaps where the fixed asset in question could be leased or rented (e.g., an office building, but not the Washington Monument). He believes that it would be too difficult to measure capital consumption accurately and that basing the charge on an arbitrary depreciation standard (e.g., ten-year straight-line depreciation) would be worse than useless. (Personal correspondence, 21 June 1990, 8 September 1990, see also Anthony, 1990). While I agree that there is no point to cascading an arbitrary depreciation charge forward, I do not believe it would be prohibitively expensive to measure capital consumption properly. Dennis Carlton and J. M. Perloff (1990, p. 226) show how to convert the replacement price of a durable asset into a periodic rental price.

5. I mean in comparison with commitments (obligational authority) or resource consumption (expenses). What government buys and, perhaps, where or for/from whom matter a great deal; but the timing of cash outflows (outlays) is matter of limited macroeconomic significance, in part because it is not a matter of great individual significance. See Barro, 1987; Kotlikoff, 1992.

6. This statement should not be read as an endorsement of the capital budgeting proposals that are going around in the federal government, most of which are modeled on the so-called capital budgets used by state and local governments (for example, Financial Management Service, 1991). Most of these proposals make two fundamental errors. First, they apply principles developed for purposes of *ex post* financial reporting to *ex ante* budgeting, i.e., they ignore the distinction drawn here between capital and operating budgets and between plans and performance reports (see Phaup, 1990a). Second, they ignore the valuation problem, the identification of liabilities, and the measurement of resources consumed, where consumption does not give rise to cash flows through the public fisc (Phaup, 1990b).

References

Anthony, Robert N. "New Frontiers in Defense Financial Management," *The Federal Accountant* 11 (June 1962): 13–32.

Anthony, Robert N. "The AICPA's Proposal for Federal Accounting Reform: It Should Focus on the Budget System, Not the Accounting System." *Management Accounting* 72 (July 1990): 48–52.

Anthony, Robert N., and David Young. *Management Control in Nonprofit Organizations.* Homewood IL: Irwin, 1988.

Bailey, M. J. "Defense Decentralization through Internal Prices," in S. Enke, ed., *Defense Management.* Englewood Cliffs, NJ: Prentice-Hall, Inc., 1967.

Barro, R. J. *Macroeconomics,* 2d ed. New York: John Wiley & Sons, 1987.

Barzelay, M., with B. J. Armajani. *Breaking Through Bureaucracy: A New Vision for Managing in Government.* Berkeley: University of California Press, 1992.

Blum, J. L. *Statement Before the Subcommittee on Readiness, Committee on Armed Services, House of Representatives.* Washington, D.C.: Congressional Budget Office, May 13, 1993.

Bower, J. *The Resource Allocation Process.* Boston: Harvard Business School, 1970.

Brooks, H. U.S. Defense: Is Reform Possible? *International Security* 14 (Winter 1989–90): 172–177.

Carlton, D. W., and J. M. Perloff. *Modern Industrial Organization.* Glenview, IL: Scott, Foresman–Little, Brown Higher Education, 1990.

Chapin, D. H. *Financial Management: Opportunities to Strengthen Management of the Defense Business Operations Fund.* Testimony before the Subcommittee on Readiness, Committee on Armed Services, House of Representatives. Washington D.C.: United States General Accounting Office, GAO-T-AFMD-93-4, May 13, 1993.

Cothran, D. A. "Entrepreneurial Budgeting: An Emerging Reform?" *Public Administration Review* 53 (Sept.-Oct. 1993): 445–454.

Doyle, R., and J. McCaffery. "The Budget Enforcement Act of 1990: The Path to No Fault Budgeting." *Public Budgeting and Finance* 11 (Spring 1991): 25–40.

Financial Management Service, Department of the Treasury, *CFS: Consolidated Financial Statements of the United States Government, Fiscal Year 1990.* U.S. Government Printing Office, Washington, D.C., 1991.

Gansler, J. S. *Affording Defense.* Cambridge, MA: MIT Press, 1989.

Gore, Al. *From Red Tape to Results: Creating a Government That Works Better and Costs Less, Report of the National Performance Review.* New York: Times Books/Random House, 1993.

Gunn, R. W., D. P. Carberry, R. Frigo, and S. Behrens. "Shared Services: Major Companies Are Reengineering Their Accounting Functions," *Management Accounting* 82 (Nov. 1993): 22–28.

Harr, D. J. "How Activity Accounting Works in Government," *Management Accounting* 72 (Sept. 1990): 36–40.

Harr, D. J., and J. T. Godfrey. *Private Sector Financial Performance Measures and Their Applicability to Government Operations.* Montvale, NJ: National Association of Accountants, 1991.

Hemingway, A. W. "Cost Center Financial Management: Training OPTAR Managers." *Navy Comptroller* 3 (April 1993): 2–26.

Hitch, C. J., and R. McKean. *The Economics of Defense in the Nuclear Age.* Cambridge, MA: Harvard University Press, 1960.

Hood, C. "A Public Management for All Seasons," *Public Administration* 69 (Spring 1991): 3–20.

Jones, L. R. "Policy Development, Planning, and Resource Allocation in the Department of Defense," *Public Budgeting and Finance* 11 (Fall 1991): 15–27.

Kennedy, J. V. "Accrual Accounting and the President's Budget," *Budget and Economic Analysis* 2 (Feb. 18, 1992): 1–4.

Kotlikoff, Laurence J. *Generational Accounting: Knowing Who Pays, and When, for What We Spend.* New York: Free Press, 1992.

Meyer, R. T. *Pay-as-You-Go Budgeting.* Washington D.C.: Congressional Budget Office Staff Memorandum, March 1990.

Monden, Y., and J. Lee. "How a Japanese Auto Maker Reduces Costs: Kaizen Costing Drives Continuous Improvements at Daihatsu," *Management Accounting* 81 (August 1993): 22–26.

Mosher, F. C. *Program Budgeting: Theory and Practice with Particular Reference to the U.S. Department of the Army.* Chicago: Public Administration Service, 1954.

Osborne, D., and T. Gaebler. *Reinventing Government*. Reading, MA: Addison Wesley, 1992.

Phaup, M. *Some Conceptual Elements of Federal Budget Accounting: The Inconsistency of Budgeting and Depreciation*. Washington D.C.: Congressional Budget Office, March 6, 1990a.

Phaup, M. "Federal Financial Reporting," *Public Budgeting and Finance* 10 (Summer 1990b): 221–26.

Pitsvada, B. T. "The Executive Budget: An Idea Whose Time Has Passed," *Public Budgeting and Finance* 8 (Spring 1988): 85–94.

Redburn, F. S. "How Should the Government Measure Spending? The Uses of Accrual Accounting," *Public Administration Review* 53 (March-April 1993): 213–221.

Rhodes, R. A. W. "The New Public Management," *Public Administration* 69 (Spring 1991): entire issue.

Scott, G., P. Bushnell, and N. Sallee. "Reform of the Core Public Sector: The New Zealand Experience," *Public Sector* 13 (1990): 11–24.

Stedry, A. *Budget Control and Cost Behavior*. Englewood Cliffs, NJ: Prentice-Hall, 1960.

Thompson, F. "Management Control and the Pentagon: The Strategy-Structure Mismatch," *Public Administration Review* 51 (Jan.-Feb. 1991): 52–66.

Thompson, F. "Matching Responsibilities with Tactics: Administrative Controls and Modern Government," *Public Administration Review* 53 (Aug.-Sept. 1993): 303–318.

Wildavsky, A. "Toward a Radical Incrementalism," in A. De Grazia, ed., *Congress: The First Branch of Government*, pp. 96–98. Washington D.C.: American Enterprise Institute, 1966.

Section I.C

EVALUATION OF BUDGETING FOR PERFORMANCE

10

BUDGETING AND PRODUCTIVITY IN STATE GOVERNMENT: NOT INTEGRATED BUT FRIENDLY

Thomas P. Lauth

Budgeting is about the allocation of scarce resources, and productivity is about the efficiency with which goods and services are produced from available resources. Logically, there would seem to be some connection between the two. This article is about the nature of the connection between budgeting and productivity in state government.

Budgeting and Productivity Improvement: The Logical Connection

A public budget is a technique for allocating scarce resources among competing agencies, activities, and programs. Scarcity is, of course, endemic to budgeting; if resources were not scarce, there would be no need to budget (Schick, 1980). However, it is in part because of perceptions that resource scarcity in the states has become more acute in recent years (Schick, 1980) that there has been a growing interest in productivity improvement. A public budget is also a device through which a chief executive attempts to direct and control agencies within the executive branch. Acting through a central budget office, chief executives may attempt to integrate productiv-

1987. Budgeting and productivity in state government: Not integrated but friendly. Lauth, Thomas P. **Public Productivity and Management Review** 41 (Spring): 21–32.

ity data into the budget process, so that budget debates over the allocation of resources among and within state agencies are based on information about agency productivity (Lucey, 1972, 1978).

Productivity is a somewhat elusive concept. In general, it refers to practices and procedures that aim at improving the performance of an agency's personnel and the quality of the goods and services the agency provides. The term *productivity* is also used, in a more precise way, to denote the relationship of certain inputs (for example, labor and capital) to outputs (for example, goods and services). That relationship is usually expressed as a ratio of the amount of work accomplished for a number of dollars or employee hours expended. Improvements in productivity, or technical efficiency, are achieved when increased output is obtained from the same volume of input, or the same volume of output is obtained from a lower volume of input (Burkhead and Hennigan, 1978). Productivity is conventionally distinguished from effectiveness, which is the relationship of inputs to outcomes, usually expressed in terms of consumer satisfaction (Burkhead and Hennigan, 1978), but at least some definitions of productivity intertwine the concepts of efficiency and effectiveness (Jarrett, 1985; Leathers, 1979).

Although efficiency or productivity in government is not a new objective (Newland, 1972; Balk, 1978; Downs and Larkey, 1986), productivity improvement has become one of the most significant concerns of public managers during the 1980s. At the state level, sluggish economies have led to declining revenues and budget shortfalls, while at the same time economic downturns have increased the number of clients for state services. These conditions have been exacerbated by taxpayer revolts, which have constrained state revenue-raising efforts, and by federal funding cutbacks, which have made states more dependent on their own source revenues. Faced with doing the same with less, or doing more with the same, many states are seeking ways to improve government operations and performance (Jarrett, 1985). It was perhaps inevitable that we would come around to considering the budgetary process as a potential vehicle for encouraging productivity improvement efforts. The budget is where basic decisions are made about the allocation of resources, and productivity improvement is one way of dealing with the difficult problem of declining resources.

If budgeting and productivity improvement efforts in state governments are logically connected, what should be the nature of the relationship? One alternative is comprehensive budget reform aimed at integrating productivity information into the central budget process of state governments. A second alternative is more modest—encouraging the development of productivity improvement efforts parallel to, but not integrated with, the budget process while simultaneously ensuring that budget practices in the states are friendly to productivity improvement efforts. The purpose of this article is to assess these alternatives.

Integrating Productivity and Budgeting

There is little doubt that the budget is the most unified and comprehensive decision-making framework available in most state governments. Forty-seven states have some form of executive budget; only South Carolina does not. In Mississippi and Texas, both the executive and legislative branches take budget initiatives. During the past four decades, there have been notable efforts to integrate program and performance information into the budget processes of state governments. In the years after World War II, the performance budgeting movement sought to structure budget categories according to activities performed, rather than things purchased, and to focus managerial attention on the operational efficiency of government agencies. In 1961, the Planning-Programming-Budgeting-System (PPBS)—the prototype of program budgeting—was introduced in the U.S. Department of Defense and was extended to domestic agencies of the federal government in 1965. Budget debates about alternative policy goals and means for achieving those goals were to be informed by quantitative analysis. PPBS was subsequently adopted by a number of state governments. Zero-Base Budgeting (ZBB), adapted from Texas Instruments and introduced in Georgia in 1971, was adopted in varying forms by approximately twenty states and a number of local governments before the end of the decade (Schick, 1979). By arraying alternative funding levels for decision makers, it sought to inform budget decisions and reduce funding for unproductive programs.

Following in these traditions, budgetary reform might seek to integrate productivity information in a systematic and comprehensive manner into the central budget process (see Havens, 1983). Productivity measures and performance agreements might be negotiated with state agencies (Polivka and Osterholt, 1985), and, after a reasonable phase-in period, in which difficult measurement problems are addressed, agencies could be required each year to submit productivity improvement data (out-year goals as well as past-year accomplishments) as part of the annual (or biennial) budget preparation and review process. In addition to financial information, agency budget requests would also include quantitative information about past agency productivity as well as productivity targets. Productivity indices might be developed to justify staffing requirements. Although this approach is likely to require a great deal of effort initially, it might be worth the effort if it signaled a commitment by the governor (and perhaps by legislative leaders) to the goal of improved government productivity and if it provided usable information to the governor and the central budget office regarding the amount of useful work being performed in state agencies. If agencies understood that the size of their budgets depended at least in part on their productivity, then they might be motivated to undertake productivity improvement efforts and to find valid and reliable ways to measure and report improvements.

What are the prospects of achieving such integration? Given experience with past efforts to integrate program and performance information into the budgetary process, the prospects do not appear to be very good. Whether one believes that the rational budget reforms of the 1960s and the 1970s failed entirely to achieve their objectives or that—even though they did not survive as systems—they left a legacy of new procedures and greater awareness of the value of analysis, the conclusion is much the same. Attempts to alter the traditional budget fundamentally by changing the rules of evidence that decision makers consider have not been very successful. Schick (1973) has analyzed the "demise" of federal PPBS and the disappointing fate of performance and program innovations in the states (Schick, 1971). We have addressed the "myth and reality" of ZBB in Georgia (Lauth, 1978). Schick (1978) reported that at the federal level "ZBB changed the terminology of budgeting, but little more." Draper and Pitsvada (1978) concluded that "ZBB did not have a major impact on reducing spending nor did it change the way agencies budget." The extensive literature on the fate of PPBS and ZBB need not be recounted here; it is likely to be well known to readers of this symposium. In general, we learned from that literature that the measurement problems associated with government activities and services, as well as the multiple and complex program goals pursued by government agencies, confounded rational analysis. Further, we learned of the frequent and often irreconcilable conflict between economic rationality and political criteria in determining the worth of programs and activities. In short, attempts in recent decades to integrated program and performance information in a systematic way into traditional budgetary processes met with substantial resistance and were at best moderately successfully. Any scheme to integrate productivity improvement into the central budget process of state governments is likely to encounter the same obstacles and suffer much the same fate.

In a recent study of productivity improvement efforts in state governments, Poister and others (1985) reported that although some productivity improvement activities were going on in virtually all states, the potential for productivity improvement exceeds performance (Poister and McGowan, 1984). Of particular interest for our purpose here was the finding that only ten states reported programs that could be classified as centralized productivity efforts. If states are unwilling to centralize their productivity improvements apart from the budget, then that does not bode well for the prospects of integrating productivity improvement into the central budget process.

Only a few studies have addressed directly the connection between productivity analysis and state budgeting. Lee and Staffeldt (1977) reported that the number of central budget offices conducting productivity analysis increased between 1970 and 1975, from fourteen to thirty-one. However, they also pointed out that executive budget decisions were based substantially on productivity analysis in only seven states in 1970 and in just thirteen by 1975. Thus, a gap was found to exist between the conduct of analysis and its actual use in policy deliberations. We reported (Lauth, 1985) that the efforts to obtain performance evaluation measures for all agencies each year, as part of the budget preparation and review process in Georgia, has not been successful. Central budget office analysts and planners indicated that they do not take performance measures into account during budget preparation and review because of their perception that state policy makers do not use such information in budgetary decision making.

In a survey of state executive budget officers, Abney and Lauth (1986) found that only 23 percent of their respondents ranked "providing assistance to agencies to do their work efficiently" as one of the two most important functions performed by their office (only 2 percent ranked it as the most important function they performed). Less than half the executive budget officers surveyed (42 percent) reported that an "agency's reputation for efficiency in management of its activities" is a factor they consider when recommending agency budget requests to the governor, and 47 percent of the state budget officers reported that the "efficiency with which an agency carries out its activities" is a piece of information in which the governor is interested during review of agency budget requests, while only 33 percent reported interest in agency efficiency on the part of the legislature during its consideration of agency requests.

Not only have the rational budgeting systems installed in state governments met with very modest success, but efforts to integrate productivity analysis into state budget decision making have also had limited success. Further, agency efficiency is not a very important consideration for state executive budget officers, and they do not perceive governors and legislatures as according it a great deal of weight.

Wildavsky (1974) argued that PPBS was politically irrational because it assumed agency objectives to be determined apart from the political process and economic rationality to be the best standard for determining the utility of programs and activities. Efforts to integrate productivity information into the central budget process would be guilty of the same political irrationality. It is naive to think that governors and legislatures will make resource allocation decisions primarily on the basis of productivity data—even if measurement problems can be overcome and agencies can be induced to generate valid and reliable data. On such an important matter as resource acquisition, agencies would no doubt prefer to make their case on the basis of workload data, rather than on the basis of work-load efficiency data. Programs that meet broadly agreed-upon social needs or have strong political constituencies will be continued and probably enhanced, no matter what the data indicate about agency productivity. Economic rationality is not the only criterion for assessing the worth of programs and activities. Not only are productivity improvement data likely to be difficult to interpret when they are aggregated at organization levels well above agency operating levels (where services are delivered and the bulk of agency work performed); on balance, productivity is just not so important for top-level decision makers as it may be for agency managers. Speaking to the manner in which governments subject to tax and expenditure limits will respond, Downs and Larkey (1986) have written: "While it is true that obtaining greater efficiency may offer officials cost savings, these savings are apt to be small relative to yield from revenue raising and broad-stroke expenditure cutting responses. Efficiency gains solve less of the larger, primal budget problem." Although in recent years there has been a growing interest in productivity improvement as an antidote to resource scarcity in the states, the integration of productivity improvement efforts into the central budget system is not likely to be much of a solution.

Productivity-Friendly Budgets

If the prospects of integration are not good, what connection between budgeting and productivity improvement efforts is feasible? Quinn (1978) has drawn a distinction that is helpful in answering this question. He has pointed out that a major problem facing the productivity movement is that everyone does not share a common definition of the term *productivity*. He notes that for economists and industrial engineers, *productivity* means the ratio of outputs to inputs. As applied to government organizations, the objective is to increase the technical efficiency of organizational work flow. In contrast, administrators tend not to view productivity in such process input/output terms. According to Quinn, "For them productivity is usually an ambiguous, shifting concept centered on over-all performance or functioning of the organization." For administrators, productivity improvement may be as much about employee motivation and agency performance, in specific situations, as it is about quantitative measures of organizational yield.

Although integrating productivity improvement efforts (as conceptualized by economists and industrial engineers) with budget preparation, review, and approval processes is likely to be problematic, budget execution practices and procedures can be made productivity-friendly for administrators. By being productivity-friendly, budget systems can facilitate productivity improvement efforts.

At times, public managers find themselves facing changed fiscal conditions, and their productivity improvement efforts are essentially reactive. When the central budget office and the governor recommend to the legislature a funding level for an agency that is substantially below what the agency has requested (even after normal agency padding has been removed), and no change in agency mission has been made, agency managers face a serious problem. One way to respond to the situation of being expected to provide the projected level of services with fewer resources than requested is to achieve greater efficiency in performing the work of the agency. (Unfortunately, a diminished quality of services is also a likely result of insufficient resources.) Agencies face a similar problem when state revenue collections fall short of revenue estimates and when midyear adjustments have to be made in operating budgets to accommodate revenue shortfalls. At times like these, managers seek flexibility in positioning their available funds, so as to accomplish as much of the agency's mission as possible with limited resources. Frequently, budget transfers are part of this effort. When state procedures governing the transfer of funds from one object of expenditure class (line item) to another are restrictive, it is likely to be difficult for managers to implement cost-saving budget changes in a timely manner.

Appropriations are made to state agencies by object class, lump sum, and program (usually within organizational units). Many states appropriate by both object class and lump sum, and a number of program budgeting states also appropriate to object class (Council of State Governments, 1975). Most state budgeting systems are hybrids, with even program budgeting states retaining traditional control elements (Schick, 1971).

In a few states, budget transfers require the approval of the legislature or an agency of the legislature. When the legislature is not in session and its agent meets infrequently, agencies may have to forgo opportunities to obtain cost savings. Purchasing supplies and materials, or undertaking repairs and maintenance earlier rather than later, or taking advantage of discounts for advance payments can achieve savings only if funds are available for spending in the appropriate object classes. Restricting the funds in a particular object class may turn out to be a false economy. For example, as financial managers pointed out in one state where legislative approval of fund transfers between object classes is required, if managers are unable to transfer funds into a "publication and printing" object class for the reproduction of needed forms, they are likely to photocopy them with funds from another object class, at several times the cost of printing (State of Georgia Fiscal Management Council, 1983). The objective of limiting the funds spent for publication and printing is achieved, but because the agency mission requires that forms be available, a way will be found to make them available. However, this may be done in a manner that results in a net inefficiency. Some degree of budget flexibility in such a case could curtail the inefficient use of public funds. In many states, fund transfers from one object class to another can be approved by the governor or the head of the budget office (Council of State Governments, 1975). Although these budget changes can usually be accomplished in a more timely manner than when legislative approval is required, the line-item budget stands as a potential impediment to productivity improvement efforts.

The major purposes of a budget-control mechanism, such as the line-item budget, are to ensure that public funds are spent in accordance with legislative intent and in conformity with gubernatorial objectives, to produce operational efficiency by discouraging unnecessary expenditures, and to attempt to limit the total amount of government outlays (Schick 1964; Howard, 1968). These, of course, are valued goals in a democratic society. Unfortunately, the very inflexibility of that budget control mechanism can also lead to less rather than more operational efficiency when managers do not have the discretion to transfer funds as environmental conditions change and unforeseen circumstances develop (Pitsvada, 1983).

Object-of-expenditure classification systems are usually applied uniformly to nearly all agencies of state government. In general, this is a sound principle. However, when an object class or subobject class is intended primarily to monitor particular costs in only selected agencies, there is no reason to impose it on all agencies. Selected application of such object classes can achieve the intended effect while at the same time maintaining the budget flexibility of other agencies.

An agency may also be permitted to transfer some portion of its funds—for example, 2 or 3 percent, or a fixed dollar amount—without legislative or top-level executive approval. Such actions would, of course, be reportable to the appropriate officials, but this flexibility would enhance managerial ability to achieve efficiencies in agency operations. In these ways, fund transfers within line-item budgets can be made more productivity-friendly.

Proactive managerial efforts to achieve productivity also need a friendly budget system in order to accomplish their objectives. Jarrett (1985) reports that a number of people-oriented approaches to productivity improvement have been attempted in the states. These approaches include quality circles, management/executive training, health-cost containment, incentive systems, and employee appreciation programs (including rewards to employees who make productivity-enhancing suggestions). The effect of some of these approaches—such as management/executive training and employee appreciation activities—on productivity is likely to be indirect and exceedingly difficult to demonstrate. In contrast, the effect of health-cost containment plans may be relatively easy to document. Incentive systems have the most symbiotic relationship with budget systems. They are intended to bring about cost savings, which can be translated either into budget reductions or into release of funds that can then be used for other purposes. They also need a budget system that is friendly to this form of productivity improvement.

Group incentive pay programs authorize payment of a certain percentage of a verified program saving to the employees of the agency unit achieving the saving. North Carolina established an incentive pay plan in 1978 (U.S. General Accounting Office, 1983). Work units within agencies were able to propose cost-saving projects (decreased budget with no decrease in services, or increased service level with no budget increase), which, if approved, became eligible for pay-incentive consideration. If savings were actually documented to the satisfaction of Office of Budget and Management and legislative reviewers, each member of the work unit would share equally in a portion (approximately 25 percent) of the savings. The incentive pay program was abolished without fanfare during the 1985 legislative session. Among the reasons for the termination were a belief on the part of some legislators that some projects were chosen more for their pay-incentive opportunities for employees than for their cost-saving utility to the state; a sentiment in some legislative quarters that it was the responsibility of state employees to perform their work efficiently without special incentives to do so; and a concern that although all work-unit employees shared equally in the pay-incentive plan, not everyone contributed equally to the work effort. During the years in which the plan operated, work crews in the Department of Transportation tended to be among the major beneficiaries of the program. Because ability to document savings is an important criterion in receiving incentive pay, agencies with well-developed cost-accounting systems and responsibility for tasks that lend themselves well to measurement are likely always to benefit more than other agencies in incentive pay programs.

The Georgia Division of Vocational Rehabilitation/Department of Human Resources operated a pilot individual employee incentive program as part of its Counselor Performance Appraisal System during the 1983 and 1984 fiscal years. Performance goals were set for each counselor through negotiation between the counselor and his or her supervisor. Counselors were eligible to earn incentive pay based on their levels of goal achievement (for example, successful rehabilitation-case closures, according to agreed-upon criteria). Incentive pay did not become a part of base salary and had to be earned each year. Funds for incentive pay came from internal management and salary savings (realized from increased employee productivity). Plans to expand the program to the entire division have not been implemented.

Although pay-incentive systems have been difficult to establish, because they run counter to traditional classification and compensation procedures, they offer some possibility for productivity improvement. The principal feature of budgetary systems, which has to be accommodated in order for pay-incentive systems to work, is the provision that funds lapse at the end of the fiscal period if they are not spent. (As one former budget officer said, "At Texas Instruments [where he was formerly employed], when you achieved cost savings, you at least got a pat on the back. Here [in Georgia], you get a kick in the backside as someone takes your money.") The rationale for letting funds lapse is a sound one. If agencies were able to carry over unspent funds from year to year, within a short time they would be in a position to expand existing programs or under-take new ones without specific legislative approval. This could severely threaten legislative prerogatives to authorize programs and control the scope of their operations through annual or biennial appropriations.

However, in order for incentive systems (which enable employees to share a percentage of documented cost savings) or pay-incentive systems (which reward goal achievement) to work, the lapse provision would have to be interpreted in a manner friendly to the objectives of those kinds of productivity improvement efforts. Such was the case in the two instances just described.

Landau and Stout (1977) provide an interesting way of thinking about the relationship between budget flexibility and budget control. They have argued that to manage is not to control—despite the fact that those concepts are frequently thought to be synonymous. The requirement for control in public organizations, they suggest, derives from the principle of accountability. This notion is clearly evident in budgetary requirements that funds not be transferred from one object classification to another without legislative approval and that funds not spent at the end of the fiscal period lapse to the state treasury. However, when an agency faces circumstances that did not exist when the budget request was originally formulated— such as changes in the economy that have an adverse effect on revenue yield, require reduction of funding levels, and increase demand for services—budget flexibility is needed, if agency managers are to use their available resources in an efficient manner. Further, proactive managerial efforts to establish pay-incentive systems for productivity improvement need to be held immune from statewide policies for lapsing all unspent funds. Efficient financial management requires a sensible balance between flexibility and control—flexibility bounded but not proscribed by centralized budget control.

Conclusion

In summary, the argument presented here is straightforward. It is important to ensure that state budgets are productivity-friendly. Even though selected productivity data may be able to inform some budget decisions, it is doubtful that productivity information can be successfully integrated in a systematic and comprehensive manner into the central budget process. Attempts to do so are likely to serve neither productivity improvement nor budgeting very well.

References

Abney, G., and T. P. Lauth. "Determinants of State Budget Success." Paper delivered at the American Society for Public Administration National Conference, Anaheim, California, April 1986.

Balk, W. L., ed. *Public Administration Review*, 1978, *38*, entire issue.

Burkhead, J., and P. J. Hennigan. "Productivity Analysis: A Search for Definition and Order." *Public Administration Review*, 1978, *38*, 34.

Council of State Governments. *Budgetary Processes in the States (A Tabular Display)*. Table XII. Lexington, Ky.: Council of State Governments, 1975.

Downs, G. W., and P. D. Larkey. *The Search for Government Efficiency: From Hubris to Helplessness*. New York: Random House, 1986.

Draper, F. D., and B. T. Pitsvada. "ZBB—Looking Back After Ten Years." *Public Administration Review*, 1978, *38*, 178.

Havens, H. S. "Integrating Evaluation and Budgeting." *Public Budgeting and Finance*, 1983, *3* (2), 102–113.

Howard, S. K. "Budget Execution: Control vs. Flexibility." *Midwest Review of Public Administration*, 1968, *2*, 20–27.

Jarrett, J. E. "An Overview of Productivity Improvement Efforts in State Government." *Public Personnel Management*, 1985, *14*, 385.

Landau, M., and R. Stout Jr. "To Manage Is Not to Control; or, The Folly of Type II Errors." *Public Administration Review*, 1977, *39*, 148–156.

Lauth, T. P. "Zero-Base Budgeting in Georgia State Government: Myth and Reality." *Public Administration Review*, 1978, *38*, 420–430.

Lauth, T. P. "Performance Evaluation in the Georgia Budgetary Process." *Public Budgeting and Finance*, 1985, *5* (1), 67–82.

Leathers, C. G. "Language Barriers in Public Productivity Analysis: The Case of Efficiency and Effectiveness." *Public Productivity Review*, 1979, *3*, 65.

Lee, R. D., and R. J. Staffeldt. "Executive and Legislative Use of Policy Analysis in the State Budgeting Process: Survey Results." *Policy Analysis*, 1977, *3*, 395–405.

Lucey, P. J. "Wisconsin's Productivity Policy." *Public Administration Review*, 1972, *32*, 795–799.

Lucey, P. J. "Wisconsin's Progress with Productivity Improvements." *Public Administration Review*, 1978, *38*, 9–12.

Newland, C. A. *Public Administration Review*, 1972, *32*, entire issue.

Pitsvada, B. T. "Flexibility in Federal Budget Execution." *Public Budgeting and Finance*, 1983, *3*, 83–101.

Poister, T. H., H. P. Hatry, D. M. Fisk, and J. M. Greiner. "Centralized Productivity Improvement Efforts in State Government." *Public Productivity Review*, 1985, *9*, 5–22.

Poister, T. H., and R. P. McGowan. "The Use of Management Tools in Municipal Governments: A National Survey." *Public Administration Review*, 1984, *44* (3), 215–223.

Polivka, L., and B. J. Osterholt. "The Governor as Manager: Agency Autonomy and Accountability." *Public Budgeting and Finance*, 1985, *5* (4), 91–104.

Quinn, R. E. "Productivity and the Process of Organizational Improvement: Why We Can't Talk to Each Other." *Public Administration Review*, 1978, *38*, 41–42.

Schick, A. "Control Patterns in State Budget Execution." *Public Administration Review*, 1964, *24*, 97–106.

Schick, A. *Budget Innovation in the States*. Washington, D.C.: Brookings Institution, 1971.

Schick, A. "A Death in the Bureaucracy: The Demise of Federal PPB." *Public Administration Review*, 1973, *33*, 146–156.

Schick, A. "The Road from ZZB." *Public Administration Review*, 1978, *38*, 178.

Schick, A. *Zero Base '80: The Status of Zero-Base Budgeting in the States*. Washington, D.C.: Urban Institute, 1979.

Schick, A. "Budgetary Adaptations to Resource Scarcity." In C. H. Levine and I. Rubin, eds., *Fiscal Stress and Public Policy*. Beverly Hills, Calif.: Sage, 1980.

State of Georgia Fiscal Management Council. Statement regarding consolidation and realignment of line items and object classes, October 1983.

U.S. General Accounting Office. *Increased Use of Productivity Management Can Help Control Government Costs*. Washington, D.C.: U.S. Government Printing Office, 1983.

Wildavsky, A. *The Politics of the Budgetary Process*. Boston: Little, Brown, 1974.

11

Linking Performance to Funding Decisions: What Is the Budgeter's Role?

Gloria A. Grizzle

Using the budget allocation process to increase productivity seems like a good idea. In practice, as Earle Klay's article in this symposium demonstrates, most budget allocation decisions do not now take productivity into account. In terms of incentives, we may have something of a chicken-and-egg phenomenon.

On the one hand, agency staff may claim that budget decisions are politically motivated, and so they wonder why they should spend time developing performance information to justify budget requests (Donohue, 1982; Lauth, 1985; Hackbart and Ramsey, 1979). On the other hand, budgeters may claim that performance information is not available to them. In her study of the budget documents for ten Houston-area local governments, MacManus (1984) found that 80 percent did not report measures of effectiveness or efficiency. She concludes that without performance information linking inputs to outputs, "any justification of spending cuts or reordering priorities is extremely difficult and likely to subject those doing the cutting

1987. Linking performance to funding decisions: What is the budgeter's role? Grizzle, Gloria A. **Public Productivity and Management Review** 41 (Spring): 33–44.

and reordering to charges of political favoritism." Indeed, in Moore's (1980) survey of 205 city budget directors, they reported that lack of information about the effectiveness and performance of programs was the most severe problem they faced, and 41 percent rated this lack of performance information as being either a severe or a very severe problem, with another 35 percent rating it as more than a minor problem.

Two studies tracking the utilization of analytical work that provided performance information suggest that decision makers do frequently take such information into account when it is available. In studying utilization at the local level of government, Weeks (1979) asked the person who had primary responsibility for each of fifty-seven outcome evaluations of human resource programs to assess the evaluation's degree of utilization. The degree of utilization was rated on a ten-point scale, with 1 indicating that the evaluation report was probably not even read and 10 indicating that enough of the recommendations were adopted and implemented so that the evaluation report could be said to have effectively made the program decisions. Of the evaluations, 53 percent scored 7 or higher. A score of 7 means that "evaluation results were an important, but not the most important, source of information used by the decision participants in reaching decisions about the program." Another 47 percent scored 8 or higher. A score of 8 means that the evaluation report "was probably the single most important piece of information the decision participants used. It was very instrumental in reaching decisions about the program." Interestingly, those evaluations that recommended changes in the program's budget support averaged higher utilization scores that those that did not.

In a second study, Grizzle (1986) tracked twenty-one analyses in a county government and thirty-one in a state government. In the county, 29 percent of the analyses affected program decisions, either by changing the focus of the problem, generating alternatives that otherwise would not have been considered, or prompting a decision where otherwise there would have been none. In studying the effect of analysis on the state budgeting outcomes, participants in the budget process were specifically asked whether the issue analyses resulted in budget decisions that were different from what they would have been had no analysis been conducted. For 29 percent of the issues, the conclusion was that the analysis did in fact change the decision.

While no budgeter would expect performance information to negate the political environment in which budgets are made, these studies do indicate that when decisions are not already foreclosed by politics, performance information, if available, may frequently be the dominant factor influencing funding decisions.

Given that budgeters perceive performance information to be inadequate, what should be their role in generating this information? At one extreme, we might argue that their only role, when provided performance information by agencies, is to take this information into account as they make funding-level decisions for agencies and/or programs. At the other extreme, we might argue that funding decisions cannot be economically rational without performance information, and that therefore designing performance information systems and collecting the pertinent data should be the responsibility of the central budget office. This article assumes that budget offices do have a role to play in generating performance information, but that budgeters do not have much time for collecting performance data. It explores ways that the central budget office for a state or local government might leverage the effort it can invest in generating performance information by reallocating its time and by creating incentives for others to ascertain agency and/or program performance. Not all, or possibly not even the majority of these ways would be practical for any single state or local government. It is hoped, however, that the list discussed here contains enough ideas so that central budget offices can use it as a starting point for designing performance information strategies suited to their own resources and environments.

Workload Shedding

If budget analysts currently play no role in generating performance information and also have no time to invest in such efforts, the first step that should be taken is to create such time. Reporting on a 1984 survey of state governments, Botner (1985) concludes that "computerization of the mundane aspects of budgetary procedures permits budget analysts to devote more time to policy analysis and program evaluation." Information that is routinely required during budget preparation and that might be computerized includes the previous year's actual spending, the current year's estimated spending, agency requests, budget analysts' recommendations, the chief executive officer's recommendation, and legislative appropriations. All these data could be stored in computer files instead of on paper forms. As the budget moves through the stages of preparation and adoption, the computer can incorporate changes made in amounts for individuals budget codes, as well as across-the-board changes for classes of expenditures. The computer can also show aggregate amounts to fund, programs, and organizational unit totals, thus eliminating much of the drudgery of budget spreadsheet preparation. Some state governments already use mainframe computers for this function. For medium and small local governments, microcomputers may be a more practical alternative for budget preparation.

A second way of creating the needed time is for the government to convert from annual to biennial budgeting. There are two disadvantages of this approach. First, the budget office does not have the authority to change its budgeting period; the legislative body must act to change to a biennial budget cycle. Obtaining legislative approval requires some investment of time, but the effort may be successful. Among state governments there has in fact been considerable shifting back and forth from annual to biennial budgets over the years. The second problem concerns the need to revise budget decisions because of uncontrollable events in the economy. As the planning phase has been lengthened at the beginning of the budget cycle, increased economic uncertainty has occasioned revising the revenues estimated and the funds appropriated for the second year of the biennium. Thus, with preparation of supplemental budgets during off years, which takes almost as much time as preparing the biennial budget, the free time created by the move to a biennial budget cycle disappears.

A third possible workload-shedding technique requires abandoning the assumption that the performance of all programs should be re-examined every budget cycle. Havens (1983) has suggested a multiyear budget/policy review as a way to avoid spending a significant amount of scarce time on a review of programs when there has been no major policy shift. Fogarty and Turnbull (1977) have suggested a rotating schedule, whereby a program would come up for extensive review once every few years. In terms of linking performance information to resource allocation decisions, this rotating process might work as follows. During every budget cycle, agency requests would be justified in terms of demand for services, quantity of services to be provided, and unit costs for services. If an agency or a program were selected for more extensive review, then performance information would also be provided to relate the quantity of services to outcomes, or program results.

A fourth workload-shedding technique would be to relax the central budget office's control over agency transfers of funds during budget execution. This option is not readily available to jurisdictions where law dictates either the flexibility agencies have for shifting already appropriated funds or the procedures for getting transfers approved by higher authorities. Even in jurisdictions where the central budget office has authority to give agencies more leeway in transferring funds, legislative attitudes about holding bureaucrats accountable may make such moves inadvisable. Finally, the central budget office itself may not trust the management capacity or intentions of agency heads enough to give them freer rein.

Generating Efficiency Information

Measuring efficiency requires relating an activity's outputs to its inputs in order to calculate unit costs of services rendered. A unit of service must be defined for each activity, the number of units provided must be counted, and the cost of providing outputs must be calculated. Few would suggest that the central budget office's role should be to collect the data necessary for measuring efficiency. It is important, however, that agencies have the capacity to calculate unit costs and that the central budget office provide incentives for agencies to exercise that capacity.

Grafton and Permaloff (1985) point out that in performance budgeting, the managers responsible for service delivery need to forecast, monitor, and analyze unit costs. They suggest that the major effect microcomputers may have on budgeting is a "resurgence of performance budgeting with its emphasis on the collection of workload statistics and their relationship to agency productivity." The microcomputer can give first-line managers the capacity to measure efficiency on a regular basis. Therefore, the central budget office might do well to encourage investment in this technology.

On the incentive side, the central budget office may use its guidelines for developing agency budget requests to encourage efficiency measurement. It could stipulate that agencies justify the amount of work to be done and the unit cost of that work. For the guidelines to be effective as an incentive, however, it is essential that budget analysts take this productivity information into account when they work up their funding recommendations. To ignore such information is to ensure that agencies will not bother supplying it in future years. If the central budget office is serious about wanting efficiency information, then it also needs to be serious about making the funds available for training managers and developing and implementing the necessary performance measurements and cost-accounting or cost-determination systems.

Privatization may also provide an opportunity to encourage performance contracting between public agencies and organizations in the private sector. Central budget offices could encourage agencies to develop contracts that would pay organizations for the number of units of service actually delivered, multiplied by the unit cost stipulated in the contract. Again, the best incentives that the central budget office can provide are funds for developing contract-monitoring capacity and budget decisions that take performance information into account.

Generating Outcome Information

In responding to surveys, a majority of cities (with populations greater than 25,000) and states claim that they do program budgeting (Poister and McGowan, 1984; Botner, 1985). A perusal of budget documents, however, suggests that most of these jurisdictions do not report program results with any regularity. While adopting program budgets has become increasingly popular during the last decade, generating information about program outcomes is much less prevalent—and with good reason, for outcome data require a higher order of resource investment. Collecting data to measure outcomes is much more expensive than counting the amount of work that public servants do. Measuring outcomes may require following up clients after they complete a program; surveying citizens; and making observations of physical phenomena, such as the level of pollution in the air or water. Because other factors in addition to a given program can affect these conditions, the necessity of demonstrating what portion of changes in these conditions was a result of the program, and not of other factors, vastly complicates the measurement problem.

The U.S. General Accounting Office now allocates half its time to benefit-cost analysis and evaluation. Even if the workload-shedding techniques already suggested could result in a similar reallocation of time on the part of state and local budget analysts, this infusion of resources is nowhere near enough to determine, on a regular basis, the outcomes of programs over a whole jurisdiction. How, then, can enough outcome information be generated so that program results can be taken into account in making budget decisions?

Expecting that agencies can regularly provide outcome information on all programs is, for the foreseeable future, unrealistic. It is important to be selective in asking for outcome information; asking for the impossible is a sure disincentive. Because of the long time required for measuring some program results, the central budget office's ability to anticipate which programs will need review in any given year is important. The budget office will need to adopt a multiyear perspective in order to have outcome information on hand when budget decisions are made.

Several tools for encouraging outcome evaluations may be available to the budget office. Projects initiated on a demonstration or pilot basis provide an opportunity for evaluation. A part of the funding for these projects might be earmarked for outcome evaluation. Participation in the demonstration project might be limited to administrators who commit themselves to supporting an evaluation design that permits their learning what portion of changes in the outcomes monitored was caused by the program being evaluated. Another way of encouraging evaluation on a selective basis would be to have the legislature write an evaluation requirement as a special condition attached to the appropriations of a few programs.

Purchasing services may provide another opportunity for getting needed evaluation information. An arrangement might be made with the purchasing office so that the budget office would have the opportunity to review all requests for proposals, in order to conduct evaluations before these requests are finalized. The purpose would be to increase the likelihood that the type of information generated would be useful for making budgeting decisions.

As is true in all budget-reform processes, the chief executive's posture is important to the reform's success. Polivka and Osterholt (1985) report that one state used performance agreements between the governor and agency heads as a means of encouraging agencies to develop and report outcome information. For a few selected outcome measures of each agency, the governor monitored progress at quarterly policy-review meetings with agency heads. These researchers explain that "the governor's routing review and assessment of agency performance, based on the quarterly performance agreement status reports, now requires agency managers to focus on the measured impact of agency programs and to develop an organizational capacity to create, implement, and monitor corrective action plans."

As with incentives for measuring efficiency, none of these incentives is likely to be effective unless agencies have the capacity to do the evaluation work (or the resources to contract for it) and unless agency administrators believe that providing the information to the central budget office will be more beneficial to them than not providing it.

We have made the point that central budget offices cannot undertake much outcome evaluation themselves but can create incentives for getting agencies to do selective outcome monitoring and impact evaluation. Budget offices might also capitalize on two other resources for doing outcome measurement.

First, the trend toward increased staffing of legislative bodies has in some states resulted in well-qualified legislative analysts who do evaluations as legislative auditors or as staff members of legislative oversight committees. In jurisdictions where the legislature is willing to share information with the executive budget office, these evaluations may be helpful to budget analysts who review agency budget requests. This source of information is not available in all states; in one state with which the author is familiar, for example, the legislative auditor reports only adverse findings and includes in the report little explanation of the methods used. Findings that are not adverse remain hidden in the auditor's working papers, which the legislature has excluded from the open-records act. The effect is that executive-branch analysts must do evaluations to get outcome information, even when that information has already been collected by legislative analysts.

A second and often overlooked resource is the group of two hundred or so colleges and universities that are members of the National Association of Schools of Public Affairs and Administration. Almost all these schools have graduate programs, and a number have doctoral programs. Budget offices could establish relationships with whichever public affairs/administration schools are in their geographical areas. Graduate students who, through evaluation and analytical coursework, have attained the competence to contribute to evaluation work could boost a budget office's capacity to undertake outcome evaluations. One arrangement might simply be to assign a graduate student as an assistant to a budget analyst, who would have the primary responsibility to conduct the evaluation. Another arrangement might be to have several students form an evaluation team headed by a professor, who would take the responsibility for ensuring that the evaluation work was properly conducted and completed on schedule. Under both arrangements, the students would benefit from the experience of working on a real-world evaluation, and the budget office would be able to increase the size of its evaluation agenda.

Cost-Effectiveness Information

Almost a decade ago, Moran (1978) wrote in this journal that focusing evaluation "on the connection between units of service received and resulting client benefit (while ignoring cost) is inadequate since it does not tell . . . agency managers what service priorities to establish in the face of agency expenditure limitations." When resources are expanding, it is easy for agency managers to assume that if outcome evaluations show programs to be effective, then these programs ought to be continued at their present levels or even expanded. When resources are contracting, the relationship of outcomes to costs becomes more important. When there are more things to be done but fewer resources with which to do them, cost-effectiveness information can help budget analysts judge the levels at which to fund programs.

Outcome evaluations frequently do not provide cost information. The following example (Grizzle, 1976) of an outcome evaluation conducted by a state education department is typical. A special pilot reading program for grades one through three was implemented in 108 classrooms. Pre- and posttests of student reading ability were obtained for these demonstration classrooms, as well as for an equal number of classrooms that did not have the benefit of the special reading program. Both tests (the reading parts of the Comprehensive Tests of Basic Skills and the Prescriptive Reading Inventory) showed that students in the demonstration classrooms averaged a larger gain in reading ability during the year than did students in classrooms without the reading program. The gain attributable to the resources allocated to the demonstration classes, but not to the comparison classes, is seven points for the Comprehensive Tests of Basic Skills (CTBS) and three points for the Prescriptive Reading Inventory (PRI) (see Table 11.1).

Given unlimited resources, this outcome evaluation supports the agency's request to expand the demonstration reading program statewide to grades one through three. To help the budget analyst decide upon the appropriate level at which to fund the reading program, however, these outcomes need to be weighed against the cost of achieving them.

Fortunately, it is usually much easier to measure program costs than to measure program outcomes. The budget analyst can frequently determine costs with only a small investment of time. Continuing with the reading evaluation example, the budget analyst determined that the direct cost of a

TABLE 11.1   Reading Achievement for Special Reading Program Compared with Achievement for Regular Program

	Pretest	*Posttest*	*Gain*	*Gain Difference*
CTBS Standard Scale Scores, *Grades 1–3*				
Special reading program	265	327	62	7
Regular program	263	318	55	
PRI Average Number of Items Correct, *Grades 2–3*				
Special reading program	81	107	26	3
Regular program	80	103	33	

classroom that did not receive the special reading program was $13,798, as compared to a direct cost of $19,285 for a classroom that received the special reading program. Using the CTBS score as the measure of effectiveness, we can relate this cost to the reading scores in order to calculate the cost-effectiveness of the two program alternatives. Classrooms without the special reading program achieved an average gain of one point in reading ability for each $251 spent. The special reading program produced gains beyond those of the regular program, but it did so at a cost of $784 for each point of additional gain in the CTBS score. Using the PRI score instead of the CTBS score gives similar results. The cost per point gained is $600 in the regular program and $1,829 for each additional point gained through the special reading program (see Table 11.2). Thus, the marginal return for each dollar spent in the special reading program is lower than that for the regular reading program.

Given this cost-effectiveness information, the budget analyst is still left with judging whether the increase in reading ability is worth the additional cost. The cost to the state in this example was $50 million per year. It would be more helpful for the analyst also to have cost-effectiveness information on alternative ways of spending $50 million per year; but even without information on alternatives, the budget analysis can be more informed with this cost-effectiveness information than with outcome information alone.

Summary and Conclusion

Table 11.3 summarizes actions that central budget offices might take to encourage generating and using performance information in budgeting. How

TABLE 11.2   Cost-Effectiveness of Special Reading Program Compared to the Regular Program

	Gain	Total Cost per Classroom	Cost per Unit Gained per Classroom
Gain Due to			
Regular Program			
CTBS	55	$13,798	$251
PRI	23	13,798	600
Additional Gain Due			
to Special Program			
CTBS	7	5,487	784
PRI	3	5,487	1,829

many of these actions are politically feasible for a given jurisdiction will obviously vary, and no attempt to assess their political feasibility has been attempted here. In making rough estimates of the amount of staff time that budget offices would consume by taking each of these actions, we see that most actions do not take much time.

In assessing how much additional money (as opposed to time reallocations for existing staff) the government should allocate to implement these actions, we see that the cost impact on the central budget office is negligible for most actions. When it comes to developing and implementing performance information systems and doing outcome evaluation, however, the cost to agencies can be substantial. It is important that the central budget office balance the data collection requirements it imposes on agencies against the resources that it is willing to allocate to agencies for this purpose. Also, it cannot be said too often that when the central budget office requires agencies to generate performance information, it must then use that information in reaching budgeting decisions. To do otherwise discourages agencies from complying with future central budget office guidelines.

For the majority of the alternatives explored here, the central budget office has the authority to act unilaterally. For about a third of these actions, however, the central budget office must obtain the cooperation of the legislative body, the chief executive officer (CEO), or the central purchasing office.

Moore's (1980) survey set this author to thinking about how to address what municipal budget directors say is the most severe problem they face: the lack of information about the effectiveness and performance of programs. This author hopes that this limited (and perforce general) explo-

TABLE 11.3 Actions That Central Budget Offices (CBOs) Might Take to Increase the Availability of Performance Information

	Assessment of Action's Feasibility		
Action	Amount of CBO Time Required	Out-of-Pocket Cost	Primary Decision Locus
Workload Shredding			
Computerize budget-preparation routines	Moderate	Moderate/ CBO	CBO
Shift to biennial budget	Little	Negligible	Legislature
Rotate program reviews	Moderate	Moderate/ CBO	CBO
Increase agency autonomy during budget execution	Negligible	Negligible	Legislature
Generating Efficiency Information			
Invest in technology to improve agency capacity	Little	Moderate/ Agency	CBO
Use budget guidelines to require unit costs	Little	Moderate/ Agency	CBO
Use productivity information when making decisions	Moderate	Negligible	CBO
Generating Outcome Information			
Ask for outcome information selectively	Little	Substantial/ Agency	CBO
Tie evaluation requirements to pilot projects	Little	Substantial/ Agency	CBO
Attach evaluation requirement to appropriations	Little	Substantial/ Agency	Legislature
Review RFPs for evaluation work	Moderate	Moderate/CBO/ Agency	Purchasing Office
Performance agreements between agency heads and chief executive officer	Moderate-Substantial	Substantial/ Agency	CBO/ CEO
Acquire legislative staff evaluations	Little	Negligible	CBO/ Legislature
Enlist graduate students to do evaluations	Moderate	Moderate/ CBO	CBO
Cost-Effectiveness Information			
Convert outcome evaluations	Little	Negligible/ CBO	CBO

ration will set directors to thinking about how they can develop realistic strategies for getting this information and putting it to use.

References

Botner, S. B. "The Use of Budget/Management Tolls by State Governments." *Public Administration Review,* 1985, 45 (5), 618.

Donohue, L. "You Can't Take Politics Out of Budgeting." *Public Budgeting and Finance,* 1982, 2 (2), 67–72.

Fogarty, A. B., and A. B. Turnbull III. "Legislative Oversight Through a Rotating Zero-Base Budget." *State and Local Government Review,* 1977, 9 (11), 18–22.

Grafton, C., and A. Permaloff. "Budget Implementation with Microcomputers." *Public Productivity Review,* 1985, 9 (2-3), 212.

Grizzle, G. A. "Analysis of the Primary Reading Program Evaluation." Unpublished paper, 1976.

Grizzle, G. A. "Building Analysis into the Budget Process: Lessons from Two Experiences." *JAI Research Annual in Public Policy Analysis,* 1986.

Hackbart, M. M., and J. R. Ramsey. "Budgeting: Inducements and Impediments to Innovations." *State Government,* 1979, 52 (2), 65–69.

Havens, H. S. "Integrating Evaluation and Budgeting." *Public Budgeting and Finance,* 1983, 3 (2), 102–113.

Lauth, T. P. "Performance Evaluation in the Georgia Budgetary Process." *Public Budgeting and Finance,* 1985, 5 (1), 67–82.

MacManus, S. A. "Coping with Retrenchment: Why Local Governments Need to Restructure Their Budget Document Formats." *Public Budgeting and Finance,* 1984, 4 (3), 61, 64.

Moore, P. "Types of Budgeting and Budgeting Problems in American Cities." *International Journal of Public Administration,* 1980, 2 (4), 504–507.

Moran, R. A. "The Economics of Resource Use in Vocational Rehabilitation: A Case Study of Labor Input Allocation." *Public Productivity Review,* 1978, 3 (2), 73.

Poister, T. H., and R. P. McGowan. "The Use of Management Tools in Municipal Governments: A National Survey." *Public Administration Review,* 1984, 44 (3), 215–223.

Polivka, L., and B. J. Osterholt. "The Governor as Manager: Agency Autonomy and Accountability." *Public Budgeting and Finance,* 1985, 5 (4), 91–104.

Weeks, E. C. "The Managerial Use of Evaluation Findings at the Local Level." Paper presented at the American Society for Public Administration annual meeting, 1979.

12

MANAGEMENT THROUGH BUDGETARY INCENTIVES

William Earle Klay

The power of the purse is the power to bestow or withhold resources. Its exercise establishes a framework of incentives, which affects the actions of those who seek its resources. There is, however, a fundamental irony associated with the power of the purse. Methods and practices that have been devised to enhance leaders' control over budget expenditures have themselves created a number of severe disincentives. In other words, the power of the purse has been exercised in a way that has perverted its incentive effects. What follows is a review of the literature that deals with this framework of incentives and a proposal for altering incentive patterns in order to achieve some of the recurring objectives of reform, especially productivity and foresight.

Pervasive Disincentives

Two decades ago, the observations of Davis, Dempster, and Wildavsky (1966) led them to conclude that officials in the federal government "uniformly believe" that the exercise of political skills and proficiency in exploiting opportunities are "more important in obtaining funds than demonstration of agency efficiency." The wisdom of these officials was supported in an important study by Warren (1975) of budget appropria-

1987. Management through budgetary incentives. Klay, William Earle. **Public Productivity and Management Review** 41 (Spring): 59–71.

tions for the Securities and Exchange Commission during the years 1945–1969. Warren was testing two alternative hypotheses regarding the response of the budget process to improvements in agency workload, relative to costs. According to Warren (1975), one hypothesis, advanced by Niskanen, was that agencies would become successful in increasing their budgets if they became more productive; the other, advanced by Wildavsky, suggested "that the appropriations process may penalize agencies which perform better than expected." The data supported the Wildavsky hypothesis, rather than that of Niskanen. The SEC's appropriations tended to grow more slowly after its more productive years and to grow more rapidly after its less productive years.

In the classic study of state budgeting by Anton (1966), he observed that failure to spend all of an appropriation in a given fiscal period can lead to a reduction in the next, while Wildavsky (1964) noted that substantial end-of-year surpluses for federal agencies could signal to reviewing officials that the agency did not need such appropriations, thereby justifying their being cut from future budgets. This writer remembers well that, when he was a junior officer in the Army, he was given a direct order by his commanding officer to purchase large quantities of supplies that were not needed at the time, in order to protect the level of spending authority that the unit would receive for the following year. That such situations are quite common is evidenced by a report of the U.S. General Accounting Office (1979), which found that agencies obligated a disproportionate amount of their money during the last quarter, and especially during the last month, of the fiscal year. The report stated that such spending patterns occurred even in multiyear and no-year fund situations, when agencies do not have to return unused funds to the treasury but still fear that substantial unobligated balances will raise unwanted questions about whether programs are overfunded or not being accomplished on time. The report concluded that "a significant underlying problem is that there are no incentives not to spend the funds appropriated."

Budgetary disincentives may thwart many organizational reforms. American efforts to adapt some of the elements of Japanese management, such as the so-called Theory Z approach, are especially important because our ability to adapt Japanese methods will reveal our own level of talent in learning from the success of others, a talent that Japan has exhibited for centuries, but which the United States has never had to develop before. One of the first reviews of efforts to try such productivity-oriented reforms in a public setting, however, has found that the efforts are foundering. Contino and Lorusso (1982) have found that the savings achieved through a Theory Z effort "are removed from the bureau's budget with no corresponding return of benefit." The employees who were responsible for achieving the savings, they say, have developed feelings of frustration and futility as a result of their efforts. They conclude that the success of such group-oriented productivity reforms is related to the ability of the budget process "at all levels" to develop positive incentives to reward such efforts.

Current practices in exercising the power of the purse include serious disincentives for anticipatory planning, as well as for efficiency. Compare, for example, the incentives for cash-flow planning that confront public and private sector administrators. It is not common for a private business with good long-term prospects to fail because of inadequate cash-flow planning. If a manager of such a firm fails to provide a contingency reserve of cash or an ability to borrow cash on short notice, then, unforeseen cost increases or revenue shortfalls can cause a severe liquidity crisis. It is the foolish stockholder who does not demand that the manager develop and maintain contingency reserves.

The public administrator faces similar uncertainties regarding levels of both demand and costs. The budget is, after all, a plan for the future when it is enacted, and uncertainty is an inescapable feature of any plan. The public manager, therefore, is also in need of some contingency reserves, but any efforts to request these explicitly or to overtly retain cost savings for such purposes may be construed as evidence of "fat" that should be cut. Not to request sufficient funds, and then to request supplemental appropriations, is likely to reflect badly on the administrator as either a poor manager, a poor forecaster, or both. The most logical behavior in the face of such contingencies is to request enough to cover some of the possible cost and demand increases and then to spend all that was received, even if the higher costs and demands do not occur, simply to ensure that sufficient funds to cover such contingencies will again be appropriated.

Environmental conditions greatly affect budgeting, yet substantial disincentives exist under conditions of both fiscal constraint and fiscal growth. This pervasiveness of disincentives, irrespective of fiscal conditions, has been summarized by Straussman (1979). When times are good, observes Straussman, "the incentive for self-evaluation as a part of budget reform is minimal, since, in a generally favorable fiscal environment, the agency will receive its base and increment anyway." Nevertheless, when confronted with fiscal constraints, agency managers fear that efficiency-oriented reviews will expose their agencies even more to the cuts at hand. Levine (1979) points out that the manager who willingly exercises frugality when his or her government is faced with constraints may be penalized, because the savings created are often shifted to support the programs of other, less conscientious managers. Thus, cutback efforts are frustrated by attitudes that have been shaped by previous misuse of the incentive power of the purse. As Levine writes, "To change this attitude, *managers will have to be shown that saving has rewards. In most government organizations this will require fundamental reforms in budgeting and personnel practices*" (emphasis in original).

One of the weaknesses of public administration is its continuing compartmentalization of such matters as budgeting and personnel administration. When one begins to look at incentives, however, and to trace their causes and consequences, the relationships between these become apparent. Any efforts to develop positive incentives within personnel systems, for example, are likely to be confounded if the personnel system is trying to reward behaviors that are penalized by the budget system. Organizational incentives and personal incentives are incontrovertibly linked.

Productivity improvement has to do with the propensity of people to analyze problems and to seek out innovative means to deal with these problems. It is especially troubling, then, that their study of innovations in the public sector led Bish and Nourse (1975) to conclude that the political system governing the power of the purse offers few incentives for improved performance and substantial penalties for innovations that fail. Similarly, Wildavsky (1979) has observed that an inherent tension exists between policy analysis, which seeks to identify error and promote change, and organizational behavior, which seeks to protect and promote the interest of the organization and its members. The only way to promote better analysis, he concludes, is to make it in the organization's interest to do so. Thus, Wildavsky writes, "Struggling with organizational incentives, therefore, is a perennial (perhaps paramount) problem of policy analysis."

The Paradox of Budget Reforms

The major budget reforms of the twentieth century have, for the most part, ignored the question of incentives. The earliest reforms were essentially oriented toward the establishment of financial control over operating agencies and were accordingly characterized by mandates issued by superiors to subordinates. Later reforms were concerned more with the achievement of improved managerial performance and with answering Key's (1944) challenge to find a rational way for policymakers to choose from among competing claims for resources, but these reforms were also issued as mandates by superiors, with little thought given to the incentive structure of subordinates. The zenith of budgetary reforms that purported to be based on what Diesing (1962) has called "economic rationality" was PPBS. This reform and others, however, have strangely ignored the long tradition in economics of building theory on the individual actor and on the incentive structure he or she faces.

That tradition is exemplified by the writings of Adam Smith, who approached the problems of providing such things as transportation, education, and legal services from the standpoint of the incentive structure as it actually existed for the persons who provided the goods and services. Smith, as Rosenberg (1960) has observed, set about to devise institutional structures that would provide the best possible incentive patterns. A century after Adam Smith, Laughlin (1892) wrote that political economy was "a means of analyzing the play of economic motives . . . and of ascertaining their causes and effects." In our time, Simon (1957), who was not trained as an economist, was awarded the Nobel Prize in that field because he had done so much to enlighten scholars and practitioners about the thought processes and incentive structures confronting individual decision makers, particularly under conditions of bounded rationality.

Simon argued that administrative theory should try to identify the decision premises that confront the members of organizations. In a sense, any proposal to use the incentive potential of the budgetary process in a more positive fashion is a proposal for a fuller integration of economic and administrative theory, especially theory concerned with the decision premises confronting individuals. Space constraints do not permit a full investigation here of the degree to which budget reforms have been weakened through their neglect of the incentives question, but a brief review is illustrative.

Wildavsky (1964) concluded that the primary role of agency people is to be advocates. The reasons for the emergence of this role are easily understood, from an incentives point of view; nevertheless, reformers have repeatedly ignored, decried, or attempted to suppress the reality of agency advocacy, but not to harness its motive force. Efforts to deny or suppress the agency role of advocacy were especially evident in the Zero-Base Budgeting (ZBB) reform effort.

In order for ZBB to work well, agency managers must think hard in order to develop information that will show reviewers how reductions in budget authority can be achieved with minimum impact on services to the public. Agency managers, of course, are motivated to show reviewers that even small cuts in funds will lead to substantial cuts in services; and that is apparently just what they did. If a manager broke stride and provided the information reviewers desired, while other managers continued to defend their programs, the maverick would likely be rewarded with fewer funds, and little else. While ZBB professed to carry a big stick, it was notably lacking in carrots. One of the most revealing and critical observations about ZBB was made by its early proponent, Phyrr (1973), when he reviewed the experiences of the ZBB system in Georgia: "There is little incentive in government to be cost effective, and most cost savings were made by agency directors or the Budget Bureau by eliminating packages rather than by improving the effectiveness of the operation."

In essence, what this means is that alleged savings occurred through the denial of authority to carry out certain discrete functions or levels of activity for which agencies had requested budget authority. Whether these cuts would have occurred anyway is open to question, and this possibility must be considered in light of the fact that post-implementation reviews of ZBB efforts have generally found no substantial reordering of priorities that could be attributed to ZBB. Of particular importance here, though, is the admission that the reform failed to alter the incentive patterns for managers to use the money appropriated to their programs more efficiently. In short, ZBB offered managers no inducement to work toward greater efficiency during the budget preparation phase, when they developed information for the reviewers to use, nor during the execution phase, once they had received their spending authority.

The thrust of PPBS was similar to that of ZBB in many ways, even though PPBS was considerably more ambitious, especially with regard to the planning function. PPBS was also designed primarily for the benefit of the budget reviewer, and here, too, the same dependence on the quality of information provided by the agencies was evident. Even though PPBS was accurately perceived by agencies to be something the reviewers would be tempted to use to cut appropriations, the PPBS format lent itself more readily to use by astute agency managers to advance their advocacy. Thus, in the federal government, the level of agency effort to do PPBS analysis was found to be related to the degree of personal support for it by top agency leaders. In his review of PPBS efforts in several federal departments and bureaus, Doh (1971) concluded that leadership support was a function of the degree to which managers saw opportunities for the organization or for themselves in PPBS. He then recommended that, if such policy analysis "is to be an effective aid to decision-making many more incentives will have to be built into the bureaucratic structure."

The fate of Management-by-Objectives (MBO), as it has been applied to budget reform, is especially telling. Conceived by organizational theorists as a method of open dialogue between superiors and subordinates, through which organization and individual needs might better be understood in order to tap the motive forces of the individual, MBO became something quite different in the hands of budgeters. Schooled to think only of the needs of those who review and decide the budget and whose authority it is to mandate whatever budgetary practices they desire, budget officials turned MBO into a unilaterally mandated system of forced accountability. Little or no thought was given to the needs and incentives of the operating persons on whom budgeters are utlimately so dependent. Nevertheless, if the tendency to make MBO into a paperwork-oriented system (in which far more objectives are identified than could possibly be funded or achieved) can be avoided, and if its original duality can be regained, MBO can be a useful mechanism for bestowing positive incentives for performance.

The Search for Congruence

The goal of an incentives-based approach is to achieve a greater congruence between personal and public interests. In fact, the search for such congruence is very much within the tradition of American political and administrative theory, as is evidenced by the famous passages of the fifty-first *Federalist Paper,* where Publius argued that our system of divided powers was fashioned to control the abuse of power by harnessing the ambition of officials, so that "the private interest of every individual may be a sentinel over the public rights" (Hamilton, Jay, and Madison, 1976). In his famous seminal treatise, Woodrow Wilson ([1887] 1978) spoke of "energizing government" and raised the very question that management through budgetary incentives seeks to address: "How shall such service be made to his commonest interest by contributing abundantly to his sustenance, to his dearest interest by furthering his ambition, and to his highest interest by advancing his honor and establishing his character?"

Wilson prescribed a set of institutional structures that would enable government employees to fulfill these ambitions in service to the public. His failure was to assume that it was merely necessary to remove the constraints of partisan controls and political obligations and to "streamline" government for the congruence between personal and public interest to occur. He, and countless others who followed, failed to recognize that the execution of political functions of the purse carried within itself the makings of a pervasive set of disincentives that would obstruct the attainment of the desired congruence. This continues to be the case with budget reform efforts that have shared Wilson's error.

Rewarding Agency Outputs

Management through budgetary incentives is based on the assumption that a cause-and-effect relationship exists between an agency's behaviors and the framework of incentives confronting that agency and its members. The enhancement of performance, therefore, requires the development of a more positive framework of incentives. This, in turn, means the identification and elimination of disincentives, insofar as possible, and the construction of positive reinforcements when too few exist.

Simply awarding some sort of monetary award to top administrators for demonstrated agency efficiency and effectiveness does not address the nature of the disincentives, which may continue to prevail for the agency itself and therefore for most of its members as well. An alternative is a retained-savings strategy, variations of which have been proposed by a number of persons (Niskanen, 1971; Doh, 1971; Roessner, 1977; Boynton, Medina, and Covello, 1977; Klay, 1978). This alternative would allow agencies to retain amounts saved from appropriations, rather than being required to return them to the general treasury. Proposals vary on whether any of the retained savings could be paid directly to employees or merely be retained and spent on other things the agency would like to do. Retained savings might be accumulated in what amounts to agency "savings accounts" and could be spent later on things legislatures have given permission to do, contingent upon the accumulation of sufficient savings. Group payments could be administered in a way that helps to provide a positive fiscal tool. Emphasizing group rewards better recognizes the collective effort that would be essential to achieving substantial efficiencies (Klay, 1981).

In addition to recommending retained savings, Boynton, Medina and Covello (1977) recommended greater degrees of freedom from restrictive controls (that is, awarding lump-sum appropriations) to reward well-managed agencies. Their proposal deserves close attention, as it may be more politically feasible than the retained-savings strategy. In their important review of exemplary practices in the public sector, Bryant and Joyce (1984) recommend both administrative autonomy and monetary incentives to stimulate productivity.

Before good performance can be rewarded, however, it must somehow be identified. The problem of measurement is one of potentially gargantuan proportions, which has overwhelmed such previous reforms as PPBS and ZBB. One strategy is to limit most of the analysts' limited time and capacity to measuring the quality of performance in agencies that supply essentially the same or very similar services (Niskanen, 1971). This strategy neglects the fundamental dilemma of budget analysis: There is no shortage of interagency competition for the budget dollar; the overriding problem is that most of the competition in the budget process is between programs that involve very different kinds of services. The proponents of PPBS recognized this comparability problem, but the best they could do was to suggest creative ways in which selected portions of agency outputs could be transferred into monetary terms. The best that the PPBS proponents could suggest for the magnitude aspect of the measurement problem was to buy more analysts and computers.

The error that PPBS, ZBB, and similar reform efforts have made is to have looked upon the evaluation of agency performance as a technical and analytical problem, rather than as an inherently social problem. Our goal in applying an incentives approach is to enhance production of public services through the differential rewarding of individuals and groups of public servants who live in a very complex social and political environment. What we must seek, first, is their willingness to participate in the necessary review and evaluation process, continue to make efforts toward improvement, and continue to be willing to submit information that can be used to judge the quality of their efforts. The first criterion, therefore, to be met in order to achieve their continuing willingness to participate is for those who are being reviewed to be persuaded that the process is fair.

The development and maintenance of a decision process for incentives must take precedence over the more purely technical issues of analysis and evaluation. It is beyond human capacity to develop an irrefutable calculus, and no amount of analysis will overcome legitimate differences in opinions and value preferences. Elected and career officials must believe that the system for reviewing performance and arriving at judgments about the quality of agency performance is reasonably accurate but above all fair. It must be an effort to which managers will be willing to submit themselves and their agencies on a continuing basis.

Fairness, Measurement, and Commitment

What might cause agencies and their administrators to conclude that an incentive review process is unfair? There are at least two possible reasons, and the existence of either would be sufficient to doom the reform effort. The first would be present if enough agency managers came to believe that the review process would not make it possible for their agencies to compete equally with others for the rewards. The second reason would be present if they felt that their performance reviews were reasonably well done and that the recommendations for subsequent treatment were fair but that the holder of the power of the purse penalized the best performers anyway. The first reason, then, has to do with measurement, and the second has to do with the degree of ultimate commitment to making the incentive power of the purse work.

What must be done first is to admit that the review process that must be developed in order to exercise the incentive power is inherently judgmental. What we are faced with is the necessity of developing judgments about the quality of agencies' efforts in achieving their assigned goals. The dilemma in developing such judgments is that the substantial human capacity to integrate numerous perceptions must be utilized as much as possible, while our information-processing limitations must not be ignored. The critical test is not whether the review process is subjective, for such subjectivity is inescapable, but whether the exercise of this subjectivity is perceived as being sufficiently fair.

In order for this to happen, there must be a review process that is capable of independent judgment, open to criticism, able to learn, and able to change itself when better ways to judge agency performance become evident. Some of these better ways will be suggested by the agencies themselves, and a review process that is not open to criticism by those being evaluated runs a much greater risk of becoming unfair. If the reviewers decide not to change their practices in response to agency criticisms, then they should carefully explain their reasons for not doing so. Agencies must be genuinely challenged, but they must also believe that it is within their power to demonstrate someday a quality of achievement that will be rewarded when milestones are reached.

The State of North Carolina has developed an incentive-pay program that has not addressed most of the fundamental measurement and comparability problems, but its experiences are nevertheless instructive (Jarrett, 1981). It essentially ignores interagency competition and comparisons by restricting reviewers' attention to each individual operation's performance against its own past record. It allows up to 25 percent of demonstrated savings to be retained and divided among a unit's employees. Participation is voluntary, and agencies that do not deal in tangible products have generally declined. Dealing only with small units (ten in 1980–81, employing about 880 persons) and only with those that have easily measured outputs, the reviewers still have had difficulty defining allowable costs and documenting outputs. Such detailed scrutiny was apparently felt to be necessary by the reviewers, but it is clear that the detail with which they have been involved could not be maintained if the reviewing program were to be expanded to encompass most of the state's agencies, including those without readily measurable outputs. Thus, the North Carolina plan, which is widely heralded, reveals severe obstacles: It appears biased toward agencies whose outputs are easily measured, it has not dealt with the possibility that the legislature may penalize the more efficient organizations, and its implementation would quickly bog down if attempted on a very large scale.

In developing the incentive power of the purse, we are plowing new fields. Technical considerations of cost measurement and output identification are vitally important if the review process is to be fair, but these considerations must not be allowed to sink the review process in mire. The fundamental question, then, becomes clearer: How much and what kind of measurement is necessary in order for the reviews and recommendations to be perceived as fair? This is as much a social as a technical question, for the respect that the officials who are reviewed have for those who exercise final judgments about relative quality of effort is probably a key factor in determining how much and what kind of measurement must be done.

A promising avenue to explore is the possibility of some sort of peer evaluation in developing the necessary judgment. Schultze (1970), for example, has proposed the use of peer review panels in comparing the performance of hospitals for incentive rewards. Numerous studies have revealed the aspirations of public employees to be professionals, and the concept of peer review of performance is one of the basic elements of professionalism. For the process to be perceived as fair, it is probable that those who are reviewed must feel that their reviewers have faced similar managerial problems themselves; this may be the most important underlying reason for peer review. In addition, the process must also be perceived as one in which the reviewers are not only eminently qualified but also free from programmatic bias and political pressure.

One strategy that might satisfy such exacting criteria as these would be to appoint a special commission to oversee the review process, to obtain information from all possible sources (including budget analysts and the agencies themselves), and to render final recommendations. The review commission members could be chosen from among the best of senior career servants and could serve under appointment and service conditions not unlike those applicable to the U.S. Comptroller General. They might even be given control over some appropriated funds, to be distributed directly to agencies and their employees.

Direct control over incentive-pay funds could enhance the prestige and influence of the incentive review effort, and this influence would be vital in the delicate relationship that the commission and its staff would have with executive and legislative budget officials. In addition to directing or recommending the distribution of incentive funds, the commissioners would have to work closely with budgeters to protect against subsequent cuts of agencies found to be most cost conscious. Eventually, they might even have to suggest moving program responsibilities from one agency to another. If the incentive power of the purse is to be developed to its fullest, then relative changes in the size of agency appropriations should occur, to reward the best performers. At the very least, well-managed agencies should be rewarded with greater administrative discretion, enhanced employment security, employee development opportunities, and so on.

Full exercise of the incentive power, as suggested here, can be expected to create political difficulties. If an agency fares less well in budget competition as a result of unfavorable evaluations, its constituents can be expected to press for additional funds anyway. If the political leadership routinely provides such funds without first requiring demonstrated proof of improved performance, then pervasive disincentives will triumph. If the political leadership attacks or stacks the review apparatus it has created, then the reform may continue in law, but not in spirit or in intended effect. If political leaders explain the reasons for their actions to the leaders of the constituent groups, however, and invite them to assist the political leadership in pressing agency management for reforms, then the incentive power may yet triumph. Incentives can ultimately be fashioned only by those who hold the power.

Rewarding Agency Inputs to the Budget Process

Considering how the problems of measurement and political will can confound the incentives approach, budgeters would be well advised to begin the approach by first rewarding agencies for good-quality inputs to the budget process itself. It has been observed that budget reviews are vitally dependent on the quality of information provided by the agencies. Improving the quality of such information may improve the quality of decisions. Furthermore, the budget staffs themselves are in a position to make reasonably sound judgments about the relative quality of information provided and can adjust their budget recommendations to give something of a comparative advantage to agencies that provide good information.

To start, a relative advantage can be created for agencies whose requests are justified through sound foresight efforts. Agencies can be induced through budgetary incentives to think more systematically about trends in client populations, about problems that might be averted with sound programmatic efforts, and about opportunities for long-term economies through investment in new technologies. If analysts and decision makers would respond more favorably to agencies whose requests reflect anticipatory and investment-oriented justifications, then others might be prompted to follow those agencies' example.

Similarly, favorable budget recommendations might be withheld from agencies that fail to monitor and evaluate their outputs conscientiously and to submit such data with their budget requests. The determination of what constitutes a conscientious effort is admittedly judgmental, with all the accompanying problems mentioned previously; nevertheless, it is within a budget office's power to make such judgments and to withhold favorable responses from agencies that fail to submit acceptable evaluation data. If that office can convince the agencies that its judgment is fair, and if it can convince the political leadership to support its recommendations, then, a positive framework of incentives can emerge. Finally, however, only the political leadership can determine whether sufficient political will exists to make management through budgetary incentives succeed.

References

Anton, T. J. *The Politics of State Expenditures in Illinois*. Urbana: University of Illinois Press, 1966.

Bish, R. L., and R. O. Nourse. *Urban Economics and Policy Analysis*. New York: McGraw-Hill, 1975.

Boynton, R. P., W. A. Medina, and L. S. Covello. "How You Always Wanted to Manage But Were Not Allowed to Try." *The Bureaucrat*, 1977, 6, 131–151.

Bryant, S., and R. Joyce. "Federal Productivity Lessons." *The Bureaucrat*, 1984, 13, 42–47.

Contino, R., and R. M. Lorusso. "The Theory Z Turnaround of a Public Agency." *Public Administration Review*, 1982, 42, 336.

Davis, O., M. Dempster, and A. Wildavsky. "A Theory of the Budgetary Process." *American Political Science Review*, 1966, 60, 530.

Part II

Performance-Based Budgeting

Introduction

This section probes several issues related to performance-based budgeting, often covered in the larger management literature. In one set of articles we delve into strategic planning and management, looking at what it is in Denhardt's "Strategic Planning in State and Local Governments." We also develop issues related to the fit of strategy with the public sector in the article "Strategy, Values, and Productivity" and in Nutt and Backoff's "Strategy for Public and Third-Sector Organizations." Finally, Poister and Streib reveal current practice and cases in "Strategic Management in the Public Sector: Concepts, Models, and Processes."

In a second set of articles, performance management and budgetary analysis issues come to the fore. Bart Hildreth looks at the link between productivity analysis methods and traditional financial disclosure goals in "Applying Professional Disclosure Standards to Productivity Financial Analyses." Burstein, in "Designing Appropriate Control Mechanisms for Managing Performance in the Federal Sector," relates management and financial control to managing performance in a specific federal context. Haven's classic article on the role of evaluation in budgeting, "Integrating Evaluation and Budgeting," then follows. Next, Gloria Grizzle explores the link between performance measures and budgeting in "Performance Measures for Budget Justifications: Developing a Selection Strategy." Wisniewski conducts a cost-benefit analysis on contracting out—an approach to competition—in "Analyzing the Contracting-Out of Government Services: Relevant Cost-Benefit Considerations." Still another approach, privatization, receives a surprising treatment in Miranda and Lerner's "Bureaucracy, Organizational, Redundancy and the Privatization of Public Services." Brown and Pyres describe the importance of the Government Accounting Standards Board's pursuit of performance measure disclosure in financial statements in "Service Efforts and Accomplishments Reporting: Has Its Time Really Come?" Ammons probes the motive underlying one approach to instilling competition in government in "A Proper Mentality for Benchmarking." Finally, Frederickson's "Can Public Officials Be Said to Have Obligations to Future Generations?" analyzes the generational dimension of performance analysis and management, an issue of growing concern, particularly in budgeting and taxation.

In a third set of articles, we broach an extremely complicated and emotional issue—pay for performance in government. Individual incentives have a central role to play in the success of most conceptual schemes related to performance. Yet, as Halachmi and Holzer argue in "Merit Pay, Performance Targeting and Productivity," such plans, while very difficult, have large possibilities; seemingly insurmountable obstacles can be overcome if the emphasis moves to "the employee's relative needs for power, affiliation, and achievement." Kellough and Lu, in "The Paradox of Merit Pay in the Public Sector: Persistence of a Problematic Procedure," look at the persistence of the pay-for-performance proposals, given its difficulties and the lack of evidence of its working as designed in public organizations. Finally, Ingraham looks at the recent experience with pay for performance in the United States and abroad in "Of Pigs in Pokes and Policy Diffusion: Another Look at Pay-for-Performance" and predicts how this approach will evolve.

Section II.A

STRATEGY

13

STRATEGIC PLANNING IN STATE AND LOCAL GOVERNMENT

Robert B. Denhardt

While strategic planning has become an essential part of the management of most private corporations and even many federal agencies, few state and local governments have yet become involved in such activities. Several reasons account for this situation, ranging from the traditional political discomfort with planning activities to recent cutbacks in planning and analysis capabilities of many agencies. However, given the success of strategic planning in the private sector, more and more state and local leaders are expressing interest in planning programs. Indeed, planning activities have recently been initiated in cities, regional governments, state agencies, and university systems (Eadie 1983; Jensen 1982; Preble 1982).

This article is written as a guide for managers who would like to know more about strategic planning and who anticipate beginning a planning program in their community or agency. We will begin with a basic definition of strategic planning, especially noting differences between strategic planning and the more familiar long-range planning. Next we will examine circumstances under which strategic planning can be effectively utilized in state and local government. Finally, we will construct a generalized model of the strategic planning process—who is involved, what they do, and how they do it.

This general guide is not comprehensive, nor do the processes outlined fit all situations readily. Indeed, a considerable variety of approaches to

1985. Strategic planning in state and local government. Denhardt, Robert B. **State and Local Government Review** 17 (1): 174–179.

strategic planning exists and planning processes should always be carefully adapted to local circumstances. However, with these caveats in mind, we can review some basics of strategic planning so managers can make more informed decisions about whether to undertake such an activity and if so how to proceed.

Development of Strategic Planning

A number of writers have commented on the rapidity of the social and technological changes we are now experiencing and on the turbulence and complexity which such changes generate (Toffler 1980; Naisbitt 1982). In an effort to recognize and respond to such changes, many private corporations began programs in the 1960s and 1970s to systematically plan for their future development. The success of these programs is now confirmed by the fact that more than half of publicly traded companies use strategic planning in some form. Studies show that companies employing strategic planning are more successful than their competitors and that those that begin strategic planning become more successful than they were before using such planning (Andrews 1980; Glueck 1980).

What is strategic planning? A dictionary definition indicates that military strategy, the obvious root of the term, is the art of deploying one's forces so as "to impose upon the enemy the place, time and conditions for fighting preferred by oneself" (Cannon 1968). Strategy suggests that actions taken today be designed to enable us to face the future on our own terms, not on those imposed from the outside. As Peter Drucker (1974) puts it, the relevant question is not simply what shall we do tomorrow? but rather what shall we do today in order to get ready for tomorrow?

Strategic planning activities are designed to help members of an organization match their objectives and capabilities with the anticipated demands of the environment so as to produce a plan of action that will assure that their objectives are achieved. In his helpful book *Strategic Management and Business Policy*, William F. Glueck (1980, 9) points out that a strategy is a plan that is unified (ties all the parts of the enterprise together), comprehensive (covers all aspects of the enterprise), and integrated (all parts are compatible with one another and fit together well). Similarly Robert Shirley (1982, 262) writes that "strategy (1) defines the relationship of the total organization to its environment and (2) gives guidance to administrative and operational activities on an ongoing basis."

Strategic Planning/Long-Range Planning

Strategic planning may be differentiated from more familiar long-range planning activities in several ways. Traditional planning activities are concerned primarily with establishing goals or objectives for performance over a period of time, but less concerned with specific steps that should be undertaken to achieve those goals. Strategic planning, on the other hand, implies that a series of action steps will develop as part of the planning process and that these will guide activities of the organization in the immediate future. Strategic planning takes the future into account, but in such a way as to improve decisions in the present.

A second way in which strategic planning differs from long-range planning is its attention to environmental complexity. The organization is not assumed to exist in a vacuum, but rather both the organization's objectives and steps to achieve those objectives are seen in the context of the resources and constraints presented by the organization's environment.

A final distinction between the two types of planning is that strategic planning, especially in the public sector, is a process that must involve many individuals at many levels of the organization. As most managers know quite well, effective changes in organizational practices are most readily accomplished with the involvement of all those who will be affected by the change. This general rule is especially applicable to those changes generated through a process of strategic planning.

Strategic Planning in the Public Sector

In considering the use of strategic planning, state and local officials should keep in mind several important circumstances unique to planning in the public sector. Among these are the following: (1) beginning with the postwar fear of a (presumably socialist) "planned economy," a fear of governmental planning has long existed, (2) the public has properly been wary of the tendency of bureaucratic organizations, including government agencies, to be concerned with their own continuance rather than with the public benefit, and (3) many governments and government agencies, faced with budgetary reductions, have reduced or eliminated planning and analysis staffs.

On the other hand, the reasons for public organizations to undertake strategic planning efforts are many—to give clarity and direction to the organization, to choose from among competing goals and activities, to cope with expected shifts in the environment, and to bring together the thoughts and ideas of all participants in the work of the organization. Most importantly, planning activities in the public sector provide an opportunity for widespread substantive involvement of leaders and citizens in defining the direction of the community or the agency as it moves into the future, thus building trust and commitment. However, communities or agencies will want to consider several questions before beginning a strategic planning program.

Is Strategic Planning Appropriate?

Managers may wonder if such activities are appropriate for their jurisdictions or their agencies. Certainly precedents for such work at all levels of government are now being established. Many federal, state, and local agencies have begun strategic planning programs over the past several years. Moreover, they have been recently joined by jurisdictions such as cities, counties, and school districts. The key seems to be that any organization is a candidate for strategic planning if by allocation of resources it can significantly influence either the formulation or the implementation of public policy.

Is Strategic Planning Worth the Costs?

Many managers question whether strategic planning is worth the costs—in terms of consultant fees, research and data analysis, and time away from other duties. While costs of planning can vary tremendously depending on the extent of the work undertaken, in all cases costs will be incurred. The best gauges for assessing these costs would seem to be two questions: Is it likely that a careful planning effort would lead to reduced operating costs or increased productivity over the long run? And, what might be lost to the organization in the absence of a more comprehensive and integrated approach to the future?

This latter question has become increasingly important to those in local governments who now realize that they stand in a competitive position with respect to other communities in attracting industry, providing amenities, and maintaining the population base. The issue, however, must be treated differently when planning is being considered by an administrative agency such as a state government department. While strategic planning might put such an agency in a better competitive position with respect to attracting resources from the executive or legislature, this clearly should *not* be the purpose of a strategic planning effort. Rather the agency should use strategic planning to involve all important "stakeholders" in an assessment of the unit's work and the possibilities for improvements in its services (Ackoff 1981). Such a process may indeed lead to requests for further funding, but it may also suggest ways of more effectively utilizing existing resources or even ways the agency might reduce the scope of its activities.

When Is the Right Time for Strategic Planning?

Managers may question whether the "time is right" for planning activities because of budgetary uncertainties. The argument seems to be that planning can't take place without more certain information about funding levels. I would argue exactly the opposite—that planning is most essential in times of uncertainty, for these are exactly the times when you most need to be in control of your own destiny. Times of uncertainty do not mitigate the need for planning efforts; they intensify that need.

A related argument voiced by managers in the public sector is that periodic changes in political leadership make planning more difficult than in private industry. This concern can be answered in several ways. First, managers in the private sector are held perhaps even more accountable than those in the public sector. Compare the industrial manager who must face a quarterly or an annual report to the elected political leader who must face the voters every four years. Second, managers in business change periodically just as they do in the public sector. In such transitions, planning can provide a new sense of continuity. Even when the new leadership wishes to change the directions specified in an earlier planning effort, such changes can be made with greater clarity and can be aimed more readily toward critical concerns. In this way, strategic planning may improve the general quality of public dialogue.

Is Strategic Planning Consistent with Participatory Process?

Managers in the public sector may wonder whether strategic planning efforts are consistent with their commitment to democratic or participatory processes. Here lies the most significant difference between strategic planning in the public and private sectors. While planning in the private sector may involve many people throughout an organization, it remains centered and directed at the top, for it is there that the private interests of the firm are most clearly articulated. In the public sector, however, every effort must be made to involve significantly all those who play an important role in the jurisdiction or the agency. For example, a local government planning effort should involve not only elected leadership and city staff, but also many others with a stake in the outcome—unions, neighborhood associations, chambers of commerce, civic organizations, etc. Similarly, a planning effort conducted by a state government agency should involve persons from all levels of the organization, members of constituent groups, elected officials, persons from other agencies and other levels of government, and representatives of the general citizenry. Strategic planning in the public sector must be a highly participatory process, but this participation opens the possibility of building new understanding among various groups about the work of the organization. Many communities that have engaged in strategic planning have found that the process brought various groups together in a way not previously possible. Strategic planning may be undertaken, therefore, to achieve both direction and commitment.

Starting Strategic Planning

Obtaining a Consultant

Assuming that a decision is made to start strategic planning in a community or agency, what ingredients must be brought together to begin? Once a firm commitment has been made by the top management, most public organizations, lacking an ongoing planning staff, employ an outside consultant to guide or facilitate the strategic planning process. Such consultants may be located either through a major management consulting firm or a university department of public administration.

In any case, the consultant should demonstrate both expertise and experience in *public sector* planning activities. As with any consultant, the manager should be certain the person hired is familiar with local or state government administration and able to interact effectively with government officials. It should be remembered that, in order to build internal commitment to the eventual plan, the consultant should only *guide* the planning process, not develop the plan. Be wary of prospective consultants who imply they will "do a plan" for you.

Consultant costs are difficult to specify given the variety of tasks involved in any particular situation. For example, arrangements must be made to provide a significant research capability, either through the consultant, a local university, or the organization staff. While the scope of the research needed will vary depending on the organization and range of its interests, some research will be needed and cannot simply be assumed to be available. If the consultant is expected to complete the research as well as to design the process and facilitate its implementation, not only will costs be increased but different skills and capabilities will be required. Remember that organizations are notorious for letting planning slide while giving attention to seemingly more pressing matters. A good consultant, hired for the duration of the planning and involved in most major aspects of the project, can provide a special impetus to keep the process going.

Outlining the Planning Process

Once the consultant has been retained, usually the administrative leader working with the consultant will construct an outline of the planning *process* itself. Who will be involved? What will be the scope of the project? Which groups will participate through the entire process? Which groups will be involved in only some portions of the process? How long will the planning effort be expected to take? What will be the expected outcomes (planning documents, lists of action steps, etc.)? What assurance is there that the plan will be implemented? (You will likely find that the first few of these questions can be answered fairly readily; the others should properly be answered only as the community or agency moves into the process itself.)

Obviously, the planning process can proceed in a number of different ways. However, in most cases, a central planning group will form the nucleus of the planning effort, working most closely with the consultant to obtain information and make commitments to various new directions. In a local community, this group would include the city's political leadership, representatives of the city administration (for example, the city manager), representatives of business, industry, labor, members of neighborhood associations, etc. For a state agency, on the other hand, the major planning group would be comprised of the agency director, managers from the next organizational level below, and selected program directors. In either case, the planning group would be specifically involved in working through various components of the planning process.

In making determinations of direction and objectives, the planning group will seek the broadest information possible. Indeed, the organization of the planning effort should be directly related to efforts to obtain the most complete information and the most creative ideas about the organization. In some cases, at either the local or state level, subgroups or task forces may be formed, even at the lowest levels of the organization, to discuss the direction of the organization and how the various parts of the organization might work together more effectively (Ackoff 1981, 67). In other cases, citizen surveys or public forums may be used to generate input from community groups about the directions the community or the organization should take. Throughout the process, techniques such as brainstorming, expert panels, nominal group studies, or simulations may be employed to help generate better information about the future. Similarly, techniques such as organizational mirrors or team building may be used to help those involved in the planning effort work together more effectively (Preble 1982).

Defining the Scope of Strategic Planning

Just as the organization of the planning effort will vary, so will the scope of the project. Some communities, for example, may choose very early to restrict their planning activities to priority issues, for example, economic development. Others may wish to focus on relationships among the many services offered by the government. In agencies of state government, some may urge improvements in services to clients, while others may prefer to focus on issues of internal organization and management. At whatever level of government, a likely choice will be to develop a comprehensive and integrated plan giving some attention to all these areas and more.

The time required for planning must be considered. The major event in most planning activities is a strategic planning session attended by members of the planning group and facilitated by the consultant. This session need be no longer than a day or two (preferably in a retreat setting). However, both preceding and following that meeting are a number of activities designed, on the one hand, to get the most complete and accurate picture of the organization and the aspirations of its members, and, on the other, to specify in action terms how the plan will be implemented. The length of these activities will vary considerably depending on the history and maturity of the agency, the type of research currently available, and capacity and experience of the planning group members in working with one another. For a small community or agency, 3 to 6 months may suffice; for a larger community or agency, 9 to 12 months may be required.

Concerns of the Planning Group

Once it has been brought together, the planning group will want to give its attention to four primary concerns: (1) the mission or objectives of the organization, (2) an assessment of the environment in terms of both opportunities and constraints, (3) an examination of the organization's existing strengths and weaknesses, and (4) the values, interests, and aspirations of those important to the organization's future. Consideration of these issues will lead to the development of several strategic alternatives, perhaps stated as scenarios for the future, and to the choice of a particular direction in which the organization should move. Finally, a set of action steps or implementation items will be developed to indicate what must be done immediately to put the organization in the proper position to face the future most effectively (Porter 1981).

Organizational Objectives

Arriving at a concise yet inclusive statement of the *objectives of the organization* is a difficult step in the planning process. While most organizations have a general sense of their mission, questions often arise which cannot be readily answered in terms of stated objectives. Having specific goals, however, provides an identity for the organization, as well as guidelines for future decisions, and a standard against which specific actions can be measured. Since arriving at a set of objectives may imply certain strategies to be detailed later, a great deal of care should be taken to consider alternative approaches to the organization's goals. A statement of mission, for instance, might indicate whether a city wishes to seek a broad industrial base or focus on particular types of businesses, such as tourism or high tech industries. Similarly, a university mission statement might indicate whether the institution seeks a broad range of programs in all areas or a limited number of exceedingly high quality programs. The objectives statement of a state agency might comment on its desired range of clientele, its responsiveness to changes in the environment, or the quality of its service. If there is doubt or debate about such items, however, they should be carried forward as elements of strategy to be considered later.

Environmental Analysis

After developing a statement of objectives or mission, the planning group should move to an *analysis of the environment* within which the organization operates. Such an assessment would likely include legal and political considerations, social and cultural trends, economic circumstances, technological developments, and, where appropriate, the competitive or "market" position of the organization. In each area, an effort would be made to show both how the environment looks at present and how it is likely to change in the future. From such an assessment, the group can determine the opportunities and constraints which the environment presents now and will present in the future and can also begin to identify possibilities for reducing constraints and extending opportunities.

One interesting way to approach the relationship between mission and environment is to examine the implicit assumptions upon which the organization currently seems to be operating. Even without a specifically formulated strategy, organizations appear to follow certain guidelines or "implicit" strategies (Mintzberg 1978, 935). It is often instructive to identify the existing strategy, even if implicit, and then to ask upon what assumptions about the environment that strategy rests. Having examined the assumptions upon which existing strategy is based, the planning group can then more readily assess the impact of changes in the future.

One environmental concern of special importance to public organizations is the relationship between one's own organization and the many other organizations with which the "focal" organization interacts. The formulation and implementation of public policy today is marked by complex networks of organizations interacting both vertically (federal, state, and local) and horizontally (public works, fire, etc.). What happens in the state legislature or in the state's administration of a block grant program is of great importance to cities; similarly, the administration of nearly any state agency requires coordination with other agencies in the state. For this reason, taking into account the current status and likely development of those organizations with which the focal organization interacts is of special importance.

Existing Capabilities

At this point, the planning group can turn its attention inside, to assess the organization's *existing capabilities,* its strengths and its weaknesses. Such an analysis should obviously be as forthright and as inclusive as possible, taking into account the financial resources of the community or agency (including changing patterns of funding), the human resources of the organization (including its political and managerial strengths and weaknesses), the operation of both its technical and its organizational systems, and the quality of its work. This assessment of the organization's capabilities should be made in terms which relate as directly as possible to the previously stated mission of the organization. For example, an agency involved in design and construction development might want to consider the age and condition of its facilities, the number and abilities of its architects and engineers, the number and frequency of design projects, and the standing of the unit among other similar organizations. Again, an examination of the strengths and weaknesses of the organization should be accompanied by some attention to programs that might significantly improve the capabilities of the organization in one or more areas.

Standards of Organizational Leaders

A final step in preparation for the development of strategic alternatives is to take into account the *values, interests, and aspirations* of those who will guide the organization into the future. Clearly, different people will respond to the same environmental and organizational analysis in different ways. In business, for example, some will be perfectly satisfied with the security of a stable market share, while others will be willing to take greater risks in the hope of greater payoffs. Leaders will vary in terms of their creativity, their energy, and their commitment to the organization. Yet in order for a plan to be effectively implemented, it will need to reflect their concerns and their interests.

At this point, the planning group can move to formulate alternative strategies for the future. These strategies can take several forms; however, one useful way to proceed is to draw up alternative "scenarios of the future," indicating what the organization might look like 5 years, 10 years, or 20 years into the future. Such scenarios should indicate new directions the organization might take; pessimistic, realistic, and optimistic interpretations of its future; and factors likely to be most influential in establishing these future patterns. In most cases, it is helpful to develop more than one scenario, then use these as competing viewpoints from which to debate the merits of various alternatives. From a thorough discussion of the scenarios, one or more strategies will emerge. The strategy should be chosen that most effectively moves the organization toward its mission, given environmental opportunities and constraints, organizational strengths and weaknesses, and the values, interests, and aspirations of the leadership.

Specific Action Steps

One final step remains—the translation of strategies into plans for action. As we noted earlier, strategic planning is of greatest benefit where it can help groups make immediate decisions in light of their future impact. For this reason, a final step in the strategic planning process is to arrive at a series of specific action steps to be taken in the near future, that is, in the next six months, the next year, or the next two years—who does what, when, and to what effect. These steps, which may detail new policy positions or new organizational processes, will form a new action agenda for the community or the agency. This point cannot be over-emphasized. Strategic planning is only helpful as it provides guidance for the day-to-day operation of the city or the agency. To be useful, planning must ultimately be action oriented.

Conclusion

Planning is certainly not something new to those in public organizations. Indeed, in the late 1930s, Luther Gulick began his acronym outlining the functions of the executive (POSDCORB) with "P" for "planning" (1937, 13). Over the years, many political leaders and managers have prided themselves on their success in intuitively predicting the future and moving in the right direction. Today's strategic planning simply carries forth that same effort in a more systematic and inclusive fashion. This last point is of considerable importance: strategic planning produces both a plan and a process. While the plan is of obvious importance, many have found that the process of planning itself, especially a process that is broadly based in the community or the agency, is of equal importance. As various groups participate in the planning effort, they will come to realize both the opportunities and constraints faced by the organization and they will develop a greater sense of commitment to the organization's future. This alone may be of great significance.

References

Ackoff, Russell L. 1981. *Creating the corporate future.* New York: John Wiley and Sons.

Andrews, Kenneth R. 1980. *The concept of corporate strategy.* Homewood, Ill.: Richard D. Irwin.

Cannon, J. Thomas. 1968. *Business strategy and policy.* New York: Harcourt, Brace & Co.

Drucker, Peter F. 1974. *Management.* New York: Harper and Row.

Eadie, Douglas C. 1983. Putting a powerful tool to practical use: The application of strategic planning in the public sector. *Public Administration Review* 43, no. 5 (September-October): 447–52.

Glueck, William F. 1980. *Strategic management and business policy.* New York: McGraw-Hill.

Gulick, Luther. 1937. Notes on the theory of organization. In *Papers on the science of administration,* 1–46. Edited by Luther Gulick and L. Urwick. New York: Institute of Public Administration.

Jensen, Daniel R. 1982. Unifying planning and management in public organizations. *Public Administration Review* 42, no. 2 (March-April): 157–62.

Mintzberg, Henry. 1978. Patterns in strategy formation. *Management Science* 24, no. 9 (May): 934–48.

Naisbitt, John. 1982. *Megatrends.* New York: Warner Books.

Porter, Michael E. 1981. The contributions of industrial organization to strategic management. *Academy of Management Review* 6, no. 4 (October): 609–20.

Preble, John F. 1982. Anticipating change: Futuristic methods in the public sector. *American Review of Public Administration* 16, no. 2/3 (Summer/Fall): 139–50.

Shirley, Robert C. 1982. Limiting the scope of strategy: A decision-based approach. *Academy of Management Review* 7, no. 2 (April): 262–68.

Toffler, Alvin. 1980. *The Third Wave.* New York: Morrow.

14

STRATEGY, VALUES, AND PRODUCTIVITY

Gerald J. Miller
Jack Rabin
W. Bartley Hildreth

Recent scholarship on financial management in the public sector has advocated that strategy—the use of strategic planning and management techniques—can be used to improve public-sector productivity. Strategy provides a method through which a financial manager analyzes the larger organizational environment in order to detect patterns and trends and gain insight that enables the manager to predict opportunities for the reduction of risk in managing cash, using debt wisely, and generally making more productive use of scarce tax and revenue resources.

The use of strategy heralds a reconsideration of values. This paper argues that the values underlying strategy tend to differ in many ways from the values now prevailing in the profession of government financial management. For strategy to be useful, the concept and its advocates must confront the problems for productivity in changing value systems, however small these changes may be, as well as the inherent productivity problems when strategy is used in a governmental, as opposed to a private-sector, setting.

1987. Strategy, values, and productivity. Miller, Gerald J., Jack Rabin, and W. Bartley Hildreth. **Public Productivity and Management Review** 43 (Fall): 81–96.

245

This paper is organized into four sections. The first section outlines the position of the advocates of strategy. The second section suggests the values that may lie behind a broader definition of strategy. The third section uses legal, empirical, and deductive work to give one reading of the values that underlie current government financial management. The fourth and last section argues that current values and the values underlying strategy conflict when the future productivity of the public service is the criterion used for comparison.

Strategy's Approach to
Government Financial Management

The primary vehicle for our examination of the values underlying strategy comes from the establishment organ of the government financial management community, *Government Finance Review,* the journal of the Government Finance Officers' Association, the largest and best-known professional organization of people involved in public financial management in the United States. The explication by Wetzler and Petersen (1985) follows lines typical of those in the general, proselytizing literature on strategy (Rabin, Miller, and Hildreth, in press) as well as the by now familiar litany that has historically preceded normative reform. That is, past management efforts and techniques have been appropriate for their times, but they are not appropriate for present times, which are different. Strategy is planning and analysis, and both are good and fit to deal with the problems of present times. Strategy's track record so far is generally mixed, but the bad marks come from incompetent or inappropriate application. Strategy is a, if not the, serious effort needed, but profound change comes with the acceptance of strategy as a mode of operation, change that might alter organization and procedure, to say nothing of politics.

But, is this reform, strategy, indeed unique? Is it indeed a new way of looking at management work? The development of strategy is not a short history, although its recent rise to prominence suggests otherwise. After all, strategy has always been a management device for war making.

Wetzler and Petersen (1985) recognize another connection with the past in their outline of the steps in the strategic planning process. That is, their model of strategy, which is shown in the left column of Table 14.1, closely parallels the basic model of the rational decision-making process, which is shown in the right column of Table 14.1.

Finally, Wetzler and Petersen (1985) use strategy as a springboard to acceptance in government circles of applied microeconomics and finance theory. They argue that strategy can help one to choose between capital markets and internal sources of financing, projects with different rates of return on investment, investments with different levels of risk, and portfo-

TABLE 14.1   A Comparison of a Model of Strategy and a Model of Rational Decision Making

Models of Strategy	*Models of Rational Decision Making*
Examine the environment	Observe the appearance of opportunities and needs in the larger world outside the organization
Assess the current situation	Determine the level of threat or reward
Set goals	Determine the basic long-term goals and objectives of the enterprise
Identify the alternatives	Design the organized activities to administer the enterprise
Analyze and select financial alternatives,	

Sources: Wetzler and Petersen (1985); Chandler (1962, pp. 13–15).

lios of various assets (resource or tax bases). Their model of strategy tends to blend the two basic components of rational decision-making theory and applied microeconomics to advocate an approach to planning and management for finance officers.

The Values Underlying Strategy

The values that seem to underlie Wetzler and Petersen's (1985) model of strategy—those related to rational decision making in general (Fischer, 1980)—do not necessarily underlie all models of strategy. In fact, one model of strategy looks quite different (Greiner, 1983, p. 13): "Strategy is a nonrational concept stemming from the informal values, traditions, and norms of behavior held by the firm's managers and employees—not a rational, formal, logical, conscious, and predetermined thought process engaged in by top executives." If strategy has a great deal to do with organizational culture (Weick, 1985), strategy requires far greater depth of support and development than proselytizers for procedural changes may understand.

While Wetzler and Petersen (1985) hint at the depth of change required, they suggest only the intervention's effects. Greiner's (1983) point differs fundamentally; it seems likely that he would agree with Burgelman (1983, p. 66) that strategy is "the more or less explicit articulation of the firm's theory about its past concrete achievements." This theory has deep roots. Managers in the organization tend to rise through the ranks and, during that time, to develop highly reliable frames of reference that they can use to evaluate strategies and resource allocation proposals (Burgelman, 1983). Wetzler and Petersen (1985) ignore the depth and meaning of the organizational strategy by creating and advocating a replacement for it.

Strategy, if anything, is not a created focus for action, a place to go, or a direction in which to move. A more useful view lies in seeing strategy and planning as internal communication devices (Waterman, 1987). As such, a plan has very little importance except for the information that the process of developing it reveals, as individuals talk and negotiate, opening up new vistas and flagging potential crises or opportunities for the organization and its members. More important, strategy is an emerging manifestation of basic agreements among people in a work organization, agreements that may never be recognized as such. These agreements arise through simple interactions, such as conversations or meetings, in which each person confirms whether the meaning that he or she attaches to objects and processes is similar enough to the meanings that others attach to get through work relations appropriately (Gregory, 1983).

The manifestation of basic agreements appears in a number of symbolic ways. These ways can include procedures, programs, and budgets that routinize and categorize everyone's shared experience in working together. Again, these manifestations appear to be more deeply embedded in organizational life than Wetzler and Petersen (1985) suggest. If anything, strategies serve as manifest culture. As Weick (1985, p. 383) remarks, "culture can substitute for plans more effectively than plans can substitute for culture."

The Values of Government Financial Managers

In what culture do financial managers immerse themselves? The question of culture should be answered broadly, of course, since we are speaking here of a profession and a culture that may both exist in another culture, namely, that of the government organization in which the professional practices. This section examines the general values of government financial managers.

Legal Analysis. The values of government financial managers can be gleaned from the broad group of values defined for them by the law and the courts, especially the law on torts.

One of the values that emerges from this broad group is the role of trustee or fiduciary. The fiduciary relationship (*Robins* v. *Hope,* 57 Cal. 497) is one in which "neither party may exert influence or pressure upon the other, take advantage . . . , or deal . . . in such a way as to benefit himself or prejudice the other except in the exercise of the utmost good faith and with the full knowledge and consent of that other, . . . shrewdness, hard bargaining, and astuteness to take advantage of the forgetfulness or negligence of another being totally prohibited."

Expanding on the trusteeship role, we note that the liability of local, state, and federal public officials (Rabin, Hildreth, and Miller, 1979; Rabin, Miller, and Hildreth, 1980; Miller, 1980–1981; Hildreth and Miller, 1985) has developed in the courts along four major lines, each of which presents ethical rules of conduct for governmental decision making but each of which also serves as the container within which the financial manager's culture develops. These issues are first, liability for intentional deprivation of constitutional rights when acting in bad faith and unreasonably; second, liability for violation of rights specifically outlawed by case law; third, liability for negligent acts that constitute deliberate indifference to constitutional rights; fourth, direct participation or knowing disregard for subordinates' illegal deprivations of rights (Rabin, Miller, and Hildreth, 1981).

Standards arise from these four bases for liability suits. These standards reflect values of the larger polity that public officials represent. The courts, in effect, require public officials to act responsibly, that is, reasonably and with good faith that their actions are constitutional. They must also accept responsibility for knowledge of the law. Moreover, while negligence may perhaps be unavoidable in isolated incidents, it constitutes misconduct when a pattern of practices reveals disregard for constitutional rights or when a particular incident has such grave consequences that it resembles "indifference that can offend 'evolving standards of decency'" (*Estelle* v. *Gamble*, 429 U.S. 308). Finally, as supervisors, public officials have responsibility for the acts that subordinates commit either in their presence or, in some cases, without their prior knowledge if those acts are part of a pattern of prior misconduct and disregard for constitutional rights.

The ethical rules that emerge from liability case law elaborate the notion of fiduciary. That is, liability case law blunts the dehumanizing effects of the administrative state (Rosenbloom, 1987). The law forces officials to recognize the constitutional rights of individuals inside and outside the organization by following the notion that Madison (1937) articulated in *The Federalist*: Preserve liberty and freedom by promoting and maintaining diversity in the population.

Empirical Work. What do financial managers themselves think about the values that underlie what they do? In a survey of almost 850 financial managers serving in various public capacities, we explored three important dimensions to determine the managers' receptivity to strategic action. The first dimension was related to fiduciary responsibility and the perception of openness and vulnerability. Presumably, as the manager becomes more open and vulnerable, the manager becomes less willing to stake everything on a strategic move. The second dimension covered dependency, especially negative dependency—the extent to which actions by other organizations leave choices open to them, whatever the area might be. The third dimension directly probed the manager's understanding of major economic strategy devices and the circumstances under which it was appropriate to use them.

Openness and Vulnerability. We asked managers a series of questions relating to their own indemnification, their employer's willingness to defend them for liability suits, and the availability of insurance to cover losses. The three questions deal directly with the various levels of vulnerability. That is, the employee who is indemnified never faces the problem of liability suits. The employer who is willing to defend the financial manager does not provide indemnification but at least some protection before judgment. Finally, insurance is a backstop for the employee without indemnification who loses a court judgment. Table 14.2 shows the responses of 850 financial management experts to questions relating to indemnification, employer willingness to defend, and insurance protection.

For financial managers, the evidence is quite strong that many are open to the consequences of a liability suit. While the evidence suggests that managers can be held as liable for timid action (Miller, 1987) as they can for overt, even hasty, action that fails to contemplate untoward consequences, vulnerability to suit leads managers to restrict their activities to well-marked paths and well-known methods—hardly the paths or methods expected for strategic action.

Negative Dependence. The ability to act in strategic ways assumes the independence to do so. Mandated programs and spending tend to create problems for strategic actors in state and local government. Diminished discretion inhibits strategy building. Our survey asked managers to articulate the degree to which a major indirect mandate, borrowing by the federal government, inhibited action by the organizations to which they belonged. Table 14.3 tabulates financial managers' reactions to the proposition "The rate of growth of the national debt will affect the financial condition of my employing organization."

Since a large number of the respondents in our sample felt that federal borrowing would have a negative impact on their organizations, we inferred that borrowing has a tendency to create organizational dependency, a negative financial trend in this case. Such a dependency, then, would minimize the effect of a strategic planning and management program.

Willingness to Use Tools of Strategy. Finally, we surveyed respondents about their knowledge of prominent and legal tools of economic development strategy—general obligation bonds, revenue bonds, leasing plans, private-purpose bonds, and advance refunding stratagems—and about their willingness to use these tools. Table 14.4 tabulates the results.

As Table 14.4 shows, the agreement about appropriate tools and uses tends to decline quite amazingly as the conservatism of the method decreases. Thus, general obligation bond borrowings elicit broad agreement.

TABLE 14.2 Openness and Vulnerability

Statement	Strongly Agree	Agree	Moderately Agree	Moderately Disagree	Disagree	Strongly Disagree
Law indemnifies me against suit for actions taken on the job.	88	108	123	134	151	176
My employer will defend my on-the-job actions in court.	284	224	122	53	65	48
My employer's insurance will protect me.	137	133	111	123	107	133
Clients can't pinpoint my role in the bureaucracy.	38	50	64	76	201	368

Source: Study by the authors of attitudes and job attributes of 850 professionals in the field of public budgeting and financial management.

TABLE 14.3   United States Government Borrowing as an Inhibiting Effect

Statement: The rate of growth of the national debt will affect the financial condition of my employing organization.

Response	Number	Percent of Total
Strongly agree	307	37.3
Agree	215	26.1
Somewhat agree	129	15.7
Somewhat disagree	64	7.8
Disagree	61	7.4
Strongly disagree	35	4.2

Source: Study by the authors of attitudes and job attributes of 850 professionals in the field of public budgeting and financial management.

TABLE 14.4   Willingness to Use Tools of Strategic Financial Management

Question: Which of the following instruments do you believe government should or should not use as a long-term financing tool?

Instrument	Government Should Use	Government Should Not Use	Not Familiar
Revenue bonds	701	45	20
General obligation bonds	701	45	28
Leasing	556	113	85
Advance refunding	469	173	116
Private-purpose financing	436	255	59

$N = 824$

Source: Study by the authors of attitudes and job attributes of 850 professionals in the field of public budgeting and financial management.

Indeed, nothing else approaches its level of acceptance. Private-purpose financings had great notoriety at the time when we conducted the survey. Now, this notoriety has given way to codified limits on its use. Yet, the limited capacity to employ the technique underlies a contemporary reading of reaction to the technique.

We understand the empirical findings as indicating that financial managers are buffeted by those who advocate advanced management techniques. Financial managers certainly can tell that they are vulnerable to court action if they do not understand adequately the consequences of their actions. Moreover, conditions outside their control tend to inhibit their ability to take strategic action. Finally, understanding of strategy's tools has its limits, at least in the area of economic development and rehabilitation of the infrastructure. Financial managers are not yet ready to take a chance at having to defend themselves against charges of profligacy.

Inferential Data. Inferential data from a study of the government cash manager's willingness to accept recent financial products, particularly futures and options contracts, provide further evidence on the value base of financial management practice and the potential reaction of financial managers to the values that underlie strategy (Miller, 1998). The futures and options contracts available to government financial cash managers would appear to contribute in important ways to cash productivity, and they have utility primarily as a conservation device. As such, government financial managers might be expected to embrace them willingly. However, both futures and options have met with widespread rejection, because of the profligacy with which these devices are associated. That is, while it is certainly possible to use these contracts to hedge—conserve taxpayers' resources by guarding against rising borrowing costs or falling investment yields—many also use them to speculate. In fact, the notoriety of such contracts derives from the association between futures and options and their use as speculative devices. The recognition that cash managers can pursue either a conservative (hedging) strategy or a risky (speculative) strategy by investing in financial futures creates a very basic problem of understanding financial futures and options.

Futures and hedging also get caught in the trade-off between two of the goals of investment. Guarding the safety of principal has always held the highest rank among public managers' investment goals, and maximizing income has always been a distant second. But, if the goal of guarding safety is taken to its ultimate extreme—not investing to produce interest income at all—the outcome has the very opposite effect of its intention: As the value of money diminishes over time, the principal decreases just as if its safety had been left unguarded. On the other hand, allowing the principal value to erode through interest rate swings by doing nothing violates the very dictum of guarding principal. In fact, risk the value of a portfolio. As a result, the practice of hedging with financial futures, which may seem to be an extremely risky business to the uninitiated, becomes a fairly simple and direct way of doing nothing risky.

The paradox—a conservative strategy is rejected because it seems to be risky, and a risky strategy is accepted because it appears to be conservative—emerges because of various long-lived impressions, coincidences, and problems involved in the symbols attached to this area of financial management. The use of futures has become a sign of speculation by those involved in the market, although the basic futures hedging strategies now in use tend toward conservatism—of ensuring against calamity. Nevertheless, the notion of speculation or of gambling through arbitrage and spread, fueled by scandal in financial markets involving public entities, has recast the symbols affixed to management decisions to create barriers to the quick acceptance of futures as orthodox financial techniques.

Inappropriate Language and Symbols. Beyond the talk of speculation, which can be controlled, and of scandal, which is limited to isolated incidents, there lies an even more important barrier to public-sector acceptance of the financial products discussed in this section: The fiduciary background that influences public cash managers tends to create word associations that blur useful distinctions. This ideological element of financial practice evidently leads some, if not many, in the profession to view all but the safest investments for idle funds as speculation. Thus, state legislatures and city councils and commissions often refuse to give cash managers the leeway they need in order to avoid loss, much less produce investment earnings or gain. Therefore, while the use of financial futures in local government finance gives the cash manager a way of safeguarding potential gain through a very conservative, traditional method of reducing potential losses of principal, the practice finds rare acceptance. The popular literature does not help. Lurid stories on financial futures portray them as the stuff of gamblers. Nevertheless, at least three language and symbol problems stand in the way of acceptance of financial futures: public financial management's emphasis on safety rather than on value, the limited elaboration of risk and loss in the language of public financial management, and the inappropriate and limited guardianship symbol that public financial management upholds.

One major problem is created by the fuzziness that surrounds the very basic notion of what it is that a cash manager should do. Obviously, the goal definition that managers use affects their receptivity to innovative financial products. Two basic conceptual views prevail. Van Horne (1981, p. 328) applies the orthodox private-sector financial management definition of the purpose of cash management to public-sector managers: "A number of studies have shown that many local governments carry cash balances in excess of those necessary for immediate transactions. There is a cost involved in carrying excess cash funds: the loss of earnings forgone on the investment of idle funds in marketable securities." Thus, the cash manager protects against lost opportunities or threats to the value of investments.

In contrast, speaking for the more conservative, fiduciary-oriented government finance officers who are actually involved in the practice of cash management, Boldt (1984, p. 19) states that "the duty of all financial officers, particularly those responsible for the public's money, is to safe-guard the principal first and to maximize income second." The cash manager, in all cases according to Boldt, guards the safety of principal.

Many not very naive observers confide the possible reasons for the emphasis on safety, not value. For some, including organizational theorists, one truism runs that in bureaucracy rules serve as points of comparison so that variance, or more simply error, leads to punishment; in less bureaucratically inclined organizations, rules serve to inspire performance (Gouldner, 1954; Golembiewski, 1965). For the investment manager of a bureaucratic or control-oriented public system, highly structured, less discretionary statutory investment authority increases the specificity of rules; reduces the chance of miscalculation, variance, and error; and therefore decreases the chance of political repercussions for poor performance (Bleakney, 1980).

The high-structure approach places the highest value on the short-term investment performance that managers exhibit. According to Bleakney (1980, p. 719), public-sector cash managers "must constantly be looking over their shoulders at what the public may say about a market decline that temporarily drives down the value of the funds they are managing. . . . In the private sector, aggressive investment managers will generally have the opportunity to explain the dips and valleys in their investment results. If they are doing a good job in the long run, they need not be concerned about short-term deficiencies." While accountability prompts short investment time frames, it also dampens an emphasis on value. Accountability imposes an artificial restriction on investments: "Managers influenced by the prospect of adverse publicity and public criticism tend to opt for the same route" (Bleakney, 1980, p. 720). They disregard ventures that tend toward shorter-term volatility.

The professional language used by financial managers and decision makers reflects inbred attitudes that are both deeply and genuinely felt and thought to be useful. This language has led many involved in public financial affairs to greet financial product innovation with a wary eye. Despite the efforts of many public administration theorists (Methe, Baesel, and Shulman, 1983), the public and private sectors differ in the definition of key terms used in cash management. Two particularly important words, *loss* and *risk*, have altogether different meanings given the context.

First, one view of loss—the only public definition but only one part of the private-sector definition—rests on the notion that something is no longer possessed or is parted with. The other aspect—an important part of the private-sector definition—refers to the failure to take advantage of a potential gain or optimizing situation. The notion of opportunities lost has never gained a hold among public decision makers (Clark and Ferguson, 1983).

Likewise, in corporate financial theory, risk is conceived of as an opportunity that, when exploited, defines gain; it is assumed that this risk affords a corresponding gain (Copeland and Weston, 1979). In the literature on bureaucracy, which informs both public and private sectors, risk refers to the chance of mishap, the avoidance or prevention of which has primacy (Schwartz, 1981). In public administration theory, risk carries ethical connotations, one of the most traditional of which regards risk taking as a violation of a fiduciary relationship to the polity (Lovrich, 1981).

Public-sector and bureaucratic definitions limit the scope of cash management. Thus, the language breeds a passive response to chance and opportunity. Hedging with futures, an active rather than a passive response, never appears to be reasonable to such financial managers, simply because language blinds them to recognition of its merits.

Public financial managers are also mired in role conflict and afflicted by symbols that constrain their acts. Consider three of these clashing sets of roles and symbols. The first and most obvious clash is the clash between the vision of the financial manager as the wise and careful (read *conservative*) steward of government finances and the view that financial innovations, such as futures and options contracts, are nothing more than institutionalized gambling.

Related to the traditional role of guardian of the treasury that most financial managers play is the role of hedger. In a sense, the hedging strategy is one that uses some form of insurance to offset possible losses from a catastrophe. Financial products offer this hedging service, but they also offer the chance of vast financial windfalls through arbitrage and spreading. The chance of a windfall besmirches the hedging image and implants the image of riverboat gambler or the ubiquitous trader waiting for the next hot tip. Ironically, proponents of financial innovation view public managers who do not hedge as speculators because these managers simply gamble with the future.

In many ways, the traditional role of a government financial manager—indeed, of any fiduciary—is the guardian of principal. In many other ways, the modern financial manager must play the role of making the most of scarce revenues in a period of fiscal stress. With financial products, the manager's choice gets a tough test. If the manager chooses not to use futures or options, she or he runs afoul of those who see that additional money must be gained by taxation to replace the funds ravaged by interest rate volatility and time. Should the manager choose to use futures, he or she is thought of as gambling or at least as not being very careful.

Does Strategy Present a Value Conflict for Public Financial Managers?

The model of strategy presented by Wetzler and Petersen (1985) appears to conform to a basic model recognized as rational decision making. That model typically resembles basic components of bureaucracy (Gerth and Mills, 1946; Pfeffer, 1981). Both models tend to promote centralized control; single-value, maximizing choice; and consistency of goals and preferences across situations and individuals.

We argue that Wetzler and Petersen's (1985) model has at least four productivity problems: First, it is not a widely shared view of strategy. Second, it cannot cope with the ethical values that financial managers must obey, particularly those from liability law. Third, it fails to contemplate financial managers' own preferences for strategies. Fourth, it sides with a view of risk that differs from the view held by financial managers.

Whether finance theory and concepts of applied microeconomics apply to public-sector problems or not (Methe, Baesel, and Shulman, 1983), Wetzler and Petersen (1985) believe that finance theory offers hope for financial managers who need it. Yet, the bigger problem lies not in transferring theory but in theory's single-minded insistence on setting a course of action, *one* goal, to stand as a criterion with which every other action is compared.

Wetzler and Petersen (1985) and the strategists have committed themselves to the road in the public sector that leads nowhere. That road—the assumption that agreement will exist long enough to plan—has never failed to surprise its advocates as failure prone, and it has also never failed to show that its advocates are at best idealists and at worse naive (Seidman, 1970).

What is there about public-sector financing that allows recycled reforms to emerge and die? Is there an inelegance in the thinking that allows "circular discovery-neglect-rediscovery sequences that recycle more than they build cumulatively" (Golembiewski, 1969, p. 191)? If the problem in Wetzler and Petersen's (1985) notion of strategy exists anywhere, it may be solved with Selznick's (1957) distinction between organizational engineering and institutional leadership. According to Selznick (1957, p. 137), strategy operates much like engineering; that is, "when the goals of the organization are clear-cut and when most choices are made on the basis of known and objective technical criteria, the engineer rather than the leader is called for." Rather than employing engineering concepts—or applied microeconomics, as in the case here—Golembiewski (1969, pp. 218–219) has argued the need to adapt to unique missions and roles, "to infuse technical structures with value" so that even "technically identical units of organization . . . have distinctive commitments to program, method, or clientele."

Culture embodies the idea that technical structures have value. To implant one culture in another way may be a bit more difficult than Wetzler and Petersen's (1985) argument envisions. In fact, the effort may be quite unproductive, since culture and organization can develop deep structures (White and McSwain, 1983), and at the very least, they operate on the basis of what Weick (1979) calls *double interacts*. Both the notion of deep structure—"individual consciousness . . . through which individuals experience and construe reality in different ways" (White and McSwain, 1983, p. 294)—and the notion of double interacts—the evocation of one person's behavior by another to create basic units of interpersonal influence—lead us to accept the pluralism of organizational life.

The tendency toward centralization that is inherent in rational decision making may also inhere in Wetzler and Petersen's (1985) view of strategy. Their offering may be classic confrontation between basic views of organizational life. The question of the suitability of applied microeconomics to the culture in which public financial managers operate is an open question.

Rational decision making stands as antithesis to Madison's notion of promoting diversity. Bureaucracy, as the foremost promoter of one form of rationality, fundamentally opposes diversity. The law of liability seems to stand on the side of diversity. Thus, the organizational environment of litigous citizens and the courts, as well as the organizational culture, may impede the use of Wetzler and Petersen's (1985) brand of strategy.

Finally, at the level at which we understand public financial theory, the raging controversy over the distinction between control and planning and over the use of hedging devices is analogous. Should we manage to minimize cost given fixed or stable production, or should we encourage production given fixed or stable costs? Theory provides little help (Bozeman and Straussman, 1982; Schick, 1966; Stedry, 1960). However, the resolution of this dilemma, tentative or not, directly affects the paradox of risk taking on which the hedging or no-hedging debate focuses. That is, strategic planning tends to favor hedging, but control tends to discourage it. We suggest that the value base of financial managers favors control: Minimize cost given fixed or stable production. Wetzler and Petersen's (1985) model of strategy must confront this very basic value. In fact, it must confront the entire belief system that financial managers use in their work.

References

Bleakney, T. P. "Municipal and State Pension Plans." In S. N. Levine (ed.), *Investment Manager's Handbook*. Homewood, Ill.: Dow Jones–Irwin, 1980.

Boldt, H. E. "Do You Know the Way to San Jose? Or Would You Like to Invest City Funds in Long-Term Government Bonds?" *Missouri Municipal League Journal*, September 1984, pp. 17–19.

Bozeman, B., and J. D. Straussman. "Shrinking Budgets and the Shrinkage of Budget Theory." *Public Administration Review*, 1982, 42, 509–515.

Burgelman, R. A. "A Model of the Interaction of Strategic Behavior, Corporate Context, and the Concept of Strategy." *Academy of Management Review*, 1983, 8, 61–70.

Chandler, A. D., Jr. *Strategy and Structure: Chapters in the History of the American Industrial Enterprise.* Cambridge, Mass.: MIT Press, 1962.

Clark, T. N., and L. C. Ferguson. *City Money.* New York: Columbia University Press, 1983.

Copeland, T. E., and J. F. Weston. *Financial Theory and Corporate Policy.* Reading, Mass.: Addison-Wesley, 1979.

Fischer, F. *Politics, Values, and Public Policy: The Problem of Methodology.* Boulder: Westview, 1980.

Gerth, H. H., and C. W. Mills. *From Max Weber: Essays in Sociology.* New York: Oxford University Press, 1946.

Golembiewski, R. T. *Men, Management, and Morality: Toward a New Organizational Ethic.* New York: McGraw-Hill, 1965.

Golembiewski, R. T. "The Wages of Methodological Inelegance Is Circularity III: Simon's 'Decision Making' as Intent and Content." In R. T. Golembiewski, W. A. Welsh, and W. J. Crotty, eds., *A Methodological Primer for Political Scientists.* Chicago: Rand McNally, 1969.

Gouldner, A. W. *Patterns of Industrial Bureaucracy.* New York: Free Press, 1954.

Gregory, K. L. "Naive-View Paradigms: Multiple Cultures and Culture Conflicts in Organizations." *Administrative Science Quarterly,* 1983, *28,* 359–376.

Greiner, L. E. "Senior Executives as Strategic Actors." *New Management,* 1983, *1*(2), 11–15.

Hildreth, W. B., and G. J. Miller. "State and Local Officials and Their Personal Liability." In J. Rabin and D. Dodd, eds., *State and Local Government Administration.* New York: Dekker, 1985.

Hinings, C. R., D. J. Hickson, J. M. Pennings, and R. E. Schneck. "Structural Conditions of Interorganizational Power." *Administrative Science Quarterly,* 1974, *19,* 22–44.

Lovrich, N. P. "Professional Ethics and the Public Interest: Sources of Judgment." *Public Personnel Management,* 1981, *10*(1), 87–92.

Madison, J. "The Federalist, No. 10." *The Federalist,* Mead edition. New York: Modern Library, 1937.

Methe, D., J. Baesel, and D. Shulman. "Applying Principles of Corporate Finance in the Public Sector." In J. L. Perry and K. L. Kraemer, eds., *Public Management: Public and Private Perspectives.* Palo Alto, Calif.: Mayfield, 1983.

Miller, G. J. "The Liability of Federal Officials: Administrative Malpractice Policy Before and After *Butz v. Economou.*" *The Bureaucrat,* 1980–1981, *9* (4), 25–32.

Miller, G. J. "The Timid Manager: A Slow-Moving Target for Civil Suits." *Public Administration Quarterly,* 1987, *10* (4).

Miller, G. J. "Will Governments Hedge Interest Rate Risks?" *Public Administration Quarterly,* 1998, 11(3).

Pfeffer, J. *Power in Organizations.* Marshfield, Mass.: Pittman, 1981.

Rabin, J., W. B. Hildreth, and G. J. Miller. "Suing Federal Executives for Damages." *The Bureaucrat,* 1979, *8* (1), 54–56.

Rabin, J., G. J. Miller, and W. B. Hildreth. "The Liability of Public Executives: Implications for Practice in Public Personnel Administration." *Review of Public Personnel Administration,* 1980, *1* (1), 45–56.

Rabin, J., G. J. Miller, and W. B. Hildreth. "Administrative Malpractice Suits: Tort Liability of Public Officials." *Public Personnel Management,* 1981, *10* (1), 119–125.

Rabin, J., G. J. Miller, and W. B. Hildreth, eds. *Handbook on Strategic Planning and Management.* New York: Dekker, in press.

Rosenbloom, D. "Public Administration Liability: Bench Versus Bureau in the Contemporary Administrative State." *Public Administration Quarterly,* 1987, *10* (4).

Schick, A. "The Road to PPB: The Stages of Budget Reform." *Public Administration Review,* 1966, *26,* 243–258.

Schwartz, E. "Inventory, Purchasing, and Risk Management." In J. R. Aronson and E. Schwartz, eds., *Management Policies in Local Government Finance.* Washington, D.C.: International City Management Association, 1981.

Seidman, H. *Politics, Position, and Power: The Dynamics of Federal Organization.* New York: Oxford University Press, 1970.

Selznick, P. *Leadership in Administration.* Evanston, Ill.: Row, Peterson, 1957.

Stedry, A. C. *Budget Control and Cost Behavior.* Englewood Cliffs, N.J.: Prentice-Hall, 1960.

Van Horne, J. C. "Cash Management." In J. R. Aronson and E. Schwartz, eds., *Management Policies in Local Government Finance.* Washington, D.C.: International City Management Association, 1981.

Waterman, R. H. "In Search of Renaissance." *New York Times,* March 31, 1987, p. D2.

Weick, K. E. *The Social Psychology of Organizing.* Reading, Mass.: Addison-Wesley, 1979.

Weick, K. E. "The Significance of Corporate Culture." In P. J. Frost, L. F. Moore, M. R. Louis, C. C. Lundberg, and J. Martin, eds., *Organizational Culture.* Newbury Park, Calif.: Sage, 1985.

Wetzler, J. W., and J. E. Petersen. "The Finance Office as Public Strategist." *Government Finance Review,* April 1985, pp. 7–10.

White, O. F., Jr., and C. J. McSwain. "Transformational Theory and Organizational Analysis." In G. Morgan, ed., *Beyond Method: Strategies for Social Research.* Newbury Park, Calif.: Sage, 1983.

15

STRATEGY FOR PUBLIC AND THIRD-SECTOR ORGANIZATIONS

Paul C. Nutt
Robert W. Backoff

According to Miles et al. (1978) organizations should continuously reexamine their strategy and its fit to the demands posed by the environment. The effective organization aligns its strategy to these demands. In the past decade, considerable research has been devoted to studying how organizations adjust their strategy to changes in the environment. This article continues this tradition, showing how strategic adaptation can be carried out for organizations with public features.

Organizations with public features include many private-nonprofits or third-sector organizations, such as hospitals, trade associations, professional societies, and museums, as well as governmental agencies. According to Bozeman (1987) third-sector organizations have characteristics that make them more like a public organization than a business. Public organizations are similar to the *large* third-sector organizations, which are considered in this article. Nutt and Backoff (1993a) draw on Bozeman's publicness idea and show how public-private differences in markets, constraints on action, aims, amount of authority, authorization to act, accountability, and performance expectations identified by Levine et al.

1995. Strategy for public and third-sector organizations. Nutt, Paul C., and Robert W. Backoff. **Journal of Public Administration Research and Theory** 5 (April): 189–211.

(1976) call for a different approach to strategy and its management for the public and third-sector organization.

This article presents a framework that shows how organizations with public features can carry out strategic adaptation. Building on the work of Miles and Snow (1978) and Acar et al. (1987), the proposed framework offers a typology of strategies that can be used by public and third-sector organizations to cope with the demands that arise from the organization's environment. Using a contingency perspective, environmental features described by need and responsiveness are used to identify appropriate strategies for various types of task environments.

The prescriptions that flow from the framework call for strategic leaders to match responsiveness with the need for action. We describe strategies that balance these factors as an organization moves from low to high levels of action, and we identify ineffective strategies in which these factors lack alignment. We show how negative feedback is produced when an ineffective strategy is used and how adjustments to more effective strategy can be carried out. The framework provides leaders with generic types of strategy that can be used and with ways to evaluate the fit of a strategy to various types of task environments.

The most effective strategy calls for sustaining need recognition and responsiveness at high levels, both internally and externally. When this is possible a *mutualist* strategy should be used. The mutualist strategy offers leaders of organizations with public features a way to deal with the turbulence predicted for the future. Using the concept of a mutualist strategy and the proposed framework, we outline a research program for the study of strategy in organizations with public features. The framework can be applied prescriptively, offering guidelines for organizations with public features to fashion strategy, or descriptively, suggesting ways to promote and sustain effective strategy.

The Political Context of Organizational Strategy

Public leaders work with many actors (e.g., legislatures) to deal with policy issues (e.g., budget) in a variety of substantive areas, such as health and housing (Wildavsky 1969 and 1979a). In this milieu, public opinion is forged from multilateral adjustments in which claims about needs are made by elected officials, legislative bodies, the courts, interest groups, the media, and the public. These claims are used to make needs seem salient, create budget requests, and get political support to deal with needs thought to have priority (Wildavsky 1979b). An agenda for action emerges from incrementalism (Lindblom 1959 and 1975) in which some needs develop good currency. Wildavsky (1965 and 1979a) and others discuss tactics that can be used to make needs seem compelling in order to garner support. In this article, we deal with the response to this activism by organizations with public features, concentrating on strategy development from the organizations' points of view.

An extension of the incremental approach of Braybrook and Lindblom (1963) to strategy development at the organizational level misses important opportunities for leadership. In today's climate, the leaders of organizations such as children's services and libraries are expected to develop new strategic initiatives within broad mandates. The public management literature suggests that leaders are not limited to a bureaucratic strategy in which an organization's initiatives are limited to a strict reading of its mandate (Lewis 1980). These mandates are often broad and call for considerable interpretation, which creates a dilemma: How proactive should a leader become? One response is an entrepreneurial posture, like that of Admiral Hyman Rickover (Hewlett and Duncan 1974) when he promoted the "Nuclear Navy." We attempt to expand on this idea and develop other strategies as well as conditions under which each can be used effectively.

We believe that the tension between incrementalism at the system level and strategic initiatives at the organizational level provides opportunities to take action that promotes the public interest. Under appropriate mandates, leaders can champion a new strategy for their organizations. We offer some prescriptive arguments to support this view of strategic steering for leaders of organizations with public features.

Identifying Strategy Types

Most people who discuss strategy distinguish strategic content (the organization's products/services, markets, etc.) from process, or how the strategic content was created. Description and assessment of organizational strategy (content) have received considerable attention in the private sector strategy literature. Topics such as strategies for declining industries (Harrigan 1980), strategies for dealing with competitive forces and aggressive competitors (Porter 1985; MacMillan 1980), promotion of innovation (Lodahl and Mitchell 1980), and mergers (Reed 1988) have been considered. Typologies have been developed to suggest when to use particular types of strategies. Table 15.1 provides a short list of these typologies, the strategic types considered, and the dimensions that form contingencies used to select among the types. Miles and Cameron (1982) consider domains and identify strategic types of domain offense, domain defense, and domain creation, selecting among the strategies using market orientation and pressure for innovation. Galbraith and Schendel (1983) select between harvest, build, continue, climb, niche, and cashout strategies using level of investment and specialization. Meyer (1982) uses leader attitude to select among experiment,

TABLE 15.1   Contingency Approaches to Selecting a Strategy

Miles and Cameron (1982)	Domain offense, domain defense, domain creation DIMENSIONS: Market orientation and innovativeness
Galbraith and Schendel (1983)	Harvest, build, continue, climb, niche cashout DIMENSIONS: level of investment and specialization
Meyer (1982)	Weather the storm, ignore the storm, experiment DIMENSIONS: Leader attitude
Mintzberg (1978)	Entrepreneurial, adaptive, planning DIMENSIONS: Source of idea
Paine and Anderson (1977)	Adaptive, planning, entrepreneurial DIMENSIONS: Amount of control over desired changes
Harrigan (1980)	Early exit, milk the investment, shrink selectively, hold position, increase investment DIMENSIONS: Amount and timing of investment.
Lawrence and Dyer (1983)	Readaptive, prospector, defender, analyzer DIMENSIONS: Resource scarcity and information scarcity

weather the storm, and ignore the storm strategies. The strategic types offered by Mintzberg (1978), Paine and Anderson (1977), Porter (1985), Harrigan (1980), and Lawrence and Dyer (1983) all call for variations on a theme of economic gain. Each identifies profit from competitiveness as a key consideration. To make such an approach useful for organizations with public features the approach must be adapted to consider the cooperation that is demanded in these settings to enable delivery of services.

Examination of strategy content is comparatively new to the public sector, with only a few notable efforts to date. For example, Rubin (1988) develops interesting strategic types around the leadership posture of a top manager. Weschler and Backoff (1988) trace the evolution of strategy in state government, showing how strategic change occurs over time and with changes in administration and the party in power. These efforts have provided many useful insights but, unlike efforts at the policymaking level, do not provide a contingency perspective that matches strategic types to environmental challenges. This article adapts contingency-based strategic types, developed for the private sector, to public and third-sector organizations.

A framework that has been accepted widely and seems adaptable to organizations with public feature was developed by Miles and his colleagues

Environmental Types

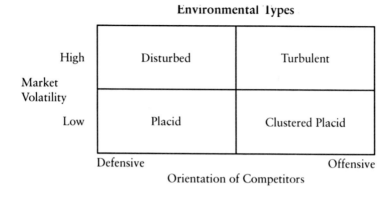

	Disturbed	Turbulent
High	Disturbed	Turbulent
Low	Placid	Clustered Placid

Market Volatility

Defensive — Offensive

Orientation of Competitors

Strategy Types

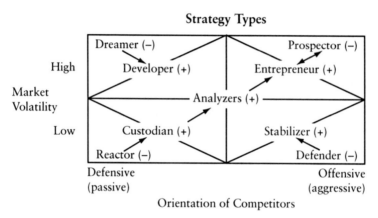

Dreamer (−) Prospector (−)
Developer (+) Entrepreneur (+)
High
Market Volatility
Analyzers (+)
Low
Custodian (+) Stabilizer (+)
Reactor (−) Defender (−)

Defensive (passive) Offensive (aggressive)

Orientation of Competitors

FIGURE 15.1 Matching Strategy to Private Sector Environments

(Miles et al. 1978; Miles and Snow 1978). In their industry studies, four types of strategy called defender, prospector, analyzer, and reactor were identified and aligned to environmental conditions. Drawing on ideas formulated by Emery and Trist (1965) the task environment was defined in terms of market volatility and orientation of competitors, as shown in the top half of Figure 15.1. Strategies were fitted to these environmental types suggesting how domains should be selected, technologies marshalled, and innovations promoted when these four conditions are believed to exist. Defenders protect their domains, prospectors search for new opportunities, and reactors try to delay action until forced. Reactors have no clear strategy and respond to environmental jolts as they are recognized. Analyzers operate as defenders in placid environmental segments and as a prospector in more turbulent environmental segments.

This framework has been applied successfully to study a number of industries and has found that a match of strategic type to environment improves organizational performance (Hambrick 1983). Miles and Cameron (1982) carried out a penetrating, long-term study of the tobacco industry with this model. Shortell et al. (1988) examined profit and nonprofit hospitals as they responded to an environmental jolt that brought price controls. In both cases the researchers gained major insights into ways to successfully carry out strategic adaptation.

Acar et al. (1987) offer a useful extension to the framework. They note that just two of the strategic postures were viable—the prospector and the defender. Analyzers, defined as combinations of other types, match none of the environments. Reactors are found to produce poor results. This leaves the disturbed and placid environment without a viable strategy (see Figure 15.1). Acar et al. also question the defender and prospector types, contending that these strategies seem to overreact to environmental conditions. Different types of strategic options seemed desirable.

In response to these criticisms, a modified framework was proposed in which both a more effective and a less effective strategy were suggested for each type of environment, as noted in the bottom half of Figure 15.1. A *custodian* strategy was suggested for placid environments. Custodians maintain distinctive competencies and nurture markets in which these competencies can be applied (e.g., U.S. Steel). A reactor strategy would be less effective because action merely is delayed. *Stabilizers* respond to a clustered placid environment by taking steps to deal with shifts in demands and market share (e.g., General Motors and Ford in the '70s). The defender becomes committed to fending off competitors and may fail to deal with market volatility. *Developers* take a defensive posture toward a changing market. Competitive moves that can jeopardize market share or erode profits are used to signal when innovation is needed (e.g., IBM's response to competitors in the '80s). The dreamer clings to tradition by vigorously selling nonviable ideas to a changing market (e.g., carbon paper manufacturers after Xerox). *Entrepreneurs* are successful in turbulent markets by taking measured action (e.g., Intel, Disney, and 3M Company). Prospectors react to competitors and weak signals that suggest changes in taste or preference, creating new ideas. This strategy is useful for producing innovations. Switching from an entrepreneurial to a prospector strategy is useful for creating innovations and then assimilating them. A prospector strategy is ineffective when new ideas are created at a rate that makes assimilation difficult.

Strategies for Organizations
with Public Features

Drawing on the work of Harmon (1981), we find that concerns about market volatility and competition should be replaced by need determinations and decisions about organizational responsiveness (Figure 15.2). Responsiveness occurs when someone in a leader role takes steps to change the organization's strategy in response to emergent client needs that seem important. These dimensions, shown in Figure 15.2, have two crucial features. First, the need for both action and responsiveness can have external *and* internal origins. For example, the need for action can be recognized by an organizational leader or by a key person in an oversight body. The perceived need for action grows as calls for action to deal with these needs increase in intensity (Figure 15.2). This is analogous to market volatility in the private sector. Responsiveness also can have internal or external origins. Needs that seem real and are widely recognized create opportunities for someone to respond by taking a leadership role. This is analogous to pressure from competitors in the private sector that prompts a leader to take action (Figure 15.1).

The second feature stems from the notion of enactment (Weick 1979). Both organizational leaders and oversight bodies enact the task environment as needs are recognized. As these perceptions change, public and third-sector organizations will experience periods of high and of lower responsiveness. The perceptual nature of needs distinguishes the public and the third-sector organization from the private organization. In private organizations, facts that characterize the task environment are more available. With good intelligence, the task environment confronting an organization can be identified. In both settings, signals that describe market conditions can be misread and needed action can be deferred.

The responsiveness to perceived needs takes shape as the organization determines its prerogatives. The type of action thought to be useful moves the organization from avoidance to compromise or collaboration, depending on how the leader responds to pressure for action. The need for action that is recognized and for responsiveness thought to be appropriate suggests which of the strategies in the bottom half of Figure 15.2 to use. Successful strategy moves toward and up the diagonal in Figure 15.2, matching the perceived needs of claimants with responsiveness of organizational leaders.

A strategy far off the diagonal in Figure 15.2 is less effective because it fails to balance responsiveness with perceived needs (Nutt and Backoff 1992). When responsiveness goes beyond what an oversight body will authorize or stakeholders will support, the organization becomes politically

Environmental Types

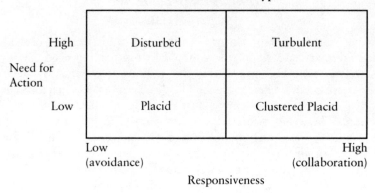

Low
(avoidance)

High
(collaboration)

Responsiveness

Strategy Types

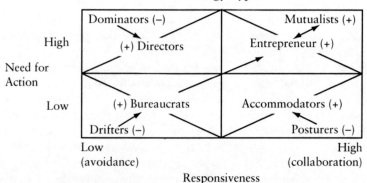

Low
(avoidance)

High
(collaboration)

Responsiveness

FIGURE 15.2   Matching Strategy to Public Sector Environments

exposed. Anyone who objects to what is being done and has connections (e.g., has the ear of someone who serves on the oversight body) effectively can pressure the organization to change its strategy. Also, organizational leaders have short tenures when the demands for action from an oversight body or from important stakeholders are ignored. In both cases, there is considerable incentive to balance perceived needs with responsiveness.

Debates that attempt to dictate what public and third-sector organizations must do are continuously underway. These discussions create various interpretations of needs and how the organization should respond. A more proactive posture by the organization will recognize this turbulent environment and will seek a strategy that calls for collaboration between oversight bodies, internal stakeholders, and other key players.

High Action Strategy

Dominators produce a strategy that takes action with little responsiveness to legitimate authority or to stakeholders, as shown in the upper left quadrant of Figure 15.2. The motivation is to produce discretion in the choice of action and divorce it from accountability. For example, the IRS promulgates rules that create such a strategy. The MPAA (Motion Picture Association of America), which gives to motion pictures the ratings that control viewing by certain age groups, has had a similar impact on film producers. Both organizations use coercive power to define need for action with little accountability. The IRS changes and implements tax rules as it sees fit; it can be challenged only through lengthy and costly litigation. To force film producers to remove what it perceives as objectionable scenes in a movie the MPAA uses the threat of an "R" rating. This rating would keep a film from being seen by those thirteen to seventeen years old, unless accompanied by an adult. This age group is the largest market segment for most films. Film producers let the MPAA censor their products so that they can reach their primary market.

In a disturbed environment, attempts should be made to move a dominator strategy to a director strategy. This change brings an increase in the responsiveness to needs perceived to be significant, as shown in Figure 15.2. A *director* strategy calls for action and accepts some modest formal accountability. For example, the Great Society programs of the Johnson administration created thousands of nonprofit organizations with a social change agenda; these organizations called for roles and missions outside most normal channels of governmental accountability. Organizations with a director strategy include mental health centers, regulatory agencies, and area health education centers (AHECs). Such organizations have been called *paragovernments* because their authority to act seldom has clear legal grounds and their formal accountability is limited to self-appointed boards and rules in the disbursement of federal funds.

Organizations can survive for long periods of time with a director strategy if their task environment allows action without full accountability. A shift in which accountability increases would force movement toward a mutualist strategy, moving toward and up the diagonal in Figure 15.2. The need for such a movement often is signaled by new legislation or a change in the party in power, which creates new missions for public and third-sector organizations. Agencies are called upon to adopt a compromiser or mutualist posture when their environments become turbulent. For example, a state department of education had an oversight board whose members were appointed to six-year terms by the governor. Key people in the department believed that a public school system should insure that its graduates have a basic set of skills. The department interpreted its mandates broadly and took on the task of reforming the state's public school systems with proficiency tests. Rules for high school graduation set minimum levels of proficiency for reading, mathematics, and so forth. The department of education threatened to withhold state funds from school districts that did not adopt these new rules. Each new appointee to the board was indoctrinated by the department staff and the continuing members as to the value of proficiency testing. School districts complained, contending that the department of education had overstepped its authority and used tests that failed to capture the full spectrum of human development. Each complaint was ignored and the argument was made that acting on it would take the department back to the days when it was a low-action and ineffective agency (a drifter strategy).

With the election of a more conservative governor, complaints from school systems increased and were directed toward the governor's office. Legislation was introduced for the purpose of checking what was perceived as an oppressive bureaucracy and enlarging the membership of the oversight board. The governor then appointed to the board people with his reform agenda. The new oversight board initiated studies into the cost of education, looking for ways to cut the state subsidy. Note how the task environment was shifted from disturbed to turbulent, making a director strategy ineffective. To maintain an orientation toward need, a compromiser strategy must replace the director strategy. The department of education had to refocus its energies toward these new mandates. Note how the mandate is more broadly shared under a compromiser strategy, which increases the level of responsiveness and moves the organization toward and up the diagonal in Figure 15.2.

Low Action Strategy

A strategy of minimal action is called a *posture*. Leaders following this approach indiscriminately read every signal to see if a call for action seems warranted, and they make statements about planned responses. These responses never materialize because action is preempted by a preoccupation with reading issues. Such a strategy lacks closure and any sense of priorities, making it less effective than one that couples responsiveness with the true level of need. However, a posture can be an effective strategy when it first raises consciousness and helps to get an important issue on the public agenda.

Some third-sector organizations adopt a posture strategy. Illustrations include AARP, NOW, and NAACP. Organizations that adopt a posture strategy make a list of issues that are brought to the attention of others to deal with. This lack of closure can make the organization seem inconsistent and even irresponsible. The inconsistency stems from ignoring the gap between what is wanted and what can be realized. Issues that pose questions that are irresolvable or resolvable only at prohibitive cost create frustration. The frustration is magnified by the organization's apparent unwillingness to seek solutions, which creates an image of irresponsibility.

Organizations faced with the termination of federal funds often use a posture strategy. The list of unresolved issues that the termination of funding would leave unattended is used to call for a restoration of funds and a continuation of the program. The Head Start program and the Office of Economic Opportunity successfully used a posture strategy to head off program termination. The Partnership For Health Acts of the '60s and '70s also used this strategy, but it was unsuccessful. Success depends on having a large and vocal constituency to trumpet the list of issues. OEO and Head Start had such a constituency, and the health programs did not. In congressional testimony, spokespersons for the Partnership For Health came across as arrogant physicians who advocated only self-interest and resisted any change that would influence their personal prerogatives and money making. Cutting off funds for agencies with this kind of image is the dream of politicians and is good politics.

Strategy as *accommodation* has many of the same ingredients as a posture, but it incorporates some commitment to action in the agenda of issues. This makes the accommodator strategy more effective than the posture strategy, as shown by the movement toward the diagonal in Figure 15.2. Trade associations, like the American Hospital Association (AHA), use such a strategy. Such an organization serves a particular constituency, as the AHA serves the interests of America's nonprofit voluntary hospitals. The concerns of this constituency make up the issues that the trade association must pursue. When changes are proposed, such as reimbursement plans that cut margins in nonprofit hospitals, the AHA is expected to take the lead in testifying in front of Congress and promulgating the point of view of hospitals.

During periods of low need for public relations, trade associations must have something to do. Many adopt service programs that benefit their constituencies. The AHA, for example, provides to its members data services that compare costs and margins by hospital size, service intensity, and geographic region. Data describing individual hospitals is provided by the subscribing hospitals and combined for a fee into reports. The data also allows the industry access to information that can be used selectively to defend its position on various issues. The fees for these services supplement membership charges to keep the trade association well-budgeted.

Organizations with an accommodator strategy can be effective if they exhibit moderate responsiveness and their environment remains predictable. A series of activities is undertaken to manage known clusters. A shift toward a compromiser strategy would be needed if the environment shifts to more turbulent conditions. Organizations adopting a compromiser strategy and moving toward a mutualist strategy are more apt to be effective. For example, HRET (Hospital Research and Education Trust), a research arm of the American Hospital Association, moved from a passive data collection agency to an aggressive grant seeker after budget support was reduced by the AHA. HRET sought out partnerships with university faculties. HRET used the faculty members' names to promote its staff team's capability when responding to grant and contract RFPs; it also retained all of the overhead payments (a compromiser strategy). In the future HRET may be called on to deal with significant societal problems that will require true partnerships, creating a mutualist strategy.

Strategies that Match Need and Responsiveness

A diagonal line running from lower left to upper right in Figure 15.2 captures the movement called for to improve the strategic effectiveness of public and third-sector organizations. At the lower left corner in Figure 15.2, an organization is functioning without much of an agenda. The aim is to move this organization to an appropriate point up the diagonal. The movement forces the organization to become more proactive in recognizing and responding to needs.

Drifter Strategy. Some organizations are in placid environments that call for little action. *Drifter* strategy can be followed in an environment that makes few demands on people, which allows the equivalent of organizational "goldbricking." Many organizations founded with vague missions that stem from legislation with unclear goals, such as the coordination of education programs in an area health education center, develop such a strategic posture. People become comfortable in roles that call for little effort. Makework programs and routines are followed to create the aura of action. New leadership or the fear that makework will be discovered periodically prompts such an agency to search for a strategy that will give it a new sense of purpose.

Drifter strategy also represents a state that some organizations pass through during periods of recovery after intense campaigns in which considerable energy was expended. Low periods of activity can be used to reward people who were expected to work at overload levels during budget shortfalls. However, this "easy life" game (Bardach 1977) can be an insidious trap for the organization when it tries to return to normal operations. The lower level of activity can become a norm that is used to justify a slower pace and less effort.

Bureaucratic Strategy. Organizations operating under modest pressure to meet a few clear-cut needs should employ a bureaucratic strategy. This approach is the minimal acceptable posture in a placid environment (Figure 15.2). The strategy calls for an organization to demonstrate moderate responsiveness by using programmed routines and standardized responses. For example, a state bureau of employment services can perceive its role as the maker of decisions about who qualifies for unemployment compensation and the processor of checks for successful claimants. The task of finding jobs for the hard-core or temporarily unemployed is avoided because finding jobs requires a more proactive posture in which environmental turbulence must be recognized and dealt with. Only token efforts at employment are mounted in a bureaucratic strategy. Periodic contacts are made with employers, following long-established routines such as sending out available people without attempting to match skills with employer needs.

Bureaucratic strategy depends on routinized programs and standard procedures, much the way the custodian strategy does for firms. A defensive posture protects these routines by maximizing budgets and hiding unused funds for the recurring periods of decline in public funding. Routines and procedures are treated as distinctive competencies that are defended in budget hearings and the like, and the need to maintain such qualities as computer capability or work-force skills is stressed. The equivalent of protectionism for firms is sought. In an attempt to seal off the organization from budget cuts, rules are promulgated that treat the funding of routines and procedures as sacrosanct.

Compromiser Strategy. Organizations that are experiencing many distinct calls for action will be pushed into a proactive posture that moves them away from operating in a rule-bound bureaucracy. The *compromiser* strategy attempts to prioritize these needs and the actions each implies by playing one constituency against another. One tactic is to meet the needs of important constituents; another is to deal with needy constituents. For example, a mental health agency can choose to treat the mentally ill, with very limited reimbursement by third-party payers, or it can deal with court-assigned substance abusers who have very high recidivism rates, and thus receive payment for all services rendered. This type of choice creates serious dilemmas for the mental health agency. A compromise often is struck to follow certain rules that balance people's needs with revenue generation that keeps the agency solvent.

A turbulent environment can bring out competitive behavior by which a public or third-sector organization must protect its turf. Attempts to serve *our* clients or offer *our* services are resisted strenuously. For example, state-assisted universities with a research mandate attempt to block new Ph.D. programs and research funding proposed for lower-rated sister institutions. Privatization initiatives (Donahue 1989) produce competition among public organizations as they bid for the right to provide valued services. Also, some public organizations such as state-assisted universities must bid regularly for grants and contracts to remain financially viable. In each case, one or more of the clusters that must be managed takes on competitive features.

Compromiser strategy deals with several clusters of need that emerge in a turbulent environment. Within each cluster, stakeholders with significant needs can be identified, but not all clusters can be managed with available resources. The compromiser strategy allocates resources among the clusters, using criteria that reflect the agency's mission. These criteria often become quite complex and identify key strategic considerations. The compromiser strategy calls for steps to defend decisions that deal with some clusters and not others by involving oversight bodies in decision making. Each cluster may call for special programs and services, which makes the compromiser strategy much more complex than the bureaucratic strategy. This match of clusters of needs and programmed responses, such as services, makes up the strategic content. Only strong signals to change clusters would be recognized, making strategic change long term.

Organizations that are pulled into a turbulent environment often treat emergent needs as just another cluster to be managed. If sufficiently compelling, these needs must be met through the allocation of resources and the development of programs. When new needs emerge at an ever-increasing rate, the clamor for action becomes strident and the understandings that set priorities among clusters are upset. At first, attempts are made to meet these new demands by reallocations and use of slack resources. Another approach, the mutualist strategy, is required when new needs emerge at a rate that makes reallocation infeasible and when slack has been depleted.

Mutualist Strategies. The most proactive strategy in the typology is called a *mutualist* strategy. This strategy is needed for turbulent environments in which needs are changing rapidly and collaboration is required to respond, as shown in Figure 15.2. Mutualist strategy responds to a diverse and ever-changing set of needs through strategy development to meet those needs. Collaboration is substituted for the more competitive orientation of the compromiser strategy, in which the organization fends off any agency that encroaches on its domain. If mandates to meet the needs of people are adhered to, competition has little if any relevance in public and third-sector organizations. Instead, cooperation should be emphasized.

To avoid duplication of effort, agencies with overlapping service areas or mandates, such as home health agencies supported by United Way and city health departments, are called on to develop a collaborative approach to strategy (Evan 1966). This collaboration can be difficult to achieve, pushing strategy to a *compromise* position in which each agency becomes competitive and serves its own perception of important clusters. This approach can leave some clients with important needs unmet or underserved and other clients with a surplus of services. The mutualist strategy calls for collaboration, serving client needs by devising consortia or other kinds of umbrella organizations (Nutt 1979). This merges the interests of organizations that have overlapping and complementary mandates or missions. This type of collaboration is focused by topic and is not interorganizational (Evan 1966). Examples include the National Kidney Foundation and the highway safety program.

The National Kidney Foundation created a consortium to manage the activities required to treat end-stage kidney disease. These activities had been under the control of various medical delivery organizations such as tissue-typing centers and hospitals that offer transplantation and dialysis. The foundation promoted organ donation laws and data bases for patients undergoing dialysis who were candidates for transplantation. The foundation ensured that the interests of patients, especially the most needy and best matched for transplantation, were considered before they considered the desires of providers for treatment revenues and large patient volumes to justify a "center designation." The highway safety program also merged the interests of many disparate agencies, such as technical centers that offered training for people who operate emergency vehicles and hospitals that provide emergency care. The consortium pushed legislatures to enact laws to ensure that all ambulance attendants were trained and vehicles were properly designed; it promulgated standards for hospitals that offer emergency care and categorized them by level of care; and it organized communication networks to dispatch emergency vehicles.

In both of these illustrations, a collaborative approach ensured that needs in a changing environment would be met. In each case, the environment had become turbulent because longstanding needs suddenly were recognized. For the National Kidney Foundation, the opportunity to improve the survival of people with end-stage kidney disease called for action. For the highway safety program, the awareness that untrained ambulance drivers often caused serious additional injury to accident victims caused a public outcry. The mutualist strategy ensured that this kind of turbulence, stemming from changing attitudes about needs in these areas, would be managed with resources and programs drawn from appropriate agencies. The self-interest of these agencies was subordinated to peoples' visible and compelling needs.

A mutualist strategy is analogous to a prospector strategy in a firm. Rapid changes in consumer taste create a volatile market for firms that call for a prospector strategy. The leader of a public organization following a mutualist strategy responds to volatile needs that emerge with the same amount of urgency and force as a dramatic change in consumer buying behavior. As in firms, an organizational structure and policy are fashioned to deal with the volatility. Signals, such as changing attitudes that permitted organ donation laws to be enacted, are read and interpreted. Developmental activities that produce strategy based on these needs are initiated by seeking novel arrangements.

The mutualist strategy makes novel arrangements to meet emergent needs. The tactics call for finding key people to set the tone by subordinating personal and organizational interests; developing an issue-centered focus of effort; establishing a consortium that draws key stakeholders into a body seeking to address emergent needs; using the consortium to create a vision and/or shape a vision to meet needs; seeking win-win arrangements for all affected parties; and promoting trust so stakeholders will cooperate in meeting needs and shepherding the consortium members toward high levels of cooperation. For example, the highway safety program was initiated by physicians who were appalled at the sorry state of emergency services in the United States. Legislation was enacted after years of effort to provide states with the funds to set in place an EMS (emergency medical service) system. Successful states formed consortiums which forged into an issue-centered body stakeholders involved in training, vehicle design, vehicle dispatch, emergency vehicle operation, and hospital emergency room categorization by levels of care. The successful consortium mediated disputes and set in place services such as "911" dispatch and emergency vehicles staffed with trained people. All parties could play an appropriate role because the available resources were shared.

The mutualist strategy periodically may give way to a compromiser strategy as an organization attempts to consolidate gains or reconnect with its traditions. Organizational leaders can feel pressure to serve their traditional clients by allocating more of the organization's resources to this group, or the organization may have the actions called for by a mutualist strategy, which takes it beyond its charter, questioned by an oversight body. Either development will pull the organization away from a mutualist strategy toward a compromisor strategy. Like the prospector and entrepreneurial strategies for a firm, both the compromiser and mutualist strategy can be useful. However, the mutualist strategy and prospector strategy are more apt to produce breakthroughs.

Research Questions

The strategy applied by organizations with public features merits several kinds of study, ranging from empirical to descriptive. Table 15.2 lists the key propositions.

Empirical studies would attempt to validate the propositions for the strategic types identified in Figure 15.2. For example, a particular type of organization, such as an acute care hospital or an academic program at a university, could be rated in terms of effectiveness. The ratings can be sorted into categories, identifying organizations with high or low effective-

TABLE 15.2 Propositions About Public and Third-Sector Organization Strategy

1. Effective organizations apply different strategies than ineffective organizations.

2. An imbalance between responsiveness and the need for action leads to the use of dominator or posture strategy, which is less effective than a director and accommodator strategy. Director and accommodator strategies are more effective because needs are better aligned to responsiveness.

3. The bureaucratic strategy is superior to drifter strategy in placid environments, the director strategy superior to dominator strategy in disturbed environments, and the accommodator strategy superior to posturer strategy in clustered placid environments.

4. In turbulent environments, both compromiser and mutualist strategy can be effective.

5. The mutualist strategy is essential under conditions of extreme turbulence and this strategy is more apt to produce visionary breakthroughs.

6. Necessary conditions tht consolidate and sustain a mutualist strategy stem from leader traits, organizational culture, and threats to cooperation and innovation.

7. A breakthrough strategy can be created by planning to involve stakeholders or by getting stakeholders to buy into the leader's vision. Both call for a mutualist strategy in which the leader subordinates personal interests, creates a consortium, and promotes innovation in which the interest of all stakeholders can be served.

ness. This would create clear-cut differences and pose sharp questions about the origin of these differences. We expect organizations with low effectiveness to use different strategies than organizations with high effectiveness.

If differences emerge, the organization's ratings can be correlated with the type of strategy that was used by each organization. Such an analysis would seek to verify the contention that drifter, posturer, and dominator strategy are less effective than director, bureaucratic, and accommodator strategy. Such a study could explore the proposition that balance between responsiveness and perceived need for action in the organization's strategy is desirable. If true, bureaucratic strategy would be superior to drifter strategy in placid environments, director strategy superior to dominator strategy in disturbed environments, and accommodator strategy superior to posturer strategy in clustered placid environments. The compromiser and mutualist strategies have a different relationship. Each is postulated to be effective in a turbulent environment, but the mutualist strategy is thought to be the better approach because of the increased level of responsiveness. We expect correlations of organizational effectiveness and strategy type to reveal that the mutualist strategy becomes more desirable as turbulence increases.

We contend that the mutualist strategy should be used to promote "breakthroughs," a new vision that can deal with high levels of environmental turbulence. Particularly innovative organizations of a type (e.g., university hospitals) must be identified to study this proposition. The strategy applied by these organizations would be explored to determine the extent to which mutualist tactics of consortiums, creativity, leaders who subordinate their personal and organizational interests, and the other predicted features of a mutualist strategy were present. The tactics used by leaders in visionary organizations should be enlightening.

The conditions under which an internal or an external push for action can be successful are of interest, as is the consideration of whether leadership should arise internally, from the titular leader, or from the outside. Such a study would differentiate the success of strategy that was prompted by the leader or members of the top management team from strategy prompted by people in a legislature or an oversight body, and it would note contextual factors that influence the prospects of success for the insider and outsider as change agents.

Empirical research requires the development of instruments that can identify the strategy of an organization with public features, measure organizational performance, and determine environmental turbulence. Classification schemes are needed to determine which strategy an organization uses. To determine the strategy used, Shortell et al. (1988) had top managers answer questions in a survey that used 7-point scales. Responses that fell at one end of the scale represented highly proactive strategy, those in the middle represented modestly proactive strategy, and those at the other end of the scale represented strategy with minimal effort. The responses were combined to several such questions that dealt with the extent to which current or new products/services were being developed or diversified across relevant lists of product/service lines. Test/retest reliability was determined by comparing responses across time and among members of the top management team. High reliability scores are typically reported in these studies (e.g., Miles and Cameron 1982; Shortell et al. 1988). A similar scheme could be developed for the proposed strategy types.

Organizational performance typically is measured with a multiattribute approach. For example, Shortell et al. (1988) combined financial indicators and quality measures, such as quality assurance activities and severity-adjusted death rates, to create their productivity indicators. Organizations that face accreditation have their performance assessed periodically, providing another source of information. Also, several rating agencies now regularly provide rankings—of university programs, hospitals, symphony orchestras, and so forth—that can be used to provide performance indicators.

Environmental turbulence can be determined by following the procedures developed by Miles and Cameron (1982), Shortell (1988), and others who have pioneered this type of research.

Empirical studies also suggest research design issues. For example, either cross-sectional or longitudinal approaches can be used to assess the data. Cross-sectional approaches put particular types of organizations into categories that depict their strategy and other factors of interest, such as size or resource base, to contrast like organizations with those that differ. Longitudinal approaches can be used to identify shifts in a given organization's performance over time to correlate changes in strategy with performance shifts, such as new clients served or new programs offered.

The importance of strategy with breakthrough or visionary features suggests several *descriptive* studies. The conditions surrounding the emergence of such a strategy merit study. The barriers to breakthrough or visionary strategy seem to be a crucial issue. Comparing organizations of a type (e.g., acute care hospitals) with compromiser and mutualist strategies may suggest what blocks the visionary from being given or acting a leadership role.

Also of concern are the causes of shifts between mutualist and compromiser strategy. Such a study would seek to identify conditions that might cause a mutualist strategy to unravel. The prior state of the organization which prompted a mutualist strategy merits study. Also, the role of the organizational leader seems to be crucial. Leaders promoting a mutualist strategy may have certain characteristics that standard instruments such as the Myers-Briggs Type Indicator (MBTI) can reveal (Nutt 1988). The organization's culture also may be a factor. Some cultures may enable and others may prohibit the emergence of mutualist strategy. Finally, the role of formal procedure seems critical. For instance, does a mutualist strategy depend on the vision a leader brings to an organization or to the development of a vision through careful planning? (Nutt and Backoff 1993b)

Inter- and intraorganizational studies also might reveal conditions under which a visionary or breakthrough strategy is used. Such a strategy may be initiated infrequently and survive only under special conditions. Comparisons of the strategy used in subunits (e.g., divisions of a state department of natural resources) with that used by the parent organization may suggest conditions under which a mutualist strategy can survive, gain momentum, or be stifled. The within and between features of particular organizational types also may reveal these conditions. Such studies could be conducted for university hospitals, state departments of transportation or commerce, symphony orchestras, public school systems, regulatory agencies, and many other organizations with public features.

Descriptive studies call for a qualitative research approach (e.g., Patton 1990; Denzin 1989). To conduct this type of research, the CEO and members of a top management team would be interviewed to identify how the organization responded to environmental shifts. The interviews would reconstruct historical events by tracing outcomes back to antecedent conditions. Responses then would be triangulated to find the most plausible interpretation of events and actions. Simulations involving people who work in these organizations could be used to test the impact of factors that emerged from such studies (Nutt 1989).

Summary

Developer, entrepreneur, custodial, and stabilizer strategic types that are useful in firms were modified to fit environmental conditions pertinent to organizations with public features. The authority network of public and most third-sector organizations define their market, which is made up of priority needs that call for action as seen by organizational leaders, oversight bodies, legislators, elected officials, and other stakeholders who make up the authority network to which a public or third-sector organization must respond. These needs can be stable or shifting. Competitiveness for organizations with public features is translated into responsiveness to perceived needs. Using these definitions, public sector strategies with positive features (directors, bureaucrats, accommodators, compromisers, and mutualists) and negative features (dominators, drifters, and posturers) were identified. We use these strategies to show how organizations with public features can move toward high responsiveness coupled with appropriate action. Using this framework, several research questions were suggested.

References

Acar, W., A. J. Melcher, and K. E. Aupperle. 1987. Organizational Processes and Strategic Postures." *Academy of Management Proceedings*, J-70 to J-94.

Bardach, E. 1977. *The Implementation Game*. Cambridge, Mass.: MIT Press.

Bozeman, B. 1987. *All Organizations Are Public*. San Francisco: Jossey-Bass.

Braybrook, D., and C. E. Lindblom. 1963. *A Strategy for Decision*. New York: Free Press.

Bryson, J. 1988. *Strategic Planning for Public and Non-Profit Organization*. San Francisco: Jossey-Bass.

Denzin, N. K. 1989. *The Research Act*. Englewood Cliffs, N.J.: Prentice-Hall.

Donahue, J. B. 1989. *The Privatization Decision*. New York: Basic Books.

Emery, F. E., and E. L. Trist. 1965. "Casual Texture of Organizational Environments." *Human Relations* 18(1): 21–32.

Evan, W. M. 1966. "The Organizational Set: Toward a Theory of Interorganizational Relations." In J. D. Thompson, ed., *Approaches to Organizational Design.* Pittsburgh: University of Pittsburgh Press.

Galbraith, C., and D. Schendel. 1983. "An Empirical Analyzing of Strategy Types." *Strategic Management Journal* 4: 153–73.

Hambrick, D. C. 1983. "Some Tests of the Effectiveness and Functional Attributes of Miles and Snow's Strategic Types." *Academy of Management Journal* 26: 5–26.

Harmon, M. M. 1981. *Action Theory for Public Administration.* New York: Longman.

Harrigan, K. R. 1980. *Strategies for Declining Industries.* Lexington, Mass.: Heath.

Hewlett, R. G., and F. Duncan. 1974. *Nuclear Navy: 1946–1962.* Chicago: University of Chicago Press.

Lawerence, P. R., and D. M. Dyer. 1983. *Renewing American Industry.* New York: Free Press.

Levine, C. H., R. W. Backoff, A. R. Cahoon, and W. J. Siffin. 1976. "Organizational Design: A Post Minnowbrook Perspective for the 'New' Public Administration." *Public Administration Review* 36 (July/Aug.): 425–35.

Lewis, E. 1980. *Public Entrepreneurship.* Bloomington: Indiana University Press.

Lindblom, C. E. 1959. "The Science of 'Muddling Through.'" *Public Administration Review* 19 (Spring): 79–88.

_____. 1975. *The Intelligence of Democracy: Decision Through Adjustment.* New York: Free Press.

Lodahl, T. M., and S. M. Mitchell. 1980. "Drift in the Development of Innovative Organizations." In J. R. Kimberly and R. H. Miles, eds., *The Organizational Life Cycle.* San Francisco, Calif.: Jossey-Bass, 184–207.

MacMillan, I. C. 1980. "How Business Strategies Can use Guerilla Tactics." *Journal of Business Strategy* 1(2): 63–5.

Meyer, A. D. 1982. "Adapting to Environmental Jolts." *Adminstrative Science Quarterly* 27: 515–37.

Miles, R. E., and C. C. Snow. 1978. *Organizational Strategy, Structure, and Process.* New York: McGraw-Hill.

Miles, R. E., C. C. Snow, A. D. Meyer, and H. J. Coleman. 1978. "Organizational Strategy, Structure, and Process." *Academy of Management Review* 3(3): 546–71.

Miles, R. H., and K. Cameron. 1982. *Coffin Nails and Corporate Strategy.* Englewood Cliffs, N.J.: Prentice-Hall.

Mintzberg, H. 1978. "Patterns in Strategy Formation." *Management Science* 24: 147–58.

Nutt, P. C. 1979. "On the Quality and Acceptance of Plans Drawn by Consortiums." *Journal of Applied Behavioral Science* 15(1): 7–21.

_____. 1988. "The Impact of Culture on Decision Making." *Omega: The International Journal of Management Science* 16: 553–67.

_____. 1989. *Making Tough Decisions.* San Francisco: Jossey-Bass.

Nutt, P. C., and R. W. Backoff. 1992. *The Strategic Management of Public and Third-Sector Organizations.* San Francisco: Jossey-Bass.

_____. 1993a. "Organizational Publicness and its Implications for Strategic Management." *Journal of Public Administration Research and Theory* 3(3): 209–31.

_____. 1993b. "The Strategic Leadership of Public Organizations." *Journal of Management* 19(2): 229–347.

Paine, F. T., and C. R. Anderson. 1977. "Contingencies Effecting Strategy Formation and Effectiveness." *Journal of Management Studies* 14: 147–58.

Patton, M. E. 1990. *Qualitative Evaluation and Research Methods.* Los Angeles: Sage.

Porter, M. E. 1985. *Competitive Advantage.* New York: Free Press.

Reed, S. R. 1988. *Mergers, Managers, and the Economy.* New York: McGraw-Hill.

Ring, P. 1989. "Strategic Issues: What Are They and Where Do They Come From?" In J. Bryson and R. Einsweiler, eds., *Strategic Planning.* Chicago: APA Planners Press.

Rubin, M. S. 1988. "Sagas, Ventures, Quests, and Parleys: A Typology of Strategies with the Public Sector." In J. Bryson and R. Einsweiler, eds., *Strategic Planning.* Chicago: APA Planners Press.

Shortell, S., E. M. Morrison, and B. Friedman. 1988. *Strategic Choices for America's Hospitals: Managing Change in Turbulent Times.* San Francisco: Jossey-Bass.

Weich, K. E. 1979. *The Social Psychology of Organizing,* 2d ed. Reading, Mass.: Addison-Wesley.

Weschler, B., and R. W. Backoff. 1988. "Policy Making and Administration in State Agencies: Strategic Management Approaches." *Public Administration Review* 48 (July-Aug.): 321–27.

Wildavsky, A. 1969. "Rescuing Policy Analysis from PPBS." *Public Administration Review* 29 (Mar.-Apr.): 189–202.

_____. 1979a. *The Politics of the Budgeting Process,* 3d ed. Boston: Little, Brown.

_____. 1979b *Speaking Truth to Power.* Boston: Little, Brown.

16

STRATEGIC MANAGEMENT IN THE PUBLIC SECTOR: CONCEPTS, MODELS, AND PROCESSES

Theodore H. Poister
Gregory D. Streib

Effective public administration in the age of results-oriented management requires public agencies to develop a capacity for strategic management, the central management process that integrates all major activities and functions and directs them toward advancing an organization's strategic agenda. Strategic management is concerned with strengthening the long-term viability and effectiveness of public sector organizations in terms of both substantive policy and management capacity. It integrates all other management processes to provide a systematic, coherent, and effective approach to establishing, attaining, monitoring, and updating an agency's strategic objectives. Strategic management is integrative in nature in the sense of (a) focusing attention across functional divisions and throughout various organizational levels on common goals, themes, and issues; (b) tying internal management processes and program initiatives to desired out-

1999. Strategic management in the public sector: Concepts, models, and processes. Poister, Theodore H., and Gregory D. Streib. **Public Productivity and Management Review** 22 (March): 308–325.

comes in the external environment; and (c) linking operational, tactical, day-to-day decisions to longer run strategic objectives. Particularly given the dynamic political and institutional environment within which many public agencies operate, an effective strategic management capability is essential for maintaining or strengthening the fit between the organization and its external stakeholders and managing for results within a clearly defined context of mission, mandates, values, and vision.

Strategic management has been addressed in the public administration literature (Koteen, 1989; Nutt and Backoff, 1992; Rabin, Miller, and Hildreth, 1989; Steiss, 1985) but by no means as extensively as has its most critical component, strategic planning, or other management approaches such as total quality management. However, a more recent article by Vinzant and Vinzant (1996a) goes a long way toward refocusing appropriate attention on the role of strategic management in the public sector and discussing implementation issues and strategies in an instructive manner.

The purpose of the present article is to raise awareness of the central importance of strategic management in government, define the critical elements in a holistic model of strategic management, discuss the strategic management process, and clarify the relationship between strategic management and other management processes. Brief examples drawn from a few state and local government units are presented to illustrate strategic management concepts and processes and making them more accessible to practicing public managers.

Managing Strategically in Government

In the ongoing rush of activities, competing demands for attention, and the press of day-to-day decisions, focusing on a viable and responsive strategic agenda as the central source of direction, initiatives, and priorities is of fundamental importance. A strong strategic management capability is essential because it provides both a short-term and a long-term sense of direction for a governmental agency relative to its internal and external environments, which could be shifting continually. Changes in societal needs, political trends, intergovernmental relations, fiscal conditions, and citizen expectations are likely to alter the mix of programmatic responsibilities and resource requirements facing local governments. Anticipating these possibly substantial changes and adapting to them productively requires the type of forward-looking, flexible, and effective responses that a strong strategic management capacity can help to provide.

Strategic Planning and Strategic Management

Although strategic management often is discussed as an extension of strategic planning, and the two terms often are confused and used interchangeably, they are by no means synonymous. Strategic planning has been defined as "a disciplined effort to produce fundamental decisions and actions that shape and guide what an organization is, what it does, and why it does it" (Bryson, 1988, p. 5). It blends futuristic thinking, objective analysis, and subjective evaluation of goals and priorities to chart future courses of action that will ensure the long-run vitality and effectiveness of the organization. In contrast to the more closed-system orientation of traditional long-range planning and conventional program planning, strategic planning is a "big picture" approach that

- is concerned with identifying and responding to the most fundamental issues facing an organization;
- addresses the subjective question of purpose and the often competing values that influence mission and strategies;
- emphasizes the importance of external trends and forces as they are likely to affect the agency and its mission;
- attempts to be politically realistic by taking into account the concerns and preferences of internal and especially external stakeholders;
- relies heavily on the active involvement of senior-level managers and sometimes elected officials, assisted by staff support where needed;
- requires the candid confrontation of critical issues by key participants to build commitment to plans;
- is action oriented and stresses the importance of developing plans for implementing strategies; and
- focuses on implementing decisions now so as to position the organization favorably for the future.

Strategic management shares these same attributes, but it is a much more encompassing process that is concerned with managing an organization in a strategic manner on a continuing basis. Strategic planning is a principal element but not the essence of strategic management, which also involves resource management, implementation, and control and evaluation (Halachmi, Hardy, and Rhoades, 1993, p. 165; Steiss, 1985, p. 9). Vinzant and Vinzant (1996b) characterize strategic planning as the cornerstone of strategic management, but they go on to say that "successful implementation of strategic management requires an assessment of organization capacities in such areas as managerial capability, power structure, culture, leadership, and organizational structure" (p. 203). Strategic management must provide a process for developing strategic plans and updating them periodically, which may involve a "strategic planning systems" approach layered down through functional divisions and operating units, but it also must provide the means for ensuring that strategic plans are implemented and monitored effectively.

Koteen (1989) defines strategic management as a broad concept that "embraces the entire set of managerial decisions and actions that determine the long-run performance of an organization" (p. 18), whereas Toft (1989) portrays it as "an advanced and coherent form of strategic thinking, attempting to extend strategic vision throughout all units of the organization, encompassing every administrative system" (p. 6). Strategic management does not occur when top executives micromanage operations to ensure uniformity; rather, it occurs when decisions and actions at all levels are driven by a few fundamental strategies or policies that are strongly endorsed as being critical for improving an agency's performance over the long run. A strategically managed public agency is one in which budgeting, performance measurement, human resource development, program management, and other management processes are guided by a strategic agenda that has been developed with a buy-in from key actors and communicated widely within the organization and among external constituencies. Strategic management is concerned with implementing strategies and measuring performance as well as monitoring trends and identifying emerging issues that might require strategic responses.

Strategic planning has gained widespread currency in government. Agency managers now view it as a valuable tool for charting future directions in changing and sometimes turbulent environments. What was an exciting new tool for public managers 15 years ago has become orthodox public management. A recent survey of state agencies found that 60% of them report using some form of strategic planning (Berry and Wechsler, 1995). Similarly, a 1993 survey of municipal managers found nearly 60% of the respondents indicating that their jurisdictions used strategic planning, with nearly 40% using it on a citywide basis and the other 20% using it in selected departments or programs (Poister and Streib, 1994).

Governmental units have been slower to implement full-fledged strategic management processes, in part because they require a substantial investment in time and resources as well as a sustained commitment over time. However, as public managers have recognized that the implementation of strategies and the ongoing management of an agency's strategic agenda are just as important as the initial planning, they have begun to embrace the holistic concept of strategic management. Moreover, many public agencies are now being required to develop a strategic management capacity. At the federal level, the Government Performance and Results Act of 1993 (GPRA) requires federal agencies to develop (a) strategic 5-year plans that identify missions, goals, and objectives and describe how they will be achieved; (b) annual performance plans, tied to proposed budgets, that also identify indicators for measuring the outputs, service levels, and outcomes produced by each program; and (c) annual performance reports comparing actual program performance to previously set goals and objectives. Most state governments have passed similar legislation (Broom, 1995; Melkers and Willoughby, 1998), and statewide programs such as Oregon Benchmarks, Texas Tomorrow, and Minnesota Milestones, typically led by a centralized budget or planning office, both require and assist operating departments in developing their own strategic management capacity.

Implementing Strategies

As effective public managers know, organizations move into the future by decisions and actions, not by plans. If plans are not implemented in a very purposeful way, then the strategies will not take hold, no matter how compelling or inspiring the planning process. Strategic management must provide for the implementation of strategies through vehicles such as action plans, the budgeting process, the performance management system, changes in organizational structure, and program and project management. These and other "management levers" are used by effective strategic managers to drive macro-level strategies down into their organizations to ensure that major decisions are designed to advance these strategies or, at the very least, are consistent with them.

The Role of Strategic Management

Strategic management is not a linear process of planning, implementation, and evaluation. Rather, it entails managing a public agency from a strategic perspective on an ongoing basis to ensure that strategic plans are kept current and that they are effectively driving other management processes. Strategic management requires the following:

1. continual monitoring of the "fit" between the organization and its environment and tracking external trends and forces that are likely to affect the governmental jurisdiction or agency;
2. shaping and communicating to both internal and external audiences a clear vision of the type of organization the governmental unit is striving to become;
3. creating strategic agendas at various levels, and in all parts of the organization, and ensuring that they become the driving force in all other decision making; and
4. guiding all other management processes in an integrated manner to support and enhance these strategic agendas.

The overall purpose of strategic management is to develop a continuing commitment to the mission and vision of the organization (both internally

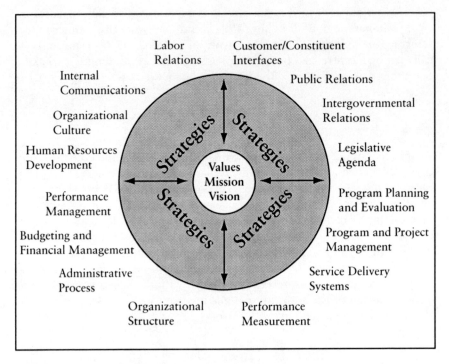

FIGURE 16.1   A Proposed Strategic Management Model

and in the authorizing environment), nurture a culture that identifies with and supports the mission and vision, and maintain a clear focus on the organization's strategic agenda throughout all its decision processes and activities.

A Strategic Management Model

Figure 16.1 presents a model of strategic management that might be useful for many public managers. At its core are the underlying values that are most important to the agency, its mission within the governmental system and the communities or constituencies it serves, and a vision of what the agency should look like in the future. For strategic management to be successful, there must be a shared commitment to the values, mission, and vision both within the governmental unit or agency (including elected officials or appointed executives, professional managers, and employees) and among the relevant external stakeholders. Thus, an important part of strategic management entails developing and refining a clear sense of values, mission, and vision and working to build and maintain widespread ownership of them.

Around the outer ring of the model are a number of management responsibilities that must be coordinated in terms of their strategic implications to develop a strategic management capacity. These functions, which are meant to be illustrative rather than exhaustive, are organized roughly in accordance with the competing values model of organizational performance (Quinn and Rohrbaugh, 1981). The elements shown in the upper right quadrant of the model all concern external relations including customer/constituent interfaces, public relations, intergovernmental relations, and a legislative agenda. In the lower right quadrant are management responsibilities concerning the programs and services provided by the agency or governmental unit including program planning and evaluation, service delivery systems, program and project management, and performance measurement. The lower left quadrant of the model concerns internal management functions including performance management, budgeting and financial management, administrative processes, and organizational structure. The upper left quadrant contains human relations elements concerning human resources development, organization culture, internal communications, and labor relations.

As indicated in Figure 16.1, there is a two-directional relationship between all these elements and the values, mission, and vision that are at the core of the strategic management process. This model is best thought of as a constellation of key management functions revolving around the core values, mission, and vision of any public sector organization. The force that keeps them in orbit consists of the strategies that are being formulated, assessed, implemented, and evaluated on an ongoing basis. For example, strategic managers must be concerned with the relationships between external stake-holders and the organization's values, mission, vision, and strategies. External relations must be conducted with an eye to soliciting input for strategic planning or updating as well as building cooperative relationships for implementing and evaluating strategies. The strategic management team must ensure that its vision and strategies are communicated effectively to external constituencies to build and maintain public support for the department or agency and its strategic agenda. Also, there must be mechanisms and processes in place for soliciting and assessing feedback from these external stakeholders, including customers and constituents, the media and public at large, other governmental units and jurisdictions, and the relevant legislative bodies, to monitor trends and forces and to anticipate changes in the agency's environment that might affect its policies or the ability to serve its mission.

Regarding the lower right quadrant of the model, programs, projects, and service delivery systems often are the vehicles used for implementing strategic plans. On the other hand, the current status of programs, projects, and services on any number of dimensions such as priorities, targeting, quality, and efficiency and effectiveness often is a critical consideration in the identification of strategic issues and the development of strategies. Thus, the strategic management process must ensure that systems for program planning and evaluation, service delivery, program and project management, and performance measurement are driven by the agency's values, mission, and vision and that strategizing at various levels is informed by the feedback provided by these systems.

Similarly, those who are responsible for strategic management must ensure that budgeting and financial management systems, performance management, and other administrative processes are designed to facilitate the implementation of strategic plans and to reinforce the focus on strategy throughout the governmental unit. Designed and used appropriately, these systems also can provide information that is indispensable for further strategic planning, assessment, and evaluation. Strategic managers also need to be aware of the linkages between strategy and structure. They must recognize that purposeful structuring can facilitate strategy implementation and that the reporting relationships inherent in structure could facilitate or impede the feedback of information that could be vital for further strategic planning and evaluation.

Finally, in the upper left quadrant of the model, the strategic management team must be critically concerned with the human resources and the internal relational aspects of the agency or jurisdiction. A primary challenge for strategic managers is to monitor the organizational climate continually and to nurture a culture that is responsive to purposeful change and attuned to the values, mission, and vision that are at the core of the process. Strategic managers also need to establish performance management systems and human resource development programs that are conducive to implementing new strategies in terms of both motivation and capabilities. Moreover, successful strategic management requires the development and dissemination of innovations and encourages the flow of useful feedback from managers and employees regarding the viability and effectiveness of strategies. These communication channels also can be used to "sell" new initiatives and develop a strong shared commitment to strategies and their underlying premises throughout the organization.

The Georgia Department of Administrative Services

To a large extent, strategic management is concerned with managing these various functions in a coordinated fashion at the highest levels so that they will complement and reinforce each other in moving the public organization in a particular direction. For example, the Georgia Department of Administrative Services (DOAS) is a large, multifunctional agency that provides a wide range of support services, from "blue collar" services such as motor vehicle rentals and mail and courier services, to high-tech services such as local area network support, data communications networks, and a distance learning program, to other operating departments in the state government. Under Commissioner Dotty Roach, DOAS has reviewed its strategic priorities and determined to strengthen customer service and increase customer satisfaction as its principal strategic direction, reinforcing a commitment made under former Commissioner Dave Evans as the agency was beginning to "reinvent" itself by replacing its self-concept as a largely regulatory department with a vision of a customer service agency. With an overarching vision of making the department "the best business run by a government," strategic initiatives that have been undertaken to move faster and further in this direction work through many of the managerial elements shown in Figure 16.1.

For example, DOAS has substantially reorganized by creating a new Information Technology (IT) unit that consolidates the former Telecommunications and Computer Services divisions to provide customers with a "seamless web" of these often interrelated services. Rather than the service-based sections in the prior structure, the new IT unit is functionally organized around technology research and development, product management, service delivery, and customer account managers to provide the central point of contact for all IT services. Each customer agency will work with a specific account representative, who will handle service requests and interface with the technical units to design information and telecommunications systems to meet the customers' needs. Furthermore, the various "help desks" that provide support for IT services have been streamlined in a more customer-friendly fashion.

More generally, DOAS is emphasizing frequent and structured interactions with customers to better understand what customer agencies want and need from the department, their evaluation of current services, and suggestions for improving service delivery. Whereas in the past most customer communications arose around complaints, the department now uses a number of forums such as customer advisory groups and conferences, focus groups, and periodic surveys to solicit customer input and feedback in a large number of program areas on a regular basis. The customer conferences, and in some program areas customer training programs, also provide DOAS with an opportunity to provide customers with information regarding these services, department operations, and what customers can expect from the department in particular service areas.

DOAS has used other management levers to advance this overall customer service strategy. To provide customer agencies with greater flexibility in their purchasing operations, for example, the department developed a legislative proposal to raise the level of "delegated authority" from the previously existing $5,000 limit so that state agencies can now make purchases of up to $50,000 in cost on their own. The institution of plastic "purchase cards" is another innovation that is enabling state agencies to make needed purchases more efficiently. With the implementation of these and other program changes, the department's purchasing unit is now emphasizing its training and consulting services for customer agencies as opposed to its former primary role as purchasing agent.

Throughout its operations, DOAS has been using quality management principles and techniques to improve the mechanics of service delivery. For example, the department's central office supply function has totally reconfigured its warehouse, reengineered work processes, and forged more productive relationships with suppliers to improve the quality of service to the state agencies, school districts, and local governments it serves. The result has been a drop in the average shipping time of items to customers from 5 days to 2 days while at the same time improving the accuracy of shipments and the accompanying documentation. At present, DOAS also is reengineering its service delivery mechanisms to create a department-wide order fulfillment process that is designed to simplify the ordering process for customers and dramatically shorten turnaround time in responding to requests for products or services.

One more example of a programmatic initiative to strengthen customer service in DOAS concerns the state's workers' compensation program. As the rising cost of risk management has resulted in much greater visibility in recent years, the department has evaluated its program and planned substantial changes in its approach to workers' compensation. Perhaps most important, the department has identified employees who are injured on the job as primary customers of the program in addition to the employing agency. This will result in more careful attention being paid to the needs of injured employees and the implementation of an aggressive return-to-work program designed to substantially reduce the number of employee workdays that are lost due to on-the-job injuries. In addition, DOAS is planning a transition to a managed care approach to the medical services provided to injured workers in the interests of both improving service and reducing costs.

Undergirding these structural and programmatic initiatives are the human resources and cultural changes that have been taking place at DOAS. Although Roach has brought in a few key individuals from outside the department, she has filled most high-level managerial positions by promoting people from within who had demonstrated a commitment and the ability to strengthen customer service. The focus on customer service is a principal theme in weekly meetings of the top leadership team, periodic retreats involving a broader base of managers, and communications issued by the commissioner. All this has helped to engender an organizational culture that prizes quality and customer service. This is reinforced by the department's use of the state's new performance management system, Georgia Gain, which uses a management by objectives (MBO)-type approach for providing direction for individual managers and employees and evaluating their performance based on the extent to which they achieve personalized objectives. At DOAS now, many of these objectives refer to quality and customer service.

Coordinating this multiplicity of strategies, which have been initiated at different times and sometimes fall to different managers to implement so as to maximize their impact on improving customer satisfaction, is the job of strategic management. Many of these activities are being pursued in parallel, often by different individuals in different parts of the organization, but to be effective they need to form a coherent whole. By setting these initiatives up as specific projects with realistic action plans, identifying them as critical responsibilities of various senior-level managers, tracking progress in these areas on a regular basis in top leadership team meetings, and identifying problems early on and resolving them effectively, the commissioner and leadership team constantly attend to these initiatives to ensure that they are being pursued relentlessly to strengthen DOAS's performance in the near term and the long run.

The Strategic Management Process

Essentially, strategic management is a vehicle for providing forward-looking leadership regarding the most fundamental issues of concern to an organization and its environment in a very purposeful, systematic, and effective manner. At the heart of the process is "the collective management of a strategic agenda that changes as an organization's problems and opportunities change. Effective strategic management requires intensive, continuous, and collective involvement of senior management" (Eadie and Steinbacher, 1985, p. 425).

Effective strategic management requires the formation of a strategic management group to provide leadership for the process. Typically, the makeup of this group will include the chief executive, top-line managers, and key executive staff members. In a small municipal jurisdiction, for example, the strategic management group might consist of the mayor or the city manager and the heads of several operating departments. In a large urban county government with numerous operating departments, the strategic management team might include the county manager, the deputy managers who over-see clusters of operating departments, and the heads of staff units such as planning and finance. In many state and federal agencies, the strategic management group includes the secretary, commissioner, or administrator along with the heads of the major divisions or bureaus. Whereas strategic management is properly a line management function, the strategic management group often will require staff support from various areas to gather and synthesize relevant information, analyze options, formulate plans, and evaluate strategies.

It is the responsibility of the strategic management team to provide the structure for developing and updating strategic plans and for guiding their implementation in all areas. Because strategic management is a continuous process, the strategic management group should meet on a regular basis to discuss strategies, monitor progress, evaluate effectiveness, and generally maintain a collective focus on the strategic agenda. This includes identifying newly emerging strategic issues, gauging problems and opportunities as they develop, modifying strategies, and providing direction and control over implementation plans to advance the strategic agenda effectively. Periodically, it may result in the development of new strategic initiatives.

The strategic management process also may involve a strategic planning systems approach in which planning efforts at various levels are centrally coordinated within the framework of an organization-wide or a jurisdiction-wide strategic planning process. For example, a city's strategic management group could develop an overall strategic plan that identifies strategic goals and objectives, the outline of strategies for achieving them, and the assignment of implementation responsibilities. Although department heads and certain other staff officers have been involved in this effort, the focus appropriately has been on citywide issues and strategies. With the adoption of this overall plan, the strategic management group might well direct the operating departments to formulate their own strategic plans, which respond to mandates established in the overall plan and also address strategic issues at their own level.

At the same time, the city's overall plan might have established goals for a few "key results areas" that cross departmental lines such as the revitalization of several satellite retail and commercial centers or the "reengineering" of the jurisdiction's procurement processes. The strategic management group might then convene cross-departmental task forces or action teams to formulate more specific strategies for achieving these goals and to develop plans for their implementation. In addition, the strategic management group might be requiring, reviewing, and approving action plans for moving both the departmental and citywide initiatives forward. Over time, the strategic management group also would be monitoring the results of all this activity, assessing new issues, and structuring plan update efforts as might be necessary.

In addition to strategic planning activities, the strategic management process clearly requires a commitment to using the organization's decision processes to focus attention and effort on the strategic agenda to achieve

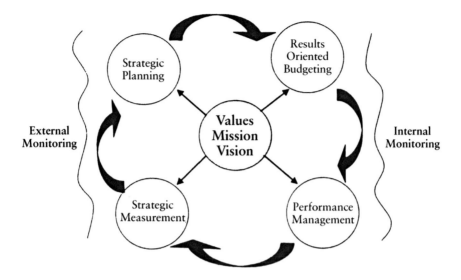

FIGURE 16.2   The Strategic Management Process

strategic goals over time. Thus, the strategic management process, as illustrated in Figure 16.2, places heavy emphasis on implementation as well as on planning. To ensure that strategic plans will indeed become the driving force behind operating-level decisions and activities in an organization, the strategic management team must develop processes for allocating resources, managing people, and measuring performance that are geared to moving the strategic agenda forward.

Once strategic plans have been adopted, the necessary resources for implementing them must be identified and committed. As indicated in Figure 16.2, some type of results-oriented budgeting system in which funding can be tied to particular programs, projects, or activities and directly related to planned outputs and impacts can facilitate the allocation of budgets so as to maximize their impact in advancing the strategic agenda. Such a budgeting process can be used to ensure that specific strategic initiatives are adequately funded and to provide incentives for directing ongoing programs to support the strategic agenda wherever possible.

Similarly, strategic management requires assigning implementation responsibilities for strategic initiatives to specific individuals and organizational units and holding them accountable for the results. An MBO-type performance management system, for example, can be used to incorporate lead and support responsibilities regarding particular strategic initiatives in performance contracts for specific senior-level managers, often members of the strategic management group themselves. These individuals can, in turn, use the performance management process to link these responsibilities to their subordinate managers, and so on down through the ranks, with their efforts on these tasks weighing in heavily in annual performance appraisals, recognition programs, and the rewards system in general. By incorporating strategic plans into this type of performance management process, the strategic management group can establish clear lines of accountability for implementing strategies, and managers at all levels of the organization become personally invested in advancing the strategic agenda.

Finally, it is essential that the strategic management process include the identification and tracking of valid measures of the organization's performance in achieving strategic objectives. To the extent that these strategic objectives relate directly to improvement in the performance of ongoing programs or activities, appropriate measures may already be imbedded in existing performance monitoring systems, but qualitatively new strategic initiatives often will require new or additional performance measures. Periodically tracking such measures will allow the strategic management group not only to tie results to budget allocations but also, more important, to track the agency's progress in achieving strategic objectives. This results-oriented feedback is critical for confirming success, revising next steps, and/or developing alternative strategies.

Whereas this cyclical process usually occurs in sequential steps on an annual basis, perhaps with some elements recurring more frequently on shorter cycles, the strategic management group should constantly be involved with the overall process through monitoring both the internal organization and its external environment on an ongoing basis, as indicated in Figure 16.2. This involves keeping informed about trends and issues regarding the political and governmental arenas, partnering and competitive organizations, customers, constituents, and other stakeholders as well as ongoing service delivery and concerns ranging from administrative processes, organizational climate, internal communications, and the like as they relate to strategic issues and initiatives. The internal monitoring may be accomplished in part through regular management information systems, periodic employee surveys, and other structured data collection efforts, but it also takes place less systematically through debriefings, informal conversations, site visits, brown bag lunches, and "management by walking around." Similarly, the external "intelligence gathering" is likely to require synthesizing information from a variety of sources including published reports, professional associations and "industry" groups, customer feedback, advisory committees, and interactions with a variety of external stakeholders. Whereas a structured process involving the steps shown in Figure 16.2

is essential, an agency's strategic managers can be truly strategic in their thinking and decisions only if they really understand what is going on in their organization and its environment.

The Pennsylvania Department of Transportation

With the advantage of remarkable continuity in leadership through three very different gubernatorial administrations, the Pennsylvania Department of Transportation (PennDOT) has been able to strengthen its capacity for strategic management and make it the driving force for decisions made throughout this agency of some 12,000 employees. Former Secretary of Transportation Tom Larson initiated strategic planning at PennDOT, created a strategic management committee (SMC), and tied it to the budget process some 15 years ago (Poister and Larson, 1988), and his two successors have broadened and deepened the process along the way.

Whereas strategic planning originally was limited to the top management team, the most recent round of strategic planning 2 years ago (led by current Secretary of Transportation Brad Mallory) involved 150 PennDOT managers and 50 external stake-holders including representatives from metropolitan planning organizations, federal agencies, private trucking companies, and a contractors association. This effort produced eight strategic goals geared to "Moving PennDOT Forward," emphasizing themes such as "maintenance first," intermodalism, customer-driven service delivery, strategic leveraging of available investment funds, and the use of leading-edge technology and written in broad form so that they apply to all transportation modes and all parts of the department.

PennDOT's SMC consists of the secretary, six deputy secretaries, the director of policy, the legislative affairs director, the communications and customer service director, the press secretary, and the chief counsel. Whereas the department's Executive Committee, which includes these individuals along with a few others, meets for an hour each Monday morning for a more operationally oriented staff meeting, the SMC has a half-day meeting once each month. This group reviews progress on ongoing strategic initiatives, discusses "hot" issues facing the department, reviews special reports and proposals brought by various divisions, and makes PennDOT's most fundamental decisions regarding both substantive policy and management strategies.

The SMC provides guidelines for the annual budget process and determines the budget that is forwarded to the Governor's Budget Office and eventually to the state legislature. In preparing the budget, central office bureaus present proposals to their respective deputy secretaries while the 67 highway maintenance units present proposals to their respective district engineers. The deputies, in turn, present budget proposals to the secretary and the deputy secretary for administration, and the 11 district engineers, whose organizations account for the great majority of PennDOT's employees and activity, present their budget proposals to the entire SMC. These presentations are based largely on demonstrating what these units accomplished in the preceding year in terms of advancing PennDOT's strategic goals and showing how their proposed business plans are keyed directly to the initiatives involved in "Moving PennDOT Forward." Major issues that arise in the internal hearings with the secretary are forwarded to the SMC to be resolved before the entire budget package is pulled together. In past years, budget proposals have been "sent back to the drawing board" because they failed to adhere to the department's strategic priorities, but the process has been deeply institutionalized by now, and budget proposals do tend to be highly responsive to the strategic goals. Currently, the SMC is emphasizing the need for operating units to have a means of monitoring progress along these lines and revising business plans throughout the year accordingly.

Regarding performance management, the deputy secretaries and other executives develop sets of special initiatives on a quarterly basis that are designed to advance "Moving PennDOT Forward." These quarterly initiatives, which are arrayed around the department's strategic goals and objectives, are negotiated as short-term performance contracts with Mallory, who holds these individuals accountable for completing these planned actions. The executives, in turn, drill responsibilities for these projects down through the senior- and middle-level managers who report to them, using the department's MBO process, and their performance on the initiatives is incorporated into the annual process of appraising individual managers' performance.

PennDOT monitors the performance of its ongoing programs, quarterly initiatives, and longer term projects in advancing the strategic plan through a monthly progress report that is designed exclusively for this purpose. The progress report, which is distributed to all senior managers, is organized according to the department's eight strategic goals and employs a mix of project milestone, program accomplishment, and outcome measures to track performance in these areas. This report is reviewed in the monthly SMC meetings, and the relevant sections are reviewed by the individual executives with their respective staffs, with problems noted and corrective actions taken. The progress report is supplemented by a more data-intensive statistical digest that is used to monitor operations and the performance of ongoing programs in greater detail on a monthly basis. This statistical digest is used primarily by the deputy secretaries, bureau chiefs, district engineers, and county maintenance managers to track the operations they supervise, but because many of the department's strategic initiatives are intended to improve service delivery quality and routine program performance, these data also serve in some ways to track PennDOT's progress in pursuing its strategic agenda.

The City of Charlotte

The City of Charlotte, North Carolina, is in the process of developing an approach to strategic management that eventually will incorporate all the elements shown in Figure 16.2. As an organizing tool for integrating various performance criteria in its strategic management process, Charlotte is using the balanced scorecard (BSC) model developed by Kaplan and Norton (1992, 1993). Created originally for private sector use, the BSC model focuses on performance from a customer perspective, an internal process perspective, and a learning organization perspective in addition to the financial perspective. Whereas the tool initially was developed as a means of linking various types of performance measures to provide a balanced picture of a company's performance, 2 years ago Charlotte began using the four perspectives as a framework for integrating goals and objectives, strategies, and performance measures across the broad spectrum of city operations.

Charlotte's BSC process is being led by City Manager Pam Syfert, assisted by budget and evaluation staff members, but the active involvement of the city council has been critical to its success so far. Figure 16.3 shows the city council's priorities from each of the four perspectives. Clear objective statements have been developed for each of these priorities, and "lead" and "lag" performance measures have been identified to track intermediate results and outcomes, respectively. The customer-oriented priorities reflect desired policy outcomes, whereas the priorities from the other perspectives are further linked to these outcomes to define thematic packages at the corporate level. For example, the community safety theme focuses on crime prevention and increasing the public's perception of safety by leveraging city and community resources to fight crime more effectively. All city council priorities concerned with expanding non-city funding, improving productivity, increasing positive contacts in the community, enhancing management capabilities, closing the skills gap, and achieving a positive employee climate are seen as being essential elements of an overall strategy to increase community safety.

Whereas the city council feels ownership of these corporate priorities and objectives, the city manager and administrative structure take ownership of the strategic management process, which at this point still is a work in progress. With the city council's priorities established, each department or business unit has been charged with developing a 1-year business plan in support of the corporate objectives. These business plans are intended to clarify the linkages by addressing the following questions: "What do you

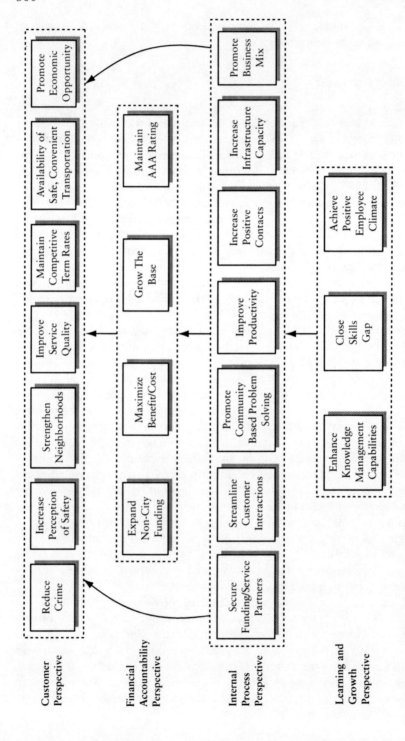

FIGURE 16.3 Corporate-Level Linkage Model Reflecting the Charlotte City Council's Priorities

do, what programs do you have, and what strategies can you develop to support our corporate priorities and objectives?" As one of the units to pilot this process, the Charlotte Department of Transportation (CDOT) has developed a strategically targeted fiscal 1998 business plan organized around the BSC framework. Designed to advance the city council's priority on the availability of safe and convenient transportation, the plan identifies the department's mission and vision, strategic "rudders" or basic values, strategic initiatives, objectives, and high-impact programs of various divisions along with attendant performance measures. Figure 16.4 shows CDOT's objectives and lead and lag performance measures organized around the four BSC perspectives.

Charlotte's planning department recently developed an annual cycle for incorporating the BSC plans and measures into the city's overall performance management process. With departmental business plans in place, the city intends to drill responsibility for them down to the operating level. Through its management by results system, performance targets and appraisals for individuals (or, in some cases, for groups or teams) will be tied to the city's overall strategic plan. At this point, there are no formal links between the BSC planning process and Charlotte's budgeting process, but the intention is to gradually transition from the current line item budget to results-based budgeting by building BSC objectives and performance measures into the budget system. At that point, the city of Charlotte should have a comprehensive strategic management system in place.

Conclusion

This article has sought to raise awareness of the crucial importance of strategic management in government and to overview the critical concepts and components of strategic management processes in public agencies. A model reflecting the integrative nature of strategic management was presented, and the essential elements of a generic strategic management process were discussed. A few real-world examples were provided in brief to illustrate the model and to bring the process alive to public managers.

In response to growing demands for public accountability, fiscal conservatism, and increased legislative oversight as well as professional imperatives for proactive leadership, improved performance, and a customer service orientation, public management scholars and practitioners have been coalescing for quite some time around the theme of managing for results. This article argues that in public agencies of any size and complexity, it is impossible to manage for results in the long or short run without a well-developed capacity for strategic management. Indeed, on a macro level, strategic management, with its emphasis on developing and implementing a strategic agenda, is synonymous with managing for results.

Perspective	Objective	Lead Measure	Lag Measure
Customer	C-1 Maintain the transportation system C-2 Operate the transportation system C-3 Develop the transportation system C-4 Determine the optimal system design C-5 Improve service quality	C-1 Repair Response: repair response action C-1 Travel Speed: average travel speed by facility and selected location C-2 Commute Time: average commute time on selected roads C-2 On-Time Buses: public transit on-line C-3 Programs Introduced: newly introduced programs, ??, or program specifications C-5 Responsiveness: % of citizen complaints and requests resolved at the CDOT level	C-1 High Quality Streets: condition of lane miles ?? 90 rating C-2 Safety: city-wide accident rate; no. of high accident locations C-3 Basic Mobility: availability of public transit C-4 Plan Progress: % complete on 2015 Transportation Plan
Financial	F-1 Expand non-City funding F-2 Maximize benefit / cost	F-2 Costs: costs compared to other municipalities and private sector competition	F-1 Funding Leverage: dollar values from non-City sources F-1 New Funding Sources: dollar value from sources not previously available
Internal Process	I-1 Gain infrastructure capacity I-2 Score funding/service partners I-3 Improve productivity I-4 Increase positive contacts with Community	I-1 Capital Investment $ allocated to capital projects in targeted areas I-2 Leverage funding/service partners: new funding/resource partners identified I-3 Cost per Unit: cost per unit I-3 Competitive Sourcing: % ofBudget bid I-3 Problem Identification: sourve & action I-4 Customer Communications: no. type, freq.	I-1 Capacity Ratios: Incremental capacity built vs. required by 2015 Plan I-2 No. of Partners: number of partners I-3 Street Maintenance Cost: cost/lane mi. I-3 Transit Passenger Cost: cost/pass'ger I-4 Customer Surveys: survey results concerning service quality
Learning	L-1 Enhance automated information systems L-2 Enhance "Bold" technology L-3 Close the skills gap L-4 Empower employees	L-1 IT Infrastructure: complete relational database across CDOT L-3 Skills Identified: key skills identified in strategic functions L-4 Employee Climate Survey: results of employee survey	L-1 Information Assess: strategic information available vs. user requirements L-2 Information Tests: strategic tools available vs. user requirements L-3 Skills Transfer: skill evidence in task or job performance L-4 Employee Goal Alignment: training/career development aligned with mission

FIGURE 16.4 Charlotte Department of Transportation Lead and Lag Measures

Whereas treatments of more specific tools such as strategic planning, performance measurement, quality improvement, work process reengineering, and results-based budgeting have been more prevalent in the public administration literature, strategic management is the central integrative process that gives the organization a sense of direction and ensures a concerted effort to achieve strategic goals and objectives. A strategically managed public agency is one in which budgeting, performance management, human resource development, program management, and other management processes are guided by a strategic agenda that has been developed with a buy-in from key stakeholders and communicated widely within the organization and among external constituencies.

Public managers have a number of levers at their disposal for influencing people and programs and bringing about organizational change, but they cannot be used effectively without a clear sense of mission, values, vision, and overall strategy. The model presented in Figure 16.1 conveys the essence of strategic management as the integrative force that guides and disciplines a wide array of management processes to move in a unified direction in a number of different arenas. The two-directional flow of influence and sensitivity between an agency's strategic agenda and the constellation of processes and associated stakeholders surrounding it reflects the dynamic nature of strategic management. As portrayed in Figure 16.2, strategic management is an iterative process in which planning generates a strategic agenda that must be not only implemented but also evaluated and updated through continued external and internal monitoring.

Strategic management in the public sector is concerned with strengthening the long-term health and effectiveness of governmental units and leading them through positive change to ensure a continuing productive "fit" with changing environments. However, strategic management should not be confused with leadership itself. Strategic management will not transform otherwise poor leaders, and public managers who lack leadership skills will find it very difficult to implement effective strategic management processes. Rather, strategic management provides a vehicle that skilled leaders can use to involve stakeholders in creating a vision for the agency, build commitment to strategic objectives, and focus organizational resources and energies on advancing the agency's strategic agenda. The abilities to identify emerging issues and understand their implication for the organization, craft viable strategies and mobilize support for them, communicate a vision for the future in a compelling manner, and build teams and authentic relationships that will be conducive to bringing about desired organizational change all are essential for managing public agencies strategically. Thus, strategic management supports good leadership and may provide a context for developing leadership skills, but basically, it takes good leaders to create effective strategic management processes.

More than any other single approach in the public manager's tool kit, strategic management is the most fundamental, and the most critical, process for producing results in the challenging and increasingly competitive environment in which most public managers work. Many governmental units and agencies have some of the pieces in place, but relatively few actually have developed full-fledged strategic management systems that truly integrate all major functions and management processes and direct them toward defining and advancing an organization's strategic agenda. Thus, public managers who are committed to results-oriented management will have to get serious about developing an effective capacity for strategic management in their agencies.

References

Berry, F. S., and B. Wechsler (1995). State agencies' experience with strategic planning: Findings from a national survey. *Public Administration Review* 55, 159–168.

Broom, C. A. (1995). Performance-based government models: Building a track record. *Public Budgeting and Finance* 15(4), 3–17.

Bryson, J. M. (1988). *Strategic planning for public and nonprofit organizations: A guide to strengthening and sustaining organizational achievement.* San Francisco: Jossey-Bass.

Eadie, D. C., and R. Steinbacher (1985). Strategic agenda management: A marriage of organizational development and strategic planning. *Public Administration Review* 45, 424–430.

Halachmi, A., W. P. Hardy, and B. L. Rhoades (1993). Demographic data and strategic analysis. *Public Administration Quarterly* 17, 159–174.

Kaplan, R. S., and D. P. Norton (1992). The balanced scorecard: Measures that drive performance. *Harvard Business Review* 70(1), 71–79.

Kaplan, R. S., and D. P. Norton (1993). Putting the balanced scorecard to work. *Harvard Business Review* 71(5), 134–142.

Koteen, J. (1989). *Strategic management in public and nonprofit organizations.* New York: Praeger.

Melkers, J., and K. Willoughby (1998). The state of the states: Performance-based budgeting requirements in 47 out of 50. *Public Administration Review* 58, 66–73.

Nutt, P. C., and R. W. Backoff (1992). *Strategic management of public and third sector organizations: A handbook for leaders.* San Francisco: Jossey-Bass.

Poister, T. H., and T. D. Larson (1988). The revitalization of PennDOT: A case study in effective public management. *Public Productivity Review* 11(3), 85–103.

Poister, T. H., and G. Streib (1994). Municipal management tools from 1976 to 1993: An overview and update. *Public Productivity and Management Review* 18, 115–125.

Quinn, R. E., and J. Rohrbaugh (1981). A competing values approach to organizational effectiveness. *Public Productivity Review* 5(2), 122–140.

Rabin, J., G. J. Miller, and W. B. Hildreth (1989). *Handbook of strategic management*. New York: Marcel Dekker.

Steiss, A. W. (1985). *Strategic management and organizational decision-making*. Lexington, MA: D. C. Heath.

Toft, G. S. (1989). Synoptic (one best way) approaches of strategic management. In J. Rabin, G. J. Miller, and W. B. Hildreth, eds., *Handbook of strategic management*. New York: Marcel Dekker.

Vinzant, D. H., and J. C. Vinzant (1996a). Strategy and organizational capacity: Finding a fit. *Public Productivity and Management Review* 20, 139–157.

Vinzant, J. C., and D. H. Vinzant (1996b). Strategic management and total quality management: Challenges and choices. *Public Administration Quarterly* 20, 201–219.

Section II.B

PERFORMANCE MANAGEMENT

17

APPLYING PROFESSIONAL DISCLOSURE STANDARDS TO PRODUCTIVITY FINANCIAL ANALYSES

W. Bartley Hildreth

Municipal finance officers have a critical role to perform in productivity analysis. The cost of a service or activity is inextricably part of any productivity study. The finance (or budget) officer often has the responsibility of costing-out existing service provisions and estimating alternative service options. In those cases where the total cost of a particular service is difficult to determine, the finance officer is required to make assumptions about both cost behavior and forecasts of future fund flows.

The finance officer's role in productivity analyses raises at least two questions. Does a finance officer have a special professional responsibility in doing productivity-related financial analyses? Are there professional standards which might provide guidance to finance officers in conducting productivity analyses? This essay answers each question. Support for the answers is provided by an examination of the disclosure responsibilities of public finance officers in doing productivity analyses.

1983. Applying professional disclosure standards to productivity financial analyses. Hildreth, W. Bartley. **Public Productivity and Management Review** 7 (September): 269–287.

A public finance professional is a person responsible for developing budgets and maintaining the integrity and accuracy of public funds in their receipt, recording, and reporting. Professional responsibility of finance officers can be demonstrated through a review of applicable professional accounting criteria. This paper reviews the accounting profession's qualitative disclosure standards as a model for assessing a productivity financial analysis used in a case study. Since the context at issue is productivity analysis, a case study is presented of a common productivity enhancement effort—contracting out of solid waste collection services.[1] The results illustrate the fit between professional disclosure standards and productivity analysis.

Professionalism

An efficient and effective public service depends to a great degree on responsible, professional public officers. Responsibility relates, in part, to a set of standards, or codes of behavior, to guide professional actions. Peer group acceptance flows from acceptance of these behavioral decision-rules while peer group sanctions result from non-compliance. As such, codes of behavior constitute one attribute of a profession.[2]

A professional's reputation is determined by the nature of relationships achieved between the professional and his or her client. The application of inaccurate or poorly conceived advice subjects the professional to the risk of malpractice or peer group sanction.

A professional has responsibility not only to a client but also to the public. Are professionals merely hired guns? Does confidentiality dictate that client or employer desires overshadow a responsibility to report to the public? In her new book, *Secrets,* Sissela Bok confronts this issue.[3] Bok notes that while the prevailing ethic is confidentiality on behalf of the client, formal codes of ethics are more insistent that the professional has a responsibility to the public. On the same point, a proposed "Certified Governmental Accountant" profession calls for a professional code of ethics which would "increase the confidence of society in government and its participants."[4]

Professionals cannot explain away responsibility by relying on the "problem of many hands."[5] As presented by Thompson, the "problem of many hands" arises through the "actions of many different people whose individual contributions may not be identified at all, and certainly cannot be distinguished significantly from other people's contributions." Rather than collective responsibility, professionals face personal responsibility for their actions. This is a problem in the public sector where political demands can conflict with professional norms. Dennis F. Thompson illustrates the point by reviewing the fiscal crisis of New York City. The mayor, at the time, Abraham Beame, had tried to use the "problem of many hands" to explain past fiscal actions, but as Thompson points out, the Mayor's past positions in the city had included serving as controller and budget director.

Uncertainty Absorption

Decisions rendered under conditions of doubt are susceptible to error and mistake. Using inference rather than evidence to guide decisions leads to "uncertainty absorption."

According to James G. March and Herbert A. Simon "uncertainty absorption" applies when "inferences are drawn from a body of evidence and the inferences, instead of the evidence itself, are then communicated."[6] As data are taken from a data base (e.g., accounting ledgers) and used in a financial report (e.g., a financial analysis supporting the desire to contract-out refuse collection services) accuracy can be diminished and uncertainty can be absorbed by inferences. March and Simon summarize the point:

> . . . (T)he recipient must, by and large, repose his confidence in the editing process that has taken place, and, if he accepts the communication at all, accept it pretty much as it stands. To the extent that he can interpret it, his interpretation must be based primarily on his confidence in the source and his knowledge of the biases to which the source is subject, rather than on a direct examination of the evidence.

Uncertainty absorption involves a power relationship. The person summarizing the data occupies a position of influence especially if the assertions are "accepted as premises of decisions."[7] In other contexts, this is referred to as the power of agenda-setting, that is, controlling information plays a basic role in structuring the agenda of decision making.

The power relationship is exacerbated when the language used is not common to all, as is the case when non-professionals do not understand the professional's technical language. For example, finance officers utilize a technical vocabulary of funds, transfers, depreciation, etc. The language barrier does little to limit uncertainty absorption.

The Efficient Market

Uncertainty absorption is reduced by disclosure. Disclosure of basic evidence or data permits others to make independent judgments regarding the quality of the decision at hand. This practice of decision oversight promotes an "efficient market." As used in corporate securities:[8]

... the efficient market hypothesis maintains that the market equilibrium prices of securities fully reflect all publicly available information, and that these prices react instantaneously and in an unbiased fashion to new information. In simpler terms, the market price of securities reflects all present public information, and adjusts accurately and immediately to new information.

The efficient market in publicly-traded corporate securities relies upon disclosure standards promulgated and policed by the Securities and Exchange Commission (SEC). Thus, insider trading of a firm's stock is subject to careful disclosure; otherwise, those closest to a corporate change have a disproportionate advantage over others in the stock market.

As applied here, an efficient market of information or data is one way to deal with uncertainty absorption. When an efficient market is operating, assertions are taken for what they are and not for conclusions based on substantiated facts.

A case study is presented below and then reviewed against a set of professional disclosure standards. The case study points out some of the problems with accepting unsubstantiated assertions about financial data.

Case Study:
"Productivity Proposal"

In the case study, a metropolitan central city[9] proposed to convert residential refuse collection services from public collection to private, contracted-out collection. The avowed purpose of the city administration's proposal was to achieve certain cost savings while maintaining or improving productivity.

All city wards received residential refuse collection services by city crews until 1978. In November 1977, a private refuse collection firm was awarded a contract to serve approximately 15,200 households (essentially two city wards of white, middle and upper-income households). City crews provided refuse collection services to the remaining city wards. Both the city and the private contractor were to pick up refuse once a week per household. The private firm received a five-year contract (January 1978 to December 1982) to provide residential collection services for a contracted price per household.

As the city's fiscal condition tightened in 1980, one response was the Mayor's convening of a financial advisory committee. The committee, composed of prominent business and civic leaders, made several recommendations in a December 1980 report.

One recommendation encouraged the city to investigate an expansion of its use of private firms in "areas where they can provide services at a lower cost than the city can provide them." The committee also recommended

TABLE 17.1   Financial analysis of first quarter, 1981

	Expense Item
$267,422.00	Permanent employee wags and overtime from Finance Department
23,814.00	Insurance from Finance Department
41,631.00	Calculated Retirement and Worker's Compensation payments
3,681.00	Calculated temporary employee wages and benefits
65,398.00	Calculated C.E.T.A. employee wages and benefits
17,134.00	Miscellaneous expense from Finance Department
39,570.00	Calculated tipping fees paid to Recycle Energy System
118,172.00	Calculated payments to Motor Equipment
56,090.00	Calculated vehicle depreciation
$632,912.00	Total expense, First Quarter, 1981

Dividing this total by 13 weeks and then by 46,946 customers, we arrive at $1.037 per house per week.

Approximately $46,750.00 for billing has been excluded since the city will continue to provide this service regardless of whether the city or a contractor is handling refuse collection.

the city retain a portion of these services "in order to maintain the city's delivery capacity and to avoid a private sector monopoly."

The city administration took action on the recommendation. By the end of the first quarter of 1981, a cost analysis had been prepared on the estimated cost of city refuse collection services. Table 17.1 provides an itemized listing of the cost calculations. The cost of providing city refuse collection services to 80 percent of the city in the first quarter of 1981 was calculated at $632,912. Based upon providing city services to 46,946 customers, the cost during the 13-week quarter was calculated at $1.037 per house per week.

To determine yearly costs, the first quarter figures were revised to reflect assumptions about future cost behavior. The finance department estimated that the remaining three-quarters of 1981 would cost the city $1,999,600, or $1.10 per household per week. As shown in Table 17.2, two assumptions were employed, namely an 8 percent salary increase and a 20 percent increase in vehicle operating costs.

Combining the first quarter's estimated actual costs with the forecasted figures for the last three quarters resulted in a yearly city collection cost of $2,632,512. Since city refuse collection was supplemented with an existing private collection service for two wards ($692,640 for 12,000 customers), residential refuse collection costs (public and private) in the city were projected at $3,325,152 in 1981.

TABLE 17.2   Financial Analysis of Yearly Costs (1981 and 1982) and Contracting-Out Alternatives

I.   A calculation of the 1982 cost for refuse collection follows:

<u>With 20 percent contracted on 7-1-81</u>

A.   City collection (46,946 customers)

1)	1-1-81 to 3-31-81 (see Table 1)	$ 632,912
2)	4-1-81 to 12-31-81 This is calculated using three times the cost of the first quarter plus an additional 8 percent for salaries and 20 percent for vehicle operating costs and equals $1.10/household/week.	1,999,600
	City subtotal	$2,632,512

B.   Contractor collection   692,640
($1.11/customer for 12,000 customers)

                                    Total 1981 $3,325,152

<u>With 50 percent contracted on 7-1-81</u>

A.   City collection (46,946 customers)

1)	1-1-81 to 3-31-81	$ 632,912
2)	4-1-81 to 6-30-81	666,533
3)	City collection (29,473 customers for the 7-1-81 to 12-31-81 period)	842,956
	Subtotal	$2,142,401

B.   Contractor collection

1)	1-1-81 to 6-31-81 $1.11/customer for 12,000 customers	$ 346,320
2)	7-1-81 to 12-31-81 $1.11/customer for 12,000 customers .75/customer for 17,472	346,320 340,704
	Subtotal	$1,033,344
	Total	3,175,745
	Savings	$ 149,407

<u>With 100 percent contracted on 7-1-81</u>

A.   City collection

1)	46,946 customers at $1.04 1-1-81 to 3-31-81	$ 632,912
2)	46,946 customers at $1.11 4-1-81 to 6-30-81	666,533

TABLE 17.2 (continued)

3)	City collection (29,473 customers for the 7-1-81 to 12-31-81 period)	842,956
	Subtotal	$1,299,445

B. Contractor collection

1)	1-1-81 to 6-30-81 $1.11/customer for 12,000 customers	$ 346,320
2)	7-1-81 to 12-31-81 $ .75/customer for 46,946 customers	915,447
	$1.11/customers for 12,000 customers	346,320
	Subtotal	$1,600,087
	Total	2,907,532
	Savings	$ 417,620

II. A calculation of the 1982 costs and savings are:

20 percent Contracted

A. City collection

1-1-82 to 12-31-82 46,946 customers at $1.20/household (this assumes 10 percent inflation in 1982)	$2,953,842

B. Contractor collection

1-1-82 to 12-31-82 12,000 customers at $1.19/household	742,560
Total	$3,696,402

50 percent Contracted

A. City collection (1-1-82 to 12-31-82)

$1.20/household for 29,473 customers	$1,839,115

B. Contractor collection

$1.19/household for 12,000 customers	$ 742,560
$ .81/household for 17,473 customers	735,962
Total	3,317,637
Savings	$ 378,765

100 percent Contracted

A. Contractor collection

$1.19/household for 12,000	$ 742,560
$ .81/household for 46,946 customers	1,977,366
Total	$2,719,926
Savings	976,476

TABLE 17.3   Contract Bid Prices (per household per week)

Period	Bid #1	Bid #2	Bid #3	Bid #4
July-Dec. 1981	$ .75	$ .869	$ .99	$ .969
1982	.81	.918	.99	1.061
1983	.88	.926	1.18	1.162
1984	.94	1.014	1.30	1.272
1985	1.02	1.113	1.45	1.393
1986	1.09	1.225	1.59	1.525

The finance department then compared city costs to contract prices. The comparisons, also in Table 17.2, show cost savings for three options: 20 percent contracted services (the current figure); 50 percent contracted; and, 100 percent contracted residential collection service. The saving to the city for 1981 by having 50 percent of the residential refuse collection performed by city crews was estimated to be $149,407; for totally contracted services, the 1981 saving was estimated to be $417,620. Cost savings in 1982 and thereafter also were calculated to be substantial, as indicated in Table 17.2.

Bids were accepted from four private hauling firms. Table 17.3 indicates the bid price per household. The bid labeled number one is from the private firm with the existing refuse collection contract (for 20 percent). The price per household bid by this firm was used by the city in calculating the estimated savings to accrue from contracted services. Either the bid price was known prior to formal bid solicitation or the private firm had excellent luck or financial acumen in costing-out its bid.

The Mayor's proposal to contract-out residential refuse collection services was not acted upon by the City Council. Not surprisingly, the affected union contested the figures and the need for contracted services. Some members of the Council opposed the Mayor's proposal. In the end, the Mayor did not force the issue. Subsequently, the contracting-out proposal arose during union negotiations and again during a city administration request to the City Council for higher user charges for residential refuse collection. As of this writing, no further action has been taken on the contracting-out proposal.

Accounting Disclosure

While this case study might serve as an interesting example in the political realities of productivity proposals, it is used here only to determine how financial officers can (and do) practice uncertainty absorption as opposed to the efficient market model of professional practice.

Disclosure operates to minimize uncertainty absorption. The accounting profession has addressed the disclosure issue by adopting standards for members to observe in communicating an organization's financial operations and condition. A well-developed body of "generally accepted accounting principles" (GAAP) and "generally accepted auditing standards" (GAAS) have evolved to ensure that financial reports fairly and completely present the entity's financial position and operations.

The adequacy of financial disclosure and reporting is assessed by certain criteria. Outlined here are the qualitative criteria of financial disclosure[10] as opposed to the specifics of handling accounting entries (the quantitative characteristics of financial disclosure). Each of six qualitative criteria of adequate disclosure is first defined. Under each of the criteria, the above case study is analyzed in terms of how disclosure as practiced fell short on the respective criteria. Brief illustrative examples are presented to show the potential for using disclosure criteria in evaluating financial analyses of productivity proposals.

Criterion One: Relevance

Information is relevant if it directly bears on user decision making processes. Information must be timely and pertinent to users for it to be relevant. Users differ in their needs and "information which is relevant for one purpose is not necessarily relevant for an alternative purpose."[11]

Who are the users and what financial information do they need? Users of public financial information include, among others, investors, employees and legislators.[12]

Participants in the municipal securities market have an almost insatiable need for data and information on public issuers of bonds. Data on the financial and economic characteristics of a public jurisdiction as well as extensive details on projects to be funded and debt repayment provisions are required by investors and bond rating agencies. Moreover, detailed disclosure guidelines have evolved.[13]

Employees and their union representatives are becoming more interested users of financial information for contract negotiation and for following the jurisdiction's financial condition. Some unions have experienced fiscal experts on their staffs or under consulting contracts.

Legislators also need financial information because of their responsibility to the electorate for allocating public resources for services and activities along public interest guidelines (however difficult to define and generalize). A periodic flow of financial information is necessary for legislators to make informed decisions on matters affecting taxes and services.

In applying the criterion of relevance to the case study, the city's contracting-out proposal gives the appearance that city collection costs—especially pay and benefits—were uncontrollable. A contrary picture emerges by reviewing relevant sections of the city's past budgets. For the period in question, the personnel service percentages of the total sanitation service budget declined (from 53 percent in 1981 to 47 percent in the 1982 budget) while non-personnel costs increased (from 47 percent to 53 percent). Thus, pay and benefit costs of refuse collection were not the costs deserving the most attention. Rather, administrative expenses increased over the period. Despite the need for sufficient cost controls in areas not affected by any proposed private contracting-out arrangement, attention was focused on already controlled budget items. Users of the financial analysis were not given such pertinent facts.

Criterion Two: Materiality

Information is "material" if its appearance, omission, or misstatement is likely to influence user decision making. In contrast, something immaterial would not motivate action regardless of its disclosure.[14]

The amount of savings to result from contracting-out services is a material factor, but what if the assumptions upon which the "savings" were calculated were questionable? The case study provides several examples.

The city's past record of keeping contracted refuse collection services to a fixed price is material. That is, can the city enforce the contract price with some certainty that over the contract period refuse collection will cost only the contracted price per household?

The city does have past experience to enlighten analysis in that residential refuse collection services in one part of the city (about 20 percent of all residential pickups) were contracted-out. Under the so-called fixed contract, the city and the contractor adjusted the contract price to reflect changes in the city's desired level of service—e.g., to have the contractor pick up large items discarded by residents. Table 17.4 shows the original contract price, the revised price, and the percent increase of the revised price over the "fixed" five-year contract price. The average price increase under the revised contract was 14 percent per year.

A review of the city's May 1981, cost analysis (see Table 17.1) provides several examples of material data: (1) inclusion of indirect and overhead costs (e.g., tipping fees) in estimates; (2) use of assumptions in projecting future costs; (3) existence of unsubstantiated costs; and, (4) other important items.

1. *INDIRECT AND OVERHEAD COSTS.* The sanitation services budget did not reflect overhead or indirect costs. To arrive at the total cost of city-provided refuse collection services requires a determination of indirect costs. The indirect costs itemized in

TABLE 17.4 Contract Revision History

Contract Year	Contract Price	Revised Price	Percent Increase
1978	$ .76		
1979	.80	$.84*	5%
1980	.85	.93*	9
1981	.92	1.11	21
1982	1.00	1.19	19

*Converted from fixed dollar amounts

Table 17.1 appear quite specific when, in fact, the figures were only estimates. In addition, the city neglected to show indirect cost determination assumptions.

One principle of contract cost estimating is to include only direct and measurable costs associated with the service to be contracted-out.[15] Furthermore, each cost item should either increase or decrease with the contract decision. If the cost item stays the same regardless of the decision, then the particular item should not be factored into the "total" cost of an option.

The case study provided an example of how the contract cost estimate rule was violated: the inclusion of "tipping fees" in the financial analysis. The city misleadingly stated that the city-imposed tipping fee would be saved. In fact, a private firm had no choice but to pay the city fee since a city ordinance mandated all private waste haulers deposit certain types of refuse in the city-financed Recycle Energy System (RES) which was designed to produce energy out of burned refuse. This cost was the same whether the city contracted-out the service or maintained city crews (since the city would use internal transfers from the sanitation collection service to the RES). Following a pre-bid conference between potential private bidders and city officials, the city revised bid specifications to exclude tipping fees. Private firms recognized that the city could later revise the tipping fees and make the firm cover the higher fees out of the fixed contract price.

2. *PROJECTION ASSUMPTIONS.* To use one quarter of costs to estimate a yearly cost assumes that the first quarter is a true reflection of cost behavior for the remainder of the year. An analysis of cost for each quarter (or month) for the past several years may or may not justify this cost assumption. It is possible that vehicle expenses, overtime, etc., during the winter months do

not mirror the costs of other quarters of the year. This was not addressed explicitly in the financial analysis.

3. *UNSUBSTANTIATED COSTS.* Not substantiating estimates leads to questions. For example, the city's financial analysis showed transfers to the Motor Equipment unit (an internal service fund) of $118,172. The sanitation service unit operated thirty-four vehicles, most of which were no older than two years. More disclosure is needed to substantiate the reasons for the costs, whether the costs are the result of driver misuse (a responsibility of sanitation services), mechanic mistakes (a responsibility of the motor equipment unit), or the equipment (perhaps a function associated with the purchasing department's lack of bid specification monitoring).

4. *OTHER IMPORTANT ITEMS.* The analysis disregarded other items which might be material. A cost-benefit analysis, if conducted, would have indicated that the city would incur certain costs as well as benefits from contracting-out refuse collection services, many of which are not easy to measure.[16] For example, the city would incur the loss of flexibility in responding to emergencies or other "quick response" situations. In an emergency, the city might need to mobilize all of its employees.

Another material impact is illustrated by the city's liquidity problem. The city faced a cash flow problem at the time of the contracting-out controversy. The questionable remedy was to change the wage and salary period to effectively delay paying employees. The city administration used its management flexibility, however improper, to overcome the immediate liquidity crisis. Under a contract, the city might find the loss of such questionable practices very material in the larger scheme of things.

Another area which might become material is related to contract pricing strategies by private firms. Contractors have an incentive to price bids as low as possible to obtain business (called "low balling"). During contract implementation, however, contractors face cost pressures. A costing-out analysis should consider carefully how these factors can affect the financial analysis. For example, contractors might achieve some startup savings over municipal collection by hiring new employees at lower wages than city employees receive for years of city service. Thus, a contractor's personnel costs could well be lower initially than the city's personnel costs. In an related manner, contractors benefit from lower maintenance expenses since new equipment often is purchased to service the contract (often required under the bid specifications).

In both cases, however, as employees gain seniority and equipment ages, a contractor faces a decreasing profit margin on a fixed contract. A contractor has significant economic incentives to pass on the costs to the city through contract revisions. Cities unable to require a contractor to adhere to contract prices, the situation in the case study city, could find initial economies evaporating under economic pressures. How does this affect the initial financial analysis? A contingency analysis is needed to make sure such situations do not result in a material finding.

Criterion Three: Meaningfulness

A third criterion of adequate disclosure is "meaningfulness" and it refers to information that is "understandable, clear, concise, and succinct."[17] Yet, users possess varying degrees of knowledge about and ability to understand disclosed information. On the one hand, the American Institute of Certified Public Accountants (AICPA) states that:[18]

... (a)ccounting information should be presented so that it can be understood by reasonably well-informed, as well as sophisticated, users. In effect, presenting information understandable only to sophisticated users establishes a bias.... (Users) with means to do their own research already have an advantage over others. The form and content of financial statements should not add to this advantage.

On the other hand, the AICPA argues that:

... (n)o valid users' needs should be ignored. Information that can be understood, and is needed, by sophisticated users should not be diluted to eliminate what less able users cannot understand. Instead, it should be ordered and arrayed to serve a broad range of users.

While the assumed level of user knowledge complicates the preparation of "meaningful" reports, it is agreed that "(i)n all cases, information is more useful if it stresses economic substance rather than technical form."

The financial analysis used by the city in the case study relating to contracting-out falls short of meeting the criterion of meaningfulness. An implict assumption of the financial report was that users, whether in the city council or in an union, could ascertain the underlying assumptions in the financial analysis and the implications of such assumptions. For example, the city estimated a 20 percent increase in vehicle operating costs for the remainder of the year (see Table 17.2). When annualized, however, the price increase would be much higher than 20 percent to compensate for different price levels in the earlier part of the year.

Compounding the disclosure problem, the financial analysis relied on depreciation figures which were not generally understood by users. Users deserve more disclosure to enable them independently to test assumptions against their own decision criteria. More disclosure on these meaningful areas was warranted.

Criterion Four: Reliability

Financial information must be "reliable". This does not mean necessarily that the information is completely accurate. Financial information is subject to uncertainties, imprecise measurements, and error. The AICPA states that[19] users ". . . should be informed about data limitations and the magnitude of possible measurement errors" and that financial information should not "imply a misleading degree of precision or reliability."

Financial information should stand the test of collaboration by independent sources. As in any "scientific" analysis, a lack of reliability serves as a sign of questionable work and questions about the validity of any findings.[20] The more reliable information is, the higher the quality. However, reconciling the criteria of relevance and reliability can present problems. Robert N. Anthony notes that the most relevant information may not be the most reliable.[21]

The city's cost analysis and projections lacked precision and detail. Assumptions about future cost behavior presumably were based on past cost behavior, yet such data were not presented. Moreover, the financial officer did not provide any clues as to the degree of confidence assigned to the savings projections.

Perhaps, an independent review of the facts might have rendered a different result. Finance officers seldom submit their analyses other than to internal debate and council deliberations. As a result, competing assumptions and figures receive little or no attention until late in the policy process. Alternative assumptions, of course, may render different results.

Criterion Five: Neutrality

Lack of bias in the reporting of financial information is important. As AICPA (1973) observed:[22] "While any information affected by judgments necessarily has some bias, there should be no *purposeful* bias favoring any group." Information must be truthful and presented fairly. Any chance for misleading information should be minimized. Again, quoting AICPA: "If financial statements do communicate information about varying degrees of uncertainty, about the judgments made and the interpretations applied, and about the underlying factual information, then the impact of surprises—pleasant or unpleasant—will diminish greatly."[23]

Proposals to contract-out public services can be something other than a desire to achieve cost economies. Edward H. Weseman, a city manager who wrote a book on contracting, notes that . . . "it is not unheard of for an employer to view contracting as a form of reprisal against a troublesome employee or union,"[24] Financial analyses designed to achieve objectives; such as union busting; conflict with the criterion of neutrality. While not stated, some close to the contracting-out case study believed that the criterion of neutrality was not central to the administration.

Criterion Six: Comparability

The disclosure of information should facilitate comparisons by users. According to AICPA[25] "(c)omparability means to have like things reported alike, and unlike things reported differently." The degree to which a financial statement fulfills this criterion depends upon how consistent in nature and format information is from one time period to another and among entities.

The need for consistency includes the use of a consistent accounting base from which to draw information. "Obviously the more comparable the information, the more valuable it is and its usefulness increases. Noncomparable information between entities and between periods significantly reduces its usefulness in decision making."[26]

The financial analysis prepared for contracting-out refuse collection services did not provide any comparisons to similar efforts in other jurisdictions. Also not shown were cost efficiencies likely to result from contracting-out other municipal activities (e.g., accounting, billing, legal services, etc.).

Adherence to a comparability criterion requires more analysis than is typically found in most contracting-out analyses. Disclosure principles suggest that the issue should be addressed in greater detail than has been the practice to date.

Disclosure Strategies

How much should be disclosed? It is difficult to provide a clear, empirical response, yet there are two basic strategies: tactical and systematic disclosure.

Tactical, selective or ad hoc disclosure by finance officers (or management) can result in selective use of data. For example, selective disclosure practices may focus on delaying the dissemination of negative information while quickly using positive information.[27] Selective disclosure fuels the fire of skepticism about management presentations. Several surveys reveal that union leaders, for example, suspect the veracity of management figures showing little or no money for economic settlements.[28]

Employing a systematic disclosure strategy also presents problems. Does systematic disclosure merely require the availability of highlighted financial "bottom lines" or does it necessitate timely, full disclosure of alternative assumptions and data factors?

An even more sweeping definition of systematic disclosure would require "full access to the system generating" management financial information.[29] Municipalities with integrated financial information systems perhaps could accomplish systematic disclosure with a read-only computer terminal available to interested parties (users). The users then could conduct their own "what if" analyses with access to the same public data.

Short of giving users (e.g., unions) limited interactive access to the financial data system, an independent auditor might be given the responsibility to check the veracity of the data and to attest to the financial analysis and the results from alternative scenarios. As B. J. Foley and K. T. Maunders note[30] ". . . to render information credible, it is not independence *in fact* which is important but independence as *perceived* by the information user." Since accountants can be viewed as "tools of management" elected officials are cautioned about accepting financial analyses as objective reporting of facts. Values can and do get reflected in the financial analyses of productivity decisions.

The Pygmalion Syndrome

Absorbing organizational uncertainty through questionable data, assumptions and/or assertions leads to possible erroneous decisions. Professionals—such as finance officers—have a responsibility to ensure that financial data represent the facts, and that assumptions about future financial happenings are premised on acceptable conditions and are fully and fairly disclosed.

Neglecting to observe such issues results in the Pygmalion Syndrome. When presenting the syndrome in the context of disclosure, Ted J. Fiflis[31] noted that model builders have problems when their models are not based in the real world. To avoid the Pygmalion Syndrome, finance professionals involved in productivity enhancement efforts have a responsibility to ensure that financial analyses succeed in meeting or exceeding qualitative disclosure standards.

Conclusions

Since public finance officers serve as gatekeepers of financial records, there should be professional attention on proper disclosure standards. A professional code of ethics for public finance officers might provide a general statement with more detailed standards contained in a set of recognized practice guidelines.

The qualitative criteria used in this paper—relevance, materiality, meaningfulness, reliability, neutrality, and comparability—are part of the general body of knowledge of the accounting profession. The accounting profession, however, does not require application of the disclosure criteria for judging interim financial reports, such as a cost analysis of contracting-out refuse collection services.

At least in the public sector, the benefits of applying disclosure criteria to financial analyses of contracting-out proposals may outweigh the costs. Avoiding disclosure opens the financial officer to the charge that he or she is a willing participant in using (and potentially misusing) data to support only one policy argument while ignoring a potentially more important position: what is best for the public interest.

Notes

1. See Frederick O'R. Hayes, *Productivity in Local Government* (Lexington, MA: Lexington Books, 1977) and George J. Washnis, editor, *Productivity Improvement Handbook for State and Local Government* (New York, NY: John Wiley and Sons, 1980).

2. Frank Marutello, "The Semantic Definition of a Profession," *Southern Review of Public Administration,* V (Fall 1981), 246–57.

3. Sissela Bok, *Secrets: On The Ethics of Concealment and Revelation* (New York, NY: Pantheon Publishers, 1983).

4. Don E. Giacomino and Dennis L. Knutson. 9It's Time for a 'Certified Government Accountant,'9 *The Government Accountants Journal,* XXXIIII (Spring 1983), 23–31.

5. Dennis F. Thompson, "Moral Responsibility of Public Officials: The Problem of Many Hands," *American Political Science Review,* LXXIV (December 1980), 905–16.

6. James G. March and Herbert A. Simon, *Organizations* (New York, NY: John Wiley and Sons), 165.

7. March and Simon, *Organizations,* 166.

8. Marshall S. Armstrong, "Disclosure: Considering Other Views," *Financial Executive,* XLIV (May 1976), 37–38.

9. While the name of the city is not reported, the events and details are related as nearly as possible to actual circumstances. The author served as an outside analyst to one user group during the contracting-out controversy.

10. See the American Institute of Certified Public Accountants (AICPA), *Objectives of Financial Statements* (New York, NY: AICPA, 1973).

11. Stephen L. Buzby, "The Nature of Adequate Disclosure," *The Journal of Accountancy,* CXXXVII (April 1974), 41.

12. Allan R. Drebin, James L. Chan, and Lorna C. Ferguson, *Objectives of Accounting and Financial Reporting for Governmental Units*, II (Chicago, IL: National Council on Governmental Accounting, 1981).

13. Municipal Finance Officers Association, *Disclosure Guidelines for State and Local Governments* (Chicago, IL: Municipal Finance Officers Association, 1979).

14. Norton M. Bedford, *Extensions in Accounting Disclosure* (Englewood Cliffs, NJ: Prentice-Hall, Inc. 1973), 70.

15. Edward H. Wesemann, *Contracting for City Services* (Pittsburgh, PA: Innovations Press, 1981).

16. Wesemann, *Contracting for City Services*.

17. General Accounting Office, *Elements of Accounting and Financial Reporting in the Federal Government: Exposure Draft* (Washington, DC: U.S. General Accounting Office, 1980), 36.

18. AICPA, 60

19. AICPA, 58

20. Bedford, *Extensions in Accounting Disclosure*, 70.

21. Robert N. Anthony, *Financial Accounting in Nonbusiness Organizations: An Exploratory Study of Conceptual Issues.* (Stamford, CT: Financial Accounting Standards Board, 1978).

22. AICPA, 58.

23. AICPA, 59.

24. Wesemann, *Contracting for City Services*, 33.

25. AICPA, 59.

26. General Accounting Office, 36.

27. Victor Pastena and Joshua Ronen, "Some Hypotheses on the Pattern of Management's. Informal Disclosures," *Journal of Accounting Research*, XVII (Autumn 1979), 550–64.

28. W. Bartley Hildreth, "Collective Bargaining: Impacts on Local Government Management," Robert T. Golembiewski and Frank Gibson, editors, *Readings in Public Administration: Institutions, Processes, Behavior, Policy* (Boston, MA: Houghton Mifflin Co.), 271–81.

29. B. J. Foley and K. T. Maunders, *Accounting Information Disclosure and Collective Bargaining* (London, England: The Macmillan Press, Ltd.), 183.

30. Foley and Maunders, *Accounting Information Disclosure*, 185, 186.

31. Ted J. Fiflis, "Economic Analysis as One Phase of Utilitarianism," Deborah A. DeMott, editor, *Corporations at the Crossroads: Governance and Reform* (New York, NY: McGraw-Hill Book Company), 70–108.

18

DESIGNING APPROPRIATE CONTROL MECHANISMS FOR MANAGING PERFORMANCE IN THE FEDERAL SECTOR

Carolyn Burstein

The implementation of performance appraisal systems for all federal employees in accord with the provisions of the Civil Service Reform Act of 1978, coupled with a new era of budgetary austerity, has resulted in perceptible changes in the federal management environment. Top managers are more closely scrutinizing the use of scarce human and financial resources often by relying on productivity data for performance evaluations of both managers and employees. Although decisions concerning the allocation of resources within agencies are only partially contingent on efficient and effective performance, critical choices are forcing managers to demonstrate that their work units are performing effectively.

In the past, especially during periods of growth, federal managers were frequently judged and rewarded on their ability to create and develop new programs and policies. Managers nurtured in a growth-oriented environment often fail to concentrate on sound personnel and performance management since access to additional people and financial resources is rela-

1983. Designing appropriate control mechanisms for managing performance in the federal sector. Burstein, Carolyn. **Public Administration Quarterly** 7 (Summer): 183–198.

tively easy and centralized personnel systems may appear to compensate for a lack of attention to important performance management functions. The present period of fiscal constraint is now reinforcing the role of **performance management** for federal managers in addition to their usual role of program management.

Performance management involves a systermatic attempt to direct organizational behavior toward task or goal accomplishment. Assuming that people within the organization possess adequate ability to perform goal-relevant tasks (an important part of the performance equation not addressed in this article), the central task in performance management is to design appropriate organizational control mechanisms so that employees' goal-directed behavior is increased.

The term "control" may seem coercive in tone and may suggest an outdated managerial approach in which workers must be closely supervised to ensure that they adhere to organizational policies and meet production standards. In fact, "a group of people constitute an organization only if there is some coordination among the activities they perform; some type of control is an inevitable result of the need to coordinate activities." (Lawler and Rhode, 1976:2) Control systems try to influence behavior by specifying what kind of behavior is appropriate (providing **information** to employees) and by rewarding or punishing goal-directed behavior (providing **incentive** to accomplish goals). Implicit in the design of any control system is a set of assumptions about what causes human behavior. (Lawler and Rhode, 1976)

Since the organization ultimately depends on people to achieve its goals, the most powerful control mechanisms organizations use are those which provide employees with the motivational impetus to direct their own behavior toward the organization's goals. (Lawler, 1973; Ouchi, 1981) When this occurs one can say that employees are committed to the organization since their goals are congruent with those of the organization. The paradox in the design of control mechanisms is that organizations may be able to ensure greater self-directed behavior and thus greater control by using mechanisms and techniques that actually **give employees greater control** (i.e., more autonomy) over various aspects of their work. Control is not a zero-sum game. Overall organizational control can increase as employees gain more direction over their work and employees may benefit from the increase in overall control.

The central issue for managers is to determine what specific methods of control are appropriate to their organizational conditions, work environment, and structure. Ouchi (1979) provides a framework for considering control systems appropriate for coping with the problems of evaluating and controlling performance under three different organizational conditions: markets, clans, and bureaucracies. Markets deal with the control problems through their ability to measure and reward individual contributions precisely. Market conditions, however, seldom prevail in the federal government. Clans rely on a relatively complete socialization process among employees who share similar values and beliefs which, in turn, should effectively eliminate the need for external controls. While these conditions obtain in major parts of some federal agencies (e.g., the CIA, FBI, DOD) and specialized work units in most agencies, they are not representative of the majority of work conditions throughout the federal government.

Bureaucracies, the most prevalent type of organization in the federal government, need control mechanisms with a mixture of close evaluations and a socialized acceptance of common objectives. Ouchi's framework indicates that the type of work performed and the organizational structure are significant contingencies affecting the methods of control used by a manager. While this framework is helpful in setting parameters to the general types of control systems that may be appropriate in federal bureaucracies, the framework provides few details about the **specific array** of control mechanisms that can be appropriately used in particular organizational work settings and their relative effectiveness.

Kerr and Slocum (1980) identified specific methods that are considered critical to effective organizational control. Many of these methods are appropriate for bureaucracies which, using Ouchi's framework, must be concerned with imparting information about agency goals and objectives, gaining commitment of employees to these goals, evaluating the adequacy of employee's goal-directed behavior, and rewarding or punishing that behavior. The methods are: role clarification, goal-setting, feedback, leader initiation of structure, consideration and stroking, employee participation in decision-making, and administration of formal rewards (monetary and non-monetary) and punishment. The authors also suggest alternative mechanisms for controlling performance that are non-manager initiated or actually may serve as "substitutes" for leadership. These mechanisms include: formal role descriptions, training programs, tasks, groups, and professional norms and values. This array of methods and techniques is well-known and frequently used within organizations to achieve a variety of ends; however, they have seldom been considered together as constituting a series of control mechanisms which can be used to direct the performance of employees toward management-desired goals. Several of these methods operate as cognitive factors for employees providing them with **information** about goals and tasks, while others operate as motivational factors providing employees with **incentives** to accomplish these goals and tasks. All are inducements that can be used by an organization to direct and control the performance of its members.

Improved or even adequate performance requires that federal managers develop and implement a cluster or set of organizational control mechanisms that "fit" the specific conditions of their work environment. Research in this area is critical to management so that the impact on performance of different methods of control under varying conditions can be determined. The Productivity Research Division (PRD) in the U.S. Office of Personnel Management initiated three separate field studies at various federal agencies to begin to examine the possibilities inherent in this key issue area for federal managers. This article will describe each of these research studies, explain how the control mechanisms are being implemented at each research site, and indicate the expected outcomes.

Two of the studies are using experimental designs and are examining management-initiated control mechanisms; the third is using descriptive qualitative methodologies and is exploring non-management or "substitute" controls. All studies are in the data collection/analysis phase at the time of this writing, which means findings cannot yet be reported, but the major hypotheses, the study design, the implementation plan, the intervention activity, and the role of management can be discussed.

Study One:
Group Incentive Pay Experiment at
the Social Security Administration (SSA)

Incentive systems are effective control mechanisms since they operate to develop, maintain, and enhance employees' goal-directed behavior. From a manager's perspective, a well-planned incentive system can be instrumental in shaping (i.e., controlling) subordinate's performance by reinforcing desirable behaviors and helping to reduce those that are undesirable. Incentives do this by making valued, organizationally-controlled rewards contingent on effective performance. Rewards help provide the motivation essential to a viable control system. To be effective, incentives must be perceived by employees as valuable rewards and must be clearly linked to the attainment of goals that are, in turn, viewed as achievable if sufficient worker effort is expended. (Lawler, 1973; Campbell and Pritchard, 1976)

Despite our knowledge of the general effectiveness of incentive systems, we know very little about the types or amount of incentives that are most conducive to improved performance among specific types of workers in actual work settings. Research does indicate that managers who use performance contingent rewards appropriately experience increases in performance and employee satisfaction, particularly the satisfaction expressed by high performers. (Greene, 1976; Hunt and Schuler, 1976; Sims, 1977; Sims and Szilagyi, 1978; Sziligyi, 1980) But there is also evidence that extrinsic incentives do not motivate in all circumstances and may even demotivate workers who are intrinsically motivated to perform their work. (Deci, 1975; Notz, 1975)

A key purpose, therefore, of examining incentive pay systems at the Social Security Administration's (SSA) Office of Disability Operations is to test the effectiveness of financial incentives among relatively low-graded claims examiners/processors in a highly bureaucratic federal work environment. Since the processing of disability claims is a group activity involving the interaction of many employees performing different functions to produce an end product, **group incentives** were chosen as the most appropriate incentive vehicle. The incentive program involves the payment of financial incentives to each module (workgroup of approximately 85 persons) based upon savings derived from increased productivity by the module. A primary goal of the group incentive program is to motivate employees to work together effectively as a team to improve performance and to reward them equally for their roles in increasing the organization's productivity.

Employment Involvement

For maximum effectiveness, financial rewards must be tied to performance goals or standards that are set neither too high nor too low and are established with the active involvement of both management and employees. There is a clear danger that unilaterally set goals will not motivate. Moderately difficult goals mutually established are probably optimal in terms of overall motivation and performance. (Lawler, 1976) For these reasons the PRD research team began its work by helping to form three working groups at SSA to assist in the implementation process. These groups consisted of 1) a policy guidance group to assure top management support for the program; 2) a working group consisting of multiple levels of management and the union; and 3) an employee committee consisting of those directly affected by the experiment who were closest to the work environment and could provide their views about implementation decisions and identify potential problems.

Based on the efforts of the PRD research team and the SSA working groups, three basic activities have been completed toward the implementation of group incentive pay. These include:

1. The development of a client-oriented measurement system and realistic performance standards;
2. The development of procedures to insure the availability of funds sufficient to pay monthly incentives of up to $25,000 per participating module;
3. The development of an experimental design to evaluate the impact of the incentive program on productivity, employee

motivation and job satisfaction, and on general organizational effectiveness. (Cohen, Eveland, and Raben, 1981)

Measurement System and Performance Standards

Several information systems used by SSA to measure workgroup performance have been refined and integrated into a system that currently measures approximately 88% of the module work in terms of quantity, timeliness, and quality. Four productivity measures have been developed: 1) workload clearance count (quantity); 2) mean processing time (timeliness); 3) average age of pending cases (timeliness); and 4) percentage of error-free cases (quality).

The standards are currently the subject of negotiations between SSA management and the union. Baseline data indicate that the standards have been set at levels that will allow employees to obtain significant rewards for improved productivity. Three standards have been set at the baseline mean while the quantity standard is 10% above the mean which prevents SSA from paying substantial amounts for current levels of productivity. In order to qualify for incentive pay, a module must meet the minimum standards on **all four measures** of productivity. This assures that quality and timeliness will not suffer by employees' attention to quantity. Thus, the standards meet the two criteria of an acceptable financial incentive system for controlling performance: moderate difficulty and mutual establishment.

Incentive Pay

The funds for incentive payments are based upon savings derived from increased productivity by the module. Each workload clearance currently costs SSA about $30 in personnel expenditures. Each additional workload clearance produced at the current personnel expenditure level, therefore, represents a cost savings of $30 which will be shared equally by the government and the employees directly responsible for producing the savings.

Procedures have been developed by the research team to determine a module's eligibility for incentive pay each month. While a full elaboration of these procedures is too lengthy for inclusion in this article, some indication of the processes required for equitable distribution of rewards is possible.

Net time and attendance figures are determined for the module each month with adjustments made for trainees' time. Workload totals are adjusted for the number of cases transferred in and out of the modules. Each of the four performance measures are valued at a certain percentage of cost savings with sliding scales developed to calculate additional pay beyond the minimum. Finally, policies have been developed for changing the performance standards in the future.

Experimental Design

The design selected for testing the impact of incentive pay combines several research strategies in order to identify real changes in productivity and isolate factors other than incentive pay which might have influenced the indicators of productivity during the course of the experiment.

The incentive program will be implemented in six modules on a staggered basis with two modules entering the experimental condition at two month intervals. This strategy will provide a multiple baseline on the performance of six modules. Some of the change in productivity during the experiment will undoubtedly represent a continuation of pre-intervention trends. Time series will enable the research team to identify trends in the pre-intervention data and estimate what would have happened during the experimental period had the intervention not occurred.

The staggered implementation of the program limits the probability of attributing the observed change to the wrong cause. If incentive pay has a real effect on module performance, we would expect to see a gradual increase in productivity for each pair of modules following entry into the incentive program. On the other hand, a simultaneous change in all six modules would suggest the possibility that some other factor in their common environment caused the increase.

As an additional check on the possibility of changes in the environment, the performance of a control group will be examined. The control group shares the same characteristics and environment as the experimental group but is not receiving incentive pay during the experiment.

The measures used to award incentive pay will also serve as the primary indicators of productivity change in this experiment. Every possible step will be taken, including the use of several control procedures, to protect the integrity of the measurement system. Employee attitude surveys will also be utilized to explore participant perceptions of the validity of the measurement system. These precautions have been taken since previous research indicates that the effectiveness of financial reward systems in influencing performance largely depends on the trust of both employees and managers in the measures being utilized.

The outline of this project points out that the role of managers in establishing an incentive pay system is a key to its ultimate success. Managers must work with employees and their unions to develop and pilot test performance standards, determine levels of pay commensurate with federal incentive awards policy, establish pay procedures, provide periodic performance feedback, and actually reward employees. Because the federal government has many jobs involving case management and claims processing, there is considerable potential for applying this incentive mechanism (i.e., control mechanism) in the federal sector if the experiment at SSA proves successful.

Study Two:
Effectiveness of Quality Circles Among
Workers at the Internal Revenue Service

The name "quality circles" derives from the basic process wherein a small group of employees doing similar work usually in the same work unit meet periodically with their supervisor to discuss their production, identify quality problems, investigate causes, and recommend solutions to higher management. The group first receives training in problem-solving techniques, data analysis, quality control, and methods of presenting data to management.

The desirability of quality circles (QCs) as a control mechanism derives in part from the participative role they provide to employees in improving the work process. Participation allows employees a degree of direct control over their work in that they are involved in decisions relating to modifications of jobs, task assignments, work or procedure, yet it does not change the central structure of organizing in the organization. (Dachler and Wilpert, 1979)

At the same time, QCs can be a useful organizational control mechanism because they are likely to motivate employees to become partners with management in problem identification and problem solving. They help to focus employee energy on issues that affect the quantity and quality of output. As a result, the manager's ability to direct and control employee performance is enhanced since his influence attempts are more effective and greater self-control exists among workers. (Tannenbaum, 1968) It is a classic win-win situation for both managers and employees. Thus, paradoxically, through participation both employees and the organization gain more control.

Research has demonstrated that participation can result in improved performance because of its effects on several cognitive and motivational factors. (Locke and Schweiger, 1979) In the cognitive area, participation results in greater upward communication, better utilization of information, and improved understanding of jobs by employees. This can result in more creative ideas and improved decision quality. In the context of motivation, participation increases trust, a sense of control and self-direction, develops group pressure and support, increases ego involvement and commitment to the organization. This can result in less resistance to change and greater acceptance of decisions and ultimately increased productive efficiency and decision quality. Research by Rosenberg and Rosenstein (1980) also confirms that increased productive efficiency is the output of participation activity in the sense that participation consists of organized problem identification, problem solving, and joint decision-making that can result in increased productivity.

This is an impressive array of benefits, but the participation literature also makes clear that the positive effects of participation are mediated by such factors as the content, process, and structure of tasks; supervisor and subordinate characteristics; participatory arrangements used; and situational conditions. (Turney and Cohen, 1980; Singer 1974) At this time, little solid evidence exists about the contributions of QCs to improved work unit performance beyond testimonials and anecdotes.

The emphasis in the study initiated by PRD researchers at the Internal Revenue Service (IRS) is clearly evaluative–the goal is to examine the implementation of QCs and their impact on a number of performance-related outcomes. Implementation is an important focus of this study since it is a major moderator of success and extensive research on participatory techniques demonstrates that the participation context is a major determinant of effects on productivity. (Locke and Schweiger, 1979)

An experimental research design is being employed. Thirteen work units in the Atlanta Service Center and District Office of the IRS are serving as the experimental QC groups with an equal number of control units (equivalent matches) at the same sites. In addition, the research team is also comparing QC units with non-QC units throughout the IRS national system of Service Centers. Since QC efforts have been initiated most frequently among blue collar workers, a key question in this research is to determine what results are achieved in a white collar and quasi-white collar working environment.

The selected experimental units, therefore, range along a continuum of work from low task autonomy/least complexity to high task autonomy/most complexity in order to test QCs in variable work environments found throughout the federal government. The work units will remain in the experimental condition for one year.

Several hypotheses relating to the impact of QCs and the participative processes used are being tested in this study. Changes in a positive direction are expected in these loci: job satisfaction and attendance, labor-management communication, worker-supervisor relationships, group cohesiveness, and work and performance (measured by cost, quality, efficiency, and effectiveness). Moderators of these changes are expected to be the degree of management support for QCs and the amount of job autonomy in the work setting.

The measurement devices being used are a combination of output and perceptual measures. The former consists of productivity data normally collected by IRS management, absenteeism and grievance data, the number and nature of changes accepted by management, and the cost-savings associated with changes implemented due to QC suggestions. Perceptual data are being collected from all employees on dimensions relating to organizational climate, supervisory behavior, job characteristics, work unit functioning, and QC interaction processes. In addition, facilitators are keeping logs on atypical external events that may affect the QC process and OPM researchers frequently observing QC sessions. (Deming **et. al.,** 1981) The results of this study should be helpful to federal managers as they select and develop the performance management strategies that might work most efficaciously in their work settings.

Study Three:
Other Factors Influencing the Effectiveness
of First-Line Supervisors

The previous two studies described above involve manager-initiated methods for controlling employee performance. Alternative mechanisms, however, that are non-manager-initated or actually "substitutes" for leadership frequently operate in an organization to control employee performance. A major part of this third study is examining how other persons or things act for or are used in place of—"substitute" for—the control supervisors exercise.

These non-managerial or organizational controls might include other individuals, tasks, and features of the organization which may strongly influence employee performance and even interfere with managerial attempts at control. It is important for managers to understand how "substitute" controls operate because their awareness of existing substitutes and their impact on employees are closely related to their own behavior and ultimate effectiveness. It is possible that the kind of control used by a manager might be incongruent with the values held by the organizational membership.

For example, in a research and development unit where task performance is inherently ambiguous, a manager's use of close surveillance for controlling performance may be highly dysfunctional since the unit's control may operate by means of shared professional norms and values on what constitutes proper behavior. This is a prime example of a "substitute" control serving to direct performance. "Substitutes" may enhance supervisory effectiveness by providing additional sources of control and, indeed, may compensate for inadequacies on the manager's part. Of course, care must be taken that "overcontrol" does not impede employee motivation or stifle initative.

Some preliminary empirical support for the existence of "substitutes" for leadership has been provided in a study by Kerr and Jermier (1978). This study developed nine subscales that yield data which plausibly described the presence or absence of substitutes for leadership in work situations. Using these subscales in a field experiment, the researchers found that, when powerful "substitutes" such as intrinsically satisfying work and task-provided performance feedback existed, the leader's controlling behavior failed to contribute significantly in predicting organizational commitment. But further research is needed to learn more about how and under what circumstances "substitute" controls operate.

PRD's current study into the phenomenon of "substitutes" for leadership is being conducted in three phases. The first is an exploratory phase which is directed toward learning more about how other sources compensate for the supervisor and how organizational barriers limit supervisory discretion in the use of control. Testable hypotheses will be developed from this analysis. At the time of this writing, the study is in the data analysis state of this first phase.

During the second experimental phase, the research team will examine specified relationships between the practices and policies of the organization and the performance of supervisors and their work units. The team will develop diagnostic instruments for assessing organizational and work unit factors which contribute to and detract from supervisory effectiveness. Finally, the third implementation phase will apply the techniques developed during the earlier phases for the improvement of supervisory and work unit performance.

The specific research design being used in this study will be described only for the first phase. Data are being collected in several work units of the Government Printing Office through semi-structured interviews, observations, examination of archival records, and existing indices of productivity. Comparisons are being made between work units and individual supervisors and, when a second research site is selected, comparisons will also be made between the two agencies' organizational policies and practices. Both individual and group interviews have been conducted. These interviews are yielding information on the organization, the work groups, the type of work, relationships between supervisors and employees, perceptions of constraints on supervisory discretion that may be substituting for formal supervisory controls.

Detailed description of the participants, observed behavior, and the environmental context are significant parts of the exploratory study since the way "substitutes" control performance has to be examined from the perspective of the organization members being studied. Thus, organizational and managerial processes are being examined interactively.

A content analysis of data from the interviews will permit the researchers to develop a typology of substitutes which will form the basis for more explicit quantitative examination in the next phases of research.

Conclusion

This article has attempted to point out the vital and functional role that control systems play in organizations. It highlights the importance of answering the question: how can a collection of employees be moved towards cooperative action to achieve organizational goals? As federal managers assume greater responsibility for managing the performance of their subordinates, the proper design of organizational control mechanisms will become a key concern for solving evaluation and performance issues. Managers will need to know the kinds of control mechanisms that are appropriate to the work they direct, to the type of employees they supervise, and to the structure of the organizational component in which they are located.

In response to this need, the Productivity Research Division has undertaken major field studies to determine if incentive pay and quality circles are controls which improve performance under certain highly specified conditions that can be generalized to similar government settings. If successful, products from these studies will provide specific guides to managers about how to implement these control mechanisms and how to apply them to achieve perceptions of equity among organizational members.

It is already clear that incentive pay should only be used in a work environment where performance can be assessed with accuracy. It is also strongly suspected that quality circles will operate at their maximum potential in a work environment where there is sufficient job autonomy to allow changes in procedures/methods and with a sufficiently high volume of relatively standardized output to enable suggested improvements save greater costs than the financial outlay of the circles themselves.

Finally, a third study, of a more exploratory nature, has the potential for identifying ways in which employees' performance is influenced by sources and mechanisms other than formal managers. The purpose is to provide managers with an understanding of how these "substitutes" may enhance managerial effectiveness or, on the other hand, reduce a manager's ability to influence subordinates' performance.

References

Cohen, S. A., L. Eveland, and C. Raben (1981). *OPM/SSA Group Incentive Pay Experiment*. Washington, D.C.: OPM, OPM Internal Project Plan.

Campbell, J. P., and R. D. Pritchard (1978). "Motivation Theory in Industrial and Organizational Psychology," in M. D. Dunnette, ed., *Handbook of Industrial and Organizational Psychology*. Chicago: Rand McNally.

Dachler, H. P., and B. Wilpert (1978). "Conceptual Dimensions and Boundaries of Participation in Organizations: A Critical Evaluation." *Administrative Science Quarterly* 23 (March):1–35.

Deci, E. (1975). *Intrinsic Motivation*. New York: Plenum Press.

Deming, B., et al. (1981). *Final Project Plan for QC Intervention*. Washington, D.C.: OPM, Productivity Research Division.

Greene, C. N. (1976). "A Longitudinal Investigation of Performance Reinforcing Leader Behavior and Subordinate Satisfaction and Performance." *Midwest Academy of Management Proceedings* pp. 157–185.

Hunt, J. G., and R. S. Schuler (1976). "Leader Reward and Sanctions Behavior Relations with Criteria in a Large Public Utility." Working paper. Carbondale: Southern Illinois University Press.

Kerr, S., and J. M. Jermier (1978). "Substitutes for Leadership: Their Meaning and Measurement." *Organizational Behavior and Human Performance* 22 (December):375–403.

Lawler, E. E. (1976). "Control Systems in Organizations," in M. D. Dunnette, ed., *Handbook of Industrial and Organizational Psychology*. Chicago: Rand McNally.

_____ (1973). *Motivation in Work Organizations*. Monterey, Cal.: Brooks/Cole.

Lawler, E. E, and J. G. Rhode (1976). *Information and Control in Organizations*. Pacific Palisades, Cal.: Goodyear.

Locke, E. A., and D. M. Schweiger (1979). "Participation in Decision-Making: One More Look," in B. Shaw. ed., *Research in Organizational Behavior*. Greenwich, Conn.: JAI Press.

Notz, N. W. (1975). "Work Activities and the Negative Effects of Extrinsic Rewards." *American Psychologist* 30 (September):884–891.

Ouchi, W. G. (1979). "A Conceptual Framework for the Design of Organizational Control Mechanisms." *Management Science* 25 (September):833–848.

_____ (1981). *Theory Z: How American Business Can Meet the Japanese Challenge*. Reading, Mass.: Addison-Wesley.

Rosenberg, R. D., and E. Rosenstein (1980). "Participation and Productivity: An Empirical Study." *Industrial and Labor Relations Review* 33 (April):355–367.

Sims, H. P. (1977). "The Leader As A Manager of Reinforcement Contingencies: An Empirical Example and A Model," in J. G. Hunt and L. L. Larson (eds.). *Leadership: The Cutting Edge*. Carbondale: Southern Illinois University Press.

Sims, H. P., and A. D. Szilagyi (1978). "A Causal Analysis of A Leader Behavior Over Three Different Time Lags." *Eastern Academy of Management Proceedings*.

Singer, J. N. (1974). "Participative Decision-Making about Work: An Overdue Look at Variables which Mediate its Effects." *Sociology of Work and Occupations* 1 (November):348–371.

Szilagyi, A. D. (1980). "Reward Behavior of Male and Female Leaders: A Causal Inference Analysis." *Journal of Vocational Behavior* 16 (February):59–72.

Tannenbaum, A. S. (1968). *Control in Organizations*. New York: McGraw-Hill.

Turney, J. R., and S. L. Cohen (1980). "Participative Management: What Is the Right Level?" *Management Review* 69 (October):66–69.

19

INTEGRATING EVALUATION AND BUDGETING

Harry S. Havens

The budget is the only reasonably comprehensive framework available in which to make decisions about what government should be doing, and how. Program evaluation is one of the few sources of potentially reliable information available on what government is doing, and how well. Logically, the two should have something to do with each other. Unfortunately, there is little evidence of such a connection. The purpose of this paper is first to offer some observations about the causes of this situation and then to suggest some courses of action which might alter it.

The concept of budgeting as a means of deciding how to allocate resources has a long history. In this country, however, at least at the federal level, the idea of an integrated central budget process is a relatively recent innovation, dating to the 1921 Budget and Accounting Act. Its evolution from an expenditure control process to a policy formulation process is even more recent, being an outgrowth of the movement of the Budget Bureau from Treasury to the Executive Office of the President under Roosevelt. But the full potential of this role only became apparent in the 1960s.

Program evaluation, too, is a relatively recent innovation. The underlying concepts have been evolving for some time in the research methods of the social and physical sciences. But, evaluation, too, emerged only in the 1960s as a broadbased institutionalized application of these research meth-

1983. Integrating evaluation and budgeting. Havens, Harry S. **Public Budgeting and Finance** 3 (Summer): 102–113.

ods for the purpose of answering decision-relevant questions about public programs and policies.

There was an early recognition of the potential value of linking these two developments, a policy-focused budget process and a decision-relevant research methodology. We called it the Planning-Programming-Budgeting System, or PPBS for short. Originated in the Department of Defense under MacNamara in the early 1960s, PPBS was mandated for application throughout the executive branch by 1966. It was one of the early casualties of the incoming Nixon Administration. There is substantial literature examining its demise, but otherwise PPBS has largely disappeared from the vocabulary.

In itself, that would be no great loss. Unfortunately, however, nothing has come along to replace it as an approach to integrating analytical and evaluative information with the budget process. The concept disappeared from discussion as soon as the clearly flawed approach to implementing it was written off. Subsequent efforts to strengthen the budget and related policy processes—Management By Objectives (MBO) and Zero-Based Budgeting (ZBB)—have moved in a markedly different direction, one which tends to minimize the role of systematic analysis in the budget process.

MBO focused on the achievement of specified objectives. To the extent that these were program-related, and many were not, they focused attention on outputs rather than the relationship between resources and outputs. The result was a dichotomy between a budget process, which determined resource levels, and an MBO process, which established process or output objectives largely independent of resource allocation decisions.

In some degree, ZBB can be seen as a move back in the direction of integrating resource allocations with output levels. Each ZBB decision package was supposed to reveal the output that could be obtained with various levels of budget resources. In principle, this relationship could have been based on evaluative data and, thus, could have been an excellent vehicle for integrating evaluation with the budget process. Indeed, there were rhetorical nods in that direction.

It was quickly apparent, however, that the rhetorical interest in analytical support for the budget process did not carry much weight in the design of the ZBB system. The number of decision units, the necessary rapidity of decision-making, and the frequency of the decision cycle could not help overwhelming the existing process, to say nothing of attempting to link it to other, inherently slower, analytical processes. The adjustments made to adapt ZBB to reality moved the process even farther from this potential analytical link. The number of alternatives was reduced, and, in some agencies, major segments were excused from the ZBB process. This may have succeeded in reducing the number of separate decisions to manageable proportions, but it certainly did nothing for the analytical content of those remaining.

President Reagan, too, has made significant changes. Most obvious has been his willingness to commit the political power of his office to the enactment of his budget, reflecting sharp departures from recent policy directions, and his remarkable success in doing so. Within the executive branch, however, the machinery by which the policies were translated into specific budget proposals has been relatively traditional in nature (albeit very compressed and accelerated in timing). But this traditional orientation to the mechanics of budget formulation is clearly not matched by a traditional approach to the basis upon which budget decisions are made.

Budget formulation necessarily involves a blend of analysis and political judgment. Analysis has rarely (if ever) been an overwhelmingly dominant factor, but there has usually been a place for it, to the extent that it was available. There is little evidence, however, that budget formulation in the Reagan Administration has been based to any significant degree on the results of analysis as that term is usually employed. On the contrary, the external evidence suggests quite strongly that the major budget decisions are based overwhelmingly on deeply held philosophical views of the proper role of government. If an activity is viewed as inappropriate, it matters little whether or not the activity is being pursued efficiently and effectively.

To say that the Reagan budget decisions were based on a markedly different view of the role of government is not to suggest that the change is somehow improper. After all, the ability to make basic changes of this sort in a peaceful way is one of the hallmarks of a democratic society. But even in the context of a radical restructuring of roles there should be room for analysis, both of likely consequences and of the relative efficiency and effectiveness with which particular objectives are being pursued. There is little evidence that this sort of analysis is wanted or, when available, has any bearing on budget decisions—at least on those being made in the Office of Management and Budget (OMB).

In the absence of further candid interviews, such as those given by Mr. Stockman, it seems unlikely that we will have a reliable picture of budget formulation in the Reagan Administration until it leaves office. In the meantime, given the propensity of recent administrations to alter the budget process, it is worth considering the possibility of change, either by this Administration or a successor. One hopes that such changes will grow out of a careful assessment of the real strengths and weaknesses of the system rather than a mechanistic application of techniques which, whatever their value in another environment, have ultimately added little to the policy process in Washington.

The real strength of a unified budget process lies in its awesome power to force decisions on the allocation of scarce resources. That strength, of course, is under constant attack from those who see themselves as potential losers in the trade-off. The attackers pursue any of a number of avenues to escape from the discipline of the budget process (off-budget status, use of guaranteed loans, tax expenditures, back-door spending, etc.). These attacks must be a source of continuing concern and must be periodically fended off, lest the central strength of the process be dissipated.

Assuming that a strong and unified budget process can be maintained, however, there is a need to consider seriously how to remedy its several notable shortcomings. Among these is the weakness of the analytical base for making the trade-off decisions which lie at the heart of the process.

The weakness of the analytical base is not the only shortcoming of the present budget process, of course, and evaluation is not the only related process with which budgeting should be linked. The federal government badly needs to achieve effective integration of a wide diversity of systems and processes involved in making policy, executing decisions, and overseeing the results. In the final analysis, we should be seeking full integration of planning, policy, program and financial systems and processes. That long-term goal, however, is fully consistent with efforts to take somewhat more modest interim steps. One of those could be the greater integration of budgeting and evaluation.

In this regard, what the budget process lacks is precisely what PPBS sought, unsuccessfully, to provide. What is needed is a flow of analytic information which reaches decision-makers at the time and in the form best suited to support them in making resource allocations and other policy judgments.

Efforts to accomplish this linkage have thus far failed because of a series of impediments. These impediments fall into several categories. Once identified, it should be possible to assess whether or not they can be overcome, and if so, how.

Organizational Structure

One evident impediment lies in the fact that those in an operating agency who are charged with the function of evaluation and analysis are commonly housed in an organizational entity which is separate from those charged with resource allocation. The evaluation function is commonly a separate unit in executive branch agencies, often with its own assistant secretary. When linked to another unit, the partner is most commonly the research function.

Budgeting, on the other hand, is traditionally viewed as an adjunct of administration or finance and is most commonly housed under the assistant secretary for administration. Organizational separation of this sort automatically creates impediments to communications. Sometimes it yields unhealthy competition and conflict. Even in the best circumstances, however, there is a tendency for the separate units to develop independent agendas, each responsive to its own view of priorities. The most sincere desire to be mutually supportive will be frustrated when conflicting agendas produce a situation in which one unit has little of value to provide the other.

Conflicting Perceptions of Time

In the federal government, the budget process functions on a rigid annual cycle. The decisions associated with it are (at least in the executive branch) equally rigidly fixed in time. The budget *must* be submitted to the Congress each year at a particular time. Once that is given, the decisions leading up to the submission must occur on a very rigid schedule, and the material required for making those decisions must be developed and supplied on a similarly rigid schedule.

Tolerable slippages in the process are measured in days, not weeks or months. If a decision point is missed, there is a high probability that material prepared for that decision will be irrelevant until the next year. At that point, the material may well be considered dated and be disregarded. In the rigid schedule of the budget process, time is a constant. Decisions *must* be made at a particular time. Thus they *will* be made, and they will be based on whatever information is available at that time.

The evaluation function, on the other hand, tends to operate with a very different view of time. Many practitioners view the schedule as being properly determined by the question being examined and by the resources available for addressing it. These factors, together with a relatively fixed concept of professionally acceptable standards of quality, establish the time required to complete the evaluation task. However, evaluators are rarely able to predict the time requirements with confidence because of the many unknowable problems which will emerge in the process of carrying out the evaluation. Slippages of months or even years may well be considered tolerable, provided the final product meets acceptable levels of quality.

Different Intellectual Frameworks

There are some noteworthy similarities between budgeteers and evaluators. Both groups are comprised, by and large, of intelligent people committed to making government work better; both see that mission being carried out by influencing decisions on program policy and operations.

On closer examination, however, these similarities rapidly give way to striking differences in the fundamental intellectual framework of the two groups. Budgeteers view their role as helping to manage the day-to-day operations of the organization of which they are a part. The budget process forces concentration on the immediate—decisions which must be made to-day, problems which can be solved this year. These immediate concerns are too large in number and too difficult in substance to afford most bud-geteers either the time or inclination to worry about longer-term issues which do not have to be addressed today and toward the solution of which today's action would make, at best, only a marginal contribution.

The evaluator, on the other hand, has his intellectual roots in the re-search community. The research paradigm pushes the evaluator in two di-rections which often contribute to other difficulties. One is the pursuit of the elusive ideal of absolute truth. The experienced evaluator recognizes the impossibility of reaching that goal, but retains it as the goal toward which he should strive. The other pressure of the research paradigm, deriv-ative of the first, is to isolate the phenomenon being examined from sur-rounding events which might otherwise contaminate the evaluation results.

What to Do?

There are undoubtedly other important factors contributing to our failure, thus far, to integrate evaluation and budgeting. Lest the agenda of prob-lems become so long as to be intolerable, however, it seems reasonable to turn at this point to the question of what can be done to overcome these impediments.

In thinking about solutions, it is preferable to start at the level of the de-partments and agencies. If functional integration is to occur, it should start at this point where the trade-off decisions are initially addressed. In addi-tion, most evaluation activity is preformed by or for the agencies. If the ba-sic evaluation agenda is to be adjusted, that will have to be accomplished by the agencies. OMB and Congress can encourage and support such a shift, but they cannot actually control it.

Reconciling Organizational Separation

Of the three identified impediments, organizational structure would seem, on the surface, the easiest to handle. When problems arise because func-tions are housed in separate organizational units, the simple, direct, and traditional answer is to combine them in a single organizational unit. That may well be the appropriate answer in this case. In some places where it has been tried (e.g., the Department of Education), it seems to have been at least somewhat successful. But one can also anticipate problems with such an approach.

In the policy apparatus of a major agency, individual functions are rarely related to other functions in a uniquely bilateral fashion. Rather, each function is related in important ways to almost every other function. Evaluation, for example, is (or should be) related to budgeting. But it is equally true that evaluation is (or should be) related to a number of other functions. It is related to the research function because evaluation, itself, is a research activity and because it should participate in setting the agenda for other parts of the research process. Evaluation should be related to the legislative development function because it is a source of ideas for that process, which is the most likely avenue for achieving the fundamental program changes often identified as necessary in evaluations. Evaluation should also be related to the non-budgeting aspects of the administrative management function, because administrative processes are frequently the subject of evaluation or the source of problems identified during the evaluation of a program.

Thus, organizational linkage of related functions may or may not be the appropriate solution to the impediment created by organizational separation. It should be considered, if only because it is an obvious alternative. If it becomes evident that organizational linkage would create more problems than it would solve, however, other avenues should be explored. One of these might well be a reconsideration of the way in which the budget is formulated within the agency.

Traditionally, the budget process in a civilian operating agency is dominated by the budget office. Often, the agency budget officer has established such control over the process and such an intimate working relationship with the agency head as to hold a virtual monopoly over the information which reaches the agency head concerning the budget. In extreme cases, other agency officials enter the process only as supplicants, seeking resources for their own activities. To some degree, this is understandable when the only stake these other officials have in the process is their own budgets. It is less defensible, however, when one acknowledges, first, that budget formulation involves basic policy direction as well as the allocation of resources, and second, that many of these other officials (such as those representing the program evaluation function) have a great deal to contribute to the development and direction of basic agency policies.

This suggests the possibility of a different context within which the budget process can be viewed. This would be an integrated policy formulation process in which budgeting, the development of legislative proposals, and the consideration of major regulatory and administrative actions would be seen as multiple facets of a single process. Various officials in an agency would be in a position to contribute to the process, but none (other than the agency head or his deputy) should dominate it.

With this concept of a policy formulation process, of which the budget process is an integral part, it is much easier to see it being managed in a more collegial fashion. If all those having a legitimate role in an integrated policy process actually participate in the management of the process, organizational separation becomes a much less serious impediment. Indeed, from the agency head's perspective, it could become a valued attribute, since it would permit a diversity of information flowing from independent sources with varying perspectives, each with some established base of credibility. This minimizes the danger that a single perspective—that of the budget officer—may come to dominate the entire policy process by controlling the flow of information and analysis.

Making such an integrated process work obviously requires more than instructing people to cooperate. One of the essential ingredients is that it be led by someone with the time, commitment, understanding, and stature to keep it from disintegrating into bureaucratic warfare. In cases where the agency head or his deputy is able to and interested in focusing on policy formulation and broad management, this sort of integrated process may tend to develop naturally. Given other demands on these officials' time, however, this happens rather infrequently. Nowhere, to the best of my knowledge, has it been institutionalized to the point of surviving the replacement of those who created it.

The basic approach could be extended to OMB. There, the integrated policy process would need to involve the budget divisions, the legislative clearance staff, the program evaluation staff, and other components of the management side. If extended to the White House itself, the concept might lead to more effective and orderly integration of OMB with other elements of the Executive Office, such as the Domestic Policy staff, the National Security Council staff, the Council of Economic Advisers staff, and the Office of Science and Technology staff.

Reconciling Different Perceptions of Time

As with organizational separation, there is a simple—and probably wrong—answer to the problem of conflicting perceptions of time. Given the rigidity of the schedule for the budget, it is tempting to say that the problem would disappear if only evaluators would learn how to do their work faster. No doubt this is true; no doubt there are elements of the evaluation process which could be accelerated.

But this sort of tinkering (e.g., cutting the time required to write a report) will not begin to close the gap between what the budget process now demands and what evaluators are now capable of providing. The nature of the budget process forces those involved in it to demand virtually instantaneous response. The Reagan rewrite of the Carter budget for fiscal year 1982, accomplished in a month or so, exemplifies this situation. In these circumstances, budgeteers have no alternative to operating on the basis of information which is readily at hand. To ask evaluators to supply new information within the timeframes of such a process is to ask them to throw away precisely those characteristics which make evaluation valuable—the careful, deliberate collection and analysis of data.

One way of beginning to shorten the evaluation lag is to build evaluation data requirements into the plans for implementing a program. It is obviously not possible to anticipate all the possible data requirements necessary to respond to all possible evaluation questions. Indeed, it would be a waste of resources to attempt such a voluminous data collection effort on every program. It should be possible, however, to design a monitoring system which is adequate to provide current, reliable information on certain key evaluative variables which are likely to be of continuing interest.

This sort of monitoring system should be developed as a joint effort between the budgeteers, the evaluators, and the policy development staff. The budgeteers should contribute knowledge of the key questions which are likely to arise on a continuing basis during the annual funding debate. The policy staff should contribute knowledge of the issues likely to arise in connection with the periodic reauthorization or legislative amendment process. The evaluators should contribute their knowledge of what it will take to answer those questions in a credible fashion.

The outcome will necessarily involve a good deal of compromise since reliable information is not a free good. But, if the effort receives sufficient emphasis from the top management of the agency, it should yield a monitoring system which, with a reasonable investment of resources, produces reliable, timely, and increasingly comprehensive answers to at least some of the key decision-relevant questions. Important questions which cannot be answered adequately or economically through a monitoring system should become part of the agenda for separate evaluation studies, scheduled (insofar as possible) for completion when major decision points are anticipated, such as reauthorization.

In addition to helping resolve the problem of differing perceptions of time, this sort of joint effort to design an effective monitoring system can be part of a strategy for overcoming organizational barriers. It might represent an important step, for example, in developing the integrated policy formulation process discussed previously.

There are other steps which might be taken to overcome the problem of time. Most discussions of the issue focus on the need for others to respond to the rigorous schedule of the budget process. It seems worthwhile to consider the possibility of changing the schedule itself. It is not self-evident, for example, that the public good is served by reconsidering every budget decision on every program, every year. Indeed, it is reasonably apparent that we pay a substantial price in doing so. First, there is a high degree of stability which can be observed in the budget estimates for most programs from one year to the next. In some cases, this stability reflects the pro forma na-

ture of the budget review. But even a pro forma review involves a significant expenditure of scarce time and talent. In other cases, of course, the review is not pro forma. In these cases, the stability of the budget reflects the
fact that circumstances simply do not warrant a substantial change. In the
absence of a major policy shift, the outcome of the budget review is predictable—the estimates will change only marginally in real terms (if at all)
from the previous year. In these cases, it is reasonable to question the cost-
effectiveness of an annual budget review process.

It is possible to conceive of a budget process which operates on quite a
different schedule. Thinking about alternatives, however, requires one first
to accept that an annual budget process is not preordained and immutable.
We have an annual cycle because we chose to do so. Others have chosen
different cycles. Some states, for example, seem to function adequately
with a biennial budget, an option which is already being discussed at the
federal level. Some governments—and not just in East Bloc countries—
build their planning around a five-year cycle.

Shifting to a two-year cycle would clearly permit a more deliberate approach to budget formulation in the executive branch and might well be
attractive from a congressional viewpoint. There has been some discussion,
for example, of a congressional schedule in which one session of each Congress would be devoted to oversight and authorization activities and the
other session to the budget and appropriations process.

It might also be worth exploring the possibility of a four-year budget cycle geared to the presidential election cycle. The quadrennium might start,
for example, with the beginning of the fiscal year following a presidential
election.

Changing to a longer cycle, however, would require careful thought. For
one thing, the estimating process would become more difficult and, at the
same time, estimating errors would be of even greater significance because
they tend to cumulate geometrically as the estimating period lengthens. An
effective mid-period adjustment process would be needed to meet changing
needs as well as to compensate for estimating errors. Yet the adjustment
process must not become a vehicle for the wholesale reopening of decisions, lest the benefits of multi-year budgeting be lost.

Annual budgeting has obvious advantages in terms of the potential for
increased flexibility and control. But that potential is used rather rarely for
anything more than marginal changes and entails a significant cost. This
cost shows up in other ways besides the time and effort devoted to the budget process itself. The potential for change, even if it goes unexercised, creates an environment of uncertainty which is a source of inefficiency in program operations. Among other things, it is another factor emphasizing
concentration on very short-term issues to the detriment of rational mid-

term and long-range planning and of effective oversight of program operations and budget execution.

Reconciling Intellectual Frameworks

There are at least two possible explanations for the differing intellectual frameworks of budgeteers and evaluators. One is that the differences are inherent in the people, either genetically or by virtue of the training they receive before becoming practitioners. An alternative hypothesis is that people adopt the intellectual framework of the activity in which they are engaged. One learns to think like a budgeteer by being a budgeteer. If one becomes an evaluator, one learns to think like other evaluators. Truth probably lies somewhere in between. Some budgeteers and evaluators would find the other intellectual framework so alien as to be intolerabe. But among the best people in each field there is also a substantial number who could make (and have made) the switch relatively painlessly.

The success of those who have moved from one activity to the other can be reasonable explained. Despite the vigorous (and frequently quite noisy) conflict between the two functions, they have a great deal in common. Both focus on the collection and analysis of information for purposes of making decisions about programs. Both operate from a basis of assumed rationality in the decision process. The two groups also share some significant behavioral characteristics. At least some evaluators are as frustrated as anyone else by their difficulties in being responsive to the time-critical needs of decision-makers. Similarly, some budgeteers are very uncomfortable about making policy on the basis of information which they recognize as being incomplete and unreliable.

A good budgeteer would like nothing better than to have a solid, relatively conclusive evaluation on which to base his recommendations, and a good evaluator would like nothing better than to provide it. But both are trapped by institutional impediments and the traditions of their own fields. It is difficult to break out of those traps, and except at the very senior level, it can be professionally hazardous to attempt to do so. Good budgets have "always" been comprehensive and annual; budgeteers have "always" operated on partial, unreliable, and impressionistic data. Good evaluators have "always" been carried out in the form of discrete, self-contained studies; evaluators have "always" worried more about reliability and precision than about timeliness. None of these statements is totally accurate, but each is part of the tradition of the field and, thus, part of its intellectual framework.

Both activities have yielded important results by remaining within their own traditions and intellectual frameworks. Neither is under direct assault for its insularity from the other. Each, of course, is subject to severe criticism, but in isolation. Budgeting is criticized for its increased politicization and for its lack of analytical support. Evaluation is accused of irrelevance. Few seem to recognize that these criticisms, when taken together, are the inevitable result of the insularity.

Failure to recognize the underlying cause of the criticisms of the two professions means there is little incentive for individual practitioners to make the modest effort to break through that insularity or to make the mutual compromises necessary to do so. Thus, even though it is relatively easy to design models which would overcome the institutional impediments and which would be at least arguably useful in themselves, they are unlikely to be implemented because there is little pressure (or perceived need) to do so.

Why Bother?

The model toward which this paper points is an integrated policy development process built around a multi-year budget and policy review process. The analysis to support this process would involve a jointly developed system for monitoring key indicators of efficiency and effectiveness and a jointly developed schedule of discrete studies on major issues timed around specific decision points.

There are obviously arguments against such a model. Suppose, however, that these arguments can be overcome or that a different model can be developed that would minimize those problems and still accomplish the desired degree of integration. Even in these circumstances, is there any compelling reason to exert the effort required to put the model in place? After all, it does require substantial effort, not only to overcome institutional inertia, but to design the operating systems and procedures in sufficient detail to make them work. That investment should not be undertaken unless there is some evident reason to do so.

The search for intellectual neatness is frequently at the heart of proposals for procedural and organizational change, whether the change involves structure or systems. It is the wrong reason for change, because the world of management and policy is not (and cannot be made) neat and orderly. Change should be sought, not because it makes an organization chart look better or a system diagram look more orderly, but because it can be expected by reasonable people to yield a different outcome in the real world.

It seems reasonable that an integrated policy development process will lead to a different and more useful policy focus. This, in turn, will permit the policy apparatus to consider a different set of choices. Changing the set of policy choices is essential because the present set—dictated, in part, by the systems, processes, and institutional structures in which the choices are being made—is increasingly unacceptable. Note some of the characteristics of the existing executive budget formulation process. It is dominated by decisions concerning actions in the next twelve to twenty-four months and by consequences expected to occur within that same time period. Trade-offs among programs are based on highly sketchy information. Constraints are imposed by overall fiscal policy objectives deemed appropriate for the achievement of short-run economic policy objectives.

Contrast this characterization of the budget decision process with the fact that in the 1982 Carter budget, more than 75% of the outlays were "uncontrollable," resulting from prior commitments and statutorily mandated payments. Much of the remaining 25% represents the cost of activities which few would wish to see totally abandoned. Thus, any effort to reduce the budget totals significantly in the short-run requires either radical surgery of that small portion which is truly discretionary, or bloody political battles to alter the uncontrollables, or both.

The Reagan budget adjustments have been representative of this approach. Whether or not one agrees with the policy priorities underlying the Administration's decisions, the structure of the process forced them—unnecessarily—to make the choice between radical surgery and the status quo. Solutions which might, four years from now, reach the same budget policy goal as the radical surgery approach tend to be discounted in this context. They take time to develop and implement and, thus, do not show the immediate results demanded in the one-year focus of the annual budget process. One can speculate, for example, that the choice of what to cut, when, where, and how might well have been different if the focus had been the 1982–1986 quadrennium, taken as a whole, rather than fiscal year 1982 alone.

Under normal circumstances, it is very difficult to gain enactment of legislation within the timeframe of a single budget cycle, to say nothing of doing so early enough in the budget cycle to affect outlays significantly during the budget year. Yet this is what must be done to reduce outlays for the uncontrollable programs. Presidential budgets have often contained proposals of this nature, but rarely (in the past) was there serious expectation of enactment. (Events associated with the reconciliation process in 1981 are clearly inconsistent with this assessment. Whether they represent a new pattern or simply an anomaly in the old one remains to be seen.)

Usually, the political costs of enactment exceed the benefits, in the form of budget reductions, in part because the only visible benefits are the budget reductions which will be accomplished in the first year. If, instead, the proposal were considered in the context of a four-year budget, or even a two-year fiscal period, there would be two substantial advantages. First, the budgetary consequences themselves would be much more visible and dramatic. Second, it would be possible to allow time both for the development of a solid evaluative and analytical basis for new proposals and for careful congressional consideration, while still contemplating enactment in time to have substantial budgetary effects during the period.

There are much more basic reasons, however, for seeking the sorts of changes suggested in this paper. Despite the best efforts of able and dedicated professionals, the way we now go about the budget and policy development process is no longer adequate to the problems we face. The experiences of the 1970s and the prospects for the 1980s make it clear that a short-term focus supported by competent seat-of-the-pants analysis just will not suffice.

The nation faces economic and social problems which are too complex and intractable to be solved by simple, quick fixes, no matter how radical. Notwithstanding our fondest wishes to the contrary, the problems of high inflation, high unemployment, high interest rates, inadequate investment, and low growth rates will not be solved quickly and painlessly by a single set of easily explained actions. They can only be overcome by a carefully developed and necessarily complex long-term strategy, diligently implemented over a number of years. That strategy can only be developed, explained credibly, and sustained politically for the necessary period if it focuses on the long-term consequences and the actions necessary to achieve them, rather than on an inevitably futile search for immediate payoff. Our own recent experience suggests, for example, that the adverse social impacts of the policies necessary to combat inflation may not be politically tolerable in the context of a short-term focus.

By changing the terms of the debate to a longer time horizon, the beneficial effects can be made more visible and the policy changes necessary to accomplish them can be made more deliberately, more gradually, and less disruptively. To return, in the end, to the earlier focus of this paper, they can also be made on the basis of a more coherent body of evaluation and analysis than is presently available.

20

PERFORMANCE MEASURES FOR BUDGET JUSTIFICATIONS: DEVELOPING A SELECTION STRATEGY

Gloria A. Grizzle

This paper explores developing a tool that agency administrators can use for deciding what performance measures to use. While it focuses upon providing information for budget preparation, the strategies discussed are equally applicable to selecting performance measures for other administrative activities, such as monitoring program implementation. The first two sections review why performance information is important for budget justification and the extent to which different types of performance measurements appear in budget documents. The next two sections describe how a measurement selection tool was developed; summarize the results of the experience, using three variations of the tool; analyze strengths and weaknesses of the tool; and suggest alternative strategies for choosing performance measures, using the assessment tool as a guide.

1985. Performance measures for budget justifications: Developing a selection strategy. Grizzle, Gloria A. **Public Productivity and Management Review** 9 (Winter): 328–341.

The Importance of Performance Data
to Budget Reform

Budget reform proponents believe that the type of information presented in proposed budgets affects budget outcomes. For example, Schick notes that the two most important aspects of budgetary technique are "the data used for making program and financial decisions and the form in which the data are classified."[1] Performance budgets, program budgets, Planning Programming Budgeting Systems (PPBS), Management by Objectives (MBO), and Zero Base Budgeting (ZBB) are all budget reforms that require information about agency or program performance. These reforms cannot be expected to produce the results their proponents anticipate when performance data are lacking.

The Extent to Which Performance Data
Currently Appear in Budget Documents

A sampling of budget documents from jurisdictions that have implemented one or more of these budget reforms will convince the reader that changing the budget's format is more often accomplished than changing the information presented in the budget. Many of these documents still rely heavily on workload measures as evidence of agency or program performance, to the near exclusion of information about efficiency, cost-effectiveness, equity, and quality of service delivery. A survey of 88 cities, for example, revealed that 74% used a performance budget format, but only 31% used efficiency information when making spending choices.[2] As a further case in point, consider Lauth's findings of the status of performance measurement in Georgia after ten years of Zero Base Budgeting:

> A perusal of the evaluation measures actually submitted by agencies indicates that with few exceptions they are workload or output measures ... Far less frequently ... do the measures provide evidence about the degree to which a program economically manages the workload associated with meeting its objectives by identifying anything resembling per unit cost of production, activity or output. Rarely, if ever, are the measures indicators of program effectiveness in the sense of identifying the impact of a program on the target population or clientele.[3]

One reason[4] for relying on workload statistics rather than efficiency or cost-effectiveness measures is that someone is already regularly collecting workload data, but no one is regularly collecting service quality, efficiency, equity, and cost-effectiveness data. Collecting these other types of performance data can be expensive. The potential cost of collecting and reporting performance information suggests that agencies must be selective when collecting performance data, choosing only those measures that are worth their cost.

On what basis should agencies choose which performance measures to include in their budget justifications? Some budget offices in their budget preparation guidelines have included specific criteria that agencies should use when evaluating the suitability of potential performance measures. The State of Wisconsin and the City of Tallahassee, Florida, provide two examples. Wisconsin's guidelines for its program budget in 1971–73 stipulated that performance measures should be output oriented, relevant to program objectives, capable of meaningful quantification, thoroughly defined, simple but informative, and available on a continuing basis, and should test the validity of objectives and recognize different levels of performance.[5] Tallahassee's guidelines for its 1979 productivity budget suggested that potential measures be evaluated in terms of validity, utility, timeliness, acceptability, simplicity, and availability.[6] Most budget offices, however, provide no specific selection criteria.

A Tool for Choosing Performance Measures

The objective of this research was to develop a tool that agencies can use to screen potential performance measures systematically in order to choose measures worth including in their budget request justifications. The tool developed should be capable of discriminating among measures in terms of specific criteria. It should also be fairly easy and quick for agency personnel to use.

The first step in developing this tool was to identify the criteria against which performance measures should be evaluated. To determine whether a consensus existed about the appropriate criteria to use when choosing "good" measures, we reviewed 24 books and articles on performance measurement.[7] Table 20.1 lists those criteria cited in more than one article. Validity was the most frequently cited criterion, occurring in 15 of 24 articles. Clarity and reliability were also cited in over half the articles.

Next, the most frequently cited criteria were classified into four categories: technical adequacy, practicality, and two utility categories. The criterion "precision," although cited six times, was believed to be a function of sensitivity and reliability and was therefore not included as a separate criterion. Two criteria, completeness and uniqueness, were considered components of the criterion "validity." Except for these modifications, all criteria cited five or more times were included in the assessment instrument.

Table 20.2 lists these criteria and includes a question or two that should be answered in order to evaluate each potential measure against a specific

TABLE 20.1   Most Frequently Cited Criteria for Choosing Good Measures, Based on Literature Survey

Criterion	Number of Times Cited
Validity	15
Clarity	14
Reliability	13
Relevance to objectives, decisions	11
Accuracy	10
Sensitivity	8
Cost	7
Ease of obtaining data	7
Precision	6
Controllability	6
Timeliness	6
Completeness	5
Uniqueness	5
Comparibility	5
Consistency	3
Credibility	3
Usefulness	3
Ability to monitor quality of data	2
Privacy	2
Flexibility	2
Representativeness	2
Importance	2

criterion. Criteria used to evaluate technical adequacy permit assessing potential measures in terms of how valid, reliable, and accurate the measurements are likely to be. Criteria for practicality address concerns about the cost and ease of obtaining data.

Utility criteria need to be divided into two categories. One category can be applied without knowing who will use the measure being assessed and the purpose for which it will be used. This category permits assessing the extent to which the measures are clear, sensitive, and comparable. A second category of utility criteria cannot readily be used unless one first knows something about the user and the purpose to which the measurements will be put. This category assesses a measure in terms of its relevance to the decision to be made; whether the information can be provided before the decision is made; and whether the aspect of performance indicated by the measure is susceptible to control by the program, agency, or government whose performance is being measured.

TABLE 20.2   Criteria Included in the Assessment Tool

I. TECHNICAL ADEQUACY

   A. Valid
Does the measure logically represent the concept or construct to be measured?

     1. Complete
Does the measure cover the entire concept or construct?

     2. Unique
Does the measure represent some concept or construct not covered by any other measure in this set?

   B. Reliable
If a measurement is repeated, will the results be identical? Are there fluctuations in the characteristic to be measured, changes in transient personal or situational factors, or inconsistencies in the measurement procedure that cause variation in the measurement obtained?

   C. Accurate
Is the measurement free of systematic error or bias?

II. PRACTICALITY

   A. Cost
How much will data collection or analysis cost?

   B. Ease of data collection
What is the anticipated ease or difficulty of obtaining data needed to make the measurement?

III. UTILITY-USER INDEPENDENT

   A. Comparable
Can this measure be used to compare different programs with each other?

   B. Sensitive
Is the discriminating power of the measurement procedure sufficient to capture the variation that occurs in the object, event, or situation being measured?

   C. Clear
Can the meaning of the measure be understood?

IV. UTILITY-USER DEPENDENT

   A. Relevant to Decision
Does the measure provide information needed to make a decision about the performance of a program or agency?

   B. Timely
Are changes in the objects, events, or situations being measured reflected quickly enough in the measurements to be available before the decision must be made?

   C. Controllable
To what extent can the user of the measure affect the measurements, providing resources are made available?

TABLE 20.3   Performance Measures Assessment Instrument: Characteristics of Three Versions

Characteristics of Each Version	Version of Assessment Instrument		
	Version A	Version B	Version C
Criteria Used	Instrument stipulates criteria used	Instrument stipulates criteria used	Rater supplies own criteria to substantiate his holistic rating
Method for Criterion-Specific Ratings	Rater must apply 3-point scale for each criterion based on defined categories supplied with instrument	Rater must judge each measure as being satisfactory or unsatisfactory on each criterion	None
Total Score for Each Measure	Overall ranking is by summing scores on individual criteria	Holistic rating made after rating for each criterion	Holistic rating is first step in the assessment process
Subjectivity of Rating	Lowest	Intermediate	Highest
Average Time Required to Rate a Measure	3 minutes	1.8 minutes	1.4 minutes

Three versions of a performance measures assessment instrument were developed. Table 20.3 summarizes each version's major characteristics. In version A, a three-point scale was developed for each criterion, borrowing heavily from the assessment tool reported by Blair.[8] For each criterion, three categories were defined. For example, a measure for the criterion "accuracy" would be judged to fall within one of these three categories:

High = measurement has little or no systematic error.

Medium = Size of systematic error is known and constant across time periods.

Low = Systematic error is known to be present. Its size is either large or unknown, and constancy across time periods is undetermined.

Using this scale, a person must judge the degree to which a proposed measure meets each criterion as being either high (scored 2 points), medium (1 point), or low (0 points). A total overall score for each measure can therefore range from 0 (if the rater judges the measure as being low on all 12 criteria) to 24 (if the rater judges the measure as being high on all 12 criteria). The resulting overall scores can then be used to rank a list of performance measures in terms of overall adequacy.

An advantage of version A is that the categories defined for each scale encourage a consistent thought process across different raters and across different measures. Nevertheless, this version, as is the case for the other two versions, is subjective. Depending upon their knowledge of the measure being assessed, two people might assign a different score to the same measure. Two possible problems—imperfect rater knowledge and lack of rater diligence—could limit the usefulness of all three assessment instrument versions.

Version B is similar to version A in that the rater first assesses a measure in terms of the same 12 criteria and afterwards gives the measure an overall numerical score. Version B differs from version A in two respects. Instead of using a three-point scale, the Version B user judges each measure as being either satisfactory or unsatisfactory on each criterion. Definition of the terms "satisfactory" and "unsatisfactory" is left to the rater. A second difference is how the rater determines the overall score. After considering a measure's adequacy according to each criterion, the rater assigns the measure a rating from 0 to 10. Version B therefore allows the rater to assign an overall rating that reflects his opinion of the relative importance of the various criteria. It also allows the rater to base his rating on other factors in addition to the criteria stipulated in the assessment instrument.

Version C reverses the steps in the rating process. The rater first considers a measure and assigns an overall numerical rating from 0 to 10. The rater then lists his reasons for the rating assigned. The instrument does not stipulate the criteria that the rater must use.

Experience with the Assessment Instrument

In order to test this assessment tool, several groups of people used one or more versions of it. Six students in a graduate program evaluation class used version A. Each student generated his own measures as a part of an evaluation design for a public-sector program. After about four hours of discussion about performance measures and measurement criteria, each student used version A to rank the performance measures that he developed. This ranking was done during whatever time the student chose the week following the discussions. Total rating time ranged from 2[fr1/2] to 4 hours, averaging 3 minutes for assessing each measure.

Two groups of people used version B, 8 being students in another graduate program evaluation course and 12 being staff members in a Federal prison. The majority of the students were full time employees of a state government. Both groups used a list of proposed measures that the researcher furnished them. The students individually rated 10 performance measures for a probation program for which they were developing an evaluation design as a class project. As was the case for version A, about 4 hours of discussion about performance measurement and measurement criteria preceded the rating session.

The prison staff used version B to rate 12 performance measures for a prison. Each staff member was approached individually, the purpose of the instrument was explained to him, and the definition of each criterion was given him in writing. A researcher was present and available to answer questions when the staff person assessed the measures.

Two groups of people also used version C. Eleven students who used version C include the 8 who used version B. They applied version C to the same set of probation performance measures used in version B. They used version C a week before they saw the version B instrument. At the same Federal prison, a different group of staff members used version C to rate the same prison measures rated by the other group with version B. Prison staff also used version C individually in the presence of a researcher after listening to an oral explanation.

Based on these five trials, we found little difference among the three versions in either the time required or the level of satisfaction with the instrument the users reported. Two additional fators that need to be explored in more detail, however, are the instrument's discriminating power and its subjectivity. If people assign most measures similar scores, then the instrument is not a useful tool for choosing adequate measures. To evaluate the discriminating power of each version, we constructed histograms showing the distribution of scores; assigned measures in each trial; and calculated the range, median, and first and third quartiles for each distribution. For all three versions, both the histograms and summary statistics showed enough spread in the scores to discriminate among potential performance measures.

As noted previously, assigning scores is a subjective act. Saaty states that objectivity means shared subjectivity in interpreting experience.[9] Accepting this definition of objectivity permits measuring an instrument's objectivity by the extent to which different individual's scores for a given measure agree.

Why do people differ in the scores they assign a given measure? There are four major sources of disagreement: (1) People may consider different attributes of a measure when scoring it. (2) People may differ in terms of the relative importance they ascribe to the attributes they consider. (3) People may have imperfect knowledge about a measure's attributes. (4) People may inconsistently apply the criteria by which they assess a measure's attributes. These sources of subjectivity suggest that one might follow several strategies in order to reduce the tool's subjectivity when using it to choose performance measures.

Using version A should eliminate the first two sources of disagreement because it prescribes the attributes (*i.e.,* the criteria) upon which its users assess measures and, also, through the three-point scale for each criterion, prescribes that all attributes receive equal weight. Another approach to eliminating the first two sources of disagreement is to have the same person or team rate all the measures being considered. The amount of disagreement found among raters using version B and C during the trials suggests that it would be inappropriate when using these versions to have one person score part of the measures, someone else to score the rest, then combine both sets and choose the measure with the highest scores. If, when scoring measures, the first two sources of disagreement are not controlled for, measures should not be compared with each other on the basis of the scores unless the same person or group scored them all.

When people using version A were unsure of how to score a measure in terms of the three-point scale, they tended to assign the middle point in the scale. The effect of this tendency is that lack of information about the measures' attributes results in measures' receiving similar scores. It may be possible for some agencies to have their staff specialize when assessing measures in order to make more informed judgments. One basis for specialization might be to have one person assess the technical adequacy of the proposed measures, another person assess their practicality, a third assess their utility, and a fourth give the measures an overall score based on the ratings of the other three.

The last source of disagreement, inconsistent application of the criteria, may occur when a person does not understand how to use the instrument or is not diligent when using it. Appropriate explanation and training should solve the first problem. When agency staff understand the use to which their assessments will be put, they may feel they have enough stake in the outcome to understand the task with reasonable diligence.

We have already noted that people may vary in the relative importance they ascribe to different measurement criteria. As a case in point, we gathered the opinions of a convenience sample of two groups—staff in a state planning and budgeting office and staff in a Federal prison. Both groups believed that reliability, accuracy, clarity, sensitivity, and timeliness were highly desirable attributes of performance measures. The planning and budget staff, however, believed that the attributes of cost, ease of data collection, and comparability were more important than did the prison staff. In turn, the prison's staff believed completeness and uniqueness to be more important than did the planning and budget staff. This small sampling can in no way be generalized to broader groups of people, but it does show that people may differ in the relative importance they accord the criteria stipulated in versions A and B of the assessment tool. When such is the case, they are unlikely to find implementing version A (which accords equal weight to each criterion) a satisfactory approach.

Developing a Strategy for Choosing Performance Measures

Using this assessment tool, agencies may tailor a strategy for systematically deciding which measures are worth including in their budget justifications. For example, when agencies believe some criteria are more important than others, they can modify the assessment tool to economize on the assessment task. By using the most important criteria as a screening device, the total number of measures can thereby more quickly be reduced to a subset that merits further assessment. Versions A and B have in fact been adapted in this fashion. In one instance, version A was adapted to screen about 1,100 potential measures for corrections programs.[10] In the first step, measures that scored low on the validity criteria (completeness and uniqueness) were discarded. In the second step, the remaining measures were further assessed in terms of reliability, accuracy, comparability, sensitivity, and clarity. In another instance, version B was adapted to rate about 500 potential measures being considered for a state's social programs (education, health, social services).[11] In this instance, a two-person team assessed each measure, again using a two-step procedure. In the first step, the team selected measures on the basis of completeness and clarity. They next took those measures rated satisfactory in terms of these two criteria and rated them in terms of accuracy, uniqueness, and cost of data collection.

Potential measures need to be assessed by people who understand the context in which performance measures submitted in budget justifications will be used. Questions of practicality and relevance to resource allocation decisions may need to be weighed more heavily than would be the case for research applications. The tool described in this paper gives one a systematic way of thinking about factors that render a potential measure adequate or inadequate for a given situation. As the applications mentioned demonstrate, the tool can be adapted to develop an assessment strategy appropriate to an agency's concerns, staff skills, and resources available for data collection. Applied systematically, such an assessment instrument can identify from a list of potential measures those worth including in agency budget justifications. As such, it can be a helpful tool in facilitating budget reform implementation.

Conclusion

If budget reforms are to lead to improved budget outcomes, the presence of two conditions is critical. First, information changes that permit budgeters to analyze requests in terms of the performance criteria that the reform proponents advocate must accompany format changes. Second, policy makers must take this information into account when making budget decisions. This paper has focused upon a tool for facilitating the first of these conditions.

While this paper has focused upon strategies for systematically assessing the technical merits of potential performance measures, agency staff cannot ignore the political and behavioral dimensions of the budgetary process. Both agency administrators and budgeters must accept the measures that agencies use to justify their budget requests as being credible indicators of agency performance. Without such acceptance, performance measurement cannot provide the basis for tying changes in productivity to funding level decisions.

One way of obtaining such acceptance may be for teams of agency and chief executive and/or legislative staff to use a version of this assessment tool for jointly selecting performance measures. Agencies might then use the measures to justify their budget requests, and oversight staff might use them to analyze these requests and evaluate agency performance. Whatever strategy an agency develops should be tailored to the political and behavioral realities of its own environment.

Notes

1. Allen Schick, "The Road from ZBB," *Public Administration Review,* 38:2 (March/April 1978), 178.
2. Lewis Friedman, "Performance Budgeting in American Cities," *Public Productivity Review,* 3:4 (Spring/Summer 1979), 50–51.
3. Thomas P. Lauth, "Performance Evaluation in the Georgia Budgetary Process" (paper presented at the American Society for Public Administration National Conference, April 1981), 7.
4. Others have ably documented the many political, organizational, economic, and behavioral problems that can also hinder collecting and reporting performance information for budget review. See, for example, "Creative Budgeting in New York City: An Interview with Former Budget Director Frederick O'R. Hayes" (Washington, D.C.: The Urban Institute, 1971); Merlin M. Hackbart and James R. Ramsey, "Budgeting: Inducements and Impediments to Innovations," *State Government,* 52:2 (Spring 1979), 65–69; Frederick O'R. Hayes, "The Budget and Its Problems," *Urban Affairs Papers,* 2:2 (Spring 1980), 7–18; Thomas P. Lauth, "Zero-Base Budgeting in Georgia State Government: Myth and Reality," *Public Administration Review,* 38:5 (September/October 1978), 420–430; Perry Moore, "Zero-Base Budget-

ing in American Cities," *Public Administration Review,* 40:3 (May/June 1980), 253–258; A. Premchand, "Government Budget Reforms: Agenda for the 1980s," *Public Budgeting and Finance,* 1:3 (Autumn 1981), 16–24; A. Premchand, "Government Budget Reforms: An Overview," *Public Budgeting and Finance,* 1:2 (Summer 1981), 74–85; Richard Rose, "Implementation and Evaporation: The Record of MBO," *Public Administration Review,* 37:1 (January/February 1977), 64–71; Allen Schick, "A Death in the Bureaucracy: The Demise of Federal PPB," *Public Administration Review,* 33:2 (March/April 1973), 146–156; Allen Schick, "The Road from ZBB," *Public Administration Review,* 38:2 (March/April 1978), 177–180; Allen Schick, "The Road to PPB: The Stages of Budget Reform," *Public Administration Review,* 26:4 (December 1966), 243–258; Elmer Staats, "The Continuing Need for Budget Reform" (address to the American Association for Budget and Program Analysis, 1980); Jeffrey D. Straussman, "A Typology of Budgetary Environments: Notes on the Prospects for Reform," *Administration and Society,* 11:2 (August 1979), 216–226; Paul T. Veillette, "A Public Accounting: Reflections on State Budgeting," *Public Budgeting and Finance,* 1:3 (Autumn 1981), 62–68; Aaron Wildavsky, "The Political Economy of Efficiency: Cost-Benefit Analysis, Systems Analysis, and Program Budgeting," *Public Administration Review,* 26:4 (December 1966), 292–310; and Aaron Wildavsky and Arthur Hammond, "Comprehensive Versus Incremental Budgeting in the Department of Agriculture," *Administrative Science Quarterly,* 10:3 (December 1965), 321–346.

5. State of Wisconsin, "Manual on Program Budget Preparation" (S. Kenneth Howard and Gloria Grizzle, eds. *Whatever Happened to State Budgeting?* Lexington, Ky.: Council of State Governments, 1972), 255–256.

6. City of Tallahassee, Florida, "Productivity Measurement Worksheet," (1979).

7. See William Ascher, *Forecasting: An Appraisal for Policy-Makers and Planners* (Baltimore: Johns Hopkins University Press, 1978); Louis H. Blair, et al., *Monitoring the Impacts of Prison and Parole Services: An Initial Examination* (Washington, D.C.: The Urban Institute, 1977); Milton M. Chen, J. W. Bush, and Donald L. Patrick, "Social Indicators for Health Planning and Policy Analysis," *Policy Sciences* 6:1 (March 1975), 71–89: Thomas J. Cook, "Performance Measures for the Courts System" (Triangle Park, N.C.: Research Triangle Institute, 1978), grant application submitted to Law Enforcement Assistance Administration; George S. Day and Burton A. Weitz, "Comparative Urban Social Indicators: Problems and Prospects," *Policy Sciences* 8:4 (December 1977), 423–435; John J. Dinkel and Joyce E. Erickson, "Multiple Objective in Environmental Protection Programs," *Policy Sciences* 9:1 (February 1978), 87–96; Allan R. Drebin, "Criteria for Performance Measurement in State and Local Government" *Governmental Finance,* 9:4 (December 1980), 3–7; Gloria A. Grizzle *et al.,* "Performance Measurement Theory for Corrections" (Raleigh, N.C.: The Osprey Company, 1978), grant application submitted to the Law Enforcement Assistance Administration, 1978; Owen P. Hall, Jr., "A Policy Model Appraisal Paradigm," *Policy Sciences,* 6:2 (June 1975), 185–195; Harry P. Hatry, "Performance Measurement Principles and Techniques: An Overview for Local Government," *Public Productivity Review,* 4:4 (December 1980), 312–339; Peter J. Hunt, *Program Evaluation Manual* (Madeira Beach, Fla.: Personnel Research and Training Institute, 1978); E. Gerald Hurst, Jr. "Attributes of Performance Measures," *Public Productivity Review,* 4:1 (March 1980), 43–49;

Joan Jacoby, "Theory of Performance Measurement for Prosecution and Public Defense" (Washington, D.C.: Bureau of Social Science Research, Inc., 1978), grant application submitted to Law Enforcement Assistance Administration; Abraham Kaplan, *The Conduct of Inquiry: Methodology for Behavioral Science* (San Francisco: Chandler, 1964); Helmut Klages, "Assessment of an Attempt at a System of Social Indicators," *Policy Sciences* 4 (1973), 249–261; Delbert C. Miller, *Handbook of Research Design and Social Measurement,* 2nd ed. (New York: David McKay Co., 1970); Jum C. Nunnally and Robert L. Durham, "Validity, Reliability, and Special Problems of Measurement in Evaluation Research," in Elmer Struening and Marcia Guttentag (eds.), *Handbook of Evaluation Research,* Vol. 1 (Beverly Hills: Sage 1975), 289–352; Dale K. Sechret, "The Development and Implementation of Standards for Correctional Systems" (College Park, Md.: American Correctional Association, 1979); Claire Selltiz, *et. al., Research Methods in Social Relations* (New York: Holt, Rinehart and Winston, 1959); Robert L. Thorndike and Elizabeth P. Hagen, *Measurement and Evaluation in Psychology and Education* (New York: John Wiley, 1977); Gordon P. Whitaker and Elinor Ostrom, "Performance Measurement in the Criminal Justice System: A Police Perspective" (Chapel Hill: University of North Carolina), grant application submitted to the Law Enforcement Assistance Administration, 1978; Marshall H. Whithed, "Toward the Development of a Set of World Criminal Justice Indicators" (Virginia Commonwealth University, unpublished manuscript, March 1969); Harold L. Wilensky, *Organizational Intelligence* (New York: Basic Books, 1967); and Joseph W. Wilkinson, "The Meaning of Measurements," *Management Accounting,* 57 (July 1975), 49–52.

8. Louis H. Blair, et al., *Monitoring the Impacts of Prison and Parole Services: An Initial Examination* (Washington, D.C.: The Urban Institute, 1977).

9. Thomas L. Saaty, *The Analytic Hierarchy Process: Planning, Priority Setting, Resource Allocation* (New York: McGraw-Hill, 1980), 15.

10. Ann G. Jones, "The Rating of Corrections Performance Measures" (Raleigh, N.C.: The Osprey Company, 1980).

11. Gloria A. Grizzle and Karen S. Minerva, "Measuring the Cost-Effectiveness of Florida's Social Programs" (Tallahassee, Fla.: Florida State University, 1980).

21

ANALYZING THE CONTRACTING-OUT OF GOVERNMENT SERVICES

Relevant Cost-Benefit Considerations

Stanley C. Wisniewski

In recent years there has been a great deal of discussion about the proper role and size of government. Some of this debate has centered on what services local governments *should be* providing in their jurisdictions and what service responsibilities *should be* returned to the private sector (i.e., the "privatization" issue).[1] Other discussions and studies have focused more narrowly on whether public services should be produced by a public workforce or by hired private agents (i.e., the "contracting out" issue).

This article is concerned with the contracting-out decision. In other words, it assumes that the decision to assign responsibility to local government for providing a particular service to the public has already been made, and that a rationale for making that decision has been articulated, usually in the form of a legislative mandate.[2] Therefore, the issue that remains for local government is how best to effectuate this mandate. Local government must decide how it can best fulfill its responsibilities—either through the use of its own employees or by retaining a contractor to carry out some or most of the tasks necessary for service delivery.

1991. Analyzing the contracting-out of government services: Relevant cost-benefit considerations. Wisniewski, Stanley C. **Public Budgeting and Finance** 11 (Summer): 95–107.

The contracting-out decision is not a simple matter of technical economic efficiency. Because legislative mandates are rarely formulated in a vacuum, public service production decisions often have to deal with several objectives at the same time. For example, trash collection may be designed to satisfy public health goals and an aesthetic goal of cleaner streets, while simultaneously meeting specific minority employment goals or minimizing adverse environmental consequences stemming from the disposal of refuse.

Government managers, then, must evaluate the different means available for achieving those objectives by weighing the benefits against the costs of each alternative method. This article offers a review of various approaches to analyzing the contracting-out decision and distills a set of cost-benefit considerations which must be addressed in order to ascertain whether there is an advantage to contracting with private sector service providers as compared to performing the work "in-house."[3]

The article begins with a brief discussion of the fundamental notion that an analysis of a contracting-out decision must start with an unambiguous, comprehensive statement of service goals which facilitates the measurement of outcomes. That discussion is followed by an examination of the considerations on the cost side of the equation which are basic to a proper measurement of relevant direct, indirect, and social costs.[4]

A Clear and Comprehensive
Statement of Service Goals:
Facilitating the Measurement of Outcomes

The first and most important task facing any public manager is a clear specification of the service goals to be attained and a description of the level of effort to be employed in their attainment. Making a rational choice about the means to be employed is impossible *without* a specific end in mind. McKean cautions that "Overlooking any relevant objectives could lead to poor choices."[5]

Too often, however, comparisons between private and public sector alternatives define the objectives of service delivery too vaguely. As a result, tasks which the public considers part of service delivery are not clearly identified for potential contractors. For example, contracting for refuse collection in some cities may traditionally involve clean-up activities in alleys and side streets littered with refuse. Unless such clean-up activities are specifically tasked, there can be no meaningful cost comparison between in-house refuse collection efforts which do provide these ancillary clean-up services and private sector contractors who do not. Similarly, to make a cost comparison under the assumption that *all* refuse collection services are identical in terms of desired objectives is a heroic and, often, unwarranted assumption. Apples and oranges are compared as if the same standard of measurement applied. Such serious distortions can be avoided and meaningful analyses can be developed if in-house and contractor cost comparisons proceed from a common starting point in terms of specified objectives. As Buchanan has recently noted, ". . . unless the same scalar is employed, how can relative 'failure' or 'success' be judged at all?"[6]

A similar problem is produced by studies which fail to adjust for differences in the quantity or quality of outcomes. The failure to adjust for quantitative or qualitative differences in outcomes means that different service objectives are, in fact, being compared. There must be a common outcome measured to permit meaningful comparisons between public sector and private sector service delivery. As Jarrell and Skibniewski point out: "For a valid cost comparison to be possible, the contractors' and government's bids must be based on an identical work requirements and specifications document. This document must be an in-depth description of the required quality and quantity of work, level of service and time restrictions on the work."[7] Sometimes an accurate identification of all service objectives may be difficult, e.g., the delivery of social worker services which may have some intangible outcomes. Yet, even in such cases, some standards can be specified in terms of proxy variables such as intensity of effort, access, timeliness of intervention, and the characteristics or qualifications of the persons actually delivering the services in question.

Attempts to take into account different outcomes may still fail to do so adequately because the measurement techniques employed are inappropriate for the objectives being addressed by service delivery in the public sector.[8] For example, Berenyi and Stevens recently compared public and private sector service delivery costs with respect to eight municipal services and claimed to control for differences due to scale, level of service, and quality of service delivery.[9] However, while noting that all the cities studied had both curbside and alley refuse collection, the authors made *no* effort to test for cost differences with respect to each of these two different processes. Rather, both were lumped together as if they were equivalent services and measured against the same performance standard (i.e., tons of refuse collected).[10]

Berenyi and Stevens made no effort to ascertain whether or not private contractors were meeting the actual quality standards employed by the city. Instead, quality was defined in terms of the authors' own perceptions of what quality of service should mean. Their subjective view *may or may not* correspond to the quality of service standard employed by *either* the public entity *or* by private contractors. Berenyi and Stevens do start at the right place in emphasizing that, for each of the services studied, measures should be developed to see how well service delivery goals are being met. However, in designing their measures they have defined the goals for service delivery, instead of *ascertaining* what the publicly mandated goals for service delivery may have been in each jurisdiction and, then, attempting to find quantitative standards by which the achievement of those objectives could be measured.[11]

One cannot assume that all outputs are homogenous and that, therefore, any outcome of the same general type is consistent with the public mandate.[12] This caution is especially relevant in evaluating alternative delivery of services, because service outcomes may prove to be slippery concepts.[13] Starr argues that: "Public and private schools, hospitals, and social services rarely have the same kinds of students, patients, or clients ... any simple comparison of costs, income, and productivity puts the public sector organizations at an unfair disadvantage ... most studies comparing public and private organizations lack any evidence about the quality of services, thereby making it difficult to judge whether lower costs result from greater efficiency or reduced service."[14] A clear specification of tasks, then, both as to the quantity and quality[15] of the service delivered is the critical starting point for evaluating alternative service delivery mechanisms.

In short, specifications must be accurately written to avoid poor quality and inappropriate work.[16] Only after the objective has been clearly identified can meaningful cost estimates of alternative delivery mechanisms be prepared.

Measurement of Relevant
Direct, Indirect, and Social Costs

A fair cost-benefit analysis of contracting-out is one which considers direct costs, indirect costs, and social costs (including quality-of-life considerations and intangibles) in measuring the differences in total costs between performing work in-house as compared to contracting-out.

Direct and Indirect Costs

Direct costs are those associated with the main service objectives of a project.[17] In other words, direct costs encompass the cost of resources used in delivering a particular service or in undertaking a specific project. Indirect costs can be defined as resource costs which are spread across several services or projects and are allocated on a percentage basis among them. Both must be reviewed to obtain a full picture of production costs.

Levin identifies the major categories of resources as personnel, facilities, equipment and materials, other inputs (such as training costs), and client costs (contributions required of the service user to facilitate delivery).[18] The cost of using these resources in production can be allocated as a direct cost or assigned to "overhead" as an indirect cost of production.

The first four categories of resource costs are familiar ones. Use of resources can result in direct or indirect costs in any of these familiar cost categories. However, the notion of client costs is not always considered in cost-benefit evaluations, although it is an easily understood concept. Examples of client costs are the requirements that a family provide its own transportation in order to take advantage of educational services offered by the government or that a family place its garbage in uniform containers on the curb for pick-up. Such client costs may vary with service delivery alternatives. Where they do vary, such costs are relevant to evaluating the price tags of in-house and contracted service delivery. Since client cost differences effectively reflect variations in service quality, it should be noted that including such costs in comparative evaluations need only be done if the public mandate requiring the service permits the government sufficient latitude to engage in some cost shifting to the actual user. If, on the other hand, the objectives of the service are spelled out with such particularity as to forbid government discretion in the area of client costs, then client cost will not be incurred. Similarly, client costs can be ignored if *all* service delivery alternatives—in-house as well as contractors—impose the same burden on service users.

Focusing on the first four kinds of resources costs—personnel, facilities, equipment, and materials, and other miscellaneous inputs—requires the collection of data on direct and indirect costs including salaries and fringe benefits, service-specific supplies, service-specific utility and insurance, capital facilities and equipment, overhead, and general and administrative expenses (such as payroll administration costs, marketing, executive salaries, general training costs, and taxes). Collecting such data is not necessarily a simple accounting exercise.

Sometimes all these data are just not readily available. Moreover, if available, such data often must be carefully scrutinized to assure accuracy and the absence of misrepresentation. For example, a study of Canadian refuse collection used estimates of capital expenditure, vehicle maintenance, fuel and lubricant expenses, and fringe benefit costs in order to supply missing information, where public sector respondents to a survey did not provide the data. Rent and utility costs were ultimately left out of that study's calculation of the cost of in-house refuse collection services because such costs could not be adequately quantified. As a result the public and private sector cost estimates in the study are not completely equivalent.[19] The data availability problem may be especially acute where a contracted service is being considered for the first time and the service is *not* identical to some service already being performed by the contractor in the private arena. In such cases, the lack of baseline data on contract costs makes it difficult to compare contractor and in-house costs in a meaningful way.[20]

Berenyi and Stevens suggest the use of actual costs rather than budget data to estimate the cost of publicly delivered services, citing earlier studies which provide some evidence that municipal budgets understate the actual cost of delivering the service.[21] However, if the value of equipment purchases related to the delivery of a specific service is listed as an expense in the year of acquisition, it may result in overstated costs in that year and understated costs in the out year when compared to an accounting approach which depreciates the cost of equipment over its useful life. In making adjustments to governmental costs to reflect depreciation, the adjustment should be made in terms of the method of depreciation employed by prospective private contractors in order to yield comparable data.

Actual cost data is also sometimes preferable to official budget data because budgets sometimes reflect larger expenditure amounts for politically popular services which, in practice, may be shifted by indirect means to less popular spending categories having immediate needs.

Salary and fringe benefit cost data may have to be adjusted to determine actual expenditures on the service when the same group of employees is diverted temporarily to other service functions. For example, if refuse collection employees are routinely engaged to supplement snow removal efforts, then that portion of salaries and benefits attributable to the latter category should be subtracted from the cost of publicly delivered refuse collection services before cost comparisons are made with private refuse collection activities.[22]

Costs implicit in a contracting-out proposal also must be made explicit if in-house and contractor costs are to be meaningfully compared. Such costs include contract administration and inspection costs, conversion costs, and the gain or loss on the government's disposition of capital assets.[23]

Contract administration and inspection efforts, while crucial to the contracting-out process, can be expensive.[24] Jarrell and Skibniewski define such costs to include personnel costs for contract administration and inspection, transportation costs to perform contract inspection and liaison, and office costs including facility, supplied communications, and furnishings.[25] This list could also be supplemented to include legal support services and general support services extended to contract administrator and contract negotiators.

An example of contract administration costs that may be significant and critical to the effectiveness of the effort, is the cost of maintaining the expertise of contracting officers with respect to operational issues. If they do not know how a service works they cannot adequately monitor contractor performance. All of the advantages of a pre-award specification of contractor tasks may well be lost in such cases.[26] Also important to the monitoring function is the training of contract managers to prepare for monitoring responsibilities such as the processing of contractor reports and citizen complaints.[27] The cost of all such training for contracting officers should be added to the contracted price of the service. Such training is important, not only from an efficiency point-of-view, but because weak contract monitoring may provide an incentive for contractor abuse.[28]

Contract administration costs may include expenses well beyond those associated with routine contract issuance and monitoring because it is often difficult to pin down information on production costs relative to specific service attributes.[29] This also is a consideration when the alternative market for the service must be made more efficient.[30] To the extent that government has to spend money on improving its information bank or on making the alternative market conform to the most efficient organizational form, these costs become part of the overhead associated with the maintenance of the contracting system.

Another cost implicit in a contracting out proposal is the cost of conversion from in-house to contractor performance. Jarrell and Skibniewski break down conversion costs into three categories: (1) labor-related conversion costs flowing from the transfer, retraining, or dismissal of government employees who are part of the in-house workforce; (2) material-related conversion costs resulting from the transfer or disposal of government-owned materials that are no longer needed; and (3) production losses and inefficiency costs associated with the transition to contract performance.[31]

Some of the impacts of conversion are more easily quantified than others. Severance pay, accrued vacation pay and sick leave cash-out costs, retraining costs, and relocation costs attributable to the displacement of public employees by contract employees are costs which are relatively easy to calculate. The ripple effect of relocation and training caused by more senior displaced employees seeking to bump less senior employees in the public workforce cannot be ignored and, with some difficulty, may be estimated. These latter estimates will be higher if employees who bump into new positions are red-circled at their old pay rates. For example, the Congressional Budget Office has noted the chain of downgradings that requires payment of higher salaries (under save-pay arrangements) in each job impacted by the process. Downgrading offsets about half the potential savings from abolished federal positions.[32]

Roehm, Castellano, and Karns show the realities of public management practices with regard to contracting out: when government workers face displacement, layoffs and/or discharges are employed less frequently than other adjustment mechanisms.[33] Consequently the cost of retraining and relocating employees in its fullest dimension must be estimated as a cost of contracting out. Even when terminations do occur, costs such as the impact on public employee retirement systems need to be recognized and measured along with more obvious ones such as severance pay.

Another cost of contracting-out is the impact on the morale and productivity of the affected in-house workforce immediately prior to conversion. Timmins found evidence that public employees anticipating layoffs used accrued leave for job searches and agency facilities for copying resumes and making long-distance job search telephone calls.[34]

Contracting-out, particularly for professional services, also raises a question as to what is an adequate nucleus or core of experienced employees. Such a core furnishes the range of skills necessary to deal with long-run needs and the more immediate contingencies, while preventing government from being a captive of the contractors it seeks to direct. For example, engineers may find it difficult to maintain their skills or may never develop certain important skills due to the lack of opportunity to work on significant, complex projects. This means that current government understaffing due to contracting out may well lead to higher contractor-associated costs in the future, particularly given the likelihood of the absence of a viable competitive in-house alternative.

Another conversion cost is the cost of preparing and implementing a plan for alternative service delivery in the event of a contractor's voluntary or involuntary withdrawal of services. Some of this cost is reflected in performance bonds or may be ultimately recouped in the form of termination penalties, but not having a plan on hand to deal with such contingencies is a luxury few governments can afford.

Finally, in addition to labor-related conversion costs, material-related conversion costs must be quantified and added to the contractor's costs. While some of these costs such as inventory preparation and shipping will clearly result in more costs being assigned to the contractor, the actual disposal of surplus materials and excess capital assets by the government may conceivably produce a net revenue gain for the government which can be attributed to the contracting-out alternative.

Social Costs

Social costs may be defined as negative externalities, that is uncompensated damage to the nonproducers of a good or service that results from the actions of the producer of the good or service. A classic example is air pollution from an unregulated industrial smokestack which inflicts damage on others, yet the amount of the damage is not counted as part of the cost of industrial production. Failure to calculate and assess social costs means the price of the responsible product or service is artificially low. The prescribed remedy for this problem is to charge the producer for the negative external effects, that is, to force him to internalize the externalities.

It is often difficult to measure adequately all social costs. Some social costs may deal with intangibles such as the destruction of an asethetically pleasing sight, sound, or taste. These kinds of costs, at best, may be listed, rather than quantitied. Musgrave and Musgrave[35] and Squire and van der Tak[36] suggest that while intangible costs are more difficult to measure, they should still be included in any cost-benefit analysis. The failure to consider such costs in evaluating contracting-out proposals would produce uninformed decisions.

Some of the more important social costs of contracting-out can be defined in terms of concerns over **equity, participation,** and **accountability** losses. Each is discussed in more detail below.

Equity can be an important performance criterion. Perry and Babitsky point out that research has shown that public transportation agencies "have not increased fare levels to cover rising operating costs, while private firms have consistently increased fares to keep pace with rising costs."[37] They hypothesize that "[b]ecause two major goals of transit are to increase mobility within urban areas and to provide transportation to the transit dependent," the distributional effects of the difference between public and private fare trends could have important equity implications.[38]

Moreover, Ross argues that equity "can be interpreted and measured in many reasonable ways," for example, some minimum level of benefits.[39] If equity considerations have not been explicitly addressed in the stated objectives of the service function, then these aspects of the difference between governmental and private service delivery must be captured to permit informed decisions about which mode of providing the service imposes more costs.

Equity concerns are often concerns about equal access. For example, does contracting-out diminish gains made by minority groups? Minorities, who are among the most recently hired government employees, may bear the largest burden of contracting's employee replacement effect. Minority economic advancement has been heavily concentrated in the public sector, given the proportionately larger number of minorities employed by government. Therefore, expanding contracting-out may reduce this important route to economic improvement for minorities.

Access to greater opportunities for minority-owned business does not necessarily materialize with the expansion of contracting-out.[40] Contractors may not compete on a "level playing field," notwithstanding the absence of corruption, because some enjoy the advantage of familiarity.

A social cost sometimes associated with contracting-out is a reduction in community **participation.** Ross describes the harm arising from diminished participation in terms of alienation as frustration at not being involved in a choice-making process which affects the community.[41]

Morgan and England argue that the criterion for evaluating the opportunity for citizen participation is the existence of avenues for the redress of grievances.[42] To the extent that contracting-out reduces the citizenry's ability to obtain responses from service providers, a social cost is incurred. A practical way of gauging this aspect of participation is to determine if a method for handling complaints has been developed by the contractor and how effective it is likely to be. If the contractor simply passes complaints on to government representatives for handling, then the government is providing an important element of the service without being compensated for its efforts. Worse still, the contractor could simply ignore complaints, compounding the negative impact of the original problem by adding this frustration for users.

Finally, another social cost of contracting-out may be a loss of **accountability**. Ross defines accountability as "the extent to which mechanisms and processes function to evaluate and assure that program actors carry out their functions effectively and responsibly."[43]

Accountability is a coupling of service functions with the responsibility for effective service delivery. Contracting-out services often decouples the service function and the responsibility for it. Day-to-day reporting and quick feedback responses seem unlikely to be the hallmark of a service delivery alternative which divorces service delivery from the public managers ultimately responsible for it. Concern over loss of managerial control has been identified as a major reason why more contracting out of service has not occurred.[44]

A breakdown in managerial control can result in more than mere temporary inefficiencies. It can also produce outright fraud and corruption that is difficult to detect and correct because of the absence of public information and direct methods of public scrutiny. Moe asserts that case studies of many federalized services suggest a shift to full public sector performance that was prompted by the exposure of a pattern of corruption.[45]

Kolderie states that ultimate managerial control can be maintained through the veto power of contract renewal.[46] But that type of managerial control may not avoid day-to-day social costs.

Contracting-out may produce these types of social costs because, as Timmins points out, it "replaces civil service rules and requirements with something considerably less in terms of employee and general public personnel protection."[47] Timmins cites the following examples of the rules which are not operative in a contracted environment: public worker ethics or conflict-of-interest laws, nepotism statutes or ordinances, and political activity laws.[48]

Both Moe[49] and Sullivan[50] argue that contracting-out may involve a broader loss of control for government—one where government sovereignty is extended to private contractors and citizens' legal rights and remedies are effectively diminished. If this happens, then the public is incurring damages for which it is not being compensated. Loss of due process is an example of one such heavy social cost.

Sullivan points out that the due process requirement presents an onerous burden for government.[51] Yet, if service delivery is in private hands an employee often can be dismissed or a citizen denied service without due process. This loss of fundamental rights is perhaps most economically harmful for citizens in cases where contractors make eligibility determinations as part of service delivery, e.g., health care services, but fail to accord due process review. To some extent, this problem may be alleviated by contract terms or regulatory legislation requiring the contractor to extend to the client the same constitutional protections which government must guarantee. But doing so raises the question of whether or not government thereby sacrifices some of its sovereignty by extending to contractors its governmental immunities. Clearly, important societal values are at stake in such situations and should be explicitly considered as part of the evaluation process.

Conclusion

Among the considerations this article identifies as basic to a proper cost-benefit evaluation of a contracting-out decision is an unambiguous, comprehensive specification of service objectives (i.e., the benefits desired), so as to facilitate the measurement of the comparable outputs of alternative delivery mechanisms. The production of a certain quantity of services can be clearly specified and subsequently measured by looking at: (1) physical outputs or (2) other outcome data. The production of a particular quality of service can also be specified in ways that permit comparisons through the use of such measures as: (1) timeliness, (2) level of effort, (3) access, (4) characteristics or qualifications of persons delivering the service, (5) citizen complaints, or (6) surveys of citizen satisfaction. An unambiguous, comprehensive statement of service goals will help assure the delivery of services of like quality in the broadest sense and will minimize unanticipated social cost impacts.

On the cost side of the equation, basic to any proper evaluation of the contracting-out decision, is an analysis of comparable contractor versus in-house costs of production. The relevant categories of costs which should be examined include such direct and indirect cost of production as: (1) personnel costs, (2) facility costs, (3) equipment costs, (4) material costs, (5) client costs, (6) contract administration and inspection costs, (7) conversion costs, and (8) gains or losses on the government's disposition of capital assets. In addition, relevant social costs incurred by contracting-out should be examined such as equity losses, reduced community participation, and diminished managerial control or diminished government sovereignty. An economic cost-benefit evaluation of contracting-out should take into account all these relevant direct, indirect, and social costs in order to ascertain whether there is any advantage to contracting-out as compared to performing the work in-house. Such comparisons enable public managers to determine which means of attaining a particular set of service goals will maximize benefits relative to the real costs of production.

Legislation permitting contracting-out, without any built-in safeguards against exaggerated cost-savings, invites abuse and ultimately results in the taxpayer being short-changed. Analyzing the contracting-out decision with respect to the cost-benefit consideration outlined in this article can provide meaningful safeguards for oversight of the contracting process.

Notes

1. Indeed, debates over whether certain government activities should be privatized are not merely confined to whether certain services should be publicly or privately provided—but often raise questions about the extent of government involvement in an activity in any form. For instead of providing services directly—running a postal service, conducting research, or operating an atomic stockpile—government may simply tell private persons what to do to achieve the same objectives through regulation, direct coercion, and attempted inducement of private conduct.

2. The "provision" decision requires a different type of analysis than the "production" decision. Analyzing the provision of a service to determine if it should be provided by government requires a careful investigation of such questions as why responsibility for the activity was given to the government in the first place and what conditions may have changed so that a different decision may be reached by the public in assigning that responsibility today (i.e., do the services at issue meet the public goods criterion?). Answers to these broad, difficult, and often philosophic questions are not required when dealing with the "production" decision (i.e., whether to contract out or not), because the responsibility for providing the service has *already* been assigned to the government. What remains is the still difficult, but more narrow, question of whether production will be publicly or privately organized.

3. Contracting can, and often does, occur *between* different governmental entities. See James Ferris and Elizabeth Graddy, "Contracting Out: For What? With Whom?" *Public Administration Review* 46 (July/Aug. 1986): 332–344.

4. If a fixed benefit level is identified *and* if both public and private sector efforts are capable of delivering the services that yield those benefits, then the question at hand reduces to the search for a least-cost solution to the problem.

5. Roland N. McKean, "Cost-Benefit Analysis" in *Managerial Economics and Operations Research: Techniques, Applications, Cases,* 3rd ed., Edwin Mansfield, ed., (New York: W.W. Norton, 1975). 551.

6. J. M. Buchanan, "Market Failure and Political Failure." *Cato Journal* 8 (Spring 1988): 1–13.

7. David A. Jarrell and Miroslaw J. Skibniewski, "Cost Comparison Model for Contracting Out Government Services." *Journal of Management in Engineering* 4 (July 1988): 260–271.

8. Some studies look impressive or technically proficient, using commonly-accepted measures of efficiency such as "unit costs," but they do not tell the reader what bundle of services is associated with the cost data. Higher unit costs may well be warranted for a higher quality bundle of services. For an example of a largely polemical exposition offered as a comparative analysis of private sector and government service delivery see Reason Foundation and the University of Miami, *Savings A.S.A.P.: An Analysis of the City and County of Los Angeles*, (commissioned by the Southern California Tax Research Foundation, Nov. 1988).

9. Eileen B. Berenyi and Barbara J. Stevens, "Does Privatization Work? A Study of the Delivery of Eight Local Services," *State and Local Government Review* 21 (Winter 1988): 11–20.

10. For a discussion of outcomes measures which attempt to take into account different quality considerations such as timeliness of collection and a range of responsibilities broader than just emptying trash containers, see Marc Holzer, "Productivity In, Garbage Out: Sanitation Gains in New York," *Public Productivity Review* 11 (Spring 1988): 37–50.

11. Nevertheless, Berenyi and Stevens do at least share most of the relevant data they have collected as well as the results of their statistical analysis, so that a critical evaluation of their methodology can be undertaken and the results of their study can either be intelligently accepted or rejected. Too many other studies in this subject area simply report higher costs for in-house service delivery after purportedly adjusting for service levels, scale of output, and environmental factors, *without* sharing any information about how these crucial adjustment factors were designed or measured and *without* providing the relevant statistics from their regression analyses from which they draw their inferences.

12. Ross, in *Government and the Private Sector: Who Should Do What?* (New York: Crane, Russak & Company, 1988). 36–64, provides another example from contracting-out of public school transportation services, of how the different conditions under which services may be produced affect relative cost comparisons.

13. For example, suppose government is faced with evaluating whether hospital services would be better provided directly through a publicly staffed and managed institution or through contractual arrangement with private providers. Should outputs be defined in terms of measures of process efficiency, for example number of pounds of laundry processed, etc.? See W.W. Carpenter. "Developing a Unit of Service to Measure Productivity," *Hospital Financial Management* 22 (July 1978): 14–18. Or should outputs be defined and measured in terms of functional output, for example a day of hospital care? See Martin Feldstein, *The Rising Cost of Hospital Care* (Washington, D.C.: Information Resources Press, 1971). Or should outputs be measured in terms of a hospital's contribution to systemwide health status? See J.R. Griffith, "A Proposal for New Hospital Performance Measures." *Hospital and Health Services Administration* 23 (Spring 1978): 60–84. And doesn't each of these output measures require further adjustments to deal with quality differences and case-mix variations?

14. Paul Starr, *The Limits of Privatization*. (Washington, D.C.: Economic Policy Institute, 1988), 6–7.

15. This may also encompass special constraints under which the service must be delivered, such as minority hiring requirements, bonding requirements, etc. James

L. Lammie, "Lending Opportunities in Privatization." *The Journal of Commercial Bank Lending* 71 (Sept. 1988): 4–12, claims that the private sector works more efficiently than the public sector *if* there are no legal constraints on how the service must be provided: 'I was involved in a privatization effort. It looked great until I got into the specific conditions of the proposal . . . this client wanted the benefit of the private sector taking the risk, but he imposed many of the contracting and building constraints associated with the public sector." Lammie further asserts that "[p]rivatization may not achieve desired social objectives such as disadvantaged business enterprise, minority business enterprise, and so forth."

16. Clear specification of tasks in the contract does not assure their adequate performance by contractors—experienced and knowledgeable contracting officers monitoring the contract are crucial to contract execution. See *infra*, 11.

17. Richard A. Musgrave and Peggy B. Musgrave, *Public Finance in Theory and Practice*, 3rd ed. (New York: McGraw-Hill, Inc., 1980), 174.

18. Henry M. Levin, *Cost-Effectiveness: A Primer.* (Beverly Hills, Calif.: Sage Publications, 1983), 54.

19. James C. McDavid, "The Canadian Experience with Privatizing Residential Solid Waste Collection Services," *Public Administration Review* 45 (Sept./Oct. 1985): 602–608.

20. John A. Rehfuss, *Contracting Out In Government*, (San Francisco: Jossey-Bass Publishers, 1989). 54.

21. Berenyi and Stevens, "Does Privatization Work?," 13.

22. Similarly, to the extent that private contractors must rely on public resources to deal with special situations, the use of those resources must be charged against the contractor.

23. Jarrell and Skibniewski, "Cost Comparison Model," 263–266.

24. Rehfuss, *Contracting Out In Government*, 48–49, 95–96.

25. Jarrell and Skibniewski, "Cost Comparison Model," 263.

26. The so-called "veto-power" of contract renewal may not be an effective substitute for good contract monitoring because its effectiveness rests on the implicit assumption that a contractor who performs in an unsatisfactory manner will be automatically eliminated as a potential bidder in future rounds of contracting. In fact, low-bidder requirements in public contracting law and/or the absence of any other private sector providers in the area may allow the poor performer another bite at the apple.

27. Rehfuss, *Contracting Out In Government*, 98.

28. The GAO's 1981 report on military contractor-operated stores contracts provides an classic example of the consequences of a loss of adequate managerial control. See U.S. General Accounting Office, "Military Contractor-Operated Stores' Contracts Are Unmanageable And Vulnerable To Abuse," *Report To The Congress*, MASAD–81–27 (July 8, 1981), iii.

29. L.R. Jones and Fred Thompson, "Reform of Budget Execution Control," *Public Budgeting & Finance* 6 (Spring 1986): 33–49.

30. Rehfuss, *Contracting Out In Government*, 117, notes that "[i]f an agency wants to contract for a reasonable fee and yet retain control over the contracting out process, it will have to look at ways of maintaining competition, such as (1)

contingency contracts, (2) partial contracting, or (3) retaining an agency work force."

31. Jarrell and Skibniewski, "Cost Comparison Model," 263–266.

32. Congressional Budget Office, *Contracting Out for Federal Support Services: Potential Savings and Budgetary Impacts* (Oct. 1982).

33. Harper A. Roehm, Joseph F. Castellano, and David A. Karns, "Contracting Services to the Private Sector: A Survey of Management Practices," *Government Finance Review* 5 (Feb. 1989): 21–25, 52.

34. William M. Timmins, "Impacts of Privatization upon Career Public Employees," *Public Administration Quarterly* 10 (Spring 1986): 50–59.

35. Musgrave and Musgrave, *Public Finance in Theory and Practice*, 174.

36. Lyn Squire and Herman G. van der Tak, *Economic Analysis of Projects*, (Washington, D.C.: The International Bank for Reconstruction and Development, 1975), 22.

37. James L. Perry and Timlynn T. Babitsky, "Comparative Performance in Urban Bus Transit: Assessing Privatization Strategies," *Public Administration Review* 46 (Jan./Feb. 1986): 57–66.

38. Ibid.

39. Ross, *Government and the Private Sector: Who Should Do What?*, 16.

40. Britt Robson, "When Private Companies Do Public Work." *Black Enterprise* 16 (Feb. 1986): 140–144.

41. Ross, *Government and the Private Sector: Who Should Do What?*, 16.

42. David R. Morgan and Robert E. England. "The Two Faces of Privatization," *Public Administration Review* 48 (Nov./Dec. 1988): 979–87.

43. Ross, *Government and the Private Sector: Who Should Do What?*. 18.

44. See, for example, *Privatization in America: An Opinion Survey of City and County Governments on Their Use of Privatization and Their Infrastructure Needs.* (Touche Ross & Company. 1987). 6: and Ferris and Graddy. "Contracting Out: For What? With Whom?", 332–344.

45. Ronald C. Moe. "Exploring the Limits of Privatization," *Public Administration Review* 47 (Nov./Dec. 1987): 453–460.

46. Ted Kolderie, "The Two Different Concepts of Privatization," *Public Administration Review* 46 (July/Aug. 1986): 285–291.

47. Timmins, "Impacts of Privatization," 55.

48. Ibid., 55–56.

49. Moe, "Exploring the Limits of Privatization," 453–460.

50. Harold J. Sullivan, "Privatization of Public Services: A Growing Threat to Constitutional Rights," *Public Administration Review* 47 (Nov./Dec. 1987): 461–467.

51. Ibid., 464.

22

Bureaucracy, Organizational Redundancy, and the Privatization of Public Services

Rowan Miranda
Allan Lerner

A common theme in the platforms of political candidates from presidents to big city mayors is a promise to consolidate fragmented systems, reduce needless duplication of services, and streamline public bureaucracies upon election to office. Although a cardinal premise in the thinking of many current reformists, this view is actually quite consistent with some very traditional—and limited—thinking in public administration: that the government which functions best is one with zero redundancy. In this view, government agencies should strive to be "lean and mean."

This notion has motivated numerous government reorganization efforts throughout the past century. When two government units are performing the same function, conventional wisdom suggests that one unit be eliminated, or consolidated within the other, to minimize the duplication of functions and overlapping of jurisdictions. Although appeals are made to scientific management and common sense, the theory that supports this

1995. Bureaucracy, organizational redundancy, and the privatization of public services. Miranda, Rowan, and Allan Lerner. **Public Administration Review** 55 (March-April): 193–200.

conventional wisdom is never explicitly stated. Yet the benefits of reorganization and consolidation are widely touted—cost reduction and better service to the public.

However, not all forms of duplication and overlap constitute waste.
Some forms of duplication and overlap can increase organizational efficiency, effectiveness, and reliability. These points were made in Landau's
(1969) seminal essay that challenged those in the discipline of public administration to rethink whether zero redundancy is indeed *the* measure of
both economy and efficiency. Landau urged that:

> there are good grounds for suggesting that efforts to improve public adminis-
> tration by eliminating duplication and overlap would, if successful, produce
> just the opposite effect. That so many attempts have failed should perhaps
> alert us to what sociologists would call the "latent function" of this type of re-
> dundancy. This possibility alone is sufficient warrant for transforming a pre-
> cept into a problem (1969; 349).

American political culture has long stressed the virtues of competitive redundancies in the constitutionally described governing process, embodied
in such precepts as federalism, checks and balances, separation of powers,
and competitive political parties. Why then did public administration, focused on the organizational dynamics of modern, bureaucratic government, "condemn competition in our public bureaucracies in a one-sided
fashion?" (Bendor, 1985; 33).

Although the virtues of competitive interorganizational arrangements
for both public and private sectors were discussed by early political economists, the fascination of early writers in public administration with getting
government to operate more like business led to an emphasis on restructuring of the type occurring at that time in the private sector. More than a century ago, privately held corporations were consolidating "horizontally to
reduce competition and vertically to coordinate specialized and interdependent processes" (Bendor, 1985; 34). Early public administration reformers
sought to do the same for government. Ironically for government, the deliberate reintroduction of competition, eventually a great concern for governance of the private sector, seemed not to have surfaced as an imperative
for the public sector itself until far more recently. Perhaps the redundancies
built into governance by the Constitution obscured the monocratic logic
elaborated in routinized administrative activities.

As the authors of *Reinventing Government* acknowledge, "it is one of
the enduring paradoxes of American ideology that we attack private monopolies so fervently but embrace public monopolies so warmly" (Osborne
and Gaebler, 1992; 79). In *Breaking Through Bureaucracy*, Barzelay similarly comments that for "Americans supporting the reform and reorganiza-

tion movements, bureaucracy meant efficiency and efficiency meant good government" (Barzelay and Armanjani, 1992; 4).

In this context, it might be said that the current "reinventing" brand of reform thinking represents an interesting combination of two kinds of efforts. One is to reduce the internal duplication and overlap—to streamline government organizations—in order to increase their efficiency. The second is to increase the satisfactoriness of their output to their environments by creating interorganizational duplication and overlap as the structure for competition. The reinventing outlook discourages intraorganizational redundancy but encourages interorganizational, usually cross-sector, redundancy.

Thus, the framework of prevalent assumptions from which we proceed would appear to have several prominent, albeit discontinuous, features. Recent as well as past reform thinking seeks to stream-line bureaucracy, including the reduction of duplication and overlap, or bureaucratic redundancy. However, one of the associated values, competition, involves the deliberate introduction of redundancy. Recent reform thinking places high value on competition as well as high value on privatization. However, some common forms of privatization do not necessarily allow for competition so much as for the replacement of an organization in one sector with an organization in another. Furthermore, while there are classic economic and public choice theoretical arguments for the preference of privatization even as simple sector substitution, the empirical justification for such a radical sector preference is unclear.

As in many such situations, complementary and contradictory assumptions overlap an important policy and administrative domain. In such cases, it is sometimes prudent to begin the search for improved understanding by probing for a coherent middle ground among the relevant normative and empirical positions.

In what follows, we use theory and empirical findings to argue the relative merits of an intermediate form of privatization: *benchmarking*. We present arguments for benchmarking as an approach to organization and service delivery that enhances reliability, increases competition, allows for measurement of comparative benefits, and avoids ideologically driven extremes. We contend that benchmarking represents an informed pragmatism in the search for improved organizational forms for the delivery of public services.

The first section reviews the theoretical literature on redundancy and applies it to the problem of organizing municipal service production. In it, we explore Landau's redundancy theory, and extensions of it by Bendor (1985) and Lerner (1986), for insight into the variety of strategies available for the introduction of controlled competition in the delivery of services provided by municipal bureaucracies. By "controlled competition," we mean competition that is planned to reduce the dysfunction of monopoly bureaucracy while preserving the benefits of organizational redundancy. Thus, Niskanen's (1971) argument that rivalries between government agencies can reduce monopoly effects is also examined.

One of our aims is to improve understanding of how service delivery arrangements that introduce intersector redundancies of various types compare to those using the public or private sector alone. A *redundant service delivery arrangement* is defined here as the use of more than one organization to deliver the same service. The second section examines findings from past studies to assess existing support for this line of theorizing.

The third section uses data on alternative forms of municipal contracting from a large sample of cities to assess evidence for the theoretical position taken here. We focus our empirical examination on the particular form of redundancy which we described above as a prudent middle-ground approach to privatization: benchmarking. Under benchmarking, a government contracts out a portion of the service while producing the remainder through in-house production.

Designing Service
Delivery Arrangements

Recent efforts to improve the delivery of public services have called for greater use of alternative service delivery arrangements in service production (Savas, 1977). Contracting out, vouchers in public schools, volunteers in welfare agencies, franchises, and citizen coproduction can all be viewed as an indirect means of undermining the monopoly position of public bureaus and their employees. At the municipal level, service contracting represents the most likely alternative to government production (Donahue, 1989; Miranda and Andersen 1994). Often in practice, calls for greater involvement of the private sector in service production lead managers toward the complete contracting out of a service to the private sector. Under this scenario, government maintains responsibility for ensuring that the service is provided and monitors contractor performance. This all or nothing approach to service contracting is consistent with the two major economic theories seeking to explain the efficiency differences between public and private production—the property rights and public choice approaches.

Empirical studies in both the property rights and public choice traditions are motivated to some extent by the desire to seek out universal patterns: Is the private sector more efficient at producing services than the public sector? With the question posed as such, the evidence is generally claimed to support the contention that greater efficiency can be attained by contracting production to the private sector (Miranda, 1994).

Thus, for example, the property rights theory, associated with the work of Alchian (1965), Alchian and Demsetz (1972), and DeAlessi (1969), predicts that the performance of government organizations is inferior to that of private firms conducting the same activity. Those subscribing to this view argue that the practical difficulties associated with the assignment and transfer of ownership rights to the "citizen shareholders" of public organizations in comparison to the "investor shareholders" in the private organizations, reduce the motivation of public managers to organize production to maximize the wealth of citizens.

Similarly, studies such as those by Ahlbrandt (1973) on fire protection, and Davies (1971) on Australian airlines, are two of many examples cited in favor of the property rights approach because both find that the private sector produces services at a lower cost, or has a higher productivity rate, than the public sector.

The public choice approach also predicts superior performance of the private sector, but the reasons are hinged on either the monopoly environment of public bureaus (Niskanen, 1971) and/or "rent seeking" pressure for bureau expansion from legislators and public employees (Bush and Denzau, 1977; Borcherding, 1977; Miller & Moe, 1983). Conclusions drawn from the empirical studies in the public choice tradition also support the hypothesis that public bureau production is inferior to delivery by contract. Thus, empirical studies in both traditions advocate greater use of the private sector. But these studies have generally ignored situations in which competition within government, or between governments and private firms, in the delivery of the same service might be preferable to using a single sector by itself.

Niskanen (1971) examined the theoretical implications of redundancy within governments as a means of undermining a bureau's monopoly position. Public bureau-sponsor relationships are modeled as a bilateral monopoly in this theory. Under these conditions, bureaucrats are assumed to act as budget maximizers who succeed in exploiting informational asymmetries facing legislative committees on service production costs. The legislative committees have "neither the incentive nor the possibility to acquire information about the minimum level sufficient to enable the bureau to provide the prescribed quantity of services in an efficient manner" (Jonsson, 1985; 72). In arguing that government bureaus will always produce output greater than competitive industry operating under similar circumstances, Niskanen outlines several reform measures to constrain the oversupply tendencies of budget maximizing bureaucrats.

One reform possibility is to have bureaus compete with one another—what public administration would view as duplication, overlap, or redundancy. Niskanen recognized that such a proposal went against the conventional wisdom:

The most important change in the present structure of bureaucracy would be to increase the competition among bureaus in the supply of the same or similar service. Competition among bureaus is generally regarded as undesirable or, at best, in deference to certain institutional traditions, as tolerable (Niskanen, 1971; 195).

Competition in bureaus, however, continues to develop, contrary to the canon of public administration, and only interrupted by periodic structural reforms. And even more competition would develop if it were not artificially constrained by public policy (Niskanen, 1971; 196–197).

Niskanen proceeded to conjecture that the efficiency gains of implementing such redundancies may be contingent on motivations of the legislative committees (i.e., high versus low demand).

Landau's (1969) essay was concerned primarily with the virtues of redundancy as a means of increasing the reliability of organizations. Landau asked:

> Is it possible to take a set of individually unreliable units and form them into a system with any "arbitrarily high reliability?" Can we, in other words, build an organization that is more reliable than any of its parts? (Landau, 1969; 350).

System reliability is a paramount concern when catastrophes might result from organizational failures. Certainly, redundant systems, even when they impose higher short-term costs than nonredundant systems, are desirable when organizations must meet *failsafe* criteria (LaPorte & Consolini, 1991; Perrow, 1984). However, organizations that do not aspire to failsafe standards may nonetheless seek to improve reliability significantly. What failsafe criteria illustrate in the extreme, *be safer* criteria illustrate in proportion. Thus, incremental improvements in reliability can be purchased with incremental improvements in redundancy.

As Bendor has argued, "far from being an exotic structure unknown in American bureaucracies," examples of redundancy abound (Bendor, 1985; 3). Interservice rivalries in the armed forces, overlapping governments characterizing metropolitan areas, and multiple welfare programs seeking to reduce poverty are but three examples of organizational redundancies. Using multiple organizations to produce the same municipal service is another.

From our perspective on local government, the question is not whether service delivery is improved with redundancy *per se* (which we would assume is problematic), but whether it is improved with redundancy of a given specifiable type. For, when left as an aggregate, undifferentiated concept, the wrong mode of redundancy in a given organizational context can increase unreliability and inefficiency. Thus, as Bendor (1985) has also noted, there is a case against redundancy which focuses on three major concerns:

1. *Efficiency*—redundancy defined as "excess" leads to a greater expenditure of resources than needed. Consolidating duplicate activities produces economies of scale.
2. *Gaps and overlaps*—in zero-sum budgetary climates, redundancies necessitate that some nonredundant agency activities go unfunded.
3. *Pinpointing responsibility*—redundancy here is viewed as fragmentation. The greater the redundancy (e.g., overlapping jurisdictions), the more difficult it is to isolate blame, which has negative consequences for organizational performance.

If some redundancies can promote inefficiency, can attempts to eliminate them promote cost savings? Several studies on the effects of government re-organizations do not find cost savings associated with such measures. The question remains, however, whether the right strategy of elimination was applied to an appropriately targeted redundancy, properly identified as in-efficient. Meier's study of reorganizations at the state level, in particular, finds that reorganizations "rarely account for significant reductions in em-ployment or expenditures" (Meier, 1980; 396). Indeed, others have argued that formally fragmented systems provide services quite reliably, and do so even in the face of stress, because they are successfully coordinated through informal networks (Chisholm, 1989).

Is redundancy equivalent to competition? Bendor points out that "all competitive structures are redundant but the converse is not true; there are noncompetitive types of duplication" (Bendor, 1985; 54). The concept of competition is valued in public administration because it speaks to the prospect of increased value of organizational outputs to their users. The concept of redundancy speaks to the prospect of increased reliability in the provision of organizational outputs. Although intimately related, the two concepts are not identical. In seeking to assess the implications of the re-dundancy literature for municipal service delivery, system reliability *per se* is less of an issue than it would be in organizational designs for managing nuclear power plants.

Put differently, the issue of failsafe design is an aspect of redundancy the-ory which is of less immediate concern here than is what Landau identified as the latent benefits of redundancy. Nevertheless, stating that reliability is less immediate a concern in organizing typical municipal production than it is in other contexts should not, by any means, suggest that reliability is-

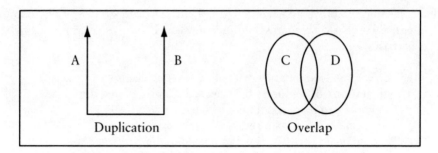

FIGURE 22.1   Duplication and Overlap in Government Bureaucracies

Source: Adapted from Lerner (1986, pp. 337, 342).

sues are unimportant. After all, one of the greatest fears of local officials contracting a service is that they will lose control over it.

Some research suggests that the emphasis placed by wary local officials on control when contemplating the prospect of privatization, is closely related to their anxiety over the reliable delivery of services under such circumstances (Miranda 1992b). In general, at the stage of contemplating adoption, particularly of something that is recognized as a relative innovation, concerns with the possibility of failure may very well be keener than would be objectively warranted. Certainly such concerns are likely to loom larger at this stage, contemplating the initial adoption of a new structural arrangement, than they would be on the occasion of, for example, evaluating a traditional practice after a substantial period of experience with it. Thus, the ease with which psychological issues can be put aside in the control of organizational redundancies is also partly a function of the structural features of particular redundancies under consideration at any given time, including their perceived innovativeness.

To facilitate understanding of the theoretical case for the value of benchmarking as a preferred form of privatization, we now explore some of the issues in choosing alternatives for redundancy. Lerner's (1986) study sought to examine the specific implications of redundancy theory for organizational design. Following the approach taken there, Figure 22.1 distinguishes duplication from overlap.

Under duplication, agencies A and B both provide the same services through identical systems. It is possible that A and B compete in the same geographic region or have different regions assigned to each. In the case of overlap, both C and D have a different core set of activities, but also produce some of the same services. As Lerner notes "duplication provides redundancy by emphasizing parallelism. Overlap provides redundancy by emphasizing ambiguity" (Lerner, 1986; 336). Much of the analysis here will focus on duplication, although issues of optimal levels of overlap are

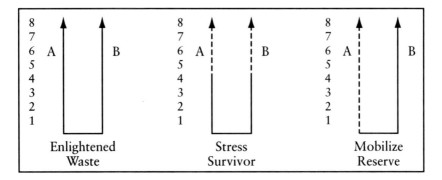

FIGURE 22.2   Alternative Designs for Redundancy

Source: Adapted from Lerner (1986, pp. 337, 342).

also appropriate in analyzing service delivery, especially in discussions of metropolitan organization (Ostrom, Tiebout, & Warren, 1961; Oakerson, 1987).

Lerner outlines three ways to introduce redundancy (Figure 22.2). Under *enlightened waste,* he writes that "excess capacity will be wasted or inventoried rather than viewed simply as a potential; the excess capacity is knowingly made manifest" (Lerner, 1986; 341). Agencies A and B produce a total of 16 units, when 8 may be optimal. This approach is certainly one of the most costly forms of introducing redundancy but is useful if it is desirable to have each channel serve as "a simulation laboratory for investigating the properties of the other" (p. 341). Under *stress the survivor,* A and B normally operate at the capacity of 4 units each. A breakdown in A could be compensated by "stressing" B for 4 more units of output. Finally, under *mobilize reserve,* the reserve unit "is essentially a shadow unit that can be quickly activated" (p. 346). Lerner argues that this form of redundancy costs less than the enlightened waste approach. Hybrid forms of these redundancies can also be designed (e.g., stress the survivor with some enlightened waste).

Local government privatization strategies are placed on a continuum in Figure 22.3. Vouchers, volunteers, and so forth are excluded for analytical convenience. As such, the continuum ranges from government monopoly to private monopoly. Intermediate approaches include intragovernmental redundancy which is similar to Niskanen's recommendation of splitting bureaus and having them compete for budgetary allocations. Under this arrangement G1 produces 4 units and G2 produces the 4 others. If some functions are "inherently governmental" (General Accounting Office, 1991), this is one means of introducing competition without the abdication of governmental authority. Under private/private competition, government

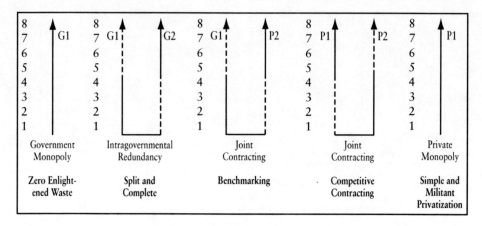

FIGURE 22.3   Alternative Designs for Introducing Redundancy in Service Delivery

focuses on "steering" and allows two or more private sector firms to "row" (Osborne and Gaebler, 1992).

Both intragovernmental redundancy and private/private competition allow government oversight authorities to reduce the monopoly power of producers. However, collusion under both arrangements is also possible. In theory, competitive bidding procedures could allow governments to contract with one private firm rather than two. Nevertheless, a transaction cost economics perspective would suggest that for reasons such as "asset specificity" and "first mover advantages," governments might get "locked in" to a particular contractor. Thus, a competitive situation during ex-ante contracting might turn into a "small-numbers condition" during ex-post contracting (Williamson, 1975; 1985). With benchmarking, governments maintain some service production capacity in-house and contract the rest to one or more private organizations. It is this latter arrangement that is compared with exclusive public and private production in this study, in an effort to assess partial validity of the redundancy argument.

Redundancies can occur at different phases of the service production process. As Bendor notes:

> Redundancy is most palpable when it occurs in the operation of a system or the delivery of a service, such as parallel transit lines, redundant missile systems, and the like. But, plausibly, if bureaucratic monopoly risks unreliable performance during operations, then monopolistic planning risks unreliable

design of operation. Monopoly during planning may be no more benign than monopoly during operations (Bendor, 1985; 22).

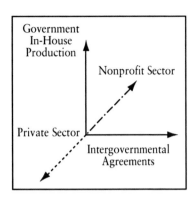

FIGURE 22.4 Sector Choices for Service Contracting

Another means of introducing redundancy is by contracting different portions of the service to different sectors, although they represent distinct choices (Figure 22.4). Throughout this study, nonprofit, intergovernmental, and private sectors are collapsed as "external production" (Ferris and Graddy, 1988; 1991). Contracting with different sectors is a choice available to municipalities in several of the approaches to redundancy discussed above. However, since it does not change the argument examined here, no distinction between the relative efficiencies of contracting with different sectors will be made.

Evidence from Past Studies

If there exists an idea common to both privatization theory and evidence, it is that the simple transfer of a service from a public monopoly to a private one is unlikely to yield improvements in either quality or cost savings (See Miranda 1994a for review of contracting studies). A middle ground suggests that organizational redundancies in service delivery are perhaps a means for averting monopoly outcomes. This section reviews existing evidence to support this point.

Several recent studies on military procurement show that competition between government producers and private sector environments improve the performance of public agencies. Carrick (1988) examined the Navy's Commercial Activity (CA) program and found that government is as efficient as the private sector at least 21 percent of the time. Carrick concludes that the "Navy experience with CA competitions demonstrates that putting managers in competition with their private counterparts effectively elicits use of market-appropriate incentives" (Carrick, 1988; 526). Leitzel reviews the procurement literature and argues that procurement reforms "such as prototype competition, that reduce the informational advantage of the DOD and defense contractors relative to outsiders, have the best likelihood of improving defense procurement" (Leitzel, 1992; 53).

Caves and Christensen (1980) compared the Canadian National (CN) and Canadian Pacific (CP) railroads (the former being a government enterprise). Both railroads were insulated from competition for a lengthy period because of government regulation. CN had a level of productive efficiency that was 90 percent as high as CP during that time. When deregulation was instituted, the CN railroad was exposed to competition to the extent that the productive efficiency gap was closed. Caves and Christensen interpret this as evidence against the property rights argument stating that "any tendency toward inefficiency resulting from public ownership has been overcome by the benefits of competition" (Caves and Christensen, 1980; 958).

Studies by Savas (1977, 1981) also support the view that property rights considerations are less important in determining efficiency compared to the extent of competition in the supplier market for local public goods. Savas' (1977) study of Minneapolis compared refuse collection performance by a city department and with that of a consortium of private firms. The city department serviced one section of the city and the consortium serviced the rest. When the public monopoly position of the city department was undermined through the introduction of this system, although the cost per ton for contract collection was lower than municipal collection, the city closed the gap both in terms of cost and performance (i.e., tons collected per shift by municipal crews). Moreover, citizens were equally satisfied in the two collection areas, and the number of telephone complaints about city collection declined when competitive pressures were introduced.

McDavid and Schick (1987) compared contract and government residential solid waste collection in two municipalities in greater Vancouver. The city with a contract for waste collection witnessed only "periodic competition" through the competitive bidding process whereas the other city had a public monopoly. Nonetheless, McDavid and Schick found that regional competitive pressures in the form of periodic unsolicited bids from private firms kept government cost and productivity indicators closely in line with those in the private sector.

Mehay and Gonzalez's (1987) study implies that Niskanen's intragovernmental redundancy or "bureau splitting" strategy for undermining public monopolies is not the only way to reduce the asymmetries of information facing legislative bodies. By examining the Lakewood Plan, the authors compared county departments that serviced other municipalities and those that did not. They found that county departments providing contracted services to municipalities, in having established a price that would cover costs, indirectly relinquished their informational advantages. Consequently, legislative committees in these cities were able to curtail their rate of expenditure growth compared to county departments that did not contract services. Mehay and Gonzalez conclude that by "generating a flow of information on production costs for a given service, the Lakewood system eases the trustees' task of monitoring the performance of county departments and increases the overall efficiency of local production" (Mehay and Gonzalez, 1987; 72). It is important to note, however, that the authors do not show that this approach at reducing costs is actually superior to the Niskanen intragovernmental redundancy proposal.

All of these examples illustrate how competitive organizational redundancies can be used to improve the performance of public bureaus. There are numerous other examples of cities using such approaches. Phoenix's decision to first contract out refuse collection and then allow city agencies to bid on the process, led to a situation in which the city ultimately won the contract back with significant cost savings resulting to taxpayers. Newark, New Jersey, has used benchmarking in solid waste collection, street sweeping, demolition, sewer cleaning, capital construction, and computer services, while also witnessing significant cost savings (International City/County Management Association, 1990). More generally, Ferris and Graddy (1986) show that "joint" contracting approaches (i.e., benchmarking) are used in a broad range of city and county functions, including numerous redistributive programs such as child welfare, programs for the elderly, and public health.

In summary, extant literature shows that some forms of duplication and overlap can lead to greater cost efficiencies. As Landau suggested, some of the benefits of redundancy are latent (i.e., unintended and beneficial). Nevertheless, because the concern here is with organizational designs for service production, several reasons to intentionally introduce redundancy can be stated. Competition is an obvious one because it can yield improvements in cost efficiencies and service quality. The term benchmarking was used to signify the idea that joint contracting allows sponsors to play service producers against one another. Such redundancies introduce rivalries. Maintaining in-house capacity to produce a service allows the city to "have a yardstick against which to measure the performance of the private sector [and] by having contract collection, the city has a yardstick against which to measure the performance of its own municipal agency" (Savas, 1981; 48). Maintaining in-house capacity reduces the bargaining power of the contractor during renegotiation and thus the threat of "lock-in." By contrast, having some production capacity through external providers reduces the impact of municipal employee strikes and work stoppages. Sufficient competition in the private sector alone may reduce the gains from redundancy. Yet when the market structure of service suppliers resembles monopoly or oligopoly, some government production in-house is desirable. The next section examines the effects of benchmarking on aggregate expenditures, employment, and wages in a sample of U.S. municipalities.

TABLE 22.A   Methodology and Research Design

Data: The data used in this study were based on the International City/County Management Association (ICMA) survey conducted between March and June of 1982. This national survey collected information on services that cities and counties provide and the way these services are delivered to residents. This study only uses information on cities. All other data were obtained from the U.S. Bureau of Census.

ICMA mailed survey instruments to chief administrative officers of 4,700 local governments. Cities with population sizes of 10,000 or more were surveyed, along with counties with population sizes of 25,000 or more. Cities with population sizes under 10,000 were surveyed at a rate of one in eight. The overall response rate was 38 percent (1,780 of 4,700 local governments). Cities had an overall response rate of 46 percent, while counties had an overall response rate of 24 percent. This study uses a sample of responding cities over 25,000 in population.

Model: A core model based on past studies using this data by Ferris (1988), Stein (1991), and Miranda (1944b) was constructed. Dependent variables in this study include expenditures, employment, and wages. The key independent variables of theoretical interest are the percentages of services contracted out jointly and the percentage of services contracted out completely. Regression analysis was used to estimate the effects of joint and complete contracting on the dependent variables.

Source: Bureaucracy, Organizational Redundancy, and the Privatization of Public Services.

Does Benchmarking Promote Cost Savings?

Several studies using data from the 1982 ICMA Survey of Alternative Service Delivery Approaches have shown that greater contracting yields reductions in aggregate expenditures and employment (Ferris, 1988; Stein, 1991; Miranda 1992a). Deacon (1979) finds similar results using data on Lakewood Plan cities. Using a sample of all cities over 25,000 in population from the ICMA survey, this study builds on past work to examine whether benchmarking is associated with lower expenditures. Although private/private competition also provides a yardstick to compare costs, this study adopts a more narrow definition of benchmarking. The concern here is with those arrangements that maintain some government capacity to produce services in-house with the rest being contracted out. This arrangement is compared to the level of services contracted out completely, in which no in-house capacity to produce the service is retained. If redundant arrangements are cost efficient, benchmarking should be associated with lower expenditures.

Results of a core model regressed on expenditures, employment, and average wages are shown in Table 22.1. The measure of benchmarking used here is the percentage of services contracted jointly (i.e., government and contractor production), which is found to be negatively related to expenditures, consistent with the redundancy argument. By contrast, the percentage of services contracted completely (no government bureau production with the use of private, nonprofit, or governmental vendors), has a negative coefficient but is statistically insignificant in explaining expenditures. The opposite results hold true for employment. Complete contracting has a statistically significant negative effect on the size of work force; the sign for joint contracting also has a negative effect, but it is statistically insignificant. As one might expect, transferring a service completely to private contractors does more to reduce employment than an arrangement that transfers only part of the service to contractors. Finally, although the effects are statistically insignificant, both complete and joint contracting, are positively associated with average wages, which suggest that contracting changes the input mix to a smaller but better paid municipal work force.

A few of the other statistically significant effects also deserve comment. Population, intergovernmental aid, and the functional responsibility score (i.e., range of services a city is responsible for providing) are found to be statistically significant in explaining expenditures in a positive direction, as one might expect. The council-manager form of government is negatively associated with wages and employment, but positively related to average wages. This pattern suggests that in council-manager systems a smaller number of higher paid jobs are chosen as a substitute for reductions in employment.

The results here support the argument that benchmarking is associated with reductions in expenditures. However, it would be premature to suggest that this approach is superior to complete contracting in its aggregate effects because alternative specifications of the model may change the results. Unfortunately, the data did not permit the separation of private monopoly from private/private competition, or public monopoly from intragovernmental competition. Moreover, the data did not permit one to control for the extent of joint contracting (e.g., 50 percent municipal/50 percent private or other combinations). Nevertheless the results are suggestive and merit further systematic examination.

One extension would be to assess the impacts of benchmarking by service function to inquire whether competition within the private sector is sufficient to promote cost savings without the need for duplication and/or overlap by instituting a production role for government.

TABLE 22.6 Effects of Complete and Joint Contracting on Expenditures, Employment, and Wages

Independent Variable	Expenditures			Employment			Average FTE Wages		
	B	SE	t	B	SE	t	B	SE	t
Population 1980	0.164	0.031	5.28***	1.101	.052	20.98***	.031	.009	3.38***
Mean per capita income 1980	0.158	0.104	1.52	.143	.176	.82	.186	.031	5.99***
City located in SMSA (1 = Y)	0.029	0.071	0.42	-.046	.119	-0.38	.038	.021	1.81*
Intergovernmental aid 1982	0.969	0.217	4.46***	-.368	.367	-1.00	-.117	.065	-1.82*
Age of city dummy variable	-0.060	0.047	-1.28	-.287	.079	-3.61***	.075	.014	5.23***
City manager-council government (1 = Y)	-0.101	0.047	-2.12**	-.259	.080	-3.23***	.084	.014	5.94***
Average private sector monthly pay 1982							.032	.019	1.66*
Percent of public employees unionized 1982	0.130	0.097	1.35	-.240	.163	-1.47	.400	.029	13.91***
Functional responsibility score for 64 services	0.763	0.098	7.78***	.733	.166	4.43***	-.029	.029	-0.98
Percent of 64 services contracted out completely	-0.500	0.321	-1.56	-1.411	.543	-2.60***	.187	.096	1.96**
Percent of 64 services contracted out jointly	-0.770	0.268	-2.88***	-.727	.453	-1.61	.143	.080	1.80*
Constant	-1.039	1.102	-0.94	-9.321	1.863	-5.00***	4.976	.344	14.48***
Number of cases	539			539			539		
R^2	.24			.53			.70		
Adjusted R^2	.23			.52			.65		

Note: *** $p < .01$; ** $p < .05$; * $p < .10$. Average private sector wage is used to explain public wage levels but excluded otherwise. Age of city is a binary variable that equals one if city reached population of 50,000 prior to 1928; otherwise, 0. Functional responsibility is measured by the percent of 64 services listed on the ICMA survey that the city delivers. All variables are logged to a Cobb-Douglas specification.

Source: Bureaucracy, Organizational Redundancy, and the Privatization of Public Services

Conclusion

In this study, we asked whether organizational redundancies in service delivery are a useful means for averting monopoly outcomes. By applying Landau's (1969) discussion of redundancy and Niskanen's (1971) analysis of public bureaus, the conventional wisdom in public administration that zero redundancy in service delivery arrangements constitutes optimal efficiency was challenged. Using data from a large sample of cities, it was demonstrated that benchmarking can be cost effective. In some instances, such arrangements may be more cost effective than exclusive production by the private sector alone.

Our intention in this study was not to prove a universal assertion that redundancy in organizational service delivery is always desirable. It is sufficient here to show, consistent with past theoretical work, that the conventional wisdom in public administration is misled. As Bendor notes, the conventional wisdom's tendency to "argue against bureaucratic duplication, is of course, to argue *for* organizational monopoly . . . " (Bendor, 1985; 30). In summary, we suggest that forcing one to choose between markets or governments (Wolf, 1988) may be an imposition of a false dichotomy. In some instances, it may be better to ask how both markets and governments may be used to improve performance in service delivery.

By identifying some forms of privatization as forms of redundancy, we were able to evaluate strategic choices in approaches to privatization, assessing them for the improvements they offer in reliability of services and cost-efficiency. The choices are made all the time; the issue is to make them consciously and with purpose.

Additionally, we have sought to illustrate how further research on the vital issue of increasing the responsiveness and effectiveness of government while controlling costs can benefit from a broadening of the theoretical framework guiding such research. The incorporation of redundancy theory can enhance the current frame of reference defined by public choice and economic theory, particularly concerning the appropriate use and form for the privatization of public services and the streamlining of public bureaucracies.

References

Ahlbrandt, Roger, 1973. "Efficiency in the Provision of Fire Services." *Public Choice*, vol. 16, no. 1, pp. 1–15.

Alchian, Armen A., 1965. "The Basis of Some Recent Advances in the Theory of Management of the Firm." *Journal of Industrial Economics*, vol. 14, no. 1, pp. 30–41.

Alchian, Armen A., and Harold Demsetz, 1972. "Production, Information Costs, and Economic Organization." *American Economic Review*, vol. 62, pp. 777–795.

Barzelay, Michael, with Babak Armanjani, 1992. *Breaking Through Bureaucracy.* Berkeley: University of California Press.

Bendor, Jonathon, 1985. *Parallel Systems: Redundancy in Government.* Berkeley: University of California Press.

Borcherding, Thomas E., ed., 1977. *Budgets and Bureaucrats: The Sources of Government Growth.* Durham, NC: Duke University Press.

Bush, Winston, and Arthur Denzau, 1977. "The Voting Behavior of Bureaucrats and Public Sector Growth." In T. Borcherding, ed., *Budgets and Bureaucrats: The Sources of Government Growth.* Durham, NC: Duke University Press.

Carrick, Paul, 1988. "New Evidence on Government Efficiency." *Journal of Policy Analysis and Management,* vol. 7, no. 3, pp. 518–528.

Caves, Douglas W., and Laurits R. Christensen, 1980. "The Relative Efficiency of Public and Private Firms in a Competitive Environment: The Case of Canadian Railroads." *Journal of Political Economy,* vol. 88 (December), pp. 958–976.

Chisholm, Donald, 1989. *Coordination Without Hierarchy: Informal Structures in Multiorganizational Systems.* Berkeley: University of California Press.

Davies, David, 1971. "The Efficiency of Public versus Private Firms: The Case of Australia's Two Airlines." *Journal of Law and Economics,* vol. 14 (April), pp. 149–165.

Deacon, Robert T., 1979. "The Expenditure Effects of Alternative Public Sector Supply Institutions." *Public Choice,* vol. 33, no. 3–4, pp. 381–398.

DeAlessi, Louis, 1969. "Implications of Property Rights for Government Investment Choices." *American Economic Review,* vol. 58, pp. 13–24.

Donahue, John D., 1989. *The Privatization Decision.* New York: Basic Books.

Ferris, James M., 1988. "The Public Spending and Employment Effects of Local Service Contracting." *National Tax Journal,* vol. 41, no. 2, pp. 207–217.

Ferris, James M., and Elizabeth Graddy, 1986. "Contracting Out: For What? With Whom?" *Public Administration Review,* vol. 46, pp. 332–344.

———, 1988. "The Production Choices for Local Government Services." *Journal of Urban Affairs,* vol. 10, pp. 273–289.

———, 1991. "Production Costs, Transaction Costs, and Local Government Contractor Choice." *Economic Inquiry,* vol. 29, pp. 541–554.

General Accounting Office (GAO), 1991. *Government Contractors: Are Service Contractors Performing Inherently Government Functions?* GAO/GGD-92-11. Washington, DC: Government Accounting Office.

International City/County Management Association (ICMA), 1982. "Is Contracting the Answer? The Newark Experience." Distributed by the ICMA, Report #40178, Washington, DC.

Jonsson, Erik, 1985. "A Model of a Non-Budget-Maximizing Bureau." In Jan-Erik Lane, ed., *State and Market: The Politics of the Public and the Private.* Beverly Hills, CA: Sage Publications, pp. 70–82.

Landau, Martin, 1969. "Redundancy, Rationality, and the Problem of Duplication and Overlap." *Public Administration Review,* vol. 39, no. 6, pp. 346–358.

La Porte, Todd, and Paula Consolini, 1991. "Working in Practice But Not in Theory: Theoretical Challenges of 'High Reliability Organization.'" *Journal of Public Administration Research and Theory,* vol. 1, pp. 19–47.

Leitzel, Jim, 1992. "Competition in Procurement." *Policy Sciences*, vol. 25, pp. 43–56.

Lerner, Allan, 1986. "There Is More Than One Way to Be Redundant." *Administration and Society*, vol. 18, no. 3, pp. 334–359.

McDavid, James, and George Schick, 1987. "Privatization Versus Union-Management Cooperation: The Effects of Competition in Service Efficiency in Municipalities." *Canadian Public Administration*, vol. 30, no. 3, pp. 472–488.

Mehay, Steven L., and Rodolfo A. Gonzalez, 1987. "Outside Information and the Monopoly Power of a Public Bureau: An Empirical Analysis." *Public Finance Quarterly*, vol. 15, no. 1 (January), pp. 61–75.

Meier, Kenneth J., 1980. "Executive Reorganization of Government: Impact on Employment and Expenditures." *American Journal of Political Science*, vol. 24, no. 3, pp. 396–412.

Miller, Gary J., and Terry M. Moe, 1983. "Bureaucrats, Legislators, and the Size of Government." *American Political Science Review*, vol. 77, pp. 297–322.

Miranda, Rowan, 1992a. *Privatizing City Government: Explaining the Adoption and Budgetary Consequences of Alternative Service Delivery Arrangements.* Doctoral dissertation. Chicago: Irving B. Harris Graduate School of Public Policy Studies, University of Chicago.

———, 1992b. "Privatization in Chicago's City Government." *Research in Urban Policy*, vol. 4, pp. 31–53.

———, 1994a. "Governments or Markets? The Privatization of Municipal Services." *Research in Governmental and Nonprofit Accounting*, vol. 8, pp. 235–264.

———, 1994b. "Privatization and the Budget Maximizing Bureaucrat." *Public Productivity and Management Review*, vol. 27, no. 4.

Miranda, Rowan, and Karlyn Andersen, 1994. "Alternative Service Delivery in Local Government, 1982–1992." *Municipal Yearbook*, Washington: International City/County Management Association, pp. 26–35.

Niskanen, William A., 1971. *Bureaucracy and Representative Government.* Chicago: Aldine Atherton.

Oakerson, Ronald, 1987. "The Organization of Local Public Economies." In *The Organization of Local Public Economics*. U.S. Advisory Commission on Intergovernmental Relations (ACIR). Washington, DC: Government Printing Office.

Osborne, David, and Todd Gaebler, 1992. *Reinventing Government.* New York: Addison-Wesley.

Ostrorn, Vincent, Charles M. Tiebout, and Robert Warren, 1961. "The Organization of Government in Metropolitan Areas: A Theoretical Inquiry." *American Journal of Political Science*, vol. 55, no. 4, pp. 831–842.

Perrow, Charles, 1984. *Normal Accidents: Living with High-Risk Technologies.* New York: Basic Books.

Savas, E. S., 1977. "An Empirical Study of Competition in Municipal Service Delivery." *Public Administration Review* (November-December), pp. 717–724.

———, 1981. "Intracity Competition Between Public and Private Service Delivery." *Public Administration Review* (January-February), pp. 46–52.

Stein, Robert M., 1991. *Urban Alternatives.* Pittsburgh: University of Pittsburgh Press.

Williamson, Oliver, 1975. *Markets and Hierarchies: Analysis and Antitrust Implications*. New York: Free Press.

———, 1985. *The Economic Institutions of Capitalism: Firms, Markets, and Relational Contracting*. New York: Free Press.

Wolf, Charles, Jr., 1988. *Markets or Governments: Choosing Between Imperfect Alternatives*. Cambridge, MA: MIT Press.

23

SERVICE EFFORTS AND ACCOMPLISHMENTS REPORTING

Has Its Time Really Come?

Richard E. Brown
James B. Pyers

With the release in April 1994 by the Government Accounting Standards Board (GASB) of *Concepts Statement No. 2, Service Efforts and Accomplishments Reporting,* SEA left the realm of a possible, far-off, and fanciful idea and entered the realm of being a likely additional financial reporting requirement within perhaps a decade.[1]

As recently as August 1996 in its *Action Report,* GASB indicated that we are now about halfway through the experimentation period specified in the 1994 Concepts Statement.[2] This article raises some fundamental questions about the experimentation phase, as well as several issues which may not be receiving needed coverage in GASB's ongoing research on SEA. These issues, it is argued, are so fundamental to the SEA process that lack of considerable attention to them may jeopardize the public financial community's acceptance of the concept, and thus GASB's efforts related to SEA reporting.

1998.   Service efforts and accomplishments reporting: Has its time really come? Brown, Richard E., and James B. Pyers. **Public Budgeting and Finance** 18 (Winter): 101–113.

Background

GASB's 1994 *Concepts Statement No. 2* dealing with service efforts and accomplishments reporting was in many ways a natural outgrowth of its initial report establishing the objectives of financial reporting in the public sector. Those objectives were delineated in GASB's *Concepts Statement No. 1, Objectives of Financial Reporting,* released in 1987, only a few years after GASB's creation. GASB made it clear in *Statement No. 1* that in addition to the more usual objectives of financial reporting relating to financial condition, position and stewardship, public sector financial reporting must include information to assist users in assessing service efforts, costs, and accomplishments of the governmental entity.[3] *Concepts Statement No. 2* dealt with SEA alone, focusing in much greater detail on the specifics of the SEA concept, including definitions and categories of measurement, possible limitations of SEA, and the uses of such measures.

Between 1987 and 1994 when the two concepts statements appeared, GASB conducted a large research project on SEA measures using academics from across the U.S. This research, in turn, led to the publication in 1990 of the GASB's *Service Efforts and Accomplishments Reporting: Its Time Has Come,* which served as a solid technical review of the state of the art of SEA both overall and in several functional areas of government.[4] But this research and document were not by themselves so remarkable, since the concept of SEA and the literature surrounding it go back many, many years. Indeed, a review of the *Journal of Accountancy,* going back to its origins in 1905, found references to performance and program measurement dating back to 1912, 1914, and 1917.[5] As any student and practitioner of performance measurement and SEA knows, the relevant literature of the 1930s through the current time is filled with papers on related topics. In the 1930s the studies were often couched in terms related to performance and program budgeting.[6] Later, especially in the 1960s and after, these discussions were also tied to performance, comprehensive, or operational auditing, culminating in the incorporation of performance audit standards in the first, 1972 version of the GAO's *Yellow Book,* now simply dubbed *Government Auditing Standards.*[7] With the advent of GASB in 1984, performance measurement has moved in the direction of tying such measurement to the third and missing link of the accountability cycle of planning, budgeting, accounting/recording, and auditing/evaluation—the accounting system and financial reporting.

It is thus important to also place SEA into this larger framework of a public sector financial accountability cycle. SEA, that is, is but one key element of a much greater concept. In 1971 Robert Anthony wrote a landmark piece in the *Public Administration Review* called "Closing the Loop Between Planning and Performance" and described this comprehensive cycle of financial accountability. In the 1980s the U.S. General Accounting Office adopted the theme, issuing a report which was to help focus and guide much of the agency's future work. Today, the concept of the full financial and managerial control structure including planning, budgeting, accounting and measurement, and audit and evaluation is standard fare in management accounting textbooks.[8]

Thus, GASB's release in 1994 of *Concepts Statement No. 2* not only represented both a logical extension of its own work in the area of SEA reporting, but also helped move forward a completion of the public sector's cycle of financial accountability.

GASB's efforts to help fulfill the financial accountability cycle is no small matter and a most welcome boost for public financial management. It is also long overdue. For at least a generation, performance auditors have had to help develop the performance-related data. They then proceeded to audit the data. This reality was virtually guaranteed to drive up audit costs, usurp managerial prerogatives, create controversy, and help confuse those public officials ordering the audit in the first place. In such an environment, performance audits often provided more heat than light.[9]

Similarly, for perhaps two generations, those involved in performance-based budgeting have been without essential feedback data on budget execution because the accounting system often did not capture relevant, performance data. This in turn tended to reduce the impact and usefulness of several pioneering budget concepts involving performance measurement. Programmatic performance data at the state and local levels of government are either nonexistent altogether, of a limited nature, or sporadically and unsystematically collected and reported. Some state and local governments have excellent performance-based financial systems, but most do not. Few have fully integrated systems with performance measures established and agreed upon by all interested parties. Illustrative of this situation is the recent paper in this journal by Robert Lee, "The Use of Program Analysis In State Budgeting." Among his conclusions, he states:

> Numerous states are going against the trend that would make greater use of program information in budgetary decision making. At a time when there is nationwide interest in program measurement . . . many states are bucking the trend and cutting back on effectiveness and productivity analysis.[10]

Thus, GASB's concern for SEA reporting, as stated, is an important, if long overdue development in helping to solidify the creation of a full public financial accountability cycle. It is, however, anything but a new idea. It is rather the extension or continuation of a series of well-developed public financial administration concepts. The question, however, is, will GASB's effort to establish performance measurement as a financial reporting requirement prove to be the long-awaited completion of this reporting cycle; or will it be, at best, simply another in a series of helpful but only partial reforms or, at worst, just another costly fad?

GASB's SEA Experiment

GASB's 1990 statement and title of its publication "Its (SEA's) Time Has Come," grabs our attention, as it was surely designed to do. It is almost as though GASB hopes to will SEA into existence. And yet, performance measurement has been coming for most of the 1900s, and it has still not fully arrived. Despite the somewhat flamboyant title of the 1990 publication, GASB appears to have sensed it must move cautiously for a number of reasons. First, it would be unlikely that GASB would fully tackle SEA reporting until its work was completed on other, more fundamental reporting issues—including the basic reporting model for state and local governments and, as of the early 1990s and, indeed, even today, much work remains to be done on this model. That is to say, it would be hard to visualize GASB issuing formal pronouncements on SEA reporting when fundamental issues involving the basis of accounting (accrual vs. modified accrual), the concept of depreciation, and the structure, presentation, and display of funds in the Comprehensive Annual Financial Report (CAFR) still needed to be resolved.[11] Second, GASB apparently judged that the simple passage of more time might help ease the opposition that was developing to SEA reporting. In June 1992, for example, the national Government Finance Officers Association (GFOA) issued a policy statement opposing certain aspects of the SEA concept.[12] Thus, for a number of valid reasons GASB decided to have an extended period of experimentation with SEA reporting. *Concepts Statement No. 2* demonstrates this note of caution by stating that:

> Before the GASB considers establishing SEA reporting standards for inclusion in GPEFR (the general purpose external financial reports), it is important that there be extensive experimentation in measuring and reporting SEA. This experimentation should consider whether SEA measures are developed that are relevant, understandable, comparable, timely, consistent, and reliable. Further analysis should explore how externally reported SEA information is used and its effect on users' ability to assess accountability and make decisions as well as its effect on the quality, effectiveness, and efficiency of the agencies, departments, programs, and services being reported on.[13]

One must ponder this statement carefully to appreciate its full impact. First, GASB is underscoring the belief that, at this point, much remains to be known about the use of SEA measures. Second, the statement suggests something resembling a controlled experiment is needed. After all, if a wide variety of state and local entities have been using performance measures for decades, what was to be learned by further uncontrolled use by these units?

In fact, the GASB "experiment" was not designed to be an "experiment" in the usual sense of that term, at least not one including many of the formal controls and systematic follow-up often associated with an experiment. Rather, GASB was issuing a call for volunteers, state and local governments willing to cooperate with GASB in providing needed information at appropriate points in time. *Concepts Statement No. 2* repeatedly refers to already ongoing experimentation in state and local governments and encourages the continuation of such experiments.[14]

Between 1994 when *Concepts Statement No. 2* was released and 1997 contact and discussion between GASB and officials which could be in any way deemed to be part of an experiment was at best sporadic and unsystematic. It would be fair to state that for the first half of GASB's experimentation period little progress was made, or at least formally reported to GASB or others.

Indeed, one of the most significant comments made by GASB on the status of the SEA experiment period was included in an August 1996 *Action Report:*

> When *Concepts Statement No. 2, Service Efforts and Accomplishments Reporting,* was released in April 1994, the GASB entered into a five-year experimentation period for SEA. As the half-way point is nearing for this experimentation period, the staff is attempting to identify who is experimenting with SEA measurement. A more detailed survey, to be mailed at a later date, will identify what measurements are being used and how results are being utilized.[15]

Again, one must consider this statement carefully. The statement confirms the view that GASB is not so much shaping and leading the SEA experimentation, but is rather attempting. to assemble what a variety of governmental units have learned from their ongoing SEA-related work. These jurisdictions will likely run the gamut from state, county, city, and other local units, cover both executive and legislative branches of government, and include budgeting, controllership, audit, and other organizational areas of government. GASB will uniformly collect such data, but GASB has not designed an experiment to systematically use specific SEA measures and then monitor the SEA efforts of a handful of selected jurisdictions. Rather, it appears GASB is instead now trying, first, to identify entities using SEA measures and, second, enlist their cooperation in collecting needed data. In truth, the several-year period since the release in 1994 of *Concepts Statement No. 2* suggests that this has been more of a "cooling off period" than one of true experimentation. This is demonstrated by the survey instrument itself, dated September 1996. The letter accompanying the survey form states that the survey will have two phases, the first seeking general information and the second seeking more comprehensive information.[16] Two very recent announcements further confirm that GASB has a long way to go in its SEA experimentation phase. In January 1998 GASB announced it was seeking to recruit an assistant project manager for SEA-related work. In February 1998 it was announced that GASB had received a $350,000 grant from the Alfred P. Sloan Foundation to fund GASB's SEA experimentation process.[17]

Questions Which Need Answers:
Suggestions to GASB

The limitations of GASB's SEA experimentation phase offer both good and bad news. The bad news is that, as with any experiment with built-in deficiencies, there is always a question as to how much one can rely on and use the results. After all, despite any protests, this is GASB's experiment and not that of a collection of state and local units of government. It is, in the final analysis, GASB who has the authority to issue SEA reporting requirements. The good news is that, while it is late in the process, GASB still has time to restructure and improve upon its experiment. As it does so, there are a number of questions which arise. The answers to these questions might help alleviate influential resistance to the concept, and avoid some of the controversy SEA required reporting will inevitably bring. These questions are raised in the spirit of constructive advice and by authors who have long been strong supporters of SEA reporting and the auditing of such performance data.

Why Has SEA Been So Long in Coming?

As mentioned above, performance reporting, budgeting, and auditing have been with us a very long time in a variety of shapes and forms. The concept has been discussed in the modern literature since the early 1900s. Program and performance budgeting go back to at least the 1930s when studies began to describe the early work of the Tennessee Valley Authority and other federal agencies. The U.S. General Accounting Office and many state governments began conducting performance audits in the 1950s and 1960s, usually at the insistence of elected legislators. More recently, this demand has spread to a number of larger American cities. Thus, the obvious question arises: if SEA reporting is as inevitable as GASB seems to suggest in the statement, "Its (SEA's) Time Has Come," where has it been for the last several decades? These were decades in which federal, state, and local audit and budget officials were truly "in the trenches," often persuading reluctant public managers to welcome or at least use the concepts, and encouraging ambitious elected officials to use, but not misuse the relevant performance reports. One possible response argues that, after all, the evolution of governmental accounting has been slow in its progress—the GASB was only established in 1984. But to a considerable extent that response is misleading: the origins of modern U.S. state and local governmental accounting can be traced to the work of the National Committee on Municipal (later Governmental) Accounting in the 1930s. In 1968 the then Municipal Finance Officers Association released the "Blue Book" on governmental accounting, auditing, and financial reporting, the forerunner to current GAAP for state and local government. Thus, to date, governmental accounting (and accountants) appears to have been most reluctant to tackle SEA reporting.

If one accepts the premise that indeed, the past tells us much about the present and future, then the great delay in the coming of SEA reporting is puzzling, and also very important. Does the more rapid adoption of SEA in the budget and audit environments stem more from special demands placed on them by their clientele groups? Is it instead perhaps due to differences in training or other traits of those who serve as budget and audit officials, rather than as accountants charged with external reporting? Or does this great delay instead suggest something about inherent shortcomings of reporting SEA data through the accounting system? Might it be that the external and systematic reporting of performance data engenders substantial and even insurmountable resistance from politicians and professionals alike? If so, why, and what can be done about it? Clearly the possibilities are many. Nonetheless, it would appear that some attention by GASB researchers to this historical issue might shed some light on when, and even, whether, SEA's time has indeed come. This long and slow development process may suggest underlying and still existing barriers to successful implementation of SEA reporting. Identifying and easing these barriers may be essential if SEA reporting is to one day be accepted as "generally accepted accounting principles."

What Can We Learn About the
Behavioral Implications of SEA Reporting?

At a recent regional meeting of about eighty members of the Ohio Government Finance Officers Association (GFOA) the participants were asked to fill out a written questionnaire on their views on SEA reporting. The good news is that about 42 percent of respondents seemed to favor required SEA reporting. However, the balance of the respondents are either clearly against such reporting or are undecided, and have basic unanswered concerns.[18]

Any professional who has been intimately involved in using SEA-type data knows of the power and potential such data have for use, misuse, and abuse, and for stirring up controversy. Early in the career of one of the authors, while serving as a management intern in the Tennessee Valley Authority (TVA), a discussion took place at a meeting of the presidentially appointed Board of Directors, attended by the managers of power, navigation, engineering and construction, forest development, recreation, etc. In response to a request for added program funds, a TVA board member asked the manager what it would cost to construct and develop feeding areas for the wildlife on their north-south flight paths. The manager responded the cost would be about one million dollars. The manager was then asked by a second board member how many fowl would be served by such a program, and he responded about 500,000. At this point the third board member, not known to be a supporter of this part of TVA's mission, commented, "Good Lord, that's two bucks a duck!" The board member had reduced the budget request to a single measure and, in doing so, cast the debate in a new and controversial light.

The possibilities and problems associated with SEA reporting are further illustrated by two audits of the Kansas Public Employees Retirement System. The traditional *financial* audit resulted in a clean audit opinion. The Retirement System officials were relieved. However, the *performance* audit raised fundamental questions about management decisions and the accomplishments of the system, including the investment earnings realized by the system in comparison to other public retirement systems. Before the dust settled legislative hearings were held, a management shake-up occurred, and some New York investment advisors were fired.[19]

SEA does approach the notion of the "bottom line" for governmental programs. Such data are extremely difficult to gather and present correctly, and this is especially so of outcomes or quality measures. This may explain in part the opposition of the national Government Finance Officers Association (GFOA) which has issued a policy statement calling upon GASB to exclude outcome measures from any further consideration as a part of required external reporting.[20] Even if such data are technically solid, they are very powerful and lend themselves to misuse, even outright abuse. Elected officials are often not as well versed in the use of "bottom line" data as their private sector counterparts. This may be due to the nature of electoral politics and the traits of those able or willing to run for office. It may be due to a lack of experience in using such data. Or, it may result from the temptation to use SEA data for political advantage. Regardless, the stakes are very high. If members of a city council, state legislature, or school board, decide that "two bucks a duck" is too much and fire the manager producing that proposal or program result—which often occurs—the results can be chilling to governmental program performance and morale.

Creativity will be stifled. Good managers will either leave or refuse to enter public service. There would be a reluctance to put forth good program ideas. No one denies the right of a democratically elected body to try to make needed program and personnel changes. What is at stake is the wisdom and timing of such actions. Prior to drastic program changes by responsible officials the following steps are first in order. The policy-setting body needs to clearly establish overall program and monetary guidelines. Specific objectives ought to be set for managers and programs. SEA measures ought to be agreed upon. And SEA data ought to be carefully assembled and audited, including relevant comparisons to peer organizations or standards. In the absence of such a complete accountability system, and appropriate behavioral patterns, SEA data may prove to be more dangerous than helpful to public programs, managers, and even the taxpayers.[21]

There is a story attributed to a number of legendary football coaches in which the coach was asked, "Why do you run the football so much?" The coach responded, "When you throw the football, several things can happen to you, and most of them are bad. I don't like the odds." Public managers' views of SEA reporting may be similar: they do not like the odds. If the results of the data are positive, they get to keep their jobs. They can not buy an equity position in the enterprise. Bonuses are rare. There are no partnerships. If the results are mixed, or even negative, they may be demoted or even fired. Or they may be embarrassed personally and professionally by the media. There would seem to be far more disincentives than incentives for being a willing participant in accurate SEA reporting. Indeed, this reality may help explain why SEA external reporting has been so slow in coming. The City of Wooster, Ohio has been hard at work in the beginning stages of SEA reporting for several years. Managers report limited SEA data, exclusively input, output, and efficiency measures. A couple of these measures, in turn, are included in the Letter of Transmittal in the Comprehensive Annual Financial Report. Wooster has been working loosely with GASB on the SEA project for several years. However, the SEA data are not audited, and are not yet used extensively by the City Council in budgetary or other policy deliberations. And, significantly, outcomes data are not reported. The true test of a SEA experiment is where the entity moves beyond the reporting of limited data to the public discussion and use of a full array of reported SEA data.

GASB, it would appear, may face practical and ethical reasons for having to devote more attention to these issues as a part of its experimentation program. In short, what do we know about these behavioral issues surrounding the use of performance data and what can be done to improve this uncertain environment? In the absence of such answers, continued opposition to SEA reporting in many influential circles may be a totally rational response.

Who Will Do the Audits, And at What Cost?

A strong argument can be made that, assuming a reasonable amount of required SEA reporting, there are limited additional costs associated with SEA reporting. Again, assuming reasonable data requirements, this is, after all, data which the responsible program manager should have available for his/her own needs. Regarding the overall performance of the fire department, for example, GASB's 1990 research report calls for many measures, including: total operating and capital expenditures and total full-time personnel and hours worked (inputs); the population served and property value protected (outputs); and percentage of citizens rating performance satisfactory, independent insurance rating, and total dollars in fire losses (outcomes).[22] It would be difficult to argue that limited amounts of such data are an *added cost* of doing business. Rather, they would seem to be an *essential* part of doing the public's business.

The difficulty arises when such data are no longer used exclusively for internal management purposes but are reported externally. What can be said of the audit costs associated with SEA reporting? How much attention has this area received? A reasonable argument might be made that the financial statements generated by the profit-seeking enterprise (and perhaps the resulting financial ratios which may be derived from those statements) depict the firm's "bottom line" and thus are the parallel to SEA reporting in the public sector, as illustrated by the fire department example offered above. However, the audit of that private entity's financial statements is a traditional financial statement or opinion audit. Its audit counterpart in the public sector if SEA data are to be audited is the performance audit.

It is hoped there is widespread agreement that SEA reporting in the absence of competent, relevant auditing would be of little value, even dangerous. Evidence of the problems associated with using unaudited SEA-type data is illustrated by a miniscandal which occurred a few years ago and is still widely reported by the print media. Colleges and universities, it was reported, were publishing glowing statistics used in a variety of college guides to help potential students choose among colleges. As it turned out the data were depicting inaccurate GPA, ACT and SAT scores. Many "innovative" approaches were used: remedial students' scores were omitted, and only the mathematics but not the verbal scores of international students were reported. These data of course are not audited.[23]

While there is some information available on the skills required for and costs associated with performance auditing, that information is not widely known or appreciated. We must begin by assuming that the auditors will be reviewing performance data reported by management, and not creating the data. If this were not the case, audit costs would be prohibitive. Still, some argue that the skills and experience required to conduct such audits more closely parallel management consulting than financial auditing. Thus, salaries for such auditors could be much higher. Also, performance auditing tends to be quite labor intensive, further driving up audit costs. Further, such work often tends to be complex and sensitive, adding time and further adding to audit costs. And it is most unlikely even these higher costs would result in a performance audit of, say, an entire city. A performance review of an entire state or local entity, if done correctly, might easily cost hundreds of thousands of dollars, perhaps even millions. This suggests the need to rotate performance audits of various programs over some kind of agreed upon cycle. In any event, a city council or school board could not digest or use a performance audit covering too many programs or activities. Finally, since performance auditing has often been conducted by governmental auditors, there are relatively few CPA firms with the needed expertise to undertake such engagements. Only the very largest firms, and a handful of specialized smaller firms, routinely conduct sizeable performance audits. While, over time, this would certainly change as more firms entered this service area, in the short term it would drive up audit costs and create a fair amount of disruption.

It might be asserted that as managers grow accustomed to SEA reporting requirements, and more comfortably report reliable data, the work of the performance auditor will also become less onerous and less costly, closer to the current attest function in the traditional financial statement audit. Still, using the fire department example again, attesting to the presentation and accuracy of the percentage of citizens rating the department's performance satisfactory, the total dollars in fire losses, etc., and probably the comparison of such measures to relevant standards, will likely remain a high cost and high skill activity.

In sum, SEA reporting without competent performance audits would be irresponsible, and there is a wide array of special difficulties and costs associated with performance auditing. In order to conclude, as GASB suggests, that SEA's time has come, GASB will need to study this item in far more depth and answer many important questions before understandable resistence will dissipate.

What Can We Learn from the Private Sector?
From Other Nations?

It is instructive to note that the more current studies and texts on managerial accounting for private sector organizations are critical of commercial enterprises for their preoccupation with costs and efficiency, and describe the efforts of the more progressive companies to report and examine critical performance measures other than costs. These include such measures as number of customer complaints, number of warranty claims, number of defects, and number of on-time deliveries. This trend is suggested by an item in a fairly recent issue of *Accounting Today* in which the writer reports on a nationwide bench marking study of best practices by the American Institute of CPAs and the Hackett Group.[24]

In the private sector such measures are usually placed in the larger context of an internal managerial accounting control system, rather than in the domain of external reporting. This internal system generally encompasses strategic planning, critical performance measures, performance standards/competitive bench marking, and feedback and continuous improvement. Again, this information is primarily for internal managerial purposes. The extent and nature of external reporting of such data is largely left to the discretion of management. It may be argued that adverse critical performance data are ultimately reflected in the income statement in the case of the private firm. Of course, the SEA reporting concept calls for the *external* reporting of basic performance data. This raises again the fundamental question of what precisely is "the bottom line" of the public entity or program. Is SEA data the domain of GASB and *external* reporting, or is it really internal managerial data? And are the answers to these questions the same for efficiency and outcome data? The private sector model may be instructive in terms of how much reporting is needed, how often, in what formats, and who the real users are likely to be. Thus before finalizing any SEA reporting requirements further study of selected private sector managerial control systems might be in order.

Additionally, it would appear that several other nations know a great deal more about reporting and auditing performance measures than does the United States. For example, Canada is one of the world's leaders in bringing government and private sectors together in reporting and auditing performance data. The same may be said of the United Kingdom. GASB may be able to learn much from a selective look at the experience of other nations. In this regard, one thing is certain: the U.S. is not a world leader in this arena, but is well behind several other countries.[25]

Conclusion

Several reasons have been presented which might suggest that, contrary to GASB's wish, the time for SEA reporting may not yet have come, at least not without much more careful and further study. Moreover, until more is known about these issues, requiring SEA reporting either might not be possible or would not succeed. Indeed, it may even do genuine harm. First, more needs to be known about why performance reporting in one form or another has been advocated for most of the twentieth century, but is still not systematically adopted. And to assert that this is because it has not been required would seem to avoid rather than answer the question. Second, performance measurement has often been surrounded by great controversy, even hostility, in the public sector. This, in turn, has led to considerable reluctance to adopt such systems. Understanding why this is so and how to influence behavioral patterns may be essential to successful SEA reporting requirements. Third, much more needs to be known about the skills and costs associated with auditing SEA data. Not requiring periodic, systematic audits of such data would be tantamount to requiring the reporting of misleading data. Finally, private U.S. companies and some foreign nations are increasingly reporting and using critical performance measures as a part of their management reporting process. Some nations are having these data audited. There may well be valuable lessons to learn from the further study of these experiences.

It is hoped that these concerns can be built into what remains of GASB's "experimentation" period. It may well be that GASB still has the time to redesign its efforts and create a genuine experiment, closely monitoring the use and results of SEA measures in a representative group of entities over a several year period. Answering the questions raised above might go a long way toward overcoming understandable resistance to required SEA reporting. It is one thing to require such reporting. It would be far better to base such a requirement on a carefully controlled period of testing. This, in turn could aid in having this reporting done willingly and at minimal cost, while also increasing the odds that such data will be used within a positive and constructive framework.

Notes

1. Governmental Accounting Standards Board, *Concepts Statement No. 2, Service Efforts and Accomplishments Reporting* (Norwalk, Conn.: GASB, 1994).

2. Governmental Accounting Standards Board, "Service Efforts and Accomplishments," *Action Report* (Norwalk, Conn.: GASB, August, 1996).

3. Governmental Accounting Standards Board, *Concepts Statement No. 1, Objectives of Financial Reporting* (Stamford, Conn.: GASB, 1987), paragraph 77c.

4. As a member of GASB's nationwide research team, one of the authors, Brown, contributed two chapters to GASB's research report, *Service Efforts and Accomplishments Reporting: Its Time Has Come*, released in 1990: Chapter 6, "Hospitals," and Chapter 9, "Public Assistance Programs." The full citation is: GASB, *Research Report: Service Efforts and Accomplishments Reporting: Its Time Has Come* (Norwalk, Conn.: GASB, 1990).

5. Gary John Previts and Richard E. Brown, "The Development of Government Accounting," *The Accounting Historians Journal*, Vol. 20, No. 2, December 1993.

6. See Jesse Burkhead's classic, *Government Budgeting* (New York: John Wiley & Sons, Inc., 1956). Chapter 6, on "Performance Budgeting," contains a brief but excellent history of the development of performance budgeting.

7. The first edition of the "Yellow Book" appeared in 1972. The latest version is: Comptroller General of the United States, *Government Auditing Standards, 1994 Revision* (Washington, D.C.: U.S. General Accounting Office, June 1994). A landmark publication in the performance audit movement was L.M. Knighton, *The*

Performance Post Audit In State Government (Ann Arbor, Mich.: University Microfilms, Inc., 1966).

8. Robert Anthony, "Closing the Loop Between Planning and Performance," *Public Administration Review* 31 (May/June 1971), pp. 388–398; Comptroller General of the United States, *Managing the Cost of Government: Building An Effective Financial Management Structure*, Vol. I, *Major Issues*, and Vol. II, *Conceptual Framework* (Washington, D.C.: U.S. General Accounting Office, February 1985).

9. See, for example, Richard E. Brown, et al., *Auditing Performance In Government* (New York: John Wiley and Sons, 1982). See especially Chapter 9, "External Relationships."

10. Robert D. Lee, Jr., "The Use of Program Analysis in State Budgeting," *Public Budgeting and Finance* 17 (Summer 1997), p. 35.

11. See, for example, Governmental Accounting Standards Board, *Exposure Draft: Basic Financial Statements . . . For State and Local Governments* (Norwalk, Conn.: GASB, 1997).

12. Government Finance Officers Association, Policy Statement: "Service Efforts and Accomplishments Reporting," Adopted June 23, 1992, pp. 17–19.

13. GASB, *Concepts Statement No. 2*, op. cit., p. 32.

14. GASB, *Concepts Statement No. 2*, op. cit., see especially p. 32.

15. GASB, *Action Report*, op, cit., p. 2.

16. Letter and Survey Instrument from James R. Fountain, GASB Assistant Director of Research. "GASB/NAPA Survey On the Use of Performance Measures by State and Local Governmental Entities," September 1996.

17. GASB, *Action Report* (Stamford, Conn: GASB, January 1998), p. 6; Association of Government Accountants, *Topics* (Alexandria, Va.: AGA, February 1998), p. 10.

18. Information gathered from questionnaires completed by training participants at Ohio GFOA Annual Meeting in Cleveland, Ohio, September 13, 1996.

19. Brown, op. cit., Chapter 2, "The Limitations of Financial Auditing."

20. GFOA, op. cit.

21. There is a vast and rich literature in this area. Illustrative of this literature is a recent paper which also includes an extensive bibliography: Vera Vogelsang-Coombs, "Governance Education: Helping City Councils Learn," *Public Administration Review*, Vol. 57, No. 6 (November/December 1997), pp. 490–509.

22. GASB, *SEA Reporting*, op, cit., "Fire Safety," Chapter 5.

23. "Educators Aim to Standardize College Ratings," *The Wall Street Journal*, September 24, 1996, p. B–1.

24. "Top Companies Compare Their 'Best Practices' in AICPA Study," *Accounting Today*, September 25–October 8, 1995, p. 12.

25. A few references indicative of the developments in other nations currently and in the past in the area of performance measurement include: Lee D. Parker, *Value-For-Money Auditing* (Victoria, Australia: Australian Accounting Research Foundation, 1986); *Value For Money In Municipalities* (Ottawa, Canada: Canadian Comprehensive Auditing Foundation, 1984); and *Effectiveness Auditing* (Stockholm, Sweden: The Swedish National Audit Bureau, 1971).

24

A PROPER MENTALITY FOR BENCHMARKING

David N. Ammons

The public sector has come a long way in measuring performance and "managing for results," but there is much still to do. Delving even modestly into the history of public management yields the discovery that performance measurement and related management initiatives have been encouraged for many years. In that respect, it has been a long haul. The seemingly slow pace, however, should not blind us to the progress that has been made.

Consider changes that have occurred over the last 25 years in attitudes toward government performance or even the possibility of creditable performance by the public sector. In the 1970s a lot of people considered *government productivity* to be an oxymoron, about as illogical as word pairs like "alone together," "peace offensive," or "fresh prunes." Some wisecracking pundits even likened government productivity to the Loch Ness monster. There were occasional sightings reported, they said, but nothing confirmed.

In the 1970s and early 1980s, it was difficult to generate much interest in performance comparison of two or more government units. "We are unique!" government officials said of their organization and its environment. "Our conditions are different; our service demands are different"

1999. A proper mentality for benchmarking. Ammons, David N. **Public Administration Review** 59 (March-April): 105–109.

(usually meaning *greater than the demands faced by any of our counter-parts*); "comparison would be meaningless."

As great as resistance was to intergovernmental performance comparison, there was even less interest in trying to adapt private sector practices. "Impractical!" proponents of adaptation were told. "Naïve!" they were called.

Notable Progress

As the century draws to a close, optimism is evident among recent converts to the measure-monitor-and-improve school of public service as well as among veterans of that movement. More than 700 people from all levels of government gathered in Austin, Texas, in 1998 for the third in a series of conferences dedicated to celebrating the successes of results-oriented management in the public sector, even as they challenged each other to do more.

The Loch Ness comparisons have faded. The sightings of government productivity are more frequent—and they are confirmed. Government agencies have established performance standards, many of which are directed toward meeting the expectations of service recipients, and service has improved in documentable ways.

Governments themselves are more receptive to performance comparisons, if they are done properly. Reasons for this newfound receptivity are not certain, but two explanations are plausible. One possibility is that government officials eventually resigned themselves to the inevitability of cross-unit comparisons. News reporters love per capita expenditure comparisons—crude as such comparisons are and devoid as they are of any sensitivity to differences among governments in the scope or quality of services, much less any differences in cost-accounting systems. "If comparisons are inevitable," some government officials may have said, "let's see if we can do them properly." By declaring their intention to "do them properly," these officials announce their resolve to report differences in the quality of service among governments and rectify accounting disparities in calculating unit costs of service delivery.

A second possibility is that government officials had their eyes opened by the corporate experience in benchmarking. Among the pioneers in the benchmarking movement were Motorola, IBM, AT&T, Alcoa, DEC, and Milliken; but none of these pioneers enjoys a more prominent role in that history than does the Xerox Corporation. In perhaps the most repeated story in benchmarking lore, Xerox confronted its own unsatisfactory performance in product warehousing and distribution. It did so not by employing the then-conventional methods of process revision or redesign, but instead by identifying the organization it considered to be the very best at warehousing and distribution, in hopes that "best practices" could be adapted from the exemplar's model. Who was judged "best in the business" at warehousing and distribution? L. L. Bean, the catalog merchant. Xerox approached L. L. Bean with its request that the two companies engage in a cooperative benchmarking project. The request was granted and the resulting project yielded major insights in inventory arrangement and the efficient processing of orders, resulting in major gains for Xerox when these lessons were adapted to its own operations.

Two aspects of the Xerox–L. L. Bean story are especially relevant to public-sector officials. First, the corporate benchmarking process—that is, the steps that emphasize the identification of practices that lead to superior results—may also be applied in the public sector. Second, and perhaps even more important, is the vivid evidence that shatters many long-held biases against comparisons with organizations that differ, even modestly, from one's own. Xerox did not select as its benchmarking partner another manufacturer of photocopying machines. It selected as its model a company from an entirely different industry. If Xerox can learn from L. L. Bean, surely the differences among city governments, among county governments, among state governments and federal agencies, and even across levels of government and across sectors are not so great as to preclude their learning from each other. Public-sector managers who followed with interest the benchmarking experience of the private sector stood to benefit directly from their observations, but even managers unfamiliar with the corporate experience often are climbing aboard the benchmarking bandwagon as it picks up speed in the public sector.

Governments are exchanging management lessons with the private sector and adapting systems and strategies that are applicable. In many cases, they are competing with the private sector for the privilege of producing public services. Sometimes they lose in that competition, but sometimes they win. The celebrated experience of Phoenix, where city employees lost refuse collection territory to private collectors, learned some important lessons from their competitive experience, and won the business back, inspired many public sector officials and advocates of a new, more aggressive, more results-oriented public service—as have more recent examples in Indianapolis, Charlotte, and elsewhere. The public sector can target the results it wants and, to a degree that surprised many detractors, it has shown an ability to compete with private companies. Governments may not always *seek out* the opportunity to compete, but, when that opportunity is thrust upon them, give them a level playing field and government can respond.

Many departments and agencies that hope to develop a strong results orientation find themselves now at the stage where they are focusing on developing or refining their performance measures. Many have decided, intentionally, not to think too much about the application of performance measures just yet. Their focus right now is development or refinement. That seems like a reasonable approach—that is, focus now on getting the measures right; worry about applications in the future. The problem is this: unless a government ties its performance measures *meaningfully* into its management systems—unless those measures are something more than decorations for the budget document, as superficial reporting practices have been called derisively—any enthusiasm for measurement will quickly lose its luster, and probably deserves to.

Officials moving toward a results orientation are well advised to think about application of performance measures right from the start. Think about application at every stage. Measurement flourishes—and deserves to flourish—only if it is used and is useful. Although many options exist, one potential use that deserves consideration is benchmarking.

Frustration of "Out-of-Context" Measurement

Until recently, most government managers faced a frustrating experience the first time they attempted to use performance measures for an evaluation with a perspective extending beyond their own backyard. After being convinced by an advocate of performance measurement that measurement was the way to go, the manager had proceeded to collect and compile the numbers. Following a year of measurement the organization had its numbers and the manager wanted to know whether these numbers reflected favorable performance.

"OK, I have done as you suggested," the manager reported. "Our result for this measure is 6.2 and our result for that measure is 87 percent. Are these results good?"

Too often the advocate was able to suggest only that the measures be collected for another year. The performance record for year two could then be compared to that of year one for a report on progress or lack of progress.

Although valuable insights can be gained from year-to-year comparisons, the documentation of progress is not what this and other officials with similar requests are seeking. They want to know how they are doing in a context external to their own organization. It is frustrating when they find themselves unable to do so. The arrival of benchmarking in the public sector is changing that.

Benchmarking

Benchmark is a term we have borrowed from surveyors. If a surveyor can mark a known position and altitude on a permanent landmark, it can serve as a reference point for other measurements and other points. In much the same way, benchmarking, as public officials use that term, features the identification of a point of reference for comparison or measurement purposes. With a benchmark, they can measure the performance gap between where they are and where they want to be and can track their progress in closing that gap.

As government officials think about applications of performance measurement, performance benchmarking deserves consideration. Benchmarking in the public sector comes in three distinct varieties. One is a direct adaptation of the corporate version. It is very analytic and very narrow in that it focuses on a single process rather than on several departments or even an entire agency. The basic steps of corporate-style benchmarking are listed below.

1. Decide what process to benchmark.
2. Study the process in your own organization.
3. Identify benchmarking partners.
4. Analyze the processes of benchmarking partners to identify differences that account for superior performance.
5. Adapt and implement "best practices."
6. Monitor and revise.

For more detail on corporate-style benchmarking see *Benchmarking Best Practices* (1997) and Keehley, *et al.* (1997).

A second form of benchmarking found in the public sector is much broader than the first. It emphasizes the articulation of a vision for a state or community and the establishment of targets to mark progress toward that vision. Typically, the vision transcends government services and addresses other facets of the state or community's quality of life. In many respects, this form of benchmarking is more akin to strategic planning than to corporate-style benchmarking.

The third form of benchmarking in the public sector features the comparison of performance statistics in one's organization to appropriate external pegs. For example such pegs can be professional standards, state or national statistics, or the performance targets and results of selected counterparts.

Success with any of the three versions of benchmarking requires public officials who possess the proper frame of mind, the proper attitude. Technical knowledge about the chosen form of benchmarking is crucial, of course, but so is proper attitude.

The required attitude is not simply an unwavering commitment to greater productivity or optimism that performance can be improved. It is more than that. It is certainly more than the pessimist's attitude that says,

"The glass is half empty." It is more than the optimist's attitude that says, "The glass is half full." It is even more than the measurement specialist's attitude regarding the efficient use of resources that says, "This glass is twice the size that is needed, given the quantity of liquid."

Benchmarking
Mentality

What, then, is the proper frame of mind, the proper mentality for successful benchmarking? Let us focus on three things. First, it only makes sense to benchmark if you recognize that you probably are not the best in everything, probably not perfect in everything you do. The whole idea is that the benchmarking organization is looking for things to improve. Successful benchmarkers cannot become defensive.

Some government officials are very proud and protective of their operations. If another government provides the same service at a lower unit cost, these officials take news of the disparity as a slap at their operation, even as an attack on their management skills and a criticism of the diligence of their employees. "This isn't a fair comparison," they say. "We operate two water treatment plants and that other government operates one large facility. Of course their unit costs are lower than ours!"

Or, "This isn't a fair comparison! You should only compare us to other governments that employ meter readers who manually read every meter every month, just like we do. How can you compare us to governments that have purchased devices that permit remote readings or automatic readings, or with governments that operate under a different strategy than we do?"

Or, "This isn't a fair comparison. You should only compare us to governments of approximately the same size, in the same region, that use crews of similar size."

Most proponents of benchmarking probably have encountered similar objections. The defensiveness of operating managers in this regard comes from pride and from a sense that the purpose of benchmarking is to render judgment on management proficiency and employee diligence. But that is not the point.

If one's benchmarking partners were selected carefully, they are going to outperform the organization initiating the benchmarking project—*by design! That is why they were picked.* If public officials could get better and less expensive services by having a combined facility rather than separate facilities, they should want to know that. If automation could make their meter readers more efficient or allow them to operate with smaller crews, they should want to know that. If managers become defensive and reject these lessons, they are missing the point.

It is perfectly all right to defend a good operation against the forced imposition of a bad idea. But before public officials construct their line of defense, they should be sure it is a bad idea.

Presumably, benchmarking partners have been selected because they get good results. Ideally, their success is attributable to good ideas and good strategies that can be imported into other organizations. If would-be benchmarkers allow defensiveness to overwhelm them, they will miss the best lessons.

Second, the best benchmarkers are eager to learn from others. When they say they don't want to reinvent the wheel, they really mean it. Some local governments resist adopting something invented elsewhere, saying simply, "It won't work here." Benchmarkers take pride in adapting it so it *will* work here.

An important point is that most successful benchmarkers *adapt* rather than *adopt*. If officials are willing to accept only those lessons they can adopt without change, they are severely restricting the pool of good ideas. Most good ideas will need to be adapted to fit a new setting.

Third, the best benchmarkers resist the tendency for benchmarking to become a beauty contest. It is a powerful tendency, the quest to claim the number one ranking and, perhaps more significantly, to avoid the embarrassment of an unfavorable rank.

A remarkable transformation sometimes takes place in government managers over the course of several months. At stage one they are enthusiastic about involvement in a benchmarking project. At stage two, anxiety sets in. If there are 20 agencies participating in the project, they begin to worry, "What if my agency is 18th ... or 20th? Will the media and the politicians have a field day?" And so the beauty contest rears its head. The precise formula for the amount of time from stage one to stage two has not yet been established, but it seems evident that proximity to election day may factor into the calculation.

Although most officials are at least moderately susceptible, stage two anxiety does not afflict every manager to the same degree. Some exhibit few outward symptoms. Their enthusiasm for benchmarking appears never to wane.

The difference in anxiety levels may have its roots in early pronouncements regarding an organization's entry into a benchmarking project. Some managers lay the groundwork for their own subsequent anxiety by announcing their involvement this way: "Oh, we are going to see how we stack up." Others never emphasize the rankings, only the lessons. They say, "We want to see what we can learn from our counterparts." This is an important point. Appropriate expectations should be established right from the start. Successful benchmarkers are intent on learning from each other, not just on seeing how they stack up.

For the past three years a benchmarking project has been underway involving 35 local governments in North Carolina. Participating cities and counties are learning valuable operating lessons from their counterparts and several are putting those lessons to use and thereby benefiting their communities. In one sense, the communities designated as top performers are stars, but in another sense the *real stars* of a benchmarking project are the ones that use the project to improve performance most dramatically.

Even after only the initial round, some local governments are crediting the project for leading them to program improvements and cost savings. For example, the city of Winston-Salem responded to benchmarking insights by implementing changes in its solid waste collection system that will save roughly $400,000 per year. That is a nice return on Winston-Salem's investment in benchmarking, its investment in managing for results. Winston-Salem's action—not its initial ranking—makes it a benchmarking star.

The idea behind benchmarking is not simply how an organization stacks up. Instead, the fundamental idea is captured by two questions: (1) What did we learn? and (2) How will we use what we have learned to make us better?

If governments make good use of performance measures, whether through benchmarking or by other applications—if they focus on results—the progress made in performance measurement and results-oriented management in recent years will accelerate and the citizens of participating governments will be the winners.

References

"Benchmarking Best Practices" (1997). *Results-Oriented Government*. Module 2. Research Triangle Park, NC: Southern Growth Policies Board.

Keehley, Patricia, Steven Medlin, Sue MacBride, and Laura Longmire (1997). *Benchmarking for Best Practices in the Public Sector*. San Francisco: Jossey-Bass.

25

Can Public Officials Correctly Be Said to Have Obligations to Future Generations?

H. George Frederickson

Consider the oath taken by citizens of the Athenian city-state:

> We will ever strive for the ideals and sacred things of the city, both alone and with many; we will unceasingly seek to quicken the sense of public duty; we will revere and obey the city's laws; we will transmit this city not only not less, but greater, better and mote beautiful than it was transmitted to us.

With this oath, citizens accepted the responsibility to conduct effectively the temporal affairs of the city. They also pledged to pass the city on to the next generation in better condition than they received it. The Athenian public service ethic called for *more* than equality between the generations.[1] My purpose in this article is to consider issues of intergenerational equality and to ask the question: can public officials correctly be said to have obligations to future generations?

1994. Can public officials correctly be said to have obligations to future generations? Frederickson, H. George. **Public Administration Review** 54 (September-October): 457–464.

It seems that issues of intergenerational fairness are all around us. The current debate over the national deficit rings with charges that the debt was incurred by a profligate generation to be paid for by their children and their children's children (Aaron, Bosworth, and Burtless, 1989). This debate is aside from the issue of which groups—lower, middle, or upper classes—benefitted most from the run-away federal borrowing of the 1980s. Proposed solutions turn entirely on the question of who will pay if much of the deficit is not passed on to coming generations (Kotikoff, 1991). The health care finance issue is also mostly about fairness and equity between the insured and uninsured in present generations; the old and those not yet old; the medical and pharmaceutical professions; and the insurance companies. It is claimed with considerable evidence, that unless health care costs are contained the deficit cannot be reduced. Much of the essential thrust of the environmental movement is to preserve the earth's resources for coming generations. The Social Security system is by definition intergenerational. These are but a few of the more visible policy issues that have mostly to do with questions of fairness and equity both between groups in present generations and between present and future generations.[2]

The economic growth of the last half of the 20th century, particularly in the United States, seemed to indicate that successive generations do better. Based on this experience it appeared that successive generations have always done better. In fact, in the longer sweep of history intergenerational well-being has never been linear. Changes in human conditions such as nutrition, education, employment, and housing have been cyclical (Neustadt and May, 1986; Smith, 1988; Schlesinger, 1986; Kennedy, 1993; Strauss and Howe, 1991).

It is now clear that the generation born from the mid–1960s through the 1970s will likely do less well than their parents at least in terms of comparative income. Indeed, in a recent review of social science research on generational differences it was concluded that the next generation will do worse psychologically, socially and economically than its parents (Whitehead, 1993). Projections are that the differences between generations will widen as the baby-boom generation retires and the children born in the late 1970s and the 1980s start to enter the work force.

There is no doubt that elected officials are now especially sensitive to intergenerational issues. This sensitivity is particularly evident in political rhetoric and symbols. Do public officials, including public administrators, in fact, have definable responsibilities to future generations?[3] If so, what are these responsibilities? Are there theories or ethics in public administration that inform our thinking about future generations? Can there be social equity between generations?

I deal with these questions, first, with a consideration of the philosophical and ideological perspectives on intergenerational equity; then with a presentation of the compound theory of social equity as a tool for working with intergenerational issues; and finally, with an application of the compound theory of social equity to intergenerational questions of fairness and equity.

Future Generations as a Domain of Equity:
Philosophical Perspectives

The possible domains of equality are endless. One thinks immediately of equal justice before the law, some level of equality in education, equality in voting, equal access to job opportunities, and other generally accepted domains of equality. I will not treat here as domains specific fields of public policy (environment, education, health care) or spheres of individual or group interests. This section is limited to a treatment of the future or future generations as a broad and generalized domain. I ask: Can future generations be regarded as a domain, or part of a domain, of equality? How is this question answered philosophically and normatively?

Classical considerations of morality and ethics often include a consideration of future generations. In Plato's "eros" (desire, striving, life as an Idea) the passion is a personal commitment to one's work, to a work that transcends the present for the uncertain future, for sacrifice not just to present others but to the remote (Hartmann, 1981). The strength in the Platonic eros is the ethos of love, not just of one's neighbor, but of the one who is to be, a love which cannot be returned. Aristotle asserted that men and women unite out of a "natural striving to leave behind another that is like oneself (Politics, p. 1252 a30). Immanuel Kant's categorical imperative, as a set of principles that defines the general condition of human life, does not presuppose temporal limitations. From this ethical perspective, time is irrelevant in moral philosophy (Rawls, 1971). If justice or equality are imperative principles of conduct in one place and at one time, they are imperative in another place and at another time. Edmund Burke accounts for a cross-generational community bound together by moral contracts. John Locke describes a state of nature in which we are moral equals, equally entitled to use the earth and its resources. In this condition, an individual may fairly possess land for his or her own use provided that the land is used rather than wasted and that he or she "leaves enough and as good for others" (Locke, 1965, p. 333). David Hume, while critical of Locke's contractarian notions, shares his view of future generations. In his account of the virtues, we are "plac'd in a kind of middle station betwixt the past and the future" and "imagine our ancestors to be, in a manner, mounted above us, and our posterity to lie below us" (Hume, 1968, p. 306; Baier, 1981).

Certainly these philosophers regard future generations to be in some general sense deserving of intergenerational justice, equity, and fairness.

They describe philosophically based domains of claims on the part of present generations toward future generations. But their considerations of morality and ethics were mostly temporal, with only very general conceptions of ethics between generations. It has been left to contemporary thinkers to fill in the details. One might wonder why considerations of intergenerational morality are much better developed in our time than they were in the past. I speculate that it has to do with the present issue of abortion, particularly in the United States, and with a wide range of contemporary environmental (natural resource depletion; endangered species; air, earth, and water pollution) and technology (particularly nuclear energy and genetic engineering) issues.

In modern moral philosophy and ethics, John Rawls (1971) is the leading advocate for including future generations in the domain of justice. His is a broadly based domain of claims. Following social contract theory, Rawls develops a principle of justice as fairness, in which "each person is to have an equal right to the most extensive basic liberty compatible with a similar liberty for all" (p. 250), and a difference principle, in which "social and economic inequalities, for example inequalities of wealth and authority, are just only if they result in compensating benefits for everyone, and in particular for the less advantaged members of society" (pp. 15–16). Choices in Rawlsian justice as fairness are made behind a veil of ignorance from which one does not know one's circumstances and cannot, therefore, make self-advantaging preferences. This part of Rawlsian justice as fairness has been the dominant subject in philosophy and ethics for the past 20 years. Rawls' concept of intergenerational equity is less well known and has seldom received consideration in the ethics literature.

When the above concepts are applied to the problem of justice between generations, Rawls holds that once the difference principle is accepted

> The appropriate expectation in applying the difference principle is that of the long-term prospects of the least favored extending over future generations. Each generation must not only preserve the gains of culture and civilization, and maintain intact those just institutions that have been established, but it must also put aside in each period of time a suitable amount of real capital accumulation (Rawls, 1971, p. 285).

This is the "just savings principle," a capital accumulation in one generation for the next, and so forth.

The criteria for justice between generations, following Rawls, are those that would be chosen from behind the veil of ignorance and in the original position. The parties do not know to which generation they belong, whether they are relatively wealthy or poor, whether their generation is wealthy or poor, agricultural or industrialized (Rawls, 1971, p. 278). Behind this veil of ignorance, people would (should) chose the principle of justice as fairness and the difference principle to guide their moral and ethical judgments both in temporal and intergenerational circumstances. Using Rawls words,

> We can now see that persons in different generations have duties and obligations to one another just as contemporaries do. The present generation cannot do as it pleases but is bound by the principles that would be chosen in the original position to define justice between persons at different moments in time. In addition, men have a natural duty to uphold and to further just institutions and for this the improvement of civilization up to a certain level is required. The derivation of these duties and obligations may seem at first a somewhat farfetched application of the contract doctrine. Nevertheless these requirements would be acknowledged in the original position, and so the conception of justice as fairness covers these matters without any change in its basic idea (Rawls, 1971, p. 293).

Rawls presents the most consistent and nuanced claim for an ethic of intergenerational fairness, although it is abstract and difficult to apply.[45]

Many other contemporary theorists regard future generations as an appropriate domain for issues of equity, justice, and fairness, but they usually do so from a less demanding contractarian perspective than Rawls does. There is, for example, the argument that future generations are members of *our* moral community (Golding, 1981). As members of the extended moral community, we have obligations at the least to do no damage to the potential interests of future generations. We can do this better in the near term because our obligations are clearer. We are, according to Golding, probably too ignorant to plan effectively for remote future generations. Callahan (1981) is more convinced of our obligations. He sets out four principles that catalog our obligations to future generations: (1) We should do nothing to jeopardize their very existence; (2) We should do nothing to jeopardize their fundamental rights to a life of human dignity; (3) We should do this in such a way as to minimize jeopardy to the present generation; and (4) We should use our moral commitment to our own children as the guide for intergenerational fairness. A host of other modern thinkers (Jonas, 1981; Goodpaster, 1979; Green, 1981; Hartshorne, 1981; Kavka, 1981; Pletcher, 1981; Dalattre, 1972; Baier, 1981; McKerlie, 1989; Partridge, 1981), often for different reasons, agree that future generations are an appropriate domain for issues of morality such as equity. Their language is often different. Some speak of possible future persons (Baier, 1981), some speak of potential persons (Warren, 1981), some speak of being and nonbeing (Hardin, 1980). All agree that there is a legitimate domain of morality between present and future generations.

Perhaps the most interesting arguments for intergenerational models of ethics are less philosophical and more empirical. We have strong evidence of a longstanding domain of allocation to future generations. Humans commonly display a concern for the future that is part of their moral psychology (Partridge, 1981). In this moral psychology, humans collectively establish moral institutions (governments, schools, foundations) and trusts (local, state, and national parks; animal and bird reserves; soil conservation programs; air, water, and land pollution controls) which serve as evidence of an instinct toward future generations. There are, Ernest Partridge argues, as many examples of the expression of positive moral instincts toward future generations on the part of present persons as there are examples of jeopardizing institutions or conditions for future generations. Thomas Sieger Derr makes a similar point in claiming that people have a kind of "moral instinct" which seems to tell them to take some responsibility for future generations (Derr, 1981). "We seem to be intuitively aware of the wrong in imposing the bad consequences of our acts on others without their acquiescence" (p. 40).

James Q. Wilson (1993) reviews the research literature on child development and identifies the emergence of the moral sense in children. Two fundamental instincts in this moral sense are sympathy, a kind of natural caring sociability; and fairness, a concern for just treatment which transcends the maximization of individual interests. These natural characteristics are passed from generation to generation. Wilson points to recent Russian history for evidence:

> After 75 years of cruel tyranny during which every effort was made to destroy civil society to create the New Soviet Man, we learn that people kept civil society alive, if not well. The elemental building blocks of that society were not isolated individuals easily trained to embrace any doctrine or adopt any habit; they were families, friends and intimate groupings in which sentiments of sympathy, reciprocity, and fairness survived and struggled to shape behavior (Wilson, 1993, p. 9).

The irony is, of course, that state imposed temporal equality is part of the logic of communism.

The stronger empirical case is found in the simple logic of decision (or action) theory. Charles Hartshorne points out that "it takes time for decisions to have their effect (therefore) all obligations in principle concern the future. Indeed the entire rational significance of the present is in its contribution to the future good" (Hartshorne, 1981, p. 103). If a decision, however instinctive or calculated, is the predicate of an action, then the processes of decisions and actions are always inclined toward the future. The question is the extent of the future—the next minute? the next day?

year? generation? or remote generations of possible people? Decision processes, by definition, cannot affect the past. We know that the cycle of decisions and actions is partly a process of informed predictions; as the future gets more distant our predictions are less well informed and our decisions and actions are less reliable. In addition, we are not only more confident in the short-term, we are more subject to pressure to serve short-term interests (Simon, 1960; Harmon and Mayer, 1986; Harmon 1989).

The contemporary challenge of intergenerational fairness appears to have taken most modern social scientists and policy analysts by surprise. On one hand contemporary social science research and policy analysis have been heavily influenced by the teleological philosophy of utilitarianism particularly associated with John Stuart Mill and Jeremy Bentham. In this tradition, decisions and actions are judged by their temporal consequences depending on the results to be maximized—security, happiness, pleasure, dignity. Presumably results can be judged on the basis of the utility of the individual, the family, the group, the neighborhood, the political jurisdiction, the nation-state or even the world. In fact much of the logic of the utilitarian perspective is individual, manifest these days by concepts such as empowerment and choice in politics, and techniques such as mathematical modeling in analysis. This work has been determinedly temporal. As yet the tools and logic of utilitarian analysis have not been effectively applied to issues of intergenerational equity or fairness.

On the other hand, most contemporary scholarship and philosophy associated with issues of generational fairness tends to be deontological, based on fundamental principles of right or wrong. Much of this work is normative and exhortative. Only now are we beginning to see a fusion of these two approaches. Both Lawrence J. Kotikoff's *Intergenerational Accounting* (1991) and Henry Aaron, Barry Bosworth and Gary T. Burtless' *Can America Afford to Grow Old?* (1989) are good examples of the wedding of deontological norms and utilitarian tools. Derek Parfit in *Reasons and Persons* (1984) builds an ethic based entirely on reason (nonreligious with no absolute moral principles) in which it is argued that in our concern for other people, including future generations, we often make mistakes based on false beliefs, particularly beliefs that individual acts can be calculated as to their particular effects. We ignore what we do together that together "impose great harm on ourselves or others. Some examples are pollution, congestion, depletion, inflation, unemployment, recession, overpopulation" (Parfit, 1984, p. 444). To remedy this, he suggests a more impersonal ethic in which we temper our concern for our own children with a broader commitment to all children. Parfit finds a Unified Theory that reduces the disagreement between common-sense morality (primarily moral idealism or the deontological perspective) and consequentialism (primarily utilitarian and teleological).

I return to the questions with which I began this section. Is there evidence of a domain requiring future allocations on the part of temporal public officials toward future persons? The answer is yes. Strong evidence exists, however, particularly in environmental and nutritional policy, of the failure to regard future generations as an appropriate domain. Are there reasonable or justifiable domains of future intergenerational claims? The answer again is yes. These claims trace to the earliest statements of morality and ethics. Claims for the interests of future generations on the part of modern thinkers are especially well developed.

The Compound Theory of Social Equity

To build a model for the treatment of issues of intergenerational equity, I use the concepts and theories of social equity, particularly in the fields of public administration and public policy. Issues of social equity are pervasive in every policy domain. A specific public policy may be in a general sense good but is seldom good or bad for everyone.

Thus far the words "equity" and "social equity" have been used without definition. Equity as used here includes conceptual and philosophical treatments of fairness (Hochschild, 1981), justice (Rawls, 1971), and equality (Rae, 1981). Fairness, following the work of Jennifer L. Hochschild (1981), is taken here to mean a more equal distribution of opportunities, costs, and benefits in social and political domains. In these domains, as compared with the economic domain, Hochschild found that Americans define equity as fairness, and generally believe that our social and political domains are too often unfair (Page, 1983; Wilson, W.J., 1987). Justice is taken here to mean distributive justice. Following Michael Walzer, (1983) I accept a pluralist conception of justice in which there are many spheres of justice and several acceptable criteria for determining what is just. Equality is not one thing but many things; equalities (Rae, 1981). These treatments of fairness, justice, and equality have been brought together in the compound theory of social equity (Frederickson, 1990; Rae, 1981) that will be used here. In the compound theory of social equity, one finds the nuanced concept of equalities rather than simpler forms or definitions of equality. In the compound theory of social equity fairness, justice, and equality are used interchangeably. There are three primary forms of equality.

Simple Individual Equalities

In simple individual equalities, there is one class of equals, for example, all who qualify to vote, and one class of equality among them, for example, each person has one vote. The rhetoric of equality often calls for simple individual equalities—that people should be treated equally. In fact, there are very few examples of the actual application of simple individual equalities in business practices or in public policy making.

Segmented Equality

Simple individual equalities are seldom practiced because people are not the same. The application of equity, fairness, or justice in everyday life is almost always in terms of segmented equality. This is the way complex social systems with divisions of labor and hierarchies accommodate human differences. Segmented equality begins with the definition of segments—all groups that are for whatever reason, treated equally. For example, farmers have a different form of taxation than do business owners, and both differ from wage earners. In segmented equality, one assumes that equality exists within the category (e.g., farmers) and that inequality exists between categories.

Segmented equality is, in fact, systematic or structured inequality, a condition in which persons are equally unequal. Segmented equality is the means by which a culture manages to accommodate individual differences while achieving a level of equality between similar individuals in a group or segment.

Block Equalities

Block equalities, on the other hand, call for equality between groups or subclasses. Blocks often occur naturally—men and women, old and young—whereas segments are usually socially constructed. In block equality there is inequality within the block, for instance between all women, and the demand for equality with another block, for instance men. Programs of affirmative action, veterans preferences, equal employment opportunity, comparable worth, and contract-setasides for minority businesses are examples of public policy applications of block equalities logic.

All forms of intergenerational equality are primarily block equalities.

Domains of Equality

What is to be judged appropriate for equal distribution? The domain of equality marks off the goods, services, costs, or benefits that are distributed. There are domains of allocation—that which is distributed to accomplish some form of equality—and domains of claims—ordinarily blocks claiming inequality with other blocks or individuals in segments claiming inequality with others in the segment. Domains can be defined broadly or narrowly. Domains of equality constantly shift, aggregate, and desegregate. It is often the case that the public policy process is the arena for those seeking equality so as to correct inequalities which result from the operation of the market or from previous governmental policies.

Equality, as described here, is much more than political rhetoric or sloganeering. Equality changes from one thing to many things—equalities (Rae, 1981). The compound theory of social equity provides both the concepts and vocabulary for the consideration of issues of equality, fairness, and justice. In applied form, significant evidence exists that both elected and appointed public officials (not to mention judicial officials) practice both segmented and block forms of social equity in virtually every field of public policy (Lineberry, 1977; Mladenka, 1978, 1981; Frederickson, 1980, 1990). Public policy is also replete with examples of intergenerational social equity.

Earlier, future generations, as blocks, were determined to be an appropriate domain of claims, although the claims are made by temporal generations on behalf of future generations. Future generations were also determined to be an appropriate domain of temporal allocation of resources.

With this grounding, we return to the question of whether public officials correctly can be said to have responsibilities to future generations for social equity.

Applications of the Compound Theory of Social Equity Toward Future Generations

When applied to the question of intergenerational equity, it was stated above that block equalities are the most logical approach to the treatment of generations. Consider the following three blocks and their definitions:

Assume that each block is generally discreet and that our primary concern is with fairness or equity between the blocks rather than with issues of fairness or equity within the blocks.

Intergenerational Social Equity

The logic of intergenerational social equity based on blocks is illustrated in Figure 25.1. The horizontal axis depicts benefits while the vertical axis depicts costs. Capital bonding for schools is the illustration. Temporal generations both benefit and pay. Near-term generations both benefit and pay, although the benefits to near-term future generations probably exceed the costs. If the capital investment is wise, future generations will continue to benefit, being obligated for only the costs of maintenance. There are many excellent examples of both public policy and public administration implementation that conform to the logic of intergenerational social equity as illustrated in Figure 25.1. Public research and development investments, particularly in health care fit this model. Virtually all public works invest-

		Benefits		
		Temporal Generations	Near-Term Future Generations	Future Generations
Costs	Temporal Generations	strong	moderate	moderate
	Near-Term Future Generations	moderate	moderate	
	Future Generations			

FIGURE 25.1   Intergenerational Social Equity: Capital Bonding for Schools

ments fit this model. Environmental protection, historic preservation, and endangered species protection also fit this model. Public education, both K–12 and higher education, fit the model, particularly if one accepts the Rawlsian concept of leaving "just institutions" in place for future generations. One could argue that democratic constitutions, democratic institutions such as legislatures and laws, and judicial institutions are just institutions that were left to us by our founders and that we pass on to future generations. One could also argue national defense as a form of commitment to the maintenance of just institutions. All of these conform to the Rawlsian "just savings principle" that define justice and equity between generations.

The single most interesting thing about the concept of intergenerational social equity is that it is so routinely and commonly practiced in policy making and public administration. The evidence appears to support the philosophical arguments of Rawls and others that just institutions constitute a form of social equity between generations and that there is a general form of the just savings principle at work. Many of the routine decisions of policy makers and the implementation of public administrators appear to support the existence of a vertical moral community in which present generations act favorably on behalf of both near-term and long-term future generations.

If there are extensive examples of block equalities between generations, what about the problems of the segmentation of policy costs and benefits in both present and future generations? Temporal equality can be segmented, as in the case of a police department deploying a disproportionate share of its resources to high crime locations at high crime times so as to attempt to make persons living in high crime areas more equal to those living in safe areas. Or temporal equity can be block as in the case of veterans preference for government jobs or affirmative action. Intergenerational equality may also be segmented or block in present generations as well as in future generations. Consider, for example, environmental protection as a domain of equity. The people of present generations may invest in environmental protection measures such as eliminating land fills or controlling the dumpling of toxic waste. Extensive segmentation may exist among those in present generations as to who pays for these policies. This will depend on tax structures, regulatory practices and/or incentives for business. The distribution of costs will be uneven—segmented. Some will pay more than others for environmental protection. The benefits to future generations may also be uneven as in the case of a broadly based future environmental protection marred by particular locations, often associated with poverty, that cannot, at least in the short run, be cleaned up.

The longest standing form of intergenerational equity in public administration is associated with the logic of capital budgeting. At the state and local levels of government, it is simply assumed that the costs of buildings, roads, and other forms of capital should be borne both by the present and by near-term (two or perhaps three generations) future generations. This is based on the logic that the benefits of capital investments will be enjoyed by approximately the same temporal generations. At the national level, large-scale debt was initially incurred to pull the country out of the Great Depression and to fight World War II, both policy decisions that presumed that the benefits of such activities would be beneficial to near-term future generations as well as temporal generations.

The logic of research and development investments, particularly as they are associated with the National Science Foundation, the National Aeronautics and Space Administration, the National Institutes of Health, and the Departments of Energy and Defense, all assume temporal investments to benefit future generations. They also assume temporal investment to benefit temporal generations often in a very segmented and uneven pork barrel.

Certainly R & D is the key to several intergenerational equity issues. Consider the case of oil, a nonrenewable resource. If it is used up by some future generation, as it is likely to be, have subsequent generations been deprived of their rights to oil? How many generations into the future are allowed to have rights to oil? "Obviously if we push the generations into the unlimited future and divide the oil deposits by the number of people, we each end up with the right to a gallon or a quart or a teaspoon or a thimble full" (DeGeorge, 1979, p. 161). We choose not to do that and assume, on the one hand, that we are entitled to use oil reserves if, on the other hand, we invest in the research and development required to find an affordable substitute by the time oil reserves are depleted. Still, it is clear that present generations are benefitting at a possible cost to future generations and that the investment in energy R & D probably does not match the temporal benefits of oil depletion.

Intergenerational Social Inequity

Figure 25.2 illustrates future generation paying for the benefits enjoyed by temporal generations. The best examples have to do with natural resources depletion and environmental degradation. Temporal generations benefit greatly by using timber, ground water, hydro-electric capacity, oil, and minerals while leaving near-term future generations and long-term future generations to pay the bills. The same can be said for environmental degradation. It is certainly the case that in the long run temporal research and development investments will (may) compensate for the imbalance between generational costs and benefits having to do with resource depletion and environmental degradation. But no amount of R & D can recreate species that have been destroyed.

Although it is speculative, it appears that an intense preoccupation with temporal equality in the absence of a market economy, such as occurred in the industrialized Warsaw Pact nations between the 1930s and the 1980s, results in a particularly pronounced form of intergenerational social inequity in the form of environmental degradation.

Backloaded
Intergenerational Equity

Figure 25.3 illustrates backloaded intergenerational social equity. The best example of backloaded intergenerational social equity is seen in the operations of the American Social Security system. While there were investments in the Social Security system by retired persons receiving benefits, those investments, on average are much less than benefits received. Therefore temporal working generations pay disproportionately for the retirement benefits of temporal retired generations. This is, of course, on the promise that when temporal generations retire they too will be supported by their children who are working.

		Benefits		
		Temporal Generations	Near-Term Future Generations	Future Generations
	Temporal Generations			
Costs	Near-Term Future Generations	moderate		
	Future Generations	moderate	moderate	

FIGURE 25.2   Intergenerational Social Inequity: Natural Resource Depletion

The most interesting feature of Social Security as an illustration of back-loaded intergenerational social equity is the interaction of the competing concepts of segmented versus block equality. Retired persons receiving Social Security are regarded as a block, all eligible for benefits. Although there is some segmentation based on contributions and other factors, benefit recipients are thought of as a block. The current entitlement debate turns on the question of whether better-off benefit recipients, say those with total retirement incomes of over $50,000.00, should be a segment that receives lower benefits than the low-income retired.

This is a most interesting twist on the question of intergenerational equity. In ordinary intergenerational social equity temporal generations must act on behalf of future generations, ordinarily as a block, because they cannot speak for themselves. In backloaded intergenerational social equity, the most senior persons among temporal generations turn out to be powerful voices in their own behalf. The irony in the debate over Social Security entitlements is that from the beginning of the system, better-off working persons paid proportionately less to support *their* retired generation(s) than did the less-well-off of their working generation (Aaron, Bosworth, and Burtless, 1989; Kennedy, 1993; Kotikoff, 1991).

	Benefits		
	Temporal Generations	Near-Term Future Generations	Future Generations
Temporal Generations	moderate		
Near-Term Future Generations	strong		
Future Generations			

(left axis label: **Costs**)

FIGURE 25.3   Backloaded Intergenerational Social Equity: Social Security

Conclusion

Should the moral and ethical responsibility of public officials be extended to future generations, to potential or possible persons, to the remote? The answer is a cautious yes. The reasons are of two types, moral and applied or practical.

In both philosophy and in the practical affairs of people, there is a pervasive concern for fairness, justice, and equity. No moral community can exist without some agreed upon arrangements for fairness, justice, or equity. These arrangements, most often manifest in government, may appear to be mostly temporal and horizontal. In fact, from the earliest practices of government, the arrangements that sustained the moral order were also intergenerational and vertical. If, in the moral order and the arrangements that sustain it, some level of fairness and equity is insisted upon, that insistence, particularly in the long run, is most probably as vertical as it is horizontal. Many examples of temporal policy makers and public administrators acting out obligations toward future generations have been illustrated here.

The instincts and intuitions of the citizens of the Greek city-state toward their fellow citizens *and* toward their posterity are probably the moral norm. That we often fall short of that moral norm, both temporally and in our attitude toward future generations, does not invalidate the norm. Not does it indicate that there have not been transcendent moments of temporal fairness and equity as well as ringing examples of intergenerational social inequity. Consider the great American public school system as a remarkable institution designed to foster learning and to facilitate temporal social justice and pass the culture from generation to generation. Consider the institution of slavery as a huge lapse in morality and the abolition of slavery as a courageous attempt to redress that evil. Consider as well contemporary programs for sustainable development and ecological balance as attempts to ensure for future generations the resources of the earth. Consider also the extreme northern-southern hemisphere inequities in temporal affairs (Chase-Dunn, 1989; Pryer, 1975; Strange, 1988). The moral community is, then, both present and future, or as Baier puts it, a "cross-generational moral community" (1981, p. 178).

This brings us to the point of seeking overarching moral or ethical principles to inform our public responsibilities to future generations. How shall we represent the future in the present? How can we tap the human instincts toward a moral community extended through time?

Following the logic of the compound theory of social equity, public officials should seek to adopt and implement policies which support intergenerational social equity, as illustrated in the cost-benefit matrix in Figure 25.1. Short of that, they should adopt policies that are likely to have a neutral effect on future generations. They should not adopt policies that support intergenerational social inequity as illustrated in the cost-benefit matrix in Figure 25.2.

We recognize that we are ignorant of the distant future and we can only imagine a little ahead. Still, we must act on what we know even at the risk of mistakes. Public policy is a world of creative problem solving. In the policy process experts and specialists often define the problems and set the agendas. If problems are *defined* as both temporal and intergenerational, then creativity will have to find policies which serve, at least to some extent, both ends. We are more knowledgeable now of the likely effects of toxic waste, pesticide overuse, overgrazing, strip mining, ground water depletion, and a host of other ecological problems. The informed and nonexaggerated articulation of the likely effects of these problems on future generations can have a powerful influence on policy.

Many intergenerational ecological problems are only marginally related to the present boundaries of countries. The World Commission on Environment and Development (1987), building on country-based studies and programs, is working toward some regional programs and solutions particularly in sustainable development. Garrett Hardin (1980) and others have described the problem of population growth and the limited carrying capacity of the earth. Large scale regional programs of education and access to birth control technology are imperative. Technology, often the source of environmental problems, is also the source of many solutions. We know about miracle rice and the reduction of famine in Asia and the Indian subcontinent. We know about antibiotics. Many of our longer range problems, such as population control, may be profoundly improved upon by technology. We now more clearly understand the limits of resources and the unlikely capacity of the earth in the long run to sustain a high- consumption definition of quality of life. Lasch (1990) and others suggest a return to definitions of well-being, moral worth, and happiness that are not linked to an acquisitive conception of success. The global village enables public officials to think of their jurisdictions and other jurisdictions as laboratories for experimenting with and testing creative solutions to temporal and intergenerational social equity challenges. Once a solution is found in one setting it may be suited to another similar setting in a diffusion of innovation.

We know these things and many others. As public officials we hold some responsibility for social equity between generations; we must act as best we can based on what we know. What are the appropriate tools? One argument is that most distributional issues that affect future generations are the result of private market transactions. In these transactions, the interests of future generations are steeply discounted (Arrow, 1983). The lack of intergenerational social equity is an example of private market failure. Government and public policy, it is argued, must intervene in the private market to regulate in favor of future generations. The problem is governmental attempts to either regulate the market or act directly in the interests of future generations have sometimes resulted in nonmarket failures such as Defense Department generated nuclear waste (Hardin, 1980). Still, we act based on what we know, using, albeit in a clumsy way, the market and nonmarket tools at hand. Whatever the weaknesses of market and nonmarket approaches, it is a considerable improvement in the prospects of future generations when their interests are explicitly considered an obligation on the part of public officials.

References

Aaron, Henry J., Barry Bosworth, and Gary T. Burtless, 1989. *Can America Afford to Grow Old?* Washington, DC: Brookings Institution.

Aristotle, *Politics,* Heinman, ed., 1967. London: Loeb Classical Library, p. 1252 a 30.

Arrow, Kenneth, 1983. *Social Choice and Justice.* Cambridge, MA: Belknap.

Baier, Annette, 1981. "The Rights of Past and Future Persons." In Ernest Partridge, ed., *Responsibility to Future Generations.* Buffalo, NY: Prometheus Books, pp. 171–83.

Barry, Brian, 1978. "Circumstances of Justice and Future Generations." In R. I. Sikora and Brian Barry, eds., *Obligations to Future Generations.* Philadelphia: Temple University Press, pp. 204–48.

Callahan, Daniel, 1981. "What Obligations Do We Have to Future Generations." In Ernest Partridge, ed., *Responsibility to Future Generations.* Buffalo, NY: Prometheus Books, pp. 73–88.

Chase-Dunn, Christopher K., 1989. *Global Formation: Structures of the World Economy.* Cambridge, MA: Basil Blackwell.

Dalattre, Edwin, 1972. "Rights, Responsibilities, and Future Persons." *Ethics,* vol. 82 (April), pp. 254–258.

DeGeorge, Richard T., 1979. "The Environment, Rights, and Future Generations." In Kenneth E. Goodpaster and Kenneth M. Sayer, eds., *Ethics and Problems in the 21st Century.* Notre Dame, IN: University of Notre Dame Press.

Derr, Thomas Sieger, 1981. "The Obligation to the Future." In Ernest Partridge, ed., *Responsibility to Future Generations.* Buffalo, NY: Prometheus Books, pp. 37–44.

Frederickson, H. George, 1980. *The New Public Administration.* University, AL: University of Alabama Press.

_____, 1990. "Public Administration and Social Equity." *Public Administration Review,* vol. 50, no. 2, (March-April) pp. 228–37.

Golding, Martin P., 1981. "Obligations to Future Generations." In Ernest Partridge, ed., *Responsibility to Future Generations.* Buffalo, NY: Prometheus Books, pp. 61–72.

Goodsell, Charles T., 1983. *The Case for Bureaucracy: A Public Administration Polemic.* Chatham, NJ: Chatham House.

Goodpaster, Kenneth E., 1979. "Ethics and the Future." In Kenneth E. Goodpaster and Kenneth M. Sayer, eds., *Ethics and Problems in the 21st Century.* Notre Dame, IN: University of Notre Dame Press, pp. 277–301.

Green, Ronald M., 1981. "Intergenerational Distributive Justice and Environmental Responsibility." In Ernest Partridge, ed., *Responsibility to Future Generations.* Buffalo, NY: Prometheus Books, pp. 91–102.

Hardin, Garrett, 1980. *Promethean Ethics.* Seattle: University of Washington Press.

Harmon, Michael M., 1989. "'Decision' and 'Action' as Contrasting Perspectives in Organization Theory." *Public Administration Review,* vol. 49, no. 2, pp. 144–149.

Harmon, Michael M., and Richard T. Mayer, 1986. *Organization Theory for Public Administration.* Boston: Little, Brown and Company.

Hartmann, Nicolai, 1981. "Love of the Remote." In Ernest Partridge, ed., *Responsibility to Future Generations.* Buffalo, NY: Prometheus Books, pp. 305–308.

Hartshorne, Charles, 1981. "The Ethics of Contributionism." In Ernest Partridge, ed., *Responsibility to Future Generations.* Buffalo, NY: Prometheus Books, pp. 103–108.

Hochschild, Jennifer L., 1981. *What's Fair? American Beliefs About Distributive Justice.* Cambridge, MA: Harvard University Press.

Hume, David, 1968. *Treatise on Human Nature,* Shelby Bigge, ed. New York: Oxford University Press.

Jonas, Hans, 1981. "Technology and Responsibility: The Ethics of an Endangered Future." In Ernest Partridge, ed., *Responsibility to Future Generations.* Buffalo, NY: Prometheus Books, pp. 23–36.

Kavka, Gregory, 1981. "The Futurity Problem." In Ernest Partridge, ed., *Responsibility to Future Generations.* Buffalo, NY: Prometheus Books, pp. 109–122.

Kennedy, Paul M., 1993. *Preparing for the Twenty-First Century.* New York: Random House.

Kotlikoff, Laurence J., 1991. *Intergenerational Accounting.* New York: Free Press.

Lasch, Christopher, 1990. *The True and Only Heaven: Progress and Its Critics.* New York: W. W. Norton.

Lineberry, Robert L., 1977. *Equality and Urban Policy: The Distribution of Urban Public Services.* Beverly Hills, CA: Sage Publications.

Locke, John, 1965. *Two Treatises of Government,* Peter Laslett, ed., Second Treatise. New York: New American Library, sect. 4. pp. 309, 328–333.

McKerlie, Dennis, 1989. "Equality and Time." *Ethics* vol. 99 (April), no. 3, 475–491.

Mladenka, Kenneth R., 1978. "Organizational Rules, Service Equality, and Distributional Decisions in Urban Politics," *Social Science Quarterly,* vol. 59 (June), pp. 192–201.

———, 1981. "Responsive Performance by Public Officials," In Charles T. Goodsell, ed., *The Public Encounter: When States and Citizens Meet.* Bloomington: Indiana University Press

Neustadt, Richard E., and E. R. May, 1986. *Thinking in Time: The Uses of History for Decisionmakers.* New York: Free Press.

Page, Benjamin, 1983. *Who Gets What from Government.* Berkeley: University of California Press.

Parfit, Derek, 1984. *Reason and Persons.* Oxford, England: Claendon Press.

Partridge, Ernest, 1981. "Who Cares About The Future." In Ernest Partridge, ed., *Responsibility to Future Generations.* Buffalo, NY: Prometheus Books, pp. 203–220.

Pletcher, Galen R., 1981. "The Rights of Future Generations." In Ernest Partridge, ed., *Responsibility to Future Generations.* Buffalo, NY: Prometheus Books, pp. 167–170.

Peyer, Cheryl, 1975. *The Debt Trap: The IMF and the Third World.* New York: Monthly Review Press.

Rae, Douglas, and Associates, 1981. *Equalities.* Cambridge, MA: Harvard University Press.

Rawls, John, 1971. *A Theory of Justice.* Cambridge, MA: Harvard University Press.

Rohr, John, 1986. *To Run a Constitution: The Legitimacy of the Administrative State.* Lawrence, KS: University Press of Kansas.

Schlesinger, Arthur M., 1986. *The Cycles of American History.* Boston: Houghton Mifflin.

Simon, Herbert A., 1960. *The New Science of Management Decision.* New York: Harper and Row.

Smith, T. Alexander, 1988. *Time and Public Policy.* Knoxville: University of Tennessee Press.

Strange, Susan, 1988. *States and Markets*. London: Pinter.

Strauss, William, and Neil Howe, 1991. *Generations: The History of America's Future, 1584–2069*. New York: William Morrow.

Thompson, Victor A., 1975. *Without Sympathy or Enthusiasm*. University, AL: University of Alabama Press.

Tuchman, Barbara W., 1984. *The March of Folly: From Troy to Vietnam*. New York: Ballantine Books.

Waldo, Dwight, 1948. *The Administrative State*. New York: Ronald Press.

_____, 1980. *The Enterprise of Public Administration*. Novato, CA: Chandler and Sharp.

_____, 1990. "A Theory of Public Administration Means in Our Time a Theory of Politics Also." In Naomi B. Lynn and Aaron Wildavsky, eds., *Public Administration: The State of the Discipline*. Chatham, NJ: Chatham House, pp. 73–96.

Walzer, Michael, 1983. *Spheres of Justice: A Defense of Pluralism and Equality*. New York: Basic Books.

Warren, Mary Ann, 1981. "Do Potential Persons Have Rights?" In Ernest Partridge, ed., *Responsibility to Future Generations*. Buffalo, NY: Prometheus Books, pp. 261–274.

Whitehead, Barbara Dafoe, 1993. "Dan Quayle Was Right." *Atlantic Monthly*, vol. 271, no. 4, pp. 47–84.

Wilson, James Q., 1993. "The Moral Sense." *American Political Science Review*, vol. 83, no. 1, pp. 1–10.

Wilson, William Julius, 1987. *The Truly Disadvantaged: The Inner City, the Underclass, and Public Policy*. Chicago: University of Chicago Press.

World Commission on Environment and Development, 1987. *Our Common Future*. New York: Oxford University Press.

Notes

1. It is important, however, to remember that temporal equality was not practiced in the Greek city-state. Women were not citizens; the Greeks kept slaves.

2. Note especially the recent organization of an interest group called Lead . . . or Leave. Put together by persons presently in the 20s, Lead . . . or Leave states that "the deficit is our Vietnam." Jon Loway, one of the founders, states: "The nation went on a vast spending spree that didn't produce anything but bills. Now we not only have a financial deficit, but a social deficit, an environmental deficit, an infrastructure deficit. We're selling out the American dream. Whether you're a liberal and want a new War on Poverty, or you're a conservative and want a capital gains tax cut, you can't do any of it." *New York Times*, Section IV, p. 3, col. 1 (March 14, 1993).

3. The phrase "public officials" is taken here to mean elected, politically appointed and merit-based civil servants. The politics-administration dichotomy is rejected (Waldo, 1948, 1980, 1990) and the practices of public administration are understood to legitimately include policy preferences, and ethical or value preferences (Goodsell, 1983). If neutrality or neutral competencies is rejected (Frederickson, 1980), then it is appropriate to describe the policy and value preferences of public administrators (Rohr, 1986). It is assumed that elected and politically ap-

pointed public officials are pursuing policy and value preferences. For a contrary view in which it is claimed that a nonneutral public administration will "steal the popular sovereignty," see Victor Thompson (1975).

4. Brian Barry (1978) is a sharp critic of Rawls on matters of intergenerational justice. He nevertheless supports concepts of intergenerational justice along the lines of "the overall range of opportunities open to successor generations should not be narrowed." It is asymmetric to attempt to make "successor generations better off, which is nice thing to do but is not required by justice, and not making them worse off, which *is* required by justice" (pp. 243–244).

5. While present decisions cannot affect the past, they can be ignorant of the past and therefore badly informed. See especially Barbara W. Tuchman (1984).

Section II.C

PAY FOR PERFORMANCE

26

MERIT PAY, PERFORMANCE TARGETING, AND PRODUCTIVITY

Arie Halachmi
Marc Holzer

Pay-for-performance has emerged as a strategy for responding to demands for increased productivity and management accountability. Merit pay is one weapon in that arsenal, which also includes bonuses, commissions, Scanlontype plans and a variety of formulas for sharing profits and savings.

In the private sector, a survey by the Conference Board reveals that ninety-two percent of the manufacturing companies in the United States have annual incentive plans for their managers (Tharp, 1986). Similarly, in the Canadian survey (*Compensation Planning Outlook 1984),* ninety-one percent of the respondents answered affirmatively when asked: "do you link pay or increases to performance?" (Luce, 1983:20). These findings suggest that private sector managers assume that "pay for performance" is a productive strategy.

In the public sector, the attractiveness of pay-for-performance has to do with similar concerns about accountability and productivity (Murlis and Wright, 1985). Furthermore, the political symbolism of public sector incentive plans makes them especially attractive. To those observers who are

1987. Merit pay, performance targeting, and productivity. Halachmi, Arie, and Marc Holzer. **Review of Public Personnel Administration** 7 (Spring): 80–91.

critical of governments for not being "business like," merit pay conveys a message: employees are under control, there is an evaluation process, and the process is used to reward productive employees and to punish those who are not productive. Despite the optimism in pay-for-performance efforts in the public sector, according to the reports of the Comptroller General, merit pay plans for federal employees enjoy only qualified successes (Comptroller General, 1981A; Comptroller General, 1981B). According to Silverman (1983: 294), "it put a previously stable employee compensation system in shambles." Luce (1983: 19) underscores that conclusion: "there is an implicit assumption that paying for performance will improve productivity and foster excellence. There is, however, considerable reason to doubt that productivity will be significantly enhanced by paying for performance." These findings are in line with other independent studies that doubt the beneficial value or the motivational justifications of merit pay plans. Speaking to the case of the public sector, Pearce and Perry (1983: 321), for example, conclude "that a diverse sample of federal managers do not appear to be more highly motivated under merit pay than under the previous time in grade compensation policies." In the same vein, the Urban Institute reports that "in three cities using monetary incentives, the evidence is strong that there were no significant improvements in productivity due to the incentives" (Hatry *et al.*, 1981:29). A similar finding is reported in a study on the influence of merit pay plans on teachers' performance (Cohen and Murnane, 1985).

Such critiques suggest that a better understanding of the limits of merit pay can help organizations avoid its shortfalls. Thus, our objectives in this article are to raise questions and issues that should be considered before making the commitment to install a merit pay system. These factors include (a) implications of expectancy theory, (b) the critical dependency of merit pay on performance appraisal, (c) problems which may cripple the opportunities for merit pay, and (d) the motivational value of performance targeting—a concept that is related to the concept of merit pay yet different from it.

The thesis of this article is, first, that most merit pay plans have limited ability to motivate employees and to enhance productivity. A second thesis is that efforts to improve productivity must include a deliberate effort to pay more attention to the motivational needs of the individual employee while avoiding the creation of de-motivators. The article cautions managers to be aware of the tendency to rely solely on the expectancy theory of motivation in designing programs for productivity enhancement. It suggests that other theories of motivation, such as Adams' equity theory and McLelland's need theory, may provide administrators with other important clues for developing such programs.

Expectancy Theory and Merit Pay

Underlying the premise that merit pay is a motivational technique is an assumption that motivation, and therefore productivity, can be improved by the use of monetary incentives (Piamonte, 1979; Mode, 1979). As Belcher (1980: 14) concludes:

> paying employees on the basis of their performance, according to the tenets of compensation administration, is the way to get performance motivation in organizations. Not only does this approach make sense intuitively, it has a solid theoretical base. Expectancy theory (in simple terms) postulates that if people want more pay and believe that working harder will result in their getting more pay, they will work harder and perform better in order to get more pay.

Similarly, Gabris and Mitchell (1986: 312) argue: "the logic that pay should be linked to performance makes a great deal of sense. Why should highly productive employees maintain high productivity if no reward is in the offing?" This type of thinking, they suggest, "undergirds Victor Vroom's 'expectancy theory'."

The elements of expectancy theory are: effort, performance, result and reward. At the core of the theory there is a basic assumption that an individual's behavior is a product of one's perception of functional linkages. First one's level of effort (over which the individual has control) is linked to the ensuing improvement in the performance level that may not occur without such efforts. Second, improved performance leads to desired rewards or the avoidance of penalties. Hence, the theory suggests that an individual is likely to change his or her behavior as a function of the strength of the desire to receive an award (or to avoid a punishment). His performance is likely to change by varying effort, and such a change would lead to the desired result. Reflecting on this point as it relates to the decision to introduce merit pay to the federal government as part of the Civil Service Reform Act (CSRA), Pearce and Perry (1983: 315–316) explain:

> Federal Merit pay is expected to increase effort and, therefore, performance by changing the probability that performance will lead to an outcome (salary increase) that is assumed to be positively valued by most managers. Therefore, the merit pay initiatives of CSRA are expected to result in higher overall performance since many, if not all, federal managers will see more benefit in striving for high performance under this program than under the previous compensation system.

Belcher's critique of the expectancy theory also underscores the conclusions of independent studies that the contributions of merit pay programs to improved performance and increased motivation or job satisfaction reveal, at best, a mixed picture (Kearney, 1979: 8). According to Belcher (1980: 15), "although studies designed to test expectancy theory explain a significant amount of the variance in employee effort and performance, they leave a large portion of the variance unexplained. Thus, the theory does explain part of what is going on, but is not a complete explanation." This skepticism, in turn, raises questions as to the instrumental value of the expectancy theory underlying merit pay, and therefore the usefulness of merit pay as a tool for improving productivity.

Expectancy theory is based on several assumptions that may not hold in all situations. For our purposes, the first of these questionable assumptions is that of economic rationality. The theory assumes that all individuals behave like "homo economicus," selecting those courses of action that are likely to maximize benefits or minimize pain. According to Pearce and Perry (1983), this assumption helps explain why it is assumed that pay for performance under CSRA is expected to result in better performance. Many individuals, however, do not purse the path of economic rationality all or even most of the time. Nor is all human behavior purposeful. There is little empirical evidence to support the claim that the individual is always mindful of what he or she is doing—that is, that a given behavior represents not only a calculated effort but a conscious choice (March, 1972). David Belcher (1980: 16) reflects on this point:

> Expectancy theory is a cognitive theory—it assumes that a conscious decision-making precedes action. More specifically, it assumes that people think about whether effort is related to performance and whether performance is related to reward before they exert effort. Thus, a legitimate question is whether people at work think about these relationships; if so, how often; and which people are most likely to do so.

Expectancy theory, which is based on external incentives, also suffers from the notion that extrinsic rewards are stronger and more lasting than the intrinsic incentives. Hertzberg's (1959) two factor theory illuminates the need to differentiate, and to place in perspective, the role of those drives that have to do with maintenance, *e.g.*, salary, working conditions, and those that have to do with inner growth. Other research (Deci, 1972) goes further to suggest that emphasis on external rewards may interfere with the motivational power of intrinsic rewards. Porter and Lawler (1968) address this weakness of expectancy theory and suggest an extension of the theory by incorporating into it such issues as role perception, traits, extrinsic and intrinsic rewards and the question of equity. This extension of expectancy theory brings it closer to other theories of management and motivation such as Barnard's (1938) concept of the equilibrium between contributions and inducements and the Equity Theory of motivation (Adams, 1963; Mowday 1983). However, Porter and Lawler have yet to capture the attention of managers and most academicians.

What are the implications of the possible weaknesses of expectancy theory as an instrumental or a prescriptive theory? It may be prudent to suggest that public managers not rely solely on the expectancy theory of motivation for designing and implementing programs of productivity enhancement. This does not mean that the manager should ignore the ideas that are offered by the theory or its potential for explaining behavior. Rather, as we see it, the implication is that the theory is not likely to hold under all conditions; thus, a manager should not develop a plan of action that is solely based on the notions of expectancy theory. A second implication is that, given the possible weakness of the theory, a merit pay program that is based solely on it may not lead to the desired results.

Merit Pay: Is It Feasible?

The major obstacles or constraints that hinder successful implementation of pay-for-performance plans are of two sorts: (1) the performance appraisal mechanism, and (2) economic and fiscal considerations.

The Performance Appraisal Mechanism

In the private sector the number of items sold, quantity of manufactured goods, percent return on investment, or the amount of a sale can be used for gauging levels of performance. Thus, the appraisal process is relatively simple. Determining the magnitude of the appropriate reward according to preestablished criteria is not difficult, and little is needed to explain the rationale behind it to the affected employee. Such measures of performance are perceived to be direct outcomes of the level of effort exerted by the employee. That is, a greater effort is assumed to lead to better results.

But in the public sector can we say that a police officer performs better if he patrols at a faster rate, but makes relatively few informal community contacts at that speed? If he issues more summons at the expense of other important activities? If he makes more arrests—which may not survive a first judicial screening? The difficulty in coming up with reliable and valid performance assessment tools is underscored by the use of performance criteria that are based on job behavior rather than job outcomes (Mihal, 1983). The perception of performance criteria as subjective or unfair in any single respect is likely to make merit pay objectionable to employees and may threaten the success of any performance pay plan.

Outcomes cannot be ascertained directly, when, for example, they are likely to materialize only in the far future, or when the measurable outcome represents the achievements of several individuals from various units. Under such conditions, secondary, or indirect, criteria must be used. Such criteria consider the level of the effort that is exerted as a good indicator of the likely organizational outcomes. One example is the number of cases processed by a social worker. However, the validity, reliability or acceptance of such a measure by employees may change over time. The implications for the manager are first that it is possible to develop surrogate performance measures that are valid and acceptable to both management and employees. Second, all such measures must be re-evaluated periodically by the manager. The re-evaluation process itself must be understood by all the concerned parties prior to the initial application of the secondary measures.

An effective performance appraisal mechanism must take cognizance of the following issues:

Inconsistency. Unfortunately, even when everything is done to eliminate intended or unintended bias of the rater, little can be done to control for the inevitable differences that occur when employees who are doing essentially the same work are evaluated by different supervisors (U.S. General Accounting Office, 1983). Given the same level of employee achievement, different managers will make different judgments about what constitutes good or bad performance (Prinz and Waldman, 1985).

Latitude. Judgmental latitude also raises questions about the possibility of using any appraisal system in connection with a merit pay plan (e.g., how much flexibility and freedom does a manager have in determining the quality of performance and/or the size of the merit award). The discretion of the evaluator can be wide or narrow, but in either case the ultimate purpose of the evaluation—rewarding the outstanding performer—can be easily compromised.

Worksite "politics." Higher evaluations may be given to maintain good working relations. Printz and Waldman (1985: 85) report that in 1979 over 50 percent of companies with merit pay plans gave merit increases to at least 95 percent of their employees. They question the implications of this finding for merit pay:

> If 95 percent of a company's employees receive merit raises, are we to assume that 95 percent of the workers are superior performers? A more realistic explanation is that companies often fear competition and bad feelings that a merit pay (plan?) can produce. Instead of rewarding superior performers only,

the company ends up paying across the board salary increments (Printz and Waldman, 1985: 85).

This observation is repeated by several writers in reference to other experiences in both the private and public sectors (Teel, 1986; Choen and Murane, 1985). The odds that supervisors would try hard to give something to every subordinate are particularly high when the superior's own performance in the future will depend on subordinates' cooperation.

Income Protection. Inflated evaluations for purposes of determining merit pay may also stem from the desire of supervisors to protect the subordinate's income in times of high inflation, or if minimal raises are likely due to cutbacks (Teel, 1980). The tendency to do so may stem from a manager's belief that he or she should "take care of" subordinates through the paternal role of the benevolent supervisor.

Retention. Inflated evaluations and oversized merit rewards may be used to induce an "important" employee to stay with the organization. Thus, more money may be allocated to those whose risk of leaving is greater (Fossum and Fitch, 1985). As Winstanley (1982: 40) concludes:

> The overwhelming evidence is that pay for salaried, non-union employees in most U.S. corporations is largely determined by job evaluations and salary surveys. Within that context salary increase budgets are funded and distributed on the basis of economics, maturity, and performance—*in that order.* Thus, an employee's performance actually plays a very small part in the determination of his or her salary. Management gets its money's worth in terms of the market for the skill. . . . While this overall salary administration process may attract and retain employees, it has little to do with their motivation. What we are observing is equitable reward for membership and for the nature of the job. This is an institutional, not a behavioral, process.

This point seems to be supported by a British study that found that skilled scientific and technical people pressure for more merit-based rewards "mainly because on the whole they expected to do well out of merit schemes." (Edwards, 1982: 9).

"Critical Unit" bias. Administrative or institutional considerations result in greater allocations for awarding performance in those units that are most crucial to the overall survival of the organization. Hence, Murlis and Wright (1985) report that the most often cited reason for favoring merit schemes was to gain greater flexibility out of a restricted budget, putting money where it was most needed.

Interpersonal Relations.   Personal bias and subjective considerations are likely to contaminate the evaluation whenever the supervisor has broad discretion in judging performance. Hence, Fossum and Fitch (1985) report that most merit pay systems neither unambigously define criteria nor insulate against the consideration of nonperformance factors in determining the magnitude of salary increases.

Inflexibility.   One remedy that is commonly used by organizations for dealing with some of the problems listed above is to reduce managerial discretion. But as the scope of discretion is reduced, the flexibility to recognize an outstanding performance is reduced with it. The direct consequence is that the supervisor cannot use discretion to correct the imperfections of the appraisal system. This, in turn, may contribute to the anxiety of both the superior and the subordinate, with possible negative implications for interpersonal and labor relations. Thus, for example, the manager would not be able to reward an employee who took the initiative and did something beyond the call of duty instead of following the safe, undemanding, and possibly irrelevant prescription for action that is called by an obsolete organizational manual. Consequently, using a rigid criterion is likely to reward the average worker as much or even more than the true performer. As Edwards (1982) points out, when medium and low performers are rewarded similarly as high performers, the organization culture quickly adopts the understanding that mediocrity is the norm and it is sufficient. Whenever true performance is not recognized, it obscures the connection between effort, results and reward. It does not matter whether one subscribes to the expectancy or equity theories of motivation. According to either one, the motivational benefit of the appraisal process is lost because of its subsequent use to determine compensation.

Matching Behavior to Narrow Evaluation Criteria.   The tendency to pay more attention to appearance rather than to the real issues that are involved in carrying out a job is not conducive to productivity improvement. That is, employees may do what is necessary for scoring higher on the evaluation form rather than what is genuinely needed for doing the job correctly. A case in point is the practice of employees in one federal agency of postponing the recording of requests from individuals until all the supporting documentation was secured by those individuals. Because the agency evaluated its employees by using the time between the receipt of the request for action and the completion of its processing as a measure of employee productivity, employees manipulated the processing time by delaying the recording of the request, keeping it to a minimum.

Extraneous Criteria. As far as management is concerned, existing methods of appraisal allow managers to differentiate between outstanding and poor performance, but not between top performers. Hence, when all, or most, employees are doing an outstanding job, considerations other than ones directly related to the actual performance are used. For example, it is reported that teachers were awarded merit raises because of their involvement in civic activity (which indicates very little, if anything, about their performance in the classroom). The reason for using such an unrelated consideration is that such involvement is the only thing that differentiates them from other top performers. The result of the appraisal is at best an increase in the motivation of the teacher whose civic activity is recognized, and no decline in the motivation of those that fail to get the merit award. In the reported study, however, not getting the merit award did lead to a negative reaction (Cohen and Murnane, 1985: 24).

Control Mechanism. Performance appraisal, particularly when it is coupled with merit pay, can be turned by supervisors into a very effective tool for controlling employees. As Fossum and Fitch (1985: 600) put it, "merit increase systems are utilized not only to reward or act as an incentive for performance. They are likely to be used by managers to influence other behaviors." However, the advantages of that prospect should not be confused or mistaken with motivation of employees. Indeed, performance appraisals can be used by a supervisor to get an employee to do what is desired, but the ensuing behavior is not going to exceed the minimum that is required. The real talent and creativity of the employee is never going to be mobilized by the use of implied threats of a low rating on the performance appraisal and/or the subsequent loss of merit pay.

What are the implications of these possible flaws in the performance appraisal process? As we see it, a merit pay plan that is riddled with any one of the above problems is not likely to be perceived by most employees as fair. It is unlikely to be conducive to improved productivity and performance. But it is likely to deprive the organization of an opportunity to provide employees with meaningful feedback that may influence their performance. Thus, by linking compensation to performance appraisal the organization may convert a situation that was meant to enhance cooperation into one of confrontation. The exchange between superior and subordinate is then not about performance but rather about pay, and it is only likely to produce de-motivators.

This point can be illustrated by reference to recent research findings. Ammons and Rodriguez (1986: 460–462) report that 60.2 percent of the respondents to a survey of municipal governments indicated that performance feedback was the primary objective of their performance appraisal practices. In comparison, 23.9 percent indicated that proper allocation of rewards was the main purpose of the system. This finding is in line with earlier findings from surveys of state personnel directors. The stated objectives of performance appraisals may not correspond to the actual practices. However, the mere need to pay lip service to "performance feedback," by itself, is an important clue in the search for an appropriate strategy for productivity enhancement. For our purposes the reference to performance feedback by supervisors in the public and private sector suggests that it is perceived to be an important, necessary, and a desired part of performance appraisal. As we see it, discrepancy between the claimed objectives of performance appraisal and the actual practices (or the way employees perceive them) may explain why some performance appraisal programs do not work.

Problems Inherent in
the Economics of Merit Pay

For merit pay to be a motivator, there must be a clear difference between the special rewards that result from outstanding performance and the normal rewards of normal pay (Kearney, 1979). Our studies suggest that this is easier to propose than to implement. Even in the private sector, many organizations seem to have difficulty coming up with the additional resources that are necessary for keeping the merit bonus or the merit increase large enough to be distinguished year after year. Also, because organizations must maintain a competitive level of salaries to sustain their manpower, the base salary that is promised to "important" employees must be guaranteed at the competitive range. The merit reward, therefore, ends up being added to the already competitive salary and may be beyond the financial abilities of many organizations. This is true, in particular, of public and private organizations operating under adverse fiscal or market conditions.

Both in the public and in the private sectors, only a few employees can be recognized as outstanding performers. When more than a few are recognized, the size of the award becomes so small that, according to expectancy theory, it may not be attractive enough to generate the drive for the extra effort. On the other hand, according to expectancy theory, when only a few employees are likely to get the merit award, the low probability of getting it would induce the same indifference. The prospect that the manager is likely to find himself in this bind is greater when dealing with a preponderance of very competent and outstanding personnel, or with as great a portion of very poor employees. In both cases there is little likelihood that too many individuals would be able to out-perform significantly the rest of the group so as to establish a clear case for giving them the merit pay award. And even when the pool of employees consists of many real achievers and only some underachievers, does it make sense to give the merit award to only a few members of the former group? When such a practice is used, the achievers that were denied the merit award may react by producing at past (or even lower) levels in the future.

Performance Targeting:
Are There Any Alternatives to Merit Pay?

Performance targeting can move the supervisor from a position where relationships with subordinates are contaminated by the prospects of rewards or punishment, to a more comfortable position of guidance, support and cooperation. Specifically, we view the relationship of the supervisor and the subordinate in terms of a mutual search for the best ways of doing a job. This entails recognition of the strengths and the weaknesses of the individual employee, by both the employee and the supervisor, in order to take advantage of strengths and remedy weaknesses. When the superior and the subordinate discuss progress and performance without the prospect that such a review must result in a penalty or an award to the employee, the communication is more likely to stay open and honest. (We are here using the term "more likely" to indicate the underlying difficulty of adults to admit their shortcomings and the psychological cost that results from such admission.) The door is then open for a genuine identification of strength and weakness, providing the employee with the necessary feedback for establishing the connection between effort and result. This assumes that, as an adult, an employee prefers the challenge of a higher achievement to an inferior one, and that he or she is willing to perform well, if given the choice.

For the manager, review of progress as part of a performance targeting effort is an opportunity to find out what makes a particular employee "tick." Piamonte (1979: 598) suggests that the incentive value of any item or condition is not an immutable property of that item, but rather is a function of the individual's personal characteristics, his "need state" for that incentive at that point of time, the absolute amount or value of the incentive, and the interactive effects of other incentives. He goes on to make the claim that new theories of motivation must accept that incentive value may be acquired, as in the case of the gold star used in grade school. Here, McClelland's theory of motivation may help the manager identify the relative importance of each need the employee is trying to satisfy. According to McClelland's (1961) "need theory," all people are motivated by the need for achievement, the need for power, or the need for affiliation. However, for each individual (at any given time or stage of life) one of those needs is stronger than the other two. Open and honest communication between the trained supervisor and subordinates relative to job performance and the reasons for it change the odds that the employee will do better in the future by helping the supervisor see what may constitute a motivator or a demotivator in a particular case.

For our purposes, performance evaluation that is not tied to merit pay and allows the supervisor to consider the broad behavior and achievement of the employee (and not just those aspects that were predetermined to be significant) has greater potential to enhance productivity. When performance targeting is not tied down by the requirements of the merit pay system, it is possible to allow the supervisor more discretion to give the employee those assignments that are likely to be in line with the employee's natural drive to satisfy personal needs. Rather than the discretion to influence salary, that might be a source for interpersonal conflicts, under performance targeting the supervisor provides the employee with the necessary conditions for doing what he or she wants to do best. The prospect that supervisors would be allowed to do just that as long as they are doing a good job may be as strong a motivator for some employees as the monetary award of the merit pay may be for others.

One of our assumptions is that the natural drive to satisfy one of the above is assumed to be more powerful than the induced or artificial drive that results from the prospect of receiving the monetary reward. The other assumption is that in many cases getting the monetary reward (which is different from securing the necessary income for subsistence) is not a motivator because of its inherent economic value. The desire to get it has to do with its instrumental value for satisfying personal needs that are not met on the job. As Kopelman (1983: 62) says: "Some individuals, those with a high need to achieve, might be expected to work hard despite the absence of reward and recognition." This approach illustrates the difficulty many researchers and managers have in seeing that without recognition even the individual with the high need for achievement may be frustrated. That is, even the inner sense of achievement is dependent on external recognition. The mistake made by Kopelman and others has to do with the unwarranted assumption that recognition and awards must always be expressed in monetary terms.

Conclusion

Given the potential problems with the motivational potential of a monetary merit award, performance targeting that is based on careful identification of the employee's relative needs for power, affiliation and achievement is likely to be more productive. Performance targeting prevents the organization from spending funds ineffectively. In contrast, ascertaining from the performance appraisal the things that are important to the employee (i.e, the need(s) he or she is trying to satisfy) is likely to be more effective than the merit award because the inducements it gives are important to the employee.

References

Adams, J. S. (1963). "Toward an Understanding of Inequity." *Journal of Abnormal and Social Psychology* 67 (November): 422–436.

_____ (1965). "Inequity in Social Exchanges," pp. 267–300 in L. Berkowitz, ed., *Advances in Experimental Social Psychology.* New York: Academic Press.

Ammons, D. N., and A. Rodriguez (1986). "Performance Appraisal Practices for Upper Management in City Government." *Public Administration Review* 46, 5 (September-October): 461–467.

Belcher, D. W. (1980). "Pay and Performance." *Compensation Review* 12, 3: 14–20.

Barnard, C. (1938). *The Function of the Executive.* Cambridge, MA: Harvard University Press.

Clark, S. A. (1982). "Linking Employee Salary Adjustments to Performance: Is It Worth the Effort?" *Governmental Finance* 11, 4 (December): 15–18.

Cohen, D. K., and R. J. Murnane (1985). "The Merits of Merit Pay." *Public Interest* 80 (Summer): 3–30.

Deci, E. L. (1972). "The Effects of Contingent and Noncontingent Rewards and Controls on Intrinsic Motivation." *Organizational Behavior and Human Performance* 8: 217–229.

Edwards, M. R. (1982). "Improved Compensation Decisions with a MRPA System." *Industrial Management* 24, 6 (November-December): 9–13.

Fossum, J. A., and M. K. Fitch (1985). "The Effects of Individual and Contextual Attributes in the Sizes of Recommended Salary Increases." *Personnel Psychology* 38, 3 (Autumn): 587–602.

Gabris, G., and K. Mitchell (1986). "Merit Based Performance Appraisal and Productivity: Do Employees Perceive the Connection?" *Public Productivity Review* 9, 4 (Winter): 311–327.

Hatry, H. P., J. M. Greiner, and R. J. Gollub (1981). *An Assessment of Local Government Management Motivational Programs: Performance Targeting with and without Monetary Incentives.* Washington, DC: Urban Institute.

Herzberg, F., B. Mausner, and B. Snyderman (1959). *The Motivation to Work.* New York: Wiley.

Kearney, W. J. (1979). "Pay for Performance? Not Always." *MSU Business Topics* 27, 2 (Spring): 5–16.

Kopelman, R. E. (1983). "Linking Pay to Performance Is a Proven Management Tool." *Personnel Administrator* 28, 10 (October): 60–68.

Locke, E. A. (1968). "Toward a Theory of Task Motivation and Incentives." *Organization Behavior and Human Performance* 3: 157–189.

Luce, S. R. (1983). "Paying for Performance." *Canadian Business Review* 10, 4 (Winter): 19–22.

March, J. G. (1972). "Model Bias in Social Action." *Review of Educational Research* 42, 4: 419–439.

Mihal, W. L. (1983). "More Research Is Needed: Goals May Motivate Better." *Personnel Administrator* 28, 10 (October): 61–67.

Mode, V. A. (1979). "Making Money the Motivator." *Supervisor Management* 24, 8 (August): 16–20.

Mowday, R. T. (1983). "Equity Theory Predictions of Behavior in Organizations," pp. 91–113 in R. M. Steer and L. W. Porter, eds., *Motivation and Work Behavior.* New York: McGraw-Hill.

Murlis, H., and A. Wright (1985). "Rewarding the Performance of the Eager Beaver." *Personnel Management* 17, 6 (June): 28–31.

Pearce, J. L., and J. L. Perry (1983). "Federal Merit Pay: A Longitudinal Analysis." *Public Administration Review* 43, 4 (July-August): 315–325.

Piamonte, J. S. (1979). "In Praise of Monetary Motivation." *Personnel Journal* 59, 9 (September): 597–599.

Porter, L. W., and E. E. Lawler (1968). *Managerial Attitudes and Performance.* Homewood, IL: Dorsey Press.

Printz, R. A., and D. A. Waldman (1985). "The Merit of Merit Pay." *Personnel Administrator* 30, 1 (January): 84–90.

Silverman, B. R. (1983). "Why the Merit Pay System Failed in the Federal Government." *Personnel Journal* 62, 4 (April): 294–302.

Teel, K. (1980). "Performance Appraisal: Current Trends, Persistent Progress." *Personnel Journal* 59, 4 (April): 296–301.

_____ (1986). "Are Merit Raises Really Based on Merit?" *Personnel Journal* 65, 3 (March): 88–95.

Tharp, C. G. (1986). "Linking Annual Incentives and Individual Performance." *Personnel Administrator* 31, 1 (January): 85–89.

U.S. Congress. (1981A). *Federal Merit Pay: Important Concerns Need Attention.* Report by the Comptroller General of the United States. FPCD-81-9 (March 3).

U.S. Congress (1981B). *Serious Problems Need to be Corrected Before Federal Merit Pay Goes into Effect.* Report by the Comptroller General of the United States. FPCD-81-73 (September 11).

U.S. General Accounting Office (1983). *Analysis of OPM's Pay for Performance in the Federal Government 1980–1982.* GAO/GGD-84-22 (October 21).

Winstanley, N. B. (1982). "Are Merit Increases Really Effective?" *Personnel Administrator* 27, 4 (April): 37–41.

27

The Paradox of Merit Pay in the Public Sector: Persistence of a Problematic Procedure

J. Edward Kellough

Haoran Lu

The idea that individuals should be paid according to their work performance is logically compelling. Pay contingent on performance, as required in merit pay systems, rests on the evaluation of individual employee accomplishments and the distribution of financial rewards to those most productive. Origins of the concept can be traced back at least to Frederick W. Taylor and the late nineteenth and early twentieth century era of scientific management (Locke, 1982, cited in Perry, 1991). As early as the 1940s, merit pay was becoming a broadly accepted way to reward outstanding employees in the private sector (Cumming, 1988).

By the 1980s, merit pay was firmly established in the public service as well. For the federal government, the Civil Service Reform Act of 1978 (CSRA) provided the catalyst. As is widely known, the CSRA established a Merit Pay System (MPS) for mid-level federal managers and supervisors

1993. The paradox of merit pay in the public sector: Persistence of a problematic procedure. Kellough, J. Edward, and Haoran Lu. **Review of Public Personnel Administration** 13 (Spring): 45–64.

(GS 13–15) to take effect in 1981. That program was revised in 1984 when the current Performance Management and Recognition System (PMRS) was created. Under the PMRS program, employees are rated at various performance levels, and those with satisfactory or higher ratings receive general pay increases and are eligible for performance awards or bonuses. The PMRS was revised and extended in 1989 and 1991 (U.S. Congress, 1989, 1991a), and current authorization is set to expire in September 1993. The common argument in support of systems such as the PMRS is that they will motivate job performance and thereby improve organizational productivity (Lawler, 1981, 1983; Perry 1988–89). By the time the PMRS was established in the federal service, similar merit pay programs were being widely adopted by state and local governments.

Now, after more than ten years of experience with merit pay in the public sector, there is a growing consensus among administrators and academic researchers that merit pay systems have failed to achieve desired results. Merit pay programs have not generally improved employee job satisfaction or reduced turnover, and there is little empirical evidence that productivity has been enhanced. Nevertheless, government seems unwilling to abandon the concept. This reluctance is most recently demonstrated in a report by a U.S. Office of Personnel Management (OPM) committee established to review the federal PMRS. The committee found that the system was "neither fair nor effective," a conclusion shared with much of the published literature, but the report also states that "the committee unanimously supports the concept of pay for performance" (U.S. Office of Personnel Management, 1991:i and 23). The committee recommended continuation and expansion of merit pay. Currently, OPM is evaluating this and other reports to develop recommendations for reform including the possible implementation of a new government-wide merit pay system for all general schedule employees. One is left to wonder why governments are apparently hesitant to abandon the idea if most of the research evidence suggests that merit pay does not work well.

This article seeks to further the ongoing discussion of merit pay in the public sector in two ways. First, the article pulls together, from numerous empirical studies of the past ten years, what is known about the effectiveness of merit pay. Some of this information may already be familiar to those who have followed the literature closely, but the purpose here is to provide a concise analytical summary of the current state of research from all levels of government. The four most common and critical problems associated with merit pay in the public service are emphasized. Second, and perhaps more importantly, the article outlines six explanations for the persistence of merit pay despite predominantly negative findings in the published record. The goal is to clarify discussion of the intriguing question of why this persistence has occurred. Such analysis has implications not only for merit pay, but also for other managerial innovations currently in vogue or under consideration in the public service.

Theoretical Foundations

Before explicitly addressing the paradox of merit pay, a brief review of theoretical underpinnings and basic problems associated with the concept is in order. At the onset, one should note that research has shown pay to be a potential motivator for many people (Lawler, 1981, 1983; Locke et al., 1980). Pay can satisfy both lower-order and higher-order needs (Gordon, 1990; Lawler, 1981, 1983; Nadler and Lawler, 1983). It provides the means to meet physiological, safety, and security requirements, and it may also serve as an indication of achievement and recognition in an organization (Latham and Wexley, 1981; Lawler, 1981; Pinder, 1984; Rainey, 1991).

Since pay is important to individuals, advocates of merit pay believe that management need only link pay to performance to motivate employees. The strongest theoretical support for this view of pay as a motivational tool is found in expectancy theory, first proposed by Victor H. Vroom (1964) and then refined by, among others, Lyman W. Porter and Edward E. Lawler III (1968). Expectancy theory assumes that people make decisions among alternative plans of behavior based on their perceptions or expectations of the degree to which given behaviors will lead to desired outcomes. More specifically, expectancy theory states that an individual's motivation to perform is greatest when:

- the individual believes that personal effort will result in a desirable level of performance (the effort-performance expectancy).
- the employee believes that performance will lead to outcomes (the performance-outcome expectancy).
- the outcomes have positive value (valence) for the individual.

The obvious implication for management is that performance can be enhanced by tying positively valued outcomes to high performance levels and making sure that employees understand the connection and have the opportunity to perform (Lawler, 1981; Pinder, 1984). Assuming that individuals value pay, motivation then depends on the perceived effort-performance and performance-outcome expectancies. When these expectancies are high, proponents of merit pay believe that employees will be motivated.

Establishing and strengthening the effort-performance and performance-outcome expectancies can be difficult, however. Tying pay to performance requires good performance measures. It also requires the ability to control the amount of pay an individual receives. For employees to perceive a performance-outcome linkage in an organization, it must be visible and trustworthy (Lawler, 1981). In fact, a climate of trust within the organization can be critical. Golembiewski (1986) contends that the absence of this kind of organizational culture or climate will significantly inhibit the success of merit pay programs.

In addition to difficulties in establishing effort-performance and performance-outcome linkages, however, other basic assumptions of expectancy theory have also been criticized. For example, the theory assumes effort-performance expectancies, performance-outcome expectancies, and perceived value of the outcome are independent, but that may not be the case. People may, for instance, place higher value on outcomes they believe are more difficult to achieve (Pinder, 1984). Furthermore, expectancy theory assumes that people are rational actors, but much of human behavior is habitual and subconscious rather than rational (Pinder, 1984). Halachmi and Holzer (1987) note that "there is little empirical evidence to support the claim that the individual is always mindful of what he or she is doing—that is, that a given behavior represents not only a calculated effort but a conscious choice." It may be the case that employees do not always think about the two expectancies or the value of probable outcomes. Halachmi and Holzer (1987) conclude that, given possible weaknesses of the underlying theory, merit pay systems may not produce intended results.

Merit Pay Experience in the Public Sector

The intuitive appeal of merit pay is so overwhelming that the public sector seems to have embraced it without carefully considering its potential. In fact, the Civil Service Reform Act of 1978 failed to provide for systematic evaluation of merit pay prior to its government-wide implementation (Ingraham, 1991). Merit pay was seen as a panacea in the 1980s, intended to cure the alleged ills of the public service (Sherwood and Wechsler, 1986).

How successful was the cure? Table 27.1 contains a list of major findings of empirical research on public sector merit pay in the federal and state and local governments. Generally, merit pay systems have had little positive impact on employee motivation and organization performance. The necessary linkage between performance and outcomes specified by expectancy theory has been very difficult to achieve. For example, in 1983, Pearce and Perry reported that federal managers were less likely to believe that higher performance would lead to increased pay under the federal MPS program than they had been under the previous compensation system. Gaertner and Gaertner, in 1984, found that few employees thought that merit pay would improve agency effectiveness. Similarly, Lovrich (1987) found that merit pay was not a salient determinant of Washington state employee motivation. More recently, Heneman and Young (1991) found that public school administrators were largely unmotivated by merit pay and that the effort-performance and performance-outcome expectancies were low.

Studies that have produced favorable results are, in fact, rare. One example, however, is Schay's (1988) research on the navy personnel management demonstration project at the China Lake Naval Weapons Center and the Naval Ocean Systems Center in San Diego. Schay reported that the "demonstration was more successful than the federal-wide merit pay system (MPS) both in strengthening the perceived link between pay and performance and in improving perceptions of equity." Turnover was also lower at the demonstration sites compared with other locations. However, changes made at the demonstration locations did not increase overall employee job satisfaction. In addition, it is not clear which of the specific reforms was most beneficial. The demonstration project included a simplified position classification system with increased managerial authority and very broad pay bands, an objectives-based performance evaluation process, and a merit pay component. Furthermore, in the early years of the project, average pay was higher at the demonstration sites compared with control locations. Also, the employees at the demonstration sites obviously knew that they were participating in an innovative personnel experiment. The extent to which that knowledge biased their responses is not known. Consequently, Schay's findings do little to dispel the overwhelmingly pessimistic conclusion of most of the literature on merit pay in the public service.

What specific problems have prevented merit pay from being more successful? Two persistent obstacles have been difficulties with performance evaluation and the lack of sufficient resources to implement a viable system. There is, however, also a question of whether public managers should exercise the discretion necessary for implementation of an effective program, and the role of financial incentives in public employee motivation is far from settled as well. The following sections more fully explore each of these four difficulties.

Problems with Performance Appraisal

Pearce and Perry (1983) conclude that federal merit pay fails as a motivational program largely because of difficulties in the performance appraisal process. From the perspective of expectancy theory, an accurate and equitable system for evaluating performance is essential to increase the perceived probability that good performance will lead to rewards. In the public sector, however, goals and performance criteria are often diverse,

TABLE 27.1   Selected Research Findings on Merit Pay in the Public Sector

Study/Year	*Agency*	*Findings*
Nachmias & Moderacki, 1982	Wisconsin Internal Revenue Service	A considerable lack of general support for the merit pay system. Most employees did not feel that merit pay was effective.
O'Toole & Churchill, 1982	U.S. Environmental Protection Agency	Performance measures are subjective. Lack of resources undermines pay-for-performance relationship.
Pearce & Perry, 1983	5 Federal Agencies	Managers were less likely to perceive that high performance would lead to increased pay than they had been earlier.
Gaertner & Gaertner 1984, 1985	2 Federal Agencies	Very few employees believed that merit pay would improve agency effectiveness. Nearly two-thirds of respondents felt that incentives were not enough to make the extra effort worthwhile.
U.S. GAO, 1984	3 Federal Agencies	Eighty percent of respondents believed that the MPS had not increased their productivity or motivation.
Pearce et al., 1985	U.S. Social Security Administration	The MPS had no effect on organizational performance.
Gabris, 1986	Biloxi, MS	Supervisors tended to support merit pay because they felt that it gave them greater control over their subordinates. Subordinates tended to view merit pay as biased, unfair, and unrelated to individual productivity.
Daley, 1987	22 Federal Agencies	Merit pay recipients neither appeared to be any more motivated nor perceived their organizations to be more effective or responsive.
Lovrich, 1987	Washington State Government	Merit pay was not a salient determinant of employee motivation in comparison with work participation and job enrichment.

TABLE 27.1   (continued)

Study/Year	Agency	Findings
Siegel, 1987	U.S. Naval Weapons Center	Only weak evidence existed that merit pay was associated with improved productivity and effectiveness. Causality, however, could not be determined.
Schay, 1988	U.S. Naval Weapons Center & U.S. Naval Ocean Systems Center	Demonstration projects are more successful than control sites in strengthening the perceived link between pay and performance.
Fox, 1989	State & Local Government	A weak positive relationship existed between merit pay and organizational commitment. The relationship was weakest among the younger employees.
Perry et al., 1989	U.S. General Services Admn.	Ninety-nine percent of managers were rated at the Fully Successful level or above; PMRS reward variables were not associated with increased performance in 1987.
Heneman & Young, 1991	Public School Administrators	Merit pay failed to motivate school administrators.

conflicting, and difficult to measure (National Research Council, 1991; Rainey, 1989, 1991). As a result, individual and organizational performance are not easily evaluated. Ultimately, performance appraisal rests on a manager's judgment of an employee's accomplishments.

Several specific problems associated with public sector performance appraisal systems may be attributed to the lack of objective data. One common difficulty is rater leniency. Performance appraisals should be able to distinguish effectively among different levels of performance, so that low performers can be identified and motivated. In reality, however, to avoid conflict and maintain good relations with subordinates, many supervisors tend to inflate ratings (Lane and Wolf, 1990). Perry and his associates (1989) found that 99% of employees in the U.S. General Services Administration received ratings of "Fully Successful" or above; those employees were then eligible for merit increases. Thus, it appears that pay increases in some parts of the federal service are still largely automatic just as in the days prior to the CSRA. It is difficult to see how the proper contingent relationship between pay and performance has been established.[1]

If supervisors do attempt to make distinctions among employees, other problems frequently occur. Often there are no standard criteria for comparing employees and distributing merit pay awards (Perry and Pearce, 1985), and such a process can be subject to numerous biases. It can also be difficult to differentiate various aspects of performance. As a result, employees may tend to receive the same rating on all items or traits under consideration. This "halo effect" could lead a supervisor who has a generally good impression of an employee to rate that employee high on all items; however, if a supervisor regards an employee as a generally poor worker, the employee may receive low ratings on all items even though the employee has performed well in some areas (Lee, 1987).

Because of problems associated with performance evaluation, such systems often have little credibility among employees (Lane and Wolf, 1990). If good performers are not effectively distinguished from poor performers, employees cannot be expected to have much confidence in the system. The lack of credibility may be exacerbated by the fact that supervisors are not well trained in evaluating subordinates (Mount, 1987; Sigel, 1987) and a supportive organizational culture/climate has not been developed (Golembiewski, 1986). There may be variation in the way performance evaluation is administered within an agency or across agencies. Ironically, the increased emphasis on performance evaluation required as part of an effort to implement merit pay can actually erode the level of trust between management and employees necessary for establishing requisite performance-outcome expectancies. One study found that only 49% of federal employees surveyed agreed with the statement "performance appraisal systems accurately rated my job performance" (Bann and Johnson, 1984). More recently, according to a report by the U.S. Merit Systems Protection Board (MSPB), forty-seven percent of federal employees surveyed lacked trust and confidence in their immediate supervisors (U.S. Merit Systems Protection Board, 1990).

Before merit pay, employee performance appraisals focused primarily on identifying the outstanding or unsatisfactory employee. Most employees received a rating "exceeded requirements, but not to an exceptional degree," and since pay and performance were not closely linked, little emphasis was placed on the appraisal process (Pagano, 1985). Now, extensive documentation and paper work are required on all employees (Silverman, 1982), and because there is a connection between ratings on performance appraisals and pay raises, conflict and dissatisfaction are more likely to result from appraisal processes. Pearce and Porter (1986) found that organizational commitment decreased for those employees who received merely "Satisfactory" ratings. The implication is that performance appraisal systems can adversely impact organizational behavior by alienating workers who do not receive high evaluations.

Problems with Funding

Merit pay programs in the public sector frequently lack adequate funding (Pearce, 1989; Perry, 1988–89; National Research Council, 1991; Siegel, 1987). The Merit Pay System established by the federal government in 1981, for example, could spend no more on merit pay than had been spent earlier under the previous general schedule system. Such a structure suggests that some individuals will of necessity receive less compensation than they otherwise would have received in order to allow for merit increases for others. According to Perry (1988–89), the requirement of budget neutrality was one factor that significantly damaged the prospect that noticeable improvements in agency performance could be achieved through merit pay. Pearce (1989: 402) observes, however, that financial constraints on pay-for-performance systems are nearly unavoidable because "the need to pay the market wage for each job and various requirements to maintain internal equity across departments and hierarchical levels results in proportionately small amounts retained for merit raises and bonuses." In addition, the political environment of public organizations makes large pay increases difficult to achieve, especially in times of fiscal stress and mandatory budget reductions.

But a pay raise is likely to serve as a strong motivator only if the amount is large enough in comparison to current income to noticeably alter the individual's pay status (Lawler, 1981; Stimson, 1980). Although many employees under either the MPS or the PMRS at the federal level have received merit pay, the amount of the increases was usually minimal (Condrey and Brudney, 1992). Perry et al., (1989) found that salary increases for most employees ranged from 1%–3%, and that only approximately 1% of employees got pay increases as high as 10%. Gaertner and Gaertner (1984) found that only 5% of those surveyed agreed with the statement, "people who deserved a big raise got a big raise under merit pay." Because the raises were so small many managers complained that the amount of paperwork and effort required were not worth subsequent monetary rewards (Pagano, 1985). Siegel (1987) concludes, "[t]rival rewards are antithetical to the idea of a merit pay system."

Managerial Discretion

Given the inherently subjective nature of performance evaluation, merit pay systems, by tying pay to the outcomes of performance appraisal processes, have the added effect of significantly increasing managerial discretion (National Research Council, 1991). That is to say, merit pay gives managers and supervisors important influence over perhaps the most fundamental condition of work—compensation. Not only do individual supervisors control work assignments and organization, they also ultimately determine an employee's total earnings.

This kind of managerial discretion can be problematic in the public service. The National Research Council (1991, p. 31) has argued, for example, that "the managerial constraints and legalistic environment that have come to characterize federal management are antithetical to the managerial discretion necessary for effective pay-for-performance processes." There is, in effect, a "tension between the principle of neutral competence and pay for performance" (National Research Council, 1991: 31). In the public sector, organizational missions and purposes are defined politically by executive and legislative action. We have, however, sought to keep public administration politically neutral in the **partisan** sense and have constructed elaborate civil service procedures based on merit principles, including neutral competence and employee protection from partisan manipulation. Because performance appraisal cannot be done objectively, however, merit pay invites political intrusion, especially when it is applied to the higher levels of the bureaucracy. Ignoring all other difficulties, this concern should itself be sufficient to call into question the application of merit pay to middle and higher level positions in the civil service.

Pay and Motivation

In addition to problems associated with performance appraisal, adequate funding, and managerial discretion, it appears that the fundamental assumption that pay is a crucial element in fostering the motivation of public employees may not be entirely well founded (Lane and Wolf, 1990; Perry and Porter, 1982; Sherwood and Wechsler, 1986). Many widely-read organizational researchers have suggested that employee work motivation relates more closely with intrinsic rewards of the work than with the level of compensation earned (Herzberg, 1966; Hackman and Lawler, 1971; Hackman and Oldham 1980). These scholars stress the importance of employee participation and the importance of the richness of the work assigned to employees.[2]

Though expectancy theory recognizes that people may differ substantially regarding what is important to them, merit pay systems do not take such differences into account. Lovrich's study of Washington state employees shows that work place participation and job enrichment are the main determinants of motivation and job satisfaction. Lovrich (1987:66) found that "little evidence exists to argue that pay concerns are primary in the minds of Washington state employees when it comes to the consideration of workplace motivation." A similar conclusion is reached by Sherwood and Wechsler (1986) in their review of pay-for-performance schemes for senior public managers in the federal and state governments, and by Daley (1987) in an analysis of the federal Merit Pay System.

Perry and Wise (1990) charge that the current trend of public motivation programs fails to acknowledge unique motives underlying public sector employment. They point out that public service motivation is commonly associated with normative orientations such as a desire to serve the public interest or social equity. Perry and Wise suggest that "public organizations that attract employees with high levels of public service motivation will not have to construct incentive systems that are predominantly utilitarian to energize and direct member behavior" (Perry and Wise, 1990:371).

Exploring the Paradox

Why Are Governments Reluctant to Abandon the Concept of Merit Pay?

The underlying problems associated with merit pay are quite unyielding. Performance appraisal, for example, can never be made wholly objective. This is especially true for career executives and the growing number of professionals employed in government. Problems associated with formal performance appraisal seem so insurmountable that a persuasive argument can be made to abolish the process (Fox, 1991). Problems of adequate funding for merit pay in the public sector do not appear to be any more tractable, and the potential use of merit pay as a mechanism of political control is ever present, but inconsistent with principles of neutral competence that currently form the foundation of classified civil service. Under such circumstances, continued reliance on extrinsic reward structures that are of questionable motivational value should be closely examined. Instrumentally, merit pay appears to have failed. Nevertheless, many governments still assume that merit pay should be a part of their compensation structures.

Why is this the case? Six probable reasons for continued adherence to merit pay are outlined in Table 27.2. To some extent, these explanations are overlapping. Policy makers may follow more than one of them, or even all of them at the same time.

Symbolic Politics

Perhaps the most compelling explanation for the persistence of merit pay is that the concept is symbolically and politically attractive. The power of symbolism to shape administrative processes has already been recognized

TABLE 27.2   Explanations for the Persistence of Merit Pay

   I. **Symbolic politics**
       Merit pay is a symbolic response to public perceptions of bureaucratic inefficiency and demands for accountability.

  II. **Business stereotype**
       Because they do it in business, we can and should do it in government.

 III. **Managerial orthodoxy**
       Merit pay is believed to enhance hierarchical control and classical notions of good management.

  IV. **Political control**
       Merit pay provides a means of strengthening political accountability in the higher levels of the bureaucracy.

   V. **Sunk costs**
       Given extensive investment in the concept, there is reluctance to admit failure.

  VI. **Perceived implementation failure**
       Difficulties associated with merit pay are the product of implementation "glitches" rather than fundamental problems with the basic idea.

(Edelman, 1964; Goodsell, 1989). Fox and Miller (1992) have gone so far recently as to argue that symbolic politics, i.e., political support for policy because of its symbolic rather than instrumental value, is a signature characteristic of our times, with implications for a wide range of personnel practices. Thompson, Riccucci, and Ban (1991) have noted that the federal employee drug testing program is in large part "a symbolic effort to reaffirm the administrative integrity of the civil service."

In a similar fashion, merit pay is a symbol of government's attempt to control the bureaucracy (Perry, 1988–89). It is a symbolic response to public perceptions of bureaucratic inefficiency and demands for accountability. Such negative impressions of the public bureaucracy are longstanding. Sixty percent of those surveyed by the Roper organization in 1981 said that government employees are not as industrious as private sector workers (Foster and Snyder, 1989). A 1982 Roper poll found that 49 percent of respondents had unfavorable opinions of "federal agency and department officials" (Foster and Snyder, 1989). When the 1989 extension of the PMRS program was under consideration on Capitol Hill, Constance B. Newman, director of the U.S. Office of Personnel Management, argued in favor of merit pay because it could be seen as a way to "make all employees more accountable for performing high quality work" (U.S. House of Representatives, 1989).

Business Stereotype

In contrast to the public bureaucracy, management in the private sector often seems to be held in high esteem. There has been a long tradition of efforts to "make government run more like a business." Indeed, the phrase became something of a cliché in the 1980s. In essence, the argument is "because they do it in business, we can and should do it in government." The universal application of such a view to all aspects of management would, however, ignore fundamental differences between the public and private sectors (Rainey, 1991). The public sector's ability to fund a viable merit pay program may be constrained by a number of political and economic factors, as noted earlier. Diverse and conflicting goals of public agencies make appraisal of individual performance difficult. But more significantly, the assumption that merit pay is a model of business management success is, itself, subject to debate. Ingraham (1991) found evidence from the private sector to be quite mixed, with little indication of clear success and some instances of unquestionable failure. Nevertheless, the view that public management should emulate private sector practices is pervasive.

Managerial Orthodoxy

Another intriguing explanation for the continued use of merit pay in the public service is that it is perceived as a control mechanism (Thayer, 1984; Gabris, 1986; Lovrich, 1987). Control can be considered a central aspect of classical management tasks associated with directing and coordinating organizational processes. It should be expected, then, that any mechanism to facilitate the performance of such tasks will enjoy support from management. Those who control the performance appraisal process also control the distribution of awards and presumably employee behavior. In this way, merit pay becomes a means of strengthening the organizational hierarchy. In fact, a major conclusion of Gabris' (1986) study was that supervisors support merit pay precisely because they believe it enhances their control over subordinates. Control aspects of performance appraisal and merit pay were considered significant enough that supervisors were willing to overlook common problems associated with those practices.

Political Control

The process of control may also be turned toward political ends. Much discussion has taken place in the public administration literature concerning the increased politicization of the federal bureaucracy following the Civil Service Reform Act of 1978, especially during the Reagan years (Newland, 1983; Ingraham, 1987). Presidential intrusion into the bureaucracy has been seen as an inevitable result of heightened public expectations for presidential leadership and accomplishment (Moe, 1985), and increased political control was an underlying motive for the CSRA. But critics have argued that bureaucratic politicization has been harmful to the career civil service (Ingraham, 1987). Aspects of the CSRA calling for, among other things, merit pay for federal managers and financial bonuses for senior executives have given political executives a new means by which to achieve influence over the career bureaucracy (Kirschten, 1983).

Sunk Costs

There is undoubtedly a certain reluctance by governments to admit that a reform such as merit pay, touted as a means to increased government efficiency and effectiveness, cannot be made to work well. Large investments have been made in the past several years in selling the concept, training employees and managers, and building expectations. As a result, it is difficult to admit the need to abandon the idea.

The Perception That Problems Are Simply Implementation Glitches

It is usually the case that policy makers, when considering problems associated with merit pay, tend to focus on technical implementation difficulties or "glitches" rather than fundamental questions concerning the viability of the underlying idea. The assumption appears to be that, "sure there are problems, but if we continue to fine-tune the program, eventually we will get it right." There is little or no discussion of the theoretical bases of merit pay or of possible dysfunctional organizational consequences. The most recent extension of the federal PMRS program is a case in point. The legislation was described in Congress as "a noncontroversial bill" that would make "minimal revisions" to the PMRS (U.S. Congress, 1991b). The central revision made was to address a glitch in the previous authorization that had the effect of causing agencies to suppress the number of high ratings produced in the performance evaluation process. Agencies were required to pay every employee with a summary performance rating two levels above fully successful an award of at least 2 percent of the employee's base pay. However, agencies were not permitted to have total payouts for performance awards in excess of 1.5 percent of their aggregate PMRS salaries. Agencies with large numbers of employees with summary ratings two levels above fully successful could easily exceed the 1.5 percent cap on total awards, and to avoid that situation agencies had to ensure that their performance evaluation process did not yield too many highly rated employees. The law removed the required 2 percent performance awards for employees with high ratings—in effect, allowing smaller awards and thereby hopefully reducing pressure to suppress ratings.

The 1991 Performance Management and Recognition System Amendments also established a committee to review the system and recommend further improvements. As noted earlier, the committee agreed that the PMRS was ineffective, but it continued to embrace the concept.[3] Specific recommendations of the committee were for improvements in training and communication, increased agency flexibility in performance evaluation and funding for merit pay, and the extension of coverage to managers and supervisors below grade 13 (U.S. Office of Personnel Management, 1991). The committee appeared to be working from the assumption that merit pay is basically a sound idea. In general, the committee wanted to fine-tune the current program and expand its coverage.

Conclusion

Despite the prevalence of merit pay in the public sector, such pay systems do not appear to be working very well. This is the predominant conclusion reached in empirical studies of the effectiveness of merit pay, but governments nevertheless continue to make merit pay a central part of their compensation structures. Possible explanations for the persistence of merit pay vary from the symbolic value of such programs to the belief that current troubles are merely the product of implementation difficulties. Implications of each of the explanations presented here vary, but it is likely that all have played some role in sustaining merit pay programs.

Interestingly, however, there are alternatives to merit pay based on individual performance. Other pay-for-performance systems have been studied and appear promising. Whether they fit the dynamics underlying past and current support for merit pay is yet to be seen. If the symbolic and control functions associated with merit pay are not served by these alternatives, chances for widespread adoption may be limited. One approach with potential, however, is the use of group incentives or gain sharing. This is a system in which rewards are based on increased organizational productivity, thus reliance on individual performance appraisals as a basis for compensation is eliminated. Lawler (1990) believes that this idea is commendable, but it must be integrated with broader participative management strategies to be effective. Presumably, this means that gain sharing will be compatible with current management strategies associated with Total Quality Management (TQM). Proponents of TQM, most notably Deming (1986), have found that merit pay based on individualized performance appraisal is inconsistent with participative management practices. The U.S. Air Force has experimented with gain sharing in the "Pacer Share" demonstration project at the McClellan Air Force Base in Sacramento. Unfortunately, a definitive assessment of that project is not yet available. In the interim, we still have merit pay.

A fuller recognition of reasons for continued commitment to merit pay should help in understanding the policy and identifying appropriate reforms. Determining the sources of commitment to merit pay and the strengths and weaknesses of those sources should help improve the process by which such programs are established, and implications may go beyond merit pay itself to a host of other management innovations ranging from budgeting reforms to drug testing and TQM. The issues addressed in this article raise questions central to the relationship between theory and practice in public management. What is the impact of research on public administration? Why are we likely to express commitment to an idea even when we lack evidence of its instrumental value in a public sector setting? These are worthwhile questions to be raised for an applied area of scholarship such as public personnel administration.

References

Bann, C., and J. Johnson (1984). "Federal Employee Attitudes Toward Reform: Performance Evaluation and Merit Pay," pp. 65–86 in P. W. Ingraham and C. Ban, eds., *Legislating Bureaucratic Change: The Civil Service Reform Act of 1978.* Albany, NY: State University of New York Press.

Condrey, S. E., and J. L. Brudney (1992). "Performance-Based Managerial Pay in the Federal Government: Does Agency Matter?" *Journal of Public Administration Research and Theory* 2, 2: 157–174.

Cumming, C. (1988). "Linking Pay to Performance." *Personnel Administrator* 33, 5: 47–52.

Daley, D. (1987). "Merit Pay Enters with a Whimper: The Initial Federal Civil Service Reform Experiences." *Review of Public Personnel Administration* 7, 2: 72–79.

Deming, W. E. (1986). *Out of The Crisis.* Cambridge, MA: MIT Press.

Edelman, M. (1964). *The Symbolic Uses of Politics.* Urbana: University of Illinois Press.

Foster, G. D., and S. K. Snyder (1989). "Public Attitudes Toward Government: Contradiction, Ambivalence, and the Dilemmas of Response." pp. 71–94 in The Volcker Commission, *Leadership for America: Rebuilding the Public Service.* Lexington, MA: Lexington Books.

Fox, C. J. (1991). "Employee Performance Appraisal: The Keystone Made of Clay," pp. 58–72 in C. Ban and N. M. Riccucci, eds., *Public Personnel Management: Current Concerns—Future Challenges.* New York: Longman.

Fox, C. J., and H. Miller (1992). *Symbolic Politics as Signature of the Postmodern Condition: Implications for Personnel Policy.* Paper presented at the annual meeting of the American Political Science Association, Chicago, Illinois.

Fox, S. F. (1989). "Intergenerational Differences, Merit Pay, and Loyalty in State and Local Government." *Review of Public Personnel Administration* 9, 2: 15–27.

Gabris, G. T. (1986). "Can a Merit Pay System Avoid Creating Discord Between Supervisors and Subordinates? Another Uneasy Look at Performance Appraisal." *Review of Public Personnel Administration* 7, 1: 70–89.

Gaertner, K. N., and G. H. Gaertner (1984). "Performance Evaluation and Merit Pay: Results in the Environmental Protection Agency and the Mine Safety and Health Administration," pp. 87–111 in Ingraham and Ban, eds., *Legislating Bureaucratic Change: The Civil Service Reform Act of 1978.* Albany, NY: State University of New York Press.

_____ (1985). "Performance-Contingent Pay for Federal Managers." *Administration and Society* 17, 1: 7–20.

Golembiewski, R. T. (1986). "OD Perspectives on High Performance: Some Good News and Some Bad News about Merit Pay." *Review of Public Personnel Administration* 7, 1: 9–26.

Goodsell, C. T. (1989). "Administration as Ritual." *Public Administration Review* 49, 2: 161–166.

Gordon, J. R. (1990). *A Diagnostic Approach to Organizational Behavior,* 3rd ed. Boston, MA: Allyn and Bacon.

Hackman, J. R., and E. E. Lawler III (1971). "Employee Reactions to Job Characteristics." *Journal of Applied Psychology* 55: 259–286.

Hackman, J. R., and G. R. Oldham. 1980. *Work Redesign.* Reading, MA: Addison-Wesley.

Halachmi, A., and M. Holzer (1987). "Merit Pay, Performance Targeting, and Productivity." *Review of Public Personnel Administration* 7, 2: 80–91.

Heneman, H. G., and I. P. Young (1991). "Assessment of a Merit Pay Program for School District Administrators." *Public Personnel Management* 20, 1: 35–47.

Herzberg, F. (1966). *Work and the Nature of Man.* Cleveland: World Publishing Company.

Ingraham, P. W. (1987). "Building Bridges or Burning Them? The President, the Appointees, and the Bureaucracy." *Public Administration Review* 47 5: 425–435.

_____ (1991). "Of Pigs in Pokes and Pay for Performance: An Analysis of Assumptions Guiding Policy Choice." Paper presented at the Conference on Public Management, The Maxwell School of Citizenship and Public Affairs, Syracuse University.

Kirschten, D. (1983). "Administration Using Carter-Era Reforms To Manipulate the Levers of Government." *National Journal* 15 15: 732–736.

Lane, L. M., and J. F. Wolf (1990). *The Human Resource Crisis in the Public Sector: Rebuilding the Capacity to Govern.* New York: Quorum Books.

Latham, G. P., and K. N. Wexley (1981). *Increasing Productivity Through Performance Appraisal.* Reading, MA: Addison-Wesley.

Lawler, E. E., III (1981). *Pay and Organization Development.* Reading, MA: Addison-Wesley.

———— (1983). "Merit Pay: An Obsolete Policy?" pp. 305–310 in J. R. Hackman, E. E. Lawler III, and L. W. Porter, eds., *Perspectives on Behavior in Organizations.* New York: McGraw-Hill Book Company.

———— (1990). *Strategic Pay: Aligning Organizational Strategies and Pay Systems.* San Francisco: Jossey-Bass Publishers.

Lee, R. D., Jr. (1987). *Public Personnel Systems,* 2nd ed. Rockville, MD: Aspen Publishers.

Locke E. A. (1982). "The Ideas of Frederick W. Taylor: An Evaluation." *Academy of Management Review* 7, 1: 14–24.

Locke, E. A., D. B. Feren, V. M. McCaleb, K. N. Shaw, and A. T. Denny (1980). "The Relative Effectiveness of Four Methods of Motivating Employee Performance," pp. 363–388 in K. D. Duncan and D. Wallis, eds., *Changes in Working Life.* New York: John Wiley & Son.

Lovrich, N. P. (1987). "Merit Pay and Motivation in the Public Workforce: Beyond Technical Concerns to More Basic Considerations." *Review of Public Personnel Administration* 7, 2: 54–71.

Moe, T. M. (1985). "The Politicized Presidency," pp. 235–271 in J. Chubb and P. Peterson, eds., *The New Direction in American Politics.* Washington DC: Brookings Institution.

Mount, Michael K. (1987). "Coordinating Salary Action and Performance Appraisal," pp. 187–195 in D. B. Balkin and L. R. Gomez-Mejia, eds., *New Perspectives on Compensation.* Englewood Cliffs, NJ: Prentice-Hall.

Nachmias, David, and Paul J. Moderacki. 1982. Patterns of Support for Merit Pay and EEO Performance: The Inherent Difficulties of Implementing Innovation." *Policy Studies Journal* 11: 318–327.

Nadler, D. A., and E. E. Lawler III (1983). "Motivation: A Diagnostic Approach," pp.67–87 in J. R. Hackman, E. E. Lawler III, and L. W. Porter, eds., *Perspectives on Behavior in Organizations.* New York: McGraw-Hill.

National Research Council (1991). *Pay for Performance: Evaluating Performance Appraisal and Merit Pay.* Washington DC: National Academy Press.

Newland, C. A. (1983). "A Midterm Appraisal—The Reagan Presidency: Limited Government and Political Administration." *Public Administration Review* 43 1: 1–21.

O'Toole, D. E., and J. R. Churchill (1982). "Implementing Pay-For-Performance: Initial Experiences." *Review of Public Personnel Administration* 2, 3: 13–28.

Pagano, M. A. (1985). "An Exploratory Evaluation of the Civil Service Reform Act's Merit Pay System for the GS13–15s: A Case Study of the U.S. Department Of Health and Human Services," pp. 161–176 in D. H. Rosenbloom, ed., *Public Personnel Policy: The Politics of Civil Service.* Port Washington, NY: Associated Faculty Press.

Pearce, J. L. (1989). "Rewarding Successful Performance," pp. 401–441 in J. L. Perry, ed., *Handbook of Public Administration.* San Francisco: Jossey-Bass.

Pearce, J. L., and J. L. Perry (1983). "Federal Merit Pay: A Longitudinal Analysis." *Public Administration Review* 43: 315–325.

Pearce, J. L., and L. W. Porter (1986). "Employee Responses to Formal Performance Appraisal Feedback." *Journal of Applied Psychology* 71, 2: 211–218.

Pearce, J. L., W. B. Stevenson, and J. L. Perry (1985). "Managerial Compensation Based on Organizational Performance: A Time Series Analysis of the Effects of Merit Pay." *Academy of Management Journal* 28: 261–278.

Perry, J. L. (1991). "Linking Pay to Performance: The Controversy Continues," pp. 73–86 in C. Ban and N. M. Riccucci, eds., *Public Personnel Management: Current Concerns—Future Challenges*. New York: Longman.

_____ 1988–89. "Making Policy by Trial and Error: Merit Pay in the Federal Service." *Policy Studies Journal* 17: 389–405.

Perry, J. L., and J. L. Pearce (1985). "Civil Service Reform and the Politics of Performance Appraisal," pp. 146–158 in D. H. Rosenbloom, ed., *Public Personnel Policy: The Politics of Civil Service*. Port Washington, NY: Associated Faculty Press.

Perry, J. L., B. A. Petrakis, and T. K. Miller (1989). "Federal Merit Pay, Round II: An Analysis of the Performance Management and Recognition System." *Public Administration Review* 49: 29–37.

Perry, J. L., and L. W. Porter (1982). "Factors Affecting the Context for Motivation in Public Organizations." *Academy of Management Review* 7: 89–98.

Perry, J. L., and L. R. Wise (1990). "The Motivational Bases of Public Service." *Public Administration Review* 50: 367–373.

Pinder, C. C. (1984). *Work Motivation: Theory, Issues, and Application*. Glenview, IL: Scott, Foresman.

Porter, L. W., and E. E. Lawler III (1968). *Managerial Attitudes and Performance*. Homewood, IL: Dorsey Press.

Rainey, H. G. (1982). "Reward Preferences Among Public and Private Managers: In Search of the Service Ethic." *American Review of Public Administration* 16, 4: 299–302.

_____ (1989). "Public Management: Recent Research on the Political Context and Managerial Roles, Structures, and Behaviors." *Journal of Management* 15, 2: 229–250.

_____ (1991). *Understanding and Managing Public Organizations*. San Francisco: Jossey-Bass.

Schay, B. W. (1988). "Effects of Performance-Contingent Pay on Employee Attitudes." *Public Personnel Management* 17, 2: 237–250.

Sherwood, F., and B. Wechsler (1986). "The 'Hadacol' of the Eighties: Paying Senior Public Managers for Performance." *Review of Public Personnel Administration* 7, 1: 27–41.

Siegel, G. B. (1987). "The Jury Is Still Out on Merit Pay in Government." *Review of Public Personnel Administration* 7: 3–15.

Silverman, B. R. (1982). "The Merit Pay System: Prognosis." *Review of Public Personnel Administration* 2, 3: 29–34.

Stimson, R. A. (1980). "Performance Pay: Will It Work?" *The Bureaucrat* 9, 2: 39–47.

Thayer, F. C. (1984). "The President's Management Reforms: Theory X Triumphant," pp. 29–41 in P. W. Ingraham and C. Ban, eds., *Legislating Bureau-*

cratic Change: The Civil Service Reform Act of 1978. Albany: State University of
New York Press.

Thompson, F. J., N. M. Riccucci, and C. Ban (1991). "Drug Testing in the Federal
Workplace: An Instrumental and Symbolic Assessment." *Public Administration
Review* 51, 6: 515–525.

U.S. Congress (1989). PMRS Reauthorization Act of 1989. U.S. Statutes at Large
103: 670–672.

_____ (1991a). Performance Management and Recognition System Amendments
of 1991. U.S. Statutes at Large 105: 71.

_____ (1991b). Congressional Record, March 19, 1991, H1814.

U.S. General Accounting Office (1984). *A 2-Year Appraisal of Merit Pay in Three
Agencies.* Washington, DC: U.S. Government Printing Office.

U.S. House of Representatives (1989). Reauthorization of the Performance Management and Recognition System: Hearing Before the Subcommittee on Compensation and Employee Benefits. Serial No. 101-16. Washington DC: U.S. Government Printing Office.

U.S. Merit Systems Protection Board (1990). *Working for America: A Federal Employee Survey.* Washington, DC: U.S. Government Printing Office.

U.S. Office of Personnel Management (1991). *Advancing Managerial Excellence: A
Report on Improving the Performance Management and Recognition System.*
Washington, DC: U.S. Government Printing Office.

Vroom, V. H. (1964). *Work and Motivation.* New York: Wiley.

Notes

1. Of course, an alternative interpretation of these findings is that ratings are not
necessarily inflated; we simply have good employees. The personnel selection
process is not intended to provide a normal distribution of employees with regard
to performance capabilities.

2. It is true that higher pay can be associated with greater intrinsic rewards when
it is accompanied by greater responsibility and recognition. Merit pay, however,
does not operate on this premise. It simply holds the promise of financial reward
for more highly evaluated performance in one's current job.

3. This was the Performance Management and Recognition System Review
Committee.

28

OF PIGS IN POKES AND POLICY DIFFUSION

Another Look at Pay-for-Performance

Patricia W. Ingraham

During the past 30 years, performance appraisal and pay-for-performance systems have become widespread in the United States. Over 90 percent of private sector firms operate with some form of pay-for-performance (Wyatt Company, 1989). The Civil Service Reform Act of 1978 created pay-for-performance systems for members of the Senior Executive Service (SES) and for midlevel managers in the federal government. The Federal Employees Pay Comparability Act of 1990 established a joint labor-management committee to investigate the possibility of extending the systems government-wide. Over 20 states currently have pay-for-performance systems on the books, and several more are considering adoption in the near future (U.S. General Accounting Office, 1990). Many counties and cities also have such systems, although data are limited on these schemes (Ammons and Rodriguez, 1986). The diffusion has also been cross-national; 13 member nations of the international Organization for Economic Cooperation and Development (OECD) now have some form of pay-for-performance (Organization for Economic Cooperation and Development, 1992).[1]

1993. Of pigs in pokes and policy diffusion: Another look at pay-for-performance. Ingraham, Patricia W. **Public Administration Review** 53 (July): 348–356.

Common sense would suggest that such an extensive presence was based on a clear record of success. In fact, however, the diffusion of pay-for-performance has been based less on careful analysis and evaluation than on a perception of success in other settings, informal communication among bureaucratic and elected decision makers, and perhaps wishful thinking. The first comprehensive examination of the effectiveness of pay-for-performance in the private sector, for example, did not occur until 1990, 12 years after its adoption in the Civil Service Reform Act of 1978. In 1990, when the Office of Personnel Management considered a proposal that would have extended pay-for-performance to all federal employees, a National Academy of Science study on the topic was commissioned (Milkovich and Wigdor, 1991). The findings did not support many of the assumptions that had surrounded initial adoption of pay-for-performance in the federal government; they demonstrated instead that many of the untested and frequently unstated assumptions held by key decision makers about pay-for-performance were without foundation. Some of these assumptions related to the transferability of private sector pay schemes to a public setting. Such assumptions have a long tradition in public administration (Perry and Kraemer, 1983).

As one of the anonymous reviewers of this analysis observed, "It is typical for a government to follow private sector examples and buy pokes without looking inside to see if there's really a good pig in there." Other assumptions build on that foundation: working assumptions related to the motivation of public employees (they are just like their private sector counterparts) and the role of financial incentives in motivation and commitment (they are the most important incentive in both cases) clearly assume easy transferability of policies and techniques. Whatever problems may exist with this transferability, the practice of looking to the private sector for public solutions is so well established as to be nearly inviolate.

A different kind of assumption is related to the nature of pay-for-performance systems themselves. There is little indication that the schemes have been viewed as anything other than a technical management tool that can easily be grafted onto any existing management system. The need for pay-for-performance systems to be accompanied or preceded by broader and more fundamental reforms has rarely been recognized in the policy adoption and diffusion process. This, in turn, assumes that fundamental management systems are in essentially good working order and modest technical fixes at the fringe will be adequate to keep them on course and to achieve desired outcomes.

Pay-for-performance is not the first public policy whose diffusion from one setting to another, whether it be private to public, state to state, or national government to national government, lacks a firm grounding in empirical evaluation and analysis. Nor is it the first to encounter inflated expectations, major problems in implementation, and harsh evaluations. It is one of many public policies to be, in Peters' and Hogwood's (1985) terms, "crippled at birth." It is important to ask how and why this crippling occurs, however, and to examine both the reality of the policy experience and the nature of the policy decisions more closely.

The analysis presented here relies on secondary analysis of existing data related to private and federal pay schemes, on my 1991 survey of those states with pay-for-performance systems, and on secondary analysis of comparative data supplemented by interviews conducted in Europe in June and October 1991 and in Washington, DC, in early 1992.

Policy Diffusion and Pay-for-Performance

The diffusion of public policies from one unit of government to another, both within and across national boundaries, has been well documented (Rose, 1976; Heidenheimer, Heclo, and Adams, 1975). Early analyses attributed policy diffusion, particularly in U.S. states and cities, to levels of socio-economic development (Hofferbert, 1968; Walker, 1969). Later studies emphasized the role of political parties, other forms of citizen participation, and social values in policy diffusion processes (Heclo, 1974). Most analyses focused on social welfare programs and policies (Flora, 1976; Ingraham and Schneider, 1984). Personnel policies, however, have also been products of broad diffusion and of some of the same influences (Tolbert and Zucker, 1983). Charles Jones (1970) terms this replication and adoption of a policy observed in another setting "analogous design." It has become a well-accepted part of American public policy processes. Use of the term "design," however, implies an analytic rigor that is often not present in analogous adoption and diffusion. Many questions are not asked, much less answered, prior to the decision to adopt the policy. In the context of organizations and organization theory, Tolbert and Zucker observe that, although initial adoption decisions may be rooted in "internal needs of the organization"—or, in the public sector, in law—" over time diffusion and adoption becomes a process . . . rooted in conformity to institutional definition" (1983, p. 37). Thus, even if some problem analysis and policy design occurs in early adopters, later adopters will utilize much less rigorous decision criteria.

Recently, scholars have argued that more attention to design and its attendant activities—clear problem specification, specific causal linkages, clear specification of policy choices, and consideration of likelihood of successful implementation—would greatly enhance chances for policy success (Schneider and Ingram, 1990; Linder and Peters, 1990). To be sure, little empirical evidence exists concerning the decision criteria applied in analogous policy choice. There are few signs, however, of the design activities specified above. Evaluation of the experience in the first setting is very limited or anecdotal; a simple assumption is made of problem commonality; issues of transferability are rarely raised. Pay-for-performance provides nearly classic evidence of this approach to policy adoption and diffusion.

The pay-for-performance provisions in the federal Civil Service Reform Act of 1978 provide a striking example. A chief architect of the legislation, Alan Campbell, was asked a decade later, in a Senate Forum, why the act had not provided for experimentation and evaluation of pay-for-performance prior to government-wide implementation. He replied, "I saw no need. It was my perception that it worked fine in the private sector" (U.S. Senate, 1988, p. 28).

This comment clearly identifies the "private to public" policy diffusion model. In the case of pay-for-performance, the model was applied despite a remarkable paucity of information and data about the relative success or failure of techniques and schemes in the private sector. It was applied despite substantial scholarly research that pointed to difficulties with pay-for-performance, particularly in large organizations (Lawler, 1981; Deming, 1986; Rainey, 1990). A brief summary of that research is useful in understanding the relationship between adoption decisions based on inaccurate assumptions and/or information and subsequent implementation difficulties.

Pay-for-Performance in the Private Sector: Theory and Practice

In both the public and private sectors, pay-for-performance schemes have the announced intention of motivating workers to higher levels of performance and productivity by linking performance to financial incentives. They can also assist in attracting and retaining employees and, to some extent, in regulating labor costs (Milkovich and Wigdor, 1991, p. 80). Given the emphasis on differentiating between employees, pay-for-performance should also be expected to *not* reward, and even to punish, those employees whose performance is not satisfactory. In most cases, a formal performance appraisal process provides the link between individual or group performance and reward. This performance appraisal provides the basis for supervisory decisions that differentiate among the employees in determining performance awards. The research of Lawler (1982) and others demonstrates that it is critical for the employee to perceive the appraisal process to be fair and objective, and to clearly link reward to effort, if pay-for-performance systems are to achieve their stated objectives. Some form of regularized performance appraisal underpins virtually all private sector efforts; the extent to which private firms have been successful in establishing the performance/reward linkage, and in documenting their success, would appear fundamental to efforts to determine overall success or failure of the policy in that setting. In fact, however, a great deal of private sector research documents the difficulties inherent in creating the necessary linkages, except under the most controlled circumstances.

Milkovich and Wigdor summarize existing research in the following way:

> These studies establish that individual incentives (for example, one time bonuses) can have positive effects on individual employee performance. But it is also important to understand the restricted organizational conditions under which these results are observed without accompanying unintended, negative consequences.... These findings suggest the dangers of using individual incentive plans for employees in complex, interdependent jobs requiring work group cooperation; in instances in which employees generally distrust management; or in an economic environment that makes job loss or the or the manipulation of incentive performance standards likely (Milkovich and Wigdor, 1991, pp. 82–83).

These difficulties and others are emphasized by theorists such as Deming (1986), who argue that pay-for-performance creates unhealthy competition and dissension among employees and should be discontinued or de-emphasized.

Pay-for-performance is, however, widespread in the private sector. Bretz and Milkovich (1989) report that between 93 and 99 percent of private sector firms use pay-for-performance plans for their salaried employees, with large firms (over 1,000 employees) slightly more likely than smaller firms to adopt the plan. They also clarify the multipurpose nature of pay-for-performance and performance appraisal when they report that, in these settings, the performance appraisal process is viewed as a means for improving organizational communication, behavior and performance, as well as for tying pay to performance and improving overall productivity.

The National Academy of Science report provides a counterpoint:

> Fewer than half the organizations participating in the surveys . . . reported any formal measurement of performance appraisal success. . . . Among those who did . . . personnel managers . . . were most likely to be questioned . . . as well as most likely to view plans as "very effective" or "partially effective".. . . . In general, less than 20 percent of personnel managers polled in recent surveys gave their performance appraisal plans an overall rating of "very effective"; another 60 to 70 percent . . . rated their plans "partially effective." Other

managers and employees were similarly unenthusiastic. On average, less than one-third rate their organization's performance appraisal plans as "effective" in tying pay to performance or in communicating organizational expectations about work" (Milkovich and Wigdor, 1991, p. 106).

Overall, little in the documented record of private sector experience with performance appraisal and pay-for-performance suggests clear success; indeed, much of the record can be read as failure. In any case, private systems do not present an unqualified success story with clear lessons for public sector organizations and managers. Given this circumstance and the likelihood that many public sector organizations will look to the private sector for guidance anyway, are there questions that can be asked by public decision makers who wish to avoid problems and to design programs with greater potential for success?

The Role of Organizational Setting and Resource Base

One candidate for such consideration is the nature of the organizational context of those systems that *are* deemed effective in the private sector. Three organizational characteristics are most significant, although others are also relevant. The first is organizational structure. The second is the nature of personnel and management systems and the degree to which they allow for managerial discretion and flexibility. The third is the nature of the resources and incentives that the organization is willing, and able, to commit to the pay-for-performance scheme.

In the public sector, organizations are generally strongly influenced by centralized civil service systems and standardized compensation rules. Rainey (1990) has observed that complex personnel rules and procedures are one of the critical characteristics of public organizations. This serves to limit flexibility and to constrain individual discretion. At the same time, these highly structured public organizations are subject to significant external influences, objectives, and standards (Rosenbloom, 1983; O'Leary and Wise, 1991). One consequence for pay-for-performance is that

> Public sector organizations may use more formal, precise performance appraisals in an effort to make management decisions appear legitimate both to employees and to other constituents. While this may be useful in satisfying some constituents (for example, Congress) it may make employees skeptical of their performance appraisals and any pay system based on them, and it may reduce management incentives to administer the systems as the organization intends (Milkovich and Wigdor, 1991, p. 133).

The experience of public sector performance appraisal systems clearly reflects this generalization. The demand of civil service systems for standardization and objectivity has forced heavy reliance by the public sector on tightly structured and quantified performance appraisals. Although this has important external symbolic value in relation to fairness and equity, it forces the manager and the organization into an area of great complexity, substantial paperwork, and potentially negative results (Murphy and Cleveland, 1991). Standardization across agencies serves to decrease flexibility and autonomy even more. Finally, the extensive role of public sector unions in demanding uniform treatment and reward is very significant. As Murlis observes in her description of "stagnant organizations," these qualities lead to the development of a ". . . more formal approach to performance awards both at the top of the organization and lower down. This move is typically accompanied by development of a simple appraisal process which carries more emphasis on the defensibility of pay decisions than on personnel development" (Murlis, 1992, p. 3).

An additional problem is created by the separation of critical personnel functions from line managers in most civil service systems. The National Academy of Public Administration (1986) and others have noted that the ability of managers to manage effectively in such systems is severely constrained. The political management structure found in many public agencies further limits and complicates managerial authority and flexibility.

In contrast, research and limited evidence from private sector schemes judged to be successful suggest the following organizational and managerial characteristics if conditions favorable to effective pay-for-performance schemes are to be created:

1. Pay-for-performance should be part of a total management system; that is, managers should have the discretion, the authority, and the resources to recognize, reward adequately, and, if necessary, to demote or fire.
2. The organizational climate should be characterized by high levels of organizational trust, based on common or shared values and objectives between executives and employees.
3. Because of these common commitments, the ability to link individual performance to organizational goals and objectives is strong.
4. There should be consensus about measures of both individual and organizational success.
5. The financial resources available for the pay-for-performance system must be adequate to ensure its significance to employees and stable enough to permit long-term payoff to the organization

(Milkovich and Wigdor, 1991, chap. 8; Ingraham, 1991, pp. 12–13).

The fit between these conditions and those found in most public sector organizations is not comfortable. Some tensions are more pronounced than others. Adequate financial resources, for example, are difficult to ensure—particularly in times of economic stress, when rewarding civil servants is not high on the priority list of most elected officials and is likely to draw public criticism if it does occur. Even more significant, the managers and executives of public organizations do not control their financial resources. They often cannot guarantee that an adequate award will be available in any given year. In addition, the presence of a satisfactory base compensation system is fundamental if pay-for-performance is not to become a remedy rather than a reward (Perry, 1992). This, too, is not present in many public sector organizations, although base pay has improved for senior executives in the federal service and the Federal Employee Pay Comparability Act of 1990 should reduce inequities more generally when it is implemented. (It should be noted, however, that funding for full implementation is not guaranteed.)

Existing public management and compensation systems, in short, do not generally create the authority, flexibility, or resources necessary to give pay-for-performance a good chance of success; careful design would have to address those issues. This is a notable gap in the diffusion of pay-for-performance.

Pay-for-Performance as Management "Technique"

The common practice of adopting pay-for-performance schemes without broader reforms to support them suggests that these techniques were viewed as mere adjustments to the base, rather than as fundamental revisions of existing management systems. Thus, civil service laws and regulations dictate the terms of recruiting, hiring, promotion, firing, demotion, transfer, training and development, and appraisal and award of individual performance.

The net effect of this complex set of directives is severe diminution of managerial authority and responsibility. It is fair to say that, for many, managing in this system means applying rules and regulations. There are few incentives for drifting from this norm (although many good managers do); there are many disincentives—including paperwork, time, lengthy appeals processes, lack of budgetary control, and inability to provide other rewards such as training and education—for doing so. This rigid maintenance of standardized behavior does not reinforce or reward the managerial behaviors associated with more flexible systems; many would argue that the primary impact is to stultify discretion. Indeed, in this setting, even "good" pay-for-performance schemes are likely to be overwhelmed. It becomes very difficult to disentangle their effects from the countervailing impacts of the larger systems.

In such settings, effective use of more flexible mechanisms and techniques is not easy; it becomes a factor of the commitment, ability and initiative of individual managers. Those managers must not only be able and willing to change but must be willing to do so in the face of rather serious systemic disincentives. From the fine stuff of civil service systems, committed and innovative managers must create and utilize rewards for flexibility. They must rely on financial incentives whose size and stability they do not control; they must apply an individual reward system in a setting noted for group tasks and activities. This is not technique-oriented management, nor, in this setting, is pay-for-performance a simple technique grafted onto a sound management system.

Overall, then, pay-for-performance schemes in the public sector proceed from a rather shaky base. Implementation has reflected this unsteadiness; at the same time, pay-for-performance has continued to expand in government. The implementation experience of pay-for-performance in the United States and in other OECD nations provides evidence of that diffusion, but raises many questions about the reasons for it.

Implementing Pay-for-Performance in Government

The experience with pay-for-performance in the federal government in the United States has been well analyzed and documented. The experience in the American states and in other nations is less well known, but, as the following summaries indicate, very similar.

The Federal Government

The Civil Service Reform Act contained two provisions related to pay-for-performance: members of the Senior Executive Service had a system and midlevel managers (GS and GM 13–15) were covered by the Merit Pay System. The experience of the Senior Executive Service is the most controversial because of the potential influence of political appointees on bonus decisions for career members of the SES. The early experience fully reflects the perils of organizational change in a political setting; provisions for bonus awards were changed dramatically within six months of initial implementation and the Reagan election profoundly changed the environment in which the career executives operated (Ingraham, 1987). There was substantial dissatisfaction with the system and a fairly high exit rate from the SES in its early years (Merit System Protection Board, 1987). Every major analysis of SES members' attitudes about their system has reported that a majority of those responding do *not* perceive a link between performance and reward (Merit System Protection Board, 1989, 1990). In 1990, the Merit System Protection Board reported that

> About one in ten SES members . . . believes that the SES performance appraisal system has improved organizational effectiveness; about six in ten do not. About one-fourth of the SES members believe that the bonus/rank system is a strong incentive; over half do not. Roughly 18 percent of the respondents believe that "there are enough bonuses so that if I perform well I have a good chance of receiving one" (Merit Systems Protection Board, 1990, pp. 22–24).

Merit pay encountered similar turbulence early in its implementation. The revenue neutral provisions of the initial legislation were problematic, as was performance appraisal. In 1984, the original program was abolished and the Performance Management and Review System was created by Congress. As with the Senior Executive Service pay-for-performance system, however, problems continue with merit pay. Although some agencies consider their program to be successful, most recent reports essentially confirm the earlier negative assessments. Rating inflation appears to be endemic (Office of Personnel Management, 1987; General Accounting Office, 1987, 1989). The size of the bonus is problematic (U.S. General Accounting Office, 1990). Employee dissatisfaction with the system is high in many agencies (Merit Systems Protection Board, 1989). In 1992, the General Accounting Office and the Office of Personnel Management (1992a) released surveys-of federal employees that found that a majority of respondents in both cases believed their performance appraisal process to be fair (Office of Personnel Management: 63 percent; Government Accounting Office: 67 percent). The OPM survey revealed, however, that less than one-fifth of the employees believed that the performance appraisal and pay system motivated employees to do their best. The GAO survey found that about 40 percent of the respondents were satisfied with monetary awards and bonuses, but an equal number were not.

The Bush administration considered expanding pay-for-performance to all federal employees; the Federal Employees' Pay Comparability Act of 1990 provided that a joint labor/management advisory committee be established to discuss expansion. That committee recommended expanding only to small, experimental efforts; its report (Office of Personnel Management, 1991) demonstrates the very significant tensions between collective bargaining and pay-for-performance. Although expansion of the system appears unlikely at this time, flexible pay schemes have been a part of every demonstration project that OPM has approved. Overall, pay-for-performance and other flexible pay programs remain very active parts of the federal personnel policy agenda.

Pay-for-Performance in the States

Two surveys have recently been completed of those states with pay-for-performance programs. The first was conducted by GAO in 1990, and included the 23 states with programs believed to be in place at that time. I completed the second in 1991. It surveyed personnel directors in the 24 states with programs at that time (North Carolina adopted the program after the GAO study was completed). Surveys were returned from 21 states. Earlier case studies of two states supplement the survey data (Ingraham, 1991; Ingraham, forthcoming).

Findings from these studies both support and expand upon the experience of the federal government and upon the findings from the states reported earlier by Sherwood and Wechsler (1986).[2] The GAO report succinctly summarized the broad range of experience found in the states:

> Although several states have adopted pay-for-performance, there is no clear consensus as to what constitutes an ideal pay-for-performance system. State pay-for-performance systems varied with regard to funding, methods for rewarding employees whose performance justified additional compensation, the number of performance levels used to assess employee performance, and the percentage of the work force covered by pay-for-performance (U.S. General Accounting Office, 1990, p. 3).

GAO also found that full implementation had not occurred in many of the states, that a general dissatisfaction existed with the total amounts of performance awards in those states that did have active programs, and that inadequate or inconsistent state funding "hindered or undermined the system's goals" (U.S. General Accounting Office, 1990, p. 23). Nonetheless, the U.S. General Accounting Office observed that there appears to be a "trend" toward adoption of pay-for-performance in state governments.

My survey reaffirmed the above findings, but also asked a different set of questions: the source of the policy "idea" in the state, the expectations for the program, the extent to which the program had been fully and consistently implemented, and the source of funding.

As in the case of the federal program, diffusion to and among the states generally occurred without analysis of the experience of pay-for-performance in other settings. Respondents were nearly evenly split in terms of the source of policy idea; about half reported an initiative from the governor, gubernatorial staff, or the legislature, while the remaining states reported that the idea had come from top state administrative personnel. Those states reporting administrative initiation linked the idea for adoption to professional affiliations and reports that the program "worked" in other states. The most common expectations included increasing governmental efficiency, reducing personnel costs, and improving communication inside state organizations.

Diffusion of pay-for-performance rarely occurred in conjunction with, or following, other civil service or compensation reforms. As with the federal program, pay-for-performance was added on to existing compensation and personnel systems. Coverage varied widely, from only the top echelon of executives to most state employees. All of the states with wide coverage operated without unionization and collective bargaining.

Three of the states discontinued their programs. Four adopted pay-for-performance twice, the second time because the first program was never implemented or funded. A large majority of the states reported problems with inadequate, inconsistent, and, in some cases, *no* funding. Of the 21 states responding, only 4 reported funding every year of the program's life. Three state programs have never been funded or implemented, but remain on the books. Nine reported no funding for at least one year of the program's life; 5 reported no funding for at least one-half of the program's total life. Four of this latter group were early adopters, which have had programs for ten years or more. Those states reporting problems with funding most often received pay-for-performance money through a special legislative appropriation, whereas other states most often relied on a percentage of the total personnel budget for funding.

Although all states reported a link between pay-for-performance and performance appraisal, a large majority of those responding expressed dissatisfaction with the appraisal process. One respondent noted that the problem was with trying to "force mangers to be more honest" in their appraisals, and another observed that her state was having problems attempting to make the appraisal process more "legally defensible." A majority of the states reported employee dissatisfaction with pay-for-performance.

Quite clearly, states with pay-for-performance systems have encountered at least as many problems as the better-documented federal schemes. They also have generally not been successful in approaching threshold conditions for effective programs. Absence of consistent and adequate funding was the most serious problem, but lack of managerial authority, performance appraisal problems, and a generalized unwillingness to differentiate among employees were noted as well. Again, however, this generally unsuccessful record is not inhibiting the diffusion of pay-for-performance programs in the states. In 1993, a queue is waiting to adopt.

Pay-for-Performance in other OECD Nations

The diffusion of pay-for-performance schemes has been international as well. Thirteen of the OECD member nations currently have some form of pay-for-performance; others are considering adoption. The international diffusion of this policy clearly reflects a private sector model. "Economic rationalism" and managerialism informed public sector reforms in many nations in the 1980s (Pollitt, 1990; Hood, forthcoming; Ingraham, forthcoming b). The reforms were described by OECD in the following way:

> These reforms have been described as the "new managerialism" because of their frequent adoption of techniques from the private sector and the elevation of managerial skills, relative to policy and advisory skills. The new managerialism has involved a comprehensive process of change to public sector organizations, with an emphasis on decentralized managerial and financial control and the fostering of what is described as a "performance culture" that places greater value on accountability and value for money (Organization for Economic Cooperation and Development, 1992, p. 8).

The report notes further that

> Across many countries and different political parties, pay for performance is seen as an exemplar of reforms modelled on practice in the private sector that are expected to lead to improved efficiency and effectiveness in the public sector (Organization for Economic Cooperation and Development, 1992, p. 11).

As much as the reforms demonstrate private-to-public policy diffusion, however, they also reflect cross-national diffusion. The clearest case of this type of diffusion is the replication of many of the components—particularly the Senior Executive Service—of the U.S. Civil Service Reform Act in the Australian reforms. Indeed, early drafting of the legislation creating the SES in Victoria was assisted by consultations with staff members of the U.S. Senate.[3]

An OECD conference in June 1991 demonstrated the wide variation in scheme design and coverage that exists outside of the United States. Some nations, such as Australia and New Zealand, have initially reformed their base civil service and management systems, adding pay-for-performance as a "capstone" reform only after more fundamental changes were in place. Others, such as the Netherlands and Sweden, adopted a decentralized approach, distributing pots of money to each of the ministries for pay-for-performance with few—or no—guidelines for standards or size of awards. Still others, such as Great Britain and Ireland, followed much the same path as the United States, distributing small amounts to senior managers and using centralized rules and procedures for doing so.

The experience of pay-for-performance in other nations has generally been less-well documented than in the United States, but there is some evidence of similar results. Further, those results appear to be similar in spite of design variations. A recent analysis of the Australian experience in Victoria reported that, in 1989, senior managers were generally satisfied with their performance appraisals and found their goals challenging, but only 41 percent believed that performance *plans* were an incentive to better performance. In addition, while 72 percent were generally satisfied with the planning system, only 41 percent reported satisfaction with performance *pay,* and 32 percent believed that it encouraged higher performance (Wood, 1991, p. 31).

The experience in the Netherlands is of special interest because of the extensive decentralization of the design. The legislation creating the scheme, however, provided that only one evaluation could be conducted by the Ministry of Home Affairs, the agency responsible for the administration of pay-for-performance. That evaluation was completed in October 1991. Findings were mixed, but one of the most significant was that managers generally wished to have some central guidelines and direction.[4] Variation existed between agencies, but use of formal performance appraisal was spotty, and the general consensus was that the amounts available for awards were too small. Some agencies reported that the system had essentially not been used. My interviews in one ministry found that awareness of the system and its intent and provisions varied dramatically from manager to manager.

OECD provides the following useful summary of the pay-for-performance experience of its member nations:

> Although a major rationale for establishing performance related pay schemes is to improve performance, there is at this point no direct evidence concerning the impact of schemes on performance. Many schemes have not been in operation long enough for a thorough assessment, and even in the case of longer running schemes, there has been very little systematic analysis of the impact on the productivity of public sector organizations. . . . It is (also) not clear whether schemes have provided managers with greater flexibility in managing their human resources toward the achievement of departmental goals. . . . A clear lesson is that performance related pay schemes must provide adequate funds for a sufficiently large number of staff to receive rewards worth striving for. Whilst there are no hard and fast rules for determining the size of awards, most schemes are currently underfunded relative to their maximum awards payable (Organization for Economic and Community Development, 1992, pp. 3–5).

Conclusion

This analysis explored the assumptions and rationales underlying the rapid diffusion of pay-for-performance as a policy innovation. It did not examine the theoretical underpinnings of the policy itself, although that has been questioned by other authors (Perry, 1986; Deming, 1986). Rather, I questioned (1) the extent to which pay-for-performance was as successful in the private sector as it was perceived to be by public policy makers, (2) the extent to which pay-for-performance techniques in the private sector are easily transferable to a public setting, and (3) the extent to which conditions for an effective pay-for-performance system exist in public personnel systems and environments. I also examined the implementation of these programs in the public sector.

Evidence of success in the private sector setting is much more limited than many decision makers involved in early adoption of this policy apparently believed. To the extent that success can be demonstrated to exist, it occurs in the context of organizational characteristics not likely to be found in most public sector organizations under existing civil service laws and procedures. Further, budget reductions and economic constraints in many public organizations render adequate and stable financial resources unlikely. Diffusion of the policy, however, proceeded in essential isolation from such information, as well as from the implementation experience of other governments.

Nonetheless, the extensive presence of pay-for-performance schemes and their apparently inexorable expansion mandate constructive attention by analysts and practitioners alike. These practices have achieved a symbolic significance to both elected officials and public managers that is very important (Ingraham and Perry, forthcoming). Simply put, it makes both political and managerial sense to reward good performers or to make an effort to do so. Further, growing evidence in many countries and in many public organizations indicates that employees themselves subscribe to a belief that their performance and productivity should be evaluated and good performers rewarded (Murlis, 1992).[5] Is it possible to create systems that are better able to do that in the public sector?

I would suggest the following:

1. Ask what public organizations *need,* not what private organizations do. This initial focus on the real nature of the problem in public sector organizations may well lead to different solutions, or at least, different designs of similar solutions.
2. Find examples of success in the *public sector.* Good management is not confined to private organizations. Many managers in many public organizations have taken ill-designed policies such as pay-

for-performance and made them work. How did they do it? What conditions were present inside the organization that supported their initiatives? Can any of these be generalized to other public organizations or to subsequent policy design?

3. Ask if threshold conditions for success are really going to be present for implementation. Essentially no evidence supports the view that pay-for-performance systems save money (at least not initially); some evidence suggests that in their early years effective systems may cost more than the more traditional practices they replaced. This reality and its budgetary implications must be addressed. What does it mean to create a pay-for-performance program, but never fund it, as some states have done? If funds are limited or new funds are not likely, should limited experiments to provide lessons for the future be the policy choice? What other policy alternatives exist that could be less costly?

4. Explore more fully how pay-for-performance really fits into a civil service system. As currently configured, many civil service systems do not provide either managers or employees with the incentives and authority fundamental to "good" and more effective performance. Pay-for-performance is not a technical add-on. It is a fundamental challenge to many of the characteristics of traditional systems. Basic reforms to those civil service systems are necessary if the fit is to be improved. The fit with other "reforms" also needs to be explored. Many public organizations now have both pay-for performance and total quality management, which have different objectives and conflicting processes.

5. Provide elected and organizational decision makers with better empirical information about how the systems really work, about settings in which they are most successful, about design options and alternatives, about necessary resource commitments, and about results. Some evidence is beginning to emerge from the OPM analyses of the China Lake Demonstration that pay-banding, for example, initially costs more but gradually levels off and then reduces costs as poor performers are not rewarded (Office of Personnel Management, 1993). Such analyses, if disseminated quickly and clearly, can be useful in shaping expectations for program performance and outcomes and for better understanding necessary resource commitments.

6. Look more carefully at other pay flexibilities and the benefits they may offer to public organizations. Group incentive plans, for example, are a better fit with the reality of work in many public organizations and are clearly a better fit with other reforms currently being implemented, such as total quality management.

More flexible base pay, nonfinancial rewards and incentives, and simple emphasis on the communication between organization, manager, and employee that pay-for-performance is presumed to foster are other candidates for consideration.

7. Finally, put personnel issues back onto the academic research agenda. The American Political Science Association reports that personnel ranks at the very bottom of the research interests of those political scientists who have an interest in public administration. That is difficult to justify, given the centrality of a sound public service to effective governance. Academic analysts can make a contribution to both theory and practice by giving critical personnel issues priority in their research agendas.

References

Ammons, David, and Arnold Rodriguez, 1986. "Performance Appraisal Practices for Upper Management in City Governments." *Public Administration Review*, vol. 46 (September-October), pp. 460–467.

Bretz, Robert, and George Milkovich, 1989. "Performance Appraisal in Large Organizations: Practice and Research Implications." Working Paper 89-17. Center for Advanced Human Resource Studies. Ithaca, NY: Cornell University.

Deming, Edward S., 1986. *Out of the Crisis*. Cambridge, MA: Center for Advanced Engineering.

Flora, Peter, 1976. "On the Development of the Western European Welfare States." Paper Delivered at the Annual Conference, International Political Science Association. Edinburgh.

Halligan, John, 1992. "The Senior Executive Service in Australia." In Patricia Ingraham and David Rosenbloom, eds., *The Promise and Paradox of Civil Service Reform*. Pittsburgh: University of Pittsburgh Press.

Heclo, Hugh, 1974. *Modern Social Policies in Britain and Sweden: From Relief to Income Maintainence*. New Haven: Yale University Press.

Heidenheimer, Arnold, Hugh Heclo, and Carolyn Adams, 1975. *Comparative Public Policies*. New York: St. Martins.

Hofferbert, Richard I., 1968. "Socioeconomic Dimensions of the American States." *Midwest Journal of Political Science*, vol. 12 (Fall), pp. 401–418.

Hood, Christopher, forthcoming. "Exploring Variations in 1980s Public Management Reform: Towards a Contingency Framework?" In Hans Bekke, Theo Toonen, and James Perry, eds., *Comparative Civil Service Reform*. Bloomington, IN: Indiana University Press.

Ingraham, Patricia W., 1987. "Building Bridges or Burning Them? The President, the Appointees, and the Bureaucracy." *Public Administration Review*, vol. 47 (September-October), pp. 425–435.

———, 1991. "The Experience with Pay for Performance in the United States." Paris: Organization for Economic Cooperation and Development.

_____, forthcoming a. "Pay for Performance in the States." *American Review of Public Administration.*

_____, forthcoming b. "Internal Stress and External Strains: The Comparative Civil Service Reform Agenda." In Hans Bekke, Theo Toonen, and James Perry, eds., *Comparative Civil Service Reform.* Bloomington, IN: Indiana University Press.

Ingraham, Patricia W., and James Perry, forthcoming. "Theory, Symbol, and Reality in Civil Service Reform." In R. Rosenbaum, ed., *Jimmy Carter: Keeping Faith.* New York: Greenwood.

Ingraham, Patricia W., and Saundra Schneider, 1984. "The Impact of Political Participation on Social Policy Adoption and Expansion: A Cross-National, Longitudinal Analysis." *Comparative Politics,* October, pp. 107–122.

Jones, Charles O., 1970. *An Introduction to the Study of Public Policy.* Belmont, CA: Wadsworth.

Lawler, E. E., 1981. *Pay and Organization Development.* Reading, MA: Addison-Wesley.

Linder, Stephen, and B. Guy Peters, 1990. "The Design of Instruments for Public Policy." In Stuart Nagel, ed., *Policy, Theory, and Policy Evaluation.* New York: Greenwood.

Milkovich, George, and Alexandra Wigdor, eds., 1991. *Pay for Performance: Evaluating Performance Appraisal and Merit Pay.* Washington, DC: National Academy Press.

Murlis, Helen, 1992. "Reward Management Strategies." Paper presented at the OECD Conference on Pay Flexibilities. Paris, November.

Murphy, Kevin, and James Cleveland, 1991. *Performance Appraisal: An Organizational Perspective.* Boston: Allyn and Bacon.

National Academy of Public Administration, 1986. "Revitalizing Federal Management." Washington, DC: National Academy of Public Administration.

Organization for Economic Cooperation and Development, 1992. "First Report of the Panel on Performance-Related Pay Schemes for Public Sector Managers." Paris: OECD, Public Management Committee.

O'Leary, Rosemary, and Charles Wise, 1991. "Public Managers, Judges, and Legislators: Redefining the 'New Partnership.'" *Public Administration Review,* vol. 51 (July-August), pp. 316–326.

Peters, B. Guy, and Brian Hogwood, 1985. *Policy Dynamics.* London: Wheatsheaf.

Perry, James, 1986. "Ment Pay in the Public Sector: The Case for a Failure of Theory." *Review of Public Personnel Administration,* vol. 7 (Fall), pp. 57–69.

_____ 1992. "Merit Pay in the Federal Government." In Patricia Ingraham and David Rosenbloom, eds., *The Promise and Paradox of Civil Service Reform.* Pittsburgh: University of Pittsburgh Press.

Perry, James, and Kenneth Kraemer, eds., 1983. *Public Management.* Mountain View, CA: Mayfield.

Pollitt, Christopher, 1990. *Managerialism and the Public Services.* Oxford: Basil Blackwell.

Rainey, Hal G., 1990. "Public Management: Recent Developments and Current Prospects." In Naomi Lynn and Aaron Wildavsky, eds., *Public Administration: The State of the Discipline.* Chatham, NJ: Chatham House.

Rose, Richard, 1976. *The Dynamics of Public Policy: A Comparative Analysis.* Beverly Hills, CA: Sage.

Rosenbloom, David H., 1983. *Public Administration and Law.* New York: Marcel Dekker.

Schneider, Anne, and Helen Ingram, 1990. "Policy Design: Elements, Premises and Strategies." In Stuart Nagel, ed., *Policy Theory and Policy Evaluation.* New York: Greenwood.

Sherwood, Frank, and Barton Wechsler, 1986. "The 'Hadacol' of the Eighties: Paying Senior Managers for Performance." *Review of Public Personnel Administration,* vol. 7 (Fall), pp. 27–41.

Tolbert, Pamela S., and Lynne G Zucker, 1983. "Institutional Sources of Change in the Formal Structure of Organizations: The Diffusion of Civil Service Reform, 1880–1935." *Administrative Science Quarterly,* vol. 28, no. 1, pp. 22–39.

U.S. General Accounting Office, 1987. "Pay for Performance: Implementation of the Performance Management and Recognition System." Washington, DC: General Accounting Office.

_____, 1989. "Pay for Performance: Interim Report on PMRS." Washington, DC: General Accounting Office.

_____, 1990. "Pay for Performance: State and International Public Sector Pay-for-Performance Systems." Washington, DC: General Accounting Office.

_____, 1992. "Federal Employment: How Federal Employees View the Government as a Place to Work." Washington, DC: General Accounting Office.

U.S. Merit Systems Protection Board, 1987. "Performance Management and Review System: Linking Pay to Performance." Washington, DC: Merit Systems Protection Boards.

_____, 1989. "Federal Personnel Management Since Civil Service Reform." Washington, DC: Merit Systems Protection Board.

_____, 1990. "Working for America: A Federal Employee Survey." Washington, DC: Merit Systems Protection Board.

U.S. Office of Personnel Management, 1987. "Performance Management and Recognition System." Washington, DC: Office of Personnel Management.

_____, 1991. "Strengthening the Link Between Pay and Performance: Report of the Pay for Performance Labor Management Committee." Washington, DC: Office of Personnel Management.

_____, 1992a. "Survey of Federal Employees." Washington, DC: Office of Personnel Management.

_____, 1993. "Broad Banding in the Federal Government" Management Report. Office of System Innovation, Office of Personnel Management.

U.S. Senate, Subcommittee on Government Affairs, 1988. "Forum on the Design of the Civil Service Reform Act of 1978." Washington, DC: Government Printing Office.

Walker, Jack, 1969. "Diffusion of Innovations Among the American States." *American Political Science Review,* vol. 63, pp. 880–899.

Wood, Robert, 1991. "Performance Pay and Related Compensation Practices in Australian State Public Sector Organizations." Paris: OECD.

Wyatt Company, 1989. "Results of the 1989 Wyatt Survey: Getting Your Hands Around Performance Management." *The Wyatt Communicator,* Fourth Quarter, pp. 4–18.

Notes

1. Although OECD is primarily concerned with economic and financial issues, its Public Management Service carefully tracks management practices and reforms. A 1992 analysis of pay for performance indicated that Australia, Canada, Denmark, Finland, France, Ireland, Italy, the Netherlands, New Zealand, Spain, Sweden, the United Kingdom, and the United States have some form of pay for performance on the books.

2. Most state programs were adopted in two time periods; the first occurred in the late 1970s; the second occurred in the mid 1980s. the two newest programs are those of North Carolina and Virginia. In both cases, programs had been adopted and terminated prior to this latest adoption.

3. In Australia, the reforms were adopted first at the state level in Victoria, in 1982. In 1991, New South Wales, South Australia, and Queensland were also ready to adopt the practice. Pay for performance is being carefully monitored and evaluated in Victoria; baseline data were collected before implementation in that state and periodic evaluations update the database. The practice was to be introduced at the national level in 1992. For additional discussion, see Wood (1991) and Halligan (1992).

4. I conducted interviews related to the pay-for-performance program and the evaluation of it at the Ministry of Finance and the Ministry of Land Affairs, the Hague, in October 1992.

5. An OECD conference in November 1992 addressed the issue of flexible-pay systems in 15 member nations. There was consensus that the development of a new performance culture was evident in many of these nations and was a cornerstone of emerging reforms.

Printed in the United States
98LVS00003B/16